The Complete
A to Z Dictionary of DREAMS

THE COMPLETE

THE COMPLETE

A to Z

D·I·C·T·I·O·N·A·R·Y of

DREAMS

OVER 12,000 DEFINITIONS

BE YOUR OWN DREAM EXPERT

IAN WALLACE

Health Communications, Inc.
Deerfield Beach, Florida

www.hcibooks.com

Cataloging-in-Publication Data is available through the Library of Congress

ISBN-13: 978-0-7573-1835-1 (paperback)
ISBN-10: 0-7573-1835-5 (paperback)
ISBN-13: 978-0-7573-1836-8 (ePub)
ISBN-10: 0-7573-1836-3 (ePub)

Publisher: Health Communications, Inc.
      3201 S.W. 15th Street
      Deerfield Beach, FL 33442–8190

Cover design by Dane Wesolko
Interior design and formatting by Lawna Patterson Oldfield

CONTENTS

INTRODUCTION

In my work with dreams and dreamers, the question I am most frequently asked is "What does my dream mean?" Although many people are interested in the dreaming process and how it can reflect a wider awareness of human consciousness, understanding the meaning of a dream is what most people want to discover. When a dreamer asks, "What does my dream mean?" he or she is actually asking a more powerful question, which is "What does my dream actually mean to me?"

Trying to find out what your dream means to you can often be a confusing and frustrating experience. Most dream interpretation sources offer a variety of meanings for a particular symbol. Although it can be interesting to explore the different viewpoints of Jung, Freud, the ancient Assyrians, and many other sources that offer dream insights, it often results in a situation where you end up spending most of your time trying to resolve contradictions between the various opinions. Using this dream dictionary is different. Instead of looking at all possible opinions, it is firmly based on taking constructive action. The symbol definitions are practical and a great way to ask yourself fundamental questions that will move you into specific action. These definitions have emerged from over thirty years of working with dreams and by consistently working with dreamers to help them identify opportunities that will lead to healthy and fulfilling outcomes. Rather than delving into the more esoteric aspects of working with dreams, this dream dictionary provides a practical method of understanding what your dreams actually mean, so you can put them into real action.

There are a number of ways to use this dictionary. You can just dive right into "The Dream Dictionary" (see page 51) and look up the definition of a dream image that has particular significance for you. You can read through "What Do My Dreams Actually Mean?" (see page 3) to find out more about the practical aspects of what dreams actually are and why we create them. There is also information on the development of dream interpretation (see page 6) and on how symbols emerge (see page

10). To understand your dreams in greater depth, you can work your way through the examples of "The Dream Connection Process" (see page 14), so you can quickly and expertly explain what you are expressing to yourself by creating a particular dream. By using examples, I show you how to define what a symbol means to you, how to ask yourself questions about its significance, and how to create an action statement.

The Dream Dictionary contains over 12,000 definitions, from *Aardvark* all the way through to *Zzz's*, and when used as the basis for The Dream Connection Process, they offer an almost infinite number of interpretations. Each of the definitions is around twenty words long and enables you to get an immediate sense of what your dream imagery means to you.

Using the definitions from The Dream Dictionary as part of The Dream Connection Process will help you to be your own dream expert. By connecting your dream meanings to the reality of your day-to-day life, you will be able to make the most of any opportunities to turn your hopes and aspirations into waking reality.

For some time now, one of my personal ambitions has been to create a modern dream dictionary that enables dreamers to connect with their unconscious power and potential. Many people have helped me put this dream into action, and I would particularly like to thank Clare Landon, Susanna Abbott, Clare Hulton, Jo Godfrey Wood, Catherine Knight, Daniel Rodger, Dagmar Kress, Caroline and Eric Cochrane, Owen Crawford, George Jamieson, Stuart Jenkinson, Marianne Garvey, Iain Banks, Carol McGiffin, Denise Welch, Shobna Gulati, Jane Mcdonald, Carol Vorderman, Alan Titchmarsh, Emil Shavila, Russell Howard, Sarah Millican, Eddie Izzard, Ryan Tubridy, Nicky Campbell, Rachel Burden, Shelagh Fogarty, Tony Blackburn, Jonathan Miles, Louise Elliott, Sally Boazman, Ricky Marshall, John Dutton, Simon Mayo, Tim Smith, and Steve Wright.

WHAT DO MY DREAMS ACTUALLY MEAN?

A Dream Is Just a Dream Until You Put It into Action

Everyone dreams. Every one of us dreams, but many of us tend to dismiss our dreams as bizarre experiences that don't appear to mean anything. Nor do our dreams seem to be of any practical use, as we often assume we cannot readily use any of our dream experiences in the real world of waking life. However, we keep being drawn back to the dreams we create every night because they may contain information that can help us realize our ambitions in waking life.

The word *dream* has two meanings for us. It can be the adventures we create for ourselves every time we sleep, and it can also represent our greatest hopes and aspirations in our day-to-day reality. Although our nighttime dreams may just seem to be a distraction from our pursuit of health and happiness in everyday life, they can provide us with vital insights that enable us to ask ourselves powerful questions about how we can turn our dreams into reality in our waking lives.

Trying to find a way to work out what your dream means can often be as bewildering as the imagery from your dream experience. There appear to be countless theories about dreams and seemingly endless debates about the function of dreams, where they come from, what they are, if they actually do exist, and so on. Although this debate and opinion are healthy, it often means that dreams end up being viewed as quirks and curiosities rather than being used as a fundamental part of human experience that can help us to live the lives we want to live.

The theories and opinions about the dreaming process have become polarized into two main areas. These two areas are the academic and esoteric approaches, which usually tend to firmly oppose each other. The academic approach often tries to work with the dreaming process by using outside-in methodologies. These methods involve studying the physiological and neurological activity that occurs during dreaming as a way of trying to understand why dream imagery is being produced. This is valuable work, but it can result in a dream being treated as a biological phenomenon rather than being seen as an opportunity for personal development.

The more esoteric approaches to dreaming tend to view the dreaming process as an experience that happens *to* the dreamer. This is also an outside-in approach that takes the ownership of the dream away from the dreamer by suggesting that the dreamer is merely a type of psychic receiver. This can result in the dreamer becoming disempowered and reliant on a process that offers little practical help in getting to a positive and healthy outcome.

Instead of trying to make a compromise between these two opposing perspectives, I take a different approach, which is to engage with the language and imagery the dreamer is creating emotionally. Rather than using the outside-in methods of the academic and esoteric approaches, mine is an inside-out process that enables a dreamer to clearly express the imagery he or she is creating, thereby taking full ownership of it and using it as a basis for practical action. This is not just an attempt to be different; rather, it is a robust process that enables dreamers to reach a specific outcome so they can take action to step into their power and positively transform some aspect of their waking lives. This inside-out approach is highly practical and has proved successful for my thousands of clients.

The basis of this inside-out process is realizing that dreams don't just happen to you; you create the dream and all the imagery and emotions you experience in it. Understanding that you are the author of your dreams immediately begins to empower you by allowing you to question why you created that particular dream experience. Instead of being unwelcome neurological intrusions or mysterious visitations, your dreams become a form of self-expression that can help you understand more about who you are, what you need, and what you believe. As you expand your self-understanding, you naturally begin to connect more deeply with your hopes and aspirations in waking life. This encourages you to step into your individual power and take action on your dreams. The guiding principle I use in working with the imagery a dreamer creates is "A dream is just a dream until you put it into action."

From this practical perspective, let's explore some basic questions about dreams and dreaming.

What Is a Dream?

A dream is how you naturally express a fundamental aspect of your self-awareness. This fundamental awareness is your unconscious self and is quite simply all the areas of yourself you are not consciously aware of. Although these may seem to be of little consequence in waking life, most of your behaviors are driven by your unconscious self and all the information you absorb with it in every waking second.

When you create a dream, you are using it as a natural way to make sense of all the information and experiences you are unconsciously aware of in day-to-day reality. This individual sense-making process can give you meaningful insights into specific challenges you encounter in waking life. The language you use to express yourself as you make sense of your unconscious awareness is the language of imagery.

As well as using visual imagery in the dreams you create, you can also use auditory (hearing), olfactory (smelling), and tactile (touching) imagery. The images you create in your dreams reflect how you see your self-image in waking life and enable you to imagine the person you have the power to become. A dream is how you imagine yourself. That's what a dream is.

Why Do We Dream?

At the most basic level, we dream because it is a natural function that has evolved. Although some people who, due to a brain injury or a congenital condition, lack the neurophysiology to dream, everyone dreams. By using our dreams to make sense of all the information we have unconsciously absorbed, we can become far more successful in identifying valuable opportunities for personal development in waking life.

Dreaming also contributes to our sense of physical well-being. If for any reason we are unable to engage in dreaming activity, we can experience a variety of unsettling physical symptoms. The human brain, however, is not just some wet organic computer that needs to be regularly decluttered and defragmented. Your brain is much more complex than the most powerful computer, and dreaming has evolved as a vital aspect of how you create your perceptions of the world around you.

The unconscious awarenesses we use our dreams to make sense of are not just the events of the previous day but are drawn from the whole of our life experience. As we recollect and reconnect with these meaningful experiences, we project them into our future lives so we can naturally position ourselves for success and fulfillment. All humans are dreamers, dreaming of brighter futures.

When we unconsciously create our dreams at night, we follow the same process we use when we imagine our ambitions in day-to-day reality by forming images of how our future might look. In waking life, however, we often tend to form an idealized future, where our dreams suddenly manifest in reality. As we know, this is highly unlikely to happen, and trying to always instantly connect to this idealized future means that we can find it difficult to take the practical steps we need to put our dreams into action.

By working with the dreams we unconsciously create every night, we start to become aware of the obstacles and frustrations we may encounter as we try to put our dreams into action in reality. In waking life, these obstacles can seem insurmountable, but by working with our dreams we can raise our level of self-awareness and understanding to realize that the obstacles are not so insurmountable after all, and we can immediately take practical steps to move toward our ambitions. If dreams are such a vital sense-making process, how can I remember my dreams, because I am sure that I don't dream?

How Do I Remember My Dreams?

You have to remember the dreams you create before you can realize their value. Even though it may seem a challenge to remember your dreams, all you have to do is remember three words: *will*, *still*, and *fill*.

As you lay your head on your pillow to go to sleep, say to yourself, "Tonight, I *will* remember my dreams." When you wake up, lie completely *still* for a minute. Don't move, don't look at the time, and don't even wiggle your toes. By staying still, images and emotions from your dreams will emerge for you. Then *fill* in the gaps between the images from the dreams you created, and your dream narrative will appear. The more you use *will*, *still*, and *fill*, the easier you will find it to work with your dreams. At first you may recall only vague images and feelings, but as you specifically engage with them, these will become clearer and more vivid.

Now you have a basic understanding of what is a dream is, why you dream, and how to remember your dreams. But the reason you are using this book is because you want to know what your dream means to you.

What Do My Dreams Mean?

Before we get into this fundamentally practical approach to understanding what your dreams mean, it is worth looking at the history of dream interpretation and some of the viewpoints and perspectives that have emerged from it.

At some point, probably around the same time language skills were emerging, early humans were trying to convey their dreaming experiences to one another. Although there is no documentary evidence of this, there are indications in the 30,000-year-old cave paintings at Chauvet-Pont-d'Arc in the Ardèche region of France. Cave paintings that appear to be inspired by dream imagery are also to be found at Lascaux and Altamira, dating from around 16,000 years ago.

The earliest known dream diaries date from 5,000 years ago and were found inscribed on clay tablets in the library of King Ashurbanipal of Nineveh, in the north of what is modern-day Iraq. Around 4,000 years ago, the ancient Egyptians documented their dreams and believed they were communications from the gods. Egyptians also created special dreaming areas, where they felt they could receive insight and healing from their deities. The ancient Greeks continued this practice of having special dream areas with their sleep temples, known as *asclepieia*. The earliest documented dream interpretation work was written by the Greek Sophist Antiphon, and although his work seemed to have had a major influence, there is no full record of it in existence today.

The first coherent work on dream interpretation was provided by another Greek, Artemidorus Daldianus. His five-volume work, *Oneirocritica*, was compiled from a variety of sources, and he used analogy as his main method for dream interpretation. He observed that "dream interpretation is nothing other than the juxtaposition of similarities." The Greek philosopher and playwright Aristotle also observed that "the most skilful interpreters of dreams are they who have the faculty for observing resemblances."

Dreams also played an important role in the emergence of most major religions, particularly regarding visions and visitations. Many religions and their spiritual inspiration emerged from the dreams of individuals; therefore, there is a great tradition of dream interpretation in all religious practices.

Until the late nineteenth century, when Sigmund Freud began to take a more methodical approach to dreams and what they might signify, dreams were still usually considered to be a phenomenon that happened to the dreamer rather than being created by the dreamer. This resulted in a situation where fortune-tellers provided dream interpretations, and a dream was an experience that foretold a predestined fate instead of being an opportunity for the dreamer to take individual action to decide the outcome. Freud's work began to move dream interpretation out of the realm of the soothsayers and into a more modern understanding.

Although Freud took a more rigorous approach to the interpretation of dreams, he often based his processes on analogies drawn from late nineteenth-century industrial chemistry. The terminology he used to describe his work with dreams included definitions such as *condensation, transference, binding, residue, discharge, sublimation, latent content,* and *mechanism.* This reflected a wider shift from the interpretation of dreaming to the analysis of dream content. Freud's method of dream analysis gave him a repeatable process he could use to consistently work with patients, but it could often result in situations where he was trying to fix them from the outside in rather than enabling them to transform themselves from the inside out.

Freud's protégé, Carl Jung, also based his work with dreams on a framework of analogies. Rather than using the technology that was contemporary to him, Jung used analogies from more ancient esoteric technologies such as alchemy, astrology, tarot, and the I Ching. His use of these esoteric traditions was inspired by Helena Blavatsky, one of the originators of the New Age movement, which began to fully blossom in the early part of the twentieth century and became much more widely accepted in the latter part.

Using contemporary technology as an analogy for the dreaming process is a trend that continues today. As personal computers became increasingly prevalent, it became more common to use computer terminology as metaphors for dream experiences. Rather than being seen as a way of expressing one's unconscious awareness, dreams became a way of defragmenting personal beliefs or refreshing and clearing the human memory cache.

The metaphors we use to describe our brains and the experience of human consciousness tend to be based on whatever technology we have available at the time. In the future, some will no doubt attempt to explain the dreaming process by using analogies from the technological marvels that may be emerging, whether they be nanodrones, sentidroids, or amoeboputers. Although analogy and metaphor are a fundamental part of understanding your dreams, using technological processes as metaphors for the experience of dreaming is an outside-in approach, whereas understanding why you are creating specific metaphors is the preferred inside-out approach.

Looking from the Inside Out Rather Than the Outside In

To understand why you create specific images in your dreams, it is much more valuable to observe how the imagery you create emerges into waking reality than to have someone else attempt to look inside your head and make assumptions about what is happening in there. The imagery we create in our dreams is based on the same images that we use in the idioms and metaphors we use in everyday life. For example, we often use the fluid and potentially turbulent nature of water to symbolize our emotions and experiences, with idioms such as "I am at a low ebb," "She was in floods of tears," and "He poured his heart out." The metaphors we use often reflect a more universal cultural awareness. Most cultures use teeth to symbolize power and confidence, as in the French idiom of *les dents longue*, which means "big teeth" and describes a person who is confident and ambitious. An individual who is considered extremely ambitious is described as having *les dents qui rayent le parque*, which literally means "teeth that are scraping the floor."

This universality of idioms and imagery can sometimes be confusing. Many dream dictionaries are translated from other languages and often lose the subtleties of particular metaphors and idioms. For example, some dream dictionaries that have been translated from French into English state that seeing an almond means you will have some regrets. This is just a subtlety that has been lost in translation rather than describing what an almond symbolizes. In French, the word for almond is *amande*, and the word for regret is *amende*, as in making amends. The imagery we consistently use in our imaginings then emerges as specific symbols that become the basis of our imaginal languages.

Dream Symbols

A symbol is often considered a simple representation of something else. This can often lead to confusion when you are trying to understand what a particular symbol might mean to you and can diminish the value of any understanding that might be associated with it. Rather than adopting a simple "this means that" approach to working with symbols, it is valuable to understand what symbols are, how to use them, and how they emerge in the first place. The word *symbol* is derived from the Greek *symbolon*, which was a way of authenticating the identity of an unfamiliar person or object.

A *symbolon* was a physical token, such as a coin, that was broken into two pieces that could form a whole only when fitted back together again. Like pieces of a jigsaw puzzle, parts of one *symbolon* would not fit with parts of a different *symbolon*. The fundamental power of a *symbolon* was not its ability to substitute for something else; its power was its ability to connect an individual to something that was unfamiliar and held potential value for him or her. This remains true today. The power of a symbol is not in its ability to be a substitute; it is the ability to make a connection.

The connection a symbol can make is powerful because it connects an individual to the universal, the known to the unknown, and the familiar to the unfamiliar. One of the main reasons there can be so much confusion in interpreting dream symbols comes from using them as substitutions instead of connections. This has led to some schools of thought that suggest all symbols are universal, and therefore everyone must experience the same meaning from every symbol. This view is opposed by other schools of thought that declare there is no such thing as a universal symbol, and any symbol is uniquely meaningful to a specific person.

The reality is that a symbol embraces both these viewpoints, and it is a connection of the individual to the universal and the universal to the individual. By understanding the meaning of a symbol, an individual can become much more aware of how what is happening in his or her inner life is reflected in the outer life.

In realizing that a symbol is a dynamic connection rather than a static substitute, we become aware that the function of a symbol is to make a connection. When we create a symbol, we are usually connecting our individual potential to opportunities that may currently seem beyond us. The meaning of a dream symbol is the connection it makes.

How Symbols Emerge

Our symbols are not consciously decided by some central authority. Instead, our symbols unconsciously emerge from the meaningful connections we make. Rather than asking how it is possible to connect a dream image with a symbolic meaning, it is much easier to turn that question around and observe how the imagery we create in our imaginations emerges in the shared symbolism we use in everyday life. The most obvious aspects of this are in the metaphors and idioms we use in our day-to-day language.

The same imagery dreamers report in the dream experiences they create is also found in the language they use every day in waking life. Although dream imagery can be identified in a number of areas in our language, it is most prevalent in the images we base our idioms and metaphors on. Like our dream symbolism, the most common of these linguistic expressions are based on the landscape and the body. For example, we use the solidity of the ground to symbolize the more practical aspects of our inner lives by using idioms such as "well-grounded" and "down-to-earth."

The meaning of a dream symbol is the connection it makes, and the first dream symbols were probably based on our experience of our bodies and the landscapes we lived in. Even today, many of our symbols are based on the physicality of body and landscape. As we grew more technologically accomplished, the symbols we used reflected the more complex aspects of our lives. For example, here is how the meaning of the dream symbol of a submarine may have emerged. The function of a symbol is what it connects us to, so we need to look at the connections associated with the image of a submarine. A submarine is a type of boat, and a boat is how we navigate across water. Let's start by looking at The Dream Dictionary definition for *water*, which is a "potential to fulfill an emotional need by immersing myself in my feelings so I can go with the flow and gain experience." So we know that a boat will have something to do with our emotional needs and how we gain experience of them.

When we look at The Dream Dictionary definition for *boat*, we see that it is an "ability to navigate complex and unpredictable feelings by using my instincts and experience to maintain my emotional stability." This suggests that creating a submarine in our dreams is somehow based on how we need to use our instincts and experiences to navigate complex feelings while maintaining our emotional stability.

A submarine goes below the surface of water, so the connection it makes as a symbol is about going deeper into the emotions. As we go deeper underwater, hydrostatic pressure increases, so a submarine also needs to guard against external emotional pressures. This leads us to The Dream Dictionary definition for *submarine*, which is an "ability to confidently explore the depths of my emotions and navigate them safely instead of cracking up under pressure."

We can then continue this process by exploring the symbolic connections of other parts of the submarine, such as the conning tower, which gives us the definition "a situation where I can take a more elevated perspective on how I can explore my emotional depths and navigate them safely."

Composite Symbols and Characters

As well as using specific imagery that may exist in waking life, we also create composite imagery in our dreams to reflect qualities and insights that have more complex characteristics. For example, you may be trying to consistently navigate your way through some complex emotions in waking life for which you need to use the power of your wisdom to illuminate the full spectrum of connections between your thoughts and feelings. One of the images you could create in your dreams to make sense of this waking-life situation would be a rainbow lighthouse, which meaningfully combines the qualities of a rainbow and a lighthouse. You might create a lighthouse with the beam as a clarifying rainbow, or the lighthouse might be painted in bright rainbow colors, or perhaps the whole lighthouse is glowing like a rainbow. However you imagine it in your dreams, it reflects how you are methodically making sense of a complex situation in your waking life.

We also create composite characters in our dreams to reflect aspects of characters that cannot simply be represented by a single person. It may be that you create a character in your dream who is a combination of an ex-lover and a new business partner. If you found your ex-lover to be unreliable, creating this dream may suggest that you have some doubts about how reliably you can connect in your relationship with your new business partner. Perhaps your ex-lover was very creative, and your new business partnership will allow you to express your emerging creativity. It might also be that your new business partner appears to be very confident, and you are blending this quality along with your ex-lover's creative qualities to explore how you can be more confident in your own creativity.

It is possible that many mythical beasts also originally emerged as composite dream symbols. For example, the centaur is a composite character of a man and a horse, embodying some of the unique characteristics of each. Different animal qualities are used in different ways to construct composite characters. A vampire is a composite creature that combines some of the qualities of bats and humans, whereas the superheroes Batman and Batwoman combine these qualities in quite a different way.

Dream Symbol Connections

Your dreams are how you imagine yourself, and the dream symbols you create are how you connect your individual potential to the opportunities you experience all around you. In waking life, you make most of these connections at an unconscious level, which results in your distributing your awareness of yourself into the world around you. Rather than unconsciously experiencing yourself as a completely separate and isolated individual, you use the people, places, events, and objects you encounter as a way of reflecting the connections you are making to a wider self-awareness. The images you create in your dreams are reflections of how you see yourself in your day-to-day reality. This process of unconscious symbolic connection is consistently used in The Dream Dictionary as a way of defining the connection each symbol describes.

Person

A person connects you to some aspect of your character. Any time you create a person in a dream, they connect you to some quality you need to be more aware of in waking life. Any symbol involving a person usually begins with "Aspect of my character . . ."

Place

A place connects you to a particular situation in your waking life, so any symbol involving a place usually begins with "Situation where . . ."

Object

An object connects you to some ability you have in waking life. Objects give you a specific ability, so the definition for an object usually starts off "Ability to . . ."

Event

Any time you create an event in your dreams, it is connecting you to an opportunity in waking life. The dictionary definitions for events usually start off as "Opportunity to . . ."

Animal

Any animal or creature in a dream is a reflection of your instinctive creativity in waking life. Any symbol definition involving an animal usually begins with "Instinctive ability . . ."

Plant

Plant imagery connects you to your ability for natural and healthy growth, so the definition for a plant usually starts with "Natural ability . . ."

Body

Dreaming of parts of your body connects you to your essential ability to take action, so body-part definitions usually begin with "Essential ability . . ."

Colors

Colors in your dreams often connect you to a particular mood that is coloring how you are viewing your position in waking life. Color definitions usually begin with "Mood that colors my perspective . . ."

Emotions

As well as creating images in our dreams, we also create the emotions we experience in them. An emotional experience usually connects us to a particular realization in waking life, so emotions are usually defined in the dictionary by starting with "Realization that . . ."

Numbers

When you create particular numbers in a dream, you are usually using them to connect to an understanding in waking life that is specific to you. While dreaming of two of something may be an indication of having to place emphasis or redouble efforts, any number beyond that usually has a personal significance in your day-to-day reality. Although there are a variety of symbolic meanings attributed to numbers in various esoteric systems, the esoteric significance is usually secondary to the symbolic connection you are making.

Dreaming into Action

The imagery you effortlessly create in your dreams is your natural way of connecting your emotional self to the realities of your day-to-day world. By connecting your unconscious insights to your conscious awareness, you have the opportunity to turn your dreams into action. In the next section, "The Dream Connection Process," we will look at some examples of how to use The Dream Dictionary definitions as a basis for taking practical action in waking life.

THE DREAM
CONNECTION PROCESS

The Dream Connection Process connects the imagery and symbols you create in your dreams to situations and opportunities in waking life, where you can use this awareness to make a healthy difference. The process uses the dictionary definitions to ask questions about the imagery you have created, enabling you to identify actions you can take. First we'll look at how to simply use the definitions. Next we'll go through some examples of how to ask questions based on these definitions, and then we'll work through examples of how to use the definitions and questions to put your dreams into action.

Using the Definitions

Every definition in the dictionary section describes a specific dream connection. For example, the dream connection for *house* is defined as "Situation where I have the security and support I need so I can comfortably explore all aspects of my inner and outer lives." Each of the dictionary definitions can be used as a dream connection, and the simplest way to use the dictionary is to recall an image from your dream and look up the definition. This will connect your dream image to its meaning and immediately give you insight into what is happening in your waking life. To make an even deeper connection, you can then create some questions about how to use this powerful understanding in your waking life.

Asking Questions

Your dreams are a natural way of making sense of all the experiences you unconsciously absorb. In waking life, our usual sense-making method is to ask a question. Your dreams do this naturally and make sense by answering questions you are not consciously aware you are asking. Although your dreams are unconsciously answering your sense-making questions, the answers you respond with are in a language of imagery. This image can sometimes be directly applied in waking life, but the best way to put The Dream Connection Process into action is to use it to create some questions. To do this, we take the definition for a particular dream symbol and turn it into a question. It is easy to think that a question is just a statement with a question mark at the end, but being able to create a good question will increase your awareness, and a great question will lead you to powerful action. There are three stages in asking a powerful question:

1. Naming the subject of the question.
2. Naming the extent of the subject.
3. Naming how you can modify the subject.

By naming the subject of the question, you identify what meaning is emerging for you. When you name the extent of the subject, you reflect on its existing value. As you name how you can modify the subject, you expand your awareness of how your situation can evolve. So by using a question to name, reflect on, and expand the subject, you can use your dream image as a basis for taking practical action.

Let's look at an example of how to use a question to connect your dream image to practical action in waking life. The question begins with the identification of the definition connected to a particular symbol. If you create the image of a ladder in your dream, then there is a situation occurring in your waking life that involves your "ability to use a particular series of steps to achieve a specific ambition so I can continue to perform at a higher level."

The first stage in creating a dream connection question is to name the most significant aspect of your dream by looking at a symbol you would like to explore further. So a first question for the ladder dream could be "What specific ambition am I trying to achieve?" or "What steps do I need to take to raise myself to a higher level?" Using naming questions like these is often enough to identify the answers you need to put your dreams into action.

To take it a step further, create a question that reflects the dream connection. The simplest way to do this is to think of the opposite of the symbol definition in the dictionary. For the ladder image, this question might be something like "Why am I currently working at a lower level than I feel I should be?" or perhaps "What is preventing me from taking the steps that I need to achieve a specific ambition?" By using reflecting questions like these, you can gain insight into some of the existing challenges you may be encountering.

The third stage of creating a dream connection question is to expand the image so that you can explore alternatives and evolve some possible actions. This expansion might involve asking questions such as "Do I actually have to go through this particular series of steps to reach the level I want to reach?" or "After I have achieved my chosen level, what are the next steps I would like to take?"

By using The Dream Connection Process to ask yourself specific questions like these, you naturally set yourself up for the possibility of attaining opportunities to put your dreams into action.

Let's create some other questions from another dream image. In this example, you have created a situation in your dream where you are naked in public. The definition from the Dream Dictionary for *naked in public* is an "opportunity to uncover my need to express my talents rather than trying to conceal them from the criticisms of other people."

So a first question that names the situation might be something like "What talents am I currently concealing from other people?" or "Do specific people criticize my unique talents?" Moving on to the reflecting part of the question, you could ask yourself, "Why am I covering up my need to express my talents?" or "Am I being too self-critical of my talents?" As you expand the question, you may further ask, "How do I want to show up to other people?" or "Why do the opinions of other people make me feel vulnerable?" These are powerful questions and directly connect the dream image you have created to possibilities in your waking life.

Let's look at the questions we can create from another dream, this time about a loose tooth. From The Dream Dictionary, the connection for a *loose tooth* is an "Essential opportunity to stay firmly connected to my fundamental power and confidence rather than feeling I can't speak up." So the first questions that name the situation might be "What might give me a firmer sense of confidence in this particular situation?" or perhaps "What is preventing me from confidently speaking up?" Reflecting questions for a loose tooth could be "What is making me feel disconnected and less confident?" or "What do I need to do so I can speak up confidently about my present situation?" Questions that expand on why you have created a loose tooth in your dream might include "What situations do I feel most confident in, and what situations do I feel less confident in?" or "What do I need to change about my situation to make it feel like I can confidently speak my truth?"

With all these dream images and questions, you can take your opportunities for practical action further by exploring the imagery you have created in your dream. For example, from this dream of a loose tooth, you could also look up the connections for symbols such as "losing teeth," which is an "opportunity to regain my self-confidence by acting in a more self-assured manner, even though I may feel a bit wobbly inside." You can take this process even further by looking up the connections associated with *loose*, "an opportunity to give myself freedom in how I approach a challenge while maintaining a firm connection to my wider ambitions," and *tooth*, an "essential ability to confidently display my power to other people rather than feeling that I have to keep it concealed from them," so you can create more questions from those perspectives. By exploring the images you have created and the possibilities they reflect, you can connect to some real actions you can take in waking life.

Let's move on to some examples of how to put your dreams into action.

Stating the Actions

Successfully putting your dreams into action requires that you have a clear understanding of the specific action you need to take. Rather than having vague ideas about what your dream might mean, you should use the image definitions and associated questions to create specific action statements. The following examples will show you how you can take the imagery from your dreams and use The Dream Connection Process to identify what the images mean, question their purpose, and decide the actions you will take.

Since there may be more than one image you would like to work with in a dream, we will start off the examples with one symbol and then add more symbols to build a more powerful understanding. Let's begin with the most common dream that everyone experiences, which is being chased.

Example 1: Being Chased

In this dream, you are trying to escape from something or someone who is pursuing you. Your pursuer may be animals, monsters, madmen, crazy women, a gang dressed in black, or anything else you can imagine. Although you may have created a number of images in your dream, we will begin by identifying the meaning of the most significant image, which is being chased. In The Dream Dictionary, the definition for *being chased* is an "opportunity to resolve an ongoing tension by turning my energies toward a pursuit that will help me to achieve my ambitions." The first awareness this definition connects us to is that we create this chase dream because of an opportunity we are becoming aware of in waking life. Rather than trying to avoid this opportunity, we are looking at ways to actively engage with it.

Because it is a chase dream, the opportunity is involved with some sort of pursuit you are engaged in or would like to become engaged in. This may be an ambition you are pursuing, such as a professional promotion, or it may be pursuing the possibility of becoming romantically involved. Whatever the nature of the pursuit you'd like to become engaged in, it is causing you some tension in waking life because you are also trying to avoid it in some way. This may be due to a lack of confidence or perhaps a feeling of being unprepared. To identify the actions you can take from this chase dream, let's create some naming, reflecting, and expanding questions.

Naming questions for this chase dream could be "What ambition am I actively pursuing in waking life?" or "What situation am I currently experiencing tension in?"

Reflecting questions for this dream might include "What ambitions do I feel most confident I will achieve?" or "Where am I not using my energies as effectively as I could?"

Expanding questions for the chase dream could be "Are there any other current opportunities that will help me to achieve my ambitions?" or "Do I need to purposefully create some healthy tension to speed up my pursuit?"

By using questions like these to name, reflect on, and expand the meaning of the dream imagery you have created, define an action statement that will help you put your dream into action. This action statement can simply be a reflection of The Dream Dictionary definition, so the statement might be "I am going to resolve an ongoing tension by turning my energies toward a pursuit that will help me to achieve my ambitions."

You can define additional action statements by simply using the questions you have created; therefore, other action statements could be "I am going to use my energies as effectively as I can" or "I am going to purposefully create some healthy tension to achieve my ambition more quickly."

Example 2: Being Chased by a Wolf

Let's study some of the other imagery you may be creating in this chase dream and imagine that in your dream you are being chased by a wolf. We know that The Dream Dictionary definition for *being chased* is an "opportunity to resolve an ongoing tension by turning my energies toward a pursuit that will help me to achieve my ambitions," so let's look at the definition for *wolf*, which is an "instinctive ability to protect those closest to me by being fiercely loyal to them, even though it may sometimes set me apart." As well as separately working your way through the definitions, you can also join them together to reach an immediate awareness. This may not always be grammatically correct, but you can easily edit and adjust it. So then the immediate definition of being chased by a wolf would be an "opportunity to resolve an ongoing tension by turning my energies toward a pursuit that will help me achieve my ambitions and by using my instinctive ability to protect those closest to me and by being fiercely loyal to them, even though it may sometimes set me apart."

Although this definition is only forty or so words, it is quite complex, so you can take the imagery that is more significant for you from these definitions and summarize it in your own way. For example, your combined definition might be an "opportunity to achieve my ambitions by instinctively protecting the people closest to me" or perhaps "setting myself apart by being fiercely loyal and causing tension."

The combined definition indicates that the tension around whatever you are pursuing in waking life is being caused by your instinctive need to protect some people close to you. This may be your family or your friends or a group of people whom you feel fiercely loyal to, such as a sports team or your colleagues at work. Your feeling a need to be fiercely protective of these people may be causing tension and may even be distancing you from them in some way. To resolve this tension and make the most of the opportunity, you can consider how your feelings of loyalty are helping them.

To identify the actions you can take from this more complex chase dream, let's create some naming, reflecting, and expanding questions.

Naming questions for this wolf-chase dream could be "How can I use my fierce loyalty to resolve an ongoing tension so I can achieve my ambitions?" and "Where am I setting myself apart from the people I feel closest to?"

Reflecting questions might include "Is my fierce loyalty causing the tension I feel?" or "When do I feel I am being taken advantage of by the people closest to me?"

Expanding questions could be "Should I be devoting all my time to the people closest to me?" or "How can I stay connected to a successful outcome without becoming so attached?"

An action statement could be "I am going to resolve an ongoing tension by using my fierce loyalty to protect those closest to me." Other action statements could be "I am going to look out for indications that my fierce loyalty is causing me tension" or "I am going to devote some of my time to looking after my needs."

Example 3: Being Chased by a Wolf Through a River

Let's take this dream a stage further and add another image you might create in it, such as being chased by a wolf through a river. The first step, which you are now becoming familiar with, is to look up The Dream Dictionary definition. *River* is defined as a "situation where I can enter my emotional flow so I can understand the source of my feelings and the course they might take." In this dream your need to be fiercely loyal as you pursue your ambition has a fundamentally emotional aspect to it. To be able to pursue your ambition and your reasons for being fiercely loyal is about being able to understand the source of your feelings and the course they might take.

By reflecting on your feelings and becoming more aware of where they come from in this situation, you can start to resolve some tensions around your fierce loyalty. You can then add this to what has emerged so far, so it gives you a more complex definition of an "opportunity to resolve an ongoing tension by turning my energies toward a pursuit that will help me achieve my ambitions by using my instinctive ability to protect those closest to me and by being fiercely loyal to them, even though it may sometimes set me apart in a situation where I need to enter my emotional flow so I can understand the source of my feelings and the course they might take."

Again, you can pick the most meaningful aspects out of the more complex definition, or you can just use it all to create some naming, reflecting, and expanding questions.

Naming questions for this dream could be "What is the source of my fierce loyalty?" or "How am I allowing the actions of other people to influence my emotions?"

Reflecting questions might include "Do I need to decisively channel my emotional flow so I don't get so attached to the people around me?" or "Is my emotional intensity causing me to feel vulnerable?"

Expanding questions could be "Can I use my emotional power to take a different course of action?" or "Am I putting all my emotional energy into protecting the people closest to me so I don't have to explore the source of my own feelings?"

An action statement could be "I am going to understand the specific source of one of my feelings so I can resolve an ongoing tension." Other action statements could be "I am going to channel my emotional flow so I won't feel my loyalties are being misplaced" or "I will share the source of my feelings with the people closest to me."

As with all these Dream Dictionary definitions, a lot of information is in each of the twenty-word definitions, so you can use your own experience and viewpoint to emphasize those that are more significant to you. This will give you a deeper awareness of the unconscious message you are expressing for yourself.

Example 4: Being Chased by a Wolf Through a River in a Flood

Although it is possible to keep adding images from your dream, doing so can sometimes obscure the imagery that is most significant for you. Let's add one more image to this dream and then move on to other examples.

As the dreamer recounted this dream, she realized that the most powerful aspect of it was that the river was actually in a flood. The Dream Dictionary definition for *flood* is an "opportunity to rise above it all by powerfully channeling my deeper emotions so I don't end up feeling too washed out," so as you pursue an ambition that involves your fierce loyalty, where you need to understand the source of your feelings, you need to rise above this emotional situation so you don't end up feeling too washed out.

To identify the actions you can take from this dream, let's create some naming, reflecting, and expanding questions.

Naming questions for this dream could be "Is it possible for me to achieve my ambitions by rising above any emotional tensions I may feel?" or "How can I consistently direct my fierce loyalty so I don't end up feeling washed out?"

Reflecting questions might include "Is my overwhelming emotional intensity causing the tension I feel?" or "Am I allowing myself to be carried away by the ambitions of the people closest to me?"

Expanding questions could be "How can I create a firm and practical boundary so my emotions don't always come flooding out unexpectedly?" or "How can I maintain a consistent level of emotional involvement?"

An action statement could be "I am going to achieve my ambitions by rising above any emotional tensions I may feel." Other action statements could be "I am going to look out for indications that my emotional intensity is causing the tension I feel" or "I am going to set consistent emotional boundaries so I can look after my needs."

Using these four simple but powerful dream images of being chased, a wolf, a river, and a flood, we have created a rich understanding of how to put this dream into action in waking life. In reality, the person who created this dream is a psychiatrist who works with disadvantaged children. Her dream reflected how her fierce loyalty to the children could sometimes result in her becoming too emotionally immersed in her relationships with them. By working through the images she had created in her dreams, asking the questions they prompted, and defining action statements, she achieved a consistent level of emotional involvement with the children. This in turn inspired the children to manage and maintain their own emotional boundaries, which led to some unexpectedly healthy outcomes.

Example 5: Being Chased by a Crazy Woman

Let's look at another chase dream, this time with different imagery. In this dream, the chase involves a crazy woman. We know from The Dream Dictionary definitions that *being chased* means an "opportunity to resolve an ongoing tension by turning my energies toward a pursuit that will help me achieve my ambitions." Let's look up *crazy woman*, which is an "aspect of my character that is driven mad when I neglect my creative wisdom and the talent it has to fulfil my aspirations." So the ongoing tension in your waking life around your pursuit of ambitions is about some aspect of your character that expresses your creative wisdom. There is a situation in your waking life where you need to express your creativity but feel you can't, and it is driving you mad.

As you work with the dream, you remember that you weren't just being chased by a crazy woman but that you had locked yourself in a bathroom and she was outside trying to smash the door down. So let's take a look at the definitions for both those symbols. *Bathroom* is an "aspect of myself that ensures my emotional privacy so I can stay relaxed when I am taking care of my fundamental needs," and *door* is an "ability to access different aspects of my character so I can develop possibilities that may have seemed closed to me." Before we move on to the naming, reflecting, and expanding questions, we can see that this dream is about the fundamental need to use your creativity, but you are trying to keep it to yourself in a private way. Your creative talent, however, can allow you to develop possibilities that may have seemed closed to you.

To identify the actions that you can take from this chase dream, let's create some naming, reflecting, and expanding questions. This time, instead of going through the dream images one by one, we are going to use the combined imagery as a basis for our questions and action statements.

Naming questions for this crazy-woman-chase dream could be "What areas of my powerful wisdom am I neglecting by always closing myself off to them?" or "How can I attend to my fundamental creative needs?"

Reflecting questions might include "How can I methodically open myself up to my creative aspirations?" or "Where can I use my powerful intuition to help me achieve my ambitions?"

Expanding questions could be "Are there other areas where I can fulfil my aspirations by showing up in a different way?" or "Why am I afraid of expressing my creativity?"

An action statement could be "I am going to attend to my fundamental, creative needs by giving myself the personal space to explore them." Other action statements could be "I am going to use my powerful intuition to decide which ambitions to pursue" or "I am going to look at a number of different areas where I can express my creativity." The dreamer who created this dream was a successful businesswoman who outwardly seemed very accomplished in her area of work but had been neglecting her huge creative talents. By using her intuitive skills, she became much more successful in realizing the practical value of her creativity.

Let's do one more chase dream and then look at some other dreams.

Example 6: Being Chased by a Monster

This is a common child's dream, and this particular version was created by an eight-year-old boy and then told to his mother. To begin with, as usual, let's look at the two main symbols so we can find their definitions in The Dream Dictionary. We know that *being chased* is an "opportunity to resolve an ongoing tension by turning my energies toward a pursuit that will help me achieve my ambitions," and from the dictionary we learn that *monster* connects us to an "instinctive ability to make the most of a huge opportunity rather than allowing my anxieties to grow out of all proportion." So when the boy created this dream, he had some tensions about a huge opportunity he wanted to pursue but made him anxious. Because this is a child's dream, the opportunity may be something that seems minor to his mother, or it can be about exciting developments in his life in general.

By using The Dream Connection Process, the boy's mother created a number of naming, reflecting, and expanding questions for him, which included "Is there a huge opportunity you are excited about but is also making you feel a little anxious?", "Are you trying to pretend that it's not really such a big deal for you?", and "Is there anything else you want to do that doesn't involve this big chance?"

Her son excitedly told her that the big opportunity was to be selected for one of the school football teams, but he had been rebuked by the sports teacher on a number of occasions about his unruly behavior. His mother helped him form an action statement, which was "I need to concentrate my energies on my football skills rather than wasting them by just messing around."

As they explored the questions and action statement, the boy described how he had also dreamed that he was taking part in a documentary as he was being chased by this monster. In The Dream Dictionary, a *documentary* is defined as an "opportunity to understand what really happened in one of my life experiences so I can investigate my motives and behaviors." His mother helped him create another action statement: "Any tensions I might feel are always a big opportunity to investigate my motives and behaviors." He then used this awareness to become more mindful of the motives and behaviors of the rest of the football team, which resulted in the team coach realizing the boy's leadership potential and quickly promoting him to team captain.

Let's move on from chase dreams and look at how to use The Dream Connection Process with some other familiar dreams. In the next examples, we will see how the characters you create in your dreams reflect aspects of your character in waking life that may hold great opportunity for you.

Example 7: Celebrity Encounter

In a celebrity-encounter dream, the dreamer creates a situation where he meets a well-known public figure. The dream often starts by the celebrity approaching the dreamer and behaving completely normally, as if they were close friends. The celebrity seems quite relaxed in the dreamer's company, and it feels like the most natural thing in the world to be spending time together. In The Dream Dictionary, the definition of *celebrity encounter* is an "opportunity to openly recognize my unique talents so I can become more widely celebrated in my chosen area of expertise." When a dreamer creates a celebrity encounter dream, he has an opportunity to have his talents more widely recognized in waking life.

A man frequently dreamed of spending time with one of the judges from a popular television talent show. Although the dreams were occasionally intimate, the dreamer mainly created situations where he was just socializing with the talent-show judge at a variety of high-profile events. The Dream Dictionary definition of *celebrity* is an "aspect of my character that I have the most respect and admiration for, even though I don't openly recognize its true value." So when the dreamer created this character in his dream, he was using it to symbolize a specific talent he was starting to develop.

All the characters you create in your dreams are aspects of your own character, no matter how famous or powerful they may appear to be in waking life. Specific celebrities connect you to particular aspects of your talents. The celebrity you create in your dream reflects an aspect of your character and helps you become more aware of how to connect to it in waking life. The unique talent you specifically associate with a celebrity is a quality you are now realizing you can express yourself. This quality may not be one you directly associate with the celebrity. For example, if you create a well-known musician in your dream, it may not be his musical skills you are drawn to. Instead, you may admire his creative approach or be attracted to a particular character trait.

If you admire this particular celebrity in waking life, then creating this dream shows your admiration for your own progress in developing a particular talent. If you are not so keen on the celebrity you've created, then there is some quality the celebrity possesses that reflects an undiscovered talent you need to own and shape to your satisfaction. One of the main challenges you may face in developing your talents is not that you don't have any talents but that you find it challenging to accept praise and recognition from other people in waking life. This can lead to a viewpoint in which you think that talent is something other people have but you never will. Although many celebrities may seem like overnight successes, most of them have had to work long and hard to develop their talents. The more you work at recognizing your unique talents and take action to develop them, the more valuable they will become to you and the people around you.

The nature of the celebrity encounter can emerge in different ways, and this dreamer developed his dream by creating a situation in which the talent-show judge initiated intimate activity with him. *Celebrity intimacy* is defined in The Dream Dictionary as an "opportunity to become more intensely aware of my unique creativity so I can begin to develop my unrealized potential." Although it may be easy to dismiss this dream as just a fantasy, creating a dream of an intimate encounter with a celebrity shows the dreamer that he is becoming aware of his unique creativity and what he can hope to conceive with it.

Naming questions that emerged from this celebrity-encounter dream included "How can I become more widely celebrated in my chosen area of expertise?" and "What do I need to do to develop my unrealized potential?"

Reflecting questions were "When do I close myself off to demonstrating my talents?" and "Do I need to make some private space so I can develop my abilities?"

Expanding questions for this dream were "How can I become more aware of how to creatively influence my chosen outcome?" and "What other talents do I have the potential to develop?"

The Dream Dictionary definition for the celebrity character the dreamer created, a talent-show judge, is an "aspect of my character that takes responsibility for showing my natural expertise instead of being critical of my efforts." The dreamer used this definition as the basis for his action statement: "I am going to confidently develop my natural creative abilities without allowing myself or other people to constantly criticize my talents."

Example 8: Meeting an Ex-Lover

In this recurring dream, the dreamer frequently created a situation in which she kept encountering an ex-lover. Although she claimed to be very happy in her current relationship, she felt guilty about this dream but also quite excited. Based on this dream, the dreamer entertained thoughts about ending her current relationship so she could invite her ex-lover back into her waking life; however, looking at the dream from both literal and imaginal points of view suggests quite different actions to take.

As we know from the process of symbol emergence, all the people we create in a dream are aspects of our own character. For example, if we create someone whose strength of opinion attracted us to him or her, we have a need to voice our opinions more strongly in waking life. Looking at the definition for *ex-lover* in The Dream Dictionary, we see that it is an "aspect of my character that embodied qualities that helped me become more intimately aware of my creative potential." This indicates that her ex-lover made her more aware of some specific qualities she had been trying to unconsciously express in a more creative manner. The specific quality the dreamer associated with this ex-lover was a feeling of control. She had experienced her lover as a controlling person. Although it had frequently frustrated her, it also made her feel quite secure.

The dreamer also described how her ex-lover sometimes appeared in her dreams as a composite character with different parts of the physical characteristics of previous lovers. Composite characters reflect how we create our dream characters based on the qualities of that experience. Creating a composite character suggests that the dreamer was drawn toward the same characteristic again and again in each of her lovers and was becoming stuck in a repetitive pattern. The quality that the dreamer was attracted to was the ability to stay in control, and this indicated that the dreamer was using the characteristics of these ex-lovers to symbolize some unresolved behaviors involving control issues.

To explore her need for this type of relationship, the dreamer created naming, reflecting, and expanding questions.

Her naming questions were "How can I become more intimately aware of my need to feel in control?" and "What qualities do I want to experience in my lover?"

Reflecting questions were "Are my relationship insecurities limiting my creative potential?" and "When do I feel distant from a romantic partner?"

Expanding questions were "Where can I take a more creative approach to resolving romantic tensions?" and "How can I make a deeper connection without feeling so dependent?"

The dreamer's action statement was "I am going to clearly identify what attracts me to a lover so I can move on from any controlling relationship patterns that may be limiting me."

After exploring these questions and defining this action statement, the dreamer decided to make a deeper commitment to her current relationship. Working through her dreams in this way enabled her to realize that she had been contributing to some of the tensions in her previous relationships. Creating the image of her ex-lover in her dreams helped identify a particular behavior that may have prevented her from consistently experiencing the deeper intimacy she desired.

When we create ex-lovers in our dreams, it usually doesn't mean that we want to be with them again. It means that we are beginning to become aware of some of the qualities that attracted us to them and are beginning to express them ourselves. It may be that our current relationship is playing out the patterns we experienced with previous lovers, and it may mean that our current lover will also become an ex-lover at some point soon. Using the characters we create in our dreams to understand our own behaviors can help us have much healthier and more fulfilling relationships.

Example 9: Ocean Mattress and Creature from the Depths

Let's look at another dream that involves some romantic concerns. In this dream, the dreamer had created a scene where she was floating on a mattress in the middle of the ocean. Although this may seem like quite a precarious position, she was very comfortable on the mattress, and the surface of the ocean was calm. As she relaxed on the mattress, a sea monster reared up from the deep and tried to drag her off the mattress. She fought the tentacles trying to wrap around her. As she was about to slide off the edge of the mattress, she woke up.

Although it might be easy to dismiss this dream as one in which the dreamer is "all at sea," we can discover much more information by exploring it further. Even though puns, metaphors, and idioms form a part of dream language, we always have to look at the wider context of the dream. The dreamer reported that she was very comfortable on the mattress, and everything around was calm. "All at sea" would suggest that the dreamer was floundering about rather than feeling happy and relaxed as she lay on the mattress. This indicates that the dreamer is not all at sea in waking life but that a challenge is lurking in her unconscious that may be potentially upsetting for her.

When we look up the definitions for the symbols in The Dream Dictionary, we can see that *mattress* is an "ability to support my need for rest and relaxation so I can stay within my comfort zone as I explore my creative urges." This suggests that the dreamer is in a situation in her waking life where she feels quite comfortable and at peace with herself. The ocean is a vast body of water, so we know that it will have some emotional content.

The Dream Dictionary tells us that dreaming of an *ocean* connects us to an understanding of a "situation where I can voyage into a wider understanding of my deeper emotional self, experiencing its moods and rhythms." This indicates that the dreamer feels quite comfortable in her current position in something in her waking life but has the opportunity to explore a wider understanding of her emotions and all the ups and downs associated with them. Although she is happy to do this, she is concerned that exploring some emotional possibilities will bring unseen tensions to the surface. These are symbolized by the sea monster, which is defined as an "instinctive ability to make the most of a huge opportunity rather than allowing myself to be overwhelmed by my emotions" and is reflected in her concerns that becoming immersed in an emotional situation in waking life will drag her down.

In waking life, she had made the choice to stay single for a while and felt very comfortable being on her own. She could, however, sense a romantic undercurrent with someone she had always wanted to be with and saw this as a huge opportunity for a fulfilling relationship. Her unconscious concern was that she tended to completely emotionally immerse herself in any romantic relationship, and this often led to jealous and obsessive behavior. As she explored her dream, she created naming, reflecting, and expanding questions.

Her naming questions included "When do I feel most relaxed and comfortable about immersing myself in my emotions?" and "What romantic situations can leave me feeling down?"

Reflecting questions for this ocean-mattress dream were "Are there specific romantic situations that trigger my feelings of jealousy?" and "How can I take a more down-to-earth approach to my relationships?"

Expanding questions included "How can I learn to disentangle myself from romantic situations I don't want to go into any deeper?" and "Can I choose the person I want to be with rather than just drifting into relationships?"

The dreamer's action statement for this mattress and monster dream was "I will use the power of my emotions to support me so I can always feel relaxed about any feelings of romantic insecurity."

The message she was creating for herself in this dream was that she could step outside her comfort zone and enter a romantic relationship, but she would have to stay aware of her tendencies toward jealousy. By taking a more relaxed approach to the ups and downs of relationships, she established a loving and supportive intimacy with the romantic partner of her choice.

Example 10: Undiscovered Room and Model Airplane

As well as using other people to express our unspoken characteristics in dreams, we use physical locations to reflect particular situations in our waking lives. In this dream, the dreamer discovered a room in his house he had forgotten about. The room was upstairs, and he described it as being almost like an attic. The dream started off with the dreamer noticing a door and realizing a room was behind it that he had not been in for years. He was sure that the door must be locked, but as he tried the handle, the door opened easily, allowing him access to the forgotten room. A variety of objects were in the room, but the one that drew his attention was a large model airplane in the center. He walked up to the model and examined it, dusting it off as he went. As he peered through the cockpit windows, the airplane grew to life-size, and he found himself sitting inside the cockpit, looking down a long, wide runway.

Looking at The Dream Dictionary definitions, we can see that an *undiscovered room* is a "Situation where I can discover my unrealized potential by realizing I have the capacity to develop a unique talent," which connected the dreamer to a realization that he had the opportunity to develop a potentially unique talent. The various objects in the room connected him to a variety of resources that may be available to him to develop his potential, but the one that attracted him most was a large model airplane. The Dream Dictionary defines *model aircraft* as an "ability to give some shape to a plan by playing around with how it might look so I can control its progress and direction." This suggested that he had a plan for developing his potential talent. It also indicated he needed to play around with this plan for a while to see how it looked and how to progress with it in a particular direction.

As he dusted off his plans and considered ways to potentially get his project off the ground, he found himself in a full-sized *cockpit*, which The Dream Dictionary defines as a "situation where I feel in full control of a particular project and can decide the best approach to reach a successful outcome." So by dusting off his ideas and playing around with his plan, the dreamer felt he was now in a position in waking life to guide his idea toward a successful completion.

Although the room, the model airplane, and the cockpit were the connections that stood out most significantly for the dreamer, it is also interesting to look at some other connections he mentioned, such as the door to the room and the dust. The Dream Dictionary defines *door* as an "ability to access different aspects of my character so I can develop possibilities that may have seemed closed to me" and *dust* as an "Ability to look beyond superficial appearances by sweeping away misconceptions so I can take a much fresher approach."

In waking life, the dreamer had recently started to make more time for himself and was unconsciously considering how he could use that time. For a number of years, he had been considering an idea for a self-employed business he had always wanted to get off the ground. To ensure that his business venture took off successfully, he asked himself these naming, reflecting, and expanding questions.

His naming questions were "What is the unique talent I specifically want to develop?" and "What is the best approach to take so I can ensure a successful outcome?"

The dreamer's reflecting questions from this undiscovered-room dream were "What is the new possibility I need to open myself up to?" and "What will prevent me from getting my idea off the ground?"

His expanding questions were "How can I use this specific opportunity to open myself up to other opportunities?" and "Where can I use my planning skills to ensure creative success?"

The dreamer's action statement for this dream was "I am going to use my creative skills to develop a plan for success so I can use my unrealized talent in a fresh and exciting way."

By working his way through these questions and basing his plan on his action statement, the dreamer developed a successful photography business. As a young man, he had been passionately interested in photography but had put it aside so he could commit himself to a more stable and secure career. Although he had fantastic talent as a photographer, he had never made a plan to use his talent successfully as a business. His dream helped him realize that he now had the business acumen and planning skills to consistently produce value from his photographic creativity.

Example 11: Zombies and Burying a Body in the Workplace

In this dream, a young man created a dream in which he was being pursued by a gang of zombies who were threatening to turn him into a zombie unless he buried a body for them. The zombies were chasing him through his workplace, and he was desperately trying to find a place to bury, or even just hide, the body so he wouldn't turn into a zombie.

Zombie dreams tend to be more prevalent among young adults—although they can happen at all stages of life. It is not because young people spend all their time watching zombie movies or playing zombie shoot-'em-up video games, but because a zombie is how we often symbolize an "aspect of my character soullessly going through the motions in my career, and it feels like I'm wasting my unique talents." So creating a zombie in a dream connects us to a feeling that we are wasting our talents in some way in waking life. It suggested that the dreamer was involved in some form of work that felt dull and repetitive, performing tasks that could routinely drain his energy.

Buried body is defined in The Dream Dictionary as an "opportunity to reveal some of my hidden creative talents so I can use my self-motivation and energy to bring them to life." This indicated that the dreamer had the opportunity to explore some creative talents he tended to conceal from the people around him. Instead of using his self-motivation and energy to bring them to life, he ended up soullessly going through the motions in repetitive tasks to keep everyone else happy. Creating a workplace in our dreams connects us to a "situation where I can experience particularly valuable aspects of my character and how they support my fundamental purpose." The dreamer felt frustrated by a situation where there was seemingly no opportunity to use his creative talents to work toward his fundamental purpose in life.

In waking life, the dreamer felt he was surrounded by other people who were also soullessly going through the motions, and he did not want to become like them. In his dream, he created a deeper awareness of how he could use his individual talents to make a difference. As he worked his way through this dream, he created naming, reflecting, and expanding questions.

His naming questions were "Where do I feel I am just soullessly going through the motions in the work I do?" and "How can I use my self-motivation and energy to bring my talents to life?"

Reflecting questions from this zombie dream were "How can I openly display my unique talents to the people around me?" and "Where can I have the courage to make my own decisions rather than trying to fit in with other people all the time?"

Expanding questions included "How can I develop my unique talents so I can make a living from them?" and "Where can I encourage other people to develop their individual abilities?"

The dreamer's action statement for this dream was "I am going to use my unique talents in a way that motivates me, even though it involves stepping outside the apparent security of a dull routine."

When he created this dream, the dreamer was working in a call center. He had taken the job as a way of earning income until he could find his ideal job as a web designer and developer. The demands of the call center job, however, left him exhausted and with very little free time to pursue his career ambitions in waking life. His questions and action statement from this dream encouraged him to leave the call center job and take a junior position at a web-design agency. He realized this was not his dream job at the moment but that he would attain his ambition within a couple of years.

Example 12: Childhood Home and Rediscovering Your Identity

Although the situations we create in our dreams often reflect what is currently happening in our waking lives, we use imagery from all our life experiences to express what we are feeling. A dreamer who had recently left a long and quite joyless marriage created a series of dreams in which she was back in her childhood home, where she was busily and joyfully exploring it. The house was exactly as she remembered it from her childhood, and she spent lots of time looking in cupboards and playing with her favorite toys.

In The Dream Dictionary, *childhood home* symbolizes the dreamer's connection to an "opportunity to rediscover fundamentally characteristic qualities of my identity so I can develop their true potential." The house is the classic symbol of the self; houses have insides and outsides, and we have inner and outer selves. Returning to a childhood house indicated that the dreamer was going back to the true source of her identity. In waking life, the dreamer was beginning to experience much more freedom than she had known for a long while. Her ex-husband had turned out to be very difficult to live with, and she always felt she had to "be" a certain way that suited him rather than having the opportunity to be herself and make her own decisions.

Exploring the different rooms in her childhood house reflected her rediscovery of different aspects of her character in waking life. The rooms in a house represent the different aspects of your character, and the rooms you visit in the house can often reflect what you are seeking in your waking life at the moment. For example, if you create a dream where you are in the basement of your childhood house even though your childhood home did not have a basement. The Dream Dictionary says that a *basement* connects us to an "aspect of myself that forms the foundations of who I really am and provides support for all the different parts of my character."

As she continued her process of rediscovering her true identity and all the different aspects of her character, the dreamer asked herself some naming, reflecting, and expanding questions.

Her naming questions were "What are the aspects of my character that make me happiest?" and "How can I bring some of my childhood ambitions into waking reality?"

Reflecting questions from this childhood-home dream were "When do I conceal my real needs so I am accepted by the people around me?" and "Are there some aspects of my childhood I should move on from?"

Her expanding questions included "What other memories can I explore to help me understand who I really am?" and "What would it feel like to visit my childhood home in reality?"

The dreamer was keen to continue outside her comfort zone and make the most of her newfound freedom, which was reflected in her action statement: "I am going to make the most of my true potential by always holding a clear and joyful awareness of who I really am."

Example 13: Being Unable to Find a Toilet

Being unable to find a toilet is the third most common dream and has a wide variety of different scenarios involved in it. It tends to be created more prevalently by dreamers who spend most of the time looking after the needs of other people rather than attending to their own needs, such as people who work in the caregiving professions.

A nurse who worked in a busy city hospital frequently created dreams involving toilets, particularly a situation where she couldn't find a toilet. *Can't find toilet* is defined in The Dream Dictionary as an "opportunity to identify my individual needs instead of thinking that I constantly have to respond to other people's needs," and *toilet* is described as a "situation where I can attend to my needs by choosing to let go of the thoughts and feelings that are no longer healthy for me."

At first the nurse decided that the only reason she was dreaming about needing the toilet was that she actually needed the toilet and should get out of bed and attend to her bodily needs. She then realized that the toilets she was trying to reach in her dreams were nothing like the toilet she was trying to get to in waking reality. This reflects that we merely use physical sensations as a way of triggering thoughts and feelings about some unresolved aspects of our waking lives. Even though we can control these physical needs in a healthy way, we use our awareness of them as a way of resolving feelings of embarrassment and vulnerability in our day-to-day lives.

The toilets that the nurse created in her dream were very different from any toilets she was familiar with in waking life. The toilets were situated in shopping centers, and in unfamiliar houses and were often flooded, with leaking walls. Sometimes they didn't have walls or they were very cramped and messy. As she considered the various toilets she created in her dreams, the nurse asked herself some naming, reflecting, and expanding questions.

Her naming questions were "What are the unhealthy thoughts and feelings I should let go of?" and "What is my most pressing individual need?"

Reflecting questions for these toilet dreams were "When can I make other people more aware of my needs?" and "How can I proudly ask for help instead of always feeling guilty about it?"

Her expanding questions included "How can I build some solid emotional boundaries?" and "How can I be more aware of the different demands of personal and professional space?"

The nurse's action statement for this dream was "I will ensure I have the private space to work through whatever emerges emotionally for me so I can let go of thoughts and feelings that are no longer healthy for me."

As she worked her way through her questions and action statement, the nurse became far more aware of how easy it had been for her to become too emotionally involved in her day-to-day professional life. By setting specific emotional boundaries and by taking better care of her own needs, the nurse found that she could take even better care of her patients.

Example 14: Missing a Train

Dreams are the language of the imagination, and it can be easy to take your dreams too literally and lose awareness of a more powerful message you are expressing. For example, a software developer regularly created a dream in which he missed his morning train to work. Although he assumed this recurring dream reflected his anxiety about missing his train in waking life, he was very punctual and always caught the train on time. Instead of his literal approach, a more imaginal approach connected him to a far more valuable awareness.

When we look up *missing a train* in The Dream Dictionary, we see it indicates an "opportunity to embark on a particular professional path instead of trying to decide where I want my career to go." We can also look at *being late*, an "opportunity to immediately commit myself to taking decisive action rather than always hesitating and using my time ineffectively," and *train*, which is an "ability to follow a set of guidelines that motivates me to progress toward my objective along a particular professional path." The deeper awareness the dreamer was creating in his dream suggested that he was not too concerned about missing his train in day-to-day reality. He did, however, have some concerns that he was spending a lot of time reflecting on where he would like his career to go rather than actually embarking on a particular professional path. Exploring his recurring missing-a-train dream, the dreamer used naming, reflecting, and expanding questions.

His naming questions were "When will I actually embark on the particular professional path I want to follow?" and "What is the first decisive action I will take?"

Reflecting questions from the train dream were "Am I letting other people make my career choices for me?" and "Do I have to follow this particular career path to get to where I want to go in my life?"

His expanding question included "Is this the career path I want to follow?" and "Should I learn other skills that will make me more valuable to potential employers?" This wider awareness also allowed him to understand his feelings of frustration that his career was not progressing as quickly and predictably as he originally hoped it might. He was using his anxieties about missing a train in waking life as a way of symbolically connecting to a deeper concern about the career direction he wanted to take.

The dreamer's action statement from this missing-a-train dream was "I am going to set out a career timetable and actively monitor my progress as I take decisive action to make it happen."

Rather than taking a tactical approach to how he organized his life, the dreamer made strategic plans so he could identify and fulfill his long-term ambitions. Although The Dream Connection Process may initially seem to be a one-way procedure, it actually works both ways. By becoming aware that his missing-a-train dream is actually about his career frustrations, the dreamer consciously started to do something about his career progression in waking life, which got it back on track and running much more smoothly. As he did this, he stopped having dreams about missing his train.

Example 15: Airplane Crashes and Premonition Dreams

Working too literally with dream imagery can result in situations in which the dreamer feels that he or she had some form of a premonition. This is often the case with airplane-crash dreams. Dreams involving crashing airplanes are very common, but actual airplane crashes in waking reality are, thankfully, quite rare. Dreaming of an airplane crash does not mean it is about to happen in reality. Rather than looking at the dream from a literal point of view, we need to understand what an airplane connects us to in our imaginations. Symbolically, the sky connects us to a wider awareness of our loftier plans and ideas. An airplane is a vehicle that navigates us through this space.

In The Dream Dictionary, *airplane* is defined as an "ability to come up with a powerful and practical plan and then get it off the ground so I can achieve my highest ambitions," and *crash* is an "opportunity to take control of a developing situation so I can choose the outcome instead of letting it all fall apart around me." Symbolically, an airplane crash is the opportunity to regain control of a powerful plan so it can be guided in a particular direction and then landed safely in a more grounded manner.

It may be that you are on the airplane in the dream and that this shows more involvement with a particular project. This dream can also often involve witnessing an airplane crash—usually seeing it crash-landing in some way. In The Dream Dictionary, we read that *crash landing* is an "opportunity to successfully complete a complex plan by taking decisive control so I can use a more down-to-earth approach." Again, this is about remaining in control of a plan rather than allowing it to spiral out of control.

It is also very common to create survivors in an airplane-crash dream who somehow manage to miraculously make their way out of the wreckage and walk away from it. Creating *crash survivors* in your dream is how you can become more familiar with an "aspect of my character that can draw on my resourcefulness to achieve my chosen outcome rather than worrying about my security."

An entrepreneur who worked with a several businesses over a number of widespread geographic locations created a recurring series of airplane-crash dreams. He spent a lot of his time traveling by air and became increasingly anxious about these dreams he was creating. Rather than worrying about the extremely rare likelihood of being involved in some form of airborne drama, he used the images he was creating in his dreams to ask himself some naming, reflecting, and expanding questions.

His naming questions from his airplane-crash dreams were "What is the powerful plan I am trying to get off the ground?" and "What are my highest ambitions?"

Reflecting questions were "When do my plans feel completely out of control?" and "Is my indecisiveness causing me anxiety about a particular project?"

Expanding questions included "Would I rather feel secure all the time than being a high achiever?" and "Should I be more rigorous in my planning process before I put it into action?"

After he worked through these questions, some surprising answers emerged for the entrepreneur, specifically concerning a particular project he had high hopes for. He had hoped this project would more or less look after itself, but he realized that it was seriously underresourced and was in constant danger of coming to an untimely end. As a result, his action statement for the dream imagery he had been creating was "I will take decisive control of this specific project by taking a much more hands-on approach so I can ensure a successful outcome."

By using the insight from the dreams he had been creating, the entrepreneur took practical action to ensure the success of one of his business ventures rather than causing himself constant anxiety about an event that would never happen.

Example 16: Children in Jeopardy and Neglected Plans

Dreaming of children in jeopardy is another type of dream whose imagery can be quite easy to work with in too literal a manner. A stylist created a series of recurring dreams in which two of her three children were in some sort of danger. The hazards facing the children evolved from dream to dream, from being abandoned in a dangerous place to being jeopardized in some horrible event. The dreamer found the dreams she was creating to be particularly distressing because looking after her children's security and happiness was her number-one priority in life. Although these could be very upsetting dreams, they had nothing to do with the safety of her children's waking lives.

When we look at The Dream Dictionary definitions, we see that *children* are defined as "aspects of my character that embody a variety of my special talents that have the potential to be developed even further," while *jeopardy* means an "opportunity to boldly play around with an uncertain outcome rather than feeling as if I am in danger of risking everything." This suggests the dreamer has special talents that have huge potential, but she has ignored developing them further because she is uncertain of the possible outcomes.

Two of her three children being involved indicate that she has taken the risk to develop one potential talent and feels happy with it, but there are at least another two she can work with and develop further. By realizing she is in danger of losing this chance to express these talents, the dreamer is drawing her attention to the opportunity of playing around with them and seeing how she can develop them. In waking life the dreamer had hoped that these other ideas would just grow and develop, even though she devoted little time and attention to them. In order to realize the value of the talents she was ignoring, the designer asked herself some naming, reflecting, and expanding questions.

Her naming questions were "Which of my talents have a huge potential to be developed further?" and "What creative situations can make me feel insecure?"

Reflecting questions from her dream were "What opportunities am I risking missing out on?" and "Who can I trust to look after my current business while I spend time developing other skills?"

Her expanding questions included "How can I test out my talents rather than hazarding a guess at the outcome?" and "How much time do I need to devote to developing my talents?"

The stylist's action statement was "I am going to regularly step outside my comfort zone so I can continue to ensure the well-being and security of my children."

As the stylist began to explore valuable opportunities outside her comfort zone, she started to develop her natural talents for set design and art direction. These skills formed the basis of a very successful business that helped ensure her family's safety and security.

Example 17: Winning the Lottery, Finding Money, and Recurring Dreams

A dreamer frequently created a dream in which he was always winning the lottery or finding money in unusual places. He would find out about his lottery success in a number of different ways, such as watching the television and seeing his lottery numbers suddenly come up, or while out shopping he sees a big billboard flashing, confirming him as a lottery winner. As well as winning the lottery in his dreams, he would also create dreams where he found money, usually high-denomination coins, as he walked down the street. As he picked up the coins, he ended up feeling weighed down by his findings and wondering how to get all the coins home so he could make the most of them.

Since dreams are the language of the imagination, dreaming of winning the lottery very rarely means you are actually going to win the lottery in waking life. It can also be easy to dismiss a lottery-winning dream as mere wishful thinking. The dreams you create every night are far more powerful than mere fantasy and can indicate how you can achieve your hopes and aspirations in waking life. In The Dream Dictionary, *winning the lottery* is an "opportunity to treasure the huge value of my unique talents instead of hoping that others will notice them by chance," and *finding* is an "opportunity to explore unfamiliar areas so I can discover a valuable aspect of my talent I was previously unaware of." *Coin* is an "ability to receive consistent recognition for my skill in taking matters into my own hands so I can create real value."

When the dreamer created these winning-the-lottery and finding-money dreams, he was actually encouraging himself to become more aware of valuable talents he may have been ignoring. To explore what these talents might be and identify his unrecognized value, he asked himself some naming, reflecting, and expanding questions.

His naming questions were "What talents do I have that I could create much more value with?" and "How can I consistently display my talents to other people?"

Reflecting questions for his dreams of financial abundance were "Why do I often hide my talents from other people?" and "How can I take a more methodical approach to having my value fully recognized?"

His expanding questions included "How can I increase my feelings of self-worth?" and "In what unfamiliar areas can I use my undoubted talents to make a big difference?"

His action statement was "I am going to methodically increase the value of my talents and openly display them so I can consistently receive financial recognition for them."

Although the dreamer did not feel particularly creative, he had a real talent for finding and restoring vintage motorcycles. By developing this skill, he soon found himself creating a healthy income from a talent he had previously dismissed as being of no real value to him.

Example 18: Mouth Cancers, Mountain Lions, and Prodromal Dreams

As well as taking apparent premonition dreams too literally, it can also be easy to think that illnesses in dreams are an indication that the dreamer or a character in the dream is ill or about to become ill in waking life. An example of this is a young woman's dream in which she created imagery of a cancer-like growth on her mouth. Rather than worrying about her health and looking for signs of a tumor in waking life, she found it valuable to look at The Dream Dictionary definition for *oral cancer*, which is an "opportunity to speak up about an unhealthy situation so I can deal with it instead of allowing it to grow out of control." This Dream Dictionary definition comes from the definition for *mouth*, which is an "essential ability to give voice to what I am presently experiencing so I can speak up and honestly express my feelings," and *cancer*, which is an "essential opportunity to get to the source of an unhealthy situation and deal with it instead of letting it grow out of control."

This suggested that there were certain circumstances in the dreamer's waking life where she needed to speak out rather than allowing the situation to grow out of control. Using her dream imagery, she asked herself the following naming, reflecting, and expanding questions.

Her naming questions were "What is the unhealthy situation I need to speak up about?" and "Why am I letting this situation grow out of control?"

Reflecting questions from her oral cancer dream were "Is always keeping my mouth shut a healthy option?" and "Why might it be painful to speak my truth?"

Her expanding questions included "Can I communicate my feelings in another way that doesn't make me feel so sensitive?" and "What triggered this unhealthy situation in the first place?"

Her action statement was "I will identify the source of any unhealthy situations so I can speak up about them and honestly express my feelings."

In day-to-day reality, the dreamer often shared confidences with her best friend, who was not particularly good at keeping secrets. Rather than ending their long-lasting friendship, the dreamer had a heart-to-heart conversation with her friend and encouraged her to be more discreet. The dreamer also used her discretion to choose which information she would share with her friend.

Although dreams of illness do not usually indicate the dreamer is ill or will become ill, we often use our dream imagery to make ourselves more aware of emerging physical unease we are experiencing. A climber who regularly participated in climbing competitions at a professional level created a series of dreams in which while on a climbing wall he was being attacked by a mountain lion. The mountain lion kept biting him without causing him any great pain, but it resulted in a lot of discomfort in his forearms as he dreamed. When we look at The Dream Dictionary definition for *mountain lion*, we see that it reflects an "instinctive ability to display my creative talents by proudly showing how comfortable I am with the heights I have achieved," while *forearm* is defined as an "essential ability to assert my power so I can prepare myself to take action and deal with any challenges."

This climber had a dynamic and extroverted climbing style that won him many admirers during climbing competitions. Even though he could achieve the same results, or better, with a more considered approach, he enjoyed being the center of attention and liked to display his talents by proudly showing them off. He asserted his power by using his finger and forearm strength. The lion biting his forearms suggested his extroverted climbing style may have been causing him some pain and tendonitis.

Naming, reflecting, and expanding questions that emerged from this dream included the following: "How can I comfortably achieve the heights I want to?" "Do I always need to openly assert my individual power?" "How can I change my climbing style while still proudly displaying my talents?"

The climber's action statement was "I am going to develop other aspects of my climbing style so that I can continue to be admired at the highest level."

Dreams that draw the dreamer's attention to health imbalances are known as prodromal dreams. Although they can be very useful in becoming aware of unspoken tensions, dreams of specific illnesses do not usually mean the dreamer will experience that illness in waking life.

Example 19: Cats, Lions, and Evolving Dreams

In the mountain lion dream, the climber reported that his attacking animal started off as a domestic cat and became a mountain lion in subsequent dreams. This is a common experience in recurring dreams. The dreamer describes a steady development of his or her created imagery. This can be seen in the following series of dreams related by a visual artist.

In the initial dreams she created, she described how she was being attacked by a domestic cat. The cat started off by being quite playful, but soon it started to bite and dig its claws in. Although the artist tried to ignore the dream, it kept recurring, and the cat in the dream evolved into a more powerful and scarier presence.

From a domestic cat, the artist's attacker evolved into a black panther, then into a tiger, and then into a lion. In The Dream Dictionary, *cat* is an "instinctive ability to gracefully assert my independence and freedom by feeling relaxed and comfortable about myself," and *panther* is an "instinctive ability to embody my need for greater independence, even though I may have to temporarily conceal my real motivation." *Tiger* is an "instinctive ability to fiercely assert my independence so other people can see the powerful difference I can make," while *lion* is an "instinctive ability to feel relaxed and comfortable about displaying my creative talents so I can take great pride in what I do."

By creating this steady evolution in dream imagery, the dreamer was reflecting on her experiences in independently developing her artistic style in waking life. At first she used her artistic skills as a way to relax and reflect on her life from an independent viewpoint. As she developed her talents, she realized the potential she had for greater independence but felt she had to conceal her long-term plans. This led to a situation in which she felt it was time to show other people the results of her individual artistic skills. Initially, she had to be quite assertive so that other people would pay attention to her talents. As she began to receive consistent praise for her work, she started to feel more relaxed about her talents and became proud of what she had accomplished.

At each stage in this evolving feline dream, the artist asked herself naming, reflecting, and expanding questions that helped her get to the next stage in developing her artistic talents. She also created an artistic action statement: "I will proudly develop my artistic talent so I can gracefully assert my independence and freedom."

Example 20: Battlements, Parapets, Fortresses, and Exploring the Dream Further

As well as unconsciously developing a series of evolving dreams, you can also consciously explore your dream imagery to become more aware of previously unseen possibilities in your waking life. This takes The Dream Connection Process a stage further and can open up a wider awareness that may not be immediately apparent in the dream, enabling you to play around with a variety of potential outcomes.

This was a valuable approach for a human resources director who frequently created a dream in which she was standing on the battlements of a castle wall. Even though she felt it was wise to keep herself concealed, she continually found herself peeking out from behind the battlements and looking out into the distance, where she could see an advancing enemy horde. She had previously attempted to work with this dream in waking life by taking it to a past-life expert, hoping that she could find resolution. The only insight the regression expert could offer her, however, was that she had been involved in a conflict in a past life and needed to make amends for it now. Although this interpretation intrigued the dreamer, she had no way of putting that viewpoint into practice.

Using The Dream Connection Process, we can simply look up the definition for *battlement*, which is a "situation in which I can resolve some inner conflicts by powerfully defending my beliefs against any criticism from others." The next stage could be to look up the definition for *horde*. Instead, we are going to use The Dream Connection Process in a different way and look up definitions for structures and objects associated with battlements, such as parapets, fortresses, and castles. For example, a *parapet* is an "ability to defend my beliefs by powerfully standing up for them rather than feeling I have to keep my head down"; *fortress* is a "situation in which I bring my practical strengths and abilities together so I can defend myself against any apparent threats"; and *castle* is a "situation in which I feel at home with my more powerful characteristics and am able to defend my beliefs against any criticism."

In day-to-day life, these associated dream images were reflected in the language the dreamer used about her workplace, such as "just keeping my head down," "trying to raise my head above the parapet," and "firing off e-mails." By connecting these associated dream connections with the emotional imagery the dreamer used in day-to-day reality, she could begin to ask some questions about what practical actions she might need to take.

In waking life, the dreamer had introduced a number of transformational initiatives that had positive and healthy effects. In recognition of her success with these initiatives, she had been promoted into a group position and faced the task of working with a much larger group of people, some of whom were apparently hostile to her methods. Although she appeared outwardly confident, she felt completely embattled at an emotional level. The dreamer now viewed every interaction with colleagues as a potential battle where she had to forcefully defend her position.

At this point, the naming and reflecting questions she asked herself included "How can I consistently defend my beliefs against the criticisms of other people?" and "Should I be more open to input from other people rather than constantly seeing it as criticism?"

The dreamer decided to implement the expanding question "Can I move beyond the situation by stepping outside my specific viewpoint?" by actively visualizing how she would feel if she changed some of the imagery in the dream and in her waking-life language. She started off by imagining she was no longer up on the battlements preparing for inevitable conflict but was instead down at the main gate of the castle in anticipation of welcoming the advancing horde and discovering its collective intentions. The dreamer also visualized standing at the castle gate with her hand on the lever of the operating mechanism, knowing that she could drop the portcullis at any time. Finally, she imagined standing in the meadows beyond the castle, looking up at the castle walls, and considering how she might accommodate a number of different beliefs. By envisioning these different possibilities, the dreamer created a wider awareness of how she saw her position in the workplace and also provided a perspective on how other people might be viewing her apparent defensiveness.

She then decided to explore the *horde* imagery she had been creating, using The Dream Dictionary definition: "Aspects of my character that can powerfully combine to make a strong, concerted effort to push through to my objective."

As she imagined herself in various situations that may have led to battles, she realized that her single-mindedness in pursuing particular objectives had led her to ignore the unspoken needs of some of her colleagues, which seemed to make her colleagues appear hostile and defensive, in turn leading her to respond in a hostile and defensive manner toward them. The dreamer then started an initiative to listen to the needs of her colleagues rather than continually trying to defend herself against their apparent criticisms, resulting in increased levels of mutual trust in her team.

Example 21: Lost in a Forest and Mythical Dreams

By going beyond how we relate the images we create in our dreams to the language we use to express ourselves in waking life, we can also see evidence of how we relate our waking reality to our dreams. The fundamental imagery from our dreams has long been used as a basis for the stories we tell each other in waking life, particularly in our fairy tales, myths, and legends.

A common folktale involves the hero or heroine being lost in a deep forest. In this type of tale the hero or heroine is trying to find the way out of the forest, but it is quite an unsettling place with lots of frustrating dead-ends and mysterious rustlings all around. This forest folktale was reflected in the dreams of an officer who had recently left the armed forces. He frequently dreamed he was making his way through a deep, dark forest toward a clearing he knew was out there somewhere. No matter how much effort he spent trying to find the clearing, he felt as if he were becoming more and more lost.

The officer's initial response to the dream was to declare, "I know exactly what this dream is about. It just means that I can't see the forest for the trees." Although this seemed like a simple and straightforward solution, it did not help him to ask any questions or state any actions he needed to take. Instead, by looking up The Dream Dictionary definition for *lost in a forest*, we read: "opportunity to make the most of my natural growth potential so I can clearly continue my journey of self-exploration."

Using this definition enabled the officer to ask himself some naming, reflecting, and expanding questions: "How can I make the most of my natural growth potential?" "Do I have any habits or behaviors that may be blocking my future journey?" "How can I open myself up to the resources that are all around me?"

Rather than going straight to an action statement, the officer was keen to explore the mythical aspect of being lost in a forest. Even though the forest he created in his dreams seemed bewildering, he also felt it had quite a magical quality. This awareness is often mirrored in fairy tales and folk stories, where the forest is enchanted in some way. The Dream Dictionary definition for *enchanted* is a "realization that I can use my imagination to create a powerful and practical transformation rather than delude myself." So rather than feeling that all his growth potential was exhausted, the officer began to use his boundless imagination to explore the huge variety of resources that were naturally available to him. His action statement became "I will use my powerful imagination to make the most of all the resources available to me so I can continue my heroic journey."

By seeing his dream forest as an area of rich possibility, the officer made a fulfilling transition from the structure of his military life to the wide range of opportunities available to him in civilian life. He also began to use a forest near to his home where he could go to ask himself questions about his direction in life and decide the actions he would take. At the beginning of The Dream Connection Process, his initial awareness was that he simply couldn't see the forest for the trees. After connecting his dream imagery to his waking reality, he became far more aware that a forest is where you can understand your true nature by simply being yourself.

Example 22: Unfamiliar Cities and Out-of-Body Experiences

We not only create natural dream landscapes with forests and mountains in our dreams, we also create urban environments. A dreamer who was a taxi driver in waking life reported that she frequently created a city in her dreams. It contained some characteristics of the city where she lived and worked in waking life, but it seemed as if all the buildings and streets were in different places. She often became quite frustrated in this dream city, because she would try to find her way to familiar destinations but without success. Even though the people in the streets seemed quite familiar, she felt uncomfortable asking for help.

Her husband suggested that this was an anxiety dream about not being able to do her job properly, but, like most taxi drivers, she had superb memory skills and great spatial awareness. By looking at The Dream Dictionary, she realized that an *unfamiliar city* is defined as a "situation in which I can connect with my wider social network so I can become more aware of previously unseen possibilities." The taxi driver realized that this dream was not about any professional anxieties she may have had. Instead, she was expressing an unconscious awareness that she could use all the contacts she had built up over the years as a way of exploring some new business opportunities.

Her naming, reflecting, and expanding questions for this unfamiliar city dream included: "What opportunities can my wider social network provide for me?" "How can I create some private space for myself so that I can explore some new possibilities?" "How can I access the knowledge I need to reach my intended outcome?"

The taxi driver's action statement was "I will use my accumulated knowledge and experience to go into new areas that will be very fulfilling for me." She then used this action statement to develop a business idea she had been thinking about for some time but had never done anything with.

In a further development of this unfamiliar city dream, the taxi driver was traveling in Europe and amazed to find a cityscape in waking life that seemed exactly the same as her dream city. Although she had been sure that her dream city did not exist in reality, she had become very familiar with its streets and sights after creating this dream for a number of years. As she explored the city in waking life, she could pick out recognizable features, such as specific buildings and junctions. When she shared her amazement with her husband and traveling companions, they concluded that she had been having an out-of-body experience as she slept.

Even though it seemed an easy connection to make, there was no real evidence that the taxi driver had been transporting herself in an out-of-body experience into this unfamiliar city. The processes we use to create imagery in our dreams are similar to the processes used in creating our perceptions of the real world in waking life. It can be easy to think we are experiencing some form of paranormal phenomenon, but it is much more valuable to realize that we often have far more power than we think we do in being able to transform how we experience our day-to-day reality.

Example 23: Abduction by Aliens and Visitation Dreams

The area where our imaginal processes coincide with reality can be fascinating to explore. Many apparent psychic and paranormal phenomena can be explained more objectively by viewing them from the perspective of our imaginal processes. A frequently reported experience is an alien abduction, whether as a dream or an apparently in waking reality.

A retired university professor had recently gone to live in another country and began to create a series of dreams in which he was being abducted by aliens. Alien abduction is a common dream, and it usually follows a fairly set procedure in which the dreamers are going about their normal business when they are captured by alien beings. They feel powerless to resist the aliens and are beamed up to some form of alien mothership, where they are examined and probed in various ways. After the aliens have finished their extensive examination, the abductees are given a tour of the spaceship and then beamed safely back down to Earth. Although the abduction may have been traumatic, abductees are keen to share their experiences with their circle of friends and family.

There are two main ways to look at the professor's dream experience. The first is that he actually was abducted by aliens, however unlikely that seems. The other way is to explore the imagery he created in his dream, so he can ask himself some questions that will lead to practical action. The alien abduction dream is often experienced by people who find themselves in a new environment that is quite unfamiliar to them. For example, they may have recently moved to a new job that requires them to learn new skills, or, as in the professor's situation, they have recently moved to a different country, where they are trying to become accustomed to the culture and the climate.

The Dream Dictionary definition for *alien abduction* is an "opportunity to be comfortable in my actions instead of feeling that unfamiliar circumstances are forcing me to behave differently." The definition for *alien* is an "aspect of my character that seems quite foreign to me but gives me the power to connect with a bigger presence than myself."

The reality of the professor's change of lifestyle was causing him to behave differently, so he often didn't feel as if he could be himself; therefore, he experienced a sense of alienation in his new surroundings. This usually made him feel powerless to resist the demands of his new environment, and he constantly felt challenged that other people seemed to be examining him about where he had come from and probing him for personal information. After the professor had established some relationships with those around him and began to feel more comfortable, he turned his awareness to investigating his new environment. As he became more familiar with it, he also became happier with his choices and started to feel as if he were at home again.

The professor's naming, reflecting, and expanding questions included the following: "What do I specifically feel I am being forced to do differently in my new environment?" "How can I familiarize myself with some of the possibilities for stepping outside my comfort zone?" "Which aspect of my character actually inspired me to make this transformation, and how can I use it to enjoy my exciting new life?"

The professor's action statement was "I will purposefully step into situations that may initially feel uncomfortable so I can continue to develop a much wider awareness of global culture."

Even before aliens and alien visitations became popular in cultural folklore, people created dreams in which they were abducted by strange beings. These mythical abductors included demons, phantoms, fairies, and other mythical creatures. The German word for nightmare is *albtraum*, meaning "elf dream," in which the dreamer is abducted by elves rather than the more contemporary aliens experienced by the retired professor.

Example 24: Vague Images and Feelings

So far in these examples of The Dream Connection Process, we have been using specific symbols and correspondingly specific definitions. There can be occasions, however, when you don't have any clear symbols to work with. It may be that you wake up suddenly, or your dream faded away quickly and you can't quite remember the imagery you were creating. As well as being a process of effortless image creation, dreaming can also be an intensely emotional experience.

If you have created a dream experience in which you can't recall the imagery but you continue to experience the emotions you felt during the dream, then you can still use The Dream Dictionary definitions to explore what may be happening in your unconscious self.

In this example, an established and acclaimed actress frequently woke up with a vague feeling of being threatened. She lived in a comfortable and safe environment, repeatedly asserting that she had absolutely no reason to feel threatened in any way. Looking at The Dream Dictionary, we can see that *vague* means a "realization that I can produce a definite outcome by having a clearer understanding of what I want to achieve." The first opportunity for the actress was to spend some time reflecting on what she wanted to accomplish in a particular situation so she could achieve a clear understanding of the actions she needed to take.

The Dream Dictionary definition for *threat* is an "ability to make the most of an approaching opportunity instead of habitually feeling that the future is filled with danger." This suggested that the actress had become quite comfortable with particular ways of working in her professional life and was feeling quite challenged about trying anything new.

Her naming, reflecting, and expanding questions included "What is the definite outcome I want to achieve?", "How can I invite more uncertainty into my life?", and "Where can I use my knowledge, experience, and talents in new roles?"

The action statement she created was "I need to spend some time getting a much clearer idea of what I want to achieve so I can make the most of any opportunities rather than feeling anxious about doing something new."

Example 25: Imagery and Emotions

You create your dream imagery as a way of making sense of all the experiences you unconsciously absorb in day-to-day reality. The most powerful way to put your dream meanings into significant action is to use the imagery you create in your dreams and apply it in waking life. Dreaming can be an intensely emotional experience, and as you create your dream imagery, you also reexperience all the emotions you associate with it. The experiences you most frequently relive in your dreams are those emotional aspects that can be challenging to make rational sense of in day-to-day life.

There are two main ways you can use The Dream Dictionary definitions for the emotional experiences you create in your dreams and in waking life. The first way is to simply look up the emotion you have been experiencing, use the definition to connect to a deeper understanding of your situation, and realize your opportunities for taking action. For example, if you wake up from a dream and experience a lingering feeling of fear, the connection The Dream Dictionary provides is an "opportunity to courageously step into my true identity so I can use my power to make a bold and transformative choice."

Naming, reflecting, and expanding questions from this connection might include: "What is the choice I really need to make?" "Why do I feel frustrated by having to show up to other people in a particular way?" "What other opportunities will open up for me as I begin to take individual action?"

An action statement could be "I am going to make a specific choice so I can become the person I want to be." This connection is a call to action that encourages you to assert who you really are rather than feeling that you always have to show yourself in a way that pleases other people. As soon as you take assertive action, you will begin to boldly transform your situation.

The other main way to use the definitions for emotions in The Dream Dictionary is to help you understand the emotional imagery you create in waking life. Using the same inside-out approach that shows how dream imagery is reflected in our everyday language, you can work with the images expressed in idioms and metaphors. When we openly express an emotion in waking life, we usually declare it in the form of an idiomatic image. For example, if someone is feeling angry, they very rarely say "I am angry." They may say "I am quite angry," but that's not true anger; it's more a statement of disappointment.

When a person wants to express his anger, he usually unconsciously uses language imagery to increase the emotional impact and intensity. For example, rather than saying "I am angry," people are more likely to use verbal imagery such as "I am boiling with anger" or "She stormed out in anger" or "He unleashed his anger." In these examples, anger is not just a rational statement, it has become a hot fluid, an unpredictable force, or an uncontrollable animal. Using language in this way is not a simple overdramatization of the situation; it is a way of creating imagery to express how we feel. We even try to communicate what we are feeling in the brief messages we communicate to each other in e-mails, texts, and instant messages by using emoticons. A picture is worth a thousand words.

Let's look at an example of how to use emotional imagery from your waking life as a way of putting your dreams into action. Imagine finding yourself saying to a close friend, "When he does that, I just want to erupt in anger!" The image you are unconsciously expressing is a volcano with fiery and potentially destructive passions bubbling just under the surface. Your anger is also an elemental force in this image, and you may not be able to contain it for much longer. Rather than continuing to seethe, you can look up The Dream Dictionary definition for *volcanic eruption*, which is an "opportunity to release pent-up emotions I've been keeping below the surface so I can positively channel my energy." So instead of waiting for someone else to trigger your behavior, you can look at other ways to use your energy to achieve your chosen outcome.

Naming, reflecting, and expanding questions from this connection could include the following: "What are the pent-up emotions I am keeping below the surface?" "What would make me feel more relaxed and self-assured?" "Why am I always trying to move mountains for other people?"

An action statement might be "I will positively channel my energy by specifically describing what I am feeling."

Although uncontrolled anger is often regarded as a destructive emotion, being able to work in a healthy way with your feelings of anger is a sign of a strong sense of self-identity. Understanding your angry emotions helps you to identify who you truly are rather than feeling that you always have to please other people in some way. If you suppress your anger just to apparently keep other people happy, it will result in your feeling frustrated and unable to take any action. When you can connect in a healthy way with your anger, you give life to your individuality, and your relationships become far more open, honest, and gentle. If you avoid your anger and try to ignore it, it can be unconsciously triggered and may burst out unexpectedly at the most inopportune moments.

As well as using The Dream Dictionary definition for a volcanic eruption, you can also look up what the emotion of anger connects you to, which is an "essential opportunity to assert my true identity and declare my real needs rather than always trying to please other people."

Naming, reflecting, and expanding questions from this connection could include the following: "What is it that I really need?" "When do I stop myself from taking meaningful action?" "How can I openly express my needs to other people?"

An action statement might be "I will declare one of my specific needs to another person instead of always trying to keep her happy."

Summary

These dream examples demonstrate how you can use the definitions in The Dream Dictionary to understand why you are creating particular dreams and how you can use the information you are unconsciously expressing to help you realize your ambitions in waking reality.

The definitions in The Dream Dictionary are not absolutes. They are intended to connect you to possibilities beyond yourself so that you have the opportunity to express the value of who you are. As you look through The Dream Dictionary definitions, you will gain a much clearer idea about the specific meaning to you in your current circumstances and how you can use these connections in a positive and healthy manner. The Dream Connection Process defines meaning, enables you to question your situation, and creates a statement to get you into action. These are the three steps:

1. Define what the image you have created means to you.
2. Ask yourself naming, reflecting, and expanding questions to explore new opportunities.
3. Create a specific action statement so you can transform your ambitions into reality.

By using The Dream Connection Process, you can quickly understand what the imagery you create in your dreams means to you. When you work from the realization that "a dream is just a dream until you put it into action," the question then becomes "How can I put my dream meanings into meaningful action?"

Your dreams are more than a series of unconscious images you somehow create. The definitions in The Dream Dictionary reflect all the opportunities, abilities, and realizations you are unconsciously aware of in day-to-day life. By working with the unconscious imagery you create, you realize that your dreams are more than distant wishes that will never be fulfilled. Your dreams are in the spaces all around you.

THE

DREAM

D·I·C·T·I·O·N·A·R·Y

Aardvark Instinctive ability to reveal a deeper understanding of my purpose by persistently delving into the vital aspects of my plans.

Abacus Ability to count on some of my old-fashioned talents so I can piece the facts together and calculate the eventual outcome.

Abalone Instinctive ability to protect the creative beauty of my inner life by presenting an invulnerable outer image to the world.

Abandoned Opportunity to rediscover a part of myself I have been neglecting so I can reconnect with all the potential it holds.

Abandoned baby Opportunity to reconnect with a labor of love I may have been ignoring as it requires effort to develop it further.

Abandoned child Opportunity to pay more attention to an idea close to my heart so I can lovingly develop it instead of avoiding it.

Abandoned city Situation where I have been disregarding wider social connections, even though they may hold great potential value.

Abandoned house Situation where I can become more aware of how to use my unique characteristics to resolve a challenge that has been occupying me.

Abandoned mine Situation where I can rediscover my depth of understanding about a subject area so I can fully realize its value.

Abandoned pet Opportunity to reconnect with my instinctive creativity so I can use it to rediscover one of my neglected natural talents.

Abandoned ship Situation where I can refamiliarize myself with my preferred course

of action rather than feeling I am drifting aimlessly.

Abandoned spacecraft Situation where I can use my expertise to move beyond any perceived self-limitations so I can rediscover my courage and drive.

Abattoir Situation where I can transform my creative power by decisively choosing what I value most and what I can safely dispose of.

Abbey Situation where I can reflect peacefully on the practical actions I take and how they can connect me to my spiritual self.

Abbot Aspect of my character that has the spiritual awareness to help me commit to experiences I always vowed I would have.

Abdication Opportunity to let go of some long-standing obligations rather than continually feeling that I am responsible for everything.

Abdomen Essential ability to feel really connected to my strongest core instincts, even though they sometimes make me feel vulnerable.

Abdominal pain Essential opportunity to use my gut instincts to confront an uncomfortable situation so I can satisfactorily resolve it.

Abductee Aspect of my character that feels I am being forced to act against my will rather than staying with my original choice.

Abduction Opportunity to remain in my preferred situation rather than feeling people are forcing me to act against better judgment.

Abhorrent Realization that I can make a worthy contribution to a situation rather than feeling ashamed about my ability to participate.

Ability Realization that I have the power to take decisive action and the full capacity to achieve what I set out to accomplish.

Able-bodied Essential ability to achieve my chosen outcome by using my creative instincts to powerfully direct self-motivation and energy.

Abnormal Realization that I can often learn more by moving away from my normal experiences and stepping into the unknown and unfamiliar.

Abode Situation where I can address all the different aspects of my inner life by relaxing and staying well within my comfort zone.

Abolish Opportunity to put an end to behavioral patterns that no longer serve me so I can choose a more positive way forward.

Abominable snowman Aspect of my character that feels very much at home in exploring a range of remote possibilities and their various ups and downs.

Aboriginal Aspect of my character that understands where I'm coming from and embodies my unique vitality and ingenuity.

Abortion Opportunity to terminate a concept I have been developing, even though it may seem unnecessarily painful and messy.

Above Realization that I can heighten my levels of awareness more than I think and can use them to gain an elevated perspective.

Abrasive Ability to shape an outcome in exactly the way I want rather than feeling that I am rubbing other people the wrong way.

Abroad Situation where I can explore a wide variety of new opportunities, even though these may initially seem quite foreign to me.

Abrupt Realization that I can continue in a calm and considered manner rather than feeling that I may have to suddenly break off.

Abscess Essential opportunity to quickly resolve unexpressed anger about an unhealthy situation instead of letting it fester.

Absent Opportunity to attend to a vital aspect of myself by staying present and engaging with some of my unspoken needs.

Absinthe Potential to fulfil an emotional need by satisfying my thirst for experience, even though it may be clouding my judgment.

Absolute zero Ability to understand how to successfully increase my levels of excitement rather than feeling I have no energy.

Absorb Opportunity to soak up any tension by using my empathy to understand the feelings that people are having difficulty expressing.

Abstinence Opportunity to fulfill my deepest desires by taking time to stand back so I can truly understand my fundamental needs.

Abstract Realization that I understand the fundamental practicalities and can take definite action rather than just being theoretical.

Absurd Realization that I can use my unique viewpoint to make sense of a situation instead of dismissing it as being nonsensical.

Abundance Opportunity to use my accumulated achievements to bring a situation to fruition and ensure I have my pick of the choices.

Abuse Opportunity to do the right thing by stepping into the real power of my own self-worth and taking ownership of my true value.

Abysmal Realization that I can make a hugely positive change by having a deeper understanding of the most profound aspects of myself.

Abyss Situation where I can go deeper in my exploration for a profound experience, even though the process may seem endless.

Academy Situation where I can become aware of what makes my talents so special by understanding the unique skills of others.

A cappella Realization that I can give voice to how I feel by understanding my beliefs rather than holding any accompanying prejudices.

A

A

Accelerant Ability to fuel a vital transformation to heighten my developing creativity instead of leaving me feeling burned out.

Accelerate Ability to speed up my plans' progression by increasing my drive and rapidly stepping up my level of commitment.

Accelerator Ability to fully step into my own power and drive my ambitions forward, even though it may involve putting my foot down.

Accent Essential opportunity to understand where others are coming from by listening for what they emphasize most.

Accept Opportunity to own my individual gifts rather than always feeling there is nothing I can do to change the situation.

Acceptance speech Opportunity to come to terms with a possible outcome by sharing my personal perspective and stating future intentions.

Access Opportunity to approach a challenging situation by giving myself permission to explore it rather than denying its potential.

Access code Ability to open myself up to wider possibilities by knowing which personal buttons I need to press to make me feel secure.

Accessorized Ability to present my self-image to the people around me by knowing what I need to include and what I can happily leave out.

Accessory Ability to offer my support to a situation that is of great significance to me rather than feeling I have nothing to add.

Access road Situation where I can smoothly join a recognized route to quickly achieve my ambitions and reach my objective.

Accident Opportunity to understand what my real intentions are so I can use any unexpected outcome as a potential possibility.

Accidental fire Opportunity to make the most of the spontaneously creative possibilities without allowing them to become an all-consuming passion.

Accidentally Realization that seemingly random events occur because I have unconsciously created the conditions for them.

Accident and emergency Situation where I can immediately take decisive action to resolve an uncomfortable feeling before it becomes too painful for me.

Accident black spot Situation where I can investigate different ways of achieving my ambitions rather than using a routinely hazardous method.

Accident compensation Ability to understand the value of creating a definite outcome rather than attempting to accommodate unforeseen eventualities.

Accident damage Ability to take action so I can improve a deteriorating situation rather than feeling an unwelcome outcome is inevitable.

Accident enquiry Opportunity to unquestioningly make the most of my unrealized abilities rather than always leaving my success to chance.

Accident investigation Opportunity to explore my self-motivation and examine my habits so I can consistently develop my individual potential.

Accident prone Realization that I can routinely avoid unexpected outcomes by ensuring I always stay close to practical considerations.

Acclimatized Opportunity to adapt to the prevailing mood, even though some of the thoughts and feelings may initially seem quite foreign to me.

Accolade Opportunity to acknowledge my achievements and be proud of them instead of always having to look to other people for praise.

Accommodation Situation where I can be more open to the beliefs of other people so I can explore their particular outlook over time.

Accompanied Opportunity to go along

with a particular action and follow a line of thinking rather than abandoning my interest.

Accomplice Aspect of my character that has the courage of my convictions rather than just feeling I am a complacent partner in crime.

Accomplish Opportunity to reach my objective and successfully reach a conclusion rather than giving up and going nowhere.

Accordion Ability to take my instinctive creativity squarely in both hands and know the right buttons to press to make myself heard.

Accountant Aspect of my character that objectively studies my self-worth and looks at how I can sum up my real value to others.

Accounts Ability to consider the stories I share with other people and how they affect my sense of self-worth and perceived value.

Accumulation Situation where I can achieve my chosen outcome by gathering my experience rather than scattering my efforts.

Accurate Realization that I understand precisely what I need to do to reach a specific outcome instead of feeling that I am at fault.

Accusation Opportunity to accept the value of my special skills rather than always feeling guilty about using them and blaming myself.

Ace Realization that I can make the most of an opportunity to display my talents by giving myself the most preferential treatment.

Ache Essential opportunity to resolve an ongoing tension in the underlying situation by relaxing and keeping things moving.

Achievement Realization that I can accomplish my chosen outcome and successfully reach my objective by consistently refusing to admit defeat.

Acid Ability to ultimately transform a situation by making the choice to neutralize any corrosive feelings I may be holding.

Acknowledgement Opportunity to recognize what I believe and accept the true value of my talents so I can share them with others.

Acne Essential opportunity to put on a brave face and clear up any powerful emotions that may be erupting just under the surface.

Acorn Natural ability to take the small seed of an idea and develop its huge potential for growth while staying rooted in reality.

Acquaintance Aspect of my character that can help me become reacquainted with some valuable qualities I may have been ignoring.

Acquire Opportunity to own my unique abilities and experiences rather than feeling I have had to yield to the taste of others.

Acrid Instinctive awareness that helps me deal with any unpleasant thoughts rather than just leaving a bitter taste in my mouth.

Acrobat Aspect of my character that embodies the strength and skill I can use to fully coordinate my intended plan of action.

Acrobatic Ability to take a routine approach that will allow me to use my flexibility rather than turning everything upside down.

Acrophobia Essential opportunity to resolve any fears I may have about elevating myself to a much higher position of influence.

Across Realization that I can make the connection between two different points of view rather than taking sides with people.

Acrylic nails Ability to enhance the apparent strength of my choices by displaying a superficial confidence and assertiveness to others.

Acting Opportunity to express parts of my character that often remain unspoken, even though they can give me invaluable insights.

Acting out of character Opportunity to make myself more aware of a potentially valuable aspect of my identity I may not be familiar with.

Action Opportunity to identify the most meaningful choice I can make in this situation and then confidently take it.

Action replay Opportunity to take a second look at a decision I made so I can understand the best choice to make in the future.

Action stations Opportunity to ready myself for the next stage of my professional progression instead of feeling that my position is under threat.

Activist Aspect of my character that has a fundamental need to oppose conventional thinking and bring wider attention to my breakthroughs.

Activity Opportunity to reach a definite outcome by taking a specific action rather than always trying to appear busy to people.

Actor Aspect of my character that can express my unseen strength and power by being more vocal about what I want to achieve.

Actress Aspect of my character that expresses my creativity and wisdom by giving voice to how I can develop my capacity for success.

Actuator Ability to put a concept into action so I can get my plans moving and achieve a successful outcome.

Acupressure Ability to achieve a healthy outcome by making a persistent effort to stay in touch with some particularly sensitive areas.

Acupuncture Ability to use my natural energy to resolve an unhealthy situation by choosing to stick to very specific points of view.

Ad Ability to display the potential value of my abilities to a wider audience so I can understand their basic needs.

Adapter Ability to remain firmly open to possibilities by making a positive connection between two apparently contradictory opinions.

Adder Instinctive ability to feel comfortable in my own skin by knowing I can count on my talents to transform the situation.

Addict Aspect of my character that I can choose to take full control of by having a healthy regard for my apparently all-consuming needs.

Addiction Opportunity to understand my most fundamental needs and take care of them rather than being consumed by what others want.

Addition Opportunity to augment my understanding of a situation by compiling what I already know and calculating possible outcomes.

Address Situation where I can track down how I felt about being part of a particular life experience and where that left me at the time.

ADHD Essential ability to use my wide-ranging awareness to focus on a specific aspect of a potentially distracting situation.

Adhesive Ability to hold it all together and stay with it, even when a potentially sticky situation is threatening to fall apart.

Adjacent Situation where I am getting close to an understanding but am still progressing toward a more fully connected awareness.

Adjudicator Aspect of my character that judges the most effective way to resolve my inner tensions rather than letting people decide for me.

Adjuster Ability to adapt to any situation by having the capacity to make small changes rather than feeling I am always unprepared.

Admiral Aspect of my character that provides me with the emotional authority and confidence to navigate my way through complex feelings.

Admiration Opportunity to recognize that my unique talents are actually quite wonderful, even though I usually tend to ignore them.

Admission Realization that only I can grant myself permission to step into new possibilities, even though I may have to own up to my fears.

Admit Opportunity to reveal any talents I have been concealing by giving myself permission to share their value with others.

Admittance fee Ability to understand my true value so I can access new possibilities instead of always feeling excluded.

Adolescence Opportunity to make responsible choices and long-term plans so I can create a more independent life for myself.

Adolescent boy Aspect of my character that has the growing opportunity to live more independently so I can demonstrate my developing power.

Adolescent girl Aspect of my character that has the developing capacity to share my creativity and potentially conceive a more independent life.

Adopted Realization that I can happily take on some of the more familiar characteristics of other people and make them my own.

Adopting Opportunity to nurture and develop a labor of love that someone else has created so I can become more familiar with it.

Adornment Ability to attract people to my point of view by looking at ways to enhance its underlying value and make it more apparent.

Adrenaline Essential ability to influence how I respond to a situation by being more aware of what triggers my feelings of excitement.

Adrift Realization that I can choose my direction rather than allowing my prevailing mood to be dependent on how others feel.

Adulation Realization that I might be devoting excessive effort to a situation, even though it may not flatter my talents.

Adult Aspect of my character that lovingly provides me with social responsibility and emotional guidance when I feel vulnerable.

Adulterer Aspect of my character that needs to have complete faith in my abilities rather than losing confidence in my attractiveness.

Adultery Opportunity to restore my trust in my talents so I can have complete faith in my ability to share them with other people.

Adulthood Opportunity to use my maturing experience to make my own decisions and have the social confidence to responsibly honor them.

Advance Opportunity to improve my current circumstances by promoting my unique capabilities and investing effort in my future progress.

Advantage Realization that I benefit from using all the experience I have gained and can use it to turn around the situation.

Adventure Opportunity to explore the unknown and unfamiliar aspects of myself by positively motivating myself to change my outlook.

Adventure playground Situation where I can discover some of the unfamiliar aspects of my development potential by being open to a range of experiences.

Adversary Aspect of my character that can often seem quite challenging but actually encourages me to fully step into my power.

Advertisement Ability to display the potential value of my abilities to a wider audience so I can understand people's deeper needs.

Advice Opportunity to open up and honestly express my beliefs rather than relying on information provided by other people.

Advocate Aspect of my character that can promote more favorable conditions by consistently judging the right time to take action.

Adze Ability to powerfully shape my circumstances by using my skills and talents to let go of old habits that no longer serve me.

Aerial Ability to tune in to what other people are really saying so I can understand how my ideas are being received.

A

A

Aerie Situation where I can use the power and strength of some of my bigger ideas to comfortably develop some fertile new talents.

Aerobatics Opportunity to push my ideas to the limits and examine them from different angles rather than indulging in flights of fancy.

Aerobics Opportunity to stay self-motivated by exercising my options in a healthy way and understanding how they fit in with my intentions.

Aerosol Ability to stay in control of how I express myself, even when I feel under pressure in an emotionally volatile situation.

Affair Opportunity to deal with any temporary loss of confidence in my own attractiveness by restoring my complete faith in my talents.

Affair with boss Opportunity to become more powerfully aware of my ability to confidently make major decisions and then successfully act on them.

Affair with colleague Opportunity to have complete confidence in my professional skills so I can continue to develop individual abilities.

Affair with friend Opportunity to become intimately reacquainted with a unique talent so I can use it to be consistently creative.

Affectation Opportunity to own my deeper expertise instead of just trying to attract other people by pretending to be different.

Affection Opportunity to honestly show my talent for doing what I love most so I can continue to nurture my special personal skills.

Affinity Realization that I can naturally attract other people to my way of working by just always being myself and enjoying what I do.

Affirmation Opportunity to declare what I believe to be true rather than denying myself the chance to communicate my viewpoint.

Affliction Opportunity to make the most of any challenging situation by always choosing to have a consistently healthy, positive outlook.

Affluent Realization that I am fortunate in having a wealth of accumulated experience instead of thinking that I am lacking in value.

Affray Opportunity to feel more at peace with any decision I make by quickly resolving any inner conflicts I may have about it.

Aficionado Aspect of my character that devotes time to one of my great passions rather than just appearing enthusiastic about it.

Afloat Realization that I can stay on top of an emotional situation and make real progress by using my enthusiasm to buoy myself.

Afraid Realization that I have the power to make a bold and transformative choice by courageously stepping into my true identity.

After Opportunity to look into the past and reflect on what has happened so I can choose how to create my future outcomes.

Afterbirth Essential opportunity to look at the circumstances surrounding a concept I brought to life so I can use it in the future.

Afterburner Ability to get fired up about a particularly powerful idea so I can ensure it moves forward even more quickly.

Aftereffects Realization that I can produce powerful results by understanding the influence of my actions on my choice of future outcome.

Afterlife Opportunity to experience a wider awareness of my everyday self by letting go of the past and being open to a different future.

Aftermath Opportunity to choose what I would like to happen in the immediate future rather than feeling a victim of circumstances.

Afternoon Opportunity to give myself time to relax and reflect on what has been recently emerging into my conscious awareness.

Aftershave Ability to create an attractive atmosphere so I can share my memories of a special experience with the people around me.

Aftershock Opportunity to resolve deeper tensions by doing groundbreaking work that can create a surprising change in my circumstances.

After sun Ability to take a gentler and more relaxed approach instead of feeling I am exposing myself to too many creative influences.

Aftertaste Opportunity to judge the flavor of a situation so I can use my refinement and experience to create my chosen future.

Afterthought Opportunity to clearly understand what really happened so I can reflect on it without getting too emotional.

Age Opportunity to draw on my growing experience so I can take a more mature approach to my continuing development.

Age allowance Ability to demonstrate my continuing value rather than expecting others to make compromises for me time and again.

Aged face Aspect of my awareness that can reflect on my accumulated wisdom and life experience so I can understand who I am.

Age discrimination Opportunity to understand the big difference that my accumulated experience makes instead of worrying about other opinions.

Ageing Essential opportunity to take a mature approach by using accumulated wisdom and life experience to choose my outcome.

Agency Situation where I can make my own decisions and act on my choices so I can continue my progress in an organized manner.

Agenda Opportunity to choose my preferred outcome by keeping an open mind so I can individually take a series of decisive actions.

Agent Aspect of my character that can make things happen by understanding my deeper purpose and what I believe in.

Aggravated Realization that I can improve my situation by softening my approach rather than becoming too exasperated by what is happening.

Aggregate Opportunity to combine my skills and talents to create something more powerful instead of relying on one specific ability.

Aggression Essential opportunity to resolve my fear of appearing vulnerable to other people by vigorously asserting my own identity.

Aggressive animal instinctive Opportunity to powerfully assert my own creativity rather than being afraid it will make me appear weak.

Aggressive person Aspect of my character that is sometimes afraid of my strength and power instead of using them in a wise and controlled manner.

Agile Essential ability to adapt my behavior to a wide range of changing circumstances so I can make the most of any openings.

Agitated Realization that I can feel more relaxed about a volatile situation by stirring myself to move so I can take decisive action.

Agony Opportunity to confront a potentially painful situation and resolve it to my satisfaction rather than prolonging discomfort.

Agreement Ability to resolve any inner tension I may be feeling by aligning myself with my chosen decision and sticking with it.

Agricultural Ability to consistently cultivate my natural value in my field of experience in a practical and down-to-earth manner.

Agricultural animal Instinctive ability to use my natural creativity to give me the motivation and energy to produce practical results.

Aground Realization that I need to work with the ebb and flow of my feelings to navigate my way through emotional realities.

Aha Realization that I can make a breakthrough in solving a particular dilemma by opening myself up to my own special talents.

Ahead Opportunity to look into the future and decide what direction I would like to take rather than just letting events happen.

Aid Opportunity to support what I want to achieve with my life instead of allowing any unresolved anxieties to hold me back.

Aid worker Aspect of my character that can develop valuable areas of my expertise by working with a variety of remote possibilities.

Aikido Ability to use my profound spiritual awareness to confidently come to grips with any challenges in a gentle and harmonious manner.

Ailment Essential opportunity to use my natural strength so I can resolve an unhealthy situation instead of just disregarding it.

Aim Ability to focus my power very specifically toward an individual goal, even though it may seem quite distant at the moment.

Aimless Realization that I need to stay focused on a particular ambition rather than thinking I will never reach my chosen target.

Air Natural awareness that I am constantly surrounded by my ideas but only notice them when I meet with any resistance.

Air bag Ability to use my mental strength to cushion the impact of any unforeseen events so I can keep my ambitions intact.

Air bed Situation where I feel most at home and comfortable with my ideas and can take a relaxed approach to exploring my thoughts.

Airbrush Ability to clearly channel my colorful ideas about the realities of a situation instead of trying to conceal any inconsistencies.

Air conditioner Ability to stay cool in a potentially heated situation by using my energy to provide some refreshing insights and ideas.

Aircraft Ability to come up with a powerful plan and then control its progress and direction so I can achieve my highest ambitions.

Aircraft carrier Ability to explore conflicting aspects of my emotional highs and lows so I can maintain my preferred way of thinking.

Airdrop Opportunity to quickly make practical use of some ideas I have been carrying around so I can sustain my progress.

Air filter Ability to take a cleaner and more refined approach by choosing the ideas I would like to keep and those I need to let go of.

Air freshener Ability to use a new way of thinking to provide a more favorable atmosphere, even though it may seem overpowering to other people.

Air guitar Ability to come to grips with the reality of some powerful ideas instead of just appearing to go through the motions.

Airlift Opportunity to get on board with a particular way of thinking so I can make much faster progress toward my goal.

Airline food Potential to use a particular way of thinking to fulfill an ambition, even though it may not be very healthy in the long run.

Airliner Ability to choose a powerful direction so I can make collective progress on a major project with a variety of other people.

Airlock Situation where I have the space to explore some different ways of thinking so I can become more comfortable with them.

Airmail Ability to communicate my ideas in a clear and concise way, even though they may appear to be lightweight to other people.

Air pistol Ability to understand the power of my ideas so I can communicate them to others without being too forceful about it.

Airplane Ability to come up with a dynamic

concept and then successfully get it off the ground so I can achieve my highest ambitions.

Airport Situation where I can embark upon a new opportunity by getting a powerful idea off the ground and then safely landing it.

Air raid Opportunity to defend my way of thinking, even though others are constantly bombarding me with their own ideas.

Air-raid siren Opportunity to respond to a sudden challenge to my thinking by taking forceful action instead of appearing defensive.

Air rifle Ability to communicate my aims by forcefully asserting my ideas at a distance instead of hurrying through my options.

Airship Ability to contain my expansive way of thinking in a more rigid framework so I can reach a higher level of understanding.

Airtight Ability to shut out unwanted influences and ideas so I can preserve a valuable concept until I have the opportunity to use it.

Air traffic controller Aspect of my character enabling me to look beyond the immediate future and resolve any conflicting thoughts.

Airy Situation where I can be more open to the prevailing atmosphere and take advantage of current thinking and fresh ideas.

Aisle Situation where I have to walk a fine line when making a big commitment so I can ensure that I stay on the straight and narrow.

Ajar Realization that I can choose whether to open up a bit more or give myself the opportunity to reflect on the situation in private.

Alarm Ability to alert myself to a rapidly emerging realization that I will need to stay calm to take decisive action.

Alarm clock Ability to give myself a wake-up call by realizing that now is the time to plan ahead and make an important life decision.

Albatross Instinctive ability to take a powerful and far-ranging idea even further, although it may seem to weigh me down and isolate me.

Albino Ability to use my unique presence to clearly understand a situation without it being too colored by my passionate emotions.

Album Ability to stay open to the idea of accumulating more knowledge and learning so I can publicly share it with other people.

Alchemist Aspect of my character that apparently has the ability to transform something seemingly worthless into something of true value.

Alchemy Ability to apparently reveal the underlying value of a precious item by transforming it from something seemingly inconsequential.

Alcohol Ability to fulfill an emotional need that can often seem confusing rather than helping me to clearly connect with my spiritual self.

Alcoholic Aspect of my character that has a fundamental need to connect with my more spiritual self so I can achieve emotional clarity.

Alcohol poisoning Opportunity to be clear about my spiritual needs instead of indulging myself in unresolved emotions.

Alcove Aspect of myself where I can withdraw from everyday activity to concentrate attention on establishing a particular niche.

Ale Potential to fulfill an emotional need by sharing some possibly confusing feelings that have been weighing me down for some time.

Alert Realization that I need to stay fully aware, as there are some aspects of a situation I may need to urgently attend to.

Algae Natural ability to use some illuminating opportunities to immerse myself in my emotions and absorb any enriching experiences.

A

Algal bloom Natural opportunity to open up to blossoming emotions without becoming too absorbed and letting them grow out of control.

Algebra Ability to make logical sense of a situation by understanding all the relationships involved and carefully working through them.

Algorithm Ability to reach a solution to an apparently complex problem by progressing through it in a rational and objective manner.

Alias Realization that I have to reveal what I need from other people instead of just revealing myself in a way that pleases them.

Alibi Opportunity to resolve an ambiguous situation by maintaining my presence of mind rather than blaming myself for my actions.

Alien Aspect of my character that seems quite foreign to me but gives me the power to connect with a bigger presence than myself.

Alien abduction Opportunity to be comfortable in my actions instead of feeling that unfamiliar circumstances are forcing me to behave differently.

Alien encounter Opportunity to become more aware of an aspect of my character that can help me explore some intriguing new possibilities.

Alignment Realization that I can be part of something bigger by adjusting my perspectives about the direction I am planning to take.

Alike Realization that I can make a difference by understanding some of the similar viewpoints I share with other people.

Alimony Opportunity to make a commitment to maintaining my sense of self-worth and independence rather than relying on others.

Alive Opportunity to revitalize an aspect of my life that passionately interests me but which I often try to leave buried in the past.

All Realization that I can feel completely at peace by drawing on my entire life experience and using everything I know.

All-clear Opportunity to move on from a potentially threatening situation by communicating what has been transparently obvious to me.

Allegation Opportunity to prove my value to other people rather than feeling that I have to take the blame for their mistakes.

Allergy Essential opportunity to sense something unseen instead of habitually overreacting to a particularly sensitive situation.

Alley Situation where I can use an informal social connection as a way of leading to a wider understanding of where I am going.

Alligator Instinctive ability to use my power to feel at home with my emotions rather than being devoured by my all-consuming fears.

Allotment Situation where I can use some collectively agreed resources to happily cultivate my relationships and interests.

Allow Realization that I can give myself permission to take my vulnerabilities into consideration instead of denying my concerns.

Allowance Ability to share my talents so I can demonstrate their value rather than having to wait for permission from other people.

Alloy Ability to combine some of my fundamental strengths so I can specifically use them to achieve a previously unobtainable result.

All-purpose Realization that I will always be able to make the most of opportunities by knowing what my fundamental needs are.

All-terrain bike Ability to use personal ambition and drive to get a solid handle on my objectives and make good progress toward them.

Allure Realization that I can attract all the attention I need from other people by being kind rather than using idle flattery.

Alluvial Situation where I can spread out a bit more and convey the value of what I have created from using my learning and experience.

All-weather Ability to feel secure in my purpose so I can continue my progress without being distracted by the prevailing atmosphere.

Ally Aspect of my character that combines a number of my talents that mutually support each other and help me to achieve results.

All-you-can-eat Situation where I can fulfill a series of ambitions, even though they may turn out not to be particularly satisfying for me.

Almanac Ability to shape events I would like to experience in the future so I can consistently make the most of my valuable time.

Almighty Realization that I always have far more power than I think and much more actual experience than I give myself credit for.

Almond Natural ability to take the kernel of an idea and use it to provide a meaningful perspective that is potentially fruitful.

Aloft Realization that I can use my thoughts and theories to lift me higher so I can raise my overall level of understanding.

Alone Opportunity to connect to an invitation to discover myself without becoming too attached to any preconceived outcomes.

Along Realization that I can choose my own direction for my continued progress rather than having to align myself with other people.

Aloud Realization that I need to openly share an important understanding with other people so I can hear it myself.

Alphabet Ability to use the fundamental aspects of my character to communicate my talents in an infinite number of different ways.

Alpine Situation where I have a more

elevated understanding of the levels of effort required to realize my higher aspirations.

Altar Situation where I can step up to a future opportunity by letting go of the past without having to make too much of a sacrifice.

Alternative energy Natural opportunity to explore other ways of keeping myself fully motivated so I can achieve my chosen outcomes in a healthy manner.

Alternative medicine Ability to remedy an unhealthy situation by looking at different ways of resolving tensions instead of feeling ill at ease.

Altimeter Ability to clearly gauge my position on a range of ideas so I can ensure a particular project does not end unexpectedly.

Altitude Situation where I can understand the potential ups and downs involved in maintaining my current levels of awareness.

Altitude chamber Situation where I can develop my awareness of my thought processes rather than making myself dizzy at the idea of it all.

Aluminum Ability to give form to some of my fundamental ideas so I can powerfully shape their value and convey their enduring strength.

Always Realization that I can rely on my inner power and strength to constantly provide support for whatever challenges I may face.

Alzheimer's Essential opportunity to remember who I am and take appropriate action no matter how unhealthy the situation seems.

Amateur dramatics Opportunity to become much more excited and emotionally engaged in my personal story without getting too carried away by it all.

Amateurish Realization that my special talent is in doing something I love rather than making half-hearted attempts in other activities.

A

A

Amazement Realization that I should never be surprised by the strength of my capabilities, even though events may seem overwhelming.

Amazon Aspect of my character that has the strength and courage to stand up for my creativity and has the power to keep it flowing.

Ambassador Aspect of my character that tries to resolve any potential conflicts by taking a more detached viewpoint about the situation.

Amber Mood that can color my perspective by making me feel cautious about becoming stuck in old ways of working.

Ambidextrous Essential opportunity to have a firm grasp of both sides of a situation so I can use it to take action and shape my future.

Ambience Realization that I can get a much better feeling for my surroundings by understanding the prevailing thoughts and feelings.

Ambiguous Realization that the viewpoints of other people are always open to interpretation rather than just doubting my own perspectives.

Ambitious Realization that I can achieve my desired success by focusing all my effort on a specific outcome until I reach my goal.

Ambulance Ability to use my drive and ambition to immediately respond to an unhealthy situation so I can quickly deal with it.

Ambush Opportunity to reveal a surprising decision, even though it means unexpectedly engaging with some previously hidden tensions.

Amends Opportunity to resolve any unspoken tension by dealing with it directly rather than trying to compensate for it in other ways.

Amenities Situation where I can venture a bit further afield while still having the convenience of staying within my comfort zone.

Amethyst Ability to attract people to my viewpoint by displaying some crystal-clear thinking that may help prevent wider confusion.

Amidst Realization that I can feel fully involved in what I am doing and have the power to influence what is happening around me.

Amiss Realization that I have the power to make my presence felt so I can do the right thing rather than feel uncomfortable.

Ammunition Ability to accumulate potentially powerful personal information that will enable me to confidently assert my particular aims.

Amnesia Essential opportunity to forgive any imagined slights and unintended hurt so I can remember the person I really am.

Amnesty Opportunity to resolve an ongoing inner tension that has been unsettling me by forgiving people rather than blaming myself.

Amoeba Instinctive ability to take a seemingly inconsequential idea and quickly develop it by adapting it to changing circumstances.

Among Realization that I can use aspects of my inner life as a way of understanding what is happening around me in my outer life.

Amount Ability to understand the value of my accumulated wisdom and experience and reflect on the effort involved in developing them.

Amphibian Instinctive ability to feel at home where I need to immerse myself in my emotions so I can work with inspiring ideas.

Amphibious vehicle Ability to reach my goal in a practical manner by using my learning and experience to support my personal ambition.

Amphitheater Situation where I need to have the confidence to place my talents center stage and have them recognized by those around me.

Amplifier Ability to increase my awareness of what I'm trying to communicate, by ensuring that people are hearing what I'm saying.

Ampoule Ability to isolate a specific feeling so I can use it to contain my emotions as I resolve an unhealthy situation.

Amputation Essential opportunity to reconnect with my fundamental strengths rather than being afraid I will lose some personal power.

Amulet Ability to take specific action to choose the best outcome in a situation instead of just hoping it will work like a charm.

Amuse Opportunity to entertain a variety of different possibilities rather than diverting my attention from my chosen objective.

Amusement park Situation where I can happily park my ambitions while I explore different opportunities and entertain a variety of possibilities.

Anachronism Realization that I can take the action I need to right now rather than always feeling as if I am running out of time.

Anaconda Instinctive ability to use my huge potential to transform an overwhelming emotional situation that may have been restricting me.

Anal retentive Opportunity to naturally work my way through any inconsistencies instead of feeling that everything has to be perfect.

Analysis Opportunity to carefully examine the fundamental aspects of my situation so I can understand how to feel more complete.

Analyst Aspect of my character that can gain a healthier outlook by constantly looking for a more detailed understanding of my situation.

Anarchist Aspect of my character that can liberate my approach to authority by choosing to take full responsibility for my own actions.

Anatomy Essential ability to understand more about the workings of my inner life by learning about the basic structure of my beliefs.

Ancestor Aspect of my character that has developed a deep understanding of my fundamental roots without dwelling too much in the past.

Anchor Ability to stay connected to a firmer understanding of my deeper emotions rather than feeling as if I'm drifting aimlessly.

Anchorage Situation where I can feel more secure in some particular sentiments by ensuring they don't suddenly sweep me away.

Ancient Realization that I can apply my accumulated wisdom and extensive experience to a unique situation happening right now.

Ancient building Situation where I can experience an older, wiser aspect of myself that has endured the test of time and still holds meaning.

Ancient monument Situation where I can recognize the long-lasting influence of a profound experience and how it always stands out for me.

Androgynous being Aspect of my character that embodies the strength and power of my masculinity and the creativity and wisdom of my femininity.

Android Aspect of my character that can embody my true humanity rather than going through the motions to keep everyone happy.

Anecdote Ability to amuse myself and maintain some wider interest by drawing attention to my particular perspective.

Anemia Realization that I can powerfully revitalize a situation by encouraging others rather than appearing fainthearted.

A

Anemone Natural ability to open up to my more colorful ideas so I can allow them to fully blossom while staying grounded in reality.

Anesthetic Ability to deal with painful feelings I encounter by healing hurt feelings instead of just numbing myself to them.

Anesthetized Realization that I can choose to deal with hurtful feelings by resolving them in a healthy way rather than appearing unfeeling.

Aneurysm Essential opportunity to stay strong and flexible in how I channel my natural passions instead of letting them go out of control.

Angel Aspect of my character that is inspired to rise above it all by embodying my essential wisdom and sharing it with other people.

Anger Essential opportunity to assert my true identity and declare my real needs rather than always trying to please other people.

Anger management Opportunity to understand that I create my emotions and can influence them instead of routinely trying to control them.

Angle Ability to gauge how inclined I might be to become involved with a situation by considering my specific degree of commitment.

Angle-grinder Ability to shape my outlook in exactly the way I choose rather than feeling that circumstances are wearing me down.

Angler Aspect of my character that is trying to land an opportunity by getting a line on what I feel is happening below the surface.

Angling Opportunity to look at a variety of ways of connecting with an emerging possibility rather than quietly reflecting on it.

Angry Realization that I can take individual action and create a positive outcome instead of feeling resentful about other people.

Angry boss Aspect of my character that enables me to become more aware of my frustrated ambitions so that I can take decisive action on them.

Angry colleague Aspect of my character that helps me to understand my professional frustrations so I can take action to deal with them.

Angry dispute Opportunity to resolve an ongoing conflict by taking constructive action rather than just trying to keep the peace.

Angry husband Aspect of my character that enables me to maintain my strength so I can confront my fears about a challenging situation.

Angry outburst Opportunity to calmly say what I need to rather than venting my frustrations in an uncontrolled manner.

Angry parent Aspect of my character that helps me to move beyond any disappointments by giving me the authority to develop my unique potential.

Angry stranger Aspect of my character that enables me to voice some unfamiliar frustrations so I can move into exciting new opportunities.

Angry wife Aspect of my character that helps me develop the empathy and wisdom I need to challenge fears I have about the future.

Anguish Realization that I can maintain a deep inner calm about an unexpected challenge rather than becoming overly agitated about it.

Animal Instinctive ability that embodies all aspects of my creative nature and gives me the motivation to express my natural wisdom.

Animal in garden Opportunity to use my instinctive creativity in a social situation instead of feeling that I am acting unnaturally just to fit in.

Animal in house Opportunity to become more aware of the instinctive aspects of my nature so I can use them to develop my creative capacities.

Animal noise Opportunity to be clear about what I am trying to communicate rather than responding impulsively to others.

Animal teeth Instinctive ability to display my power and confidence in my creativity so I can be more assertive with my unique talents.

Animated Realization that I can bring my passions to life by taking action rather than just getting overexcited at the thought of them.

Animation Ability to bring a more colorful aspect of myself to life so I can revitalize a creative talent I may have been neglecting.

Animatronic Realization that I have independent control of my choices instead of feeling that someone else is making my decisions for me.

Animosity Realization that I can choose a kinder, more gentle approach, even though others may be antagonizing me for no reason.

Ankh Situation where I can achieve a more structured understanding of my life by simply having the presence to stand up for who I am.

Ankle Essential ability to stay connected to my deeper values by always taking a flexible approach as I move forward with my beliefs.

Annihilated Realization that I can create something of lasting importance by using inner resources rather than thinking I have nothing to offer.

Anniversary Opportunity to recognize the consistency of my creative achievements so I can celebrate my success with other people.

Announcement Opportunity to publicly express my needs by having the courage to confidently speak up so people can hear my true voice.

Announcer Aspect of my character that can express my fundamental needs by speaking up and having them heard by a wider audience.

Annoying Realization that I can make a positive change in a consistently irritating situation by behaving in a pleasant manner.

Anointed Realization that under the surface, other people feel the same way as I do, instead of believing that I am the chosen one.

Anomaly Opportunity to achieve a wider understanding by exploring different perspectives rather than conforming to expectations.

Anonymous Realization that I can name how I feel about a situation instead of thinking I am a nobody whose opinion doesn't count.

Anorak Ability to comfortably present my self-image to people in a warm, relaxed manner rather than appearing dull and nondescript.

Anorexic Essential opportunity to restore my appetite for life by giving myself the permission to indulge my need for love and affection.

Answer Opportunity to step into new possibilities so I can discover my unknown potential by questioning what I really need.

Answering machine Ability to pick up on how I habitually ignore my own needs because I feel I have to answer to the demands of others.

Ant Instinctive ability to work with the people around me so we can create an outcome that benefits us all as individuals.

Antagonist Aspect of my character that complements my natural drive rather than continually opposing my ambitions and causing problems.

Anteater Instinctive ability to fulfill a number of ambitions by delving more deeply into the specific details of my particular plans.

Antelope Instinctive ability to use my intuition so I can make a creative leap, even though I am wary of a potentially risky outcome.

Antenna Ability to pick up on something in the air that might convey vital information, rather than tuning out of conversations.

Anthem Ability to instinctively communicate a profounder feeling by collectively giving voice to a beautiful and deeply felt message.

Anthill Instinctive ability to raise my level of awareness by participating in a range of activities that will widen my perspective.

Antiaircraft gun Ability to powerfully defend myself against apparently threatening thoughts and ideas by forcefully communicating my aims.

Anti-aliasing Opportunity to smooth out any apparent inconsistencies in how I see a situation so it seems clearer and more familiar to me.

Antibacterial Ability to clearly resolve a potentially unhealthy situation by using my infectious enthusiasm to develop the germ of an idea.

Antibiotic Ability to use my natural perceptiveness to resolve an unhealthy situation rather than always resisting my instincts.

Anticipation Realization that I have the power to decide my chosen outcome rather than feeling I always have to live up to expectations.

Antics Opportunity to take meaningful action so I can step into a new future instead of feeling that I'm up to my old tricks.

Antidepressant Ability to clearly identify specific actions I can take to raise my spirits instead of continually downing outside advice.

Antidote Ability to make myself feel less ill at ease by making the decision to resolve any tensions so I can remedy an unhealthy situation.

Antigravity machine Ability to release myself from any weighty obligations by lightening up instead of relying too heavily on my forceful nature.

Antihero Aspect of my character that always chooses to do the right thing, even though I may often conceal my courage from others.

Antilock brakes Ability to stay in control of my drive and ambition by knowing just the right time to deal with any pressure that I'm feeling.

Antimatter Realization that I can make a colossal difference in my situation instead of thinking that circumstances are always against me.

Antiperspirant Ability to guard against any emotional frictions by choosing to control my feelings so that I don't show any outward anxiety.

Antique Ability to recognize the true value of my accumulated wisdom and experience so I can see how it has withstood the test of time.

Antiseptic Ability to take a healthy approach to resolving any underlying conflict so I can decisively deal with any harmful influences.

Antisocial Realization that I can find out more about my needs and beliefs by spending time with other people and finding out about theirs.

Antlers Ability to display the underlying power of my thinking and the strength of how I instinctively structure my plans and ideas.

Anus Essential ability to take control of my own needs by choosing to exert decisive control of what is no longer useful to me.

Anvil Ability to add some real weight to my point of view by providing myself with a firm basis for hammering out a definite result.

Anxiety Realization that the best way to understand what I need is to honestly share my fears and concerns with others.

Apart Realization that I can create real value by bringing some of my different skills together rather than keeping them separate.

Apartment Situation where I can retain my full independence, even though I may have to fit in with some of the needs of other people.

Apathy Realization that I can make most progress by enthusiastically sharing what my ambitions are and how they motivate me.

Ape Instinctive ability to understand my natural creativity by copying other people and then intelligently adapting their methods.

Ape-man Aspect of my character that may seem quite primitive but has the capacity to quickly adapt to a variety of circumstances.

Aperture Ability to look deeper into what really motivates me by opening up to what is actually going on rather than closing myself off.

Aphrodisiac Ability to conceive an idea by honestly engaging with a really seductive opportunity that has captured my imagination.

Apocalypse Opportunity to completely transform my life by stepping into my power instead of thinking that this is the end of everything.

Apology Opportunity to proudly assert what I need rather than leaving my personal ambitions in a neglected and sorry state.

App Ability to have a range of powerful thought processes at my fingertips so I can apply them to a variety of situations.

Apparatus Ability to produce an outcome of great practical value by bringing together a range of my skills and using them purposefully.

Apparition Aspect of my character that has the opportunity to embody a unique talent rather than just appearing to have that expertise.

Appearance Opportunity to deepen my understanding by looking beyond first impressions and seeing what is happening below the surface.

Appendix Essential ability to expand my awareness by fully digesting what I learn so I can always add to my accumulated knowledge.

Appetite Essential opportunity to achieve an ambition by understanding what type of success will make me feel most fulfilled.

Appetizer Opportunity to make a start to my anticipated success by taking in small considerations before continuing to bigger rewards.

Applause Opportunity to connect more successfully with others by displaying my talents and having them widely recognized.

Apple Natural ability to fulfill an ambition by having a healthy awareness of my own attractiveness when making a romantic choice.

Apple pie Potential to fulfill a long-term romantic ambition by sharing how I feel about someone in a wholesome, healthy way.

Appliance Ability to work more efficiently by applying myself to a specific task and ensuring that I do it to the best of my ability.

Appointment Opportunity to come to a definite realization of what I need to do so I can fully meet my hopes and aspirations.

Appraisal Opportunity to assess how satisfied I am with my progress on my own terms instead of letting others judge my performance.

Appreciation Realization that gratefully acknowledging my abilities and expertise actually increases their value in others' eyes.

Apprehensive Realization that I can resolve my anxieties by making a firm decision rather than getting caught up in my worries.

Apprentice Aspect of my character that takes the opportunity to master a specific skill and always has the openness to learn something new.

Approach Opportunity to arrive at a more valuable perspective by making a definite choice to see the situation in a different way.

Approval Opportunity to acknowledge my expertise and abilities rather than feeling I have to look to other people for recognition.

Approximate Realization that I can get much closer to what I need by not always having to do everything perfectly.

Apricot Natural ability to fulfill an ambition by using my mature wisdom and well-rounded awareness to make a potentially fruitful choice.

Apron Ability to carefully deal with a

A

potentially messy situation so I can protect the self-image I normally show to other people.

Aptitude test Opportunity to become aware of my inclinations in a challenging situation instead of feeling that other people are judging me.

Aqualung Ability to keep thinking clearly by using a rational perspective, even though I may be deeply immersed in an emotional situation.

Aquarium Situation where I am able to safely observe all the different aspects of my emotional life in a calm and detached manner.

Aqueduct Situation where I can channel my emotional support without any interruptions so I can convey the value of what I am feeling.

Arachnophobia Realization that I can release myself from an emotional entanglement by using my power to make a bold and transformative choice.

Arc Ability to rise above it all so I can connect with my all-encompassing wisdom and describe where it is eventually taking me.

Arcade Situation where I can use my expertise and playful opportunism to take a variety of chances and see how I might profit from them.

Arch Ability to be more open about stepping into a new opportunity by framing any number of well-balanced and constructive viewpoints.

Archaeologist Aspect of my character that seeks to understand my deeper needs by carefully making a sustained effort to gently uncover them.

Archaeology Ability to understand the various layers of my behaviors by digging deeper into the past and unearthing what I value.

Archaic Realizing I can use my accumulated wisdom to resolve a current tension rather than feeling it may be outdated.

Archegyre Ability to powerfully understand the fundamental aspects of who I am, what I need, and what I believe.

Archer Aspect of my character that can successfully achieve my aims by firing off a quick decision rather than seeming high-strung.

Architect Aspect of my character that creates the space for fundamentally new opportunities by artfully structuring my practical resources.

Architecture Situation where I have the space to explore some aspects of my inner self so I can understand how I structure my world.

Archive Ability to maintain the value of my learning and experience by consistently taking care to remember its true significance to me.

Archrival Aspect of my character that may seem overly competitive instead of combining my abilities so that I can be even more powerful.

Arch villain Aspect of my character with the overarching power to take my good intentions and transform them into wonderful results.

Archway Situation where I can move into a new area of expertise without being too concerned that it will all go over my head.

Arctic Situation where I can attempt to cool down a potentially emotional situation by offering clear and consistent thinking.

Area Situation where I can fully step into my own power so I can define my personal boundaries and give myself space to develop.

Arena Situation where I have the opportunity to display my expertise and have it appreciatively received by a much wider audience.

Argot Ability to evocatively express my emotions so other people will always be open to what I need to communicate to them.

Arguing Opportunity to resolve a tense situation by specifically understanding what I might be contributing to the confusion.

Argument Situation where I can understand

the value of a different perspective rather than feeling I have to defend my viewpoint.

Arid Opportunity to use my fertile imagination so I can be emotionally receptive to some views that may seem unnecessarily hostile.

Aristocrat Aspect of my character that allows me to express my more noble qualities rather than always lording it over everyone else.

Arithmetic Ability to understand what my real value is to other people instead of thinking that I am there just to make up the numbers.

Ark Ability to navigate seemingly over-whelming emotional challenges by looking after all my creative instincts and artistic urges.

Arm Essential ability to assert my individual power by confidently taking action so I can signal my intentions to other people.

Armadillo Instinctive ability to defend my creative expertise so I can dig deeper and find a sense of long-lasting fulfillment.

Armageddon Opportunity to make a transformative decision by understanding the grounds for any fundamentally opposing viewpoints.

Armband Ability to display to other people how I feel so I can confidently take action and assert my individual power.

Armchair Ability to relax in my habitually comfortable opinions when I could be standing up for a viewpoint that I believe in.

Armed Opportunity to powerfully assert my beliefs so I can feel confident in how I can exert my influence over other people.

Armed guard Aspect of my character that has the power to defend my deepest values and provides me with control of my personal boundaries.

Armed robbery Opportunity to have the value of my expertise recognized rather than allowing people to forcefully influence me.

Armor Ability to robustly defend my self-motivation and vitality instead of making myself vulnerable to the criticism of others.

Armpit Essential ability to confidently take action in an unpleasant situation, even though I may have to sweat it out until I succeed.

Arm wrestling Opportunity to have a firm basis for making a powerful personal decision by balancing two fundamentally opposing needs.

Army Aspects of my character that have the organized power to defend my basic needs and resolve my self-destructive behaviors.

Army uniform Ability to present my self-image to people in a way that displays my combination of skills and the power of my self-discipline.

Aroma Instinctive awareness that encourages me to naturally follow my nose so I can clearly identify the mood in the air.

Aromatherapist Aspect of my character that can naturally connect with my deepest instincts to apparently create a healthier atmosphere.

Arousal Opportunity to stimulate my levels of self-motivation so I can always rise to the occasion and heighten my awareness.

Arranged marriage Opportunity to make my own choices about meeting my fundamental needs instead of feeling I am being forced into a compromise.

Arrangement Situation where I can come to an understanding of what I need by examining the different aspects and how they are related.

Array Ability to organize my considerable talents in a particular way so I can use them most effectively and impressively.

Arrested Opportunity to slow down an out-of-control and fast-moving situation by reflecting on my personal responsibilities.

A

Arrival Realization that I am getting close to achieving my chosen outcome and that my imminent success will be fully acknowledged.

Arrival information Ability to gain a clearer understanding of an emerging possibility so I can use it to achieve a successful outcome.

Arrogant Realization that I need to be more confident in my own abilities instead of always exaggerating the skills of other people.

Arrow Ability to swiftly reach my target by completely understanding my long-term aims so I can get straight to the point.

Arrowhead Ability to use a particular idea to make a very specific point rather than spending time thinking about other possibilities.

Arsenal Situation where I can gain access to all the influence I have accumulated and use it to powerfully assert my beliefs.

Arson Opportunity to avoid creative burnout by recognizing my responsibilities instead of being overwhelmed by all-consuming passions.

Art Ability to instinctively express who I am and what I value so I can share my fundamental perspectives.

Artery Essential ability to channel my natural passion and vitality to where it is needed so I can keep my rich creativity flowing.

Art gallery Situation where I can openly reflect on the value of what I create so I can confidently invite people to recognize my expertise.

Arthritis Opportunity to resolve discomfort by avoiding inflammatory remarks and staying flexible in my relationships with others.

Artichoke Natural ability to fulfill an ambition in a healthy way by opening up my heart to new possibilities and committing to my future growth.

Articulated Realization that the best way to form a strong and flexible connection is to communicate exactly what I need from others.

Articulated lorry Ability be quite flexible in how I negotiate any obstacles so I can use my powerful drive to convey the value of my abilities.

Artifact Ability to remind myself of some of the individual tools and skills that I have used to help me shape my current circumstances.

Artificial Realization that I have an opportunity to use my natural talents rather than feeling I have to fake enthusiasm.

Artificial horizon Ability to have a realistic opportunity to be more down-to-earth, to my way of thinking, so I can maintain progress.

Artificial insemination Ability to take assertive action in a consistently detached manner so I can make the most of any fertile opportunities.

Artificial intelligence Realization that I have much more natural expertise than I previously thought instead of feeling I may be ignorant.

Artificial limb Ability to use my inner strength to reach out to other people so I can take the necessary steps to connect with them.

Artificial sweetener Ability to make an unpleasant situation more palatable by saying how I feel rather than trying to disguise my real emotions.

Artillery Ability to resolve a conflicting situation by displaying the power of my ideas and ensuring that their potential impact is understood.

Artist Aspect of my character that uses my natural ingenuity and creative instincts to display my fundamental life perspectives.

Artwork Ability to display how I openly express my creativity so other people can recognize its value and appreciate my efforts.

Ascending Opportunity to raise my awareness to a higher level so I can keep making positive progress toward a lofty ambition.

Ascension Situation where I can achieve greater spiritual clarity by making the effort to heighten my fundamental understanding of myself.

Ascent Realization that I can lift my spirits and elevate my understanding to a higher level by letting go of any weighty obligations.

Ascetic Aspect of my character that can choose to fully embody my creative urges rather than trying to serve an abstract ideal.

Ashamed Realization that I need to be proud of my achievements instead of feeling embarrassed about them and regretting my actions.

Ashes Ability to discard the less useful aspects of my creative process rather than raking through them to find something of value.

Ashore Situation where I can securely establish a firmer and more grounded understanding of the continual ebb and flow of my emotions.

Ashtray Ability to stub out the root cause of an unhealthy personal situation instead of remaining in an atmosphere of uncertainty.

Ash tree Natural potential for my long-term spiritual growth by sharpening my awareness so I can always reflect on my memories.

Asking Opportunity to discover my unknown potential by having the courage to question what I need and what it might involve.

Asleep Opportunity to be completely relaxed about the future so I can open my eyes to exciting new possibilities.

Asp Instinctive ability to transform how I feel about some past experiences so I can move on from potentially poisonous behaviors.

Asparagus Natural ability to fulfill an ambition by understanding the delicacy of the situation so I can commit to my healthy growth.

Aspect Realization that what I believe about a particular situation really depends on how I look at it and the attitude I take.

Asphalt Ability to use my skills to ensure a smooth journey toward my goal without getting bogged down in any rough patches.

Asphyxiate Opportunity to open up and clearly express thoughts and feelings instead of letting others continually cut me off.

Aspirational Realization that I can breathe new life into my most powerful ambitions rather than thinking they're beyond me.

Ass Instinctive ability to kick-start an opportunity by harnessing my unconscious energy, even if it involves baring my cheeky side.

Assailant Aspect of my character that needs to trust in my abilities and look after my interests rather than being so self-critical.

Assassin Aspect of my character that has chosen to try to kill off one of my vital ambitions in an attempt to keep others happy.

Assassination Opportunity to revitalize one of my most powerful talents so I can use it to fundamentally transform my quality of life.

Assault course Situation where I can resolve a conflict by following a series of recognized procedures, even though they may seem challenging.

Assaulting Opportunity to resolve a conflict by vigorously protecting my personal boundaries so I can achieve a peaceful solution.

Assembling Opportunity to piece together the various resources I need to help me feel fully present when I participate in any activity.

Assembly line Situation where I am just going through the motions and feel unable to express my unique skills and abilities.

Assembly-line worker Aspect of my character that appears to be very efficient but could be employing my skills much more industriously.

Assertive Realization that I could have much more confidence in my abilities without feeling that I am forcing my beliefs onto other people.

A

Assessment Opportunity to evaluate my performance in an everyday situation instead of allowing other people to judge my abilities.

Assets Ability to have enough confidence in the value of my own expertise rather than feeling that I have nothing to really offer.

Assistant Aspect of my character that consistently supports my ambitions and helps me make continued progress in a much easier way.

Assisted Opportunity to cooperate with other people so I can make easier progress by having my ambitions consistently supported.

Assisted suicide Opportunity for me to make a healthy life transformation by trusting in the support of others and committing to my future.

Association Ability to make the best use of my professional relationships to connect my wider talents together so I can achieve my goals.

Assortment Ability to take a variety of resources and abilities to produce a unique result rather than trying to do it all on my own.

Assumption Realization that most opportunities emerge unexpectedly from the unknown instead of always taking everything for granted.

Assured Realization that I can be comfortable with the possibilities that uncertainty brings rather than becoming overly complacent.

Asteroid Situation where I can attract some rare resources into my sphere of influence so I can use them to make the most impact.

Asthma Essential opportunity to resolve an uncomfortable situation by opening up to my inspiration and letting go of restrictive beliefs.

Astonishment Realization that I should be a lot more excited about my unique talents instead of thinking that they are unremarkable.

Astray Realization that I can follow my natural instincts to stay firmly on track rather than allowing other people to distract me.

Astrocompass Ability to choose which creative direction I need to take by understanding my attraction to a variety of powerful influences.

Astronaut Aspect of my character that has the ability to raise my awareness to a much higher level by exploring my boundless curiosity.

Astronomer Aspect of my character that observes my creative patterns by studying my fundamental connection to bigger influences.

Asylum Situation where I can choose to speak out freely and take positive action about something that has been driving me crazy.

Asylum seeker Aspect of my character that is searching for a way to speak out honestly rather than feeling I may never fit in.

Athlete Aspect of my character that embodies the power to fulfill my heartfelt ambitions and dedicates all of my energy to achieving them.

Atlas Ability to use a more global perspective to navigate my way through a remotely familiar and potentially complex situation.

ATM Ability to know the right buttons to press to gain recognition of my value and ensure that it is acknowledged by other people.

Atmosphere Situation where I can surround myself with prevailing thoughts and moods so I can get a better feeling for them.

Atom Ability to understand the tiniest details and the attraction they hold so I can use them to create a much bigger result.

Atom bomb Ability to safely contain the potential energy needed for enormous individual transformation so I can choose how I use it.

Atomizer Ability to subtly influence the mood by paying attention to the tiniest details that can change the overall atmosphere.

Atom smasher Ability to make a major breakthrough I can feel really happy about by ensuring I pay attention to the tiniest details.

Atonement Realization that I can feel more at one with other people by taking time to make amends for any upset I may have caused.

Atrium Aspect of my character that is open to more expansive thoughts and theories so I can use them to illuminate my understanding.

Atrocious Realization that the most effective way to achieve what I desire is to be kind and gracious to other people.

Atrocity Opportunity to be on my best behavior instead of always feeling compelled to ruthlessly pursue what I really desire.

Atrophied Opportunity to build up my capacity to take creative action and nourish it, rather than just letting it waste away.

Attachment Ability to add to my experience by connecting to possibilities beyond myself rather than becoming fixated on a certain outcome.

Attack Opportunity to engage with a challenge by taking forceful action to assert my ambitions instead of always being defensive.

Attacked Realization that I can take forceful action to assert my personal boundaries rather than feeling like a victim of circumstance.

Attacked by an animal Opportunity to engage with a challenge by having the confidence to use my instinctive creativity instead of trying to ignore it.

Attacked by a stranger Opportunity to assert what I need from other people, even though it requires me to use unfamiliar communication methods.

Attacking Opportunity to forcefully work my way toward my intended result instead of feeling I always have to defend my actions.

Attempt Opportunity to use my inner strengths in an effort to achieve my ambitions instead of thinking that they will end in failure.

Attend Opportunity to become more fully present in my own awareness so I can pay closer attention to how I look after myself.

Attendant Aspect of my character that looks after my well-being and can take care of some of my basic needs that I often disregard.

Attention Realization that I need to focus my awareness on what is of most interest to me rather than ignoring my fundamental needs.

Attic Aspect of myself in which I can accumulate plans and ideas for future use, even though they may be currently gathering dust.

Attire Ability to gear myself up for an event by choosing what I am happy to display and deciding what I prefer to conceal.

Attorney Aspect of my character that can be stuck in habitual beliefs rather than taking the opportunity to turn events to my advantage.

Attraction Realization that I can bring valuable resources into my life by letting my creativity shine so it can be more fully appreciated.

Aubergine Natural ability to fulfill an ambition by making the most of a fertile opportunity and committing to my future healthy growth.

Auction Opportunity to raise wider awareness of my individual expertise in a bid to have my value fully recognized by other people.

Auctioneer Aspect of my character that can choose the opportunity that holds the greatest value for me and is prepared to hammer out a deal.

Audible Realization that I need to speak up and make myself clearly heard rather than thinking I should just continue in silence.

Audience Aspects of my character that are receptive to my speaking up and sharing my unique perspective so everyone can hear it.

A

A

Audiobook Ability to listen to my inner voice so I can open up to the wealth of my accumulated knowledge and learning.

Audiovisual Ability to clearly see the bigger picture so I can successfully sound out the viewpoints of a variety of other people.

Audition Opportunity to develop my talents by listening to my own performances and judging how they might be perceived by other people.

Auditorium Situation where I can give myself the space to speak up and be heard so other people might possibly entertain my beliefs.

Auger Ability to take a wider perspective so I can go deeper into the practicalities and see what they actually consist of.

Augmentation Realization that I can increase my influence by developing my expertise rather than allowing my role to become diminished.

Aunt Aspect of my character that helps me become more familiar with my capacity for creative wisdom and intuitive understanding.

Au pair Aspect of my character that can become more comfortable in an unfamiliar situation by looking after the needs of others.

Aura Ability to surround myself with an atmosphere of compelling ideas and intentions whose qualities attract people toward me.

Aurora Situation where I naturally attract some very creative thoughts and theories I can use to illuminate my understanding.

Austere Realization that I can achieve much more by using my wealth of experience rather than being too strict and uncompromising.

Authentic Realization that honestly showing how I feel is invariably the most powerful way to have my talents recognized by other people.

Author Aspect of my character that understands the power of my motivation and can create the circumstances to achieve my ambitions.

Authority figure Aspect of my character that gives me permission to fully step into my own power and make the decisions I need to.

Authorization Realization that I can step into my own power to make my ambitions happen rather than waiting for permission from others.

Authorized access Situation where I can choose what intimacies I want to share with others and those I prefer to keep to myself.

Autobahn Situation where without any apparent limitations I can use my individual drive to efficiently fast-track a personal ambition.

Autoclave Ability to take a clean and considered approach in a high-pressure situation rather than just blowing off steam.

Autocomplete Ability to predict what someone else is going to say by having the opportunity to clearly understand his or her unspoken needs.

Autocorrect Ability to resolve an apparent mistake by taking the time to understand what I want rather than constantly judging myself.

Autocosm Situation where I can become fully aware of what is going on all around me by understanding how I create my perceptions of it.

Autocue Ability to remind myself about what I need to say to clearly get my message across instead of just trying to improvise.

Autodial Ability to instantly communicate what I need to say by facing up to the facts rather than just going round and round.

Autoerotic Opportunity to make myself emotionally aroused about a situation so I can get more excited by its creative possibilities.

Autofocus Ability to naturally center my awareness so I can give my full attention to a particular point I want to emphasize.

Autograph Ability to express my creative

skills in a unique, personal way so that evidence of my talent can be validated by others.

Automatic Ability to understand how I habitually respond to particular situations so I can take decisive action to be more independent.

Automaton Aspect of my character that may appear to be going through the motions instead of expressing my need for independence.

Automobile Ability to use my motivation and drive to make my own choices so I can decide what I need to progress with my ambitions.

Autopilot Ability to follow a prescribed course of action so I can consistently get my ideas off the ground and then successfully land them.

Autopsy Opportunity to examine the more soulful aspects of my creative talent I may have been neglecting until quite recently.

Auto tune Ability to communicate with other people in a way that will resonate with them rather than trying to sound authentic.

Autumn Natural opportunity to use my accumulated wisdom to realize what I no longer need so I can transform it into new beginnings.

Avail Realization that I can demonstrate my actual expertise to other people by using an emerging opportunity to my full advantage.

Avalanche Opportunity to safely release an accumulating mountain of unexpressed feelings so I don't continually feel overwhelmed.

Avenger Aspect of my character that vindicates my approach to dealing with a specific situation without judging my actions too harshly.

Avenue Situation where possibilities for my future progress are largely defined by

my natural potential for long-term spiritual growth.

Average Realization that I have some unique skills and experience I should use instead of trying to fit in with everyone else.

Aversion Opportunity to look at different options so I can fully engage with all the possibilities rather than avoiding them.

Aversion therapy Opportunity to relieve an unhealthy tension by carefully attending to a situation I may have been avoiding.

Avocado Natural ability to have a healthy awareness of the choices I make and how they can fulfill my need for a feeling of well-being.

Avoidance Opportunity to fully engage with a difficult situation and confront any challenges that may have been plaguing my progress.

Awake Opportunity to be conscious of my potential choices by staying alert to the possibilities in what is happening.

Award Ability to have other people recognize the merits of my unique talents so I can prize my skills and abilities.

Award ceremony Opportunity to have my individual achievements prized by a wider audience that fully appreciates and acknowledges my value.

Aware Essential opportunity to realize what is happening around me so I can direct my attention to emerging possibilities.

Awe Realization that I have an overwhelming admiration for my unique qualities, even though they may seem very familiar to me.

Awe-inspiring Realization that I can use my sense of wonder to powerfully convey my most influential thoughts to the people around me.

Awesome Realization that I should never be too overcome by the extent of my capabilities instead of being astonished by my achievements.

A

A

Awful Realization that I can feel reassured by my own abilities rather than feeling bad about events that are outside my control.

Awkward Realization that I can perform a skill in a graceful and elegant manner instead of feeling as if I'm somehow out of place.

Awning Ability to comfortably approach a situation so I can see different shades of meaning rather than just feeling burned out.

Ax Ability to take a series of powerfully decisive actions that will enable me to let go of old habits that no longer serve me.

Axle Ability to stay centered and connected so I can keep things rolling along and have some stability in the direction I take.

Azure Mood that can color my perspective by helping me to become genuinely aware of how I can naturally use my wider potential.

Babble Essential opportunity to express myself clearly by letting my feelings flow instead of thinking I have to chatter on incessantly.

Baboon Instinctive ability to always grab an opportunity so I can use it to increase my status within my immediate social circle.

Baby Aspect of my character that embodies a labor of love and requires careful nurturing to fully develop to its true potential.

Baby carriage Ability to use self-motivation to take some definite steps and make progress with a new concept I care deeply about.

Baby clothes Ability to present my developing self-image to other people so they can become more aware of my individual characteristics.

Baby monitor Ability to observe what is happening in a project that is close to my heart so I can ensure its continued development.

Baby seat Ability to maintain a safe, secure perspective on one of my developing talents so I can make comfortable progress with it.

Babysitter Aspect of my character that trusts my fundamental creativity and recognizes the real value of my developing plans and ideas.

Bachelor Aspect of my character that is usually up for making creative commitments so I can demonstrate my particular strengths.

Bachelorette Aspect of my character that is often open to asserting my individual talents so I can see what chances might emerge for me.

Back Essential ability to maintain my continued forward progress by being supportive about what I may need to leave behind me.

Backache Essential opportunity to leave any ongoing anxieties behind me so I can resolve a continuing tension in the underlying situation.

Back alley Situation where I can use an informal social connection as a way of leaving the past behind so I can continue my progress.

Back at school Opportunity to realize that I never stop learning and will always be open to increasing my levels of knowledge and self-awareness.

Backbone Essential ability to demonstrate the underlying strength of my character by being able to stand up for what I believe in.

Backdoor Ability to maintain a less formal boundary between private and public life so I can be more open to emerging opportunities.

Backdraft Opportunity to deal with a potentially explosive thought without feeling that I have to exclude all other possibilities.

Backdrop Ability to let go of any attachment to a particular outcome by understanding what is actually happening behind the scenes.

Backer Aspect of my character that provides valuable support in an unobtrusive way by giving me a number of options to fall back on.

Backfire Opportunity to take a more methodical approach to achieving my chosen outcome rather than getting fired up prematurely.

Backgammon Opportunity to decide an unpredictable outcome by taking some apparently backward steps so I can keep moving forward.

B

Background Realization that the wider context can provide a much more significant meaning to what is happening.

Backhanded Opportunity to have a firm grasp of my inner power so I can eliminate potential ambiguities in how I plan to take action.

Backlog Opportunity to realize that building frustrations may be caused by the habitual behaviors I have accumulated over time.

Backpack Ability to maintain my motivation by being as self-contained as possible without feeling too weighed down by responsibility.

Back room Aspect of myself that can draw on my accumulated experience so I can be up-front about what I need to move forward.

Backseat driver Aspect of my character that can control my future direction instead of being driven by the previous expectations of others.

Backside Ability to directly understand what is happening so I can become more aware of how I can continue to support my position.

Backstage Situation where I can gather the resources I need to openly display my talents so I can progress to the next level.

Backtrack Opportunity to make progress by understanding where I want to go instead of feeling I am covering the same old ground.

Backward Opportunity to work my way through a sequence of events so I can continue to make forward progress toward my chosen objective.

Backwoods Situation where I can explore the natural resourcefulness and deeper growth potential of the undiscovered aspects of my character.

Backwoodsman Aspect of my character that has the experience and expertise to make the most of my natural potential for healthy growth.

Backyard Situation where I can give myself the space to consider the extent of my personal ambitions and the resources I may need.

Bacon Potential to fulfill an ambition by using my practical power and strength to happily provide a wealth of comfort and abundance.

Bacteria Instinctive ability to take the germ of an idea and develop it so I can use it to resolve a potentially unhealthy situation.

Bacteriological warfare Ability to set definite personal boundaries so I can make myself immune to any hostile feelings and unwelcome criticism.

Bad Realization that I can use my good judgment to do the right thing instead of feeling that everything has gone wrong for me.

Bad breath Essential opportunity to express in a healthy way the value of some of my most inspiring ideas in a fresh and attractive manner.

Bad deed Opportunity to gain a much clearer understanding of my fundamental needs so I can explore them in a positive manner.

Bad feeling Realization that I can achieve much greater success by being more aware of my emotions rather than always being overly objective.

Bad food Opportunity to look after my own needs instead of continually feeling unfulfilled by looking after the needs of other people.

Badge Ability to confidently display my talents so I can have them formally recognized and understood by the people around me.

Bad man Aspect of my character that gives me the strength and power to use my good judgment, even though the situation may be challenging.

Badger Instinctive ability to take powerful action by continuing to be persistent so I can have a deeper appreciation of events.

Badly fitting Opportunity to decide how I want others to see me rather than feeling I have to show myself in a way that doesn't suit me.

Badminton Opportunity to knock ideas back and forth so I can raise specific points that will help decide the outcome.

Bad result Opportunity to become more aware of my preferred outcome so I can work through possible consequences of my actions.

Bad situation Realization about my potential for personal transformation by understanding how I can change my immediate surroundings.

Bad woman Aspect of my character that gives me the wisdom and empathy to achieve the best outcome in a potentially challenging situation.

Baffle Ability to clearly communicate my ideas by removing any barriers that may be preventing my message from getting through.

Baffled Realization that I have the power to express myself clearly, without any barriers to communication getting in the way.

Bag Ability to take good care of the personal resources I regularly need so I can always be open to any new opportunities.

Baggage Ability to convey the unrealized hopes and ambitions I carry around with me, even though they can often weigh me down.

Baggage carousel Situation where I can look out for emerging possibilities that will help me to fulfill my unrealized hopes and ambitions.

Baggage claim Situation where I can reconnect with my unrealized hopes and ambitions after having recently been brought back down to earth.

Baggage handler Aspect of my character that can firmly grasp the value of my unrealized hopes and ambitions so I can always keep them in mind.

Bagpipes Ability to take my instinctive creativity in both hands so I can use it to explore the edges of my wilder hopes and ambitions.

Bail Opportunity to make a commitment to my responsibilities by declaring my confidence in my actions and the choices I make.

Bailiff Aspect of my character that helps me to seek out my true value and ensures I can proudly declare it to other people.

Bailing bucket Opportunity to provide space and support to those who need it by methodically dealing with any potentially overwhelming emotions.

Bail out Opportunity to take a more down-to-earth approach by moving away from a project that is no longer heading in my chosen direction.

Bait Ability to provide a seemingly minor incentive that may lead to the eventual fulfillment of a much more valuable ambition.

Baked potato Potential to fulfill my ambitions by taking my time to become comfortable with my talents so that I can sustain my progress.

Baker Aspect of my character that can steadily raise my value to other people by planning ahead and taking my time to produce results.

Bakery Situation where I can consistently produce a variety of fresh ideas that allow other people to recognize my increasing value.

Baking Opportunity to transform my value by taking the time to plan ahead so I can sustain my consistently creative activity.

Balaclava Ability to present my self-image to people in a way that may make me feel less vulnerable but can conceal my valuable ideas.

B

Balance Realization that I can reflect on the stance I've been taking and observe how I've been distributing my responsibilities.

Balcony Situation where I can use my inner awareness to gain a more elevated perspective on what is happening around me.

Bald Essential opportunity to freely go beyond everyday thinking so I can feel comfortable thinking about exposing my thoughts to other people.

Bale Ability to collect a number of practical skills together and package them in a way that will provide me with continued support.

Ball Ability to play around with a potentially successful outcome and share some valuable activity with people who are close to me.

Ballast Ability to maintain my balance and stability so I can progress without feeling too weighed down by my heavier responsibilities.

Ball bearing Ability to make a situation run more smoothly by understanding the precise details that will provide a successful outcome.

Ball boy Aspect of my character that is happy to pick up on a particular ambition other people have been playing around with.

Ballerina Aspect of my character that embodies my creative talents and can gracefully bring them to life in a powerful and uplifting manner.

Ballet Opportunity to coordinate the various aspects of my natural creativity so I can display them in a balanced and disciplined way.

Ballet shoe Ability to display my unique status by using my powerful talent to make a creative point in a balanced and precise way.

Ball game Opportunity to play around with both sides of a situation and explore different strategies for achieving a successful outcome.

Ball girl Aspect of my character that can quickly pick up on a creative idea that others have been going back and forth with.

Ball gown Ability to present my self-image to other people in a way that celebrates the length and splendor of my accomplishments.

Ballistic Realization that I will inevitably have to come back down to earth at some point rather than leaving my decision up in the air.

Ballistic missile Ability to powerfully assert my beliefs and exert influence without getting too fired up about the gravity of the situation.

Balloon Ability to play around with an attractive idea, even though it may appear insubstantial and might just suddenly collapse.

Ballot box Ability to feel safe and secure about expressing my individual decisions to other people instead of trying to hide how I feel.

Ballot paper Ability to consistently make my mark with the people around me by using my layers of experience to make the right decision.

Ballpark Situation where I can play around with a potentially uncertain outcome and confirm the likeliness of my eventual success.

Ballroom Situation where I can take some steps to feel more comfortable and secure in confidently developing my emerging expertise.

Ballroom dancing Opportunity to demonstrate the steps I might need to take to have my talent recognized by those around me.

Balm Instinctive awareness that helps me to identify the mood in the air so I can continue to stay calm and relaxed.

Balmy Natural ability to sense the prevailing atmosphere so I can enjoy the warmth and comfort of the current circumstances.

Bamboo Natural ability to keep growing successfully in a rapidly developing situation by remaining flexible and staying strong.

Bamboo flute Ability to take my instinctive creativity in both hands so I can channel my spiritual beliefs and express them gracefully.

Ban Opportunity to continue displaying the personal behaviors I am happy with so I can choose to let go of any others.

Banana Natural ability to have healthy optimism about achieving a fruitful outcome rather than worrying that I will just slip up.

Band Aspects of my character that can work together harmoniously so that I can use my variety of talents to create a unique outcome.

Bandage Ability to successfully wrap up the outcome of any ongoing tensions so I can resolve a potentially hurtful situation.

Band-Aid Ability to quickly resolve any superficial conflicts by sticking to surface impressions rather than going any deeper.

Bandana Ability to present my self-image to people by taking a more open view instead of allowing my style of thinking to get in the way.

Bandit Aspect of my character that often disregards traditional etiquette and can find it challenging to recognize my true value.

Bandolier Ability to accumulate potentially powerful personal resources that will enable me to confidently assert my particular aims.

Bandwagon Ability to use my drive and ambition to convey the value of my accumulated expertise rather than just following everyone else.

Bane Ability to use my individual power to do what I need to instead of thinking that people are spoiling things for me.

Bang Opportunity to make a positive start that will have a real impact rather than just sounding off about my circumstances.

Bangle Ability to draw attention to how I shape my outcomes so I can attract people to the variety of opportunities I create.

Banished Opportunity to reconnect with a valuable aspect of my identity by recognizing my talents rather than trying to disown them.

Banister Ability to provide a source of constant support and security so I can continue my steady progress in a step-by-step manner.

Banjo Ability to take my instinctive creativity in both hands so I can use it to communicate in a clear and simple way how I feel.

Bank Situation where I can draw on my accumulated wealth of experience so I can have my true value recognized by other people.

Bank account Ability to accumulate a sense of self-worth so I can feel more secure in displaying the value of my talents to others.

Bankbook Ability to have my wealth of accumulated knowledge recognized by others so I can feel safe about opening up a bit more.

Bank card Ability to communicate the wealth of my accumulated wisdom to others so they can publicly acknowledge my value.

Banker Aspect of my character that may prevent access to my accumulated wisdom and experience by trying to lock my talent away.

Bank loan Opportunity to acknowledge the real value of my skills and expertise rather than feeling that I owe my success to other people.

Banknote Ability to recognize my levels of self-worth so I can have them positively validated by others when I exchange my views.

Bank robber Aspect of my character that needs to honor the value of my accumulated wealth of knowledge rather than losing confidence in it.

Bankruptcy Opportunity to transform my fundamental feelings of self-worth by choosing to release myself from time-wasting habits.

Bank statement Ability to make a worthwhile contribution to a specific cause so other people can understand the value of my opinion.

B

Banner Ability to display my thoughts and feelings on a much larger scale so I can successfully draw others' attention to them.

Banquet Opportunity to fulfil a personal ambition by lavishing attention on my special skills so I can have them formally acknowledged.

Banshee Aspect of my character that can express some scarily powerful ideas and that is screaming out for creative transformation.

Banter Opportunity to play around with what I want to say so I can happily tease out what appears to be most meaningful.

Baptism Opportunity to connect with my spiritual beliefs at a deeper level by allowing myself to become immersed in my emotions.

Bar Ability to raise my awareness to a certain level so I can give myself permission to enjoy my sense of freedom.

Barb Ability to get really stuck in a situation and stay connected with it rather than making pointed criticisms of it.

Barbarian Aspect of my character that fundamentally sees no real limits to my powerful ambitions so I can choose to use them wisely.

Barbecue Opportunity to heighten my developing creativity by cooking up some ideas and using my raw power to fulfil an ambition.

Barbed wire Ability to clearly define my personal boundaries without having to be too pointed in how I communicate them to others.

Barbell Ability to use my inner strength and personal power to take individual action and deal with some heavy responsibilities.

Barber Aspect of my character that helps me shape my thoughts and ideas so I can present them to people in my own inimitable style.

Bar code Ability to communicate my fundamental value in a clear and succinct manner by being straight about my contrasting feelings.

Bard Aspect of my character that can stay composed as I express my deeper feelings so I can evoke some profound emotions.

Bare Ability to be honest and open about my intentions, even though it can make me appear quite vulnerable to other people.

Barefoot Essential ability to feel fully connected to my deeper values so I can be open and honest about who I really am.

Bargain Opportunity to use my experience to negotiate an unexpected situation so I can have my true value recognized by other people.

Barge Ability to powerfully navigate my way through a potentially complex emotional situation by strongly asserting how I really feel.

Barge pole Ability to make my way through a potentially emotional situation by keeping my distance as I communicate how I feel.

Barium meal Opportunity to resolve an unhealthy situation by understanding my instinctive gut reaction so I can work my way through it.

Bark Natural ability to protect my potential for long-term spiritual growth while staying rooted in everyday practicalities.

Barking Opportunity to bring my attention to how I show my unconditional loyalty to other people, even though it may seem irrational.

Barley Natural ability to sustain my ambitions by shaking up some ideas I have accumulated over time so I can reap their benefits.

Barn Situation where I can carefully maintain my energy so I can feel comfortable with some of my more familiar instincts.

Barnacle Instinctive ability to hang on tightly to my fundamental beliefs rather than being swept away by any powerful emotions.

Barometer Ability to sense the prevailing atmosphere in a situation so I can become aware of any pressures that may emerge in the future.

Baron Aspect of my character that has the potential to hold great power and can use it wisely in one particular area of my life.

Barracks Situation where I can marshal my wider resources so I can bring them together in a more assertive and disciplined manner.

Barrage Opportunity to protect my personal boundaries by forcefully displaying the power of my thoughts and feelings to other people.

Barrage balloon Ability to keep my ideas firmly grounded in reality so I can defend my way of thinking against any potential criticism.

Barred Opportunity to set specific personal boundaries instead of feeling that other people are excluding me from their activities.

Barred window Ability to clearly see through a number of my self-imposed limitations so I can have more freedom in expressing my point of view.

Barrel Ability to get to the bottom of a situation by using my accumulated experience to provide a more mature source of insight.

Barren Realization that I can use my fertile imagination to do something far more productive and useful instead of feeling empty.

Barricade Situation where I can establish firm personal boundaries, even though they may close me off to potential growth opportunities.

Barrier Opportunity get over a self-limiting belief so I can continue my progress toward successfully fulfilling an individual goal.

Barrister Aspect of my character that can understand what a specific situation represents for me so I can communicate its significance.

Barrow Ability to use my self-motivation and energy to convey a weighty issue to other people so that it can be firmly laid to rest.

Bartender Aspect of my personality that openly listens to my feelings and helps serve my need for emotional and spiritual exploration.

Base Situation where I can use my fundamental integrity to provide the essential resources I need to explore my deeper awareness.

Baseball Opportunity to play around with both sides of a situation so I can explore different strategies for striking a successful outcome.

Baseball bat Ability to connect with an approaching opportunity so I can use my individual expertise to make a definite impact.

Baseball cap Ability to present my self-image to other people in a way that shows the type of ideas I am often most attracted to.

Base camp Situation where I can get more comfortable as I prepare myself for a major challenge that may involve a range of ups and downs.

BASE jump Opportunity to quickly commit myself to taking a more down-to-earth approach rather than jumping to a premature conclusion.

Basement Aspect of myself that forms the foundations of who I really am and provides support for all the different parts of my character.

Bash Opportunity to be open to new ways of fulfilling my ambitions rather than letting other people give me a hard time about them.

Basha Ability to feel relaxed and comfortable in a hostile situation by using my natural resourcefulness to help me feel more secure.

Basic Realization that I have a fundamental understanding of what I need instead of feeling distracted by nonessentials.

Basin Ability to contain my feelings so I can keep myself open and receptive to the different ways in which I might appear to others.

B

Bask Opportunity to feel relaxed and comfortable about my achievements without feeling that I need constant praise from others.

Basket Ability to gather the resources I need to create the space I require to satisfy a particular personal ambition.

Basketball Opportunity to play around with both sides of a situation and achieve some collective goals by rising above any opposition.

Basket weaver Aspect of my character that creates opportunities for personal fulfilment by weaving together various strands of my story.

Basking shark Instinctive ability to feel relaxed and comfortable about my ambitions by opening myself up to the wider flow of my emotions.

Bass guitar Ability to take my instinctive creativity in both hands so I can pitch some ideas that explore a range of deeper issues.

Bassoon Ability to take my instinctive creativity and use it to shape my deeper ideas so I can express them more profoundly.

Bat Instinctive ability to listen to some of my darker ideas so I can understand my motivations and take action on them.

Bated breath Natural opportunity to be more moderate in my thoughts and theories rather than becoming too carried away by them all.

Bath Situation where I feel most relaxed and at home with my emotional life and am happy to immerse myself in my feelings.

Bathhouse Situation where I feel relaxed about sharing my sentiments with other people and happy for them to share their feelings with me.

Bathing Opportunity to take a more relaxed outlook by immersing myself in my emotions and reflecting on the feelings that surround me.

Bat mammal Instinctive ability to achieve a much clearer understanding of what is happening by listening out for what is normally unspoken.

Bath mat Ability to know where I stand in a potentially emotional situation and to feel comfortable about immersing myself deeply in it.

Bathrobe Ability to present my self-image to people in a manner that shows that I feel very comfortable and relaxed in my emotional life.

Bathroom Aspect of myself that ensures my emotional privacy so I can stay relaxed when I am taking care of my fundamental needs.

Bathroom cabinet Ability to accumulate a variety of useful resources that I might require to help me take care of my most fundamental needs.

Bathroom mirror Ability to gain a clearer sense of self-awareness by reflecting on who I want to be without getting too steamed up about it.

Bathwater Ability to immerse myself in my emotional life so I can be more comfortable with it rather than wallowing in my sentiments.

Baton Ability to grasp the implications of my individual responsibility so I can help ensure that a collective ambition is achieved.

Batter Ability to assert my appetite for competitive success, even though it may be potentially unhealthy for me in the long run.

Battering ram Ability to move into new areas of opportunity by using the strength of my convictions to remove any barriers to progress.

Battery Ability to bring vital energy to a situation by getting charged up about the powerful potential it holds for me.

Battle Opportunity to take decisive action and make a stand so I can resolve an ongoing inner tension that is causing conflict for me.

Battle fatigue Ability to resolve any inner conflict by strongly asserting my power instead of going through the same tired old patterns.

Battlefield Situation where I can reveal hidden tensions and resolve a personal conflict rather than going back over the same old ground.

Battlement Situation where I can resolve some inner conflicts by powerfully defending my beliefs against any criticism from others.

Bawdy Realization that I can meet my creative needs by refining my sense of power and how I demonstrate it to the people around me.

Bawling Opportunity to show what I feel by opening up to my more powerful emotions so I can honestly share them.

Bay Situation where I can explore the edge of my experience in relative calm so I can be more receptive to my wider emotions.

Bayonet Ability to influence people by using my strongly fixed beliefs to make my point, even though my opinions may be quite outdated.

Bazaar Situation where I can acquire valuable information, even though the process may seem quite foreign and unfamiliar to me.

Beach Situation where I can connect the security and stability of my accumulated knowledge with the ebb and flow of my emotional life.

Beachcomber Aspect of my character that can find unexpected value from exploring the high and low points of my emotional experiences.

Beached whale Instinctive ability to get a huge opportunity moving again by immersing myself in my emotions instead of being isolated from them.

Beacon Ability to use my insight and understanding to illuminate an unfamiliar situation so I can guide myself safely through it.

Beads Ability to attract attention to the talents I have for piecing together the various parts of a situation into a valuable outcome.

Beak Instinctive ability to judge some of the finer points of a situation so I can clearly communicate them to other people.

Beam Ability to provide support for some thoughts and theories by staying positive so I can provide an illuminating perspective.

Beanie hat Ability to present my self-image to other people in a way that draws attention to my viewpoint and how comfortable I am with it.

Beans Potential to fulfill an ambition by gathering a variety of smaller resources together so I can use their collective energy.

Bear Instinctive ability to use my spiritual wisdom to robustly deal with any adversity so I can powerfully protect my loved ones.

Beard Essential opportunity to powerfully assert my wisdom so I can face up to the facts and use them to make a firm decision.

Bear hug Opportunity to get much closer to the power of my own wisdom by fully embracing it rather than being standoffish about it.

Bearings Realization that I can make a situation run much more smoothly by choosing how I conduct myself as I decide on a direction.

Beast Instinctive ability to embody my fundamental talent by taming my more primal urges so I can channel their creative power.

Beat Opportunity to achieve a successful outcome by listening to my deeper rhythms so I can understand what is happening.

Beatbox Ability to convey how I feel in a more individual manner rather than feeling I'm just repeating myself like everyone else.

B

Beautician Aspect of my character that can enhance my true identity by looking beyond surface appearances and revealing deeper allure.

B

Beauty Essential opportunity to share my real talents by revealing my deeper value rather than judging myself on superficial appearances.

Beauty contest Opportunity to display the value of my deeper talents to other people instead of worrying how I might appear to them.

Beauty mark Situation where I can focus on my deeper value by understanding what sets me apart from all the other people around me.

Beauty queen Aspect of my character that wisely uses my talents in a gracious manner rather than trying to draw attention to myself.

Beauty salon Situation where I can work at positively developing my deeper value instead of constantly fussing over superficial details.

Beaver Instinctive ability to resolve any gnawing anxieties I have by eagerly channeling my emotions so I can use them productively.

Becalmed Opportunity to make progress in an emotional situation by taking courageous action rather than just getting the wind up.

Beck Realization that I can call my own shots and choose my own way rather than feeling I have to attend to other people.

Beckoning Opportunity to make a gesture that will open up some new possibilities for me rather than trying to ignore the unknown.

Bed Situation where I feel most at home and comfortable with myself and can take a relaxed approach to exploring my creative urges.

Bed-and-breakfast Situation where I can gain a different perspective on my value so I can wake up to a new way of feeding my appetite for success.

Bedbug Instinctive ability to be comfortable dealing with small details rather than letting myself be constantly irritated by them.

Bed hair Ability to feel very comfortable with my fundamental style of thinking, even.

though it may take a while to get my ideas into shape.

Bedlam Opportunity to bring some calm and order to a situation rather than feeling it is chaotically descending into a madhouse.

Bedraggled Realization that I can present a clean and powerful image to people rather than feeling limp and emotionally washed out.

Bedrock Ability to understand my fundamental nature so I can always be supportive and maintain a firm and practical outlook.

Bedroom Aspect of myself that gives me the space to release any residual tensions and the privacy to feel comfortable and at home.

Bedside Situation where I can take a different viewpoint so I can get closer to what will make me feel more comfortable with myself.

Bedtime story Ability to share my unique personal perspective by understanding my deepest aspirations and the role I play in them.

Bed-wetting Opportunity to realize that I am in a relaxed environment so I can feel less anxious about releasing my innermost emotions.

Bee Instinctive ability to create a buzz by exchanging new ideas with other people and keeping myself busy and industrious.

Beech tree Natural potential for a long-term spiritual growth by gathering ideas while still staying rooted in everyday practicalities.

Beef Potential to fulfill one of my ambitions by using my strength and power to resolve a situation that may have been upsetting me.

Beehive Situation where I can participate in busy and coordinated activity that produces a sweet and satisfying outcome for everyone.

Beekeeper Aspect of my character that keeps

me busy by making sure that I have a safe place to exchange my ideas with other people.

Beep Opportunity to alert myself to a specific event and the small amount of time I may have available to take action on it.

Beer Potential to fulfill an emotional need by sharing some possibly confusing feelings I may have been keeping bottled up.

Beetle Instinctive ability to rapidly progress by making the most of emerging opportunities and being able to shrug off any criticism.

Beetroot Natural ability to have a healthy awareness of how I can use my enthusiasm to resolve a potentially embarrassing situation.

Before Opportunity to look into the future and explore what might emerge rather than leaving it to fate and letting it happen.

Befriending an animal Opportunity to become more acquainted with my creative impulses so I can instinctively sense any emerging possibilities.

Befriending a stranger Opportunity to renew my acquaintance with an unfamiliar aspect of my character that can give me a deep insight into my situation.

Befuddled Realization that the best way to resolve any tension is to keep my head clear of anything else that may be distracting me.

Beggar Aspect of my character that neglects my talents, although they are crying out to have their value truly recognized by other people.

Begging Opportunity to recognize my own talents and realize their value rather than pleading with other people to acknowledge my presence.

Beginner Aspect of my character that has an open mind about what I need to achieve and is lucky enough to have no preconceptions.

Beginning Opportunity to open myself up to a new range of possibilities so I can explore how I can use them to feel more complete.

Beguiling Realization that I need to communicate what I feel to others rather than trying to attract them toward me.

Behave Opportunity to do something really meaningful by truly identifying with my actions so I can take full responsibility for them.

Beheading Opportunity to cleanly separate my thoughts and emotions without feeling that I might lose my head and behave irrationally.

Behind Opportunity to look back into the past and see where I've been coming from so I can choose how to create my future.

Beige Mood that can color my perspective by reflecting how I like to keep things relaxed in a neutral and unthreatening manner.

Being Aspect of my character that gives me the presence of mind to step fully into my power and take the action that is needed.

Being addicted Opportunity to understand my most fundamental needs instead of constantly being attracted to situations that are unhealthy for me.

Being arrested Opportunity to decide my personal responsibilities so I can slow down a situation that is threatening to get out of control.

Being attacked Opportunity to take forceful action to assert my individual needs instead of feeling that other people are victimizing me.

Being betrayed Opportunity to have real faith in myself by trusting in my decisions rather than worrying I won't meet my expectations.

Being chased Opportunity to resolve an ongoing tension by turning my energies toward a pursuit that will help me achieve my ambitions.

Being executed Opportunity to make a fundamentally transformative choice for myself instead of thinking that I always have to follow orders.

Being forced Opportunity to use my powerful talent to exert my individual influence rather than feeling my options for action are limited.

Being frustrated Opportunity to realize that my persistence will help me make a fundamental breakthrough in how I can accomplish my ambitions.

Being injured Opportunity to develop healthier relationships with other people by being more open to showing my feelings of vulnerability.

Being intoxicated Opportunity to keep a clear head in an exhilarating situation rather than feeling overcome with the excitement of it all.

Being invisible Opportunity to make myself more visible to others so they can recognize my individual talents and unique value.

Being kidnapped Opportunity to give myself the freedom to make my own choices, instead of feeling that I have to meet other people's expectations.

Being late Opportunity to immediately commit myself to taking decisive action rather than always hesitating and using my time ineffectively.

Being left behind Opportunity to make rapid progress by continuing to develop some individual expertise I learned a while ago.

Being let down Opportunity to set my own criteria for my success instead of feeling that I don't live up to the expectations of others.

Being pregnant Opportunity to create a uniquely wonderful outcome by taking the time to develop a concept that is extremely precious to me.

Being premature Opportunity to take a more mature approach to an emerging possibility so I can make a long-term commitment to my success.

Being pushed Opportunity to overcome the resistance of other people so I can keep moving forward at a pace that suits me.

Being shot Opportunity to step into my power and assert what I need rather than feeling powerless about the actions of other people.

Being squeezed Opportunity to get a much tighter grip on what I really want to do instead of feeling that other people are always pressuring me.

Being stabbed Opportunity to make my point by asserting what I need rather than feeling cut up about the actions of other people.

Being tricked Opportunity to understand what will make me happiest instead of deluding myself about what appears to satisfy me.

Being wounded Opportunity to be comfortable with feeling vulnerable rather than always needing to be on the defensive with other people.

Belay Ability to keep myself safe and secure during a sudden period of transformation by staying connected to someone I can rely on.

Belch Opportunity to openly release pent-up thoughts and ideas, even though they may be potentially volatile and inflammatory.

Belfry Situation where I can consolidate my power and make myself stand out by clearly communicating my intentions to other people.

Beliefs Realization that I can share my particular perspectives on a situation so I can explore a number of alternative viewpoints.

Believable Opportunity to examine my particular viewpoint about a situation so I can be more open to different perspectives.

Bell Ability to increase my awareness of an emerging opportunity by striking quickly so I can clearly ring the changes.

Bellowing Ability to naturally attract the attention of other people and make myself heard by using my huge capacity for self-expression.

Belly Essential ability to guard myself against

any possible vulnerabilities by using my accumulated experience and gut instincts.

Belly button Essential ability to take specific action by staying connected to my gut instincts without becoming attached to them.

Belongings Ability to own my habitual behavior patterns so I can decide if they can help me get to where I will feel really at home.

Beloved Aspect of my character that has the potential to make a profound connection to a much deeper understanding of myself.

Below Realization that I can deepen my levels of awareness more than I think so I can use them to gain a profounder perspective.

Belt Ability to hold a situation securely together by acting in a fair and open manner so I can share what resources I have access to.

Bench Ability to share a practical and solid viewpoint with others so I can conveniently coordinate my activities with them.

Bend Situation where I can realign my perspectives by being more flexible and taking a different viewpoint of how I approach them.

Beneath Situation where I can go below surface appearances so I can gain a deeper understanding rather than just rejecting the chance.

Benefit Opportunity to take advantage of a situation where I can show the value of my talents instead of doubting my creative abilities.

Benign tumor Ability to live with the possible benefits of a slowly developing situation, even though it may potentially grow out of control.

Bent Ability to view a situation from a different angle so I can take a more honest and straightforward approach in dealing with it.

Bequest Opportunity to transform the situation by letting go of my old habits so I can realize the value of my previous experiences.

Bereavement Opportunity to let go of the past by stepping into my own power so that I can embody my unique qualities and feel revitalized.

Bereavement Counselor Aspect of my character that helps me see the wisdom in letting go of the past so I can continue to revitalize my progress.

Beret Ability to present my self-image to people in a more casual way that can make my viewpoint seem quite levelheaded.

Berries Natural ability to gather a number of ripening possibilities so I can use them to provide a more fruitful outcome.

Berserk Essential opportunity to understand the irrational aspects of my nature instead of trying to be too violent and forceful.

Berth Situation where I can seek shelter and comfort in emotionally challenging circumstances rather than trying to avoid them.

Beside Realization that I can become more centered in my awareness by observing my habitual behaviors in a calm and detached manner.

Besieged Opportunity to open up to the resources that are all around me rather than always appearing to resist any outside assistance.

Besotted Opportunity to recognize how attractive my unique talents are instead of always obsessing about the skills of other people.

Bespectacled Opportunity to study a situation more closely so I can form a clear opinion rather than appearing too introspective.

Best Realization that I can use challenging circumstances to my advantage so I can become the person I always dream of being.

Bestial Essential ability to embody the strength of my creative instincts so I can achieve a powerful outcome without going wild.

B

Best man Aspect of my character that recognizes my potential for ultimate success and fully supports my commitments to others.

Bet Opportunity to decide the definite outcome of a situation by using the power of my insight to confidently stick my neck out.

Betrayal Opportunity to have real faith in myself by trusting in my choice of actions rather than habitually letting myself down.

Betrothal Opportunity to make a deeper commitment to a developing possibility that truly excites me and which I love being engaged in.

Better Realization that I can continue to develop the value of my talents by always being open to ways of improving my performance.

Betting shop Situation where I can display the value of my decision-making process to other people instead of leaving it to chance.

Between Realization that a greater awareness often emerges from the difference between two points of view rather than just choosing one.

Beverage Potential to fulfill an emotional need by making a specific choice so I can satisfy my fundamental thirst for experience.

Bewildered Opportunity to think more clearly by observing my instinctive reactions and controlling them rather than feeling confused.

Bewitched Opportunity to understand what is happening by looking beyond my vague superstitions instead of always feeling spooked.

Beyond Realization that my most powerful development emerges from going to the edge of what I know rather than limiting my actions.

Bib Ability to protect the self-image I present to people so I can pursue an ambition that may become quite emotional for me.

Bible Ability to understand what I believe so I can use that awareness positively as a way of consistently informing my actions.

Biblical figure Aspect of my character that can communicate a wiser and more profound understanding of the spiritual connections I make.

Biceps Essential ability to use my power and strength to bend a situation more to my liking so I can take decisive action on it.

Bickering Opportunity to resolve an ongoing inner tension by making a graceful and considered decision rather than appearing petulant.

Bicycle Ability to make progress toward my chosen ambition by using my energy and self-motivation to keep my commitments balanced.

Bicycle courier Aspect of my character that has the self-motivation to quickly communicate the true value of my insights to other people.

Bicycle helmet Ability to protect my way of thinking in potentially risky situations so I can maintain my levels of self-motivation.

Bicycle pump Ability to consistently channel my ideas so I can continue to keep my commitments balanced in a high-pressure situation.

Bid Ability to free myself from any self-imposed limitations by making other people more aware of the unique value of my expertise.

Bidding Opportunity to go beyond a self-imposed boundary by raising awareness of my talents and having their value openly recognized.

Bidet Ability to have a clear and healthy awareness of my emotional needs, particularly after dealing with a potentially messy situation.

Bifocals Ability to clearly see both the short-term and long-term possibilities of a situation so I can alter my perspective accordingly.

Bifurcation Opportunity to make my own decision about which path I need to follow so I can commit to a specific ambition.

Big Realization that I can achieve a great success by understanding the scale of my ambitions and attending to the smaller details.

Bigamy Opportunity to fully commit to a situation that I find much more engaging by choosing to release myself from another commitment.

Big bang Opportunity to naturally develop my massive potential rather than feeling that I'm trying to make something out of nothing.

Big cat Instinctive ability to embody my need for much greater freedom and independence so I can feel more relaxed and comfortable.

Bigger house Situation where I can explore a variety of different aspects so I can develop my potential talent and increasing my creative value.

Bigoted Realization that I can be more open about my wide range of beliefs rather than feeling I always have to agree with other people.

Bike Ability to make self-motivated progress by balancing my energies so I can keep a handle on any emerging opportunities.

Bikini Ability to present my self-image to other people by always being very open about how I immerse myself in my deeper emotions.

Bile Essential ability to transform any self-indulgent behavior by taking a more positive approach instead of feeling angry.

Bilge pump Ability to lift my emotions so I can stay on an even keel and deliver what is needed in a high-pressure situation.

Bill Ability to balance the value of my accumulated experience against the personal cost of pursuing one of my ambitions.

Billboard Ability to bring my attention to a big opportunity I may be overlooking because of my focus on a particular objective.

Billiards Opportunity to examine all the angles in a situation so I can give it my best shot in deciding a successful outcome.

Billiard table Ability to be very open and supportive with other people by examining all the different opportunities in our social connections.

Billionaire Aspect of my character that has steadily accumulated a huge wealth of experience and has the freedom to use my talents wisely.

Billowing Realization that I can make a great surge in my progress by successfully capturing powerful thoughts and theories.

Bimbo Aspect of my character that can feel comfortable pursuing my ambitions rather than always trying to please other people.

Bin Ability to make a positive and healthy choice about what is no longer useful to me so I can ensure that I remove it from my life.

Bind Opportunity to stay fully connected without always feeling that I'm trapped in a situation that may limit my future actions.

Bindi Ability to draw attention to my unseen wisdom and compassion so I can help other people raise their level of awareness.

Binge drinking Potential to fulfill an emotional need by being positive and healthy about my feelings rather than indulging in self-pity.

Binge eating Potential to fulfill an ambition by taking a more considered approach instead of always appearing to be excessively demanding.

Bingo Realization that I can take positive action to decide my chosen outcome rather than just waiting for my number to come up.

Bin man Aspect of my character that helps keep me healthy by choosing to let go of what I no longer need and then just moving on.

Binnacle Ability to provide strong and stable support as I chart my progress so I can choose the future direction I would like to take.

Binoculars Ability to look farther into the future from two different perspectives so I can clearly understand it in much more depth.

Biochip Ability to understand a developing situation in much greater depth by instinctively using an array of my natural talents.

Biodegradable Ability to gracefully let go of what is no longer useful to me rather than breaking down at the thought of transformation.

Biofeedback Opportunity to clearly learn from my experiences and embody those lessons so I can continue to keep myself in the loop.

Biography Ability to draw on my life experience so I can understand my unique perspectives and openly share them with others.

Biological clock Ability to choose the precise moment to make the most of a fertile opportunity rather than feeling that time is running out.

Biological warfare Opportunity to deal with an ongoing inner tension by being more open to using my instinctive abilities and natural creativity.

Biological weapon Ability to exert my influence by powerfully asserting my beliefs, even though it may not create the result I was hoping for.

Biologist Aspect of my character that understands my instinctive needs and fundamental creativity so I can put them into practical use.

Biology Ability to choose my own course of action by developing my understanding of my natural abilities and fundamental creativity.

Bionic Ability to embody my unrealized power so I can use it tirelessly to achieve much more than I could ever have previously imagined.

Biopsy Opportunity to maintain my level of healthy awareness by examining some aspect of my self-motivation in much greater detail.

Bioterrorist Aspect of my character that has the surprising power to challenge my natural anxieties and potentially self-destructive behavior.

Biplane Ability to emphasize the uplifting qualities of one of my ideas, even though its practical aspects may prove to be a drag.

Bipolar Essential opportunity to understand the extremes of a situation without allowing it to make me feel too excited or depressed.

Birch Natural potential for my long-term spiritual growth by using my practical wisdom in a straightforward and graceful manner.

Bird Instinctive ability to rise above more practical concerns so I can spread my ideas by communicating them to other people.

Bird of prey Instinctive ability to powerfully connect with some potentially fulfilling ideas so I can grasp their significance.

Birdsong Opportunity to instinctively share my most uplifting and passionate ideas with other people in an inspiring and evocative manner.

Bird-watcher Aspect of my character that observes how I behave when I am sharing my ideas and communicating them more widely.

Birth Opportunity to bring a plan into life and use it to make a new beginning, even though I may have conceived it some time ago.

Birth certificate Ability to recognize my uniqueness in bringing a concept to life by having my expertise formally acknowledged by other people.

Birth control Opportunity to responsibly take full control of my creative urges and how they might potentially be conceived by other people.

Birthday Opportunity to joyfully celebrate my individual uniqueness by having the value of my creative gifts recognized by other people.

Birthday cake Ability to fulfill a potential ambition by celebrating my unique talents so I can continue to happily share them with others.

Birthing partner Aspect of my character that provides me with support and encouragement so I can successfully bring my concepts into reality.

Biscuits Ability to fulfill a potential ambition by conveniently taking a small short-term reward for behaving in a particular way.

Bisexual Essential ability to balance my masculine and feminine energies by embodying the strength and power of my creative instincts.

Bishop Aspect of my character that looks after my developing spirituality and observes how my progress is viewed by other people.

Bison Instinctive ability to gather a wide range of my talents so I can use my creativity to drive the situation forward.

Bistro Situation where I can make choices about how I can fulfill a valuable ambition without making too much of a meal out of it.

Bit Ability to confidently understand the wider situation and take decisive action by using one piece of information at a time.

Bitch Instinctive ability to show my unconditional loyalty and determination to change my situation rather than just moaning about it.

Bite Essential ability to use my power and confidence to take incisive action so I can begin to fulfill one of my potential ambitions.

Biting Opportunity to assert my confidence and power by getting stuck in and having the honesty to say what I think.

Biting animal Opportunity to confidently assert my instinctive creativity instead of feeling uncomfortable about openly expressing my talent.

Biting dog Opportunity to persistently demonstrate my loyalty and affection, even though it requires me to express myself quite sharply.

Biting snake Opportunity to be more confident so I can transform my self-image instead of trying to hang on to painful experiences from the past.

Bit part Aspect of my character that has the talent to play a leading role rather than feeling that I'm stuck on the sidelines.

Bitten Realization that I can use my strength and power to incisively resolve a challenge instead of always just chewing it over.

Bitter Essential ability to use my personal taste to get the flavor of the situation rather than behaving in an unpleasant manner.

Bivouac Ability to feel relaxed and comfortable in an unfamiliar situation by using my resourcefulness to help me feel more secure.

Bizarre Opportunity to reconcile some aspects of my life that may seem at odds with each other so I can resolve any challenges they cause.

Blabbering Opportunity to communicate how I feel by being discreet rather than chattering on and on with no real purpose.

Black Mood that can color my perspective by revealing the transformational value of unfamiliar possibilities emerging for me.

Black and white Realization that I can rationally consider the facts and figures in a much more colorful way without losing my objectivity.

Black belt Ability to masterfully resolve my inner conflicts by using any emerging possibilities in a balanced and graceful manner.

Blackbird Instinctive ability to spread my ideas by communicating them to other people in a very bright and appealing manner.

Blackboard Ability to share an important lesson I have experienced by describing it rationally and using black-and-white facts.

Black box recorder Ability to have a much clearer awareness of possible outcomes for a project rather than feeling it will end in disaster.

B

Black eye Essential opportunity to achieve my vision by looking beyond an uncomfortable situation that has made quite an impact on me.

Black hole Opportunity to use my talents to shine rather than feeling there is no escape from the gravity of my situation.

Black ice Ability to be more transparent about how I intend to make progress instead of thinking that everything is sliding out of control.

Black magic Opportunity to understand the great value of my emerging power by using it to look beyond any fearful superstitions.

Blackmail Opportunity to open up emotionally and express myself honestly so I can release myself from any guilty feelings.

Blackmailer Aspect of my character that can openly express how I feel in a clear and honest way so I can resolve any guilty feelings.

Blackmail note Ability to communicate my needs by expressing myself openly and honestly so I can free myself from any feelings of guilt.

Blacksmith Aspect of my character that can powerfully shape a situation and hammer out a result without getting overwrought about it.

Black widow Instinctive ability to release myself from an emotional entanglement so I can fundamentally transform my anxieties.

Bladder Essential ability to contain the accumulated emotions and feelings that no longer serve me so I can let them go in a healthy way.

Blade Ability to use the power and strength of my expertise to cut through any confusion so that I can get straight to the point.

Blame Realization that I need to understand my contribution to a successful outcome rather than always being so self-critical.

Blank Realization that I need to keep a clear head about emerging possibilities instead of becoming too occupied by other thoughts.

Blanket Ability to feel relaxed and comfortable by covering up my vulnerabilities and surrounding myself with a sense of loving security.

Blare Realization that I can communicate what I feel in a quiet and calm way rather than thinking I have to shout about it.

Blasphemy Opportunity to be more open to the viewpoints of other people by having the courage to question my strongest beliefs.

Blast Ability to channel some of my most powerful thoughts and theories so I can use them to make a sudden and positive impact.

Blast furnace Ability to get fired up about how I can make a creative impact by suddenly realizing how to positively channel my energy.

Blaze Opportunity to make a vital development that can illuminate my fundamental passions and resolve some powerful tensions.

Bleach Ability to change my outlook of a situation by understanding the strength of my emotions rather than feeling washed-out.

Bleak Realization that I can use the richness of my imagination to develop my talents and make myself feel much more comfortable.

Bleeding Opportunity to channel my passions by healing any old wounds rather than allowing my emotions to leak out uncontrollably.

Bleep Realization that I need to draw my attention to the significance of a specific event rather than always trying to censor it.

Blemish Ability to clear up a minor misunderstanding about a fleeting and superficial impression of a deeper and more complex situation.

Blender Ability to fulfill an ambition by taking a mix of thoughts and feelings and smoothly integrating them into a pleasing outcome.

Blending Opportunity to fit in with what might be happening around me by understanding how my unique abilities naturally stand out.

Blessing Opportunity to reflect on my unique talents and how I can count on them to make me feel good about my continuing progress.

Blimp Ability to contain my more expansive ideas in a defined framework so I can use them to observe how I communicate my intentions.

Blind Essential opportunity to look beyond the more obvious aspects of a situation so I can see what is happening.

Blind date Opportunity to become more acquainted with an unfamiliar aspect of my character so I can see my talents in a different light.

Blindfold Ability to open up to a wider perspective and understand what is happening rather than just blindly following other people.

Blind spot Situation where I need to use my instinct and intuition to understand what is going on rather than taking it at face value.

Bling Ability to attract attention by demonstrating my real value instead of trying to dazzle other people by merely showing off.

Blink Natural ability to open up to opportunities that are happening outside by quickly reflecting what is happening on the inside.

Bliss Opportunity to fundamentally experience the deepest and widest aspects of my individual spiritual awareness in any situation.

Blister Essential ability to move on from a situation that has been rubbing me the wrong way and causing repeated friction for me.

Blitz Opportunity to engage with a challenge by taking swift and vigorous action as I push forward and work at lightning speed.

Blizzard Opportunity to be much clearer about a seemingly uncontrollable swirl of emotions instead of feeling overwhelmed by them.

Bloated Realization that I need to be more definite about my chosen outcome rather than feeling that I need to keep expanding.

B

Block Ability to make progress by creating a solid piece of work without allowing myself to feel obstructed by other people.

Blockage Situation where I can open myself up to a range of different possibilities and get my creative flow moving again.

Blocked Opportunity to continue moving ahead by giving myself permission to resume progress rather than imposing any self-limitations.

Blocked entrance Opportunity to take definite steps that will open me up to a wider range of possibilities instead of feeling frustrated.

Blocked road Opportunity to explore alternative ways of pursuing my ambitions so I can successfully accomplish my chosen objective.

Blocked toilet Opportunity to open up about my own needs instead of feeling that other people are constantly dumping their problems on me.

Blog Ability to powerfully share my personal learning and experience with a wider audience by communicating as clearly as I can.

Blonde Ability to present my way of thinking in an apparently open and innocent style that other people often find very attractive.

Blood Essential capacity to convey my unique passion and vitality in any situation by naturally channeling the flow of my emotions.

Blood bank Situation where I can draw on my accumulated wealth of experience so others will recognize my unique value.

Blood-curdling Opportunity to take a fresh approach to channeling my passion and vitality rather than being terrified of new experiences.

Blood donor Aspect of my character that has the courage to be open about my passions and willingly shares them so I can inspire other people.

Blood in mouth Opportunity to speak out about powerful passions instead of allowing my confidence and vitality to drain away.

Blood poisoning Essential opportunity to choose how I react to any unwelcome emotions rather than responding in a way that causes more bad blood.

Bloodstain Opportunity to use my passion and vitality to clear up any emotional experiences that may be coloring how I see the future.

Blood-sucking insect Instinctive ability to thrive in any situation without allowing the pointed remarks of other people to leave me feeling drained.

Blood test Opportunity to judge my own levels of passion and vitality rather than letting other people decide if I make the grade.

Blood transfusion Opportunity to share my vitality and passion with other people to help them with a personal challenge they feel strongly about.

Bloom Natural ability to open up to the blossoming of a number of new ideas and how they can help creative relationships flower.

Blooper Opportunity to reflect on the unspoken value of any unforeseen outcomes rather than trying to hide my public embarrassment.

Blossom Natural ability to open myself up to an emerging opportunity in which I can attract people into a flourishing creative environment.

Blot Ability to consistently soak up criticism from other people rather than feeling they are trying to place a black mark against me.

Blotchy Ability to clear up a number of misunderstandings about some superficial impressions of a deeper and more complex situation.

Blouse Ability to present my self-image to people in a way that displays my potential creativity in a more formal and public manner.

Blow Opportunity to powerfully direct my inspirational thoughts and theories to other people without having to resort to conflict.

Blowout Opportunity to deal with an unexpectedly high-pressure situation by containing my feelings and maintaining emotional control.

Blowpipe Ability to concentrate on a particular idea so I can powerfully assert my beliefs and exert my influence over others.

Blowtorch Ability to shape my chosen outcome by concentrating on a particular aspect of the situation I need to transform.

Blubbering Essential opportunity to protect myself from emotional discomfort instead of becoming uncontrollably upset and incoherent.

Bludgeoning Opportunity to clearly state my feelings in a direct manner rather than trying to force my opinion on to other people.

Blue Mood that can color my perspective by truthfully reflecting my emotional outlook in a cool and calmly considered manner.

Bluebell Natural ability to open up to emerging ideas so I can encourage them to blossom while staying firmly grounded in reality.

Blueberry Natural ability to fulfill an ambition by gathering a number of possibilities and using them to provide a fruitful result.

Blueprints Ability to carefully plan my approach in a calm and considered manner without becoming obsessed by all the details.

Bluffing Opportunity to be open about my talents and how I display them to people rather than trying to hide my expertise.

Blunder Opportunity to keep my eyes open and proceed carefully instead of always feeling I am about to make a big mistake.

Blunt Realization that being open and honest is the best way to cut through confusion rather than being too pointed in my criticism.

Blurred Realization that I can make things much clearer for myself by moving quickly and taking action instead of just being vague.

Blush Essential opportunity to be proud of my achievements so I can openly share them with other people rather than trying to hide them.

Blustery Opportunity to resolve an unsettling atmosphere by speaking my truth so I can take a calmer and more consistent approach.

Boa constrictor Instinctive ability to transform a situation by healing hurt feelings and releasing myself from any restrictions I have imposed.

Boar Instinctive ability to unearth hidden value by rooting around in the practicalities, even though it can often seem quite dull.

Board Ability to be open and honest about my habitual patterns of behavior rather than trying to sweep aside any criticism of them.

Boarder Aspect of my character that can feel more at home with my skills by showing myself as me instead of how people want to see me.

Board game Opportunity to achieve a favorable outcome by making considered choices and working within previously agreed-upon guidelines.

Boarding call Opportunity to immediately embark on a new project so I can get it off the ground and make significant progress with it.

Boarding house Situation where I feel I should show up to other people in a particular way instead of letting them see my true talents.

Boarding pass Ability to give myself the permission to embark on my chosen opportunity and have my choice clearly acknowledged by other people.

Boarding school Situation where I can learn valuable lessons and examine what I know so I can feel more at home with my unique talents.

Boast Realization that I can make a big idea happen by understanding the practicalities and being open about my concerns.

Boat Ability to navigate complex and unpredictable feelings by using my instincts and experience to maintain my emotional stability.

Boathouse Situation where I have the security and support to feel more at home with different ways of navigating complex emotions.

Boatyard Situation where I can give myself the space to build my skills navigating complex and unpredictable feelings.

Bobsleigh Ability to use the result of my accumulated efforts to speedily make progress toward my goal in a cool and detached manner.

Bocce Opportunity to decide an uncertain outcome by keeping my feet firmly planted on the ground so I can use my steely resolve.

Bodies Ability to become more aware of all the potential ways in which I can use my natural talents so I can bring them to life.

Bodily harm Opportunity to look after my levels of self-motivation rather than allowing others to damage my feelings of self-esteem.

Body Essential ability to make sense of a situation by using my creative instincts to direct my self-motivation and energy.

Body armor Ability to robustly defend my deeper feelings of self-motivation instead of allowing other people to make me feel vulnerable.

Body builder Aspect of my character that consistently makes an effort to provide me with a healthy awareness of my power and strength.

Body double Aspect of my character that has the courage to take decisive action rather than just appearing to be involved in the outcome.

Body fluid Essential ability to express my emotions so I can stay self-motivated, regardless of what shape I feel I am in.

Bodyguard Aspect of my character that looks after my health and well-being and ensures that I am safe and secure in any situation.

Body hair Essential ability to develop ideas that emerge from my fundamental behaviors so I can use them to shape my plans for growth.

Body hugging Opportunity to present my self-image to the people around me by confidently showing off the best aspects of my character.

Body mass index Ability to indulge in my appetite for success by being motivated to take a fresh approach and exercise a healthier perspective.

Body part Essential ability to understand what I am contributing to a situation so I can take the most effective action.

Body piercing Ability to draw attention to what motivates me by going beyond superficial details so I can get to the point.

Body scanner Ability to methodically observe what motivates me at a deeper level so I can understand how to feel more secure.

Body scrub Opportunity to make a real effort and come clean about my motivation so I can take a fresh approach to a challenge.

Body search Opportunity to discover how I feel about my potential talents rather than trying to conceal my creative instincts.

Body snatcher Aspect of my character that can grasp the significance of my potential talent and how I can use it to support my future progress.

Body wrap Opportunity to maintain my individual levels of self-motivation rather than becoming too involved in the surrounding situation.

Bog Situation where I can release myself from having to deal with any messy details that are persistently slowing down my progress.

Bogus caller Aspect of my character that needs to speak my truth instead of always saying what I think other people want to hear.

Boil Essential ability to release heated emotions that are building up under the surface so I can let go of any associated guilt.

Boiler Ability to provide a warm and comfortable atmosphere by safely containing my feelings when emotional temperatures are high.

Boiler room Aspect of myself that has the ability to make everything seem warm and comfortable, even when the underlying mood is cool.

Boiling Opportunity to control my emotions by letting off some steam rather than letting my feelings bubble up uncontrollably.

Boisterous Realization that I can make a significant difference by quietly using my expertise instead of making a big noise about my skills.

Bold Realization that I need to emphasize my talents by being courageous and decisive rather than using my usual approach.

Bollard Ability to remain connected to a firm reality rather than allowing my attention to be diverted by an apparent obstacle.

Bolt Ability to feel secure about a situation and achieve closure instead of feeling that I have to immediately escape from it.

Bolt hole Situation where I can bring my talents out into the open for everyone to see rather than running away from potential criticism.

Bomb Ability to safely contain my potentially explosive feelings so I can aim to use my energy to create a positive transformation.

Bomb aimer Aspect of my character that chooses to let go of potentially explosive feelings by expertly choosing just the right moment.

B

Bombardment Opportunity to show my power by forcefully defending my personal boundaries from some potentially hostile thoughts and ideas.

Bomb-disposal expert Aspect of my character that understands the intricacies of what can trigger certain behaviors so I can safely deal with them.

Bomb site Situation where I have previously used my accumulated energy to create a huge transformation that can now be developed further.

Bond Ability to stay connected at a fundamental level without feeling trapped by thinking that I'm overly attached to the outcome.

Bondage Opportunity to release myself from any constraints about how other people see me rather than feeling I'm bound to please them.

Bone Essential ability to give a fundamental structure to what I do so I can use my inner strength to support myself in my actions.

Bone marrow Essential ability to make myself immune to criticism from other people by using my inner strength to fundamentally support me.

Bone marrow transplant Opportunity to use my inner strength to resolve an unhealthy situation instead of rejecting my ability to make a difference.

Bonfire Opportunity to draw attention to a creative transformation by heaping praise on it and openly sharing it with other people.

Bonkers Realization that I can become more intimate with the irrational nature of my creativity so I can look at practical uses for it.

Bonnet Ability to present my self-image to people in a way that draws attention to my ambitions so I can be more open about them.

Bonus Opportunity to recognize the increasing value of my unseen talents and realize that I have more to offer than I often think.

Booby trap Opportunity to release myself from any self-limiting behavior by openly

showing that I am able to learn from my experiences.

Book Ability to open up to the wealth of my accumulated knowledge and learning so I can publicly share it with other people.

Bookcase Ability to bring different aspects of my knowledge and learning together so I can feel secure in maintaining my expertise.

Bookkeeper Aspect of my character that ensures my real value can be recognized by making sure that everything adds up about a situation.

Bookmaker Aspect of my character that is fully committed to my creative success rather than always feeling at odds with everything.

Boomerang Ability to bend rules to my advantage by tossing an idea into the air and seeing what thoughts others come back with.

Booster seat Ability to raise the profile of my individual viewpoint so I can become more aware of how I can increase support for it.

Boot Ability to present my self-image to people by taking steps to protect my status so I can stamp my authority on the situation.

Booth Situation where I can feel safe and comfortable in exploring some of the wilder and less familiar aspects of my character.

Bootleg Ability to share my unique talents with people in an open and honest way without feeling that I have to ask for their permission.

Border Situation where I can give myself permission to cross a threshold so I can explore unfamiliar aspects of my character.

Bored Realization that I can increase my level of enthusiasm by going much deeper in an area that interests me.

Born Realization that I have the resources to revitalize a plan I conceived some time ago and can use it to make a new beginning.

Borrowing Realization that I owe it to myself to have my value fully acknowledged by other people instead of feeling indebted to them.

B

Bosom Essential ability to nurture other people by bringing them closer to me and openly being able to take them into my confidence.

Boss Aspect of my character that asserts my ability to make powerful decisions so I can then have the authority to act on them.

Botanic garden Situation where I can explore some of the more exotic aspects of my wider social relationships and become more familiar with them.

Botched up Opportunity to perform a task in a manner that satisfies me rather than allowing other people to spoil my enjoyment of it.

Bothered Realization that I can resolve a challenging situation by taking the trouble to understand what might be irritating me.

Botnet Ability to use my own ideas to quickly make a decision instead of feeling that I'm under the influence of how other people think.

Botox Essential opportunity to honestly express my individual feelings and insight rather than appearing blank and unconvincing.

Bottle Ability to use my courage and resourcefulness to draw on my accumulated experience instead of just trying to keep it hidden.

Bottom Situation where I can understand my deepest motivations by getting right down to what is fundamentally important to me.

Bottomless Realization that I have an apparently infinite capacity to understand my deepest motivations and their profound influence.

Boulder Ability to remain firm and strong about a heavy responsibility by staying detached from the wider implications of the situation.

Bounce Realization that I can rebound from any apparent setbacks by using my natural resilience to happily choose my own direction.

Bouncer Aspect of my character that can

help me spring back from any rebuffs by giving myself permission to be more optimistic.

Bouncy castle Situation where I can play around with my more powerful characteristics and spring back from any criticism from others.

Bound Opportunity to make a big leap forward in my progress rather than feeling committed to anything that may be holding me back.

Boundary Situation where I can get to the center of some of my self-limiting behaviors by clearly being more open with other people.

Boundless Realization that I have an apparently limitless imagination and can use it to achieve specific goals without feeling restricted.

Bounty hunter Aspect of my character that understands the value of an opportunity that has been eluding me and is going to make it happen.

Bouquet Ability to attract attention to a variety of my blossoming talents I have brought together into a beautiful reality.

Boutique Situation where I can exclusively display my special talents so other people can fully appreciate my unique expertise.

Bow Ability to cut through complex and unpredictable feelings by choosing a definite direction that maintains my emotional stability.

Bow and arrow Ability to meet my target in a tense situation by firing off a quick decision rather than always appearing high-strung.

Bowel Essential ability to process in a healthy manner the experiences I have assimilated so I can thoroughly digest my learning from them.

Bowing Opportunity to stand up for what I believe in and have it recognized by other people instead of following their wishes.

Bowl Ability to contain my emotions so I can keep myself open and receptive to different ways of fulfilling my needs and ambitions.

Bowling alley Situation where I can get all my opportunities lined up so I can skillfully make the most of them without knocking myself out.

Bow tie Ability to present my self-image to other people by neatly pulling together and formally connecting my ideas and feelings.

Box Ability to feel safe and secure by setting personal boundaries around my resources, even though it can be quite limiting.

Boxer Aspect of my character that can deal with unresolved inner conflicts by not pulling any punches and just taking it on the chin.

Boxing Opportunity to resolve any ongoing inner tension by courageously squaring up to the challenge and being firm in my stance.

Boxing gloves Ability to present my self-image to people in a way that protects my power to safely resolve any ongoing inner conflicts.

Box room Aspect of myself in which I can set personal boundaries around my resources and keep them safe and secure until I need them.

Boy Aspect of my character that embodies my playful curiosity and has the potential to assertively develop my strength and power.

Boy band Aspects of my character that can work harmoniously together so I can develop my strength and power to create a unique outcome.

Boyfriend Aspect of my character that helps me become more intimately aware of my strength and power so I can connect more deeply to them.

Bra Ability to support my capacity for nurturing other people so I am able to present it to them in a socially acceptable manner.

Bracelet Ability to directly shape my chosen outcome by drawing other people's attention to the value of what I am reaching out for.

Braces Ability to firmly support my levels of confidence so I can make decisions that are fully aligned with my personal values.

Bragging Opportunity to bring one of my big ideas into reality by understanding the practicalities and being open about my concerns.

Braid Ability to weave a number of strands of thinking together so I can integrate their different qualities into a stronger alignment.

Braille Essential ability to be sensitive about how I control my actions so I can look beyond the more obvious aspects of a situation.

Brain Essential ability to use my instinctive intelligence to understand patterns that naturally emerge in complex situations.

Brain damage Opportunity to protect my deeper self-awareness rather than worrying whether an experience will harm how I appear to other people.

Brain-dead Opportunity to bring my accumulated wisdom back to life so I can revitalize a deeper awareness that may have seemed lost to me.

Brain implant Ability to achieve a deeper understanding of my habitual behaviors rather than being distracted by intrusive thoughts.

Brain surgeon Aspect of my character that can decisively resolve a potentially unhealthy behavior by taking very specific and incisive action.

Brainwashing Opportunity to open up my natural awareness by letting go of what I no longer need so I can come clean and take a fresh approach.

Brain wave Ability to make a real difference by understanding the power of my thoughts and realizing how I can use their emerging value.

Brake Ability to stay in control of my drive and ambition instead of feeling that I am getting carried away by circumstances.

Brake failure Opportunity to relax and let go of any foregone conclusions rather than feeling I always have to be in complete control.

B

Brake light Ability to signal to myself that I may be in danger of getting uncontrollably carried away by my powerful drives and ambitions.

Braking heavily Opportunity to understand the weighty responsibilities associated with a commitment so I can decide how I approach it.

Bramble Natural ability to pick the right moment so I can achieve a fruitful outcome from a potentially thorny situation.

Branch Natural ability to develop my long-term spiritual connections so I can spread out from my more familiar roots.

Branding iron Ability to clearly identify my creative instincts without getting too hot and bothered about how I can permanently make my mark.

Brand-new Ability to make the most of an emerging opportunity by seeing myself in a different way instead of doing the same old thing.

Brandy Potential to fulfill an emotional need by distilling the wisdom I have developed from a variety of fruitful experiences.

Brass Ability to bring different aspects of my fundamental power together so I can use them to provide a valuable and honest result.

Bravery Opportunity to demonstrate my courage to other people by being confident in my talents rather than trying to hide them away.

Brawl Ability to resolve any inner tensions that I may have instead of always making a big noise about them and doing nothing.

Brawny Essential ability to feel comfortable in my strength of purpose so I can use my brain to direct my power as wisely as I can.

Brazier Ability to creatively transform my beliefs by publicly displaying my passion, even though I may only have limited resources.

Breach Situation where I can step into a big opportunity by making a stronger connection with other people and resolving any differences.

Bread Potential to fulfill my ambitions by looking after my fundamental needs and ensuring that others recognize my value.

Bread crumbs Potential to fulfill my ambitions by taking care of my basic needs rather than trying to keep track of lots of different wishes.

Breadth Realization that I can see the bigger picture by taking a wider perspective rather than appearing narrow-minded.

Break Ability to deal with one of my habitual behaviors by taking some time out and developing more integrated and useful patterns.

Breakdance Ability to embody my natural rhythms by staying grounded and taking unusual steps to bring my individual expertise to life.

Breakdown Opportunity to use my drive and ambition to break out of habitual patterns so I can create a dramatic transformation in my life.

Breakfast Opportunity to wake up to a new way of feeding my appetite for success so I can nourish my continuing growth and vitality.

Break-in Opportunity to understand the value of some of my habitual behaviors rather than allowing other people to try to change them.

Breaking Opportunity to free myself from some of my habitual patterns of behavior so I can continue to make deeper connections.

Breaking free Opportunity to let go of the past by releasing myself from any self-imposed limitations that may have been holding me back.

Breakout Opportunity to let go of some of my self-limitations so I can move beyond a situation I have been feeling trapped in.

Breakup Opportunity to let go of aspects of my character I no longer feel deeply connected with and allow myself to freely move on.

Breakwater Situation where I can set some firm personal boundaries to help me successfully deal with any deeply powerful emotions.

Breast Essential ability to look after myself and other people by opening up about how I can be of most assistance to them.

Breast-feeding Essential opportunity to nurture one of my concepts and develop it further by taking it into the bosom of my affections.

Breast implant Essential opportunity to understand that my huge capacity for looking after other people goes beyond superficial appearances.

Breath Essential ability to consistently inspire myself and other people in a healthy and vital way that makes us feel truly alive.

Breathalyzer Ability to closely monitor how I am communicating my inspiration to other people rather than using it as a form of escape.

Breathing Essential opportunity to absorb thoughts and ideas from other people so I can respond to them by sharing my plans and theories.

Breathing under water Opportunity to immerse myself in my deeper emotions so I feel more comfortable in expressing some of my ways of thinking.

Breath test Ability to examine how well I am communicating my inspiration to other people rather than continually deluding myself.

Breed Opportunity to use my creative instincts to ensure that my concepts consistently happen in reality instead of being a rarity.

Breeze Natural opportunity to use a simple idea to produce a result with much greater ease than I had previously thought possible.

Brewery Situation where I can fulfill an emotional need by methodically processing feelings I have been trying to bottle up.

Brewing Opportunity to process some possibly confusing feelings rather than concocting an explanation to avoid any trouble.

Bribe Opportunity to motivate myself by recognizing the value of the underlying issue and openly sharing it with other people.

Brick Ability to provide solid and supportive foundations for a developing situation that may have been causing me some anxiety.

Bricklayer Aspect of my character that can consistently provide a solid and supportive foundation for my further personal development.

Bride Aspect of my character that is willing to support my ambitions and make a long-lasting commitment to my enduring creativity.

Bridegroom Aspect of my character that willingly commits to supporting my talents and consistently supports all my enduring ambitions.

Bridesmaid Aspect of my character that happily supports the long-term commitments of others so they can realize their ambitions.

Bridge Situation where I can resolve a dilemma by creating a lasting connection between two apparently distinct areas of my life.

Bridle Ability to directly harness my unconscious energies, even though I may initially resist trying to make progress in this way.

Brief Realization that I can quickly convey a powerful understanding of how I really feel rather than going on about it at length.

Briefcase Ability to securely look after my knowledge so I can be open to new thinking that will carry me forward in my career.

Brigade Aspects of my character that have the power to defend my urgent needs and successfully engage with any heavy responsibilities.

B

Bright Realization that I can use my natural intelligence to illuminate a potentially dull situation and make it all seem clearer.

Brilliant Realization that I can use my creative power in a focused manner rather than trying to dazzle everyone with my talent.

Brimming Realization that I have a capacity to fulfill all my emotional needs without letting my feelings spill over uncontrollably.

Bring Opportunity to convey what I need to help me successfully achieve my ambitions rather than quitting.

Brink Situation where I can choose to take a decisive step to transform a situation instead of always feeling that I'm on edge.

Brisk Realization that I can make an opportunity happen very quickly without always having to be too abrupt with other people.

Bristles Essential ability to develop ideas that naturally emerge in day-to-day activities without becoming too rigid in my thinking.

Brittle Realization that I can achieve my deeper ambitions by being open and flexible rather than trying to present a tough exterior.

Broad Realization that I have the opportunity to use my entire range of talents instead of feeling restricted to a narrow perspective.

Broadband Ability to open myself up to a wide range of thoughts from other people so I can convey my own feelings to a wider audience.

Broadcast Ability to share my innermost thoughts and feelings on a wide variety of subjects by being receptive to people's responses.

Broccoli Natural ability to fulfill my ambitions by having a healthy awareness of how I can use my inner strengths in a fresh way.

Broken Opportunity to carefully resolve a potentially fragile situation so I can use it to successfully transform my circumstances.

Broken bone Essential opportunity to use my inner strength to make a straight decision so I can continue to support myself in my actions.

Broken-down car Opportunity to understand where I need to pay more attention to my personal drive so I can regain my fundamental motivation.

Broken-down truck Opportunity to understand my driving force so I can successfully convey the value of my ambitions to the people around me.

Broken glass Opportunity to be clear about what I need to say to other people rather than worrying they will shatter my confidence.

Brokenhearted Essential opportunity to resolve a situation in which I feel emotionally fragile by having the courage to keep my passion flowing.

Broken home Situation where I can feel more secure with all the different aspects of myself by bravely stepping outside my comfort zone.

Broken teeth Opportunity to openly display my power and confidence to other people, even though I might be feeling quite fragile inside.

Bronze Ability to integrate different aspects of my fundamental power so I can shape a successful outcome in a winning way.

Bronzed Essential opportunity to have a healthy awareness of what is happening by exposing myself to a range of illuminating ideas.

Brooch Ability to attract attention to the feelings I consider most valuable to me so that I can express them more graciously.

Brood Instinctive ability to conceive a number of new ideas so I can develop them more fully and share them with other people.

Broody Opportunity to take action and produce a number of possibilities rather than worrying about the situation and doing nothing.

Brook Situation where I can connect with my emotions without feeling that I have to always babble on about them to other people.

Broom Ability to clear up any confusion by choosing to make some sweeping changes and brushing off any criticism from other people.

Broomstick Ability to blow away the cobwebs by clearing up any flights of fancy and being very specific about any sweeping generalizations.

Broth Potential to achieve my ambitions by nourishing my continuing growth without feeling I have to involve a lot of other people.

Brothel Situation where I need to recognize my creative value so I can set some safe personal boundaries around how I use it.

Brother Aspect of my character that enables me to assert my strength and power in familiar situations without being too overbearing.

Brought Realization that I have what I need to successfully achieve a particular ambition rather than feeling I'm being left behind.

Brow Essential ability to make the effort to get to the edge of my understanding so I can easily raise my level of awareness.

Brown Mood that can color my perspective by naturally making me feel comfortable with the practicalities in a warm and grounded way.

Browser Ability to find exactly what I'm looking for rather than feeling that I always have to be trying to identify new opportunities.

Bruise Essential opportunity to resolve an uncomfortable situation that seems to have made an impact on me at a superficial level.

Brunch Opportunity to fulfill my appetite for success by being more relaxed about my ambitions so I can progress to greater achievements.

Brunette Ability to present my thinking in a way that illuminates some of my darker ideas and helps me get them clearly out in the open.

Brunt Realization that I can be at the center of a transformation that has a great impact so I can absorb any associated criticism.

Brush Ability to clear up some uncertain thinking and make it more presentable without being too dismissive of other people's ideas.

Brutality Realization that I can use my natural power in a more gracious way rather than always having to resort to strong-arm tactics.

Bubble Ability to take an emerging idea that apparently seems quite insubstantial so I can see how far it might go before it fades away.

Bubble bath Situation where I feel really relaxed and am happy to immerse myself in my feelings so I can see what ideas might emerge.

Bubblegum Ability to spit out what I really need to say to other people rather than constantly chewing it over and trying to sugarcoat it.

Bubble wrap Ability to protect a potentially fragile concept by surrounding it in different layers of meaning that may seem more substantial.

Bubonic plague Opportunity to clear up a potentially unhealthy situation by resolving some gnawing anxieties and a variety of minor irritations.

Buck Instinctive ability to value my ideas and understand my responsibility for them rather than sharing them indiscriminately.

Bucket Ability to use my accumulated knowledge and experience to consistently carry me through any potentially challenging situations.

Buckle Ability to hold a situation securely together by remaining connected, even when it may seem to be collapsing around me.

Bucktoothed Essential opportunity to confidently display my value to other people instead of feeling that I may appear too intrusive to them.

Bud Natural ability to let my creative potential blossom in its own good time rather than feeling I have to cut it off prematurely.

Buddha Aspect of my character that is comfortable with my perspective on my deeper truth and is at peace with my needs and desires.

Buddy Aspect of my character that I am well acquainted with and that I can always rely on to support me in unfamiliar situations.

Budge Realization that I can get a situation moving and continue my progress past an obstacle by understanding what really moves me.

Budgie Instinctive ability to chatter away about some ideas I have a lot of affection for, even though they may seem quite trivial.

Buffalo Instinctive ability to gather a wide range of my talents together so I can use my creativity to drive the situation forward.

Buffer Ability to bring a particular stage of my professional career to a definite conclusion so I have the space to change track.

Buffet Opportunity to fulfill my appetite for success by sharing a variety of my ambitions with other people and letting them help me.

Bug Instinctive ability to allow small details to look after themselves rather than letting myself be too disconcerted by them.

Buggy Ability to clearly convey a concept I feel very strongly about without letting myself be distracted by any minor details.

Bugle Ability to give myself a wake-up call about an approaching challenge that may potentially involve conflicting perspectives.

Builder Aspect of my character that provides me with the firm foundations to develop a solidly structured sense of who I really am.

Building Situation where I can fully step into the various aspects of my inner and outer selves and see how I can best develop them.

Building site Situation where I can lay the foundations for some solid personal growth that will provide possibilities for further development.

Bulb Natural ability to accumulate vital resources and keep them safe so I can develop them more fully when the time is right.

Bulging Realization that I have accumulated more wisdom and experience than I was aware of and can use it to open up new areas.

Bulimic Essential opportunity to understand how I can feel more fulfilled rather than indulging myself in unsettling experiences.

Bulky Realization that I can successfully deal with an apparently enormous challenge by making the time and space to handle it.

Bull Instinctive ability to remain consistently patient rather than releasing any pent-up aggression that is causing me to see red.

Bulldog Instinctive ability to show my unconditional loyalty and affection for particular people by always being patient and persistent.

Bulldozer Ability to level with myself about potentially destructive habits so I can transform them into opportunities for self-development.

Bullet Ability to take a single decisive action so I can assert my power from a distance and achieve the ambition I'm aiming for.

Bullet hole Ability to look deeper into some painful feelings so I can defend myself against any potentially wounding criticism.

Bulletin Opportunity to communicate how I feel by giving a brief account of my experiences rather than going on at length.

Bulletin board Ability to display my wider awareness of future possibilities so I can invite others to help me achieve my ambitions.

Bulletproof Ability to protect myself from any potentially wounding criticism as people try to assert their power over me from a distance.

Bullfighter Aspect of my character that can resolve my feelings of pent-up aggression by having the courage to flag my frustrations.

Bullion Ability to concentrate on my fundamental value in a more refined manner so it is simpler for people to see my strengths.

Bull's-eye Ability to take my time and carefully prepare so I can get to the center of the ambition I've been aiming for.

Bully Aspect of my character that has the power to own my vulnerabilities by courageously revealing my weaknesses to other people.

Bum Essential ability to sense what is happening so I can become more aware of how I can continue to support my position.

Bump Opportunity to dislodge myself from any feelings of complacency instead of feeling that other people are giving me a rough ride.

Bump start Opportunity to regain my momentum and drive by allowing others to keep pushing me rather than just feeling demotivated.

Bumpy Opportunity to use an apparently unavoidable confrontation to choose the direction I will take with my conflicting ambitions.

Bun Potential to fulfill an ambition by gathering together some of my emerging thoughts and ideas in a compact and tidy style.

Bunch Ability to collect a range of my abilities so I can use them to stay fully connected to a larger opportunity.

Bundle Ability to bring a wide variety of ideas together to increase my overall value rather than just feeling nervous for no reason.

Bung Ability to contain my feelings so I can allow my expertise to mature instead of feeling drained by the experience.

Bungalow Situation where I am more involved with the practical aspects of self-development rather than any of the theoretical perspectives.

Bungee jump Opportunity to decisively face my fears by having the courage to take a big step that may result in a lot of ups and downs.

Bungled attempt Opportunity to use my experience and expertise to do the right thing rather than feeling my actions will end in failure.

Bungling detective Aspect of my character that can discover my profound truths by clearly understanding what I consider to be some of my failings.

Bunion Essential opportunity to point myself in the right direction so I can elevate my status without getting too bent out of shape.

Bunk bed Situation where I can feel relaxed and comfortable with a number of my creative talents on a variety of different levels.

Bunker Situation where I can defend my thoughts and theories by using some of the deeper resources I often conceal from people.

Bunker buster Ability to make a major breakthrough by using my expertise to create a powerful transformation in my deeper understanding.

Bunker mentality Realization that I need to open up some of my ideas to others rather than feeling I need to defend my way of thinking.

Buoy Ability to continually keep my spirits up as I guide myself through an emotional situation that may have some hidden challenges.

Buoyancy aid Ability to use some helpful thoughts and ideas to stop me from sinking too deeply into an emotionally upsetting situation.

Burden Ability to release myself from a heavy responsibility instead of continually allowing it to weigh on my conscience.

B

Bureaucrat Aspect of my character that tries to fit in with everyone else's demands rather than taking time to understand my own needs.

Burger Potential to fulfill an ambition by using my strength and power to shape a situation so it will have a satisfying outcome.

Burger van Ability to employ my personal resources to make committed progress rather than doing what is convenient for others.

Burglar Aspect of my character that can undervalue my need for privacy and be far too open to the intrusive needs of other people.

Burglary Opportunity to be clear about the value of my personal boundaries instead of letting others intrude into my personal space.

Burial Opportunity to lay to rest some old behaviors and habits so I can move on to a new future in a more gracious manner.

Burial plot Situation where I can understand the circumstances surrounding a major life transformation so I can work my way through it.

Buried alive Opportunity to unearth some talents I have been neglecting so I can resurrect some of my ambitions and revitalize them.

Buried body Opportunity to reveal some of my hidden creative talents so I can use my self-motivation and energy to bring them to life.

Buried city Situation where I can uncover the deeper value of my social connections so I can access some previously concealed resources.

Buried treasure Ability to reveal the wealth of experience and knowledge I have accumulated so my value will be more fully recognized.

Buried weapon Ability to disclose one of my deeper beliefs so I can understand its powerful influence in my personal relationships.

Burlesque dancer Aspect of my character that embodies my quirkier behavioral

patterns and can take creative steps to bring them to life.

Burly Realization that I have an inner strength that can be quite forceful rather than feeling I am too weak to take action.

Burn Ability to use my creative passion to catalyze a situation and transform it, even though it might seem painful at the time.

Burned Realization that I can use my creative talent to illuminate a situation and transform it rather than feeling disappointed.

Burning Opportunity to use my creative abilities to transform a situation instead of continually ending up in a heated argument about it.

Burning house Opportunity to direct my creativity toward a more constructive outcome rather than being consumed by an all-or-nothing approach.

Burning workplace Opportunity to take some heat out of a professional situation so I can create an outcome that will accommodate everyone.

Burnished Realization that I can use my fundamental strength and power to reflect my talents so I can shine in any situation.

Burp Essential opportunity to let go of some thoughts and ideas that may have been causing me some inner tension and discomfort.

Burrow Situation where I can dig a bit deeper into the more practical aspects of a situation so I can see where it might end up.

Burst Opportunity to contain my feelings in a controlled and measured way rather than suddenly feeling I have to open up.

Burying Opportunity to respectfully lay some past commitments and obligations to rest instead of hastily trying to avoid them.

Burying a body Opportunity to proudly stand up for what motivates me rather than trying to conceal my talents from other people.

Burying treasure Opportunity to use my rich experience to take action now instead of constantly waiting for more favorable circumstances.

Bus Ability to make progress toward my professional objectives by ensuring that my colleagues are heading in the same direction.

Bus driver Aspect of my character that helps me choose my professional direction and knows the best route to follow to reach my goal.

Bush Natural potential for my short-term spiritual growth by being more open to what often seems unknown and unfamiliar to me.

Bushfire Opportunity to transform my short-term spiritual growth by opening up to how rapidly I can spread my creative talents.

Business Situation where I can formally recognize the true value of my talents and abilities so I can communicate them to others.

Business card Ability to communicate my purpose to the people around me rather than show myself as I think they would like me to.

Business jet Ability to concentrate on a powerful concept so I can add my professional input to ensure it moves forward more rapidly.

Businesslike Opportunity to make people aware of the value of my creativity and expertise rather than doubting my ability to succeed.

Businessman Aspect of my character that formally recognizes the real power of my talents and abilities so I can consistently assert them.

Business park Situation where I have a range of opportunities to develop my potential expertise so I can discover my life purpose.

Business partner Aspect of my character that helps me understand the value of my talents and how I can combine them to achieve success.

Businesswoman Aspect of my character that acknowledges the true value of my empathy and wisdom in being able to achieve my chosen outcome.

Busker Aspect of my character that has the confidence to communicate my unique talents to a wider audience without any prompting.

Busking Opportunity to use my creativity in a more structured way, rather than feeling as if i'm just making it up as I go along.

Bus lane Situation where I can take a more defined approach to developing my professional expertise, even though it may be quite limiting.

Bus shelter Situation where I can spend some time considering my career options so I can understand what will make me feel most secure.

Bus station Situation where I can choose which professional path I would like to embark on so I can make a commitment to it.

Bus stop Situation where I can embark on a particular stage of my professional progression so I can get fully on board with my ambitions.

Bust Ability to nurture other people by being proud of my experiences instead of feeling that my involvement will end unexpectedly.

Bustier Ability to present my self-image to other people in a way that helps me shape a more caring approach to my chosen outcome.

Bustle Opportunity to use my abundance of self-motivation and energy to get things moving rather than just responding too slowly.

Busy Opportunity to fully engage with the situation and take decisive action instead of indulging myself in needless activity.

Butcher Aspect of my character that uses my raw talent to identify my most powerful characteristics and cuts out unnecessary influences.

B

B

Butter Potential to fulfill my ambitions by being charmingly optimistic and smoothing over any rough patches to make them more palatable.

Buttercup Natural ability for my optimism to bloom by cheerfully opening up to my creative plans and allowing them to fully blossom.

Butterfly Instinctive ability to trust in my potential to undergo a powerful transformation that will enable me to spread my wings.

Buttocks Essential ability to sense what is happening and become more aware of how I can continue to support my powerful stance.

Button Ability to hold a situation securely together by calmly taking a specific action and then knowing when I need to stay quiet.

Buttress Ability to support a situation I have been building up to for some time rather than just letting it collapse around me.

Buying Opportunity to ensure that my value is fully recognized by other people and that I am always accountable for my behaviors.

Buzzard Instinctive ability to quickly pounce on an idea that has been preying on my mind rather than just circling around it.

Buzzer Ability to alert myself to a new opportunity that has the potential to be very exciting if I choose to take action on it.

Bygone Realization that I can use my accumulated wisdom and extensive experience to let go of the past and step into a new future.

Bypass Situation where I can fast-track an ambition by avoiding any narrow-mindedness, even though it may require a different approach.

Bystander Aspect of my character that needs to be more involved in a situation, even though I feel quite comfortable in my current position.

Cab Ability to make progress with one of my ambitions by employing someone else's specific knowledge to reach my goal.

Cabaret Opportunity to fulfill some of my more unusual ambitions by being open to displaying my talents in an informal way.

Cabbage Potential to fulfill an ambition by having a healthy awareness of the mundane tasks required to make my ideas happen.

Cab driver Aspect of my character that knows the best way to reach a successful result by having extensive knowledge of the ins and outs.

Cabin Situation where I can feel comfortable and safe in exploring some of the more unknown, unfamiliar aspects of my character.

Cabin crew Aspects of my character that help me to maintain my sense of well-being as I make rapid progress with a particular project.

Cabinet Ability to accumulate useful learning and store valuable memories so I can use them to help me make decisions at a later date.

Cable Ability to directly connect with my unconscious power so I can communicate what I really need to say in an energetic way.

Cable car Ability to use connections above me to make progress with my career so I can achieve a higher level of professional prominence.

Cable television Ability to look at a wide range of potential scenarios and decide which I find myself compelled to connect with.

Cabriolet Ability to open myself up to the prevailing thinking as I use personal ambition and drive to progress toward an objective.

Cache Situation where I can gain access to some of the individual expertise I may have been keeping concealed from other people.

Cackle Opportunity to speak honestly rather than feeling as if people will laugh at me when I share my true feelings.

Cacophony Opportunity to be extremely clear about what I need to express so I can make sure it doesn't get lost in the background noise.

Cactus Natural ability to defend my innermost feelings by being prickly and unapproachable, even though I might be quite softhearted.

Caesarean birth Opportunity to turn a precious plan into reality by taking incisive action to bring a unique concept into being.

Café Situation where I can stimulate interest in my individual ambitions by sharing them with other people in my social circles.

Cafeteria Ability to brew plans that will stimulate my feelings and help energize me so I can fulfill some of my emotional needs.

Caftan Ability to present my self-image to the people around me in a way that shows my relaxed approach to exploring my spirituality.

Cage Situation where I may feel defensive about my perceived self-limitations rather than removing any barriers to my progress.

Cage fighting Opportunity to take assertive action to deal with internal conflicts instead of feeling defensive about my limitations.

Cairn Situation where I can make heaps of practical effort so I can have my highest achievements recognized by other people.

Cake Potential to fulfill a shared ambition and celebrate collective success by working through a challenge in a relaxed manner.

Calamity Opportunity to take full control of my inner power so I can make a decisive choice rather than just leaving everything to fate.

Calculator Ability to sum up a situation by taking a more objective approach so I can see how all the pros and cons add up.

Calendar Ability to make the most of my time by using my imagination to visualize the future and my experience to look back into the past.

Calf Instinctive ability to nurture a creative talent that can take care of my needs, even though it may leave me feeling vulnerable.

Calf muscle Essential ability to have my own strength of purpose and power so I can stand up for my more fundamental viewpoints.

Calibration Situation where I can examine my motives to see how they measure up to the accepted standards of other people I trust.

Caliper Ability to strongly support my beliefs by closely looking at both sides of the situation and seeing how they measure up.

Call Opportunity to understand what moves me by taking the chance to connect with the people around me at a deeper level.

Call center Situation where I try to resolve challenges by resorting to habitual behavior instead of courageously speaking up for myself.

Caller Aspect of my character that has a powerful and timely message I need to listen to rather than screening it out.

Caller ID Ability to clearly identify one of my unique characteristics that has been calling out for me to give it more attention.

Calling Opportunity to listen to my inner voice so I can hear the emerging awareness that will help me find my true purpose in life.

Callus Essential ability to be more sensitive about how I shape my future rather than being habitually tough and indifferent.

Calm Opportunity to understand the prevailing mood by creating some space and observing what ideas and feelings emerge from it.

Calorie counting Opportunity to consider how I can fulfill a personal ambition by looking at the bigger picture rather than being too picky.

Camcorder Ability to observe a specific aspect of my life so I can use it as a way of framing the context of my other habitual behaviors.

Camel Instinctive ability to deal with a challenge by being emotionally self-contained and having enduring faith in my own motivation.

Cameo Opportunity to highlight one of my talents by having the confidence to compare and contrast my skills with people around me.

Camera Ability to frame a particular perspective and reflect on the beliefs I hold rather than making a snap decision.

Cameraman Aspect of my character that holds an objective viewpoint that can give me a great deal of insight into my current situation.

Camouflage Opportunity to show my true colors and be open about my needs instead of trying to conceal them and hoping they disappear.

Camouflage netting Ability to be open about what I need rather than trying to always hide from people as a way of avoiding conflict.

Camp Situation where I can temporarily feel at home with some unfamiliar aspects of my character so I can explore their possibilities.

Campaign Opportunity to speak my truth and help expand the beliefs of other people by taking the steps I need to transform my perspective.

Camper Aspect of my character that is happy to explore the wider value of my natural potential in a practical, down-to-earth manner.

Camper van Ability to take a more self-contained approach so I can feel comfortable as I make progress with a personal ambition.

Campfire Opportunity to go to the edge of what I know so I can share a creative transformation that will bring people closer together.

Camping Opportunity to explore aspects of my character that can be very exciting but can often seem quite distant and unattainable.

Campsite Situation where I can share some of my less familiar feelings with other people and explore my natural instincts and behaviors.

Can Ability to keep an opportunity fresh in my mind by preserving my ambitions and taking full responsibility for achieving them.

Canal Situation where I can safely channel my emotions as a way of straightforwardly navigating toward a particular ambition.

Canal boat Ability to navigate a well-defined emotional situation by narrowing my focus and proceeding in a calm and consistent way.

Canal lock Situation where I can take a series of definite steps to understand the different levels of emotion I am experiencing.

Canary Instinctive ability to check on how healthy my ideas are so I can understand how optimistic I am about singing their praises.

Cancellation Opportunity to step into my own power and make my choice rather than feeling that someone else might let me down.

Cancer Essential opportunity to get to the source of an unhealthy situation and deal with it instead of letting it grow out of control.

Candidate Aspect of my character that is open and honest about my abilities and can communicate how I plan to develop them.

Candle Ability to gently illuminate my spirituality and inner wisdom, even though I may have flickers of doubt about my value.

Candlelight Situation where I can step into my power and brighten up an apparently sad situation by being naturally warm and positive.

Candlestick Ability to support my beliefs by having confidence to let my unique spirituality and inner wisdom naturally shine through.

Cane Ability to support my natural instincts for growth by being strong and flexible, even though I feel my actions may be punished.

Canine tooth Essential ability to use my confidence to stay loyal to my ambitions by making sure that I don't bite off more than I can chew.

Canister Ability to contain my ambitions until I can secure what I need rather than having them disrupted by how I feel now.

Cannabis Natural ability to face up to the realities of a challenging situation in a relaxed manner instead of trying to escape from them.

Canned food Ability to preserve my accumulated expertise so that at some point in the future I can use it to fulfill a long-held ambition.

Cannibal Aspect of my character that feels trapped by my wilder ambitions and how they devour my resources by eating away at my confidence.

Cannon Ability to influence people by gently using my authority rather than always making heavy-handed judgments on moral issues.

Cannonball Ability to heavily influence a situation by using old power structures rather than being more specific and direct in my aims.

C

Canoe Ability to navigate an emotional situation by using my personal feelings and experience to individually motivate myself.

Can opener Ability to open myself up to new opportunities, even though I may feel that I have had to contain my ambitions up until now.

Canopy Ability to protect my ideas and beliefs by staying cool about them, even though the prevailing mood may seem unpredictable.

Canteen Situation where I can fulfill a personal ambition by letting other people work with me so we can share in a bigger achievement.

Can't find home Opportunity to express who I really am rather than always feeling I need to portray myself in ways other people expect me to.

Can't find toilet Opportunity to identify my needs instead of thinking that I constantly have to respond to other people's needs.

Canvas Ability to express unfamiliar aspects of myself in a more practical way by understanding the material resources I need.

Canyon Situation where there is a natural break in my progress, even though it may require extra effort to deal with the disruption.

Cap Ability to openly show my beliefs to people, even though continuing to hold on to these viewpoints may limit my progress.

Capacious Realization that I have access to more personal resources than I previously thought rather than feeling limited by circumstances.

Cape Ability to open up my hidden talents to other people instead of always wrapping myself up in an apparently old-fashioned image.

Caper Opportunity to play around with various aspects of a situation rather than thinking I have to behave in a specific manner.

Capillary Ability to convey my passion and enthusiasm in a very natural way, even though my influence on the situation may seem minor.

Capital Ability to attract attention to what I want to say by using my accumulated personal resources and emphasizing their value.

Capital punishment Opportunity to make a dramatic and decisive transformation in my life rather than allowing people to judge my talents for me.

Capo Ability to pitch my creative input with just the right tone instead of being too high-strung about the whole situation.

Capsized Opportunity to keep my feelings on an even keel rather than allowing prevailing events to turn my emotional life upside down.

Capsule Ability to contain my feelings by summarizing them in a concise way until I can break down barriers and really open up.

Captain Aspect of my character that has confidence in my experience to safely steer my way through an uncertain emotional situation.

Caption Ability to communicate what is happening for me in a specific situation rather than letting other people make up their own minds.

Captive Aspect of my character that may seem unable to fulfill my individual ambitions because it tends to hold self-limiting beliefs.

Captivity Situation where I have the power to break out from any self-limiting beliefs rather than blaming my plight on other people.

Captured Opportunity to recognize my natural talents so I can understand how my instinctive behaviors can limit my freedom of action.

Car Ability to use my personal ambition and drive to make my own choices about what I need so I can progress toward my objective.

Carabiner Ability to quickly make a firm

commitment that can keep me feeling connected without becoming too attached.

Car alarm Ability to alert myself to a rapidly emerging realization about some choices I need to make as I progress toward my goal.

Caravan Ability to make progress with a personal ambition by taking a more self-contained and relaxed approach for a time.

Caravan site Situation where I can take a more grounded approach so I can understand the best way to make progress with a personal ambition.

Carbohydrates Potential to fulfill an ambition by storing up personal resources so I can sustain myself over time.

Car bomb Ability to defuse any potentially explosive tensions so I can continue to make progress with my individual ambitions.

Carbon Ability to use the outcome of any creative transformation as a basis for bringing into being new plans and other projects.

Carbon dating Ability to place a series of creative transformations into a wider perspective so I can see how they shape my current behaviors.

Carbon footprint Ability to understand how I can make a distinct creative transformation by having the confidence to stand firmly in my beliefs.

Car breakdown Opportunity to use my drive and ambition to break out of habitual patterns so I can create a dramatic transformation in my life.

Carburetor Ability to mix an inrush of ideas with my creative spirit so I can continually fuel a personal ambition and drive it forward.

Carcass Instinctive ability to revitalize my natural creativity so that I can use my individual power to bring a project back to life.

Car crash Opportunity to take full control of my personal ambitions and drives rather than feeling I am a victim of circumstances.

Card Ability to communicate my true value to other people by being more open instead of keeping everything too close to my chest.

Cardboard Ability to use my natural potential by stiffening my resolve rather than appearing to be lightweight and two-dimensional.

Car dealer Aspect of my character that understands the value of my ambitions and can supply me with the necessary motivation.

Card game Opportunity to make the most of an unpredictable situation by taking a chance instead of accepting the hand I've been dealt.

Cardiac arrest Opportunity to courageously meet a challenge by slowing down a fast-moving situation that is getting out of control.

Cardiac problem Opportunity to resolve a challenge by using my passion and vitality rather than allowing it to become an obstacle to my progress.

Cardigan Ability to present my self-image in a way that seems comfortable, although it may make me appear a little complacent.

Cardinal Aspect of my character that gives me permission to choose my personal spiritual direction and has the conviction to maintain it.

Cardiologist Aspect of my character that can ensure a healthy love life without too much heartache or feeling I'm an incurable romantic.

Careful Realization that I can consistently achieve secure, successful outcomes by taking the time to step outside my comfort zone.

Careless Realization that I can achieve much more consistent outcomes by looking after myself and ensuring that I continue to feel safe.

Carer Aspect of my character that provides me with a sense of safety and security by protecting my innermost feelings from others.

Caretaker Aspect of my character that ensures I have the time and space to fulfill my ambitions by looking after personal resources.

C

Cargo Ability to convey the practical value of my expertise and experience so I can have them acknowledged to a much greater extent.

Cargo ship Ability to use my valuable experience and resourcefulness to navigate any emotional highs and lows I may encounter.

Caricature Ability to emphasize the strongest aspects of my character instead of trivializing them in the face of criticism from anyone.

Carjacking Opportunity to stay in the driver's seat and pursue my ambition rather than feeling I am being driven to act against my will.

Car keys Ability to access the resources I need to drive forward with my personal ambitions so I can open myself up to future success.

Car mechanic Aspect of my character that is familiar with all the intricacies of how I can continue to make progress with a personal ambition.

Carnage Opportunity to make a positive transformation instead of feeling I need to kill off all my aspirations to keep others happy.

Carnation Natural ability to blossom in a social situation so I can openly show my passion about becoming involved in a shared ambition.

Carnival Opportunity to proceed with a collective ambition by releasing some of my inhibitions so I can display my talents to others.

Carnivore Instinctive ability to get my teeth into an opportunity so I can use it to feed my individual power and vitality.

Carousel Situation where I'm trying to move ahead so I can feel happier, but it seems like I'm just going in circles.

Carp Instinctive ability to take courageous action by immersing myself in my emotions rather than nagging others about it.

Carpenter Aspect of my character that is skilful at using my habitual patterns to shape outcomes in a practical and solid manner.

Carpet Ability to be comfortable about where I stand in a situation without feeling that I have to conceal my beliefs.

Carpet bombing Opportunity to contain potentially explosive feelings so I can feel comfortable about my standing with people.

Carriage Ability to progress in my ambitions by using more traditional methods, even though they may seem old-fashioned to me.

Carrier bag Ability to conveniently collect all the resources I need to easily achieve one of my personal ambitions.

Carrier pigeon Instinctive ability to convey an important idea in a very natural way so it can hit home with other people.

Carrion Ability to use my natural power and strength to vitally transform a situation rather than always picking over the bones.

Carrot Natural ability to have a healthy appreciation of what is happening by seeing the real value of what I'm being promised.

Carryall Ability to get a grip on my situation so I can be more aware of all the personal experiences I habitually carry with me.

Carrying Opportunity to convey my need for immediate action rather than allowing habitual obligations to persistently weigh me down.

Car showroom Situation where I can choose the most appropriate vehicle for my ambitions by understanding what value I have to offer.

Cart Ability to work with some heavier issues by connecting them to my deeper instincts and ambitions so I can get them moving.

Car tax Ability to recognize the resources I need to further my progress, even though their influence may seem quite limiting.

Cart horse Instinctive ability to harness my unconscious strength and power as a way of steadily progressing in some larger ambitions.

Cartilage Essential ability to smoothly articulate the support I need so I can feel consistently motivated to take action.

Carton Ability to stiffen my resolve and contain my ambitions so I can secure what I need to move my situation forward.

Cartoon Ability to use simpler and more colorful language to communicate individual perspective in a fundamentally direct way.

Cartridge Ability to concentrate on a particular idea and keep it secure, even though it may contain a potentially explosive revelation.

Carve Opportunity to connect with my different characteristics by going deeper into memories and realizing how they've shaped me.

Carving knife Ability to reveal my underlying power and strength so I can cut through any uncertainty about how to fulfill my ambitions.

Car wash Situation where I can quickly become clear about my personal ambitions so I can present them in the best possible light.

Cascade Situation where I can experience a sudden emotional transformation whose far-reaching effects will be felt by other people.

Case Ability to define set boundaries so I can contain my personal involvement without needing to revert to old behaviors.

Case study Opportunity to understand any self-limiting behaviors I experience so I can move on from the patterns that hold me back.

Cash Ability to have my true value quickly and easily recognized by other people rather than feeling I have to buy their affection.

Cash machine Ability to understand the intricacies of a process so I can consistently have my value recognized by other people.

Cash register Ability to have my creative value formally recognized by others so I can give them an opportunity to ring up their own changes.

Casino Opportunity to profit from a potentially risky encounter by choosing what I want to do rather than leaving it to fate.

Cask Ability to take a more mature approach to achieving my ambitions by drawing on my accumulated experience and learning.

Casket Ability to release myself from some heavy responsibilities that may be holding me back so I can resurrect a neglected ambition.

Casserole Potential to fulfill an ambition by being able to contain my excitement as I take time to develop a combination of influences.

Cassette Ability to conveniently convey some of my ideas, although it can take time to work my way through to the most significant parts.

Cast Opportunity to throw myself into the spotlight and ensure that other people recognize my talents instead of dismissing them.

Castaway Aspect of my character that can make a transformative choice rather than feeling left high and dry by emotional circumstances.

Cast iron Ability to powerfully shape my surrounding circumstances, so I can use my fundamental strength to create a guaranteed outcome.

Castle Situation where I can feel at home with my more powerful characteristics and am able to defend my beliefs against any criticism.

Castration Opportunity to courageously assert my natural creativity rather than feeling completely cut off from my deeper inspiration.

Casual Aspect of my character that can commit to my long-term plans instead of leaving everything to chance.

C

Casualty Aspect of my character that can make healthy and life-affirming choices rather than feeling I am a victim of circumstances.

Cat Instinctive ability to gracefully assert my independence and freedom by feeling relaxed and comfortable about myself.

Cataclysm Opportunity to take control of a potentially overwhelming emotional upheaval that seems to be turning my world upside down.

Catacomb Situation where I can venture deeper into talents I've forgotten about, even though they form the basis of my character.

Catalog Ability to systematically contemplate the resources I have available so I can make the right choice from a wide range of options.

Catalyst Ability to precipitate a positive transformation by using my unique skills and qualities to bring people much closer together.

Catamaran Ability to use the prevailing mood to bring two characteristic qualities together so I can navigate an emotional situation.

Catapult Ability to use my own strength and self-motivation to make the most of a sudden opportunity to project my influence.

Cataract Situation where I can navigate my way through a sudden emotional transformation by clearly sharing my vision with other people.

Catarrh Essential ability to use my passion as a way of getting rid of any messy and unwelcome emotions I may have been concealing.

Catastrophe Opportunity to take positive action to deal with a challenging situation rather than feeling I've made a disastrous choice.

Cat burglar Aspect of my character that undervalues my independence by allowing unwanted intrusions from other people into my personal space.

Catch Ability to seize an opportunity and grasp the full significance of an ambition I have been pursuing for some time.

Catching a bus Opportunity to take on board what I need to do to make consistent progress toward my professional objectives.

Catching a plane Opportunity to actually get one of my powerful ideas off the ground so I can make rapid progress in taking it further.

Catching a train Opportunity to decide where I want to go in my career so I can embark upon on a particular professional path.

Catchphrase Ability to speak my unique truth rather than habitually saying what other people expect me to say just to keep them happy.

Cat door Ability to easily open up to emerging opportunities that will allow me to use my independence to come and go as I please.

Caterer Aspect of my character that helps me fulfill professional ambitions by understanding my unspoken needs and meeting them.

Caterpillar Instinctive ability to slowly work my way through my everyday routine, knowing that it will lead to a wonderful transformation.

Catfish Instinctive ability to immerse myself in my emotional life and enjoy my independence, even though it may sometimes appear unclear.

Catharsis Opportunity to open up my feelings to other people and let go of any unwanted emotional hurt instead of bottling it up inside.

Cathedral Situation where I can step into my higher spiritual self and trust that those around me will give me the space that I need.

Cat-sitting Opportunity to take a relaxed, comfortable viewpoint and become more aware of how I can continue to maintain my independence.

Cat suit Ability to present my self-image to others in a way that shows how comfortable I am with my independence and freedom.

Cattle Instinctive ability to gather a variety of my talents so I can use their power and strength to nurture a wider ambition.

Cattle grid Situation where I can use my kindness to move beyond traditional boundaries rather than feeling my progress is barred.

Catwalk Situation where I can hold my head up high and proudly strut my stuff so other people can recognize my unique talents.

Caught Opportunity to hold on to my natural talent for making the right choice rather than feeling trapped by my current circumstances.

Caught in a war Opportunity to decisively deal with some of my conflicting needs rather than continually trying to avoid any confrontation.

Cauldron Ability to transform my emotional life by spelling out a number of issues that have been bubbling just under the surface.

Cauliflower Natural ability to have a healthy regard for my own intelligence so I can use it to listen for fulfilling opportunities.

Causeway Situation where I can raise my professional progress to a higher level rather than getting bogged down in minor details.

Caution Opportunity to make sure that I listen to other people's advice instead of leaping at the first opportunity that comes along.

Cautious Realization that I need to be more open in how I approach challenging situations rather than staying inside my comfort zone.

Cave Situation where I can step into a more fundamental understanding of my character so I can explore the roots of my deepest self.

Cave diver Aspect of my character that enjoys immersing myself in my feelings so I can explore some of my more primitive qualities.

Cave-in Opportunity to look beyond surface appearances so I can dig more deeply into some of the primitive aspects of my character.

Caveman Aspect of my character that may seem primitive but has a profound understanding of my fundamental strength and power.

Cave painting Ability to communicate my deepest instincts by using my essential strength, even though it may seem primitive to others.

Cavernous Realization that I can step into my fundamental power at any time rather than feeling I have to keep up surface appearances.

Caviar Potential to fulfill my ambitions by using my wealth of experience and instinctive taste for exploring lots of fertile ideas.

Caving Opportunity to explore some of the profounder aspects of my existence rather than being happy with superficial appearances.

Cavity Ability to make the space to create something much more substantial instead of being content with a hollow achievement.

CD Ability to focus on the ins and outs of my creative talents so I can reflect on what makes them so special to people.

CD player Ability to share my creative skills with other people by maintaining an intense focus on what makes my talents so special.

Cease fire Opportunity to transform a period of chronic tension by accepting that other viewpoints may be as valid as my own.

Cedar tree Natural potential for my long-term spiritual growth by developing my ideas graciously, evoking pleasant memories.

Ceiling Ability to shelter a particular aspect of my character from outside criticism, even though it may end up limiting my freedom.

C

Celebration Opportunity to assemble all the valuable aspects of my greatest qualities and have them openly recognized by other people.

Celebrity Aspect of my character that I have the most respect and admiration for, even though I don't openly recognize its true value.

Celebrity affair Opportunity to have complete confidence in my own attractiveness rather than always looking to others for their approval.

Celebrity encounter Opportunity to openly recognize my unique talents so I can become more widely celebrated in my chosen area of expertise.

Celebrity friendship Opportunity to become more acquainted with my developing talents so I can openly use them more consistently.

Celebrity game show Opportunity to play around with the personal qualities that I respect and admire the most so I can recognize their value to me.

Celebrity intimacy Opportunity to become more intensely aware of my unique creativity so that I can begin to develop my unrealized potential.

Celebrity lover Aspect of my character that can help me become more intimately aware of my creative talent by being more open to my potential.

Celebrity romance Opportunity to develop one of my intriguing creative ideas by exploring an area of my expertise that really fascinates me.

Celebrity spouse Aspect of my character that embodies my commitment to developing my unique talents and having them more widely recognized.

Celery Natural ability to fulfill a personal ambition by seeking out healthy alternatives and sticking up for what I believe in.

Celestial Realization that I can raise my spirits by reaching into the unknown and going far beyond what I am consciously aware of.

Celibacy Opportunity to reflect on what I hope to conceive in the future rather than immediately responding to my creative urges.

Cell Situation where I can step into a much wider freedom by having the courage to break out of any self-limiting behaviors.

Cellar Aspect of myself where I build up my deepest experiences and treasured memories as a way of supporting my everyday activities.

Cellmate Aspect of my character that can help me express my self-limiting beliefs so I can have the courage to break out of them.

Cello Ability to take my instinctive creativity in both hands so I can feel very grounded in opening up to my performance skills.

Cellophane Ability to clearly see what ambitions I have chosen to develop rather than getting too wrapped up in my superficial beliefs.

Cellulite Essential opportunity to store up personal resources I may need for future action without getting too complacent about it.

Cement Ability to transform a situation by making a strong connection with my practical abilities rather than being too set in my ways.

Cement mixer Ability to blend my practical skills together so I can create a definite outcome rather than just go through the motions.

Cemetery Situation where I can resurrect some vital social relationships that I may have felt I had to lay to rest in the past.

Cenotaph Situation where I can fully acknowledge the monumental effort I made to achieve an ambition that once seemed distant.

Censor Aspect of my character that tries to supervise my instinctive nature, although it may diminish my apparent value to other people.

Census Opportunity to observe all the varied aspects of my character so I can understand how to express them most powerfully.

Centaur Apparent ability to harness my unconscious energies so I can balance them with my obvious humanity as a way of motivating myself.

Center Situation where I can experience the true source of who I really am and understand how far my sphere of influence extends.

Centerfold Ability to get to the heart of what is happening by clearly understanding some of my less obvious thoughts and ideas.

Centipede Instinctive ability to progress toward my chosen objective by taking things one step at a time and always moving forward.

Central heating Ability to safely channel my more heated emotions to make all aspects of my character seem warm and approachable.

Central locking Ability to maintain an overall sense of security in personal ambitions rather than feeling I am leaving myself open to doubts.

Central reservation Situation where I am able to stand back and see the bigger picture so I can safely separate two opposing ambitions.

Centrifuge Ability to separate out what is most important to me rather than feeling that I'm always going in circles.

Centurion Aspect of my character that is very experienced in being able to resolve hundreds of minor tensions I may be dealing with.

CEO Aspect of my character that has the power to make complex decisions and can give myself complete authority to act on them.

Ceramic Ability to preserve a potentially fragile situation by choosing not to overreact to any potential threats or criticisms.

Cereal Natural ability to sustain my ambitions by reaping the benefits of the many ideas I have steadily accumulated over time.

Ceremony Opportunity to celebrate how I have transformed my value so I can have my uniqueness recognized by those around me.

Certain Realization that regularly questioning my individual intentions will always enable me to achieve the results I need.

Certificate Ability to recognize my confidence and competence so I can have my unique skills formally acknowledged by others.

Cervical smear Opportunity to maintain my creative talents by preventing a potentially unhealthy situation from rapidly growing out of control.

Cesspool Situation where I have a safe and secure place to methodically deal with any messy habits and behaviors I no longer need.

Chafed Essential opportunity to reduce the friction in a tense situation by adjusting my individual perspective and opening up more.

Chain Ability to create a strong relationship by using a series of individual connections and not placing any limitations on them.

Chain mail Ability to present myself to people in a way that may make me seem invulnerable but relies on a variety of strong relationships.

Chain reaction Opportunity to create a powerful decisive outcome by building up a range of strong, interconnected relationships.

Chainsaw Ability to use the strength of my relationships to consistently cut my way through any old patterns that no longer serve me.

Chain-smoking Opportunity to keep a clear head rather than always letting myself be drawn into a series of unhealthy situations.

Chain store Situation where I can recognize the value of my connections in helping me to identify the resources I need to progress.

Chair Ability to maintain my habitual viewpoint on a situation rather than taking decisive action by stepping outside my comfort zone.

Chairlift Ability to make progress with a viewpoint that makes me feel comfortable so I can continue to elevate my level of understanding.

Chairman Aspect of my character that is comfortable with asserting my individual strength and power as a way of achieving my ambitions.

Chairwoman Aspect of my character that feels relaxed about using my empathy and wisdom as a way of fulfilling my aspirations.

Chaise longue Ability to lie back and enjoy a relaxed viewpoint while feeling completely supported by my habitual outlook on life.

Chalet Situation where I feel comfortable and safe as I make the effort to explore some of the less familiar aspects of my character.

Chalice Ability to fulfill an emotional need by being able to contain my spiritual feelings and stand up for what I believe in.

Chalk Ability to quickly communicate my emerging ideas to other people, even though my thoughts may seem quite dry and insubstantial.

Challenge Opportunity to question my deeper motives so I can move out of my comfort zone into a wider understanding.

Chamber Aspect of myself that offers me the privacy to feel comfortable and secure in developing my potential talents and skills.

Chameleon Instinctive ability to show how I feel instead of allowing my beliefs to be colored by whatever situation I am in.

Champagne Potential to fulfill an emotional need by recognizing an opportunity bubbling up so I can celebrate my future success.

Champion Aspect of my character that always wins rather than holding my progress back with any self-defeating behaviors.

Chance Realization that I have an opportunity to make my own decisions and choose the outcome instead of leaving everything to fate.

Chancellor Aspect of my character that embodies my fundamental value so I can use it to decisively make a significant transformation.

Chandelier Ability to share an elevated understanding with others so that it illuminates the situation in a grand and obvious manner.

Chandler Aspect of my character that can provide me with the resources I need to navigate an emotionally complex situation.

Change Opportunity to transform a situation by understanding how I can use my insight and ingenuity to make a real difference to it.

Channel Situation where I can contain the flow of my emotions by being definite about how I feel and the course I would like to take.

Channel-hopping Opportunity to choose one aspect of my story I would like to develop so I can stay with it until I understand the outcome.

Chant Ability to instinctively communicate my deeper truth to others without mono-tonously going on and on about it at length.

Chaos Opportunity to use my perspective to understand what is happening rather than feeling utterly confused.

Chapel Situation where I can explore some intimate aspects of my spirituality and gain more understanding of the basis for my beliefs.

Chapstick Ability to be careful about what I say so I can smooth things over with other people rather than feeling I am irritating them.

Character Ability to identify the particular qualities I find most meaningful so I can use them to really make my mark.

Charade Opportunity to behave in the way I would like to rather than feeling I am just acting out someone else's demands.

Charcoal Ability to use the results of a previous creative transformation to progressively catalyze the successful outcome of another one.

Charge Opportunity to make decisive progress by forcefully asserting my power so I can fully demonstrate my unseen potential.

Charge sheet Ability to clearly spell out where I can make best use of my powerful abilities rather than feeling guilty about using them.

Chariot Ability to harness my instinctive energies so I can use my natural power to successfully drive my ambitions forward.

Charity shop Situation where I can realize I don't always need help and kindness from other people to have my true value recognized.

Charity worker Aspect of my character that can create abundant opportunities by consistently being kind and open to the people around me.

Charm Realization that I can attract all the attention I need by being gracious to other people rather than resorting to any trickery.

Charred Realization that I can use my talent to completely transform a situation instead of just working around the edges of it.

Chart Ability to understand the bigger picture about what I believe so I can use this perspective to decide where I'm going.

Charter flight Opportunity to plan ahead and make a special commitment so I can convey some of my thoughts and ideas about a particular project.

Chase Opportunity to pursue a goal that has great personal significance by bringing my attention to what will make me feel fulfilled.

Chased by an animal Opportunity to understand the nature of an instinctive impulse so I can use its power to create a uniquely valuable result.

Chased by a gang Opportunity to assert my individuality so I can develop my skills instead of always giving in to the demands of others.

Chased by a man Opportunity to successfully realize an ambition by developing my individual strength and power so I can assert my talents.

Chased by a monster Opportunity to make the most of a huge possibility by connecting with one of my raw and powerful talents and steadily refining it.

Chased by a murderer Opportunity to create a profound transformation in my life by motivating myself to revitalize one of my neglected talents.

Chased by a woman Opportunity to passionately express my unique gift of creativity by courageously developing my individual empathy and wisdom.

Chasm Situation where I can look deeper into my motives for pursuing a specific ambition, although it may disrupt my continuing progress.

Chastity belt Ability to take control of my creative potential and decide whom to share it with, rather than trying to keep it under lock and key.

Chat line Ability to share my individual perspective with a group of other people, even if they seem to be quite distant to begin with.

Chattering Opportunity to communicate how I feel by speaking my mind rather than just going on and on with no real purpose.

Chauffeur Aspect of my character that has extensive knowledge of my personal ambitions and is comfortable with helping me attain them.

Cheap Realization of the wealth of talent I can offer to other people instead of constantly undervaluing my unique abilities.

Cheat Opportunity to recognize my fundamental value and openly declare it to other people rather than being mistrustful of my talent.

Cheat sheet Ability to clearly spell out the unique value of my individual talents instead of always trying to conceal them from others.

Check Opportunity to examine my behavior in more detail so I can investigate my motives rather than trying to restrain myself.

C

Check Ability to declare how much I value my wealth of experience so other people can acknowledge my individual contribution.

Checkered flag Ability to resolve an uncertain outcome by eventually drawing the attention of other people to my individual perspective.

Check-in Opportunity to give myself permission to embark on a project so I can have my choices acknowledged by others.

Checklist Ability to be very specific about the challenges I face so I can examine the behaviors that will provide me with success.

Checkmate Opportunity to move forward from an apparently obvious outcome by taking the time to look beyond the black-and-white aspects.

Checkout Situation where I can fully acknowledge the value of the resources I need to successfully fulfill a personal ambition.

Checkpoint Situation where I can specifically examine my progress so far and give myself permission to proceed in my chosen direction.

Checkup Opportunity to take a healthy perspective on some of my behaviors so I can examine how useful they appear to be to me.

Cheek Essential ability to express my feelings and give my side of the story, even though it may involve bending the rules.

Cheerful Realization that I can raise my spirits by recognizing my special abilities instead of feeling that everything is gloomy.

Cheering Opportunity to encourage my eventual success by displaying my talents rather than feeling I have nothing to celebrate.

Cheese Potential to fulfill my ambitions by taking a mature approach to how I nurture my aspirations so I can make them more tangible.

Cheesecake Potential to fulfill a shared ambition and celebrate collective success by working through a challenge in a mature manner.

Cheetah Instinctive ability to embody my need for much greater freedom and independence by pursuing my ambitions as quickly as I can.

Chef Aspect of my character that has the great taste and skill to transform my raw ambition rather than just making a meal of it.

Chemical Ability to separate the complex feelings that may be compounding a situation so I can provide an ideal solution.

Chemical warfare Opportunity to deal with an inner conflict by understanding its various causes instead of trying to apply an immediate solution.

Chemist Aspect of my character that can provide practical solutions to complex emotional problems rather than just dispensing advice.

Chemistry Ability to become more aware of how I react emotionally with the people around me so I can be more measured with them.

Chemotherapy Opportunity to relieve an unhealthy situation by providing practical solutions to remedy any inner tensions I may be feeling.

Cherry Natural ability to maintain a healthy awareness by choosing the best and most obvious option to achieve a fruitful outcome.

Cherub Aspect of my character that can express the more innocent and open aspects of my spiritual self in a playful manner.

Chess Opportunity to think more strategically about the specific moves I need to make to resolve an uncertain situation.

Chessboard Ability to go beyond simple black-and-white thinking so I can carefully consider how I can make some decisive moves.

Chest Essential ability to embody my inspiration and safely contain my emotions so I can proudly show off my talents to others.

Chest freezer Ability to stay cool and maintain my composure so I can safely contain my feelings about some long-term ambitions.

Chest infection Opportunity to define healthy, personal boundaries so I can maintain my levels of inspiration and feel at ease with them.

Chestnut Potential to fulfill an ambition by coming out of my shell more so I don't become stuck in the same old situation again and again.

Chest of drawers Ability to take a methodical approach to my creative abilities so I can pull them out for inspiration when I need to.

Chest waders Ability to make comfortable progress in a deeply unpredictable emotional situation by having a firm idea of where I really stand.

Chew Essential ability to break down the various aspects of a complex experience so I can fully digest what it means to me.

Chewing Opportunity to use my confidence to methodically work my way through a situation and ensure I absorb all the learning from it.

Chewing glass Opportunity to take a softer approach in clearly speaking my truth rather than feeling I should provide some sharp criticism.

Chewing gum Potential ability to go through the motions of trying to fulfill an ambition without gaining any real sense of achievement.

Chewing needles Opportunity to take a gentler approach in expressing my opinion instead of feeling I need to be pointedly critical.

Chic Realization that I can arrive at an elegant solution in my own fashion rather than having to follow the whims of other people.

Chick Instinctive ability to nurture some of my ambitions into more fertile ideas in a way that will make me feel very chirpy.

Chicken Instinctive ability to rule the roost rather than feeling anxious about laying out my ideas and hatching my fertile plans.

Chicken meat Potential to fulfill an ambition by using my raw strength and power to produce some important ideas that have great substance.

Chicken pox Opportunity to resolve an unhealthy situation by attending to irritating ideas that are starting to get under my skin.

Chief Aspect of my character that has great natural power, which I often use to openly display one of my most important qualities.

Chiffon Ability to be more transparent about my sensuality and how I can use it to fashion my feelings into something more substantial.

Child Aspect of my character that embodies my uniquely precious talents and holds all my potential for continuing growth and love.

Childbirth Opportunity to bring a plan to life and use it to make a new beginning, even though it may be a painful experience.

Childhood Opportunity to reflect on my most fundamental qualities so I can understand what experiences made me the person I am.

Childhood bed Situation where I feel most at home with my fundamental qualities and can take a relaxed approach to exploring my creative urges.

Childhood bedroom Situation where I have the space to feel more comfortable with my fundamental characteristics so I can develop my talents.

Childhood clothing Ability to become more aware of how I fundamentally like to appear to others rather than worrying about how they expect me to appear.

C

Childhood friend Aspect of my character I am becoming reacquainted with so I can begin to rediscover my fundamental sense of self.

Childhood garden Situation where I can cultivate some of my fundamental relationships and interests so they will continue to naturally bloom.

Childhood home Opportunity to rediscover fundamentally characteristic qualities of my identity so I can develop their true potential.

Childhood pet Natural ability to nurture my fundamentally creative instincts so I can develop a talent that is very close to my heart.

Childhood toy Ability to play around with some of my fundamental talents so I can understand their importance rather than just amusing myself.

Childhood wardrobe Ability to become more aware of the fundamental aspects of my self-image so I can choose how to develop them.

Child in jeopardy Opportunity to become more aware of a precious personal talent I have been neglecting so I can give it more attention.

Child-minder Aspect of my character that can look after my emerging identity and recognize the value of my developing plans and ideas.

Childproof Ability to keep my emerging ideas safe and secure by protecting them from uncontrolled criticism that may be harmful.

Children Aspects of my character that embody a variety of my special talents that have the potential to be developed even further.

Children's clothing Ability to present my self-image by choosing the playful qualities I am happy to display and deciding what I prefer to conceal.

Children's play area Situation where I can play around with the different aspects of my fundamental talents so I can understand how to develop them.

Children's ward Situation where I can take a healthier approach to dealing with any inner tensions in my fundamental sense of self.

Child seat Ability to take a more supportive viewpoint so I can securely convey some of my developing concepts to other people.

Chill Realization that I need to warm to an emerging opportunity rather than suppressing my emotions and feeling uncomfortable.

Chimera Apparent ability to create a fundamental transformation by using confidence in my ideas rather than just playing around.

Chimes Ability to raise my awareness of various emerging opportunities so I can ring some changes that will really resonate with me.

Chimney Ability to channel some of my creative output in a warm and traditional way rather than allowing it to cloud the issue.

Chimpanzee Instinctive ability to understand my natural creativity by copying other people and then playfully adapting their methods.

Chin Essential ability to maintain my strength of character by being able to open up and take direct criticism from other people.

China Ability to contain any delicate emotions I may be feeling by presenting an apparently impenetrable exterior to other people.

Chink Ability to open up more to what is going on so I can illuminate what motivates me and explore it further.

Chip Potential to fulfill an ambition and sustain my progress by using a more comfortable approach I can take one step at a time.

Chip van Ability to sustain my personal drive and resources so that I can make committed progress toward my objective in a healthy way.

Chiropodist Aspect of my character that helps me stay firmly grounded and ensures that I can take practical steps to move into action.

Chiropractor Aspect of my character that helps give me fundamental strength to stand up for my ideas and what I believe in.

Chisel Ability to use my individual power and skill to work my way through some old habit so I can shape them into something better.

Chock Ability to control how my plans and ideas can potentially develop by applying a small amount of effort in just the right place.

Chocolate Potential to indulge in a short-term ambition that seems very rewarding without paying attention to possible long-term gains.

Choice Realization that I can determine my course of action and fulfill my needs rather than always trying to please other people.

Choir Aspects of my character that help me instinctively communicate with other people in a harmonious and deeply felt manner.

Choirboy Aspect of my character that has the potential to assertively develop my strength and power in the way that I communicate.

Choirgirl Aspect of my character that has the emerging creativity and intuition to powerfully develop the way I communicate my wisdom.

Chokehold Opportunity to have a firm grasp of my thoughts and feelings so I can use them to freely voice my individual opinion.

Choker Ability to attract more attention to how I connect my thoughts and feelings, even though it can make me appear vulnerable.

Choking Opportunity to clearly connect my ideas and emotions instead of feeling that other people are inhibiting my freedom of expression.

Cholesterol Essential opportunity to increase my chances for success by taking a fresh approach and exercising a healthier perspective.

Chomping Opportunity to break down the aspects of a complex experience without feeling I have to make too much noise about it.

Choosy Realization that I need to make a firm decision so I can take decisive action rather than just making a meal of it.

Chop Opportunity to quickly take decisive action so I can use the strength of my talent to confidently step into a new future.

Chopsticks Ability to fulfill my appetite for success by staying with what I know so I can always produce a straightforward outcome.

Chord Ability to strike just the right tone in what I want to communicate so it resonates with people in a straightforward way.

Chore Opportunity to connect with my deeper purpose by taking responsibility for my talents rather than feeling obliged to other people.

Choreographer Aspect of my character that helps me embody my natural rhythms and shows me steps I can take to bring them to life.

Chorus Opportunity to express my feelings in unison with other people rather than feeling that I always have to refrain from doing so.

Chough Instinctive ability to confidently display a powerful idea so I can use it to transform a situation in a soulful way.

Christmas Opportunity to joyfully celebrate the birth of new possibilities and have the value of my gifts recognized by other people.

Christmas card Ability to clearly communicate what I need to say to the people around me rather than just using platitudes and clichés.

Christmas decoration Ability to display my emerging potential instead of trying to

C

make it seem more attractive to the people around me.

Christmas present Ability to demonstrate the value of my creative gifts to other people rather than just trying to appeal to their generosity.

Christmas tree Ability to feel more rooted in my long-term spiritual growth by becoming more healthily aware of its enduring value.

Chronic Realization that I need to step into my power and take action right now rather than feeling stuck in old behavioral patterns.

Chronic fatigue syndrome Essential opportunity to resolve an energy-sapping situation by taking the time to make a decision that will really motivate me.

Chrysalis Instinctive ability to create some personal space so I can retreat into myself prior to a major life-changing transformation.

Chrysanthemum Natural ability to have a blossoming awareness of my maturing wisdom and how it blooms from my accumulating experiences.

Chubby Realization that I can indulge in my appetite for success by taking a fresh approach and exercising a healthy perspective.

Chum Aspect of my character that is open, easygoing, and reliable to show itself in a consistently supportive way.

Chunk Ability to break down a seemingly insurmountable problem into a series of manageable challenges I can deal with one at a time.

Church Situation where I can share my spiritual beliefs with a wider community and have them enthusiastically supported by others.

Church bell Ability to raise awareness about my emerging spiritual beliefs by clearly communicating feelings without causing alarm.

Churchyard Situation where I can give

myself the space to be much more open about my personal spirituality and my creative ambitions.

Churn Ability to collect the emotional resources I need to nurture myself rather than feeling I'm pointlessly going round and round.

Churning Opportunity to take decisive control of any unsettling emotions so I can begin to channel their energy much more productively.

Chute Ability to use my accumulated experience to quickly go deeper into my emotions so I can release myself from frictions.

Chutes and ladders Opportunity to use my skill to play around with ways of raising my awareness to transform a hurtful situation.

Chutney Potential to fulfill an ambition by using a variety of influences and relishing the challenge of being able to use them all.

Cicada Instinctive ability to signal how I really feel to other people without thinking that I have to endlessly drone on about it.

Cider Potential to fulfill an emotional need by having a healthy awareness of my own attractiveness when making a romantic choice.

Cigar Ability to use my power and influence to speak up strongly instead of trying to create an atmosphere of tension and uncertainty.

Cigarette Ability to resolve an unhealthy personal situation by speaking up clearly rather than trying to hide behind a smokescreen.

Cigarette lighter Ability to use a creative spark to resolve an unhealthy situation by having the courage to take matters into my own hands.

Cinder Ability to discard some of the less useful aspects of a creative process so I can prevent myself from slipping up in the future.

Cinema Situation where I can become more aware of my personal story and immerse myself in the dramas unfolding around me.

Cinematic Realization that I have the power to create a personal story that is much wider in scope than I had previously imagined.

Cipher Ability to communicate what I need to say in an obvious and direct manner rather than trying to obscure my underlying intentions.

Circle Ability to shape my circumstances by having the presence to remain centered, even when I am reaching out to the edge of what I know.

Circuit Situation where I am continually accumulating experience, even though it seems I always come back to the same starting point.

Circuit breaker Ability to switch off from one of my current anxieties by using my power to let go of any old behaviors I no longer need.

Circular Realization that I need to express myself in a new way rather than covering the same old ground again and again.

Circulation Ability to keep a situation moving so I can continue to display my passion to other people and have it fully acknowledged.

Circumcision Opportunity to protect my creativity and what it stands for rather than letting others insensitively assert their beliefs.

Circumference Situation where I can get to the edge of some of my apparent limitations by understanding what is of central importance.

Circus Situation where I can bring changes by focusing my attention on my instinctive creativity rather than trivializing my talents.

Cirrhosis Essential opportunity to resolve an unhealthy situation by understanding the valuable, more challenging aspects of my power.

Cistern Ability to draw on my accumulated experience and learning so I can flush out any feelings that are no longer useful to me.

Citadel Situation where I can take the higher ground rather than having to retreat when I encounter a threatening social situation.

Citizen Aspect of my character that naturally connects with a wider social circle as a way of accessing the resources I need.

Citizen's arrest Ability to slow down an out-of-control situation by reflecting on my deeper responsibilities to my wider social circle.

City Situation where I can connect with my wider social network and access all the resources I need to fulfill my individual ambitions.

Civilian Aspect of my character that has the energy and curiosity to engage with emerging opportunities in my wider social circle.

Civilization Situation where I can use my accumulated experience and wisdom to develop my wider understanding so I can advance my ambitions.

Civilized Realization that I can resolve my inner tensions in a graceful, peaceful manner instead of feeling conflicted by them.

Civil war opportunity to resolve an ongoing tension by graciously declaring what I need rather than continually trying to avoid conflict.

Claim Opportunity to demand that people must pay attention to the value of my individual talents, especially when the stakes are high.

Clairvoyant Aspect of my character that can create a clear picture of the practical steps I need to take instead of deluding myself.

Clam Instinctive ability to filter out unpleasant feelings rather than withdrawing emotionally and keeping a defensive silence.

Clambering Opportunity to deal with a looming challenge by carefully choosing my direction and making sure I know where I stand.

Clammy Realization that I need to show why I feel so worked up about a situation rather than always trying to appear cool.

Clamor Opportunity to speak up powerfully and draw attention to my special abilities instead of continually staying quiet about them.

Clamp Ability to make a connection at a fundamental level rather than trying to strictly control something I should let go of.

Clandestine activity Opportunity to take specific action to show how I really feel instead of trying to conceal my intentions from others.

Clandestine operative Aspect of my character that can definitely reach a successful outcome by openly sharing my passions with the people around me.

Clang Opportunity to draw attention to a situation that resonates with me instead of worrying that I have made a huge mistake.

Clank Realization that I have the power to keep things moving smoothly, although the outcome may not always be a resounding success.

Clap Opportunity to show how I feel by taking decisive action, even though it may not meet with everyone else's approval.

Clarinet Ability to take my instinctive creativity in both hands so I can use it to shape my ideas in a clear and harmonious manner.

Clarity Realization that I can express my feelings in a clear and simple manner rather than always appearing noncommittal.

Clash Opportunity to approach a potential conflict in a graceful and considered way instead of rushing headlong into confrontation.

Clasp Ability to show the strength of my connection to other people rather than feeling completely detached from what is happening.

Class Opportunity to learn more about my unique talents and how I can use them to make myself stand out from the crowd.

Classroom Situation where I can sit down and examine the value of my life lessons rather than letting myself be judged by other people.

Clatter Realization that I can approach a situation in a smooth and positive way instead of leaping in and feeling rattled.

Claustrophobic Situation where I can be far more open about my self-limiting beliefs rather than staying closed to any new possibilities.

Claw Instinctive ability to pounce on a creative opportunity instead of feeling that other people will tear my efforts to shreds.

Clay Ability to use my instinctive creativity and my practical skills to shape a situation that other people will be very receptive to.

Cleaner Aspect of my character that may seem insignificant but maintains my ability to function in a healthy and productive manner.

Cleaning Opportunity to maintain a healthy approach to a continuing challenge, even though it may get very messy at some point.

Clean room Situation where I can shut myself away from any distracting influences and be very clear about what I want the outcome to be.

Clean-shaven Essential ability to face up to the underlying facts in a touch-and-go situation so I can be more open about what I need to say.

Clear Realization that what may appear transparently obvious to me might not seem so evident to the people around me.

Clearance sale Opportunity to make the most of my valuable skills by choosing to let go of what is no longer of any value to me.

Clear-headed Realization that I can express

my ideas in a simple, straightforward way rather than being fuzzy and vague about what I think.

Clearing Situation where I can be more open about my huge growth potential so I can see a way forward for settling any differences I have.

Cleavage Essential opportunity to show the depths of my nurturing capabilities, even though my actions might seem outwardly divisive.

Clenched Realization that I can stay relaxed in a tense situation without losing my grasp on what I would prefer the outcome to be.

Clergyman Aspect of my character that understands the more spiritual aspects of my life and provides support as I explore them.

Clever Realization that I can demonstrate my personal insight to people rather than feeling I have to play dumb to keep everyone happy.

Cliché Realization that I have the ability to express myself in a unique way instead of trying to stay popular with other people.

Click Realization that I can make an ambition come together by taking some small and deliberate steps to make it happen.

Client Aspect of my character that is inclined to seek the protection of someone more powerful rather than using my own influence.

Clientele Aspects of my character that can combine to provide a powerful influence in deciding the outcome of an unfamiliar situation.

Cliff Situation where there is a looming awareness of a sudden transformation in the sheer effort required to deal with a challenge.

Cliff edge Situation where I am on the threshold of an abrupt change in my circumstances and need to be confident in my next steps.

Cliff face Situation where I have to face up to the sheer effort required to reach my objective, even though it can make me feel insecure.

Climate change Opportunity to take decisive action to transform the prevailing mood, even though it initially causes an uncomfortable atmosphere.

Climate control Ability to choose how I respond to the prevailing mood by maintaining an even temperament and ensuring everyone feels comfortable.

Climax Opportunity to use my accumulated wisdom to build up my confidence rather than always feeling I let everyone down.

Climber Aspect of my character that raises my overall awareness by confidently stepping into the unknown and being sure of where I stand.

Climbing Opportunity to overcome an apparently insurmountable challenge by taking steps to minimize the sheer effort involved.

Climbing equipment Ability to use my accumulated expertise and experience as a way to elevate my overall level of understanding about a situation.

Climbing up building Opportunity to raise my awareness of how I appear to other people so I can continue to develop my unique characteristics.

Climbing up cliff Opportunity to confidently make the effort required to deal with a sudden transformation in my continuing progress.

Climbing uphill Opportunity to raise my level of understanding and widen my perspective, even though it may require considerable effort.

Climbing wall Situation where I can play around with how to safely raise my overall awareness rather than feeling stuck on a specific problem.

Clinch Realization that I can reach an agreement by choosing to take individual action without becoming too attached to the outcome.

C

Cling Realization that I can maintain my grasp of what is happening in a challenging situation so I can maintain my independence.

Clinic Situation where I can examine some of my potentially unhealthy behaviors rather than feeling that people will have to comfort me.

Clip Ability to quickly decide what I find most interesting in a particular connection so I can cut out any unnecessary effort.

Clipboard Ability to collect my thoughts so I have a firm basis for communicating my ideas in a rational and objective manner.

Clitoris Essential ability to become more turned on to my creative potential and its unique sensitivities rather than hiding it away.

Cloak Ability to present my self-image to others by being more open instead of becoming too wrapped up in how I might appear.

Cloakroom Situation where I can relax and attend to my personal needs by stepping out of my more formal public image for a while.

Cloche Ability to protect a potential ambition by ensuring that it is not damaged in any way by the cool response of other people.

Clock Ability to look ahead and choose the precise moment to make the most of a big opportunity rather than racing around all the time.

Clock tower Situation where I have a monumental opportunity to choose the right moment to ring the changes and fulfill a long-held ambition.

Clockwork Ability to explore the more unpredictable aspects of an event rather than getting too wound up about things not going as planned.

Clog Ability to free myself from a sticky situation by taking decisive steps rather than feeling caught in my habitual viewpoint.

Clone Ability to individually develop one of my unique talents instead of copying everyone else to keep them happy.

Close Realization that a long-held ambition is not as far away as it once seemed and I can soon bring it to a successful conclusion.

Closed Realization that I can open up and communicate how I feel about an experience rather than shutting myself off.

Close encounter Opportunity to meet with an unexpected challenge by communicating my needs in a way that may initially seem alien to me.

Close-fitting Ability to present my self-image to people in a way that enables me to reveal how a situation is shaping up for me.

Closeness Realization that I can make a deep connection with someone by having the confidence to open up and tell him or her how I feel.

Closet Aspect of myself that I tend to keep hidden away from other people in case they might see me unfavorably in a different light.

Close-up Opportunity to take a good look at how my expertise may appear to people rather than trying to keep quiet about my talents.

Closure Opportunity to be open about my needs so I can deal with a challenging situation and agree to move on from it.

Clot Essential ability to control my passion and vitality by channeling my emotions rather than appearing clumsy and stupid.

Cloth Ability to provide a substantial basis for the various threads of my story material and how I choose to weave them together.

Clothes Ability to present my self-image to people by choosing what I am happy to display and deciding what I prefer to conceal.

Clothesline Ability to freshen up my self-image by using a particular line of thinking to open myself to a variety of new ideas.

Clothespin Ability to stay connected to a

particular line of thinking by using it to help me stay open to any fresh new opportunities.

Cloud Situation where I can draw on my accumulated learning and experience to help me think clearly, without a shadow of a doubt.

Cloudburst Opportunity to release some heavy emotions that may have been over-shadowing an event and threatening the successful outcome.

Cloud cover Opportunity to brighten up my outlook by letting go of some feelings that have been obscuring the clarity of my thoughts.

Clover Natural ability to enjoy the sweet taste of success by taking a healthy approach to seeking out good fortune and happiness.

Clown Aspect of my character that can trivialize my talents by behaving predictably in an obvious attempt to please other people.

Clown fish Instinctive ability to go with the flow instead of feeling I have to belittle my talents as a way of keeping other people happy.

Club Ability to bring together the different aspects of my character so I can use their combined power and strength to hit home.

Clubhouse Situation where I can bring together the different qualities of my character and feel comfortable with their combined skills.

Clue Ability to explore the deeper and less familiar aspects of my character by choosing to point myself in the right direction.

Clueless Realization that the solution to my current challenge is a change of personal direction rather than just feeling helpless.

Clump Situation where I can bring together a number of emerging opportunities without feeling that I have to stamp my mark on them.

Clumsy Realization that I have the ability to make an independent decision rather than feeling awkward about keeping everyone happy.

Clunky Ability to bring together a number of my skills in a precise manner without feeling that I have to be too sophisticated about it.

Cluster Ability to gather a number of my ideas so I can use them as a wider basis for exploring new opportunities.

Clutch Ability to take a firm grasp of the situation rather than feeling that I'm letting it slip out of my control.

Clutter Ability to clearly identify what is of most value to me instead of feeling distracted by everything that is going on around me.

Coach Ability to make definite progress toward my career objectives by being open to guidance and insight from other professionals.

Coal Ability to take a solid creative skill that has accumulated over time so I can use it to power a personal transformation.

Coal mine Situation where I can venture much deeper into my accumulated experience as a way of accessing a rich seam of solid creativity.

Coal miner Aspect of my character that is not afraid to get my hands dirty as I bring my creative talents out into the light of day.

Coarse Realization that I don't always have to pick my way through the finer details to reach an acceptable outcome for other people.

Coast Situation where I can go to the edge of what I know and see how it shapes my experiences instead of taking things too easily.

Coast guard Aspect of my character that keeps me secure by ensuring I am not emotionally overwhelmed as I explore the edges of my experience.

Coat Ability to present my self-image in a way that makes me feel more secure by comfortably separating my inner and outer lives.

C

Coating Ability to protect my innermost feelings by having the skill to smooth over any rough patches in my close relationships.

Coat of arms Ability to have my status and power fully recognized by a wider social circle rather than just those who are familiar with me.

Coax Opportunity to push my talents to the forefront and be proud of them rather than hoping someone will notice them.

Cobbler Aspect of my character that helps me take steps to stay self-motivated and ensures that I feel comfortable in my unique identity.

Cobbles Ability to provide a definite way forward by carefully piecing together my skills instead of riding roughshod over everyone.

Cobra Instinctive ability to transform how I see myself by raising my awareness and moving on from potentially poisonous behaviors.

Cobweb Situation where I can use bright and breezy new ideas to move on from old emotional entanglements that have held me back.

Cocaine Ability to stay relaxed and be naturally confident instead of feeling I have to constantly stimulate the interest of others.

Cochlear implant Ability to clearly hear what I am trying to tell myself instead of letting the unspoken aspects of a situation get under my skin.

Cock Instinctive ability to assert my natural talents by taking full control of my creative flow and preparing myself for any outcome.

Cockatoo Instinctive ability to intelligently communicate a colorful thought rather than screaming for attention from other people.

Cockerel Instinctive ability to develop my talents by learning how to communicate my ideas and see how they are received by others.

Cockpit Situation where I feel in full control of a particular project and can decide the best approach to reach a successful outcome.

Cockroach Instinctive ability to endure a challenging situation by resolving an unhealthy aspect of my life that is bugging me.

Cocktail Potential to fulfill an emotional need by understanding some of the ways in which my different feelings influence each other.

Cocoa Potential to fulfill an emotional need by being very much at home with my feelings so I can relax instead of worrying about them.

Coconut Natural ability to have a soft center for nurturing other people, even though I seem quite tough and defensive on the outside.

Cocoon Situation where I can explore my opportunities for personal transformation rather than getting too wrapped up in other problems.

Cod Instinctive ability to immerse myself in my emotions and be genuine about how I feel, although I may seem cool to other people.

Code Ability to say exactly how I feel about a very specific detail, even though other people may not initially understand what I mean.

Code breaker Aspect of my character that expresses what I need to say rather than feeling I have to communicate more cryptically.

Coded message Ability to communicate exactly how I feel about a situation instead of assuming that people understand what I am trying to say.

Code name Ability to identify what I find most meaningful so I can communicate my talents instead of thinking that I have to conceal them.

Code word Ability to open up to my promising potential by knowing what I need to say to make myself completely understood.

Coffee Potential to fulfill an emotional need by stimulating a conversation that perks up other people and creates a real buzz.

Coffee bar Situation where I can fulfill an emotional need by being open about what I find most stimulating rather than keeping it to myself.

Coffee table Ability to fulfill an emotional need by being open and supportive in my habitual relationships with those closest to me.

Coffer Ability to keep my valuable memories and resources safe and secure by ensuring that other people respect my personal boundaries.

Coffin Ability to keep one of my neglected ambitions safe so I can resurrect it at a later date when I don't feel so boxed in by people.

Cog Ability to keep a situation moving in a predictable way, even though it may sometimes seem that my efforts are quite insignificant.

Cognitive therapist Aspect of my character that can help me to resolve any unsettling thoughts by drawing my attention to my own powers of awareness.

Cohabitee Aspect of my character I feel very comfortable and at home with, even though it may occasionally have conflicting needs.

Coil Ability to shape a situation by always being ready for action rather than feeling like I'm always going round in circles.

Coin Ability to receive consistent recognition for my skill in taking matters into my own hands so I can create real value.

Coincidence Realization that I can combine my talents to make something really special happen rather than always leaving it to fate.

Colander Ability to ensure a fulfilling outcome rather than an emotionally draining experience by controlling my feelings.

Cold Realization that I need to show how fired up I am rather than suppressing my feelings and appearing noncommittal.

Cold-blooded animal Instinctive ability that embodies all aspects of my more primitive nature and gives me energy to express fundamental feelings.

Cold fusion Opportunity to bring some of my different qualities together so I can create a powerful outcome without any dramas.

Coldhearted Essential opportunity to really warm to my passion so I can keep my creativity flowing and connect more deeply with others.

Cold sore Essential ability to take a healthy approach to what I really need to say so I can resolve any tension or distress.

Cold storage Situation where I can preserve my accumulated experience and learning so I can feel secure in accessing it at any time.

Cold sweat Opportunity to be really fired up about a situation rather than getting all worked up and causing a lot of friction.

Collaborator Aspect of my character that can work through a potentially conflicting situation by combining a number of my practical skills.

Collage Ability to piece together a variety of my ideas so I can see the bigger picture and understand how they are connected.

Collagen Essential ability to give a fuller appreciation of what I am trying to communicate, even though it may initially be uncomfortable.

Collapsed lung Essential opportunity to always draw on my inspiration so I can powerfully express it rather than feeling I have run out of ideas.

Collapsing Realization that I need to be really strong and supportive instead of feeling that I always cave in to other people's demands.

Collapsing building Situation where I can be my fundamental self rather than feeling I have to keep up a particular front for the people around me.

C

Collapsing stairs Ability to feel secure in personally taking the steps I need to take instead of feeling I always need outside support.

Collar Ability to openly communicate how I feel about myself to other people, even though it can make me feel vulnerable and on edge.

Collateral damage Opportunity to use my wider experience to specifically target what makes me feel secure rather than always distracting myself.

Colleague Aspect of my character that can support my professional ambitions and help me achieve my goals through developing my talents.

Collecting Opportunity to stay calm by gathering my thoughts so I can use my accumulated experience to understand what is happening.

Collection Ability to understand what action I should take by looking at my options so I can use the experience I have built up.

Collector Aspect of my character that can use my accumulated wisdom to identify the most meaningful action I can take right now.

Collector's item Ability to identify the unique value of one aspect of my accumulated experience and realize how I can use it most meaningfully.

College Situation where I can learn lessons and examine what I know by developing my working relationships.

Collider Ability to make a major break-through by paying attention to the tiniest details in two opposing approaches to a problem.

Collision Opportunity to use an apparently unavoidable confrontation to choose the direction I will take with conflicting ambitions.

Colon Essential ability to fully absorb the value of what I have been experiencing so I can sum up what I am happy to let go of.

Colonel Aspect of my character that can get to the center of any conflicting ambitions and deal with them in a disciplined manner.

Colonic irrigation Essential opportunity to use my accumulated learning and experience to let go of unhealthy behaviors I no longer need.

Colonist Aspect of my character that is feeling more settled in a situation that initially seemed quite foreign and unfamiliar.

Colonoscopy Opportunity to probe the results of my recent experiences so I can achieve an in-depth understanding of their value to me.

Colony Situation where I am feeling more at home about opening up to new developments that may have seemed foreign.

Colossal Realization that I need to make a big effort to fully develop my huge talents, even though other people may often belittle them.

Color Mood that can shift my perspective by reflecting the emotional intensity of a situation and how it is illuminating my feelings.

Color-blind Essential opportunity to identify the different emotions emerging for me so I can see the bigger picture and understand it.

Color code Ability to share my individual perspective in a clear way by expressing exactly how I feel about a specific detail.

Colorless Realization that I can become much clearer about an event by expressing the intensity of my emotions and how they affect my mood.

Color scheme Situation where I can shape how I feel about a possible outcome by reflecting on my emotions and how they influence my mood.

Column Ability to support some of my bigger ideas so I can stay on the straight and narrow without being too rigid in my thinking.

Coma Essential opportunity to wake up to my talent and bring it back to life, even if there is no apparent interest from other people.

Comb Ability to straighten out my thought processes by methodically working my way through some ideas that are a bit tangled up.

Combat Opportunity to come to terms with an ongoing tension so I can prevent it from spreading into open conflict with other people.

Combatant Aspect of my character that can courageously confront any conflicts I may encounter so I can decisively deal with them.

Combination Realization that my unique value is not just a result of one specific quality, but in the way that I bring all my talents together.

Combination lock Ability to know the right sequence of actions to take so I can continue to feel safe and secure in an unfamiliar situation.

Combine harvester Ability to quickly and methodically reap the rewards from a combination of ideas that I began to develop some time ago.

Comedian Aspect of my character that can resolve serious dilemmas by taking an unexpected approach that ends up satisfying everyone.

Comedienne Aspect of my character that takes a more intuitive and creative approach to gracefully resolving any unexpected tensions.

Comedy Opportunity to resolve some of my more fundamental dilemmas by entertaining a variety of outcomes to keep everyone happy.

Comet Opportunity to consistently blaze a trail by observing my flashes of higher insight and using them to influence my timing.

Comfort Realization that I constantly need to seek out new challenges rather than complacently reassuring myself that everything is fine.

Comfort eating Opportunity to satisfy my hunger for success by making more courageous choices instead of letting my anxieties weigh me down.

Comfort food Opportunity to develop my appetite for success by looking for more exotic challenges rather than feeling complacent.

Comfort zone Situation where I have the courage to step out beyond my personal boundaries so I can achieve a wider understanding.

Comic Ability to resolve a serious dilemma by taking a more colorful approach so I can reach an outcome that keeps everyone smiling.

Coming Opportunity to understand how I can make the right choice as I approach a decision that seems to be getting ever closer.

Commandeer Opportunity to seize the moment by permitting myself to take decisive action instead of agreeing to the demands of other people.

Commander Aspect of my character that can resolve conflicts by having the authority to act decisively rather than waiting for instructions.

Commando Aspect of my character that has the special skills and discipline to resolve any potential hostility in an unobtrusive manner.

Commentary Opportunity to observe what is emerging for me as a situation unfolds so I can share my feelings with other people.

Commentator Aspect of my character that listens to my inner voice so I can understand my feelings about what is happening.

Commercial break Opportunity to understand how I present my talents to a wider audience so I can profit from the knowledge in the long run.

Commercial vehicle Ability to use my personal drive as a way of conveying the value of my talents and abilities to a wider range of people.

C

Commercial venture Opportunity to take a chance so I can prove my value to the people around me rather than feeling that I will never succeed.

Commitment Opportunity to support my abilities by having much greater confidence in them instead of feeling unsupported by other people.

Committee Aspects of my character that are committed to bringing my talents together and using them to quickly take decisive action.

Common cold Essential opportunity to share thoughts and feelings with others in a healthy way rather than just appearing cool.

Commonplace Realization that I have a potentially outstanding talent, although I sometimes feel I'm nothing out of the ordinary.

Commotion Opportunity to keep calm and collected about a potential disruption rather than becoming overagitated about what might happen.

Communal Realization that I embody a unique variety of characteristics that I can bring together to create unrivaled outcomes.

Commune Situation where I can bring all aspects of my character together on an equal basis so I can understand their connections.

Communication Opportunity to instinctively express my feelings rather than thinking I have to be more formal for others to accept me.

Communication breakdown Opportunity to break out of my habitual way of thinking so I can create a dramatic transformation in how I relate to people.

Community Aspects of my character that can combine their talent and resources to provide mutual support for a variety of my ambitions.

Community center Situation where I can understand the fundamental source of my characteristics and how I can combine their unique qualities.

Community service Opportunity to bring a variety of my character aspects together so I can understand how they interact and support one another.

Community worker Aspect of my character that makes the effort to understand the unique qualities embodied by my different characteristics.

Commuter Aspect of my character that is willing to repeatedly go the distance as a way of succeeding with my long-term ambitions.

Compact disc Ability to focus on the ins and outs of my creative talents so I can reflect on what makes them appear so special.

Compacter Ability to open up to new opportunities by taking a more concentrated approach to any behaviors I need to let go of.

Companion Aspect of my character that has the courage to fully support my own decisions rather than always trying to please other people.

Company Situation where I can bring a range of my talents and resources together so I can use them to create value for other people.

Compartment Ability to maintain a rational approach to a challenging situation by separating what is of value to me so I can look after it.

Compass Ability to choose which direction I need to take by clearly understanding my unconscious attraction to a variety of points.

Compassion Opportunity to show how I honestly feel by sharing my emotions with other people instead of suffering in silence.

Compelling Realization that I can powerfully influence a positive outcome rather than feeling forced to submit to the wishes of other people.

Compensation Opportunity to have my unique qualities recognized by other people rather than having to accommodate their particular leanings.

Competition Opportunity to use my self-motivation to discover my unique talents instead of thinking everyone else is better.

Competitor Aspect of my character that drives me to seek out my best qualities rather than always comparing myself to other people.

Compilation Ability to assemble my accumulated experience and knowledge into a coherent record of how I feel about a particular subject.

Compliment Opportunity to admire the value of my own talents instead of thinking I always have to ask for the approval of other people.

Complaint Opportunity to resolve a challenging situation by openly sharing my feelings rather than ineffectively moaning about it.

Complementary medicine Ability to examine both sides of an unhealthy relationship so I can use a variety of perspectives to move it back into balance.

Complete Realization that I lack nothing and actually have all the inner resources that I need to successfully feel at one with myself.

Complex Realize that I have the power to influence the outcome of an uncertain situation without always getting too obsessed about it.

Complexion Essential ability to face up to how my personal situation really appears to me rather than continually trying to smooth it over.

Compliant Realization that I can be flexible and bend the rules a little rather than always feeling I have to follow instructions.

Complicated Realization that I can use a specific procedure to achieve what I want, even though it may become quite involved.

Complimentary Realization that praising people for their achievements takes nothing away from the value of my accomplishments.

Component Ability to assemble a number of different ideas into a coherent viewpoint so I can achieve a more practical outcome.

Composer Aspect of my character that can bring together a variety of themes from my life and use them to evocatively express how I feel.

Composite character Ability to create a better understanding of the particular qualities I find most meaningful so I can take action with them.

Composite place Situation where I can become more aware of the various factors influencing my circumstances so that I can make the most of them.

Composition Ability to combine a number of my different qualities so I can use them to communicate my wider perspective.

Compost Natural ability to accumulate heaps of practical skills that will encourage me to successfully develop a variety of new ideas.

Composure Realization that I can positively influence an outcome by arranging priorities rather than letting everything fall apart.

Compound Situation where I can combine a number of my fundamental qualities so I can feel more comfortable in an unfamiliar environment.

Comprehension Realization that I have to quickly move beyond my everyday perspectives to understand what is going on for me.

Compress Ability to bring out the essential quality of what I want to say without feeling too squeezed out by other people.

Compressed air Ability to forcefully direct the power of what I want to say, even though I may be deeply immersed in an emotional situation.

Compulsion Realization that I can have a powerfully motivating influence on a specific situation without becoming obsessed about it.

C

Computer Ability to use my mind to quickly and precisely work out the various permutations that can influence the outcome of my situation.

Computer game Opportunity to coordinate my ideas and actions so I can play around with different scenarios to achieve eventual success.

Computer network Ability to take the initiative in sharing my accumulated experience so I can powerfully connect with other ways of thinking.

Computer programmer Aspect of my character that can assemble a powerful understanding by observing my behaviors from a more rational perspective.

Computer virus Ability to understand my thought processes so I can make myself immune to any potential criticism of my thinking.

Comrade Aspect of my character that understands why I behave the way I do and supports my beliefs, even though they can be challenging.

Concealed Opportunity to be open about my intentions rather than attempting to hide them away in case others attack them.

Concealed affair Opportunity to be honest about my temporary loss of confidence so I can restore complete faith in my abilities.

Concealed evidence Ability to make my underlying feelings more obvious instead of allowing other people to influence what I am trying to prove.

Concealed explosives Ability to create a major transformation by being more open about my underlying talents rather than always trying to hide them.

Concealed weapon Ability to openly assert my beliefs so I can exert my powerful influence instead of feeling threatened by my deeper feelings.

Concealer Ability to put a new complexion on a situation by showing how I feel rather than always trying to cover up my concerns.

Conceited Realization that I can have a more favorable opinion of my talents instead of vainly trying to seek the approval of others.

Conceivable Realization that I have the instinctive power to create anything I can imagine, although it may prove quite laborious.

Concentrated Ability to fulfill an ambition by focusing on my basic skills without allowing the effectiveness of my actions to be diluted.

Concentration camp Situation where I need to focus on giving myself the freedom to develop my natural talents instead of always repressing them.

Concept Realization that my efforts will bear fruit by taking a practical hands-on approach rather than being too abstract in my ideas.

Concern Realization that I am responsible for my own actions and decisions rather than worrying too much about what others think.

Concert Opportunity to harmoniously combine a variety of different talents to orchestrate a successfully balanced outcome.

Concertina Ability to take my instinctive creativity squarely in both hands and know the right buttons to press to make myself heard.

Concessionary fare Ability to achieve one of my ambitions by being open to what people might be driving at and the value of what they have to say.

Conch shell Ability to listen to what others are saying rather than habitually presenting an apparently impenetrable appearance.

Conclusive evidence Opportunity to reach a successful outcome by basing my decisions on what I have seen rather than being influenced by other people.

Concoction Ability to blend a number of my special abilities together so I can share them with people rather than just making up a story.

Concrete Ability to take a firm stance on my viewpoint by maintaining a set opinion based on the weight of the available evidence.

Concussion Essential opportunity to clearly communicate what has been on my mind, even though it may leave me feeling a bit shaken up.

Condemned Realization that I have the resourcefulness to restore my own confidence rather than blaming other people for doubting in myself.

Condensation Opportunity to bring clarity to a situation by staying cool as I share my feelings rather than getting steamed up about it.

Condiment Potential to spice up my ambitions by paying more attention to the small details that can add to the flavor of the experience.

Condom Ability to play it safe by keeping my options open and healthy when playing around with new concepts and their potential outcomes.

Condor Instinctive ability to work with a massive idea by using the prevailing atmosphere to elevate my level of understanding.

Conductor Aspect of my character that listens to my needs and guides me to a successful outcome by encouraging me to make the right moves.

Cone Ability to shape my circumstances by defining some boundaries so I can use my accumulated wisdom to really get to the point.

Confectionery Ability to fulfill a number of short-term ambitions that seem very attractive, without paying any attention to long-term gains.

Conference Opportunity to listen to different aspects of my character so I can begin to understand their needs and how I can meet them.

Confession Opportunity to speak my truth about how I feel rather than always being concerned that I may have let others down.

Confetti Ability to celebrate that I have managed to balance some major commitments in my life without showering myself in praise.

Confidence Essential understanding that the best way to attract people is to have faith in my uniqueness so I don't betray my talents.

Confidential Realization that I should have a deeper trust in my talents rather than always trying to keep them secret from others.

Confined space Situation where I have more choices than I think instead of feeling I am being coerced into decisions that will limit me.

Confinement Opportunity to look beyond my immediate limitations so I can think outside the box rather than always behaving the same way.

Confirmation Realization that I can always justify my actions by speaking my truth instead of waiting for other people to give me approval.

Confiscated Opportunity to have a firm grasp of my talent and what it can achieve rather than giving in to the demands of others.

Conflict Opportunity to resolve a tension between two apparently opposing aspects of my character so I can achieve a lasting peace.

Conformist Aspect of my character that can uniquely shape the outcome of a situation rather than always feeling I just have to fit in.

Confusion Opportunity to be clear about my fundamental needs instead of always trying to meet the vague demands of others.

Congestion Opportunity to be clear about my goals and how I plan to reach them rather than letting people routinely block my progress.

Congestion charge Ability to realize the value of having clear objectives so I can quickly push ahead with them instead of just sitting around.

C

Congratulations Opportunity to take great pleasure in my abilities by sharing them with other people rather than always playing my talents down.

Congregation Aspects of my character that can bring together a variety of skills and talents by sharing certain beliefs and perspectives.

C

Conifer Natural potential for my long-term spiritual growth, even though it currently may seem a bit conformist and conservative.

Conjurer Aspect of my character that can sometimes play tricks on me and distract me from seeing my magical qualities.

Connecting Opportunity to establish communication with another person at a fundamental level so I can express my feelings.

Connection Ability to maintain a firm understanding of what I am trying to accomplish so I can consistently achieve solid results.

Connective tissue Essential ability to combine my deeper strengths so I can direct them without getting too attached to a specific outcome.

Connector Ability to join two quite different aspects of my character so I can enjoy the combined value they provide

Conning tower Situation where I can take a more elevated perspective on how I can explore my emotional depths and navigate them safely.

Conquest Opportunity to seek a deeper relationship by exploring what I need and fully engaging with the associated challenges.

Conscience Realization that it is up to me to decide what I think is right or wrong so I can choose my actions accordingly.

Conscientious Realization that I instinctively keep the best interests of people in mind rather than always painstakingly justifying my actions.

Conscious Opportunity to wake up to what is happening around me by having a deeper understanding of my unconscious awareness.

Consecrated Realization that I can understand my spirituality more clearly by understanding how I relate to it in the world around me.

Consequences Opportunity to successfully achieve my chosen outcome by understanding the practical aspects of my decision making.

Conservation Ability to preserve what is most important to me by taking the time to look after the sources of my energy and self-motivation.

Conservative Realization that nothing is preventing me from realizing my potential rather than always being too cautious about it.

Conservatory Aspect of myself that is relaxed and comfortable with opening up to others and letting them see more of the real me.

Consolation prize Ability to take comfort in the knowledge that my unique talents will be rewarded and other people will acknowledge them.

Conspicuous Realization that I need to explore a greater variety of more subtle choices instead of going for the most obvious one.

Conspiracy Opportunity to be open about my thoughts and ideas rather than feeling that I can only share them surreptitiously.

Conspiracy theory Ability to have enough self-belief to openly share my ideas instead of thinking that others will secretly ridicule them.

Conspirator Aspect of my character that can breathe freely about expressing my unique talents rather than feeling I need to conceal them.

Constant danger Opportunity to feel secure in decisions I make so I am content to explore any possibilities beyond my comfort zone.

Constellation Situation where I can assemble a dazzling array of ideas and explore all the different ways in which they are connected.

Constipation Opportunity to gracefully let go of habits that are no longer healthy for me instead of dumping them unceremoniously.

Constricted Opportunity to gain freedom by specifically defining my needs rather than feeling like I'm being squeezed into a decision.

Construction Opportunity to lay a firm foundation for my learning so I can build a solid understanding of what I am trying to create.

Construction site Situation where I can bring my best qualities into prominence by employing my talents to create a character-building experience.

Constructive dismissal Opportunity to fully recognize my unique qualities and how I can build on them rather than dismissing them.

Consultant Aspect of my character that can observe my behaviors as a way of understanding what I need and how I can achieve it.

Consumption Opportunity to plan how I can make best use of my resources instead of becoming caught up in an all-consuming obsession.

Contact Opportunity to communicate how I feel about a particular situation by actively staying in touch with what I really need.

Contact lens Ability to clearly focus on the most important parts of a situation rather than getting caught up in superficial details.

Contact sport Opportunity to successfully achieve my ambitions by communicating how I feel about a challenging situation.

Contagious Realization that sharing my positive approach to a challenge is far healthier than spreading unconfirmed rumors about it.

Container Ability to use my individual resourcefulness to move a situation forward, even though it may seem initially limiting.

Contaminated Opportunity to clear up confusion about my natural anxieties by taking a positive and healthy approach to my ambitions.

Contemporary Realization that I need to take prompt action in my present situation instead of revisiting the past or planning my future.

Contempt Realization that I need to look much deeper into my motives rather than dismissing other actions as being beneath me.

Contentment Realization that I have all the resources I need to be happy instead of constantly feeling dissatisfied with my situation.

Contest Opportunity to challenge my habitual behaviors so I can open myself up to playing around with my opposing drives and ambitions.

Contestant Aspect of my character that has the talent to influence a potentially uncertain outcome by openly playing with my talents.

Context Realization that the surrounding aspects of any situation are often just as important as the more obvious main elements.

Continent Situation where I can define the boundaries of my cultural influences and the possibilities they offer for exploration.

Contortionist Aspect of my character that often bends over backward to please others as I try to fit in with their convoluted needs.

Contour line Ability to give some shape to my challenges by clearly making direct connections with the levels of effort I am exerting.

Contraband Ability to use my knowledge in a variety of areas without feeling that I need to get the permission of other people to do so.

C

Contraceptive Ability to keep potential developments under control until I feel the time is right to share my new concepts and their outcomes.

Contract Ability to use my talents in an agreeable way that amplifies the opportunities rather than limiting the value of my participation.

Contradictory Realization that I can decisively reconcile my different viewpoints instead of allowing them to continually work against me.

Contra flow Opportunity to work my way through some of my opposing drives and ambitions, even though it may temporarily slow me down.

Contrail Ability to clearly track the progress of a high-flying project by looking at the learning and experience that follows from it.

Contrary Realization that I can happily bring together apparently opposing aspects of my character without caring what others think.

Contravene Opportunity to give myself direct permission to move forward instead of feeling that I'm up against a self-imposed barrier.

Contribution Realization that I have creative gifts I can share with other people, even though it can seem like I have nothing to give.

Contrived Realization that I can be spontaneously ingenious rather than having to go through an elaborate process to display my talents.

Control Realization that I have the ability to decide a specific outcome instead of feeling that other people are in charge of my growth.

Control-Alt-Delete Opportunity to take an unsatisfying situation into my own hands so I can transform it by deciding to start all over again.

Control column Ability to leverage some of the current forces influencing me so I can steer a project toward my chosen outcome.

Control freak Aspect of my character that can create a specific outcome by letting go of conventional thinking and allowing my talent to emerge.

Controller Ability to decide the result of an uncertain situation by making a definite choice rather than letting it go out of control.

Control tower Situation where I can get an overall view of the progress of a variety of projects so I can safely direct the outcomes.

Conundrum Ability to state my needs unambiguously instead of playing around with what I need to say to the characters around me.

Convalescent Opportunity to take some time out and recover my motivation rather than feeling I have to continue in an unhealthy atmosphere.

Convenience food Potential to quickly fulfill a short-term ambition without feeling that I always have to prepare an involved plan of action.

Convent Situation where I can reflect on my deeper spirituality so I can develop much stronger beliefs in my pure creative potential.

Convention Opportunity to understand my needs so I can connect some of my unique talents instead of always feeling I have to fit in.

Convergence Realization that I can bring together a number of my different practical skills so I can get my point across.

Conversation Opportunity to listen to what I'm saying so I can hear what I need to do to turn the situation around.

Converted Realization that the best way for me to make a positive transformation is to convince myself that I can make the change.

Convertible Ability to make progress toward my objective by being more open to the prevailing mood and allowing it to influence my choices.

Conveyor belt Situation where I feel I'm

endlessly going through the motions to keep up with expectations rather than making my own decisions.

Convict Aspect of my character that liberates my talents by having the courage of my convictions as I go beyond self-limiting beliefs.

Convoy Ability to make steady progress by guarding myself against emotional highs and lows as I navigate toward my chosen objective.

Convulsing Opportunity to take a calm, considered approach so I can choose my preferred outcome rather than getting agitated.

Cook Aspect of my character that takes some of the ingredients of my raw ambition and uses them to nourish my appetite for success.

Cooker Ability to use my creative powers in a warm and comforting manner so I can consistently satisfy my hunger for results.

Cookie Ability to make my own choice instead of being happy with a small and short-lived reward for behaving in a particular way.

Cooking Opportunity to use my raw talent to create a satisfying outcome so I can continue to sustain my long-term ambitions.

Cool Realization that I need to take a warmer and more welcoming approach to a situation rather than withdrawing by chilling out.

Cooling tower Ability to vent my frustration with a whole range of heated discussions so I can raise my sense of empowerment to a higher level.

Coop Situation where I can use my ability to produce fertile ideas, although I may feel limited by self-imposed boundaries.

Cop Aspect of my character that gives me permission to powerfully assert the strength of my talents in a fair and reasonable manner.

Copilot Aspect of my character that helps me see the bigger picture so I can get my ideas off the ground and successfully land them.

Copper Ability to use my fundamental strength to channel my creative flow, although it initially may not seem to be of any great value.

Copse Situation where I can cultivate the growth potential of some of my developing talents so I can share their practical value.

Copy Opportunity to use my unique talent to produce something original instead of feeling I have to duplicate the work of other people.

Coracle Ability to navigate a potentially challenging emotional situation by taking the time to look around and see the possibilities.

Coral Natural ability to simply let the ebb and flow of my feelings help me build up a complex and richly rewarding emotional life.

Coral fish Instinctive ability to immerse myself in my rich and complex emotional life so I can make the most of its ebbs and flows.

Coral reef Situation where I can use my accumulated experience from my emotional life to build up my level of attractiveness to others.

Cord Ability to stay firmly connected to the result of a situation without feeling that I am bound to act in a particular way.

Cordless Ability to move freely and choose my preferred outcome without feeling that I need to be involved in any binding agreements.

Cordon Situation where I can give myself permission to step into a new opportunity instead of thinking people are holding me back.

Core Ability to get to the heart of the matter and connect with its power rather than being content with external appearances.

Cork Ability to contain myself from uncontrollably pouring out my feelings so I can maintain my mood of buoyant optimism.

Corkscrew Ability to open up my feelings to other people so I can feel much happier and relaxed rather than just going round and round.

C

Cormorant Instinctive ability to connect with my deeper feelings and bring them to the surface so I can examine them in a logical manner.

Corn Natural ability to sustain my ambitions by listening for some abundantly fertile opportunities so I can reap their benefits.

Corner Situation where I have reached a turning point and can choose what I need to leave behind so I can step into a new future.

Corner shop Situation where I can choose to take a new direction by displaying my specific value and having it recognized by other people.

Cornflower Natural ability to have a more vivid appreciation of how to develop my talents by allowing my calmness and serenity to blossom.

Cornice Ability to draw attention to a potentially delicate situation rather than always taking it too far and just going over the top.

Cornucopia Ability to realize that I have plenty of resources and can access the continuing abundance of my natural talents at any time.

Coronary bypass Opportunity to keep my passion and vitality flowing rather than taking a different route and avoiding the heart of the matter.

Coronation Opportunity to display my accumulated power and wisdom so I can have my crowning achievements recognized by others.

Coroner Aspect of my character that helps me to examine the areas of my life that I should lay to rest to transform my future.

Corporal punishment Opportunity to transform my situation by taking action that will give me a lot of pleasure rather than always being a killjoy.

Corporate hospitality Opportunity to be more welcoming and receptive to the value of my individual talents instead of just routinely dismissing them.

Corpse Aspect of my character I am trying to lay to rest, even though it embodies an unfulfilled talent I have been repressing.

Corral Situation where I can round up my instinctive skills and put them to work for me by harnessing their unconscious energies.

Correct Realization that I can use my own judgment to do the right thing rather than worrying about making a wrong decision.

Correction facility Situation where I have the freedom to choose the right thing to do instead of feeling limited by the behaviors of others.

Correspondence Opportunity to understand how I feel by helping people to express their sentiments and observing my response.

Corridor Situation where I can make comfortable progress within clearly defined boundaries and be open to any opportunities along the way.

Corrosion-proof Ability to protect myself against caustic remarks by allowing the brilliance of my natural talent to keep shining through.

Corrosive Realization that I need to be open about what is eating away at me instead of trying to keep up surface appearances.

Corrugated iron Ability to use the ups and downs of the situation to make me feel stronger rather than always trying to smooth everything out.

Corruption Realization that it is my responsibility to be honest about my feelings instead of allowing others to influence them.

Corset Ability to present my self-image to the people around me by being able to clearly define how I feel in a contained fashion.

Cortège Opportunity to recognize a once-vital aspect of my past so I can proceed to lay it to rest in a graceful and befitting manner.

Cosh Ability to powerfully assert my viewpoint by being blunt and without giving myself too much of a headache.

Cosmetics Ability to present the aspects of myself that I think other people want to see instead of facing up to my inner beauty.

Cosmetic surgery Opportunity to be happy in my skin rather than trying to reshape how people see me so I can cut out their negative criticism.

Cosmic Realization that I have infinite potential to expand my awareness and explore all the different aspects of my uniqueness.

Cosmonaut Aspect of my character that can powerfully elevate my spirit by being boundlessly inquisitive about my wider surroundings.

Cosmos Situation where I can create a sense of order and harmony in my world so I can expand my understanding without limitation.

Cosplay Opportunity to play around with different aspects of how I appear to others without necessarily dressing it up too much.

Cost Realization that I can always increase my value to other people instead of feeling I always have to agree to their demands.

Costar Aspect of my character that is supportive of my skills and methods so I can make their brilliance shine.

Costly Realization that my wisdom and experience are always accumulating in value, even though outcomes are sometimes unexpected.

Costume Ability to show my depth of character instead of just presenting my self-image to people in a way they find acceptable.

Costume drama Opportunity to show the reality of my emotional life rather than feeling I always have to dress it up for others.

Costume jewelry Ability to show people the aspects of myself that I feel are valuable instead of appearing superficially attractive.

Cot Ability to nurture a labor of love in a simple and protective manner so I can keep it separate from my other activities.

Cottage Situation where I can take a simpler and more relaxed approach to exploring all the different aspects of who I really am.

Cotton Ability to increase my understanding of what is happening by connecting with people in a softer and more natural way.

Cotton bud Ability to maintain a clear awareness of a situation by allowing creative connections to blossom in their own time.

Cotton wool Ability to be more comfortable with my fundamental behaviors so I can feel less fragile when protecting my needs.

Couch Ability to share a relaxed and comfortable viewpoint with others so I can influence them from my perspective.

Couch-surfing Opportunity to explore a variety of outcomes for entertaining myself, while sharing an agreeable situation with others.

Cougar Instinctive ability to confidently assert my independence and freedom in a more mature way that naturally attracts people to me.

Cough Essential opportunity to clear up an irritating tension by speaking up so I can draw attention to an unhealthy situation.

Councillor Aspect of my character that supports my everyday activities by trying to ensure that I follow traditional social values.

Counselor Aspect of my character that helps me see the wisdom in what I'm doing and how my experiences can inspire other people.

Countdown Opportunity to take time out so I can look at a variety of possible outcomes instead of feeling that my number is up.

Counter Situation where I have a solid basis for my preparations so I can show my value to people and see how it all adds up.

Counterattack Opportunity to respond to a challenge by taking forceful action so I can assert my ambitions and declare their value.

C

Counterfeit Realization that I need to show the value of my unique talents to people rather than trying to copy everyone else.

Counterterrorism Opportunity to take the initiative to decisively deal with my unresolved anxieties instead of always feeling threatened by them.

Counting Opportunity to take the time to understand the value of my accumulated experience so I can have it acknowledged by other people.

Country Situation where I can define the boundaries of my wider identity and the opportunities it offers for personal exploration.

Country house Situation where I have the security and support to explore at leisure some of the unknown and unfamiliar aspects of my character.

Country lane Situation where I can take a narrower and more defined route to explore remoter and more rewarding aspects of my nature.

Countryside Situation where I can explore some of the unfamiliar and undiscovered aspects of my nature and the opportunities they hold.

Coup Opportunity to fundamentally change the power in a relationship by delivering an unexpected action that is highly successful.

Couple Aspects of my character that can connect at a fundamental level as a way of forming a whole that is greater than the parts.

Couples therapist Aspect of my character that can help me resolve ongoing tensions by combining my unique qualities at a deeper level.

Coupon Ability to clearly demonstrate my value to other people instead of always cutting myself off from new opportunities.

Courage Opportunity to demonstrate my passion and commitment by being confident in my talents rather than being shy about them.

Courier Aspect of my character that is on a mission to assist me in communicating the value of my insights to other people.

Course Situation where I can make most progress by understanding the correct direction I need to take to make further advances.

Court Situation where I can view myself more favorably by judging how attractive my behaviors appear to other people.

Court case Opportunity to examine my behaviors in a particular situation so I can release myself from guilt associated with them.

Courtroom Situation where I have some space to judge my attitudes so that can free myself from any guilty feelings I may have.

Courtship Opportunity to recognize my most attractive qualities rather than continually trying to judge how I appear to other people.

Courtyard Situation where I can be more open about my habitual behaviors so I can have space to explore bigger plans and ideas.

Cousin Aspect of my character that can bring me closer to an understanding about the wider aspects of some familiar areas of my life.

Cove Situation where I can explore the edge of my experience in relative calm so I can be more receptive to my wider emotions.

Cover Ability to reveal how I feel about a situation instead of presenting a superficial appearance to other people.

Covert activity Opportunity to make my sentiments obvious to the people around me rather than always feeling I need to disguise my true emotions.

Covert surveillance Opportunity to closely observe the actions I take, even though my original intentions may have been quite different.

Cover-up Opportunity to reveal feelings I may have been concealing instead of conspiring to keep everyone else happy.

Cow Instinctive ability to nurture the emotional life of other people in a naturally healthy way by taking time to chew things over.

Coward Aspect of my character that has the courage to stand up for what I believe, instead of being intimidated by other people.

Cowardly Realization that the best way to resolve my fears and anxieties is to directly engage with them in a bold, courageous manner.

Cowbell Ability to raise my awareness of my own capabilities for nurturing other people so I can clearly draw their attention to it.

Cowboy Aspect of my character that tames my unconscious energies and can harness them as a way of exploring the edge of what I know.

Cowering Opportunity to stand up straight and courageously declare what I believe in so I can shake off any lurking fears.

Coxswain Aspect of my character that keeps my self-motivation on track as I take the most direct route through an emotional situation.

Coyote Instinctive ability to demonstrate my loyalty and commitment in a situation where my good nature might be taken for granted.

Cozy Opportunity to move outside my comfort zone and get myself much closer to a challenge so I can feel more relaxed with it.

Crab Instinctive ability to protect my vulnerabilities by being a bit nippy and defensive rather than taking a more direct approach.

Crack Ability to make the most of an opportunity that is unexpectedly opening up, even though it may initially seem to be unwelcome.

Crackdown Opportunity to open up to what makes me feel happiest rather than cutting down on my enjoyment by being too strict with myself.

Cradle Situation where I can consistently nurture a labor of love by keeping it very close to me and gently protecting its development.

Craft Ability to use my ambition and drive to produce a unique outcome that demonstrates my special expertise and skills.

Crag Situation where I can come to grips with a sudden transformation by sticking up for myself and progressing through sheer effort.

Cramp Essential ability to stay relaxed about a tense situation by being open to suggestions rather than limiting my options.

Cramped conditions Situation where I need to start making my own decisions, even though I may feel uncomfortable about it not being my style.

Crampon Ability to confidently stand up for myself and get to the point in a dangerous and potentially treacherous situation.

Crane Ability to firmly develop my wider perspectives by making the effort to rise above it all in a character-building experience.

Crank Ability to use my unique self-motivation and energy to move a situation into action without feeling that I may appear strange.

Crannog Situation where I can feel at home by being able to reflect on my deeper emotions and what I have learned from them.

Crap Ability to take decisive action by cutting out some of my habitual behaviors that are no longer of any value to me.

Crash Opportunity to take control of a developing situation so I can choose the outcome instead of letting it fall apart around me.

Crash barrier Ability to get beyond a self-limiting belief by taking control of a situation and choosing how I would like it to progress.

Crash diet Opportunity to fulfill my appetite for success by being measured in the way I take control of my developing situation.

C

Crash dive Opportunity to immerse myself in my emotional life so I have more influence over the feelings that are emerging for me.

Crash helmet Ability to protect my individual way of thinking by confidently taking more control of my plans in a potentially risky situation.

Crash landing Opportunity to successfully complete a complex plan by taking decisive control so I can use a more down-to-earth approach.

Crash survivor Aspect of my character that can draw on my resourcefulness to achieve my chosen outcome rather than worrying about my security.

Crate Ability to convey my memories and experiences to other people as a way of helping me retain my ideas and keep them safe.

Crater Situation where I can go a bit deeper into the practical aspects so I can understand the impact they might have.

Craving Opportunity to become more familiar with my deepest desires so I can fulfill them instead of becoming obsessed by them.

Crawling Opportunity to get much closer to the practical realities, even though it may initially seem to be very slow and quite painful.

Crayon Ability to use my colorful imagination to point out what is happening rather than just sketching over the details.

Crazed Opportunity to see a deeper pattern in my apparently irrational behavior instead of just looking at surface appearances.

Crazed beast Instinctive ability to embody my fundamental talent so I can channel my creative urges in a practical, positive manner.

Crazy Essential opportunity to understand the irrational nature of my creativity so I can use it practically and consistently.

Crazy man Aspect of my character that is frustrated when I ignore my creative strength and its power to accomplish my ambitions.

Crazy woman Aspect of my character that is driven mad when I neglect my creative wisdom and the talent it has to fulfill my aspirations.

Creak Opportunity to make things run more smoothly by drawing my attention to behaviors that are beginning to let me down.

Creaking floorboard Opportunity to become more aware of how a fairly narrow set of beliefs is offering less support for me as I continue my progress.

Cream Potential to fulfill an emotional need by choosing the smoothest way to display my steadily increasing level of expertise.

Crease Ability to straighten out a situation by being able to draw a definite line around what I consider acceptable behavior.

Creating Opportunity to bring my unique talents into being by allowing my individual concepts to evolve from my thoughts and feelings.

Creativity Ability to see my unique perspective so I can use my instinctive power and awareness to make the most of an emerging opportunity.

Creature Instinctive ability to embody my vital nature so I can use my creativity to bring some new opportunities to life.

Crèche Situation where I have the time and space to take care of a number of developing projects in a safe and nurturing manner.

Credit Ability to be proud of my unique talents so I can have the confidence that their value will be fully acknowledged by others.

Credit card Ability to give myself full credit for my abilities so I can value my talents rather than feeling I owe anything to anyone else.

Credit rating Ability to have other people fully recognize the wealth of my accumulated wisdom and experience instead of being critical of it.

Creek Situation where I can understand how I naturally channel my emotions by looking to their source and the course they might take.

Creel Ability to immerse myself in my emotions so I can gather them and not get too caught up in what is happening around me.

Creep Opportunity to make steady progress by staying close to the realities of the situation rather than feeling strange about it.

Creeper Natural ability to quietly explore an opportunity without feeling that I have to cling to false hopes or spread any anxieties.

Creepy-crawly Instinctive ability to quietly make my way through some of the practical realities without causing myself too much anxiety.

Cremation Opportunity to acknowledge a once-vital aspect of my past so I can use it to completely transform my creative awareness.

Crematorium Situation where I can get fired up about letting go of unwanted habits so I can completely transform my creative talent.

Creosote Ability to preserve some of my habitual behavior patterns rather than feeling that I always need to get rid of dead wood.

Crepuscular Realization that I can clearly understand what is happening, even though others may take a dim view of my activities.

Crescent Ability to shape my circumstances by observing the edge of my awareness and seeing how I can expand its growth.

Crest Situation where I can rise to the occasion by acknowledging all the uplifting activities and emotions that got me here.

Crestfallen Opportunity to hold my head up high and be proud of my actions rather than being discouraged about one specific outcome.

Crevice Situation where I can make the most of an opening without becoming too deeply stuck in the practicalities involved in it.

Crew Aspects of my character that draw on my experience in using well-rehearsed routines to deal with challenging situations.

Crib Ability to make the space to nurture a project that is close to my heart while trying not to draw too much attention to it.

Crib death Opportunity to revitalize a project that is close to my heart by paying close attention to any limitations I impose on it.

Cricket Opportunity to make the most of an uncertain outcome by playing fairly, even though other people may behave in an underhanded manner.

Cricket bat Ability to make a satisfying connection with an approaching opportunity so I can use my skill to make an impact.

Crime Opportunity to have confidence in my good judgment rather than punishing myself when I feel I have let people down.

Crime scene Situation where I can become aware of what motivates me by having the confidence to trust in my good judgment.

Crime-scene artist Situation where I can become more confident in trusting my judgment by using my creative instincts to share my viewpoint.

Crime-scene investigator Aspect of my character that helps me examine my behaviors so I can move on rather than feeling I'm letting myself down.

Criminal Aspect of my character that tries to do the right thing, even though other people may not fully understand my deeper motives.

Criminal record Ability to acknowledge that I always try to do the right thing instead of being too self-critical of any of my perceived failures.

C

Crimson Mood that can color my perspective by reflecting my deeper passions and how they can attract me to unfamiliar situations.

Cringing Realization that I need to be proud of my talents so I can have the confidence to stand up straight and tall with them.

Cripple Essential opportunity to stand up for what I believe in so I can take decisive steps rather than coming up with lame excuses.

Crisis Opportunity to take dramatic action to make the most of an emerging possibility instead of feeling I am a victim of circumstance.

Crisp Realization that I may need to soften my approach in achieving an ambition so I can make it more palatable to other people.

Crisps Potential to fulfill short-term ambition through some habitual activity without paying any attention to the long-term gains.

Critic Aspect of my character that is always trying to improve my talents, even though it seems to voice doubts about my abilities.

Critical list Opportunity to resolve an unhealthy situation by putting it into perspective rather than seeing it as a life-or-death decision.

Criticism Realization that the most powerful learning comes from being open to failure instead of feeling I must be perfect every time.

Crochet Ability to connect a number of story threads in a bigger pattern so I can present my material to other people.

Crockery Ability to support my ambitions in a way that enables me to share them with other people and ensure things don't get too messy.

Crocodile Instinctive ability to seize the moment and powerfully express genuine feelings instead of hypocritically concealing them.

Crone Aspect of my character that can use my accumulated wisdom to resolve my vague fears rather than letting my talents wither away.

Crook Aspect of my character that always tries to do the right thing, even though it means I have to bend the rules to be successful.

Crooked Realization that I may have to bend the rules to reach a valuable outcome instead of conforming to the straight and narrow.

Crop Opportunity to realize the value of a growing ambition I have been cultivating without feeling too cut off from my roots.

Crop circle Situation where I can stay centered and realize the apparent value of a developing ambition that may seem quite otherworldly.

Cropped hair Essential opportunity to shape my ideas in a very precise style without feeling that I have to cut off my creative flow.

Croquet Opportunity to knock ideas around in a gracious and decisive manner without deliberating too much over the outcome.

Cross Ability to shape my circumstances by not getting too upset that other viewpoints may seem to be completely different from mine.

Crossbow Ability to immediately resolve a conflict by firing off a quick decision rather than thinking I've already shot my bolt.

Cross-country Opportunity to explore the wider boundaries of my comfort zone and the possibilities they offer for personal exploration.

Cross-dressing Opportunity to explore unconventional aspects of my self-image that can give me a more complete understanding of my true identity.

Cross-examining Opportunity to understand the fundamental basis of my opinions so I can be more consistent in achieving chosen outcomes.

Cross-eyed Opportunity to look at a situation from number of different angles so I can straighten out my particular point of view.

C

Crossfire Opportunity to understand the intentions behind a number of conflicting aims so I can make a choice and give it my best shot.

Crosshairs Ability to zero in on a particular idea that reflects my fundamental style of thinking so I can use it to achieve my aims.

Crossing Situation where I can resolve a dilemma between two perspectives by choosing to make a transition that goes beyond them.

Cross-questioning Opportunity to discover my unknown potential by examining different angles and asking myself what they can provide.

Crossroad Situation where I can make a definite decision to follow a particular path as a way of resolving conflicting possibilities.

Crossword Ability to resolve a complicated situation by looking at the bigger picture instead of seeing everything in black and white.

Crotch Essential ability to embody my creative potential so I can use it to take the steps I need to turn it into direct action.

Crouching Essential opportunity to spring into action so I can achieve an ambition that will enable me to stand proud and tall.

Croupier Aspect of my character that opens me up to a number of chances to have my value acknowledged so I can rake it in.

Crow Instinctive ability to pick out a powerful idea that is deeply transformative without feeling I always have to go on about it.

Crowbar Ability to open myself up to new opportunities rather than feeling I have to pry on other people's activities to succeed.

Crowd Situation where I can identify one particular aspect of my talent, even though there are a lot of demands for my attention.

Crowded Opportunity to turn my attention to one of my specific skills without feeling too pressured by what is happening around me.

Crowd-surfing Opportunity to rise above it all and celebrate my success by relaxing and allowing people to support me and push me forward.

Crown Ability to present my self-image to people by drawing attention to my greatest achievements without appearing too bigheaded.

Crucial Realization that I have the power to make an extremely important decision rather than always feeling cross with myself.

Crucible Ability to powerfully reshape the fundamental practicalities of the situation by carefully containing my heated emotions.

Crucifix Ability to display my beliefs without getting too upset that other people's spiritual perspectives may be different from my own.

Crucifixion Opportunity to rise above some conflicting beliefs, even though it means I may have to sacrifice my viewpoint.

Crude Realization that my distilled wisdom comes from being open to my raw power rather than feeling I have to be a polished presenter.

Cruelty Opportunity to be kind and gentle about my vulnerabilities instead of causing myself a lot of pain and anxiety over them.

Cruise Opportunity to keep things moving in a steady and relaxed manner without feeling that I always have to be actively involved.

Cruise control Ability to make more relaxed progress with one of my ambitions rather than feeling I have to put my foot down all the time.

Cruise liner Ability to navigate complex and unpredictable emotions in a more relaxed manner that enables me to make steady progress.

Cruise missile Ability to powerfully assert my beliefs and exert my influence by staying close to the practical aspects of a tense situation.

Crumbling Realization that I can use my inner strength and confidence to support me rather than continuing to let things fall apart.

C

Crumbling rock Opportunity to maintain a firm and practical outlook, even though I may not feel I have the fundamental support I need.

Crumbling ruins Situation where I can begin to rebuild my sense of identity so I can explore a variety of character building experiences.

Crumbling teeth Opportunity to display my power and confidence to the people around me, even though I may seem to have no obvious support.

Crumbs Potential to fulfill my ambitions by pursuing larger opportunities rather than trying to keep track of lots of smaller ones.

Crumpled Opportunity to keep things running smoothly by ironing out any problems that are making the situation appear worse than it is.

Crumple zone Ability to absorb the impact of any unforeseen events by being willing to sacrifice aspects of how other people see me.

Crunchy Potential to fulfill an ambition by having the confidence to take decisive action rather than trying to smooth things over.

Crusade Opportunity to assert the strength of my beliefs by challenging others, even though the issues may seem quite foreign to me.

Crushed Realization that I can continue to stand up for my beliefs, even when other people seem to be trying to make me feel small.

Crushing weight Opportunity to release myself from a heavy responsibility rather than allowing it to shape how I might appear to others.

Crust Ability to demonstrate my value by showing my softer, more vulnerable aspects beneath the hard edge I present to people.

Crutches Ability to support my actions and take the necessary steps to move forward, even though it seems quite an artificial process.

Crying Essential opportunity to show what I feel by opening up to an emotional release that gives me a clearer perspective.

Cryogenically frozen Opportunity to step into the future by immersing myself in my more heated emotions rather than trying to play it very cool.

Crypt Situation where I can achieve one of my deeper desires by stepping into the past and resurrecting a long-neglected ambition.

Cryptic Realization that the most powerful way to explore my own mysteries is to directly engage with them rather than being enigmatic.

Cryptologist Aspect of my character that can reveal my deeper motivations by sharing them openly instead of just endlessly analyzing them.

Crystal Ability to achieve a precious clarity by using clear and structured thinking to illuminate the full spectrum of my potential.

Crystal ball Ability to play around with my clear need to create my own future rather than thinking I have to leave it to fate.

Cubbyhole Aspect of myself that has some unique talents tucked away, even though I tend to ignore them because of other opportunities.

Cube Ability to shape my circumstances by naturally raising my power and being exact about the volume of work I feel I have to do.

Cubicle Situation where I can work on developing my influence and expanding my potential rather than feeling limited by regulations.

Cuckoo Instinctive ability to be rational instead of having the crazy thought that someone might be taking credit for my ideas.

Cucumber Natural ability to have a healthy appreciation of what is happening by keeping cool and looking for fresh opportunities.

Cuddling Opportunity to get much closer

and more comfortable with an aspect of my nature rather than trying to keep it at arm's length.

Cuddly toy Ability to get more comfortable with some of my creative instincts so I can play around with how I can feel more secure in them.

Cudgel Ability to powerfully defend my individual viewpoint without being too short-tempered or giving myself too hard a time about it.

Cue Opportunity to signal my intentions so I can act promptly in how I respond to what other people are suggesting to me.

Cue card Ability to be firm but flexible in how I respond to the suggestions of other people so I can continue to act promptly.

Cuff Ability to improvise by staying flexible about how I can use my strength and power to shape and direct my chosen outcome.

Cuff link Ability to tidy up any loose ends by staying connected to how I can use my strength and power to shape the outcome I choose.

Cul-de-sac Situation where I can progress in a new direction rather than staying stuck in a dead-end position that is going nowhere.

Cull Opportunity to transform my creative instincts by focusing on my most important aims and getting rid of my destructive behaviors.

Culmination Realization that that I can reach my loftiest ambitions by using my accumulated experience and wisdom to lift me higher.

Culpable Realization that I am less likely to judge myself too harshly if I take more responsibility for my own actions.

Culprit Aspect of my character that is open and honest about my responsibilities instead of feeling that I am always to blame.

Cult Opportunity to explore some of my wider beliefs rather than becoming overly devoted to one particular aspect of my character.

Cult figure Aspect of my character that can assume a great deal of significance, even though I have not devoted enough time to developing it.

Cultivated Opportunity to take a more civilized approach to how I develop a variety of fertile ideas so I can reap the benefits.

Cult status Opportunity to understand the power of one of my beliefs so I can use it to transform my standing with other people.

Cultural minority Aspects of my character that help me feel more secure by speaking my truth instead of being influenced by the weight of numbers.

Cultured Realization that the best way to increase my awareness is to share it with other people rather than developing it in isolation.

Culture shock Realization that I have an unexpectedly powerful opportunity to develop my understanding in a way that may seem quite surprising.

Culvert Situation where I can channel some of my deeper emotions so they continue to support my progress instead of disrupting it.

Cumbersome Realization that my opinions carry some weight, even though I may sometimes find it awkward to convey them.

Cummerbund Ability to present my self-image to people in a way that draws attention to how I connect my thoughts and feelings to my actions.

Cunnilingus Essential opportunity to become more intimately aware of how I can communicate a unique idea and how it might be conceived.

Cunning Realization that I can use my natural intelligence to solve a challenging problem without feeling I have to be too subtle.

Cup Ability to fulfill an emotional need by containing a particular feeling so I can enjoy it rather than letting it spill out.

C

Cupboard Ability to open myself up a bit so I can access personal insights and experiences I may have chosen to shut away.

Cupid Aspect of my character that can suddenly connect me with some of the qualities other people find most attractive in me.

Curb Ability to define the boundaries of my involvement in a wider ambition instead of feeling that other people are holding me back.

Curdled Realization that I need to keep my relationships fresh by nurturing other people rather than always going off on my own.

Cure Opportunity to remedy an unhealthy feeling by resolving to take action instead of trying to preserve the current situation.

Curfew Opportunity to show my authority in public whenever I choose to rather than feeling as if my time to take action is limited.

Curio Ability to value some of my more unusual talents and abilities instead of regarding them as mere curiosities.

Curious Realization that the most powerful way to accumulate more wisdom and wealth is to always be open to increasing my understanding.

Curlew Instinctive ability to sift through my feelings so I can evoke some thoughts that remind me of wild and beautiful places.

Curly Ability to shape my circumstances by taking a more rounded approach rather than trying to keep myself on the straight and narrow.

Currency Ability to immediately demonstrate my wider value to other people by staying in the moment instead of trying to save face.

Current Opportunity to influence the outcome of a situation by channeling my unconscious power rather than just going with the flow.

Curry Potential to fulfill an ambition by using a variety of influences to spice the situation up a bit so it meets with my approval.

Curse Opportunity to say what I feel in a positive way rather than thinking that other people may be the cause of my misfortune.

Cursor Ability to identify exactly where I am in a potentially confusing situation so I can direct my actions toward a specific outcome.

Curtain Ability to temporarily conceal a private situation from other people rather than permanently shutting them out of my life.

Curtain call Opportunity to be more open about the role I have been playing so people can show their appreciation of my talents.

Curtsey Opportunity to stand up for what I believe in instead of thinking I have to always bow down to the wishes of others.

Curve Ability to shape a situation by being flexible so I can stay ahead of any changes rather than feeling that I've been left behind.

Cushion Ability to make myself more comfortable in a habitual viewpoint I hold so I can absorb any criticism from other people.

Custard Potential to fulfill a short-term ambition by being very kind to other people without feeling I have to lay it on too thick.

Custodian Aspect of my character that ensures I look after my most precious memories without feeling too guarded about sharing them.

Custody Opportunity to have more self-discipline in my creativity rather than thinking that other people are limiting my activities.

Custom Realization that I can shape my habits in any way I want instead of having to conform to the traditions of other people.

Customer Aspect of my character that can stay cool and bring out my most valuable qualities when faced with a tough situation.

Customs officer Aspect of my character that examines my choices and decides what I need to do without it being too taxing.

Cut Ability to take decisive action so I can leave unwelcome aspects of the past behind and confidently step into a new future.

Cute Realization that I can continue to attract all the support I need without having to be too coy or precious about it.

Cutlery Ability to shape a potential ambition by choosing the most fulfilling aspects and breaking them down into bite-sized chunks.

Cutting out Opportunity to decisively pick out a specific quality that will help me continue my progress in a smooth and consistent manner.

Cuttlefish Instinctive ability to express my most deeply felt emotions now rather than presenting them in sepia-toned nostalgia.

Cyber Realization that I need to embody my emotions and display my most human qualities instead of behaving in such a detached manner.

Cybercrime Opportunity to do the right thing by showing my humanity rather than punishing myself for appearing so detached and uncaring.

Cybersex Opportunity to become more intimately aware of how I need to embody my talents before I can conceive something special.

Cyberstalking Opportunity to identify my concealed talents so I can bring them into the open rather than feeling too detached from them.

Cyberterrorism Opportunity to deal with my unresolved anxieties in a human way instead of constantly worrying about what might happen to me.

Cyberwarfare Opportunity to resolve an ongoing inner tension by taking a more humane approach rather than trying to avoid my feelings.

Cyborg Aspect of my character that has a fundamental need to display my human qualities by having the courage to embody my emotions.

Cycle Realization that I can use my past experience to influence future outcomes without feeling I'm just going round and round.

Cycle path Situation where I can use my self-motivation and energy to reach an outcome by taking a narrower and more defined route.

Cycling Opportunity to use my energy and powerful self-motivation to keep a number of commitments in balance and still make progress.

Cyclist Aspect of my character that has the self-motivation and energy to make significant progress by balancing my various commitments.

Cyclone Opportunity to get to the center of a powerful whirl of ideas and emotions rather than letting myself be blown away by them.

Cyclops Aspect of my character that has the strength to achieve powerful ambitions but may be limited by its narrow perspective.

Cygnet Instinctive ability to transform my way of thinking by elegantly developing the connection between my thoughts and emotions.

Cylinder Ability to shape my circumstances by having the presence to stay centered as I continue to raise my awareness to a higher level.

Cymbal Ability to use my fundamental strength and sensitive touch to clearly draw attention to a higher aspect of my spiritual self.

Cypress tree Natural potential for my long-term spiritual growth by being able to endure hardships in a gracious and resilient manner.

Cyst Essential opportunity to go below the surface and release any accumulated emotions that may be causing an unhealthy situation.

C

Dab Opportunity to use a light tough so I can take a softer approach rather than feeling that I have to be heavy-handed.

Daffodil Natural ability to open up to my creativity so I can trumpet my blossoming optimism while staying grounded in reality.

Dagger Ability to get straight to the heart of an emotional situation instead of behaving in a wounding and underhanded manner.

Daily Opportunity to become fully aware of my developing talents rather than feeling that they are commonplace occurrences.

Dairy Situation where I can bring together a variety of creative talent so I can nurture other people's needs in a healthy way.

Daisy Natural ability to wake up to a more optimistic view of my numerous creative talents while staying firmly grounded.

Dale Situation where I can gather my wider learning and experience so I can use them as a basis for more open thinking.

Dalmatian Instinctive ability to show my loyalty and affection for other people rather than seeing things in black and white.

Dam Ability to retain a huge amount of accumulated experience and learning that has the potential to be a powerfully emotive force.

Damage Ability to protect something that is of great value to me without worrying if it will harm how I appear to other people.

Damaged Opportunity to resolve a less than perfect situation by releasing myself from any unrealistic expectations that I may hold.

Damaged building Situation where I can rebuild confidence in areas of self-development rather than feeling I must be perfect.

Damaged car Opportunity to repair feelings of self-esteem so I can keep using my ambition and drive toward my objective.

Damaged house Situation where I can accommodate new possibilities by reestablishing firm personal boundaries around my needs.

Damnation Opportunity to transform any judgmental beliefs that can apparently prevent me from successfully reaching my highest potential.

Damp Realization that I can feel relaxed and comfortable about any intrusive emotions rather than responding unenthusiastically.

Damp course Ability to control rising anxieties about persistently intruding emotions so I can continue to feel safe and secure.

Damp-proof Ability to deflect any intrusive feelings by realizing I have all the evidence I need to guard against creeping cynicism.

Damsel Aspect of my character that can embody my creative power and wisdom rather than feeling distressed about a situation.

Damselfly Instinctive ability to immerse myself in my thoughts and feelings, even though they may only seem very transitory to me.

Dance Ability to embody my natural rhythms and take steps that can express my unique behavioral patterns so I can bring them to life.

Dance floor Ability to support the fundamental principles of my creativity so I can take steps to openly show my personal talents.

Dancer Aspect of my character that embodies my individual behavioral patterns and can take creative steps to share them with people.

Dance troupe Aspects of my character that I can skillfully coordinate to gracefully express my particular expertise and display it to others.

Dancing Opportunity to display my abilities by taking a series of steps that allow me to instinctively express how I really feel.

Dandelion Natural ability to open up to my creative talents and encourage them to blossom so I can spread my ideas far and wide.

Dandruff Essential opportunity to display my ideas in a healthy and positive manner so they don't always appear dry and irritating.

Danger Opportunity to go to the edge of my comfort zone so I can take control of a finely balanced situation and use it to my advantage.

Dangerous Realization that I can feel more secure by being open to taking some calculated risks rather than just hazarding a guess.

Dangerous driving Opportunity to carefully choose my direction instead of feeling I'm on a collision course with an inevitable outcome.

Dangling Opportunity to be firm and specific about the support I need rather than just hanging on for other people's decisions.

Dank Realization that I can deal with any intrusive emotions in a warm and relaxed way rather than responding in a cool manner.

Dare Opportunity to be courageous and successfully rise to an emerging challenge instead of refraining from sharing my expertise.

Daredevil Aspect of my character that can open me to some tempting new possibilities by having the courage to take some creative risks.

Dark Realization that I can positively develop my awareness by illuminating unknown aspects of myself rather than being afraid of them.

Dark basement Situation where I can examine my fundamental behaviors so I can feel more solid and secure in my foundations.

Dark forest Situation where I can become more aware of the valuable growth potential of all the undiscovered aspects of my character.

Dark glasses Ability to look deeper into my perceptions so I can clearly understand a situation that could be highly illuminating.

Dark matter Ability to understand the true gravity of the situation so I can become more aware of the difference I can make.

Darkness Opportunity to illuminate valuable aspects of myself I may be unaware of rather than just feeling my way around them.

Dark passageway Situation where I can step into emerging opportunities rather than feeling I have to follow a particular path.

Darkroom Situation where I can develop my understanding of a situation by seeing what emerges from a number of different viewpoints.

Darn Opportunity to reconnect to some of the stories I've been weaving together rather than feeling worn out and frayed at the edges.

Dart Ability to assert my ideas by aiming to meet a particular target rather than listening to the pointed criticism of other people.

Dartboard Situation where I can achieve a successful outcome by understanding my aims and calculating their potential outcome.

Dash Opportunity to move quickly so I can decisively seize an opportunity instead of thinking other people have frustrated my hopes.

Dashboard Ability to speed up a process and perform it more efficiently by taking a detached and more specific view of my progress.

Data Ability to see my own perspective and form my own opinion rather than just accepting some facts that have been given to me.

Data bank Ability to build up a wealth of practical expertise by working my way through the facts so I can understand their value.

Database Ability to look into the deeper aspects of my fundamental behaviors so I can become more aware of emerging possibilities.

Data dump Opportunity to understand the real story rather than allowing myself to be overwhelmed by meaningless facts and figures.

Data link Ability to make the connection to what I find most meaningful in a situation so I can be more receptive to the outcome.

Date Opportunity to focus on one of my future ambitions so I can make a commitment to allow it to naturally come to fruition.

Date rape Opportunity to take full responsibility for my creative power rather than being oblivious to the intentions of others.

Dating agency Situation where I give myself the power and permission to choose whom I want to be with instead of leaving it up to others.

Daub Opportunity to make constructive use of some of my less clearly defined feelings rather than thinking they are a mess.

Daughter Aspect of my character that has the potential to develop my creativity and intuition so I can become more familiar with it.

Dawdle Realization that I can achieve an ambition more quickly by deciding on my direction rather than delaying it any longer.

Dawn Opportunity to experience my emerging realization of the fundamental connection between my conscious and unconscious awareness.

Dawn raid Opportunity to respond to an emerging challenge by taking forceful action to assert my ambitions rather than being defensive.

Day Opportunity to wait for the right time so I can use my natural awareness to illuminate a situation that has been unclear for me.

Day care Opportunity to make time for myself so I can attend to some needs that will help make everything much clearer for me.

Daydream Opportunity to explore my unconscious awareness so I can understand how to achieve my most powerful ambitions.

Daylight Realization that I can understand a situation with greater clarity by using the power of my conscious awareness to illuminate it.

Daze Realization that I can achieve an overwhelming success rather than feeling I have to live up to the expectations of other people.

Dazzle Opportunity to impress other people by displaying the brilliance of my talents without overpowering them with my intensity.

Dead Essential opportunity to bring an aspect of myself back to life and reenergize a creative talent that may have seemed lost to me.

Dead animal Instinctive ability to revitalize my creative talents so I can regain the motivation to express my natural wisdom in a healthy way.

Dead baby Aspect of my character that can breathe new life into a labor of love so I can carefully develop its true potential.

Dead body Essential opportunity to use my self-motivation and energy to revitalize one of my talents so I can fully realize its value.

Dead child Aspect of my character that can

breathe new life into one of my most precious talents so I can continue to healthily develop it.

Dead end Situation where I can use my power and vitality to decide on a new direction so I can bring my ambitions back to life.

Dead fish Instinctive ability to fully revitalize my deeper emotions instead of just getting too caught up in my current circumstances.

Dead grandparent Aspect of my character that can transform my outlook on a situation so I can take a much healthier and more mature approach.

Dead heat Opportunity to bring together two of my competing ambitions so I can use them equally to raise my chances of success.

Deadline Ability to align my skills and resources so I can make a specific commitment while still maintaining my personal boundaries.

Deadlock Realization that I can revitalize my natural potential by being open to new possibilities rather than trying to stay secure.

Dead loved one Aspect of my character that can reconnect me with a deeper level of self-awareness so I can express unspoken talents.

Deadly Realization that being more serious about achieving my ambitions is the most powerful way to create a valuable transformation.

Deadly nightshade Natural ability to transform my creative talents by encouraging them to blossom while staying healthily grounded in reality.

Dead parent Aspect of my character that can help me transform how I see myself so I can make the most of my wider potential.

Dead people Aspects of my character that bring my attention to ambitions that I felt I had to lay to rest to keep everyone happy.

Dead pet Instinctive ability that can bring vital new energy to a plan that is very close to my heart so I can happily develop it.

Dead plant Natural ability to absorb the fundamental value of some deeper emotions so I can revitalize some illuminating ideas.

Dead reckoning Ability to work out the vital resources I need to transform my progress rather than using vague assumptions.

Dead relative Aspect of my character in which I can refamiliarize myself with one of my most vital talents so I develop its wider potential.

Dead spouse Aspect of my character that can revitalize my commitment to exploring and developing my unknown, unfamiliar aspects.

Dead tree Natural ability to reconnect with my spirituality at a deeper level so I can open myself up to illuminating possibilities.

Deadwood Ability to get rid of old patterns that are no longer useful to me so I can use my energy to revitalize my practical expertise.

Deaf Essential opportunity to listen deeply to the more obvious aspects of a situation so I can hear what is going on.

Deaf aid Ability to understand what is happening by keeping my ears open to some of the less obvious aspects of the situation.

Deafening Realization that I need to listen carefully to understand the subtleties of the situation rather than being overpowered by it.

Deal Opportunity to conduct myself in a way that acknowledges my value so I can agree to a beneficial outcome with other people.

Dealer Aspect of my character that recognizes the potential value of my talents and has the confidence to share them with other people.

Dear Realization that I need to cherish what is most precious to me, even though its value may not always be recognized by other people.

Death Opportunity to completely transform my habitual behaviors so I can step into a new future by naturally letting go of the past.

D

Deathbed Situation where I feel most relaxed and comfortable about releasing myself from the past so I can embrace a new future.

Death certificate Ability to clearly acknowledge the value of a transformational experience so I can feel confident in leaving the past behind.

Death mask Ability to present my self-image to people in a way that will openly reveal a fundamental transformation in how I see myself.

Death penalty Opportunity to powerfully transform myself rather than feeling others are trying to change my fundamental behaviors.

Death ray Ability to positively direct my energy so I can transform my deeper understanding of a seemingly distant opportunity.

Death row Situation where I can independently free myself from any self-limiting beliefs instead of just hanging around to see what happens.

Death sentence Ability to clearly state what I need to transform my situation rather than feeling that other people are trying to judge me.

Death squad Aspects of my character that can work in a coordinated way to provide me with a number of transformative opportunities.

Death toll Ability to be clear about the aspects of my life I need to leave behind so I can move forward.

Death warrant Ability to give myself permission to transform my life in the way I choose rather than allowing other people to decide for me.

Death wish Opportunity to use my transformative powers to achieve one of my desires rather than hoping it will happen.

Debate Opportunity to methodically explore two of my opposing needs so I can consider the most agreeable way to resolve any tension.

Debauched Realization that I sometimes need to indulge in some of my more imaginative schemes rather than letting them go.

Debilitating Realization that I can feel invigorated about using some of my special abilities instead of giving feeble excuses.

Debit card Ability to communicate the wealth of my accumulated expertise to other people rather than feeling I have to owe them.

Debris Ability to create a coherent outcome by using valuable fragments of my experiences to ensure a successful transformation.

Debt Realization that I owe it to myself to display my valuable talents so they can be fully acknowledged by other people.

Debt collector Opportunity to reclaim my sense of self-worth by encouraging others to recognize my individual expertise and how I use it.

Debug Opportunity to pay close attention to the small details rather than being too distracted by looking at the bigger picture.

Debut Opportunity to communicate how an emerging situation appears to me rather than relying on first impressions.

Decadent Realization that I can use my strength and power to develop a healthy outlook instead of letting people influence my behavior.

Decaffeinated Potential to fulfill an emotional need that could be a lot more stimulating and has left me feeling that I need to perk up.

Decal Ability to stay flexible in how I appear rather than getting too stuck in my ways and trying to transfer responsibility.

Decanter Ability to realize the value of my accumulated experience so I am confident in openly sharing it with other people.

Decapitated Realization that I can keep moving ahead by cleanly separating thoughts and feelings rather than behaving irrationally.

Decapitation Opportunity to let go of ideas I have been hanging on to without becoming too disconnected from my deeper emotions.

Decay Realization that I can use past experiences to develop a new future by nurturing my talents and building on them.

Deceased Realization that I have the power to stop any self-destructive behaviors so I can bring my creative talents back to life.

Deceitful Realization that I need to be open and honest and say what I think rather than trying to fool myself about my feelings.

Decelerate Opportunity to consolidate my progress by slowing down for a while and identifying where I may be feeling out of control.

Decent Realization that I need to respect my basic skills so I can receive the appropriate recognition for making the best use of them.

Deception Opportunity to be honest and open about my intentions rather than trying to conceal talents I often keep hidden.

Deceptive Realization that I need to be clear about what I believe instead of deluding myself about my apparent limitations.

Deciduous Natural ability to work with the ups and downs of my creative rhythms so I can continue to nourish my spiritual growth.

Deciduous tooth Essential ability to move on from childish power struggles so I can continue to develop a more grown-up sense of confidence.

Decimated Realization that I have talent of lasting importance to offer instead of allowing other people to continually cut me down.

Decipher Realization that I need to express myself in a more obvious and direct manner rather than trying to communicate obscurely.

Decision Opportunity to take determined action and show how I feel rather than procrastinating to keep everyone happy.

Deck Situation where I can move closer toward the edge of my comfort zone and understand my feelings from a different perspective.

Deck chair Situation where I can maintain my habitual viewpoint while being able to consider my feelings from a different perspective.

Deckhand Aspect of my character that has a firm grasp of my power and can take me to the edge of my comfort zone so I can shape my future.

Declaration Opportunity to announce my deeper emotions by having the courage to openly speak up, so other people can hear how I really feel.

Decline Opportunity to set boundaries around my deeper feelings, rather than becoming involved in the slippery slope of denial.

Decode Realization that I need to think clearly about the underlying details, even though other people may not understand my ideas yet.

Decomposing Opportunity to transform my physical vitality by returning resources that I no longer need so I can create something new.

Decompression chamber Situation where I can become more accustomed to intense thoughts and ideas without always feeling under a lot of pressure.

Decontaminate Opportunity to clean up some widespread misunderstandings, even though it means I have to get my hands dirty to accomplish it.

Decorating Opportunity to take a fresh look at how I elaborate on my viewpoints so I can get a better understanding of how I feel.

Decoration Ability to gracefully display a deeper level of courage rather than feeling I always have to embellish how I express myself.

Decorator Aspect of my character that can positively help me change my perspective by taking a fresh look at my habitual viewpoints.

D

Decoy Ability to reveal myself as the person I want to be instead of allowing others to influence how I should appear to them.

Decrepit Realization that I can always develop new aspects of my potential talents rather than feeling weak and worse for the wear.

Decrypt Realization that I can achieve one of my deeper desires by communicating what I need to say in an obvious and direct manner.

Dedicated Realization that I need to make a commitment to achieving a particular ambition rather than using my energy elsewhere.

Deduce Opportunity to realize what I have been looking for in my life, although I assumed it was something quite different.

Deed Opportunity to successfully achieve what I set out to accomplish, even though it may have turned into quite an adventure.

Deep Realization that I have a profound understanding of what I need and am willing to go below the surface to achieve it.

Deep end Situation where I can immerse myself in some profound learning experiences without feeling it will all go over my head.

Deep freeze Situation where I can choose to preserve some long-term ambitions rather than becoming too emotionally involved in them.

Deep-fried Potential to fulfill an ambition by taking a fresher and more profound approach so I can exercise my talent more healthily.

Deep space Situation where I can go far beyond my perceived limitations by giving myself the opportunity to expand my wider awareness.

Deep-vein thrombosis Essential opportunity to channel my passion and vitality in a healthy manner rather than feeling as if I might appear clumsy and stupid.

Deer Instinctive ability to be proud of the wilder aspects of my nature instead of thinking that other people are gunning for me.

Deface Opportunity to express my identity in an individual manner without worrying if it will damage my reputation.

Defamation Opportunity to openly recognize the value of my talents instead of being concerned about how others view my performance.

Default Realization that I have the ability to decide my outcomes rather than taking the usual route and not doing anything.

Defeat Realization that I have the inner strength and power to succeed instead of feeling like I have been a complete failure.

Defecating Opportunity to choose the moment when I can let go of possessions and memories that no longer have any real value.

Defect Realization that there is nothing wrong about looking after my own needs instead of feeling I owe an allegiance to other people.

Defection Opportunity to choose my perspectives and outcomes rather than feeling obliged to let others decide them for me.

Defense Opportunity to engage more powerfully with my own needs by realizing I have to set firm boundaries around them.

Defensive Realization that I can make myself more secure by opening myself up to new possibilities instead of protecting what I have.

Defiant Realization that I can succeed against all odds by courageously using my talent rather than feeling I have to obey convention.

Defibrillator Ability to jump-start my ambitions so I can keep my finger on the pulse and ensure that my passion and vitality continue to flow.

Deficiency Realization that I have more than enough natural ability instead of feeling I have to make up for my perceived inadequacies.

Definite Realization that my potential for growth is in the unknown and unfamiliar aspects of myself rather than in more obvious

D

places.

Deflated Opportunity to concentrate on some new ideas and get pumped up about them instead of thinking I've let myself down.

Deflected Opportunity to keep my ambitions on course by bouncing some ideas off other people without allowing them to distract me.

Defoliant Ability to strip away any unwelcome influences that may be concealing opportunities for my healthy long-term spiritual growth.

Deformed Realization that everything doesn't have to be perfect for me to succeed rather than getting too bent out of shape about it.

Deformity Ability to make a big difference by understanding the value of any inconsistencies instead of trying to ensure perfection.

Defragmenting Opportunity to piece together important parts of my learning and experience so I can assemble a more complete understanding.

Defrauded Realization that I can make a fundamental transformation in my self-worth by having the confidence to prove it to others.

Defrost Realization that I need to take a warmer approach to how I feel about a relationship in which I've been trying to play it cool.

Defuse Realization that I can resolve some potentially explosive emotions by confidently choosing just the right moment to take action.

Defy Opportunity to confidently use my abilities so I can succeed in a risky ambition instead of giving in to any anxieties.

Degenerate Realization that I can improve my situation by generating new opportunities rather than letting everything fall apart.

Degrading Realization that I need to show the richness of my understanding instead of thinking that other people will be scornful of it.

Degree Ability to achieve an ambition by taking an aspect of my unique experiences and using it with just the right intensity.

Dehumanized Realization that my most

valuable aspect is my humanity rather than feeling I have to conform to artificial limitations.

Dehumidifier Ability to become more aware of how I may be allowing my feelings to cloud my judgment in a potentially sticky situation.

Dehydrated Opportunity to use my experience and learning to bring a situation to life instead of approaching it in a dry, unfeeling way.

Deicer Ability to see a situation more clearly so I can get my ambitions moving rather than feeling I've been stuck for some time.

Déjà vu Opportunity to see a predictably routine series of events in a different way, even though I may think I've seen it all before.

Dejected Realization that I can raise my spirits by taking a positive and realistic approach rather than letting myself feel down.

Delay Opportunity to take decisive action right now instead of feeling that past circumstances are preventing me from doing so.

Delegation Aspects of my character that are collectively responsible for letting other people know how I feel about a subject.

Deleted Opportunity to decide to create something new instead of thinking that I have to restore things to the way they were before.

Deliberate Realization that I need to set firm intentions about the outcomes I would like to achieve rather than just thinking about them.

Delicate Realization that I can use my strength of character to deal with an intricate situation without worrying about it falling apart.

Delicatessen Situation where I can make a choice about how I would like to fulfill an ambition, even though it may seem quite exotic.

Delicious Realization that I should use my aesthetic awareness to do what pleases me

D

without worrying if it is palatable to others.

Delight Realization that a great way to keep other people happy is to routinely please myself and take enjoyment in what I do.

Delinquent Realization that I need to take responsibility for declaring my true value rather than always lapsing into inactivity.

Delirious Opportunity to show my feverish enthusiasm for a new idea, even though I may seem disproportionately keen to other people.

Delivery Opportunity to convey my feelings about a commitment that is of great value to me so I can continue to keep my promises.

Dell Situation where I can explore the rich diversity of my learning and develop some natural opportunities for fertile growth.

Delta Situation where I can use my long experience to drop some of the load I've been carrying so I can broaden my awareness.

Deluge Opportunity to immerse myself in powerful learning rather than allowing myself to be swept away by overwhelming emotions.

Delusion Realization that I am being honest about my abilities and know what to do instead of thinking I am somehow fooling myself.

Delve Opportunity to investigate the practical aspects of a situation in greater detail by continuing to move more deeply into it.

Demand Opportunity to ask for what I need from other people instead of always feeling I have to meet their requests.

Dematerialize Opportunity to provide a more substantial basis for my actions rather than allowing them to fade away into thin air.

Demented Realization that I sometimes have to take actions that don't make sense at the time instead of driving myself crazy about it.

Dementia Opportunity to resolve an unhealthy situation by keeping my mind on

what matters rather than allowing myself to be distracted.

Demise Opportunity to transform a situation by gracefully bringing it to a close instead of thinking that this is the end of everything.

Demist Ability to clear up any vague feelings so I can progress in my chosen direction and successfully fulfill a personal ambition.

Demolition Opportunity to firmly build on a new possibility by intentionally removing some aspect of my behavior I no longer need.

Demon Aspect of my character that can have a positive influence on a challenging task rather than becoming too fanatical about it.

Demonic Realization that I have the instinctive power and strength to achieve a successful outcome without becoming too obsessed.

Demonstration Opportunity to prove my special skills and unique expertise to others instead of protesting that they never pay attention.

Demonstrators Aspects of my character that can bring together a variety of my talents and abilities and use them to reach a successful outcome.

Demoralized Realization that I can use my courage and discipline to resolve a challenging situation instead of giving up without a fight.

Den Situation where I can feel relaxed and secure in my ability to use my instinctive creativity to make the most of any opportunity.

Denied Opportunity to give myself the freedom to make my own decisions rather than feeling people are preventing me from doing so.

Dense Realization that I can open up some brighter possibilities by taking a lighter approach rather than just feeling a bit dim.

Dense forest Situation where I can work

my way through undiscovered aspects of my character so I can open up to their full potential.

Dent Ability to fill in any deficiencies by using my accumulated knowledge to smooth over the impact of any unforeseen events.

Dental Ability to display my power and confidence to others so I can speak up and honestly express my feelings to them.

Dental bridge Ability to deal with an apparent loss in confidence by making a powerful new connection between other areas of my life.

Dental crown Ability to display a lot more confidence in what I have achieved so far by staying healthily connected to my roots.

Dental dam Ability to work on my feelings of confidence by choosing how I prefer to channel my emotions so I can learn from the experience.

Dental drill Ability to remove concerns about my lack of confidence so I can make my point, even though it feels uncomfortable.

Dental floss Ability to be flexible so I can confidently make a powerful decision rather than just scraping along by the skin of my teeth.

Dental hygienist Aspect of my character that ensures I have a healthy regard for my power and confidence and how I express them.

Dental practice Situation where I can build up my confidence by displaying my powerful skills rather than feeling that I'm repeating myself.

Dental surgery Situation where I can safely deal with my confidence issues by opening up to others so they can understand my experiences.

Dental veneer Ability to have real confidence in my own power rather than trying to gloss over challenges just to give a good impression.

Dentist Aspect of my character that helps me maintain my confidence and develop my power by understanding the roots of my behaviors.

Dentist's chair Situation where I can build levels of power and confidence by taking decisive action to step outside my comfort zone.

Dentures Ability to use my natural power and confidence to say what I mean instead of feeling toothless and ineffective.

Deodorant Ability to cover up concerns I may have about taking action, even though I might have to sweat it out until I succeed.

Department Aspect of my professional identity that enables me to understand the area where I can employ my talents most productively.

Departure Opportunity to let go of any habits that no longer serve me so I can step into a new future by taking a different approach.

Departure information Ability to gain a clearer understanding of the actions I need to take now to make the most of an emerging possibility.

Dependency Realization that I have to attend to my own fundamental needs rather than being influenced by what others seem to want.

Deposit Ability to feel more secure about the future by making a definite commitment to delivering on a promise I have made to myself.

Deported Realization that I can give myself permission to explore unfamiliar opportunities rather than banishing them outright.

Depot Situation where I can access resources that will help me embark on the next valuable stage of my professional development.

Depraved Realization that I have the moral strength to always do the right thing instead of thinking I have to abandon my principles.

D

Depreciation Opportunity to appreciate the increasing value of my accumulated experience and wisdom rather than worrying about age.

Depression Opportunity to take a positive and realistic approach to raising my spirits instead of feeling a bit hollow inside.

Deprived Realization that I have a wealth of experience and can create my own opportunities rather than feeling left out by others.

Depth Realization that I can share my profound understanding instead of trying to conceal it under a shallower perspective.

Depth finder Ability to clearly see how profound my emotions can be and the extent to which they are based on a solid understanding of myself.

Derailment Opportunity to stay right on track with one of my bigger ambitions rather than giving up control and going off the rails.

Deranged Realization that I am taking an ordered, methodical approach to a challenge, even though it may seem crazy to other people.

Derelict Realization that I may have been neglecting some unique talents that could prove very powerful in restoring my confidence.

Derelict asylum Situation where I can continue to develop my wider confidence by revisiting aspects of my life that used to drive me crazy.

Derelict hospital Situation where I can take a healthier approach to my neglected skills rather than just hoping that things will get better.

Derelict house Situation where I can pay more attention to valuable aspects of my potential development that I may have been neglecting.

Derelict mansion Situation where I am far more expansive in developing my potential value rather than abandoning wider ambitions.

Derelict school Situation where I can revisit valuable expertise I have been neglecting instead of letting it fall into disuse.

Derision Realization that I need to be commended for my achievements rather than letting other people mock my efforts.

Dermatitis Essential opportunity to stay in touch with my feelings instead of becoming irritated by them and doing something rash.

Derrick Situation where I can build on my organizational skills so I can convey my power and raise my spirits to a higher level.

Desalination plant Situation where I can apply specialist knowledge to distil a clear, healthy awareness from my emotions and experiences.

Descent Realization that I can achieve a much profounder understanding of myself by steadily going deeper into what really motivates me.

Desecrated Realization that I need to honor what is most important to me instead of letting people routinely abuse their position.

Desert Situation in which a persistent lack of emotion leaves only the harsh realities of the bare facts and hard choices.

Deserted Realization that I have abandoned vital interests that used to occupy me, and now I have the chance to bring them back.

Deserter Aspect of my character that can make a long-term commitment to resolving a chronic tension rather than trying to avoid it.

Desert fort Situation where I can guard against potential conflict by establishing firm personal boundaries so I can make hard choices.

Desert island Situation where I am happy to deal with hard decisions and can choose to remain detached from unpredictable emotions.

Design Realization that I can understand some of my deeper behavioral patterns by looking at my future plans and how I conceive them.

Designer Aspect of my character that can illuminate my unconscious behavioral patterns and understand how they can shape my future.

Designer baby Aspect of my character that can be too prescriptive about a precious plan instead of letting it develop naturally.

Designer drug Ability to resolve in a healthy way one of my fundamental needs by being more aware of my deeper behaviors and how I deal with them.

Desirable Realization that openly having more confidence in my individual talents will make me appear much more attractive to others.

Desk Ability to be supportive of the people I work with by openly sharing my feelings about our professional relationships.

Desolate Realization that I can use my fertile imagination to develop a wide range of future possibilities instead of feeling barren.

Despair Realization that my confident approach inspires new possibilities to emerge rather than feeling that the situation is hopeless.

Desperate Realization that I am happy and secure in my beliefs instead of trying to prove them to people by always acting outrageously.

Desperate for toilet Opportunity to set firm personal boundaries so I can look after my own needs rather than feeling ashamed of them.

Dessert Potential to fulfill a short-term ambition that seems very attractive, without giving any attention to the long-term realities.

Destination Situation where I can clearly see where my ambitions could take me so I can understand the path I must follow to achieve them.

Destiny Realization that I can choose where

my decisions will take me rather than feeling I always have to leave it to fate.

Destitute Realization that I have the inner resources to provide my security and comfort instead of thinking I have to rely on others.

Destroyer Ability to peacefully resolve any conflicts arising from my emotional life without resorting to self-destructive behavior.

Destruction Opportunity to create the life I want to live by choosing to leave the past behind so I can step into my new future.

Detached Realization that I can maintain involvement in a situation by staying connected rather than feeling I must be distant.

Detail Realization that I can use my curiosity to understand the bigger picture without becoming too obsessed by some minor points.

Detained Realization that instead of delaying it any longer I can liberate myself now from any self-limiting behaviors that hold me back.

Detective Aspect of my character that can discover my profounder truths by investigating my deeper motives and how I usually act on them.

Detector Ability to understand what is going on by paying attention to what is usually unseen rather than ignoring the indications.

Detention center Situation where I can make the choice to freely follow my decisions instead of feeling that others are holding me back.

Detergent Ability to achieve a clear understanding of a potentially messy problem by using a consistent solution to resolve it.

Deteriorated Realization that I can improve my situation by taking a healthy and positive approach rather than feeling worse for the wear.

Determined Realization that I can decide my chosen outcome by staying committed to my plan and tenaciously following it through.

D

Deterrent Ability to resolve any potential conflict by creating an obvious incentive that positively encourages a stronger connection.

Detonator Ability to choose just the right moment to safely let go of any potentially explosive emotions I might be holding on to.

Detour Opportunity to take a wider perspective so I can explore new directions rather than feel my progress has been disrupted.

Detoxing Opportunity to make healthy decisions so I can take positive action instead of going along with others' choices.

Devastated Realization that I have the strength and power to build the life I want rather than letting it be spoiled by other people.

Developing Opportunity to make continuing progress by widening my original perspective and using it to expand my awareness further.

Deviant Realization that I can achieve a wider understanding by exploring different paths rather than staying on the straight and narrow.

Device Ability to use a specific apparatus that will help me to fulfill my greater purpose by evoking a particular response from people.

Devil Aspect of my character that can open me up to tempting new possibilities without necessarily having any burning ambitions.

Devotee Aspect of my character that focuses on a particular pursuit so I can achieve a more intimate understanding.

Devour Opportunity to fulfill my ambition for huge success without it becoming an all-consuming passion that eats up all my time.

Dew Natural opportunity to take a cooler approach to some of my thoughts and plans so I can reflect on my feelings about them.

Diadem Ability to present my self-image to others by drawing attention to my greatest achievements and how attractive they seem.

Diagnosis Opportunity to understand the cause of an unhealthy situation so I can take positive action to resolve it.

Diagonal Ability to shape my circumstances by making some different connections rather than relying on my own judgments and biases.

Diagram Ability to plan ahead by having a clear understanding of what might be involved instead of taking a more sketchy approach.

Dial Ability to quickly communicate what I need to say by facing up to the facts rather than just going in circles.

Dial tone Opportunity to take my individual cue so I can face up to the facts and express myself clearly and honestly to others.

Dialogue box Ability to use my mind to quickly and precisely identify what I need to communicate for me to move forward.

Dialysis machine Ability to produce an outcome of great practical value by clarifying my emotions and filtering unhealthy influences.

Diamond Ability to use my unique clarity of thinking to cut through confusion and attract other people to my individual viewpoint.

Diapers Ability to contain some of my fundamental emotional needs so others don't experience my behavior as too childish.

Diaphragm Ability to keep developments under control rather than feeling I'm going too far by spreading myself too thin.

Diarrhea Essential ability to let go of possessions and memories that were once useful to me instead of becoming too emotional about it.

Diary Ability to collect some of my personal perspectives and reflect on them so I can gain a clearer understanding of who I am.

Dice Ability to achieve a successful outcome by cutting down on the possibility of failure rather than just leaving it to chance.

Dictator Aspect of my character that constantly tries to tell me what I can and can't do instead of speaking my truth.

Dictionary Ability to use a structured thinking process so I can make sense of an unfamiliar situation and understand its deeper meaning.

Didgeridoo Ability to take my instinctive creativity in both hands and voice some of my deeper feelings without droning on about them.

Die Opportunity to let go of a situation that I no longer find fulfilling so I can step into a new future and transform my life.

Diesel Ability to refine my raw creative power so I can use it to fuel my drive for success in achieving my larger ambitions.

Diet Opportunity to fulfill my appetite for success by being measured in the way I let go of weighty responsibilities.

Different Realization that I have the power to change my situation rather than feeling everything will always be the same for me.

Different city Situation where I can use my wider social network to build new relationships so I can fulfill my individual ambitions.

Different house Situation where I have the security and support I need to comfortably explore unfamiliar aspects of who I am.

Different job Opportunity to connect with my life purpose by understanding the difference I can make in creating unique value.

Different spouse Aspect of my character that is fully committed to exploring and developing the undiscovered potential of my unique talents.

Difficulty Realization that I can create most value by engaging with situations I find challenging rather than just taking it easy.

Digest Opportunity to process any recent experiences so I can fully absorb their real value in a positive and healthy manner.

Digestive system Essential ability to assimilate new experiences so I can use them to maintain my levels of energy and self-motivation.

Digger Ability to use my professional ambition and drive to get to the bottom of what is happening so I can make my own choices.

Digging Opportunity to explore the practicalities of a situation in greater depth by making the effort to go beyond surface appearances.

Digital Realization that I need more than facts and figures to understand a situation so I can point out what is happening.

Dignity Realization that I need to examine where I stand on my behavior rather than thinking it's something beneath me.

Dilapidated Realization that I need to have more confidence in my individual abilities instead of always letting others run them down.

Dilemma Opportunity to resolve a challenging situation by taking a firm grasp of it so I can understand both points of view.

Diluted Realization that I can often be much more effective by concentrating on my emotions rather than watering them down.

Dim Realization that I can use my natural wisdom to give myself a clearer view by understanding apparently contrasting perspectives.

Dimensions Ability to understand the fullest extent of my ambitions so I can ensure I measure up to what is required of me.

Diminutive Realization that I can have a big influence on small but vital details instead of thinking my views are of little consequence.

Dimmer switch Ability to let my talents shine in a way that suits the current mood rather than feeling that I always have to be full-on.

Dinghy Ability to navigate complex and unpredictable feelings in a personal situation by understanding the prevailing atmosphere.

D

Dingy Realization that I can brighten up a potentially dull experience by taking a more enlightened approach to how I feel about it.

Dining out Opportunity to fulfill some of my ambitions by sharing them with other people so they can recognize my potential value.

Dining room Aspect of myself that provides the space and resources to achieve ambitions by being open to sharing them with others.

Dining table Ability to be very open and supportive with others by sharing my thoughts and feelings about our mutual ambitions.

Dinner Opportunity to achieve my main ambitions by assimilating my recent experiences and using them to fulfill my appetite for success.

Dinner party Opportunity to fulfill some of my ambitions by celebrating my special skills and inviting other people to recognize my abilities.

Dinosaur Instinctive ability to use my primal power to transform any threatening emotions so I can respond in a much warmer way.

Diode Ability to consistently be more open to using my energy in different ways by choosing a firm direction in my current situation.

Diorama Situation where I can examine what has really been happening for me, without feeling I have to become personally involved.

Diploma Ability to have my unique skills formally acknowledged by others so I can recognize their confidence in my abilities.

Diplomat Aspect of my character that tries to resolve any potential conflicts by always saying the right thing and keeping everyone happy.

Direction Realization that I can choose to have a successful outcome by looking toward my future and deciding the path I will take.

Direction finder Ability to keep myself on track as I progress toward my chosen objective rather than straying off the straight and narrow.

Director Aspect of my character that focuses on a very specific personal ambition and is decisive about achieving a successful result.

Director's cut Opportunity to connect my most powerful life experiences in the way I find most evocative and deeply meaningful.

Directory Ability to communicate a specific message by having an initial idea about the type of response I'm looking for.

Dirge Opportunity to raise my spirits by instinctively giving voice to a beautiful and deeply felt message about how I feel.

Dirigible Ability to contain my expansive ideas in a more rigid framework so I can use them to maintain my direction toward my objective.

Dirt Ability to go beyond superficial appearances by getting closer to fundamental aspects and taking a fresh look at them.

Dirt bike Ability to make fast progress in uncertain conditions by keeping the situation balanced and not being afraid to put my foot down.

Dirt track Situation where I can make more direct progress toward my objective, even if I have to take a slightly rougher approach.

Dirty Realization that I need to make a clean start instead of allowing myself to become involved in an unpleasant situation.

Dirty trick Opportunity to take a fresh look below the surface so I can make a real transformation rather than just deluding myself.

Disability Ability to use some of the unique skills I'm often not consciously aware of instead of feeling I'm being excluded.

Disagreement Opportunity to understand my conflicting feelings about a situation rather than trying to keep everyone happy.

Disappearance Opportunity to bring an elusive idea into existence by understanding the realities instead of just knowing the theory.

Disappointment Realization that it is up to me to achieve a successful outcome rather than always feeling I am being let down by others.

Disapproval Opportunity to applaud myself for my efforts instead of feeling I have not managed to live up to others' expectations.

Disarming Realization that I can deal with any unresolved tensions by openly reaching out to other people and connecting with them.

Disaster Opportunity to use any unforeseeable circumstances to my best advantage instead of feeling that everything is falling apart.

Disbelief Realization that I can achieve a much deeper understanding of my beliefs by carefully examining individual viewpoints.

Disc Ability to shape my circumstances by using the layers of my accumulated knowledge to reach out to the edge of what I know.

Discarded Realization that being able to express my feelings is of much greater value rather than always using throwaway lines.

Disciplinary hearing Opportunity to open up to new possibilities by listening to my own intentions instead of feeling restricted by others.

Discipline Realization that I can acknowledge a deeper structure in my particular area of study rather than just proceeding chaotically.

Disc jockey Aspect of my character that can create the mood that gives voice to my talents so I can communicate with other people.

Disco Situation where I can connect with the people around me so we can take some steps to display our talents to one another.

Discomfort Realization that I can become more comfortable with my behaviors rather than continually being annoyed with my awkwardness.

Disconnected Ability to take a more detached view of what I want to achieve so I can reconnect to seemingly distant possibilities.

Discouraged Realization that I have the opportunity to inspire and encourage others instead of allowing myself to feel downhearted.

Discovery Opportunity to find out more about myself by exploring what seems uncertain rather than feeling at a loss about what to do next.

Discreet Realization that I can use my judgment to make the right decision instead of allowing other people to make it for me.

Discrete Realization that I can achieve a clearer understanding of what I need to do by simply taking a more detached view.

Discrimination Opportunity to understand the big difference I make rather than allowing myself to be influenced by existing prejudices.

Discussion Opportunity to listen closely to my range of different needs so I can understand the most agreeable way of fulfilling them.

Disease Opportunity to deal with an unhealthy situation by resolving any chronic tensions so I can feel more at ease with myself.

Disembark Opportunity to step out of a particular career path so I can decide where and when I will embark on my next opportunity.

Disembowel Opportunity to digest any recent experiences in a calm and contained manner rather than feeling I have to spill out my guts.

Disengage Opportunity to maintain my interest by reengaging with my individual needs instead of being too attached to other people's needs.

Disfigured Realization that I need to share the ugly truth rather than worrying that it might make other people see me in a different light.

D

Disgorge Opportunity to forcefully express what I am feeling instead of thinking I have to choke it back all the time.

Disgrace Realization that I need to respect my emotions and be proud of them rather than feeling ashamed of what I want to see.

Disguise Ability to be open and honest about what I need from other people rather than feeling I have to conceal my needs.

Disgust Realization that I need to share my talents so they can be admired instead of worrying that people may find them distasteful.

Dish Ability to be receptive to the variety of ways in which I can fulfill my appetite for success by attracting people toward me.

Disheveled Realization that the creative process can appear to be a messy business instead of always trying to keep it neat and tidy.

Dishonest Realization that other people will share their needs more truthfully when I can honestly express my feelings to them.

Dishwasher Ability to be clear about the ambitions I have achieved so far so I can prepare for future opportunities without too much effort.

Disinfectant Ability to clear up unseen challenges by taking a positive, healthy approach to understanding the strength of my feelings.

Disintegrating Opportunity to take a more integrated approach to achieving a long-held ambition instead of letting everything fall apart.

Disintegrating clothing Opportunity to reveal myself to others in the way I want to rather than feeling I'm coming apart at the seams.

Dislike Realization that I can state my chosen preferences in a confident way instead of constantly looking for approval from others.

Dislocated Essential ability to remain connected and take action rather than being anxious about having my feelings put out of joint.

Dislodged Realization that I can gain a much wider perspective by making a definite decision to move out of my habitual standpoint.

Dismal Realization that I can brighten up my prospects by recognizing my unique talents rather than feeling dejected about the future.

Dismantled Realization that I can piece together all the resources I need so I can use them coherently to achieve a bigger ambition.

Dismembered Opportunity to use my power to reach out to people and connect with them instead of feeling I have to cut them off.

Disobedience Opportunity to be guided by what I believe in rather than feeling that I need to comply with the wishes of others.

Disorder Realization that I can use my creativity to solve an apparently upsetting problem by using a less structured approach.

Disoriented Realization that I can understand my position by observing my emerging feelings rather than wandering around in a daze.

Display Opportunity to share my individual expertise with the people around me so they can recognize the value of my skills.

Display case Ability to show my special skills to others while still setting boundaries s I can contain my involvement with them.

Displeasure Realization that I can take great satisfaction in making my own choices instead of feeling I have to keep other people happy.

Disposal Realization that what I would like to hold on to can often depend on my mood, and I don't have to let everything go.

Disprove Realization that I can prove my abilities by authentically demonstrating them to other people instead of feeling discredited.

Dispute Opportunity to resolve an ongoing conflict by being open to debating the merits of the different opinions held by other people.

Disqualified Realization that I can explore my deeper needs and wider ambitions without having to wait for permission from other people.

Disrepair Realization that I have the power to maintain my continued progress toward long-held ambitions rather than breaking down.

Disruptive Realization that I can keep a situation running smoothly by being open about the freedom I need instead of being distracted by it.

Dissatisfaction Realization that I am responsible for my feelings of happiness instead of trying to satisfy others' needs.

Dissected Opportunity to cut to the heart of the matter and decide what I need without appearing too divisive to others.

Dissolve Opportunity to understand the emotional aspects as well as the practical ones so I can come up with a suitable solution.

Distance runner Aspect of my character that has the energy and self-motivation to pursue a personal ambition, even though it seems far-fetched.

Distant Realization that a long-held desire is much closer than it once seemed, and I will soon be able to fully connect with it.

Distant city Situation where I can explore ideas from other people, even though some of their ideas may initially seem far-fetched.

Distant land Situation where I can take a more practical, down-to-earth approach to achieving more than I thought was remotely possible.

Distant voice Ability to identify a powerful source of inspiration so I can immediately express my intentions in a much clearer way.

Distasteful Realization that I can make a situation more palatable by pleasing myself

instead of just agreeing with other people's tastes.

Distillery Situation where I can work through the essence of where my spiritual beliefs come from rather than always trying to avoid them.

Distinct Realization that there is great value in exploring my ambiguous feelings instead of always going for the more obvious solution.

Distorted Realization that I can gain a much truer understanding of my needs by being straight about how I express them to others.

Distracted Realization that I need to pay more attention to my needs instead of being diverted by the demands of other people.

Distressed Realization that I can be calm and collected about an unexpected challenge rather than always becoming agitated and distraught.

Distress signal Ability to communicate what I need to say by taking direct action instead of appearing to be upset with myself.

District Situation where I can set some personal boundaries around how I share my particular area of expertise with other people.

Disturbing Realization that without aggravating others I can make a positive change to a situation that has been bothering me.

Disused Realization that I can keep my skills up-to-date by applying them to a contemporary situation rather than letting them fade away.

Ditch Situation where I can maintain my progress by staying on the straight and narrow and not getting stuck in messy side issues.

Diva Aspect of my character that fully recognizes my uniquely creative talents and immensely enjoys attracting attention to them.

Dive Opportunity to go deeper into my understanding of a situation so I can powerfully elevate my overall levels of awareness.

D

Diver Aspect of my character that enjoys immersing myself completely in my feelings so I can explore my emotional depths.

Divergence Realization that I can achieve a wider perspective by accepting that my various beliefs may not always be completely aligned.

Diver's belt Ability to add some weight to my individual opinions so I can feel more at ease when I am exploring my deeper emotions.

Diversion Opportunity to be specific about the direction I have chosen rather than allowing myself to be distracted from it.

Divided highway Situation where I can use a recognized route as a way of quickly achieving my ambitions by separating any opposing perspectives.

Dividing wall Ability to strongly support my beliefs and maintain firm personal boundaries with others without it becoming too divisive.

Divine Realization that I can create my future by understanding who I am, what I need, and what I believe.

Diving Opportunity to fully immerse myself in my emotional life so I can explore my profounder feelings in much greater depth.

Diving bell Situation where I can keep a clear head, even when I am deeply immersed in the most profound aspects of my emotional life.

Diving board Situation where I can raise my levels of awareness before immersing myself in a potentially overwhelming emotional experience.

Diving suit Ability to present my self-image to people in a way that keeps me feeling safe and secure in a potentially emotional situation.

Divorce Opportunity to release myself from a major commitment so I can regain independence and devote time to my true purpose.

DIY Ability to use my creativity and expertise to look after my well-being rather than feeling I always need professional help.

Dizzy Realization that I can achieve a much clearer understanding by choosing a definite direction rather than going in circles.

DNA Essential ability to powerfully shape my circumstances by healthily developing a deeper understanding of my fundamental nature.

Docile Realization that I sometimes need to be determined and headstrong rather than complying with what others require.

Dock Situation where I can safely contain my deeper emotions so I can unload a number of concerns and take on a variety of new ideas.

Dockside Situation where I can work more deeply with my emotions while still having the security of feeling I am on solid ground.

Dockyard Situation where I can give myself the space to reflect on my emotional challenges and plan how to work my way through them.

Doctor Aspect of my character that rationally examines my behaviors and provides me with the healthy clarity to resolve any tensions.

Docudrama Opportunity to become more emotionally engaged with life experiences rather than feeling I've seen it all before.

Document Ability to formalize what I need to say so I can have a clear understanding of my viewpoint when I share it with other people.

Documentary Opportunity to understand what happened in one of my life experiences so I can investigate my motives and behaviors.

Docusoap Opportunity to understand what I feel by observing my behaviors rather than overdramatizing my emotional life.

Dodecahedron Ability to shape my circumstances by knowing that I can show the different sides of my character to others.

D

Dodging Opportunity to stand up for what I believe in so I can make it obvious rather than continually trying to avoid the issue.

Dodo Instinctive ability to bring an old idea back to life and use it to revitalize a creative talent that may have seemed long gone.

Doe Instinctive ability to feel proud of the gentler aspect of my nature rather than always hunting for a more assertive edge.

Dog Instinctive ability to show my unconditional loyalty and affection for particular people in a persistently determined manner.

Dogfight Opportunity to resolve a number of conflicting ideas I may have by dealing with them in a tenacious and purposeful manner.

Dog lead Ability to take control of my feelings of loyalty and affection so I can connect with other people in a more direct way.

Dog tag Ability to identify my instinctive loyalties so I can consistently display my continuing commitment to those around me.

Dog trainer Aspect of my character that can develop some instinctive talents by having the discipline to make a determined commitment.

Dog walker Aspect of my character that can lead me to success by taking a series of steps to consistently progress toward one of my ambitions.

Dojo Situation where I can resolve any inner conflicts by using the strength and power of other people in a balanced and graceful way.

Doll Ability to play around with different aspects of my character so I can see how to potentially develop them into something bigger.

Dolphin Instinctive ability to immerse myself in my feelings so I can use deeper emotional awareness in an intelligent and playful way.

Dome Ability to shape my thoughts and ideas so I can create a well-rounded perspective and open myself up a wider awareness.

Domestic Situation where I feel relaxed with the different aspects of my character rather than thinking that I have to go completely wild.

Domestic argument Opportunity to understand a different perspective instead of feeling that other people should always accommodate my beliefs.

Domesticated Realization that I am happy to stay in my comfort zone rather than feeling that I have to constantly pursue my wilder instincts.

Domestic violence Opportunity to be more accommodating with others so I can use my power to peacefully resolve a familiar conflict.

Domination Opportunity to give myself more creative freedom instead of thinking I always have to submit to the demands of other people.

Dominator Aspect of my character that tries to subjugate my creative instincts rather than yielding to the power of my intuition.

Dominatrix Aspect of my character that attempts to control my creative power instead of giving me freedom to follow my pleasures.

Domino Ability to influence something by using my skill to connect the dots rather than feeling it will inevitably fall to pieces.

Donation Realization that my sense of self-worth is well-enough developed for me to support people without asking for anything in return.

Donkey Instinctive ability to accept the burdens and obligations of other people, even though I may want to really kick up a fuss.

Donor Aspect of my character committed to providing unconditional support for other people without requiring anything in return.

Donor card Ability to communicate my value to other people by openly providing them with my unconditional support and loyalty.

D

Doodle Opportunity to draw on my wisdom and experience so I can play around with my ideas and sketch out some possibilities.

Doom Opportunity to raise my spirits by using my courage to make a positive decision rather than leaving the outcome to fate.

Door Ability to access different aspects of my character so that I can develop possibilities that may have seemed closed to me.

Doorbell Ability to alert myself to approaching opportunities so I can be more open to possibilities that once seemed distant.

Doormat Ability to welcome any new opportunities by knowing where I stand on a situation rather than letting people walk all over me.

Doorway Situation where I am on the threshold of an opportunity where I can take steps that may open up new possibilities for me.

Doping Opportunity to be clear about the value of my talents instead of trying to lay it on thick with other people.

Doppelgänger Aspect of my character that has the opportunity to express all my unrealized talent by fleshing out what I need to do.

Dormitory Situation where I can feel comfortable with different aspects of my character so I can take a more relaxed approach with them.

Dormouse Instinctive ability to stay relaxed and comfortable as I deal with any small anxieties that have been gnawing away at me.

Dose Ability to remedy an unhealthy situation by choosing to do just the right amount rather than always feeling ill at ease.

Dossier Ability to collect my thoughts and plans so I can identify any tensions and make it clear what I need to say.

Dot Ability to individually make my mark, even though my efforts may initially seem quite insignificant to the people around me.

Dot-com Ability to take a single, apparently insignificant idea and use it as a way of attracting much wider attention to my theories.

Double Realization that I can use a number of my characteristic qualities to be twice as effective in achieving one of my ambitions.

Double act Opportunity to listen to my internal dialogue so I can change my usual routine instead of always playing it straight.

Double agent Aspect of my character that can see both sides of a situation and help me reveal the hidden talents I often conceal.

Double chin Essential opportunity to take a firmer approach with other people rather than taking direct criticism from them.

Double cross Opportunity to understand that other viewpoints may be completely different from mine, instead of feeling I've been betrayed.

Double-decker Ability to make progress toward professional objectives by ensuring my colleagues understand the level of my ambitions.

Double-glazing Ability to remain clear about a potentially fragile situation rather than trying to distance myself from unwelcome insights.

Double-jointed Essential opportunity to stay flexible to the needs of other people without always bending over backward to please them.

Doubt Realization that I need to have much more confidence in my abilities so I can trust myself to make beneficial decisions.

Dough Ability to fulfill a valuable ambition by acquiring some basic resources and using them to raise my levels of practical expertise.

Dove Instinctive ability to resolve any tensions by formulating a more peaceful approach so I can put my ideas into action.

Dowdy Realization that I can use my talents to fashion my desired outcome instead of feeling that I should fade into the background.

Down Realization that I can raise my awareness by looking beyond surface appearances rather than being upset about how they may seem.

Down-and-out Opportunity to uplift my spirits by drawing on my inner resources instead of feeling I have to rely on others.

Downdraft Opportunity to deal with an apparently depressing thought so I can continue to elevate my current level of understanding.

Downhearted Realization that I can always raise my spirits by having the courage to remain centered in the power of my passion and vitality.

Downhill Situation where I can use accumulated experience to make faster progress rather than feeling my powers are diminishing.

Download Opportunity to take ownership of my actions so I can understand the value of being able to convey my fundamental ambitions.

Downpour Opportunity to openly share some emotions that have been steadily building up so I can clearly understand my thoughts.

Downstairs Situation where I can take a series of steps to steadily look deeper into a situation that is of fundamental importance to me.

Downstream Situation where I can realize the outcome of my accumulated learning and experience instead of getting swept away by my emotions.

Dowry Ability to share the long-term value of a deep, creative commitment so I can have it recognized by the people around me.

Doze Opportunity to let go and just relax as a way of starting to connect with my most powerful ambitions and highest aspirations.

Drab Realization that I can draw attention to my talents by displaying them more colorfully instead of feeling I have to conceal them.

Draft Ability to outline some of my current

thinking so I can have a firmer understanding of the resources I might need to draw on.

Draft Opportunity to deal with an apparently intrusive thought without feeling I have to exclude any other possibilities.

Drag Opportunity to convey the full weight of a subject I feel strongly about rather than allowing it to constantly hold me back.

Drag king Aspect of my character that takes a more disciplined approach to dealing with how I convey my creative responsibilities.

Dragon Instinctive ability to use my fantastic powers of imagination and creativity to get fired up about a monster opportunity.

Dragonfly Instinctive ability to take a more colorful approach and create a real buzz so I can make the most of any emerging opportunities.

Drag queen Aspect of my character that takes a more flamboyant approach to my creativity rather than allowing it to become a liability.

Drag race Opportunity to make faster progress by letting go of some of the weighty commitments that may be holding me back.

Drain Ability to get rid of any emotions that are no longer useful to me instead of allowing them to affect my feelings of vitality.

Drainpipe Ability to consistently channel any potentially overwhelming emotions rather than allowing them to pour out uncontrollably.

Drama Opportunity to become more excited and emotionally engaged in my personal story rather than feeling I've seen it all before.

Drama queen Aspect of my character that can take a more gracious approach to my personal story instead of trying to attract attention to it.

Drawbridge Ability to resolve an emotional dilemma by making a firm connection rather than shutting myself off and hiding behind my defenses.

D

Drawer Ability to tuck away a variety of experiences and memories so I can keep them safe and pull them back out when I need them.

Drawing Opportunity to outline my wisdom and experience so I can gather my resources and sketch out a vision for success.

Drawout Instinctive ability to investigate my emotions in greater depth rather than curling up and trying to hide from any threats.

Dread Realization that I need to step forward courageously and take control rather than being afraid of what might happen to me.

Dreadlocks Ability to feel comfortable with my way of thinking instead of being afraid that it will somehow limit my freedom.

Dream Realization that I can achieve my most powerful ambitions and highest aspirations by understanding my unconscious awareness.

Dreamer Aspect of my character that can fulfill my ambitions by naturally expressing my deepest feelings and sharing my highest awareness.

Dreaming Opportunity to become profoundly aware of how I can achieve my deepest ambitions rather than feeling that they seem out of reach.

Dredger Ability to work my way through a complex emotional situation by bringing concerns and potential obstacles to the surface.

Dregs Potential to fulfill an emotional need by learning from experience instead of worrying about any resulting minor anxieties.

Drenched Realization that I need to immerse myself in a learning experience rather than using a dry, dull approach.

Dress Ability to present my self-image to people in a way that gives me the freedom to display my individuality and sense of occasion.

Dressing Opportunity to choose the self-image I would like to display to other people so I can feel more comfortable with it.

Dressing room Aspect of myself that has the capacity to help me feel comfortable and secure with how I present my self-image to others.

Dress rehearsal Opportunity to understand the effects my actions have on people instead of feeling I am going through the motions.

Dribble Opportunity to carefully maintain my emotional involvement rather than continually trying to avoid expressing my feelings.

Dried flower Natural opportunity to remember my creative expertise so I can understand how it might bloom again in the future.

Dried fruit Natural opportunity to preserve my optimism and to concentrate on its fundamental value so I can use it to fulfill a future ambition.

Drifting Opportunity to choose my direction and be more self-motivated in working toward it rather than just going with the flow.

Driftwood Ability to use the flow of my emotions to guide my practical abilities and strengths so I can produce a pleasing outcome.

Drill Ability to use a prescribed method so I can go deeper and deeper into the practicalities and make a particular point.

Drink Potential to fulfill an emotional need by quenching my thirst for experience so I can satisfy my deeper desire to learn.

Drinking Opportunity to fulfill my fundamental emotional needs by being able to draw on my accumulated experience and deeper learning.

Drinking fountain Situation where I can lift my spirits by channeling my accumulated experience and deeper learning so I can celebrate their power.

D

Drinking glass Ability to fulfill an emotional need by being able to contain a sentiment and make it clear how I feel about it.

Drip Ability to contain most of my emotions and keep them under control, even though some of my less obvious feelings may leak out.

Drive Ability to use my motivation and energy to progress in my chosen direction as I actively pursue one of my ambitions.

Drive-by shooting Opportunity to take a look at what motivates me rather than trying to assertively force my opinions on others.

Drivel Opportunity to make sure of my emotions before I speak instead of feeling I have to chatter on incessantly.

Driver Aspect of my character that directs my motivation and energy so I can use my preferred way to reach my chosen objective.

Drive-through Situation where I realize that I have the power and motivation to quickly and conveniently fulfill one of my ambitions.

Driveway Situation where I can feel more relaxed about the direction I can take to connect with my wider professional ambitions.

Driving Opportunity to choose my direction so I can consistently movr forward and fulfill a personal objective.

Driving instructor Aspect of my character that encourages me to develop personal drive so I can make progress with my ambitions.

Driving test Opportunity to judge my levels of professional motivation rather than letting others decide if I can make the grade.

Drizzle Natural opportunity to let go of some insidious sentiments and feelings rather than allowing them to dampen my positive mood.

Drone Opportunity to become more aware of a fundamental challenge to my way of thinking rather than letting it fade into the background.

Droop Opportunity to take a much firmer approach to an exhausting situation by realizing the support I have from other people.

Drop Opportunity to relax by letting go of something that is no longer useful to me rather than feeling I have to carry on with it.

Drop-in center Situation where I can release myself from potentially self-destructive habits so I can experience the source of who I am.

Dropout Aspect of my character that releases me from carrying the expectations of other people so I can raise my own awareness.

Dropping Opportunity to relax by releasing any of my expectations about a specific outcome rather than having to carry on with it.

Drought Opportunity to use the prevailing mood to draw on my deep learning and experience so I can get my purpose flowing again.

Drowned Essential opportunity to revitalize a creative talent that may have seemed lost to me rather than feeling emotionally overwhelmed.

Drowning Opportunity to use the breath-taking powers of my thoughts and ideas to inspire me instead of being overwhelmed by my feelings.

Drowsy Essential opportunity to wake up to what is happening rather than allowing myself to be caught napping.

Drug Ability to temporarily avoid dealing with one of my fundamental needs rather than healthily resolving it in reality.

Drug addict Aspect of my character that can take full control of my fundamental needs by having a healthy regard for my unique talents.

Drug bust Opportunity to carefully resolve a potentially delicate situation by taking full responsibility for my fundamental needs.

Drug dealer Aspect of my character that temporarily takes care of my fundamental needs rather than dealing with them on a long-term basis.

D

Drug lord Aspect of my character that has the potential to hold great power over my fundamental needs and knows how to use it wisely.

Drug mule Aspect of my character that can clearly convey my fundamental needs instead of burdening myself with others' expectations.

Drug test Opportunity to judge my performance in a challenging situation rather than trying to delude myself about my abilities.

Drug trafficker Aspect of my character that can take responsibility for my basic needs instead of trying to fit in with others' plans.

Druid Aspect of my character that encourages my long-term spiritual growth while staying rooted in the traditions of the past.

Drum Ability to make myself heard in a distinctive, powerful manner so I can encourage people to enthusiastically support me.

Drumroll Opportunity to create a sense of anticipation for others so I can emphasize the power of what I need to communicate.

Drumstick Ability to take specific action as I pursue a particular ambition so I can bang out my message and make myself heard.

Drunken driver Aspect of my character that can pursue my ambitions in a sober and more engaging manner instead of losing emotional control.

Drunkenness Opportunity to take a more sober and disciplined approach to a situation rather than wallowing in uncontrollable emotions.

Dry Realization that I create my emotions so I can choose to use them as I please rather than just letting them happen to me.

Dry-clean Opportunity to freshen up my self-image by gaining a clearer understanding of whatever may be coloring my viewpoint.

Dry rot Opportunity to use my learning and experience to provide a firm and reliable basis for supporting my future development.

Dry suit Ability to present my self-image to people in a way that helps me keep any emotions from entering my personal comfort zone.

Dub Ability to specifically identify one of my individual talents rather than always trying to combine my efforts with other people.

Duck Instinctive ability to feel comfortable with my position as I dabble in some ideas so I can avoid any direct confrontations.

Duck-billed platypus Instinctive ability to use my creative talents and feel comfortable with them, even though they may seem primitive.

Duct Ability to consistently channel my ideas and emotions so I can convey the value of what I am thinking and feeling.

Ducting Ability to convey the flow of my thoughts and feelings so I can consistently share them in a variety of situations.

Duct tape Ability to quickly make a strong connection so I can align my thoughts and feelings, no matter what the circumstances are.

Duel Opportunity to choose the right time to resolve a conflict between two aspects of my character so I can deal with it in private.

Duet Opportunity to express my deepest feelings by inspiring two powerful aspects of my character to work in close harmony.

Dugout Situation where I can coordinate an ongoing opportunity by observing it from the sidelines instead of keeping my head down.

Dulcimer Ability to take my instinctive creativity in both hands so I can express my feelings in a quite simple and striking way.

Dull Realization that I can brighten up my situation by using my sharp observations to take a more colorful approach.

Dumb Essential opportunity to speak out and express what I need to say rather than going along with what everyone else wants.

Dumbbell Ability to use my inner strength and personal power to clearly speak out so I can deal with some heavy responsibilities.

Dummy Aspect of my character that may try to display a particular self-image rather than embody my more vital purpose.

Dump Situation where I can let go of behaviors that are no longer useful instead of allowing them to continually accumulate.

Dumped Realization that I need to have much more confidence in my unique value rather than ignoring my attractiveness to other people.

Dumpling Ability to fulfill a valuable ambition by taking a more seasoned approach to how I use my basic resources to achieve an result.

Dunce Aspect of my character that may appear foolish to others, even though they are actually mistaken in their pointed criticism.

Dune Situation where I can use my shifting perspective to see how seemingly small details can accumulate into a much larger effort.

Dung Instinctive ability to let go of creative endeavors that were once very useful but no longer have any real value for me.

Dungeon Situation where I can raise my spirits by having the courage to release myself from frustrations that appear to hold me back.

Duplicate Ability to achieve twice as much success by using my individual talents rather than thinking I have to copy everyone else.

Dusk Natural opportunity to use my creativity to illuminate a situation from a different angle so I can explore it in more depth.

Dust Ability to look beyond superficial appearances by sweeping away false conceptions so I can take a much fresher approach.

Duster Ability to clean up any small details that may be getting in the way of my seeing the bigger picture so I can take action on it.

Dusty attic Situation where I can rediscover old ideas so I can blow the cobwebs off them and put them into practical use.

Duty Ability to take responsibility for my talents and behaviors rather than obliging people to take care of them for me.

DVD Ability to immerse myself in the ins and outs of my creative talents so I can realize what makes them appear so special.

Dwarf Aspect of my character that can hold my head high instead of habitually belittling my talents and playing down my achievements.

Dwelling Situation where I can feel comfortable and relaxed with myself rather than becoming fixated on a building anxiety.

Dye Ability to colorfully express the self-image I present to people so they can see it from a different perspective.

Dying Opportunity to breathe new life into a situation by letting go of the past so I can step into a more vital future in a healthy way.

Dying animal Opportunity to revitalize my instinctive creativity so I am motivated to express the power of my natural talent.

Dying child Opportunity to increase the amount of time I devote to one of my most precious talents so I can keep developing it.

Dying dog Opportunity to question my unconditional loyalty and affection for particular people so I can completely remotivate myself.

Dying fish Opportunity to immerse myself in the deeper emotional life I fundamentally need so I can feel much more at home.

Dying loved one Opportunity to reconnect with a deeper level of self-awareness so I can create a positive and profound transformation.

D

Dying parent Opportunity to transform how I see myself so I can give myself permission to make the most of my wider potential.

Dying spouse Opportunity to reaffirm my long-term commitment to exploring and developing unknown aspects of my talents.

Dynamite Ability to transform a situation by powerfully controlling myself rather than releasing a potentially explosive revelation.

Dynamo Ability to use the power of my ideas to directly generate a great deal of excitement about my current situation.

Dyslexia Essential opportunity to figure out what is happening in a situation instead of trying to read too much into it.

Dystopia Realization that I have the power to create my best possible future rather than always imagining how bad it might become.

D

Eagle Instinctive ability to us the power and strength of my thinking to lift myself higher so I can clearly see the bigger picture.

Ear Essential ability to open up to new possibilities by listening to my feelings and hearing what I am trying to say.

Earache Essential opportunity to resolve an ongoing tension in the underlying situation by listening to what I am saying.

Early Realization that I am fully aware of all the information I need to make the most of an emerging opportunity.

Earned Opportunity to demonstrate my skills and abilities to the people around me so they can recognize my fundamental value.

Earnest Realization that I need to use my unique talents more professionally rather than appearing to be an enthusiastic amateur.

Earphones Ability to listen to my inner dialogue so I can hear what I need and direct my attention toward achieving it.

Ear protectors Ability to be more open in how I listen to the opinions of other people rather than appearing to be deaf to their needs.

Earring Ability to attract the attention of other people to what I want to say rather than saying what they want to hear.

Earth Ability to support my future growth by using my accumulated skills and abilities so I can dig deeper into my resources.

Earthquake Opportunity to deal with some deeper tensions by taking some groundbreaking action rather than feeling shaken up.

Earthwork Situation where I can defend my position by using the wide range of skills and experience I have built up.

Earthworm Instinctive ability to work my way into the more practical aspects of a situation so I can think about it more deeply.

Earwax Essential opportunity to listen deeply to what is happening rather than trying to protect myself from what is being said.

Earwig Instinctive ability to listen to what is going on rather than trying to cut out any potential criticism from other people.

Ease Realization that I am making gentle and persistent progress instead of feeling that I am being too relaxed about the outcome.

Easel Ability to support my creative processes so I can maintain a consistent viewpoint as I express my particular perspective.

East Natural opportunity to become more aware of the direction that I am taking so I can achieve greater clarity.

Easter egg Potential to transform my situation by happily indulging myself in a short-term ambition rather than just rolling along as usual.

Easy Realization that I can use my natural talent to quickly reach my chosen outcome instead of trying to overcomplicate the situation.

Easy chair Ability to comfortably maintain my habitual viewpoint in a situation rather than making things more difficult for myself.

Eating Opportunity to satisfy my appetite for success and fulfill my hunger for achievement without being weighed down by expectations.

Eating disorder Essential opportunity to understand what will make me feel more satisfied instead of constantly feeling that I am unfulfilled.

Eaves Ability to extend my feelings of individual security so I can keep exploring some of the wider aspects of my inner life.

Eavesdropping Opportunity to listen to what I'm saying so I can feel more secure about letting go of any unnecessary emotions.

Ebb Opportunity to let go of feelings I no longer need so I can be more open to connecting with my deeper emotions.

E-book Ability to instantly access the wealth of my accumulated knowledge and experience so I can share my current thinking.

Eccentric Realization that I can achieve a different level of understanding by exploring other paths rather than conforming to expectations.

Echidna Instinctive ability to fulfill a number of smaller ambitions by using my natural creativity to make a number of specific points.

Echo Opportunity to repeatedly send myself some soundly thought-out information that reflects how I feel about a situation.

Echo chamber Situation where I can clearly hear what I need to say to other people rather than just repeating it to myself again and again.

Echo sounder Ability to sound out a situation so I can achieve a much deeper understanding of what is happening in my emotional life.

Eclipse Natural opportunity to experience how a minor event can have unforeseen consequences that help me understand my brilliance.

Ecologist Aspect of my character that makes the most of my circumstances by using my natural understanding of complex relationships.

Economical Realization that I can use my resources most effectively when I don't allow myself the luxury of indulging others.

Economy class Situation where I can go far with one of my plans even though it means I have to use my resources quite carefully.

Eco-warrior Aspect of my character that can take a more natural approach in dealing with the tensions I experience in my inner world.

Ecstatic Realization that I can be extremely happy by having the courage to stand outside myself so I can observe my behaviors.

Eczema Essential opportunity to feel more comfortable by resolving an irritating situation I have allowed to get under my skin.

Eddy Ability to influence my emotions by choosing my path in the current situation rather than going with the flow.

Edge Ability to make a definite difference by understanding the extent of my ambitions while still remaining centered.

Editor Aspect of my character that helps me to clearly communicate what I feel in my heart rather than trying to censor it in any way.

Education Opportunity to use natural curiosity to accumulate a deeper understanding of my wider ambitions and how I can achieve them.

Eel Instinctive ability to navigate my way through the practical aspects of an emotional situation without causing too much friction.

Eerie Realization that I can always rely on my sense of judgment instead of allowing myself to be spooked by circumstances.

Effect Realization that I can produce powerful results by understanding the influence of my actions on all the people around me.

Effigy Aspect of my character that can bring a situation to life and transform it rather than just crudely reflecting my skills.

Effluent Ability to maintain my sense of flow by channeling emotions I no longer need and making the choice to let them go.

Effort Opportunity to persistently work my way through to achieving a successful outcome rather than just making an attempt at it.

Egg Natural ability to develop a potential talent so I can break into a fertile new area instead of just sitting on my efforts.

Egg cup Ability to hold on to a potentially fragile ambition so I can break into a new area and open up some other possibilities.

Eggshell Ability to understand the fragile nature of a new idea so I can deal with it sensitively rather than glossing over it.

Egg timer Ability to use my past experience to help me decide the best time to take action rather than running out of opportunities.

Egret Instinctive ability to work my way through a range of experiences so I can achieve success and make my point.

Ejaculation Essential opportunity to forcefully share some very powerful ideas as a way of helping to conceive a much bigger success.

Ejector seat Ability to take a more relaxed viewpoint so I can rapidly distance myself from a project I no longer feel committed to.

Elastic Ability to be flexible and accommodating in a potentially tense situation so I can always spring back and retain my power.

Elbow Essential ability to be flexible in how I use my power and strength to take deliberate action and make choices about my future.

Elder Aspect of my character that can use my extensive experience to realistically see new ways of dealing with age-old problems.

Elderflower Natural ability to open up to my variety of creative talents so I can encourage them to blossom by using my accumulated expertise.

Elderly man Aspect of my character that embodies the strength of my individual wisdom and understands what is most vital for me in my life.

Elderly pet Instinctive ability to provide unconditional love and affection by sharing vital wisdom that is very close to my heart.

Elderly woman Aspect of my character that embodies the vital creativity that enables me to fulfill my aspirations and realize my dreams.

Elder tree Natural ability for developing my long-term spiritual growth while staying rooted in the practicalities of my deeper experience.

Election Opportunity to make a long-term decision about the type of public image I would like to share with the people around me.

Electrical storm Natural opportunity to keep myself calm by using the prevailing mood to illuminate some brilliant new flashes of insight.

Electric blanket Ability to feel relaxed and comfortable by understanding my current needs so I can always surround myself with affection.

Electric chair Ability to completely transform my habitual viewpoint on a situation without it being too much of a shock to me.

Electric eel Instinctive ability to navigate my way through a highly charged emotional situation without causing too much friction around me.

Electric fence Ability to establish clear personal boundaries and defend them energetically so everyone can see exactly where I stand.

Electric guitar Ability to take my instinctive creativity in both hands so I can pitch a wide range of ideas and listen for feedback.

Electrician Aspect of my character that can skillfully maintain a powerful flow of energy to consistently supply my current needs.

E

Electricity Ability to get charged up about the potential for using my energy in an exciting way that sparks my creative flow.

Electric razor Ability to get much closer to the basis of my ideas so I can use the current situation to take precise action.

Electric shock Realization that I have an unexpected ability to energetically change my circumstances without it being a complete surprise.

Electric window Ability to clearly understand my viewpoint on a situation so I can raise or lower my expectations accordingly.

Electrode Ability to become more aware of my current way of thinking so I can decide how to conduct myself most appropriately.

Electron Ability to pay attention to a significant detail so I can understand my fundamental attraction to a particular viewpoint.

Electron microscope Ability to clearly focus my energy on some specific details so I can see how they contribute to the overall situation.

Element Ability to identify a fundamental feature of what will satisfy me so I can understand what else I might need.

Elephant Instinctive ability to use my accumulated wisdom and experience so I can remember how to deal with weighty obligations.

Elephant tusk Instinctive ability to confidently demonstrate the powerful nature of my memory so I can get straight to the point.

Elevator Ability to raise my awareness so I can reach new levels in my career progression, even though I may have to confine my ambitions.

Elf Aspect of my character that may seem quite mischievous but has the possibility to open me up to new creative opportunities.

Elimination Opportunity to completely get rid of any possessions that are no longer useful so I can concentrate on more important items.

Elixir Potential to fulfill a fundamental need by identifying the experiences that make me feel most alive so I can drink them in.

Elk Instinctive ability to be proud of the wilder aspects of my nature so I can feel comfortable in exploring my deeper self.

Elm Natural ability for developing my long-term spiritual growth while staying rooted in heavy responsibilities.

Elocution lessons Opportunity to listen to what I'm saying so I can learn to articulate my fundamental needs to others.

Eloping Opportunity to make a more balanced commitment to my needs rather than compromising by trying to run away from them.

Eloquent Realization that understanding the flow of my deeper emotions helps me far more powerfully to state my viewpoint to others.

Elusive Realization that I can successfully fulfill a long-held ambition by taking the time to understand some of my deeper mysteries.

Emaciated Essential opportunity to fulfill one of my biggest ambitions rather than wasting my time and resources.

E-mail Ability to instantly communicate my needs in a clear and concise way instead of seeming detached and distant to other people.

E-mail attachment Ability to expand my understanding in a more powerful way rather than becoming fixated on a particular viewpoint.

Emasculated Realization that I can courageously reconnect with my deeper creativity instead of feeling cut off from my source of power.

Embalmed Opportunity to transform by revitalizing my creative talents rather than trying to preserve my past achievements.

E

Embankment Situation where I can build my levels of awareness by using my practical skills to establish firm personal boundaries.

Embarrassment Realization that I need to take more pride in my individual achievements instead of feeling self-conscious about them.

Embassy Situation where I can feel more at home with an aspect of my character that may seem quite unfamiliar or foreign to me.

Ember Ability to supply fresh inspiration so I can continue my creative transformation rather than let it fade away.

Embezzler Aspect of my character that can prove my worth to other people by fully owning my need for my value to be recognized.

Emblem Ability to identify what I find most meaningful in a situation so I can openly share its significance with other people.

Embrace Opportunity to use my enthusiasm to get much closer to a powerful outcome rather than trying to keep it at arm's length.

Embroidery Ability to use my creative talents to colorfully bring some story threads together without having to embellish them too much.

Embryo Aspect of my character that develops from my fertile ideas and has the potential to embody all of my future possibilities.

Emerald Ability to attract attention to my talent for reflecting a fresh perspective in a healthy, clear, and structured way.

Emergency Opportunity to quickly choose my preferred outcome so I can immediately take decisive action to make it happen.

Emerging Opportunity to observe what is appearing in my awareness so I can raise my level of understanding about a situation.

Emigrating Opportunity to make myself feel more at home with an aspect of my character that may have seemed quite foreign to me.

Emission Opportunity to let go of thoughts and feelings that are no longer of any use to me instead of allowing them to exhaust me.

Emoticon Ability to face up to one aspect of how I am feeling so I can share my current mood with the people around me.

Emotion Essential realization that I can motivate myself by using instinctive behavioral patterns to put my feelings into action.

Emotional Opportunity to use the strength of my feelings to instinctively take action instead of feeling powerless to make a decision.

Emotionless Opportunity to instinctively understand the best course of action to take rather than endlessly analyzing the situation.

Empathy Realization that I can achieve a much deeper understanding of my emotions by observing how they are reflected in my behaviors.

Emperor Aspect of my character that has the maturity to use my power wisely so my influence can be universally acknowledged.

Employee Aspect of my character that displays the value of my talents to other people so they can reward my efforts.

Employer Aspect of my character that provides me with the opportunity to explore my different skills so I can understand their value.

Employment Opportunity to consistently express my fundamental value so I can make the effort to connect with my purpose in life.

Employment agency Situation where I can make decisions on how I like to work so I can continue to make progress in an organized way.

Empowerment Realization that I have the capacity to fulfill my needs rather than feeling that someone else should look after them for me.

Empress Aspect of my character that has the refinement to use my talents graciously so I can continue to be widely influential.

E

Emptiness Situation where I can take full advantage of all the emerging possibilities by having complete freedom to act on them.

Empty Realization that I am full of successful ideas and expertise rather than thinking that I have nothing to offer.

Empty cupboard Opportunity to understand what I need to fulfill my ambitions instead of feeling I'm being left on the shelf.

Empty house Opportunity to arrive at a fuller understanding of my fundamental identity so I can plan some character-building experiences.

Empty room Opportunity to make full use of a particular aspect of my individual talent instead of feeling I'm a waste of space.

Empty school Opportunity to make valuable use of the knowledge I have accumulated rather than thinking it is a pointless exercise.

Empty supermarket Opportunity to realize that I have a wide range of options for using my skills instead of feeling my talents are of no value.

Empty workplace Opportunity to place more value on my professional skills rather than dismissing them as being nothing out of the ordinary.

Emu Instinctive ability to keep my more powerful ideas grounded in reality so I can take a down-to-earth approach with them.

Enamel Ability to take great care in a fragile situation so I can see it in the best possible light rather than just gloss over it.

Enamored Realization that I am powerfully attracted to a particular opportunity as a way of reflecting a deeper understanding of myself.

Encampment Situation where I can establish a wider awareness of some aspects of myself so I can feel more at home with them.

Enchanted Realization that I can use my imagination to create a powerful and practical transformation rather than delude myself.

Enchantress Aspect of my character that can easily resist a variety of powerful distractions so I can create a quite magical result.

Enchilada Potential to fulfill an ambition by using my power and strength to spice up a situation without getting too wrapped up in it.

Encircle Opportunity to shape my circumstances by having the presence to remain centered even when I feel I am surrounded by challenges.

Enclosed Opportunity to be much more open about my needs so I can reach a wider awareness of what might be happening inside.

Enclosure Situation where I can open myself up to going beyond my self-limiting beliefs instead of having a specific attachment to them.

Encoded Ability to express exactly how I feel about a particular situation rather than conceal my feelings in some way.

Encounter Opportunity to become more aware of a particular aspect of my character that is proving to be unexpectedly valuable.

Encrusted Ability to display my deeper value by going beyond surface appearances rather than displaying a hard edge to others.

Encrypted Ability to openly reveal my deeper motivations to the people around me rather than endlessly analyzing my intentions.

Encumbered Opportunity to release myself from heavy responsibilities that may have been weighing on my mind for some time.

Encyclopedia Ability to open up to the wealth of my accumulated knowledge and learning so I can be consistently true to my beliefs.

End Opportunity to reach a definite conclusion so I can begin to understand what my long-term intentions are.

Endless Realization that I have the determination to reach a long-term objective, even though it may seem a never-ending task.

Endless chewing gum Opportunity to spit out what I need to say to other people instead of just chewing it over and trying to sugarcoat it.

Endless journey Opportunity to decide what will make me feel happiest rather than constantly searching for fulfillment in other people's beliefs.

Endlessly falling Opportunity to let everything drop into place so I can relax my grip on a situation and reach a comfortable level.

Endless meeting Opportunity to become more acquainted with my needs so I can take action instead of always talking about it.

Endless packing Opportunity to take immediate action to fulfill one of my ambitions rather than busying myself with activity.

Endless stairs Situation where I need to specifically define the series of steps I need to take to reach my objective.

Endless task Opportunity to take decisive action rather than feeling that I am going through the motions to please other people.

Endless war Opportunity to resolve an ongoing inner tension by declaring what I need instead of always trying to avoid conflict.

End of the world Opportunity to completely transform my view of the world so I can make the most of any upheaval in my circumstances.

Endoscope Ability to resolve an unhealthy situation by taking a long and detailed look at what is happening in my inner life.

Enema Opportunity to introduce some powerful emotions at a fundamental level so I can easily let go of what I no longer value.

Enemy Aspect of my character that can help me understand my greatest strengths and insights so I can accept them more easily.

Energetic Realization that I have the power I need to achieve my chosen objective rather than feeling I can't be bothered.

Energy Natural capacity to use all my available power to keep myself fully motivated so I can always achieve my chosen outcome.

Enforcement Opportunity to ensure that I do what makes me happy rather than limiting my enjoyment by being too strict with myself.

Engagement Opportunity to rearrange my commitments so I can understand my fundamental intentions and make long-term plans.

Engagement ring Ability to demonstrate my individual commitment to making long-term plans that will continue to develop over time.

Engine Ability to drive my ambitions forward by consistently using my creative spirit in a measured way to reach a powerful outcome.

Engineer Aspect of my character that can draw on my practical skills and planning expertise to produce consistently powerful results.

Engineering Opportunity to use the value of my practical knowledge and experience rather than contriving to reach a particular outcome.

Engine room Aspect of myself that has the ability to keep me fully motivated as I navigate my way through an emotionally complex situation.

Engraved Ability to use my creative talents to carve out a unique reputation so I can continue to employ my skills to make my mark.

Engulfed Opportunity to positively channel a sudden rush of emotions rather than allowing myself to be overwhelmed by my feelings.

Enigma Ability to explore some of the puzzling and unexplained aspects of my behavior so I can understand myself in greater depth.

Enjoying Opportunity to honestly show my pleasure so I can continue to take great satisfaction in fulfilling my fundamental needs.

E

Enlightenment Opportunity to use my creativity and wisdom to illuminate my current situation so I can deepen my understanding of it.

Enormous Realization that my potential talents are much greater than I previously thought so I can use them to create abundant opportunity.

En route Situation where I can maintain my levels of drive by continuing on my chosen path so I can reach my preferred outcome.

Ensemble Ability to see how the different aspects of my character form my wider outlook so I can coordinate them more effectively.

Enslaved Opportunity to give myself complete freedom of action instead of feeling I always have to behave in a restrained manner.

En suite Aspect of myself that allows me to conveniently deal with any potentially messy emotions in a relaxed and comfortable way.

Entangled Opportunity to work my way through some of the confusion surrounding a situation rather than getting too caught up in it.

Enter Opportunity to take decisive action by stepping fully into my power rather than trying to influence events by keeping my distance.

Entertainer Aspect of my character that can maintain a hold on other people's attention by displaying my expertise in an agreeable manner.

Enthusiastic Realization that I can increase my levels of vitality by owning my creative talents so I can fully step into them.

Entire Realization that I have all the inner resources I need to feel fulfilled rather than feel I am somehow incomplete.

Entity Ability to make my plans successfully happen in reality instead of feeling that my opportunities are nonexistent.

Entourage Aspects of my character that provide me with security and support so I can display my talents to the people around me.

Entrails Opportunity to open up about my instinctive feelings so I can fully digest the significance of my experiences.

Entrance Situation where I can make definite steps to cross a threshold that will open me up to a wider range of opportunities.

Entranced Realization that I can open up to a broader understanding by taking the time to immerse myself in my thoughts and feelings.

Entrapment Opportunity to feel truly confident that I have made the correct decision rather than being caught.

Entrenched Opportunity to openly explore the wider causes of an inner conflict instead of always taking the same defensive line.

Entrepreneur Aspect of my character that can increase my feelings of self-worth by confidently making the most of an unfamiliar opportunity.

Entry Opportunity to participate in a new experience so I can move into other areas where I can display my talents and expertise.

Entry wound Opportunity to heal painful feelings by participating more closely with the people around me.

Envelope Ability to keep an important idea safe and secure so I can convey it to other people without being too pushy about it.

Environment Situation where I can decide on the most natural action to take based on my understanding of the surrounding circumstances.

Environmental activist Aspect of my character that takes decisive action to make the most positive and healthy use of my surrounding situation.

Envoy Aspect of my character that tries to resolve my ongoing inner tensions so I can get my message across to other people.

Envy Realization that I can use my personal talents to my advantage instead of feeling that other people are more gifted than I am.

Enzyme Essential ability to create a positive transformation by using one of my unique qualities to achieve a healthy outcome.

Epic Ability to create a hugely impressive result by understanding my deeper motivations and the powerful role I play in them.

Epidemic Opportunity to quickly deal with an unhealthy situation by catching on to how I can be much more at ease with myself.

Epilepsy Opportunity to keep my attention focused on a significant task instead of feeling that I'm proceeding in fits and starts.

Episode Opportunity to choose the path I want to take so I can enter a new and fulfilling stage of my development.

Epitaph Ability to make my mark by communicating what is most significant in my life and ensuring I can continue to live up to it.

Equal Realization that balancing my commitments evenly will invariably help me to be as great as I want to be.

Equation Ability to understand the magnitude of my talents so I can have complete confidence that I am equal to the task at hand.

Equator Situation where I can embrace a much fuller awareness by remaining centered as I reach out to the edge of my understanding.

Equilibrium Opportunity to understand the opposing influences on my possible choices so I can take a more balanced approach to them.

Equinox Natural progression in which I can have a more balanced awareness of the conscious and unconscious aspects of my situation.

Equipment Ability to create an outcome of great practical value by understanding that I have all the required skills and resources.

Era Opportunity to reflect on a significant period in my life so I can make big choices about my ambitions for the future.

Eraser Ability to use my creative talents to make my mark on a more permanent basis rather than feel continually wiped out.

Erect Opportunity to steadily and progressively build up my levels of experience so I can stand up for what I believe in.

Erection Essential opportunity to channel my vitality and passion in a direct manner so I can firmly assert my creative potential.

Ermine Instinctive ability to display the ideas that emerge from my fundamental behaviors so they can be more widely recognized.

Eroded Realization that I can increase the value of my talents instead of letting the thought of any missed opportunities eat away at me.

Erotic Opportunity to become more emotionally aroused by a situation so I can get excited about its creative possibilities.

Errand Opportunity to use my energy and motivation for a specific purpose so I can successfully achieve a particular ambition.

Error Realization that I don't have to be perfect every time so I can learn from my experiences and see how to take the right action.

Erupting volcano Opportunity to let go of some of my deeper feelings of frustration rather than let them bubble below the surface.

Eruption Opportunity to release unresolved tensions that have been building up for some time so I can achieve a deeper understanding.

Escalator Situation where I can stay consistently motivated as I make progress in connecting my higher aspirations and deeper desires.

Escape Opportunity to release myself from any self-imposed constraints rather than feel trapped by any apparent limitations.

E

Escape road Situation where I have the option to follow a different route to success rather than feel I'm stuck on a particular path.

Escapologist Aspect of my character that can successfully pick my way through a number of challenges that appear to be holding me back.

Escort Aspect of my character that looks after my well-being and protects me from potential threats as I open myself up to the public.

Espionage Opportunity to be open about my underlying intentions rather than always trying to disguise my fundamental needs.

Esplanade Situation where I can pursue one of my ambitions by using my self-motivation and energy in a relaxed and level-headed manner.

Espresso Potential to fulfill an emotional need by giving it my best shot so I can stimulate a short conversation that creates a buzz.

Essay Ability to convey my deeper understanding of a particular theme rather than subject myself to endless self-examination.

Essence Ability to identify the most significant aspect of a situation so I can understand a fundamental quality of my character.

Establishment Ability to institute a firm and consistent approach to developing my unique skills rather than follow a recognized procedure.

Estate Situation where I can establish some wider personal boundaries so I can make progress in a more down-to-earth manner.

Estate agent Aspect of my character that can help me understand my value by exploring which aspects of myself I find most attractive.

Estuary Situation where I can explore the rich variety of experience that emerges from the continual ebb and flow of my emotional life.

Etched Ability to use some powerful emotions to make my mark rather than allow my deeper feelings to just eat away at me.

Eternal Realization that a part of my character is fundamentally unchanging, even during the most profound transformations.

Eternity ring Ability to demonstrate my long-term commitment to a strong, powerful partnership that will develop over time.

Ethnic minority Aspects of my character that can honestly speak my truth and share my viewpoint without being influenced by others.

Etiquette Ability to satisfy my sense of responsibility rather than feel I constantly have to be polite to other people.

Eunuch Aspect of my character that can firmly assert my natural creativity rather than feel cut off from my deeper power.

Euthanasia Opportunity to be more compassionate about my deeper needs so I can fundamentally transform one of my behavioral patterns.

Evacuation Opportunity to discharge myself of any responsibilities so I can step out of a situation that no longer serves me.

Evacuee Aspect of my character that can resolve an inner conflict by stepping out of my comfort zone rather than being too distant.

Evaporate Opportunity to raise my awareness by observing my emerging emotions rather than letting them disappear into thin air.

Evasive Realization that I need to clearly state my ambitions to the people around me rather than try to avoid looking foolish.

Even Realization that I can make smoother progress by taking a more consistent approach instead of going to extremes and appearing odd.

Evening Natural opportunity to discover a deeper understanding of myself by reflecting on what I have learned about my present situation.

Evening class Opportunity to achieve a deeper understanding of my talents and how I can use them to make myself stand out from the crowd.

Event Opportunity to become more aware of the significance of my actions so I can be more decisive about my preferred outcome.

Evergreen Natural ability to retain my creative powers so I can use them to raise awareness of my long-term spiritual growth.

Everyday Natural opportunity to consistently maintain my sense of purpose so I can continue to become more aware of my value.

Everything Ability to achieve my ambitions with the resources I have instead of feeling I never have enough.

Eviction Opportunity to feel secure and at home with who I am rather than think I am being forced out of my comfort zone.

Evidence Ability to understand my individual story by basing it on what I have seen rather than allowing other people to influence me.

Evil Realization that being completely honest with myself always results in knowing the right action to take in any situation.

Evil force Opportunity to make my own decision based on my ideas of right and wrong rather than feeling I have to behave a certain way.

Exaggerated Opportunity to have enough confidence in my talents so I can openly display them without any need for further embellishment.

Exam Opportunity to understand what I have learned so I can add it to my experience rather than be self-critical of my behaviors.

Examination Opportunity to closely observe my behavioral patterns so I can become more aware of how to share what I have learned.

Example Ability to become more aware of one of my behavioral patterns so I can understand how to make a more general transformation.

Excavation Situation where I can dig a bit deeper into my fundamental level of understanding so I can see what might open up for me.

Excavator Ability to produce an outcome of high practical value by opening up to the possibility of exploring my situation in greater depth.

Exception Realization that I have a unique talent that can make me stand out instead of feeling I'm being excluded by people.

Excess baggage Ability to clearly convey the potential value of my unrealized hopes and ambitions rather than let them weigh me down.

Excessive Realization that I am sufficiently talented to achieve my chosen result instead of feeling I have to exaggerate my skills.

Exchange Opportunity to let go of some habitual behaviors that no longer serve me so I can keep my overall progress in balance.

Excitement Realization that I have the power to influence my levels of motivation instead of feeling bored about my current circumstances.

Excluded Opportunity to welcome a new or different way of seeing a situation rather than close my mind to some emerging possibilities.

Exclusion zone Situation where I can work my way through specific areas of an inner conflict by being very definite about my personal boundaries.

Exclusive Realization that I need to be more open to emerging possibilities rather than always rely on my existing privileges.

Excrement Ability to decide what aspects of a situation might be of some use to me so I can use them to cultivate new opportunities.

E

Excreting Opportunity to naturally realize that it is often more valuable to just let some things go rather than try to retain them.

Excretion Essential ability to bring my emotions to the surface and openly show how I feel so I can let go of messy obligations.

Excursion Opportunity transform how I view a situation by motivating myself to explore a particular perspective of it.

Excuse Ability to present a clear and justifiable reason for my actions rather than feel I may have to ask for forgiveness.

Execution Opportunity to make a fundamentally transformative decision for myself instead of feeling I'm just following orders.

Executioner Aspect of my character that can transform my life rather than condemn myself to a particular course of action.

Exercise Opportunity to take a healthy approach to a real-life challenge so I can work my way through to a successful outcome.

Exercise bike Ability to work through a challenge by keeping myself motivated, even though it may feel as if I'm going nowhere.

Exercise machine Ability to produce a healthy outcome with great practical value rather than feeling I'm going through the motions.

Exertion Opportunity to use my natural talent to accomplish an ambition instead of feeling that other people always have to push me.

Exhale Essential ability to use the prevailing atmosphere as a way of letting go of feelings that have been building up inside me.

Exhaustion Opportunity to revitalize my situation by drawing on my accumulated experience rather than being consumed by anxieties.

Exhaust pipe Ability to pursue my ambitions in a powerful and healthy way by positively channeling feelings that no longer motivate me.

Exhibition Opportunity to clearly display my talents to the people around me without worrying that I will just make a fool of myself.

Exhilaration Realization that I can cheer myself up immensely by having the courage to step outside my comfort zone for an exciting experience.

Exhumation Opportunity to revitalize the practical aspects of forgotten talent rather than feel that I am digging up the past.

Exile Situation where I can feel more at home with some unfamiliar aspects of myself that may hold a truer reflection of my identity.

Existence Realization that I can be the person I want to become rather than feel my opportunities are nonexistent.

Exit Opportunity to transform my situation by leaving the past behind so I can move into other areas to realize my ambitions.

Exit wound Opportunity to heal some painful feelings by gracefully letting go of any passing discomfort so I can gain healthy closure.

Ex-lover Aspect of my character that embodied qualities that helped me become more intimately aware of my creative potential.

Exodus Opportunity to move into a whole new area so I can use my wide range of expertise and experience in a variety of ways.

Exorcism Opportunity to be far more self-possessed about my talents rather than feel that I have to get rid of my creative instincts.

Exorcist Aspect of my character that can take control of my creative drives so I can positively influence a successful outcome.

Exotic Realization that some of my unfamiliar aspects hold huge potential, even though they may initially seem quite foreign to me.

Exotic fruit Natural ability to have a healthy awareness of my less familiar talents and how I can use them for unexpected fulfillment.

E

Expanding Opportunity to freely explore a large number of possibilities so I can continue to increase my wider level of awareness.

Expansion joint Ability to keep myself comfortably aware of the prevailing atmosphere so I can always give myself enough room to maneuver.

Expatriate Aspect of my character that can use my talents to create a valuable result, even though I don't feel entirely at home with them.

Expected Realization that I need to be more open to unforeseen opportunities rather than thinking everything will turn out as planned.

Expedition Opportunity to discover my deeper purpose in life by courageously exploring some aspects of myself that may seem foreign to me.

Expelled Opportunity to fully absorb the value of a new experience rather than shutting myself off from any further learning.

Expensive Realization that I have the resources I need to achieve my goal instead of feeling that success will come at great cost.

Experience Opportunity to become more emotionally engaged with my situation so I can absorb the full value of what I have learned.

Experiment Opportunity to be open to a variety of results as I explore my options so I can understand what I need to be successful.

Expert Aspect of my character that has the confidence to use my unique talent rather than feeling I'm nothing out of the ordinary.

Expertise Ability to employ my accumulated skill and experience in productive action instead of feeling I have no value to offer.

Expired Opportunity to breathe new life into a seemingly hopeless situation so I can feel much more inspired about the future.

Explorer Aspect of my character that purposefully ventures into unknown and unfamiliar areas so I can discover their potential value.

Explorer Aspect of my character that enjoys enveloping myself in the practicalities of a situation so I can explore it in greater depth.

Exploring Opportunity to discover the wider value of my unknown potential by working my way through a range of unfamiliar viewpoints.

Explosion Opportunity to contain my potentially volatile feelings rather than releasing them in a burst of uncontrolled emotion.

Explosive Ability to control my powerful and energetic talent for creating sudden change rather than allowing it to blow up unexpectedly.

Export Opportunity to realize the value of my expertise by taking time to convey some of my experiences to the people around me.

Exposed Realization that I can feel more secure by confidently opening up to other people rather than feeling vulnerable to them.

Exposure Opportunity to reveal my deeper expertise to the people around me instead of feeling that I'm being left out in the cold.

Express Opportunity to clearly say what I need so I can move quickly and purposefully toward achieving my objective.

Expulsion Opportunity to gladly welcome genuine offers of help from other people so I can quickly banish any thoughts of failure.

Ex-spouse Aspect of my character that embodied my commitment to exploring and developing some unknown and unfamiliar aspects of myself.

Extension Aspect of myself that can build on my existing talents so I can open up a new opportunity for developing my skills.

Exterior Situation where I can become more aware of how I present myself to the world around me so I can feel more at home with it.

Extermination Ability to completely transform my current situation so I can powerfully create the type of life I want to live.

E

Extinct Realization that I can use my past experience to revitalize a creative possibility that may have seemed to no longer exist.

Extinguisher Ability to powerfully direct my emotions so I can deal with a creative challenge that seems to be getting out of control.

Extra Realization that I always have more to offer than I thought instead of feeling I am just making up the numbers.

Extra limb Ability to give myself the support I need rather than always looking to other people to give me a hand or a leg up.

Extra room Aspect of myself that has more capacity than I thought for developing my talents so I can begin to make the most of them.

Extraterrestrial Aspect of my character that can express the deeper and more universal qualities of myself, which can sometimes seem alien to me.

Extra time Opportunity to use all my experience to achieve my original goal rather than feeling that the outcome has already been decided.

Extract Ability to quickly identify what is of most significance to me rather than allowing the situation to become too drawn out.

Extradition Opportunity to make my own decision to step outside my comfort zone rather than feeling others are forcing me into it.

Extramarital Opportunity to restore a lack of confidence in my attractiveness by making a more balanced commitment to my fundamental needs.

Extraordinary Realization that I have a unique opportunity to create something wonderful rather than feeling as if I'm nothing special.

Extravagant Realization that I should spend more time looking after my needs instead of always indulging the whims of others.

Extreme Realization that I can always achieve much more than I thought was possible when I go beyond the limits of my understanding.

Extreme sport Opportunity to achieve incredible results by stepping out of my comfort zone, even though the outcome may always be uncertain.

Extremist Aspect of my character that can create a fundamental transformation in my life by being more open to the beliefs of others.

Extremity Situation where I can achieve a much wider awareness by going out on a limb and exploring the edges of my current understanding.

Eye Essential ability to see the bigger picture so I can stay focused on my personal vision and understand how I can achieve it.

Eyeball Essential ability to look around at what is happening so I can gain a well-rounded insight into my situation.

Eyebrow Essential ability to signal how I feel to others rather than trying to appear surprised or concerned to them.

Eye contact Opportunity to make a much deeper connection with one of my specific insights rather than just touching on it.

Eyeglasses Ability to look more closely at a situation so I can form a clearer opinion and understand what is happening.

Eyehole Ability to clearly look into different opportunities so I can develop possibilities that may currently seem closed to me.

Eyelashes Essential ability to take care of my point of view so I can attract other people to how I see the situation.

Eyelid Essential ability to protect my point of view so I can always take time to reflect on my deeper insights.

Eyeliner Ability to emphasize my viewpoint

so I can make my perspective more attractive to other people.

Eye shadow Ability to see the contrast between different aspects of my viewpoint so I can gain more insight into my perspective.

Eyesight Essential ability to maintain a wider awareness of the bigger picture so I can stay focused on a particular objective.

Eyewitness Aspect of my character that can objectively observe my habitual viewpoints so I can clearly make rational sense of them.

E

F

Fabled Realization that facts are sometimes stranger than fiction and that I can use them to create a fantastic practical outcome.

Fabric Ability to provide a substantial basis for my thoughts and feelings so I can fashion them into something more tangible.

Fabrication Ability to create a valuable and constructive outcome rather than making up a story as a way of pleasing other people.

Fabric softener Ability to take a more flexible approach to dealing with a tough challenge so I can understand it from a fresh perspective.

Fabulous Realization that I can create something wonderful by having the self-belief to go beyond my current level of understanding.

Facade Situation where I can openly reveal my position in public rather than feeling that I have to conceal my opinions from people.

Face Essential ability to express my true identity so I can have my unique qualities consistently recognized by other people.

Facebook Ability to stay acquainted with aspects of my character so I can develop a wider understanding of who I really am.

Facecloth Ability to always be very clear about my deeper identity, even though it may mean being open to using a fresh perspective.

Faceless Realization that I need to reveal the true nature of my unique talents to others rather than using them anonymously.

Faceless lover Aspect of my character that connects with my fundamental identity at a deeper level so I can become more intimately aware of it.

Faceless stranger Aspect of my character that may seem unknown and unfamiliar but can give me a deep insight into my true identity.

Facelift Opportunity to be comfortable with my identity rather than continually trying to raise my profile with the people around me.

Facial Opportunity to go beyond surface appearances so I can revitalize myself and take a fresh look at what makes me unique.

Facilitator Aspect of my character that makes it easier for me to maintain an inner dialogue so I can reach a successful outcome.

Fact Ability to consistently be true to my beliefs rather than feeling I have to conform to the opinions of other people.

Factory Situation where I can use my raw talent and continuing dedication to reliably produce a consistently valuable outcome.

Factory farm Situation where I can produce a valuable outcome by developing creative instincts and cultivating my abilities.

Factory ship Situation where I can use fundamental instincts to process raw emotions so I can use them more productively.

Factory worker Aspect of my character that can express my fundamental value by making the effort to connect with my true life purpose.

Fact sheet Ability to clearly display what I believe so I can feel more comfortable about sharing my perspectives with other people.

Fade Opportunity to express myself clearly and coherently to other people rather than feeling that I am appearing too intense.

Failure Opportunity to relax and let go of any foregone conclusions so I can identify what it will take for me to succeed.

Faint Realization that I have a distinct contribution to make instead of feeling I am not bright enough to make any difference.

Fainting Opportunity to become more aware of what is happening rather than feeling overwhelmed by insubstantial concerns.

Fair Realization that I always need to be aware of my own biases instead of thinking I am being treated unjustly by other people.

Fairground Situation where I can play around with different methods of achieving my targets so I can reach the most balanced outcome.

Fairway Situation where I can use my drive and vision to play around with outcomes that will be acceptable to everyone else.

Fairy Aspect of my character that may seem quite whimsical but has the possibility to open me up to new creative opportunities.

Fairy godmother Aspect of my character that uses my creativity and wisdom to produce practical outcomes from seemingly nowhere.

Fairy lights Ability to clearly see the significance of a special occasion rather than feeling I am being strung along by people.

Fairy tale Ability to share a unique insight that may seem quite whimsical, even though it displays the fantastic power of my imagination.

Faith Ability to believe in my talents and have complete confidence in my skills rather than doubting my abilities.

Faith healer Aspect of my character that can make a situation seem much healthier by having more confidence in my skills and experience.

Fake Realization that I possess a genuine talent rather than feeling I always have to conceal my imagined flaws.

Falcon Instinctive ability to rise above practical limitations so I can use my quick thinking to rapidly pursue a specific goal.

Fall Opportunity to let go of a situation that I have been trying to overcontrol so I can pick up my motivation and move on.

Fallen Realization that I can use this opportunity to achieve a more practical perspective rather than feeling down about it.

Falling Opportunity to relax my grip on a situation so I just let everything drop into place rather than trying to overcontrol it.

Fallout Ability to let my thoughts settle after experiencing a conflict so I can decide what to do in the immediate future.

Fallow Realization that I can accumulate experience by naturally absorbing what is happening rather than always having to work at it.

Falsies Realization that I need to communicate what I honestly feel instead of thinking I should try to fake some enthusiasm.

False alarm Opportunity to alert myself to the rapidly emerging realization that I need to clearly express any concerns I may have.

False boobs Ability to reveal my true capacity for nurturing and supporting other people rather than trying to attract more attention.

False eyelashes Ability to clearly understand my particular point of view rather than trying to make it more attractive to other people.

False teeth Ability to reveal my true power by honestly sharing my emotions instead of thinking I always need to put on a brave face.

Falsified document Ability to formalize what I need to say to other people instead of trying to make my viewpoint more presentable to them.

Fame Opportunity to recognize the value of my talents so I can have my achievements publicly recognized by a wider audience.

F

Familiar Realization that I need to explore some of the unknown aspects of my character rather than being complacent about my situation.

Familiar people Aspects of my character that often reflect my habitual behavior patterns without my realizing their full significance.

Family Aspects of my character that are most familiar to me and provide continuing support and motivation for my development.

Famine Opportunity to fulfill my hunger for wider success by understanding my fundamental ambitions and cultivating their value.

Famous Realization that I need to celebrate my successes and applaud my skills rather than trying to remain inconspicuous.

Famous person Aspect of my character that recognizes my unique creative talents and gives me the chance to share them with a wider audience.

Fan Ability to create some movement in my way of thinking so I can circulate my ideas more widely to the people around me.

Fanatic Aspect of my character that can use my enthusiasm to create a real transformation rather than fixating on a specific outcome.

Fan club Aspects of my character that convey the significance of my talent and support me when I need to take creative risks.

Fancy Realization that I can use the power of my imagination to create a valuable result rather than indulging in whimsy.

Fancy dress Ability to present my self-image to other people in a way that shows parts of my character I normally try to conceal.

Fancy-dress party Opportunity to invite others to recognize my hidden talents so I can become the person I want to be.

Fanfare Opportunity to proudly display my creative skills to other people rather than feeling I should be less ostentatious.

Fan fiction Ability to explore what I enjoy most about a situation instead of feeling limited by previously established facts.

Fang Ability to confidently display my power and strength to other people rather than worrying about appearing too conspicuous.

Fantasia Ability to instinctively communicate with people in a fundamentally powerful way that goes beyond the merely superficial.

Fantastic Realization that I can use my imagination to successfully produce incredibly valuable and down-to-earth outcomes.

Fantasy Ability to create a much deeper understanding by imagining how I can make a difference and then validating it in reality.

Far Realization that I am much nearer to achieving a distant ambition than I previously thought and will soon reach my objective.

Farce Opportunity to skillfully exploit a situation to my advantage rather than feeling I have to take the outcome too seriously.

Fare Ability to convey my value to other people by displaying my unique expertise and abilities as I make progress toward my goal.

Farewell Opportunity to open myself up to new possibilities by gracefully letting go of an aspect of my character I no longer need.

Far-fetched Realization that I can use seemingly commonplace knowledge and experience to successfully achieve incredible results.

Farm Situation where I can produce a valuable outcome by developing my creative instincts and cultivating my natural abilities.

Farmer Aspect of my character that can consistently use my down-to-earth nature to produce an outcome of great practical value.

Farmhand Aspect of my character that has a firm grasp of the practicalities so I can successfully develop some fertile opportunities.

F

Farmhouse Situation where I have the security and support to comfortably explore the wider potential of my practical expertise and abilities.

Farmyard Situation where I can give myself the space to be much more open about how I can productively develop my skills and abilities.

Fart Opportunity to let go of some ideas that no longer have any value for me, even though I may have been digesting them for some time.

Farthest Realization that an apparently distant ambition is much closer than it once seemed and I soon will be able to actually achieve it.

Fascia Ability to clearly define my personal boundaries so I can take a more detached and precise view of the information I share.

Fascinated Realization that I can use my unique qualities to attract others instead of feeling disenchanted with my circumstances.

Fascist Aspect of my character that tries to control my every action rather than allowing me to be more open to emerging possibilities.

Fashion Opportunity to shape my self-image so I can develop fresh new perspectives on how I see myself and my range of talents.

Fast Realization that I can quickly get a situation moving, even though I may not be able to fully control its eventual outcome.

Fastening Ability to make a firm connection with a new opportunity without feeling that there must always be a catch in it somewhere.

Fast food Potential to fulfill a short-term ambition in a deceptively convenient way without paying any attention to long-term gains.

Fast-forward Ability to quickly move into my desired future state rather than waiting for the present situation to play out at its own speed.

Fasting Opportunity to achieve my long-term ambitions by understanding my fundamental appetite for success and how it feeds my desire.

Fast lane Situation where I can be much more direct about my future ambitions and how I plan to rapidly move toward achieving them.

Fast track Opportunity to quickly achieve my objective by taking the initiative and working my way around some persistent challenges.

Fat Essential opportunity to indulge in my appetite for success by taking a fresh approach and exercising a healthier perspective.

Fatal Realization that transforming my self-destructive behaviors will enable me to take control of an apparently inevitable outcome.

Fatal accident Opportunity to revitalize my ambitions and remotivate myself by being more open to potentially transformative outcomes.

F

Fatal injury Opportunity to resolve an unhealthy situation by fundamentally transforming the way that I deal with criticism from others.

Fat camp Situation where I can begin to feel more at home with my previously concealed talents so I can comfortably embody them.

Fate Realization that I can decide my chosen outcome and take full responsibility for it rather than leaving it to chance.

Father Aspect of my character that embodies the loving power and authority that encourages me to assertively develop my true potential.

Father's death Opportunity to reconnect with a part of myself that may have seemed lost so I can embrace and embody its loving strength.

Fathomless Realization that I can achieve a much more profound understanding by taking the time to explore my emotions in greater depth.

Fatigue Opportunity to deal with some chronic tensions so I can revitalize a situation that has become very wearisome for me.

Fault Opportunity to become more aware of any possible flaws in my thinking rather than allowing other people to needlessly blame me.

Faulty brakes Opportunity to take decisive action to maintain my progress instead of feeling I am getting diverted by commitments.

Faulty computer Opportunity to explore a number of possibilities for using my ideas rather than feeling I must think in a specific way.

Faulty switch Opportunity to understand the deeper connection I am trying to make instead of expecting the same response every time.

Faulty vehicle Opportunity to take more responsibility for my individual ambitions rather than blaming others for my lack of progress.

Faux pas Opportunity to discover more about myself and others instead of being anxious that I may somehow appear foolish to them.

Favorite Realization that I can follow my preferences and make my own choices rather than doing what other people want me to do.

Fawn Instinctive ability to develop the wilder aspects of my nature instead of feeling I have to constantly flatter other people.

Fax machine Ability to express exactly what I feel so I can directly communicate it rather than copying the behaviors of others.

Fear Opportunity to courageously step into my true identity so I can use my power to make a bold and transformative choice.

Fearful Realization that I can create a bold transformation by making the first move instead of trying to stay inside my comfort zone.

Fearless Realization that I can use my courage in a wise and compassionate manner rather than rushing into an unfamiliar situation.

Feast Opportunity to fulfill some of my greatest ambitions by creating satisfying work and sharing the results with other people.

Feather Natural ability to explore my thoughts and theories by taking a softer and gentler approach to raise my level of awareness.

Feather duster Ability to let go of any minor doubts that may be getting in the way of seeing the bigger picture and taking action.

Feat of strength Opportunity to demonstrate my commitment to achieving a specific outcome, even though it may involve embracing my weaknesses.

Feature Ability to attract attention to what I have achieved so I can raise my profile and demonstrate the difference that I make.

Feces Ability to let go of possessions and memories I once found very useful but are no longer of any real value to me.

Fed up Realization that I have the resources to satisfy my appetite for success instead of always feeling unfulfilled.

Fee Ability to have other people recognize the value of my professionalism rather than thinking my work is taken for granted.

Feeble Realization that I have far greater strength than I am aware of instead of making excuses about my performance.

Feedback Opportunity to listen to what I am saying so I get a good indication of how other people might respond to it.

Feeding Opportunity to fulfill my ambitions by taking in all the information I need so I can satisfy my hunger for success.

Feelings Opportunity to become more aware of my emotions by understanding what I am intuitively sensing rather than being too objective.

Feet Essential ability to take a definite stand on an issue so I have a firm basis for deciding the next steps to take.

F

Feline Realization that I feel most relaxed and comfortable about myself when I am gracefully asserting my independent choices.

Fell Opportunity to take a more down-to-earth approach in my spiritual development rather than destructively cutting back on it.

Fellatio Essential opportunity to become more intimately aware of how I can voice my creativity and assert it firmly and strongly.

Fellow Aspect of my character that can support my professional ambitions by helping me decide how I use my strength and power.

Female Realization that I can embody the empathy and wisdom I need to fulfill my aspirations so I can fully realize my potential.

Fembot Aspect of my character that may suppress my true wisdom and efficiently go through the motions to keep others happy.

Feminine Realization that I can use my instincts and intuition to adapt to changing circumstances so I can fulfill my deepest aspirations.

Feminization Opportunity to become more in touch with my wiser, gentle nature rather than always putting on a show of strength and power.

Femur Essential ability to give a fundamental structure to my actions so I am strongly motivated to take necessary, decisive steps.

Fen Situation where I need to get on a firmer footing rather than being inundated by my emotions and feeling a bit low.

Fence Ability to establish clear personal boundaries and understand any of my self-imposed limitations so everyone knows where I stand.

Fencepost Ability to have a firm foundation for my beliefs so I can support my decision to establish clear personal boundaries.

Fence wire Ability to clearly define my personal boundaries, even though it may initially cause quite a lot of tension with other people.

Fencing Opportunity to demonstrate the thrust of my argument rather than attempting to foil any attacks on my individual stance.

Fermented Ability to use my natural enthusiasm to get excited and raise my awareness rather than appearing agitated about the outcome.

Fern Natural ability to explore the delicate intricacies of a situation so I can understand the best way to develop it in a healthy manner.

Ferocious Realization that I possess instinctive, engaging courage instead of feeling I am overly assertive.

Ferret Instinctive ability to fearlessly go deeper into practicalities so I can pursue an opportunity that may otherwise be hidden.

Ferry Ability to resolve an emotional dilemma by using my instincts and experience to connect two different aspects of my life.

Ferryman Aspect of my character that helps me to navigate complex feelings so I can consistently connect with new opportunities.

Fertility Opportunity to use my natural creative potential to produce a practical result rather than feeling I have nothing to offer.

Fertilizer Ability to enrich my practical skills so I can use them to support my future growth and realize the fruits of my labors.

Fester Opportunity to motivate myself so that I can deal with any deep-rooted anxieties that may be causing some unhealthy feelings.

Festival Opportunity to celebrate one of my unique talents by sharing it with other people so they can openly recognize my value.

Festive Gathering opportunity to display the wider range of my skills and experience by reflecting on the value of all my different qualities.

Festooned Realization that I can happily display a deeper level of independence rather than always weighing myself down with expectations.

F

Fetch Opportunity to clearly convey what I need to successfully achieve my ambitions by just going out and getting it.

Fête Opportunity to step outside my comfort zone so I can invite other people to celebrate my skills and range of talents.

Fetid Realization that I can resolve an underlying conflict by motivating myself to take a fresh approach so I can openly air my views.

Fetish Ability to clearly understand the underlying context of a situation rather than obsessing about one specific aspect of it.

Fetter Ability to become more aware of my freedom of action so I can take independent steps to release myself from any constraints.

Fetus Aspect of my character that embodies all my future possibilities and that will always continue to develop throughout my life.

Feud Opportunity to resolve some chronic tensions by embracing the unfamiliar rather than being hostile to any other suggestions.

Fever Essential opportunity to healthily resolve a situation that makes me feel hot and bothered instead of becoming agitated about it.

Few Realization that I need to focus on one of my talents so I can use it to make the best choice from a number of options.

Fiancé Aspect of my character that is prepared to make a commitment to using my strength and power so I can assert my ambitions.

Fiancée Aspect of my character that is committed to using my empathy and wisdom so I can get ready to fulfill my aspirations.

Fiasco Opportunity to take full advantage of an uncertain situation rather than being concerned it will end in a catastrophe.

Fiber Ability to take the thread of an idea and weave it into something more powerful rather than feeling I'm being strung along.

Fiberglass Ability to shape my preferred outcome by using the layers of understanding and insight I have accumulated over time.

Fiber optic Ability to focus on communicating my ideas quickly and precisely so I can clearly illuminate any emerging opportunities.

Fiction Ability to explore all the potential outcomes of a situation rather than feeling limited by previously established facts.

Fictional character Aspect of my character that helps me explore my life story so I can understand how I might continue to develop.

Fiddle Ability to take my instinctive creativity in both hands so I can honestly express how I feel about a situation.

Fidelity Ability to clearly express my expertise and believe in my ability to produce consistent results rather than doubting my skills.

Fidget Realization that I can use my energy and self-motivation to take decisive action rather than feeling nervous and impatient.

Field Situation where I can use my accumulated experience to cultivate my knowledge so I can realize its practical value.

Field hospital Situation where I can immediately attend to any inner conflicts and tensions that may have been causing me discomfort or pain.

Fiend Aspect of my character that can powerfully transform a challenging situation by stepping into my power and confronting fears.

Fierce Realization that I sometimes have to use my instinctive strength and power rather than appearing to be meek and gentle.

Fig Potential to fulfill an ambition by being very attentive to what my intentions are so I can achieve a fruitful outcome.

Fight Ability to resolve any inner tensions and conflicts I may have by standing up for my beliefs and defending them to other people.

F

Fighting Opportunity to take action and resolve any internal conflicts I am experiencing by having the courage to engage with them.

Figment Ability to bring one of my ideas into practical reality rather than continuing to play around with it in my mind.

Figure Ability to understand the value of my fundamental talents rather than always worrying about the shape I'm in.

Filament Ability to stay strongly connected to the outcome of a situation by having a fine appreciation of its eventual value for me.

Filbert Potential to fulfill an ambition by having enough confidence in my plans so I can easily open up to a variety of challenges.

File Ability to shape the outcome of a situation by applying consistent pressure and ensuring that I don't wear myself down.

Filing Opportunity to shape an outcome by being consistently organized so I have convenient access to underlying resources.

Filing cabinet Ability to have convenient access to my memories and experiences so I can use them to help me make decisions at a later date.

Fill Ability to steadily increase my levels of personal achievement rather than feeling I have reached my individual potential.

Filler cap Ability to contain my raw creative power so I can always be open to pursuing my ambitions in a more spirited manner.

Filling Opportunity to realize my capacity for learning so I can continue to add to my growing levels of experience and expertise.

Film Ability to understand the thin layer between imagination and reality so I can become more aware of my personal story.

Filming Opportunity to become more aware of my viewpoint so I can direct my efforts toward achieving my ambitions.

Filter Ability to take a cleaner and more refined approach by choosing what I would like to keep and what I need to let go of.

Filthy Realization that I sometimes need to acknowledge my less rational instincts rather than always responding in a precise manner.

Filthy toilet Opportunity to resolve concerns I have about a messy emotional situation by clearly expressing my personal needs to people.

Filtration plant Situation where I can consistently process some of my more challenging emotions so I can achieve a clearer outcome.

Fin Instinctive ability to maintain my direction as I explore my thoughts and feelings so I can align them with my wider purpose.

Final Opportunity to open myself up to some exciting new possibilities so I can decide what I want to ultimately achieve.

Financial Realization that declaring my confidence in my skills and expertise enables my value to be genuinely recognized by others.

Financier Aspect of my character that has a solid understanding of my value and can provide me with the resources to develop it.

Finch Instinctive ability to rise above more practical concerns so I can assert some apparently small but powerful ideas.

Find Ability to discover the special skill that defines my talents by methodically searching for it rather than leaving it to chance.

Finding Opportunity to explore unfamiliar areas so I can discover a valuable aspect of my talent that I was previously unaware of.

Fine Realization that I can increase my value by attending to the details rather than feeling there is always a price to pay.

Fine print Ability to clearly and boldly state any of my concerns about a situation instead of trying to resolve some minor details.

F

Finger Essential ability to control my actions and shape my future by always being able to point myself in the right direction.

Finger food Potential to fulfill my ambitions by maintaining a firm grip on reality so I can keep myself pointing in the right direction.

Fingernail Essential ability to protect my skill in shaping outcomes so I can choose my future without letting any anxieties gnaw away at me.

Fingerprint Essential opportunity to have my unique creativity identified so I can use my practical handiwork to make my mark with people.

Fingers Essential ability to count on a number of personal influences so I can use them to shape how I can grasp future opportunities.

Fingertip Essential ability to be sensitive about how I control my actions and shape my future by staying close to my feelings.

Finish Opportunity to realize that I have accomplished what I set out to achieve so I can begin to look for other possibilities.

Finishing line Situation where I can draw a line under my achievements rather than continually taking on more and more commitments.

Fire Opportunity for a vital transformation that can illuminate my fundamental passions and heighten my developing creativity.

Fire alarm Ability to alert myself to a rapidly emerging realization that I can decisively transform my fundamental creative processes.

Firearm Ability to assert my creativity in a forceful manner by confidently communicating my aims so I can take decisive action.

Fireball Opportunity to shape a creative outcome by concentrating on a fundamental transformation so I can play around with it.

Fire chief Aspect of my character that has great creative power and can use it to guide me through a period of fundamental transformation.

Fire department Aspects of my character that can help me realize my burning ambitions by courageously engaging with my creative challenges.

Fire door Ability to set safe creative boundaries so I can develop possibilities for transformation that may have seemed closed to me.

Fire drill Ability to use a prescribed method so I can become more accustomed to my creative process and feel confident in using it.

Fire engine Ability to quickly resolve any creative challenges so I can drive my ambitions forward and reach a powerful outcome.

Fire escape Ability to release myself from self-imposed practical constraints so I can deal with any apparent creative limitations.

Fire extinguisher Ability to powerfully direct my thinking so I can deal with a creative situation that appears to be getting out of control.

Firefight Opportunity to resolve creative conflicts by courageously engaging with any challenges to my beliefs so I can defend them.

Firefighter Aspect of my character that is willing to step into a transformational process and ensure I can deal with it creatively or keep my cool.

Firefly Instinctive ability to immerse myself in my creativity so I can use some seemingly trivial ideas to illuminate the situation.

Firehouse Situation where I have the security and support I need to comfortably engage with any creative challenges I may encounter.

Fireplace Situation where I can contain my creative urges so I can focus on using them to create a warm and welcoming atmosphere.

F

Fire retardant Ability to slow down a potentially volatile transformation so I have the opportunity to respond to it in a creative way.

Fireworks Ability to celebrate my brilliance by displaying my creative sparks to people and dazzling them with my spectacular performance.

Firing range Situation where I can explore a number of options for communicating my aims and then assess how accurate they are in reality.

Firing squad Aspects of my character that can help me understand my aims so I can coordinate my power and use it more confidently.

Firm Realization that I can provide myself with solid support and motivation rather than feeling I have to yield to other people.

First Realization of what I find most significant about a situation so I can use it to conceive a winning strategy.

First light Opportunity to understand a situation with much greater clarity by using the power of my wisdom to let it naturally dawn on me.

Firth Situation where I can experience a much wider and deeper understanding of the continual ebb and flow of my emotional life.

Fir tree Natural potentials for my long-term spiritual growth, which can help me thrive in conditions that may seem quite arduous to me.

Fish Instinctive ability to immerse myself in my emotions and just go with the flow without getting too caught up in my surroundings.

Fish bait Ability to use a seemingly minor sentiment to successfully reach a much deeper understanding of one of my more powerful emotions.

Fish bowl Ability to reveal my instinctive feelings by being clear and open about my emotions rather than trying to keep them concealed.

Fish egg Natural ability to develop my emotional awareness so I can move into fertile new areas and create a deeper understanding.

Fisherman Aspect of my character that can use my strength and power to successfully allow my deeper emotions to surface and employ them productively.

Fishing Opportunity to bring my instinctive feelings to the surface so I can firmly grasp their deeper emotional power and vitality.

Fishing pole Ability to clearly draw attention to a point I need to recognize so I can connect with my feelings at a deeper level.

Fishing rod Ability to use my instinctive feelings to cast my talents farther so I can extend my influence over a much wider area.

Fish ladder Ability to use a specific series of steps to raise my emotional awareness so I can use it to perform at a higher level.

Fish market Situation where I can understand the value of displaying my emotions to others so they can recognize how I feel.

Fishmonger Aspect of my character that uses my raw emotion to identify my most powerful feelings and cut out any unnecessary sentiments.

Fish sandwich Potential to fulfill an ambition by understanding my different emotional levels and what difference they make to me.

Fissure Situation where I can make the most of an opening rather than feeling as though I have no attachment to the eventual outcome.

Fist Essential opportunity to concentrate on my power and assertiveness so I can use it to shape the outcome of a situation.

Fistfight Opportunity to deal with any inner conflicts I may have by concentrating on my individual power and practical strengths.

Fit Realization that I can shape an outcome in a positive and healthy manner by using the appropriate skills and experience.

F

Fitness Ability to inspire myself so I can feel motivated to use my power and strength instead of feeling that I don't fit in.

Fitness class Opportunity to learn more about practical abilities and how can I use them to make me stand out from people around me.

Fix Opportunity to work my way through some underlying tensions instead of feeling that I am stuck in a situation.

Fixated Realization that I can easily consolidate my learning and experience rather than becoming obsessed about influencing the future.

Fixing Opportunity to resolve any upsets in a personal relationship so I can make a deeper and long-lasting connection.

Fizzing Opportunity to enjoy continuing excitement so I can see how long it will last before it eventually diminishes.

Fizzle Opportunity to maintain the intensity of my creative output instead of allowing it to slowly fade to nothing.

Fjord Situation where I can experience a much deeper understanding of my higher ambitions and the effort required to attain them.

Flag Ability to consistently draw the attention of other people to my individual perspective without their becoming too tired of it.

Flagellation Opportunity to whip up enthusiasm for one of my plans rather than worrying it will just be a painful experience.

Flagpole Ability to clearly draw others' attention to one of my ideas and my need for recognition at some higher level.

Flailing Opportunity to steadily work my way through achieving an ambition rather than always thrashing around with no real purpose.

Flak Ability to powerfully deflect criticism from other people so I can defend myself against any apparently threatening ideas.

Flake Ability to take a small aspect of an idea so I can scale it up and see the bigger picture without thinking I'm going crazy.

Flak jacket Ability to present my self-image to people in a way that allows me to protect myself from potentially wounding criticisms.

Flambé Opportunity to fulfill a potential ambition by taking a more spirited approach, even though it may result in a volatile outcome.

Flame Ability to transform a situation by getting all fired up so I can illuminate my fundamental passions and growing creativity.

Flame retardant Ability to take my time as I work my way through a creative transformation rather than feeling I have to react immediately.

Flamethrower Ability to use my creative spirit to powerfully influence events from a distance without becoming too closely involved in them.

Flamingo Instinctive ability to sift through my emotional life and find some valuable ideas, even though they may appear quite flamboyant.

Flan Potential to fulfill a shared ambition and celebrate collective success by working through a challenge in a steady manner.

Flannel Ability to provide a more comfortable basis for my thoughts and feelings so I can shape them into something more practical.

Flap Ability to easily open up to new opportunities rather than becoming overly anxious about how to take the correct action.

Flapping Opportunity to get some fresh ideas moving around instead of feeling agitated about possibly losing control of the situation.

Flare Ability to suddenly draw attention to my unique creativity so I can illuminate my passions and open up to them more.

Flash Opportunity to quickly see the most significant aspect of a situation so I can understand it in much clearer detail.

Flashback Opportunity to step back into my previous experience so I can apply it to my current situation and recognize its value.

Flasher Aspect of my character that eagerly opens up about my creative potential, even though it may seem inappropriate at the time.

Flash flood Opportunity to quickly rise above a potentially overwhelming emotional situation rather than getting carried away by it.

Flashgun Ability to direct my brilliance in a powerful way so I can quickly understand a situation that may have seemed obscure.

Flashlight Ability to clearly direct my future actions by using the power of my wisdom to illuminate a wide range of possible options.

Flash mob Opportunity to quickly identify different aspects of my character so I can bring them together and resolve any conflicts.

Flask Ability to safely contain my emotions so I can take a more measured approach to dealing with a challenging situation.

Flat Situation where I can make positive progress by regaining confidence and momentum rather than feeling too up or down about it.

Flat battery Opportunity to build up my current energy levels so I can use my accumulated experience to connect with my wider potential.

Flattery Opportunity to communicate to other people what I feel rather than trying to look good by keeping them happy.

Flatulence Essential opportunity to release unwelcome thoughts that have been building up while I have been digesting new ideas.

Flaunting Opportunity to confidently display my unique talents rather than feeling I always have to conceal them from other people.

Flavor Ability to use my good taste to create a favorable mood so I can influence how people experience my distinctive qualities.

Flaw Realization that I can make a huge difference by being prepared to fail rather than thinking I always have to achieve perfection.

Flax Natural ability to develop the basic material I need so I can weave together all the individual threads of my story.

Flaxseed Natural ability for a seemingly insignificant story to potentially grow into something much stronger and more colorful.

Flayed Ability to understand what is happening below the surface, although it may expose deeper passions and raw emotions.

Flaying Opportunity to get beyond superficial appearances and reveal what is happening, even though it may be quite uncomfortable.

Flea Instinctive ability to powerfully jump from one idea to another even though it may seem quite irritating to other people.

Fleck Ability to understand a tiny detail that gives me a clear perspective on how to understand a much bigger situation.

Fleece Ability to present my self-image to other people in an unobtrusive way that makes me feel more comfortable about fitting in.

Fleet Ability to use a number of methods to quickly navigate unpredictable feelings so I can maintain my emotional stability.

Flesh Natural ability to produce a result of great substance and importance by being more open about my raw strength and power.

Flesh wound Opportunity to use my underlying strength and power to heal some painful feelings so I can comfortably gain healthy closure.

Flexibility Realization that I can make the most of a situation by adapting my approach rather than feeling I need to shape up.

F

Flick Opportunity to quickly touch on a subject so I can decisively move it forward and successfully achieve my chosen outcome.

Flickering Opportunity to give my unwavering attention to an uncertain opportunity so I can use my ideas to create a definite result.

Flies Instinctive ability to deal with all the ideas that seem to be buzzing around rather than becoming annoyed with them.

Flight Opportunity to make a commitment to exploring my loftier thoughts and plans rather than trying to run away from them.

Flight attendant Aspect of my character that takes care of the practical aspects of a project so I can attend to some of my bigger ideas.

Flight crew Aspects of my character that draw on my knowledge by using well-rehearsed routines to deal with challenging plans and ideas.

Flight deck Situation where I have a clear view of where my project is heading and have all the resources I need to stay in full control.

Flight path Ability to understand where my current line of thinking is taking me so I can make any necessary adjustments to my plans.

Flight recorder Ability to become more aware of emerging ideas by having a clear understanding of the original basis of my previous thinking.

Flight simulator Ability to elevate my awareness by taking a definite course of action rather than appearing to go through the motions.

Flight test Opportunity to judge my performance in dealing with a challenging concept rather than letting people decide if I make the grade.

Flimsy Realization that I have substantial practical knowledge rather than being concerned about appearing inadequate to others.

Flinching Opportunity to engage with a potentially uncomfortable challenge rather than suddenly withdrawing in case it proves painful.

Fling Opportunity to connect more intimately with an exciting creative talent without feeling I have to throw everything else away.

Flinging Opportunity to use my power and strength to influence events from a distance instead of feeling I have to behave in a certain way.

Flint Ability to light my enthusiasm so I can get fired up about an idea, even though I may appear quite hard-edged to people.

Flip Opportunity to turn a situation around by making a firm and committed decision rather than leaving everything to chance.

Flip chart Ability to quickly understand the bigger picture about what I believe so I can share my perspectives with other people.

Flip-flop Ability to present my self-image to other people by always being open with them and taking steps to show my more casual approach.

Flippant Realization that I should make a more serious commitment to my talents rather than dismissing them as being of little consequence.

Flipper Instinctive ability to immerse myself in my feelings so I can naturally navigate my way through a complex emotional situation.

Flirting Opportunity to make a deeper connection to my creativity instead of just playing around with some exciting possibilities.

Float Ability to stay on top of a potentially emotional situation by keeping my spirits up and staying buoyantly enthusiastic.

Floating Opportunity to give myself more freedom to explore my feelings rather than becoming too emotionally attached to a situation.

F

Floatplane Ability to come up with a powerful and practical plan that will help me to rise above a potentially challenging emotional situation.

Flock Ability to draw the attention of other people to their collective purpose so we can work together in a harmonious and aligned way.

Floe Situation where I can achieve a more solid understanding of my deeper emotions, even though I may appear cool and detached.

Flogging Opportunity to consistently use my talents to make a real impact so I can have my creative value recognized by other people.

Flood Opportunity to rise above it all by powerfully channeling my deeper emotions so I don't end up feeling too washed out.

Flooded basement Situation where I can explore some of my foundational experiences so I can feel secure in working with my deeper emotions.

Flooded house Situation where I can take action to prevent intrusive emotions rather than allowing them to build up and overwhelm me.

Flooded toilet Situation where I can decisively let go of emotions that are no longer healthy for me instead of feeling my progress is blocked.

Floodgate Ability to powerfully channel my feelings so I can be more aware of my emotional boundaries and securely maintain them.

Flooding Situation where I can use my extensive learning and empathy to change my outlook rather than feeling drained by the experience.

Floodlight Ability to understand my feelings with much greater clarity by using the power of my experience to illuminate what is happening.

Floodplain Situation where I can see all the emerging emotional possibilities spread out in front of me in a straightforward way.

Flood tide Opportunity to experience the ebb and flow of my emotions as a natural rhythm rather than feeling overwhelmed by them.

Floodwater Opportunity to fulfill an emotional need by immersing myself in my feelings so I can gain deeper understanding and experience.

Floor Ability to support the fundamental principles I stand for so I can feel secure in sharing my viewpoint.

Floorboard Ability to support a fairly narrow set of beliefs that can help me feel more comfortable as I explore other viewpoints.

Floor cloth Ability to quickly clean up a potentially messy situation so I can continue to clearly support my beliefs.

Floor manager Aspect of my character that tries to influence how I share my beliefs so others can have a clear understanding of my value.

Florist Aspect of my character that can recognize the value of my blossoming talents and give other people the opportunity to bloom.

Floss Ability to provide a substantial basis for achieving my ambitions rather than feeling as if I have no real influence.

Flotation tank Situation where I can rise above the influence of my deeper emotions by making sure I maintain my personal boundaries.

Flotilla Ability to maintain my emotional stability by choosing a few different methods to navigate complex and unpredictable feelings.

Flotsam Ability to create a coherent outcome by using areas of my experience to stay on top of a potentially emotional situation.

F

Floundering Opportunity to take the confident steps I need to pursue an ambition rather than being overwhelmed by emotional concerns.

Flour Ability to rise to the occasion by using the fine details of some of the talents I have been cultivating.

Flourishing Opportunity to enthusiastically develop my creative talents so I can proudly display them to the people around me.

Flow Realization that I can naturally connect with my stream of consciousness by relaxing and immersing myself in my feelings.

Flower Natural ability to open up to my creative talents so I can encourage them to blossom while I staying grounded in reality.

Flower arranging Opportunity to carefully examine a range of my blossoming talents so I can choose to display them in a particular manner.

Flower bed Situation where I feel most at home and comfortable with my creativity and can take a relaxed approach to how it blossoms.

Flower garden Situation where I can display my blossoming talents to those around me and attract them toward my particular viewpoint.

Flowering Opportunity to develop my blossoming awareness so I can take a more colorful approach to attracting support for my growth.

Flowering tree Natural ability to develop my long-term spiritual growth so it continues to bloom while staying rooted in the practicalities.

Flowerpot Ability to gather together some of my accumulated experience and skill so I can take a fresh approach to fulfilling an ambition.

Flowing Opportunity to continue learning and keep my development moving by naturally adapting to whatever situation I may be in.

Fluctuating Opportunity to decisively make up my mind by fully engaging with a challenge, even though it may have its ups and downs.

Flu Opportunity to resolve an unhealthy situation by expressing myself very clearly instead of taking the situation lying down.

Flue Ability to consistently channel my creative output so I can convey my value rather than appearing to cloud the issue.

Fluent Ability to easily articulate the feelings I want to express instead of being hesitant in sharing my emotions.

Fluff Ability to take a lighter approach if I feel I have made a mistake rather than imagining it will have major consequences.

Fluffer Aspect of my character that helps me prepare myself so I can creatively conceive plans and ideas with other people.

Fluffy Realization that I can resolve a challenge by taking a tougher, harder approach rather than trying to keep everyone happy.

Fluid Ability to express my emotions in a positive way so I can keep them flowing, regardless of what shape I feel I may be in.

Fluke Opportunity to firmly connect to a deeper understanding of my creative instincts rather than leaving it all to chance.

Flume Ability to use my accumulated experience to quickly go deeper into my emotions so I can channel some powerful feelings.

Fluorescent Realization that positively brightening my outlook will naturally draw everyone's attention to my particular viewpoint.

Fluoride Ability to naturally develop my elemental feelings of strength and power so I can confidently display them to other people.

Flurry Ability to maintain clear thinking and keep myself calm instead of trying to rush around and keep everyone else happy.

Flush Opportunity to let go of some ideas and feelings I no longer need rather than appearing to be embarrassed about them.

Flute Ability to take my instinctive creativity in both hands so I can precisely channel my thoughts and express them gracefully.

Flutter Opportunity to choose a definite direction instead of switching backward and forward, leaving the outcome to chance.

Flux Opportunity to positively channel my energy rather than allowing it to be influenced by the ebb and flow of my emotional life.

Fly Instinctive ability to immerse myself in my thoughts so I can understand all the wider possibilities that are open to me.

Flyby Opportunity to observe my ideas in action so I have a more powerful understanding of how I originally came up with them.

Fly-fishing Opportunity to bring my instinctive feelings to the surface and safely land them rather than casting around for excuses.

Flying Opportunity to release myself from any weighty commitments so I have complete freedom to explore my thoughts and theories.

Flying boat Ability to maintain my stability by using a particular way of thinking to raise my awareness of a complex emotional situation.

Flying bomb Ability to use my widely influential ideas to create a positive transformation rather than blowing up at every opportunity.

Flying doctor Aspect of my character that rationally examines my thought processes and provides me with the clarity to resolve tensions.

Flying fish Instinctive ability to raise my awareness of my emotional life rather than getting too caught up in my way of thinking.

Flying machine Ability to use my thoughts and ideas to effortlessly produce an outcome of great practical value that displays my unique talents.

Flying saucer Ability to explore some apparently far-fetched thoughts and ideas that may initially seem alien and unfamiliar to me.

Flypaper Ability to be clearer in my thought processes by capturing some theories and ideas that have been bugging me for a while.

Foal Instinctive ability to develop my unconscious strength so I can use my natural enthusiasm to drive forward with my ambitions.

Foam Ability to let my ideas bubble up to the surface so I can clearly experience my underlying feelings and bring them to a head.

Fob Ability to quickly locate a method to unlock my hidden potential rather than trying to fool myself into thinking that it doesn't really matter.

Focus Ability to center my awareness so I can give my full attention to a particular point that I specifically need to emphasize.

Fodder Potential to fulfill my ambitions by satisfying my instinctive creativity and nourishing my continued growth and vitality.

Foe Aspect of my character that often seems to oppose my natural instincts but can encourage me to engage with a wider understanding.

Fog Natural opportunity to clear up any vague feelings about the prevailing mood so I can gain a much clearer perspective.

Fog bank Situation where I can get a feel for all the knowledge and experience I have accumulated so I can see its distinctive value.

Foghorn Ability to make myself more aware of the practical aspects of any looming challenges as I navigate an emotional situation.

Foil Ability to conduct myself in a powerful manner that reflects my brilliance rather than getting too wrapped up in the outcome.

Foiled Opportunity to resolve a challenging situation by taking decisive action rather than allowing it to reflect my frustrations.

F

Fold Opportunity to stand up for what I believe in so I can create a persistent feeling of comfort and security.

Folded Ability to make twice as much effort to achieve my ambitions instead of giving in to any apparent pressures around me.

Foliage Natural ability to absorb the power of my creative talent so I can use it to raise my wider awareness of my situation.

Folio Ability to shape my wide range of knowledge and experience so I can communicate to others how I see things.

Folk Aspects of my character that I am very familiar with and which give me a solid and supportive basis for my fundamental beliefs.

Folk dance Ability to embody my natural rhythms and take steps that reflect my basic behavioral patterns so I can bring them to life.

Folk song Ability to instinctively communicate with other people by giving voice to a beautiful and deeply felt message about my origins.

Follower Aspect of my character that can inspire others by adhering to a particular vision and committing to moving forward with it.

Following Opportunity to acknowledge where my ambitions are taking me so I can understand how to successfully support them.

Folly Situation where I can provide a much more substantial basis for my beliefs, even though they may appear foolish to others.

Foment Opportunity to take positive action so I can openly understand any unanswered needs and prevent any further disruption.

Fondle Essential opportunity to make the most of a situation by lovingly connecting with it and understanding how it touches me.

Fondly Realization that I can always continue to nurture my talent by affectionately showing my aptitude for doing what I love most.

Food Potential to fulfill my ambitions by satisfying my appetite for success so I can nourish my continued growth and vitality.

Food allergy Essential opportunity to understand my deeper ambitions rather than habitually overreacting to my current circumstances.

Food critic Aspect of my character that is always trying to achieve greater success, even though it can voice doubts about my accomplishments.

Food poisoning Opportunity to decisively respond to any professional challenges rather than leaving myself open to an unhealthy situation.

Food processor Opportunity to use a mix of my skills as I work my way through a situation so I can deal with any unsavory challenges.

Fool Aspect of my character that has no preconceptions about a particular challenge and that can resolve it by not taking it too seriously.

Foolproof Realization that I can consistently achieve success by understanding my more open approach and defending it against criticism.

Foot Essential ability to stay firmly grounded in my particular perspective so I can take practical steps to move into action.

Football Ability to play around with a potentially successful outcome so I can achieve some collective goals with people close to me.

Football player Aspect of my character that takes a series of specific steps to build up powerful connections so I can achieve my goals.

Football game Opportunity to play around with some fundamentally opposing approaches so I can successfully achieve my individual goals.

Football pass Situation where I can achieve a successful outcome by using a number of

F

angles to display my expertise to the people around me.

Football stadium Situation where I have a huge opportunity to play to my strengths so my achievements can be recognized by a wider audience.

Football team Aspects of my character that powerfully complement one another and work well together to help me achieve my goals.

Footbath Situation where I can feel relaxed and at home with my particular perspective and prepare myself to take the steps I need to.

Footbridge Situation where I can resolve a dilemma by taking steps to create a connection between two different areas of my life.

Foothold Situation where I have specific support for my viewpoint so I can maintain my position rather than feeling insecure about it.

Footlights Ability to understand my performance with much greater clarity by using the power of my wisdom to illuminate where I stand.

Footpath Situation where I can take definite steps to understand my direction in life and decide where it can potentially take me.

Footprint Ability to make a distinct impression by having the confidence and self-motivation to consistently stand firm in my beliefs.

Footstep Essential opportunity to use my self-motivation to take deliberate action as I engage with one practical challenge at a time.

Footstool Ability to express my viewpoint in a comfortable and relaxed manner so I can raise any steps I might need to take.

Footwear Ability to present my self-image to people by taking steps to display my viewpoint and how comfortable I am with it.

Forage Opportunity to feed my instinctive ambitions by exploring a variety of opportunities so I can achieve wider fulfillment.

Foray Opportunity to take forceful action to assert my ambitions rather than responding to any challenges by just being defensive.

Forbidden Opportunity to give myself permission to explore unknown areas of my character instead of feeling held back by others.

Force Opportunity to use the power of my talent to exert my individual influence rather than feeling I have to behave in a certain way.

Forced landing Opportunity to secure the future of a complex plan by taking a more down-to-earth approach that keeps it in touch with reality.

Force field Situation where I can use my powerful influence to focus my energy on a particular challenge and decide on my preferred outcome.

Force majeure Realization that I can use my superior strength to achieve an ambition rather than blaming any frustrations on the circumstances.

Forceps Ability to have a feel for both sides of a situation so I can take very specific and incisive action to resolve any tension.

Forcible shaving Opportunity to closely examine some of my own ideas instead of worrying that other people will expose my vulnerabilities.

Ford Situation where I can resolve an ongoing emotional dilemma by using my awareness of what is happening just below the surface.

Forearm Essential ability to assert my power so I can prepare myself to take action and deal with any challenges.

Foreboding Opportunity to use my intuitive awareness to create a positive outcome rather than being anxious about what might occur.

Forecast Ability to understand how the prevailing mood might develop so I can make the most of whatever outcomes may emerge.

F

Forefather Aspect of my character that has a profound understanding of my fundamental power and encourages me to develop my potential.

Forefront Situation where I can decisively push forward with an ambitious project by consistently staying ahead of any emerging challenges.

Forehead Essential ability to use my natural wisdom to support my emerging ideas so I can smooth out any challenges I encounter.

Foreign Realization that I can always expand my horizons by exploring unfamiliar aspects of myself so I can discover my wider potential.

Foreign body Ability to make the most of an unexpected opportunity rather than trying to avoid experiences that appear unfamiliar.

Foreigner Aspect of my character that can help me understand an unfamiliar situation so I have the chance to use my native talent.

Foreknowledge Realization that I can use my skills and abilities to create my chosen future instead of hoping it will somehow just appear.

Forelock Essential ability to develop my fundamental styles of thinking rather than feeling I have to hold them back for others.

Foremost Realization that I need to explore what appears to be more significant for me instead of being concerned where it might leave me.

Forensic scientist Aspect of my character that is constantly looking for vital clues so I can understand my situation in greater detail.

Forensic team Aspects of my character that help me achieve a wider understanding of vital details that I otherwise may have missed.

Foreplay Opportunity to explore some conceptual possibilities before following my instincts and making deeper creative connections.

Foreseeable Realization that I can use my personal vision to create a different outcome

rather than feeling as if it is predetermined.

Foresight Ability to focus on a particular objective so I can achieve my aims and be aware of what might emerge in the future.

Foreskin Essential ability to feel comfortable with my natural creativity so I am happy to open up and reveal what I believe in.

Forest Situation where I can explore the rich diversity and natural growth potential of all the undiscovered aspects of my character.

Forest warden Aspect of my character that takes responsibility for looking after my natural development and the opportunities it provides.

Foretell Opportunity to openly speak up about my specific plans for the future rather than staying quiet and leaving it all to fate.

Forever Realization that I can permanently transform my situation by taking time to understand what emerges from moment to moment.

Forewarned Realization that I can step courageously into a challenging situation rather than feeling I have to approach it too cautiously.

Forfeit Ability to assertively claim my value and have it recognized by other people instead of giving up on my contribution.

Forge Opportunity to powerfully shape a practical outcome in a heated situation by being open and honest about what I value.

Forgery Ability to clearly identify what is of real value to me rather than feeling that I have to follow everyone else's example.

Forget-me-not Natural ability to open up to my creative talents so I can encourage them to blossom by remembering what is important to me.

Forgetting Opportunity to remember my purpose in life rather than ignoring it and hoping that everything will go my way.

Forgiveness Opportunity to accept

apparent quirks and flaws in my nature instead of always blaming myself for a particular outcome.

Forgotten Realization that I have accumulated a huge amount of wisdom and experience that will always spring to mind when I need it to.

Forgotten baby Opportunity to devote precious time to developing my unique talents rather than neglecting my natural creative capacity.

Forgotten children Opportunity to pay more attention to ideas that are close to my heart instead of ignoring my future potential.

Forgotten keys Opportunity to remember how much freedom I have rather than feeling I am unavoidably stuck in my present position.

Fork Ability to work my way through a particular ambition by seeing what sticks out for me and basing decisions on those aspects.

Forklift Ability to raise the value of my practical abilities by using my drive to powerfully engage with them at a fundamental level.

Forlorn Realization that I can take great comfort in what I have achieved so far rather than feeling that my situation is hopeless.

Form Ability to shape my beliefs about a situation so I can understand the best way to display my skills to other people.

Formal Realization that I can be more effective by working with my own processes rather than having to conform to conventional methods.

Formaldehyde Ability to preserve a particular aspect of my creativity so I can achieve a clearer understanding of it at a future date.

Formation Opportunity to decisively arrange a variety of thoughts and ideas so I can use them to influence a more tangible outcome.

Formless Realization that I can become

more clearly aware of a distinct possibility by being very specific in shaping exactly what I need.

Formula Ability to consistently identify the more complex aspects of a situation so I can always achieve my desired result.

Formulation Opportunity to specifically express what I am feeling so that I can easily articulate it to the people around me.

Fornication Opportunity to become more intimately aware of my creative talents without worrying about what others may think of me.

Forsaken Opportunity to rediscover part of myself that I have been neglecting rather than feeling I have to abandon it completely.

Fort Situation where I can guard against potential conflict by understanding my strengths and establishing firm personal boundaries.

Fortification Situation where I can build my confidence and feel comfortable in my position, even though the situation may be challenging.

Fortress Situation where I bring together my practical strengths and abilities so that I can defend myself against any apparent threats.

Fortuitous Realization that I can take deliberate action to reach my intended outcome rather than hoping I will just get lucky.

Fortunate Realization that I can take the opportunity to amass a more impressive sense of self-worth instead of leaving it to chance.

Fortune Ability to accumulate an abundant wealth of experience and wisdom rather than feeling I am lacking in any real value.

Fortune-teller Aspect of my character that gives me the power to speak my mind so I can choose my future rather than leaving it to fate.

Forum Situation where I can make a decision by understanding my individual beliefs rather than listening to everyone else's opinion.

F

Forward Opportunity to work my way through a sequence of events by being openly confident about the power and strength of my talent.

Fossil Ability to use my instinctive creativity to clearly shape an outcome rather than feeling my future is set in stone.

Fossil hunter Aspect of my character that helps me revitalize my practical talents rather than feeling they are buried forever.

Fossil record Ability to observe my instinctive reactions so I can understand how to transform my habitual patterns of behavior.

Foster child Aspect of my character that embodies my uniquely precious talents, even though they may seem unfamiliar to begin with.

Foster parent Aspect of my character that provides me with a fundamental sense of security and gives me a more familiar sense of belonging.

Foul Realization that I can take a fair and clean approach to resolving a challenge instead of feeling that it will bring me down.

Foundation garment Ability to present my self-image to others in a way that lets me support my beliefs and how they shape my outlook.

Foundations Ability to provide a character-building experience by securely supporting my personal development and individual viewpoints.

Foundation stone Ability to provide substantial support so I can raise my level of awareness and steadily maintain a solid presence.

Foundry Situation where I can use my intense creativity to transform my fundamental power so I can shape a definite outcome.

Fountain Situation where I can raise my spirits by channeling my inspirational feelings so I can celebrate their abundance and power.

Fountain pen Ability to uniquely express

my talents by channeling my experiences so I can direct their flow and get to the point.

Four-leaf clover Natural ability to enjoy the sweet taste of success by taking a more healthy approach rather than relying on good fortune.

Four-wheel drive Ability to use my motivation and energy to make progress into less familiar territory and deal with challenges I encounter.

Fowl Instinctive ability to stay in my comfort zone and fulfill ambitions that are closer to home instead of spreading my wings.

Fox Instinctive ability to use my intelligence and resourcefulness to make the most of any challenges that require native cunning.

Foxglove Natural ability to open up to my creative talents so I can encourage them to blossom and stimulate my essential passion.

Foyer Aspect of myself that has the capacity to open me up to new experiences so I can develop my potential talents and skills.

Fracas Opportunity to peacefully resolve an inner conflict that has been disturbing me rather than noisily sounding off about it.

Fracking Opportunity to take a more natural approach to channeling my creative power instead of always feeling I am under pressure.

Fraction Ability to use my individual resources to help achieve a greater success rather than feeling I am being divisive in any way.

Fracture Opportunity to understand both sides of a situation and their combined potential so I can make a much stronger connection.

Fragile Realization that I have the underlying strength to respond much more robustly rather than behaving in too delicate a manner.

Fragment Ability to piece together the different aspects of my ambitions so I can have a greater understanding of what I want to achieve.

F

Fragrance Ability to create a pleasing atmosphere so I can attract other people to my perspective and share it with them.

Frail Realization that I have the power to firmly deal with a challenging situation rather than feeling weak and vulnerable.

Frame Ability to provide a clear context for a situation so I can establish some boundaries and make my position more apparent.

Frame-up Opportunity to clearly share what actually happened rather than allowing others to manipulate my personal boundaries.

Frank Realization that I need to be completely honest with myself about my deeper intentions so I can openly communicate them.

Frantic Realization that I can make most productive use of my restless energy by deciding to take a more calm, composed approach.

Fraud Opportunity to make a fundamental transformation by having the confidence to prove my worth to people so I can own it.

Fraud squad Aspects of my character that work together to clearly demonstrate my value to others so I can feel more self-possessed.

Frayed Realization that I need to maintain my personal boundaries with others rather than letting them constantly get on my nerves.

Frazzled Realization that I need to maintain my levels of energy and determination instead of allowing circumstances to wear me down.

Freak Realization that I can often encounter a monster opportunity by moving outside my normal experience into less familiar areas.

Freckle Essential ability to feel comfortable with any apparent flaws in my viewpoint rather than trying to conceal them.

Free Realization that I have the liberty to make my own choices and act on them rather than feeling constrained by circumstances.

Freedom Opportunity to make the most of emerging possibilities by using them to expand my awareness instead of always limiting myself.

Free fall Opportunity to jump at a big chance so I can decide my own outcome rather than wait for others to make a decision.

Freelance Ability to take decisive action based on my skills instead of feeling I have to conform to recognized procedures.

Free-running Opportunity to quickly motivate myself so I can take powerful steps to energetically negotiate a series of major obstacles.

Freewheel Opportunity to make a revolutionary discovery by realizing that I don't always have to exert myself to keep things rolling along.

Free will Realization that I create my own perceptions of the world around me instead of thinking I have to leave everything to fate.

Freeze Opportunity to stop for a while so that I can consider my options in a cool and detached manner, without becoming too emotional.

Freezer Ability to stay cool and maintain my composure about how I plan to successfully fulfill a number of long-term ambitions.

Freight Ability to convey the fundamental value of my expertise to other people so I can have it fully acknowledged by them.

Freight ship Ability to understand the value of my learning and experience so I can navigate emotional highs and lows.

Freight train Ability to convey the great value of my practical expertise to the people around me so I can reach my career objectives.

French fries Potential to fulfill an ambition and sustain my progress by taking a healthy approach, even though it seems quite foreign to me.

French window Ability to clearly understand my perspective so I can develop possibilities that may have seemed closed.

F

Frenetic Realization that I can successfully reach my chosen outcome by directing my energy in a more balanced and considered way.

Frenzy Opportunity to get excited about a stimulating idea without feeling that I have to drive other people crazy with it.

Frequent Realization that I can use my habitual behavior patterns to help me to connect with a rare opportunity and make the most of it.

Fresh Realization that I can make a new beginning by taking a different approach rather than tiring of the same old situation.

Fret Ability to choose how I want to pitch one of my ideas rather than worrying about the tone I should take.

Fretting Opportunity to understand the ins and outs of an intricate situation rather than allowing anxieties to gnaw away at me.

Fretwork Ability to cut my way through the potential intricacies of a situation instead of feeling I always have to embellish my ideas.

Friction Ability to gain traction for one of my ambitions rather than feeling I'm rubbing people up the wrong way.

Fridge Ability to preserve my composure and keep my cool so I can choose how to use my resources to fulfill long-term ambitions.

Fried Potential to indulge in my appetite for success by taking a fresh approach so I can exercise a healthier perspective.

Friend Aspect of my character that I am well acquainted with and can always rely on to behave consistently and supportively.

Friendly Realization that I am already acquainted with what I need to do so I can make the most of an emerging possibility.

Fright Opportunity to suddenly make a bold and transformative choice by having the courage to show myself as I would like.

Frightened Realization that I have the power to courageously confront any of my concerns so I can live the life I truly want to lead.

Frigid Realization that I can be more successful creatively by warmly opening up to new concepts rather than coolly rejecting them.

Frill Ability to enjoy being at the edge of my comfort zone rather than feeling I may be taking an unnecessary risk.

Fringe Situation where I feel comfortable with my individual perspective instead of feeling too on edge about my beliefs.

Frock Ability to present my self-image to people in a way that gives me the freedom to display my taste and sense of occasion.

Frog Instinctive ability to make a creative leap so I can immerse myself in my emotions and look beyond what I see on the surface.

Frogman Aspect of my character that has the courage to explore my emotional life in greater depth so I can understand it more profoundly.

Frog-marched Opportunity to assertively pursue one of my ambitions rather than feeling I am being forced to follow particular steps.

Frog spawn Instinctive ability to use my deeper sentiments and fertile imagination to produce a large number of transformative ideas.

Frond Natural ability to absorb the power of my creative talent so I can differentiate in a healthy way the finer aspects of my growth.

Front Situation where I can push forward with an ambitious project rather than trying to appear progressive to other people.

Front door Ability to control the connection between my inner and outer worlds so I can openly use it to maintain my sense of privacy.

Frontier Situation where I can discover wider opportunities for personal development by courageously going to the edge of what I know.

F

Frost Natural opportunity to get beyond any superficial coolness so I can clearly experience my emotions at a much deeper level.

Frostbite Essential opportunity to take confident and incisive action rather than allowing the prevailing mood to numb my senses.

Froth Ability to look below surface appearances so I can understand the more substantial feelings that are bubbling up for me.

Frowning Opportunity to open up to who I really am rather than always being concerned that other people will disapprove of my viewpoint.

Frozen Realization that the quickest way to get things moving is to use a warm and friendly approach rather than playing it cool.

Frozen food Potential to fulfill my ambitions and satisfy my appetite for success by staying emotionally cool and looking to the future.

Frugal Realization that I should welcome the opportunity to indulge my talents rather than feeling that they are a limited resource.

Fruit Natural ability to have a healthy awareness of my developing talents and how I can use them to achieve some fresh ambitions.

Fruit bowl Ability to keep myself open and receptive to the variety of ways in which I can fulfill my needs in a healthy manner.

Fruitcake Potential to fulfill a shared ambition and celebrate collective success, even though I may seem quite eccentric to other people.

Fruitless Realization that my continuing growth will eventually produce a healthy result, even though it seems unproductive now.

Fruit machine Ability to produce an outcome of great practical value by aligning my skills and resources instead of leaving it to chance.

Frustration Realization that my persistent efforts will soon make a fundamental breakthrough, rather than feeling it is difficult to succeed.

Frying pan Ability to fulfill a potential ambition by gathering knowledge and experience so I can take a fresher approach.

Fudge Potential to fill a short-term ambition that seems very attractive by taking a softer option and exaggerating its value.

Fuel Ability to refine my raw creative power so I can use it to motivate my drive for success in a more spirited manner.

Fugitive Aspect of my character that courageously confronts any challenging circumstances instead of continually running away from them.

Fulfillment Realization that the most effective way to create value is to understand my fundamental needs so I can successfully satisfy them.

Full Realization that I have an abundance of talent and experience, instead of being concerned that I have nothing to offer.

Fully clothed Ability to present my self-image to people by choosing to conceal my private life and taking control of how I appear.

Fumble Opportunity to get a grip on what is happening rather than feeling that I have no way to control the outcome I desire.

Fumes Ability to sense evidence of a fundamental transformation in my way of thinking, even though it may appear to cloud the issue.

Fumigate Opportunity to use a different way of thinking to rid myself of an annoying situation rather than allowing it to plague me.

Fuming Opportunity to use my creative talent to positively influence my immediate surroundings instead of being angry about them.

Fun Realization that I can achieve an enormous amount of pleasure by spending time on a task that may initially seem quite difficult.

F

Function Opportunity to gather a variety of my skills and talents together so I can have a wider understanding of my deeper purpose.

Functional Realization that I have all I need to achieve my chosen outcome rather than feeling I am not particularly effective.

Fund Ability to draw on my accumulated knowledge and experience so I can use it to create a valuable transformation in my life.

Funeral Opportunity to acknowledge a once-vital aspect of my past so I can peacefully lay it to rest and move on into a new future.

Funeral parlor Situation where I can be more comfortable about my neglected talents so I can be more open to ways of revitalizing them.

Fungus Natural ability to identify growth opportunities that I may have been neglecting so I can use them for personal transformation.

Fun house Situation where I have the security and support to explore the amusing and surprising aspects of my inner and outer lives.

Funnel Ability to collect my wider feelings so I can channel my emotions and direct them toward achieving a coherent outcome.

Funny Opportunity to resolve a potential drama so I can understand my deeper ambitions rather than taking myself too seriously.

Fun run Opportunity to quickly motivate myself so I can take some powerful steps to understand what will give me pleasure.

Fur Instinctive ability to develop ideas that emerge from my fundamental behaviors so I can be more comfortable with them.

Fur coat Ability to present my self-image to other people in a way that helps me indulge myself in some of my fundamental behaviors.

Fur hat Ability to present my self-image to people in a way that draws attention to my

viewpoint and gives me a warm feeling.

Furious Realization that I can use my feelings of intense passion to achieve a constructive outcome instead of appearing unreasonable.

Furnace Ability to get fired up about how I can make a creative transformation by concentrating my power and channeling my energy.

Furniture Ability to feel comfortable with my habitual behaviors so that I can rely on them for consistent support in familiar situations.

Furrow Ability to take a down-to-earth approach so that I can open up the deeper possibilities instead of being anxious about them.

Furtive Realization that I can be very open about how I feel and what I hope to achieve rather than trying to conceal it from people.

Fury Realization that I can gracefully channel my seemingly uncontrollable passions rather than punishing myself for my behavior.

Fuse Ability to take my time so I can choose exactly the right moment to share my feelings rather than blowing up about it.

Fuselage Situation where I can explore the main body of a powerful plan so I can understand what it will take to get it off the ground.

Fusion Opportunity to bring some of my different qualities together so I can transform them into something much more powerful.

Fusion reactor Ability to tap into a vital source of personal energy by understanding how to combine some of my wildly different qualities.

Fuss Opportunity to act decisively and quickly reach my chosen outcome instead of anxiously involving myself in needless activity.

F

Futile Realization that understanding my purpose always produces a valuable result rather than feeling that my efforts are worthless.

Futon Ability to support my need for rest and relaxation so I can take a more spontaneous approach to exploring my creative urges.

Future Opportunity to achieve a successful outcome by building on past experience so I can understand what is emerging in the present.

Fuzziness Realization that I can achieve a definite result by setting distinct boundaries around the particular area I am working in.

F

Gab Opportunity to show how gifted I am at communicating by speaking my mind rather than just talking with no purpose.

Gadget Ability to use my ingenuity to perform a specific task so I can consistently achieve my desired response from other people.

Gaff Ability to quickly catch on to what is surfacing in my emotional life instead of feeling that I have made a big mistake.

Gaffer Aspect of my character that consistently supplies me with the power I need to become more aware of my personal story.

Gaffer tape Ability to make some strong connections so I can convey my sense of power in a coherent and effective manner.

Gag Ability to see the funny side of a situation rather than holding myself back and not saying what I would like to.

Gagged Opportunity to honestly open up and express what I think instead of always allowing other people to put words into my mouth.

Gag order Opportunity to give myself the permission to say how I feel rather than trying to keep everyone happy by saying nothing.

Gain Opportunity to successfully develop one of my ambitions by encouraging other people to realize the value of my contribution.

Gait Ability to observe my levels of self-motivation and energy so I can clearly understand the steps I need to take.

Gaiter Ability to present my self-image to other people in a way that allows me to protect my fundamental status so I can stay motivated.

Galaxy Situation where I can open up to my much wider universal awareness and all the creative potential it holds for me.

Gale Opportunity to stand firm and stay flexible as I encounter powerful thoughts and ideas that seem beyond my immediate control.

Gallant Realization that I have the courage to openly demonstrate how I really feel rather than behaving in a timid manner.

Gall bladder Essential ability to transform my emotional life by gracefully getting rid of any residual bitterness I may be feeling.

Galleon Ability to use the prevailing atmosphere to keep myself on an even keel as I work through some of my habitual behaviors.

Gallery Situation where I can openly see the value of what I create so I can confidently invite other people to recognize my talents.

Galley Aspect of myself that maintains my energy levels and looks after my needs as I navigate an emotionally complex situation.

Gallon Ability to understand my capacity for dealing with a potentially emotional situation so I can be sure I will measure up.

Galloping Instinctive ability to harness unconscious energy so I can use natural power to make faster progress toward my objective.

Gallows Situation where I need to be more supportive of my traditional stance rather than feeling that I will suddenly let myself down.

Gambler Aspect of my character that honors my creative value by choosing my preferred outcome rather than leaving it to chance.

Gambling Opportunity to fully recognize the value of my ingenuity by deciding my chosen result instead of hoping I'll just get lucky.

Game Opportunity to use my skill to play around with ways of achieving my goals, even though the outcome may seem uncertain.

Gamekeeper Aspect of my character that has a unique understanding of my creative instincts so I can nurture their transformational power.

Game pad Ability to skillfully control the outcome of an uncertain situation, even though I just seem to be playing around with it.

Game show Opportunity to display my talents to other people by demonstrating my unique skill in working through a series of challenges.

Game show host Aspect of my character that asks powerful questions about what I'm trying to achieve and lets me find the answers.

Game warden Aspect of my character that takes responsibility for looking after my wilder instincts and the creative value they embody.

Gander Instinctive ability to take a good look at my plans and ideas so I feel fully confident in going the distance with them.

Gang Aspects of my character that I may be unacquainted with can work together to reveal undiscovered strengths and talents.

Gangland Situation where I can take a more practical and down-to-earth approach so I can openly display my range of expertise.

Gangplank Ability to follow a very specific course of action that will help me embark upon a fundamental emotional transformation.

Gangrene Essential opportunity to completely transform an unhealthy situation that has been eating away at my power and strength.

Gangster Aspect of my character that can often be intimidated by my power rather than having the confidence to assert my true value.

Gangway Situation where I can enter a deeper sense of safety and security for the best way to navigate some complex emotions.

Gannet Instinctive ability to rise above any practical concerns so I can dive right into an emotional situation and get to the point.

Gantry Ability to use an existing framework to provide me with the support I need to consistently move forward with my ambitions.

Gap Situation where I can see an opening to use my skills and abilities instead of feeling that I have to make a leap of faith.

Gaping Opportunity to open myself up to some wider possibilities rather than appearing surprised at what is developing.

Gap year Opportunity to take a long-term view so I can open myself up to using my accumulated experience in a different area.

Garage Situation where I feel that I have the safety and security to consistently maintain my progress with my drives and ambitions.

Garage door Ability to open myself up to possibilities for using my drive and ambition that may have seemed closed to me.

Garbage Ability to decide what behaviors are no longer of any value to me so I can make a clear choice to gracefully let them go.

Garbage truck Ability to employ powerful drive to provide a valuable shift in my behaviors to make progress toward my ambitions.

Garbled Opportunity to clearly communicate my intentions to the people around me rather than feeling confused about what I need to say.

Garden Situation where I can cultivate my relationships and interests so they will continue to naturally blossom around me.

Garden center Situation where I can make some firm choices about the talents I would like to develop so I can put them into practice.

Gardener Aspect of my character that makes a continuing effort to nurture my wide variety of talents and encourages them to blossom.

G

Garden gate Situation where I can make the choice to step outside my immediate interests and explore new ways to cultivate my talents.

Gardening Opportunity to cultivate the down-to-earth aspects of my fundamental relationships so they continue to flourish healthily.

Garden party Opportunity to happily celebrate my special skills and varied talents by sharing them with the people around me.

Garden path Situation where I can take steps to understand my natural talent so I can decide if it is leading me where I want to go.

Garden shed Situation where I can collect the resources I need to look after the practical aspects of my long-term relationships.

Gargling Opportunity to be consistently clear about any emotional challenges so I can speak up and honestly express my feelings.

Gargoyle Ability to protect myself from any imagined threats by confronting some of my habitual behaviors that concern me.

Garland Ability to surround myself with a variety of blossoming talent so I can encourage my own creativity to really bloom.

Garlic Ability to protect myself in an unhealthy relationship by using my good taste to guard against any potential drains on my energy.

Garnet Ability to attract other people to the value of my talents by passionately using my skills in a more vital and exciting way.

Garnish Ability to quickly get the flavor of a situation rather than feeling I always have to embellish my particular approach.

Garret Aspect of myself where I can gather together some of my more creative plans and ideas so I can expand on them in the future.

Garrison Situation where I feel more comfortable about my wider social relationships instead of feeling I have to always defend them.

Garrote Ability to create a fundamental transformation in my life by saying exactly what I feel rather than becoming all choked up.

Garter Ability to present my self-image to other people in a way that gives me the support to take smooth and individual action.

Gas Ability to let my thoughts and ideas flow so I can expand on their value, regardless of the shape I think I am in.

Gas chamber Situation where I can open myself up to fresh ideas rather than confining myself to poisonous, self-destructive thinking.

Gas-fired Ability to use my ideas to take a more passionate approach to a challenge so I can create a vital transformation.

Gash Opportunity to heal some hurt feelings by taking decisive action to look more closely at both sides of a painful argument.

Gasket Ability to smooth out any irregularities so I can feel emotionally secure about a situation that might leave me feeling drained.

Gaslight Ability to use my way of thinking to understand a situation with much greater clarity so I can illuminate what is happening.

Gas mask Ability to present my self-image to other people in a way that will reveal my real thoughts rather than trying to conceal them.

Gasoline Ability to refine my raw creative spirit so I can use it to fuel my drive for continuing success in achieving my ambitions.

Gasp Opportunity to inspire myself more consistently by opening up to my undiscovered talents so I am less surprised by their power.

Gas pipeline Ability to reliably communicate the power of my ideas to others, even though they may appear to be ideologically distant.

Gas storage tank Ability to collect my thoughts and ideas in a more contained manner so I can channel them effectively into my work.

G

Gastric band Ability to maintain a positive and healthy approach by being structured and specific in how I choose to fulfill my ambitions.

Gastropub Situation where I can comfortably fulfill ambitions by taking a relaxed viewpoint as I reacquaint myself with my talents.

Gasworks Situation where I can express the fundamental value of my thinking to others so I can continue to develop new ideas.

Gate Situation where I can make the choice to step beyond a self-imposed boundary so I can enter into a new phase of my life.

Gateau Potential to fulfill a shared ambition and celebrate collective success by working through the different levels of a challenge.

Gated community Situation where I can define some personal boundaries to gather the talent and resources I need.

Gatekeeper Aspect of my character that maintains personal boundaries and helps me decide what influences I will allow into my life.

Gatepost Ability to fully support my personal boundaries so I have a firm reference point that everything else can revolve around.

Gathering Opportunity to bring all my different qualities together so I can demonstrate the range of my expertise and experience.

Gaudy Realization that I can share my talents in a more refined manner rather than having to show them off in a brash and vulgar way.

Gauge Ability to take a more precise view of my progress so I can use that information to successfully influence the outcome.

Gaunt Opportunity to flesh out one of my ambitions by taking in a fuller awareness of what I need to move forward.

Gauntlet Ability to present my self-image to other people in a way that helps me shape my future without being too challenging.

Gauze Ability to provide a more substantial basis for any hurt feelings I may have so I can make myself feel more comfortable.

Gavel Ability to hammer out a firm decision so I can achieve an effective outcome by having a persistently forceful point of view.

Gawk Opportunity to realize that I understand more than I think I do rather than appearing surprised by what is emerging.

Gay Realization that I am very happy about how I appear to other people rather than being too concerned about what they think of me.

Gaze Essential opportunity to look more deeply inside myself so I can understand the value people see in me.

Gazelle Instinctive ability to make a graceful creative leap, even though I might be wary of jmping to a premature conclusion.

Gear Ability to decisively adjust my progress based on the prevailing conditions and the resources I currently have access to.

Gearbox Ability to move toward my objective by conveying personal power in the most appropriate manner in the circumstances.

Gear lever Ability to make a small but decisive action so I can choose the most engaging way to drive forward with my ambitions.

Gecko Instinctive ability to stick with what I feel comfortable so I can continue to express my fundamental creativity.

Geek Aspect of my character that can gracefully resolve a situation without feeling I have to become obsessed by it.

Geese Instinctive ability to align my thoughts so I can go to great lengths to ensure that other people see my way of thinking.

Geisha Aspect of my character that unquestioningly looks after the creative needs of others in a traditional and habitual manner.

Gel Ability to bring together a number of different influences so I can take a firmer approach to a potentially messy situation.

G

Gelignite Ability to mold my potentially explosive behavior to the circumstances rather than letting myself blow up unexpectedly.

Gem Ability to attract attention to one of my specific talents by displaying it to others in a clear and structured way.

Gemstone Ability to attract other people to the value of my talents by always being firm without feeling I need to be too hard-edged.

Gender Essential opportunity to become more intimately aware of the aspects of my creativity I prefer to share with other people.

Gender bender Aspect of my character that can make further creative advances by having a more flexible approach to displaying my talents.

Genealogist Aspect of my character that is familiar with habitual behavior patterns and understands where I am coming from.

General Aspect of my character that can make me feel special by commanding respect from others in a whole range of situations.

General anesthetic Ability to healthily work through any painful feelings I may encounter rather than trying to completely avoid them.

Generator Ability to use my creative flow to get charged up about the potential for using my energy in a consistently exciting way.

Generic character Ability to create a better understanding of my standout qualities so I can take meaningful action with them.

Generous Realization that sharing my creative gifts and talents usually opens up even more valuable opportunities for me to explore.

Genes Essential ability to understand the fundamental nature of my knowledge and experience so I can convey it to others.

Genetically modified Ability to understand my fundamental nature so I can work with it rather than trying to change it in any way.

Genetic engineering Opportunity to use the value of my natural talent and experience rather than contriving a particular outcome.

Genie Aspect of my character that can courageously achieve practical results rather than wishing I had the bottle to do it.

Genitals Essential ability to conceive new ideas by making fundamental connections with people so I can channel my unique creativity.

Genius Aspect of my character that has an exceptional capacity to use one of my unique talents in a hugely creative and original manner.

Gentleman Aspect of my character that behaves in a kind and sensitive manner so I can use my charm to resolve any tough challenges.

Gently Realization that I can achieve much firmer results by taking an uncompromising approach that enables me to use my sensitivity.

Genuine Realization that sharing my authentic feelings with other people is the most powerful way for them to recognize my expertise.

Geological hammer Ability to tackle a challenge by taking time to persistently use my strength and power to uncover deeper truths.

Geologist Aspect of my character that can achieve a profound awareness of the present by understanding how past experiences have shaped me.

Geometric Ability to shape my circumstances by understanding all the different angles of a situation so I can face up to any challenges.

Geostationary Ability to maintain my distance so I can continue to operate at a high level and stay on top of a rapidly changing situation.

Geothermal Ability to go much deeper into the practical aspects of a situation so I can release some profoundly creative energy.

G

Geranium Natural ability to open up to my talents so I can resolve a particular challenge while staying firmly grounded in reality.

Gerbil Instinctive ability to look after one of my pet projects so I can deal with any concerns that have been gnawing away at me.

Geriatric Realization that I can make a new start by drawing on my wealth of experience to keep myself consistently motivated.

Geriatric ward Situation where I can feel more comfortable by healthily resolving tensions that may have concerned me in my life.

Germ Natural ability to develop an apparently insignificant idea while being able to remain immune from any unwelcome criticism.

Germination Natural opportunity to help healthy ideas sprout from some of my practical skills that may have been lying dormant.

Germ warfare Opportunity to deal with an ongoing inner conflict by building up my natural resilience so I can achieve a healthy outcome.

Gestation Essential opportunity to allow a plan I have conceived to just develop in its own time rather than trying to force it out.

Gesture Essential opportunity to take an action so I can convey my deeper feelings about an event that has really moved me.

Getaway car Ability to use personal ambition and drive to quickly move on from a situation where my value is not being recognized.

Getting divorced Opportunity to be released from a major commitment so I can regain independence and devote more time to myself.

Getting lost Opportunity to explore where I want to go in life rather than feeling I always have to show up in a particular way.

Getting married Opportunity to honor my promises to others, even though it involves releasing myself from previous commitments.

Getting rescued Opportunity to feel more secure about my future by giving myself freedom to step outside my comfort zone.

Geyser Situation where I can channel my deeper, more powerful emotions so I can choose how to routinely share them.

Ghastly Realization that I can resolve a potentially upsetting situation by courageously stepping forward and taking control of it.

Gherkin Potential to fulfill an ambition by trying to preserve my healthy outlook until I can connect with some fresh opportunities.

Ghetto Situation where I can move beyond externally imposed boundaries so I can access the resources I need to succeed.

Ghetto blaster Ability to quietly communicate some of my more powerful theories and ideas rather than trying to force them on others.

Ghost Aspect of my character that I thought was dead and buried but needs to be either laid to rest or brought back to life.

Ghost animal Opportunity to revitalize my creative instincts so I can regain my motivation to express the value of my natural wisdom.

Ghost child Opportunity to reconnect with my most precious talents so I can continue to embody my potential for growth and love.

Ghostly apparition Opportunity to achieve substantial awareness of what will make me feel most alive instead of going by appearances.

Ghostly figure Ability to come to grips with the value of my fundamental talents rather than always worrying about the shape I am in.

Ghostly lover Aspect of my character that can make advances in helping me become intimately aware of my creative potential.

Ghost town Situation where I can revitalize my social life instead of always ending up in circumstances that seem hauntingly familiar.

G

Ghost train Ability to follow a set of guidelines that can motivate me to progress in my ambitions without being afraid of the outcome.

Ghoul Aspect of my character that allows other people to feed off my energy rather than contributing something more substantial for me.

Giant Aspect of my character that embodies my greater strength and power to help me be the biggest person I can possibly be.

Gibberish Ability to clearly communicate my viewpoints and ideas to other people instead of thinking I am talking nonsense.

Gibbet Ability to make decisive progress after a transformational experience rather than feeling I am just hanging around.

Gibbon Instinctive ability to understand my natural creativity by going to great lengths to copy people and adapt their methods.

Giddy Realization that I can achieve a much clearer understanding by choosing a definite direction rather than acting impulsively.

Gift Ability to recognize the value of one of my unique talents so other people can celebrate and acknowledge it.

Gift certificate Ability to have the value of my creative contribution recognized by other people so I can choose how to use my skills.

Gift wrapping Ability to take good care of my most valuable talents rather than becoming too involved in the surrounding circumstances.

Gig Opportunity to engage with a challenging creative situation so I can achieve a much wider understanding of my expertise.

Giggle Essential opportunity to be more serious about an apparently inconsequential challenge so I can enjoy the experience.

Gigolo Aspect of my character that can become more intimately aware of my creative strengths rather than trying to cheapen them.

Gilet Ability to present my self-image to other people by having the confidence to take action and clearly signal my intentions.

Gills Instinctive ability to stay inspired and keep a clear head when I immerse myself more fully in my deeper emotional life.

Gimmick Ability to attract attention to my authentic expertise rather than feeling that I have to take a more contrived approach.

Ginger Ability to use my good taste to enthusiastically get to the root of a challenge so I can add a sense of excitement to it.

Gingerbread Potential to fulfill an ambition by recognizing my fundamental need for excitement and ensuring my value is acknowledged.

Gingerly Realization that I can take a more lively approach to challenging situations instead of worrying about any deep-rooted anxieties.

Giraffe Instinctive ability to raise my overall awareness by sticking my neck out and being confident in my point of view.

Gird Opportunity to hold a situation securely together so I can prepare myself for any challenges that may be closing in on me.

Girder Ability to provide substantial support for some of my thoughts and opinions rather than always sticking to rigid beliefs.

Girdle Ability to present my self-image to people in a way that pulls all my creative powers together and attractively displays them.

Girl Aspect of my character that embodies my growing wisdom and has the potential to develop my creativity and intuition even further.

Girl band Aspects of my character that can work together harmoniously so I can use my instinctive creativity to realize my ambitions.

Girlfriend Aspect of my character that helps me become more intimately aware of my creativity so I can connect more intuitively to it.

Giveaway Opportunity to have other people recognize the true worth of my talents rather than feeling that they are of little value.

Giving Opportunity to open up to my unique gifts so I can celebrate my skills and abilities by sharing them with other people.

Glacier Situation where I feel I can move mountains by taking my time and coolly applying the experience I have accumulated.

Glad Realization that I can positively influence how I feel rather than always relying on the people around me to keep me happy.

Glade Situation where I can be more open about my huge potential for growth so I can explore the rich diversity of my learning.

Gladiator Aspect of my character that has the courage to engage with my inner conflicts rather than being a slave to habitual patterns.

Glam Ability to emphasize aspects of my talents I am particular proud of instead of feeling I should try to cover them up.

Glamazon Aspect of my character with strength and courage to stand up for my appearance, with power to keep enhancing it.

Glamorous Realization that I can attract all the attention I need from people by making the effort to go beyond superficial appearances.

Glance Opportunity to take a longer and more detailed look at my situation instead of trying to deflect any potential criticism.

Gland Essential ability to influence my emotions and convey my feelings so I can maintain my healthy and positive approach.

Glare Opportunity to display the intense brilliance of my talents without becoming too fixated on how others see my performance.

Glass Ability to remain clear about a potentially fragile situation, although it makes me feel vulnerable to be emotionally transparent.

Glassblower Aspect of my character that can use the strength and power of my inspiration to shape my perceptions and contain my emotions.

Glasses Ability to look more closely at a situation so I can form a clear opinion rather than becoming too introspective about it.

Glass eye Ability to use my unique viewpoint to see the bigger picture rather than feeling that I am unable to offer a wider perspective.

Glasshouse Situation where I can take a much more transparent view of how I can honestly open up my blossoming talents to public view.

Glazed Ability to form a clear perspective on a situation, even though my viewpoint may seem dull and tedious to other people.

Gleam Opportunity to consistently use my optimism and insight so I can quickly achieve a clearer understanding of a situation.

Glider Ability to warm to some current ways of thinking so I can get a plan off the ground and achieve one of my higher ambitions.

Glimmer Opportunity to brighten up my current situation by using my creative strength to clearly produce my preferred outcome.

Glimpse Opportunity to take a longer and more detailed look at a subject that interests me so I can truly understand it.

Glistening Opportunity to reflect on what is most valuable to me rather than becoming distracted by less rewarding activities.

Glitch Opportunity to change one of my habitual behaviors so I can be more reliable in how I communicate with other people.

Glitter Opportunity to reflect my undoubted brilliance so I can achieve greater prominence in how I pursue my professional career.

Global Realization that I can achieve a more complete understanding of my situation by opening myself to a wider range of viewpoints.

Global warming Opportunity to become more aware of my influence by taking time to understand the far-reaching effects of my actions.

G

Globe Ability to come around to a particular way of thinking that can give me a more encompassing idea of what is happening.

Globule Ability to form a more rounded perspective on what specific emotions may be causing a particularly sticky situation for me.

Gloomy Opportunity to achieve a much clearer understanding of a situation so I can illuminate some bright new opportunities.

Glop Ability to work my way through a potentially messy emotional situation so I can decisively shape my preferred outcome.

Glory Realization that I need to acknowledge the brilliance of my own achievements instead of always waiting for people to praise me.

Glossy Realization that I can easily repel any unnecessary criticism rather than feeling that my approach is deeply flawed in some way.

Glossy magazine Ability to communicate my ideas by clearly laying them out in a colorful manner to illuminate potential opportunities.

Glove Ability to present my self-image to people that comfortably protects my power to fittingly shape and direct my future.

Glow Opportunity to radiate confidence in my unique talents so I can happily surround myself with illuminating possibilities.

Glue Ability to ensure a strong bond in a close relationship rather than feeling I am stuck in old behavioral patterns.

Glue sniffing Opportunity to inspire my creativity more naturally rather than habitually trying to overstimulate instinctive talents.

Glum Realization that I can lift my spirits by really listening out for my inner voice rather than trying to play it down.

Glutton Aspect of my character that understands what will make me satisfied but often punishes me as I try to achieve it.

Gnarled Opportunity to straighten out some of my habitual behavioral patterns so I can

move directly ahead with my plans.

Gnash Opportunity to use a challenge to smoothly assert my power and confidence rather than feeling it is a continual grind for me.

Gnat Instinctive ability to deal with a large number of small annoyances so I can get much closer to what I want to achieve.

Gnawing Opportunity to use my power and confidence to successfully work through a challenge that has been causing me anxiety.

Gnocchi Potential to fulfill a valuable ambition by using some fertile ideas so I can take a more seasoned approach to achieving a result.

Gnome Aspect of my character that has a fantastic talent for looking after my self-worth rather than letting people make me feel small.

Goading Opportunity to take positive action so I can display my expertise instead of feeling that other people are provoking me.

Goal Opportunity to achieve a valuable personal objective by using my unique skills and abilities to reach the outcome I need.

Goalkeeper Aspect of my character that helps me maintain my personal boundaries so I can always achieve my individual objectives.

Goalpost Ability to support my decision to establish definite personal boundaries, so that I can clearly identify my intended objective.

Goat Instinctive ability to play around with my strength and vitality rather than feeling I am just stupidly charging around.

Gob Ability to make a massive contribution by saying exactly what I need rather than continually mouthing off about it.

Goblin Aspect of my character that can demonstrate my true value by revealing my desires instead of trying to conceal them.

Goblet Ability to fulfill an emotional need by

being able to contain my deeper feelings so I can stand up for what I believe in.

God Aspect of my character that gives me the power to fully assert my higher and wiser self so I can create my unique life.

Goddess Aspect of my character that has the power to create a unique life for me by embracing the wisdom of my more spiritual self.

Godparent Aspect of my character that embodies my fundamental sense of wisdom and lovingly provids resources to develop my potential.

Goggles Ability to protect my fundamental awareness from potentially distracting thoughts so I can see what is really happening

Gold Ability to use my special strengths to let my value shine through so I can have my winning qualities recognized by other people.

Gold digger Aspect of my character that succeeds through my own creative efforts instead of relying on others to provide my value.

Gold dust Ability to look beyond superficial appearances so I can display the value of my talents and demonstrate how precious they are.

Goldfish Instinctive ability to immerse myself in my feelings so I can access my wealth of emotions and live in the moment.

Goldfish bowl Ability to be transparent about the richness and security of my emotional life, even though it opens me up to wider scrutiny.

Gold panning Opportunity to open up to my emotions so I can sift through my practical skills and identify which are the most valuable.

Golf Opportunity to use my drive and ambition to achieve a series of objectives, even though the outcome may seem a bit of a long shot.

Golf ball Ability to play around with a potentially successful outcome by being able to focus on a particular aspect of my progress.

Golf club Ability to get into the swing of things so I can use a combination of my power and strength that really hits home.

Golf clubhouse Situation where I can bring together different character drives and ambitions so I can feel comfortable with them.

Golf course Situation where I can make progress by understanding the prevailing mood and using it to influence my chosen outcome.

Golfer Aspect of my character that uses my talents and experience to connect with my ambitions so I can drive them forward.

Gonads Essential ability to use accumulated courage and audacity to consistently conceive a whole range of fertile possibilities.

Gondola Ability to navigate the complex emotional aspects of my romantic feelings by using my self-motivation to stick with them.

Gondolier Aspect of my character that can navigate the complexities of my romantic feelings by understanding the best way to channel them.

Gong Ability to alert myself to my true calling so I can fulfill my ambitions and have my efforts openly acknowledged by other people.

Goo Ability to maintain my composure so I can resolve some potentially messy feelings rather than becoming stuck in them.

Good Realization that I can achieve much greater contentment by performing valuable work instead of feeling bad about myself.

Good-bye Opportunity to decisively leave one episode of my life behind so I can give myself the possibility to step into a new future.

Goods Ability to realize the great value of my practical expertise to other people rather than being too possessive about my skills.

G

Goods train Ability to convey the full value of my skills to the people around me so I can progress toward my professional objective.

Google Ability to continue my quest for greater self-awareness by searching for an answer within myself that only I can provide.

Goose Instinctive ability to go to great lengths to powerfully communicate my ideas rather than always feeling guarded about them.

Gooseberry Natural ability to engage with a more fruitful outcome rather than feeling sour.

Goosebumps Essential opportunity to stand up for a situation that excites me so I can make my presence powerfully felt.

Gore Ability to protect myself from any potentially wounding criticism so I can continue to convey my passion and vitality.

Gorge Situation where I can achieve a sense of great fulfillment by resolving a dilemma between two different viewpoints I hold.

Gorgeous Realization that I can attract other people to my viewpoint by displaying my wonderful talents and revealing deeper value.

Gorilla Instinctive ability to draw attention to my huge creative strengths by having the natural confidence to display them proudly.

Gospel Ability to be very clear and objective about the facts of a situation rather than just trying to preach my particular viewpoint.

Gossamer Natural ability to make a number of stronger and more permanent connections between some ideas I have had floating around.

Gossip Opportunity to express what I would like to say myself instead of being concerned about what other people might think.

Gouge Opportunity to clearly make my own mark rather than allowing other people to surreptitiously ignore my underlying value.

Gourd Ability to take a more rounded approach so I can draw on my accumulated experience when I am developing fertile ideas.

Government Aspects of my character that guide my actions and help me decide on the path I should take to make continued progress.

Gown Ability to present my self-image to other people in a manner that shows the full length and splendor of my accomplishments.

GPS Ability to use my highly elevated awareness to understand the bigger picture of where I am in life and where I need to go.

Grab Opportunity to quickly get a grip on a situation so I can seize my chance to demonstrate my value to the people around me.

Grace Realization that I can use my natural charm to attract support from other people rather than feeling awkward about my actions.

Grade Ability to make a specific step so I can achieve a degree of success instead of feeling that other people are judging me.

Gradient Situation where I can understand my degree of inclination to reach my objective and how quickly I might need to change.

Gradual Realization that I can transform my situation remarkably quickly by taking the time to carefully develop my unique abilities.

Graduation Opportunity to recognize that I have achieved a degree of success so I can have my talents formally acknowledged by others.

Graffiti Ability to clearly mark my personal boundaries so I have an opportunity to openly express my hidden artistic talents.

Graft Opportunity to make a sustained effort so I can incorporate some healthy growth into my developing skills and abilities.

Grail Ability to fulfill an emotional need by devoting my time to understanding my deepest qualities and how I can embody them.

Grain Ability to fulfill a potential ambition by taking the time to pay attention to a small but particularly significant detail.

G

Grammar Ability to organize myself in a specific manner so I can communicate what I really need to say to the people around me.

Gramophone Ability to give voice to my deeper feelings so I can share some of my most significant memories with other people.

Granary Situation where I can accumulate the valuable resources I need so I can work my way through a number of fertile ideas.

Grand Realization that I have an impressive range of expertise and experience I can use to create consistently magnificent results.

Granddaughter Aspect of my character that can develop my wisdom and empathy so I can become even more familiar with it.

Grandeur Realization that I need to take a more practical approach to using my array of talents so I can demonstrate their value.

Grandfather Aspect of my character embodying the loving wisdom and authority that encourages me to continually develop my true potential.

Grandfather clock Ability to choose the right time to make the most of a long-standing opportunity by taking a closer look at ingrained habits.

Grandmother Aspect of my character that gracefully embodies my continuing capacity for creatively providing unconditional love.

Grandparent Aspect of my character that embodies my wider sense of security and gives me the loving authority to wisely develop my potential.

Grandson Aspect of my character that has the potential to develop my power and strength so I can become even more familiar with it.

Grandstand Situation where I can establish a clear perspective so I can influence the outcome of an uncertain challenge.

Grant Ability to realize the value of my developing expertise rather than feeling that I have to make any concessions to other people.

Grapefruit Natural ability to fulfill an ambition by using an expansive and optimistic approach that will result in a fruitful outcome.

Grapes Potential to fulfill an ambition by collecting a bunch of fruitful opportunities rather than feeling sour about missed chances.

Grapevine Natural ability to communicate my deeper feelings to the people around me, while staying rooted in everyday practicalities.

Grapple Opportunity to come to grips with a challenge instead of continually wrestling with my anxieties about possible outcomes.

Grappling hook Ability to quickly catch on to what I need to do so I can make the sheer effort involved to reach a higher level.

Grasp Opportunity to take my time to fully understand a situation so I can get a firm grip on what is happening.

Grass Natural ability to help my skills grow in a healthy way so I can use them more widely, while staying rooted in everyday practicalities.

Grasshopper Instinctive ability to achieve higher awareness by settling on a particular viewpoint rather than always jumping around.

Grateful Opportunity to be more open to receiving well-deserved praise from others so I can acknowledge my individual talents.

Gratitude Realization that other people are very appreciative of the support I give, even though I may not acknowledge my own input.

Grave Situation where I can prepare the ground for a major life transformation and take it seriously without feeling too down about it.

Gravedigger Aspect of my character that can help me explore the practicalities of a major life transformation in much greater depth.

Grave goods Ability to use the great value of my practical expertise to help me to feel more comfortable about a major life transformation.

G

Gravel Ability to support my viewpoint by using a large number of individual facts, rather than feeling as if I'm on shaky ground.

Graveside Situation where I can take a more objective view of an approaching life transformation and the best way to work through it.

Gravestone Ability to respect my experiences and accomplishments by being firm and practical as I prepare for a major transformation.

Graveyard Situation where I can resurrect my talent by giving myself the space to revitalize a number of plans I had laid to rest.

Gravitational field Situation where I can use accumulated experience to understand what habitually draws me toward a way of behaving.

Gravity Ability to attract other people toward me in a consistently powerful way without relying too heavily on my forceful nature.

Gravy Potential to fulfill an ambition by understanding the richness of the emotions that are released when I use my strength and power.

Gray Mood that can color my perspective by reflecting different shades of meaning rather than making everything appear ordinary.

Graze Ability to fulfill my ambitions in a consistently positive and healthy manner rather than feeling as if I am just scraping by.

Grease Ability to make everything run smoothly by openly stating my contribution rather than feeling like I am always slipping up.

Greasepaint Ability to colorfully express my creativity without laying on my emotions so thickly that it conceals my underlying talent.

Great Realization that I have an abundance of the talent I need to prominently display to make my potential and my personality stand out.

Great-grandparent Aspect of my character embodying a deeper sense of wisdom and

gives me continuing authority to develop my abilities.

Green Mood that can color my perspective by naturally reflecting my potential for continuing growth in a fresh and healthy way.

Greenhouse Situation where I can open up blossoming talents to wider public view, even though there may initially be a cool response.

Green light Ability to feel more confident about proceeding with an ambition by using my wisdom to illuminate what is happening.

Green room Aspect of myself that has the capacity to help me feel comfortable and secure in displaying my talents to a wider audience.

Greeting Opportunity to connect with an aspect of my character that has some valuable qualities I need to reacquaint myself with.

Gremlin Ability to confidently rely on my practical abilities instead of blaming myself for apparent breakdowns in a process.

Grenade Ability to safely contain my potentially explosive feelings so I can grasp the power I have to shape a successful outcome.

Greyhound Instinctive ability to faithfully follow a particular course of action, although it may seem I am going in circles.

Grid Ability to make a number of powerful connections with other people so we can work together in a structured way.

Griddle Ability to fulfill a potential ambition by gathering some of my knowledge and experience so I can creatively transform it.

Gridlock Opportunity to be more open about my professional connections so I can quickly free up some of my frustrated ambitions.

Grief Opportunity to happily gain a deeper awareness of myself so I can create a healthier and more fundamental transformation.

Griffin Apparent ability to clearly see a monster opportunity so I can have the pride and confidence to grasp its larger significance.

Grill Ability to achieve an ambition by creatively transforming my raw talent rather than continually questioning my motivation.

Grim Realization that I can determine my chosen outcome by taking a more optimistic approach that doesn't require any compromises.

Grime Ability to go beyond superficial appearances by getting closer to fundamental realities and seeing them in a fresh light.

Grin Essential opportunity to show my wider feelings of power and confidence as I happily face up to a much broader challenge.

Grinder Ability to shape an outcome in exactly the way I choose rather than feeling that circumstances are wearing me down.

Grinding Opportunity to make steady progress and keep things moving instead of feeling that I am causing a lot of friction with people.

Grindstone Ability to produce a valuable outcome by always being firm and practical so I can steadily maintain a solid presence.

Grip Ability to get a handle on what is going on so I can confidently ensure a positive outcome for my situation.

Grist Ability to provide the raw material I need so I can use it to help me fulfill a wide variety of potential ambitions.

Grit Ability to endure a persistently challenging episode, even though it presents a great number of minor irritations for me.

Groan Opportunity to clearly voice my feelings of discomfort rather than continually moaning about them to other people.

Grocer Aspect of my character that recognizes the value of my ambitions and provides me with a healthy variety of ways to fulfill them.

Groceries Ability to provide the resources I need so I can use my raw talent to create a successful and satisfying outcome.

Grocery store Situation where I can make a healthy choice by displaying my natural talents and having them recognized by other people.

Groin Essential ability to feel connected to my core beliefs so I can confidently motivate myself and take decisive action.

Groom Opportunity to work my way through how I routinely present my self-image to people rather than just fussing over my appearance.

Groove Ability to get stuck in the direction I want to take so I can enjoy the experience and follow through with it.

Grope Opportunity to look beyond the more obvious aspects of the situation so I can get a feel for what is happening.

Grotesque Realization that I can use my creativity to shape a more desirable outcome rather than feeling I behave out of character.

Grotto Situations where I can go deeper into the profounder aspects of my character so I can explore the basis of my understanding.

Ground Situation where I can support the fundamental principles I stand for by taking a more practical and down-to-earth approach.

Ground control Situation where I can monitor my progress as I explore some powerful processes that will elevate my understanding.

Ground zero Situation where I can create a positive transformation by having a firm, solidly practical basis for my fundamental beliefs.

Group Aspects of my character that I can bring together to help me successfully fulfill a wide variety of ambitions.

Grout Ability to fill in any gaps in my practical experience so I can feel more emotionally self-contained about my situation.

Grove Situation where I can explore the rich diversity and natural growth potential of some of the undiscovered aspects of my character.

G

Grovel Opportunity to stand up for what I believe in and be proud of accomplishments rather than having to lower my standards.

Grow Opportunity to develop my unrealized potential so I can continue to increase the value of my unique skills and abilities.

Growth Ability to realize what has been emerging for me so I can become more aware of the valuable difference that I can make.

Grub Instinctive ability to consistently fulfill a series of ambitions so I can motivate myself for a fundamental transformation.

Grubby Realization that I should take a more methodical approach to accumulating my resources rather than always messing around.

Grudge Opportunity to resolve a challenging situation by taking a softer approach instead of continuing to hold on to any hard feelings.

Gruesome Realization that I can use my talents to create a beautiful result rather than thinking it will end up in a horrible mess.

Guarantee Ability to be much more consistent in my behaviors so I can successfully deliver on some promises I have made.

Guard Aspect of my character that feels responsible for protecting vulnerabilities, even though it can keep me closed to opportunity.

Guardian Aspect of my character that helps me preserve my sense of wonder so I can continue to develop my creative potential.

Guardrail Ability to protect personal boundaries so I can use them to consistently support actions and make me feel more secure.

Guerrilla Aspect of my character that has the courage to challenge authority by asserting my independence in some unconventional ways.

Guerrilla warfare Opportunity to resolve an inner conflict by recognizing my uniqueness with the discipline to challenge traditional methods.

Guess Opportunity to validate my assumptions by taking decisive practical action instead of just relying on my habitual beliefs.

Guest Aspect of my character that I may not feel completely at home with, although I am prepared to entertain its potential value.

Guesthouse Situation where I have the security and support I need so I can feel at home with my talents on a more permanent basis.

Guide Aspect of my character that uses my experience to show which direction I should be heading in to achieve my objective.

Guidebook Ability to open up to the wealth of my accumulated knowledge and experience so I can clearly decide on my future intentions.

Guide dog Instinctive ability to show my unconditional loyalty and affection so I can continue to explore the bigger picture.

Guillotine Ability to be clear-cut about a situation so I can finally let go of some beliefs I have been hanging on to.

Guilt Realization that I can take full responsibility for a successful outcome rather than continually feeling I have to blame myself.

Guilty of a crime Realization that I need to have confidence in my judgment instead of punishing myself when I have let myself down.

Guilty of fraud Realization that I need to own the value of my expertise rather than feeling I'm somehow not worth it.

Guilty of infidelity Realization that I need to strengthen confidence in my creativity instead of feeling it may no longer appear attractive.

Guilty of murder Realization that I can revitalize one of my unique talents rather than feeling that others are forcing me to get rid of it.

Guilty of rape Realization that I need to set firm boundaries around my creative concepts instead of allowing others to intrude on them.

Guilty of theft Realization that I need to

give myself permission to recognize my talents rather than letting others take credit for them.

Guilty person Aspect of my character that helps me come to terms with my deepest needs instead of allowing others to judge me.

Guinea pig Instinctive ability to experiment with something close to my heart, even though it involves trying something for the first time.

Guitar Ability to take my instinctive creativity in both hands so I can strike just the right tone as I pitch some of my ideas.

Gulf Situation where I can navigate a complex emotional challenge by understanding the wide differences in surrounding perspectives.

Gull Instinctive ability to rise above more practical concerns so I can feel more at home as I spread my learning and experience.

Gully Situation where I can quickly elevate my understanding by taking the path of least resistance when channeling my emotions.

Gum Ability to get stuck in a potentially messy challenge rather than allowing it to slide any further out of control.

Gums Essential ability to healthily support all aspects of my power and confidence so I can get my teeth into a challenge.

Gun Ability to communicate my aims to other people by confidently keeping my distance and asserting my power in a forceful manner.

Gundog Instinctive ability to show my unconditional loyalty and persistence by retrieving ideas that may have fallen by the wayside.

Gunfire Opportunity to alert myself to an emerging challenge so I can take decisive action to deflect any unnecessary criticism.

Gunman Aspect of my character that can embody my individual power by forcefully communicating my aims to the people around me.

Gunpoint Ability to be specific in how I assert my power so other people will be able to align themselves with my perspective.

Gunpowder Ability to make some dry subject matter come to life so that I can catalyze a potentially fundamental transformation.

Gunrunner Aspect of my character that can quickly take steps to assert my power and has the energy and self-motivation to succeed.

Gunshot Opportunity to quickly communicate my intentions to the people around me so that I can assert my influence in a forceful manner.

Gun sight Ability to focus on a particular objective so I can achieve my aims while continuing to stay aware of the bigger picture.

Guru Aspect of my character that can guide me through a challenge by having a positive regard for accumulated wisdom and experience.

Gushing Opportunity to naturally adapt to a sudden emotional challenge rather than responding in an sentimentally extravagant way.

Gusset Ability to reinforce the strength of my creative talents in a way that helps me feel more comfortable with how I present them.

Gust Natural opportunity to quickly respond to some prevailing thinking so I can use it to make a sudden and positive change.

Guts Essential ability to digest the full significance of what I am experiencing so I can motivate myself to take courageous action.

Gutter Situation where I can reliably let go of unwanted feelings and emotions rather than letting myself be carried away by them.

Guy Aspect of my character that can make things easier for other people by asserting my power and strength in a less formal manner.

Guy rope Ability to keep a tight hold on my sense of security so I can feel more relaxed and comfortable in an unfamiliar situation.

G

Gymnasium Situation where I can take a healthy positive approach to working my way through a challenge by staying strong.

Gymnast Aspect of my character that has the talent to be extremely flexible in any situation rather than getting bent out of shape.

Gymnastics Ability to be more flexible in my approach instead of feeling that I constantly have to jump through hoops for other people.

Gypsy Aspect of my character that enjoys my individual sense of freedom rather than feeling restricted by conventional society.

Gyrating Opportunity to become more centered in a particular perspective rather than feeling I am just going round and round.

Gyre Ability to work my way through my current way of thinking so I can transform my situation by completely turning it around.

Gyrocompass Ability to firmly choose what direction I need to take by realizing that everything does not revolve around me.

Gyroscope Ability to maintain my equilibrium by keeping the situation moving rather than letting everything spin out of control.

G

Haberdashery Situation where I can display a variety of my unique talents to other people by making sure I measure up to my own standards.

Habit Essential ability to understand my instinctive behavioral patterns and how they characterize the actions I consistently take.

Hacker Aspect of my character that permits me to tap into a different way of thinking so I can reach a more valuable understanding.

Hacking Opportunity to achieve a valuable goal, even though my specific methods may seem inappropriate to the people around me.

Hackles Instinctive ability to confidently communicate my ideas and feelings rather than feeling alarmed by any emerging challenges.

Hacksaw Ability to powerfully cut my way through old behavioral patterns so I can shape a definite outcome and fully support it.

Haddock Instinctive ability to immerse myself in my emotions so I can learn some powerful lessons about how to fulfill my ambitions.

Hag Aspect of my character that can help me heal old tensions by using my creativity and wisdom to truthfully resolve them.

Haggard Realization that I need to take a fresh look at how I am pursuing my ambitions so I can create a more healthy approach.

Haggling Opportunity to realize the value of my talents by using them to negotiate an unexpected challenge as I deal with others.

Haiku Ability to express myself powerfully and succinctly so other people can appreciate a much deeper connection with my story.

Hail Opportunity to alert myself to a variety of small but unresolved emotions that may have been causing me some discomfort.

Hailstorm Natural opportunity to let go of hard feelings that are no longer useful to me rather than leaving things up in the air.

Hair Essential ability to develop ideas that emerge from my fundamental style of thinking and use them to shape my plans for growth.

Hairbrush Ability to tidy my particular style of thinking by methodically working my way through developing ideas and aligning them.

Hair colorist Aspect of my character that can help me think in a more colorful way to highlight any potential new ideas I may have.

Haircut Opportunity to decisively let go of some beliefs that no longer suit me so I can move on from any ideas I have outgrown.

Hair designer Aspect of my character that has unique talent for shaping my thoughts and plans and visualizing their outcome.

Hairdresser Aspect of my character that can help me take care of my continually emerging thoughts and how I present them to others.

Hair dryer Ability to work my way through any emotions associated with my thinking so I am happy to take a fresh look at my plans.

Hair in throat Opportunity to grasp the value of one of my ideas by understanding its deeper significance and trusting my gut feelings.

Hairpiece Ability to enhance my style of thinking by using substantial theories and ideas that have emerged for someone else.

H

Hairpin Ability to firmly hold on to a stray thought so I can create a more stylish outcome by aligning it with my wider beliefs.

Hairpin bend Situation where I may have to quickly change my direction and rapidly realign my perspectives so I can reach my objective.

Hairspray Ability to convey the power of my ideas to others in a clear and gentle way rather than becoming overly fixated by them.

Hair straighteners Ability to quickly straighten out my ideas so I can get to the point without getting into heated argument.

Hairstyle Ability to feel comfortable with my own way of thinking so I am happy to show my ideas to the people around me.

Hairstylist Aspect of my character that helps me shape my thinking and look at how I can identify more meaningfully with my ideas.

Half Realization that I can achieve complete fulfillment by wholeheartedly embracing what makes me feel most happy and excited.

Half-life Ability to use previous experiences to achieve a whole lot more rather than feeling my skills are steadily fading away.

Halfway house Situation where I have continuing security and support so I can transform all aspects of my inner and outer lives.

Halfway there Situation where I can use the experience I have accumulated so far to help me become more aware of emerging possibilities.

Halitosis Essential opportunity to confidently speak out about the value of my most inspiring ideas in an attractively fresh manner.

Hall Aspect of myself where I have the space to explore a variety of opportunities that have the potential to open all around me.

Hallmark Ability to genuinely show the value of my expertise instead of always waiting for others to give it their stamp of approval.

Halloween Opportunity to happily celebrate instinctive and forgotten aspects of myself by inviting others to recognize my talents.

Hallucination Opportunity to be more open-minded about exploring new experiences rather than being concerned I am deluding myself.

Hallucinogenic Opportunity to open up my thinking to a different level of awareness by letting my mind both wander and wonder.

Hallway Situation that can lead to a variety of new choices and can help me explore the inner and outer aspects of who I really am.

Halo Ability to illuminate a situation with my own sense of spirituality instead of always being dazzled by other people's brilliance.

Halt Opportunity to bring proceedings to a stop so I can reflect on my progress and reach a conclusion about my choices so far.

Halter Ability to harness my talents so I can take charge of my creativity and give it direction rather than getting carried away by it.

Halting Opportunity to stay consistently motivated about my progress instead of feeling I am holding myself back in some way.

Ham Potential to fulfill an ambition by using my raw strength and power rather than just acting up to draw attention to myself.

Hammer Ability to shape an effective outcome by taking time to persistently use my power and strength to produce a definite result.

Hammock Situation where I feel supported as I explore a situation in greater depth so I can take a relaxed approach to the outcome.

Hamper Ability to comfortably convey the value of my ambitions to others so I can continue to satisfy my appetite for success.

Hampered Realization that my continuing preparations for every possible eventuality may be holding me back in a number of ways.

H

Hamster Instinctive ability to pursue a creative goal, even though it sometimes feels as though I am continually going in circles.

Hand Essential ability to have a firm grasp of my inner power so I can use it to control my actions and shape my own future.

Handbag Ability to maintain the more individual aspects of who I am so I can always show others what makes me valuable.

Handbook Ability to draw on my wealth of accumulated knowledge and learning so I can confidently put it into practical action.

Handbrake Ability to maintain my position by keeping a firm grip on my drives and ambitions rather than letting them get out of control.

Hand clap Opportunity to act decisively and show how I feel so others can appreciate how much I value their contribution.

Handcuffs Ability to release myself from restraints on my behavior by becoming more aware of my freedom to control my future.

Handhold Ability to sense specific support for my actions so I can maintain my position and feel secure about making further progress.

Handicap Ability to use my skills to the fullest extent rather than constantly feeling that other people are holding me back in some way.

Handicraft Ability to shape a successful outcome by using my practical skills so I can create further opportunities for my expertise.

Handkerchief Ability to look after the potential outcome of an emerging emotional situation by taking action before things get messy.

Handle Ability to shape a successful outcome by having the confidence to firmly grasp any opportunities and keep in touch with them.

Handlebars Ability to take my future in both hands so I can use energy and self-motivation to choose the direction I want to follow.

Handrail Ability to provide constant support so I can make continued progress as I grasp the implications of my needs.

Handset Ability to clearly communicate what I need to say to other people rather than putting my individual progress on hold.

Hands-free Ability to separate my immediate actions from my long-term thinking so I can successfully connect with new possibilities.

Handshake Opportunity to become reacquainted with an aspect of my character that will help me commit to future action.

Handsome Aspect of my character that can attractively assert my power, even though I may be sharing an unappealing truth.

Handstand Opportunity to look at a situation from a different angle so I can become more aware of how I can support my viewpoint.

Handwriting Ability to communicate my creative identity in a unique manner by ensuring I consistently make my mark with other people.

Hang Ability to successfully learn a particular technique rather than feeling that my efforts will just be a letdown for everyone.

Hangar Situation where I can maintain interest in my bigger plans and ideas until I have the opportunity to get them off the ground.

Hang glider Ability to use the prevailing mood to raise my levels of understanding so I can explore some current ways of thinking.

Hanging Opportunity to support myself as I explore a situation in greater depth instead of feeling that I always let myself down.

Hanging up Opportunity to say what I need to and decisively move on rather than feeling as if I am waiting for an immediate response.

Hangman Aspect of my character that helps me honestly voice my emotions rather than feeling roped in to other people's plans.

H

Hangover Opportunity to let go of some previous commitments that no longer serve me so I am able to do some clear thinking.

Hang-up Realization that I can let go of a situation that is making me feel down rather than always feeling I can't speak my truth.

Happiness Realization that I have more influence over my future than I think instead of just hoping for continued good fortune.

Harassment Realization that I have the power to change my situation rather than feeling persistently aggravated by people around me.

Harbor Situation where I can consistently provide emotional security for myself and other people, without retaining any bad feelings.

Hard Realization that the most challenging circumstances can often give me the solid foundations I need to make my presence felt.

Hard drive Ability to easily put my accumulated knowledge into practice rather than feeling that I'm going round in circles.

Hard hat Ability to present my self-image to people in a way that protects my individual way of thinking and makes it appear more robust.

Hard labor Opportunity to productively work my way through a set of tough challenges without feeling I am being forced into doing it.

Hard luck Opportunity to achieve ambitions through hard work and practicing skills rather than feeling everything is against me.

Hard shoulder Situation where I can gain solid support from the sidelines as I pursue ambitions and move toward my chosen objective.

Hardware Ability to consistently rely on my practical skills and abilities rather than feeling that I don't have the required resources.

Hare Instinctive ability to understand the power of my spiritual nature so I can effortlessly make a valuable creative leap.

Harem Situation where I can attend to the wiser and more creative aspects of myself rather than overindulging in my desires.

Harlot Aspect of my character that can become more intimately aware of my creative experience instead concealing its value.

Harm Opportunity to protect an aspect of my life that I greatly value rather than allowing other people to damage my self-esteem.

Harmonica Instinctive ability to channel my inspiration so I can use my natural talent to honestly express my deeper emotions.

Harness Ability to consistently control and direct my instinctive energies so I can use the vital power of my creative urges.

Harp Instinctive ability to take my creativity in both hands and create a pleasant atmosphere without going on about it at length.

Harpoon Ability to decisively get to the point so I can bring some of my deeper emotions to the surface and realize their value.

Harsh Realization that I can take a gentler and more pleasant approach rather than feeling I have to grimly keep going on.

Harvest Opportunity to reap the rewards from ideas I planted a while ago so I can continue to develop my long-term ambitions.

Harvest festival Opportunity to celebrate the mature growth of an individual talent by sharing its unique value with those around me.

Hash Ability to quickly fulfill a potential ambition by reworking some old ideas rather than muddling my way through it.

Hashish Natural ability to take a more relaxed approach to a challenging situation instead of trying to avoid facing up to it.

Hashtag Ability to sum up my more significant thinking in a very succinct style so I can communicate my ideas to a wider audience.

Haste Realization that deliberately thinking through my preferred outcome gives me the opportunity to act rapidly when I need to.

H

Hat Ability to present my self-image to other people by drawing attention to my viewpoint and making it seem attractive.

Hatch Ability to use my fertile mind as a convenient way of accessing a variety of possibilities that may have seemed closed.

Hatchet Ability to make a series of small but decisive actions so I can transform a situation by resolving it in a peaceful manner.

Hatching Opportunity to come up with a plan for developing a new talent rather than feeling I will never make a breakthrough.

Hate Realization that I can use my passionate intensity in a positive manner instead of giving in to self-destructive tendencies.

Hate crime Opportunity to have confidence in my creative judgment rather than punishing myself when I feel I have let people down.

Hate speech Opportunity to confidently share my positive outlook with other people so I can passionately state my future intentions.

Haul Opportunity to obtain what I really need by making a big effort to go out and actively convey my value to the people around me.

Haunches Instinctive ability to stand up for my creative instincts so I can feel strongly motivated to take the steps I need to.

Haunted Opportunity to revitalize some old talents that I felt forced to move on from rather than always obsessing about them.

Haunted asylum Situation where I can take steps to put my ideas into action instead of driving myself crazy by constantly thinking about them.

Haunted attic Situation where I am starting to remember ideas I had completely forgotten about and am realizing how I can use them.

Haunted basement Situation where I am becoming more aware of an unsettling issue in my fundamental behaviors that I can now resolve in a healthy way.

Haunted castle Situation where I am strongly defending fundamental beliefs, even though I am having an uneasy feeling about them.

Haunted dockyard Situation where I give myself the space to work my way through a challenging process that is emotionally unsettling for me.

Haunted forest Situation where I can explore the rich diversity of my experience and refamiliarize myself with my natural growth potential.

Haunted hospital Situation where I can take a healthier approach to dealing with a disquieting feeling rather than just feeling ill at ease.

Haunted house Situation where I have the security to explore some aspects of myself that I need to bring back to life or just lay to rest.

Haunted school Situation where I can revisit valuable lessons rather than feeling I will never accomplish what I set out to achieve.

Hauntingly familiar Situation where I can explore all the paths I could have taken in my life so I'm more certain of my future direction.

Haven Situation where I can reach a comfortable level of emotional security rather than feeling vulnerable to unpredictable feelings.

Haversack Ability to maintain self-motivation by taking responsibility for my progress without weighing myself down with obligations.

Havoc Opportunity to choose the life I want to live by understanding what is happening rather than behaving chaotically.

Hawk Instinctive ability to observe a situation carefully so I can clearly understand it and respond with some very quick thinking.

Hawthorn Natural ability to let spiritual development blossom rather than being defensive about unwelcome intrusions into my space.

H

Hay Natural ability to make the most of my creative experiences so I can use them to satisfy my ambitions whenever I need to.

Haystack Ability to rise to prominence by using creative experience I have accumulated without losing a sense of perspective.

Haywire Opportunity to make a strong connection to my creative ambitions instead of going crazy because I haven't achieved them yet.

Hazard Opportunity to have confidence in my undoubted abilities rather than feeling I have to guess what I should do next.

Hazard lights Ability to draw attention to a creative risk I am taking so I can attract assistance from the people around me.

Haze Natural opportunity to clarify the details that are coloring the prevailing mood so I can see the way ahead more clearly.

Hazelnut Potential to fulfill an ambition by having enough confidence in my ideas so I can easily open up to a variety of challenges.

Head Essential ability to create the life I want to live by envisioning a variety of possibilities and bringing them together.

Headache Essential opportunity to resolve an ongoing tension with conflicting ideas by relaxing so I can keep things moving.

Head-butt Opportunity to get my point of view across to someone else without feeling I have to be too forceful or aggressive.

Headdress Ability to present my self-image to people by feeling I have the freedom to draw attention to my viewpoint.

Headgear Ability to present my self-image to people by expressing the connections between my ideas and how I worked through them.

Headhunter Aspect of my character that tracks down my creative talents so I can identify where I can use my ideas most valuably.

H

Headland Situation where I can take a practical, down-to-earth approach as I look at how to deal with an emotionally complex situation.

Headless Opportunity to respond to an emotional situation on an instinctive level without feeling that I have think about it too much.

Head lice Instinctive ability to take a really fresh approach to my style of thinking instead of allowing other ideas merely to irritate me.

Headlight Ability to use my thoughts and theories to illuminate some less obvious aspects of a situation as I make my way forward.

Headlock Opportunity to open up to the idea of thinking in a different way rather than closing down any other possible thoughts.

Headmaster Aspect of my character that encourages me to develop power and gives me permission to continue learning about myself.

Headmistress Aspect of my character that empathizes with my creativity and gives me the self-discipline to examine what I know.

Head of state Aspect of my character that embodies my power for confident, decisive change so I can transform my overall condition.

Headphones Ability to clearly listen to my inner voice so I can observe what ideas are emerging and can decide how to act on them.

Headpiece Ability to present my self-image by proudly displaying my point of view without feeling I have to embroider it too much.

Headquarters Situation where I can bring a number of my ideas together so I can use them to spread my influence on a wider basis.

Headrest Ability to maintain my habitual viewpoint so I can take a more relaxed approach when working with plans and projects.

Headroom Ability to give myself the space I need to develop my way of thinking without feeling I am limiting my ideas in any way.

Head scarf Ability to present my self-image to others by warmly communicating my ideas rather than getting too wrapped up in them.

Headset Ability to directly communicate my thoughts and theories so I can express a definite decision about my chosen direction.

Headstand Opportunity to give myself a healthy new perspective on a situation without feeling I have to turn the world upside down.

Headstone Ability to acknowledge the value of a major life transformation so I can consistently maintain my solid, steady presence.

Head torch Ability to use the power of my thinking to illuminate an unfamiliar situation so I can decide the path I need to take.

Headway Realization that I can use a recognized method of thinking to enable me to pursue my ambitions in a characteristic manner.

Headwind Natural opportunity to understand some of my prevailing thoughts and ideas rather than feeling they are working against me.

Healer Aspect of my character that can make a situation seem much healthier by resolving my conflicting tensions and motivations.

Health Essential opportunity to resolve any inner tensions I may experience so I can use my abilities to their fullest power.

Health center Situation where I can experience the true source of my fundamental being so I can heal any inner conflicts I have.

Health certificate Ability to display the good feelings I have about my abilities so I can have my talents acknowledged by others.

Health club Situation where I can bring different aspects of my character together and use their combined power to feel good.

Health farm Situation where I can feel more at ease with myself by developing my creative instincts and cultivating my natural power.

Health food Potential to fulfill my ambitions by satisfying my need for wholeness so I can nourish my continued growth and vitality.

Heap Ability to accumulate a great deal of practical experience so I can make myself stand out from any unnecessary activity.

Hearing Opportunity to open up to new possibilities by listening to my feelings and understanding what I am trying to say.

Hearing aid Ability to listen for valuable information so I can use it to help me clearly understand my wider ambitions.

Hearse Ability to use my personal ambition and drive to lay to rest an aspect of my past so I can progress into a new future.

Heart Essential ability to have the courage to remain centered in my emotions so I can always keep my passion and vitality flowing.

Heart attack Opportunity to courageously meet a challenge by taking forceful action to fulfill my desires rather than feeling defensive.

Heartbeat Essential opportunity to listen to my deeper rhythms so I can use my excitement and exuberance to attain my ambitions.

Heart disease Opportunity to ensure a healthy love life instead of feeling I'm an incurable romantic or experiencing too much heartache.

Heart failure Opportunity to resolve an unhealthy situation by letting go of foregone conclusions so I can keep my passion flowing.

Hearth Situation where I can support the fundamental principles I stand for so I can create a warm, welcoming atmosphere.

Heart surgery Opportunity to deal with inner tensions by opening up about my passions so I can understand what is going on inside me.

H

Heart transplant Opportunity to take my courage and devotion and use them in a completely different way rather than rejecting their value.

Hearty Realization that I can use my power and strength in a warm, affectionate manner that demonstrates my passion and vitality.

Heat Opportunity to use my vitality to raise my chances of success rather than taking a cooler and more considered approach.

Heater Ability to create a warmer atmosphere so I feel more comfortable in opening up my hidden talents to the people around me.

Heath Situation where I can be more open about my particular field of expertise, even though my approach may not be so cultivated.

Heathen Aspect of my character that is happy to follow my instinctive beliefs, even though they may seem uncultured and primitive.

Heat-seeking Realization that I can reach my objective quickly by identifying the particular aspects I feel most passionate about.

Heatstroke Opportunity to work through a challenge in a cool and relaxed manner rather than allowing it to become a heated argument.

Heat wave Natural opportunity to make the most of the prevailing mood so I can enjoy taking a warmer, more passionate approach.

Heave Opportunity to make an effort so I can raise my level of commitment, even though it may involve some weighty obligations.

Heaven Situation where I have the power to fully connect with my higher and wiser self so I can create my vision of perfection.

Heavenly Realization that I have the inner power to use my creativity and wisdom to make positive transformations in everyday life.

Heavy Realization that I can resolve a serious challenge by taking a more lighthearted approach instead of letting it weigh me down.

Heavy industry Ability to make a systematic effort so I can use the weight of my experience to achieve a consistently valuable outcome.

Heckler Aspect of my character that has the opportunity to recognize my talent rather than being constantly critical of my performances.

Hedge Natural potential for my short-term spiritual growth by setting some personal boundaries so I feel less vulnerable.

Hedgehog Instinctive ability to look after myself in a potentially prickly situation rather than always curling up in a ball.

Hedge trimmer Ability to shape my spiritual growth so I feel more comfortable with it instead of worrying about how it appears.

Hedonist Aspect of my character that has a great appetite for life and can always bring me to my senses in challenging situations.

Heel Essential ability to take decisive steps to leave the past firmly behind, even though it can sometimes leave me feeling vulnerable.

Height Situation where I can attain an elevated understanding of what I have achieved and can raise my levels of ambition even further.

Heimlich maneuver Essential opportunity to clearly express my frustrations so I can spit out something that has been bothering me.

Heir Aspect of my character that uses the power of my older self to help me realize the lasting value of a fundamental transformation.

Heiress Aspect of my character that uses the wisdom of my more mature self to help me become self-possessed about using my talents.

Heirloom Ability to use the skills and abilities that are most familiar to me so I can pass on my methods on to the people around me.

Heist Opportunity to have others acknowledge the value of my talents rather than feeling guilty about openly using my abilities.

Helicopter Ability to use a powerful way of thinking to quickly rise above a challenge instead of always hovering around indecisively.

Heliograph Ability to reflect on the power of my creativity so I can signal my intentions and attract the assistance of other people.

Helipad Situation where I can safely get a powerful idea off the ground and then ensure I can continue my down-to-earth approach.

Heliophobe Aspect of my character that can more openly luxuriate in my natural creativity rather than feeling I have to conceal my talents.

Hell Situation where I can use my instinctive creativity and passion to decide an outcome instead of feeling chronically frustrated.

Helm Ability to be firmly in charge of my feelings so I can directly decide how to navigate a complex emotional situation.

Helmet Ability to protect my individual way of thinking in potentially risky situations so I can safely deflect any criticism.

Helping Opportunity to understand the value of my contribution and the level of assistance that I openly provide to other people.

Hem Ability to present my self-image in a way that shows my personal boundaries rather than feeling I'm being held back.

Hemisphere Ability to shape my circumstances so I can create a well-rounded perspective instead of being aware of half the story.

Hemlock Natural ability to take a calmer approach to unwelcome feelings rather than opening myself up to an unhealthy situation.

Hemorrhage Opportunity to channel my profusely passionate nature so I can maintain vitality rather than feeling emotionally drained.

Hemorrhoids Essential opportunity to use my rich creativity to control my needs rather than becoming twisted and frustrated.

Hemp Natural ability to use every fiber of my being to make a powerful connection instead of feeling confused about events.

Hemp seed Natural ability to support my creative abilities so I can feed my thoughts and theories and develop them more powerfully.

Hen Instinctive ability to develop a number of potential talents in fertile new areas rather than just brooding about possibilities.

Henchman Aspect of my character that tries to support beliefs even though people may not understand my strengths and may judge me harshly.

Henge Situation where I can raise my awareness of my spiritual outlook by steadily maintaining a firm grounding in everyday reality.

Hen night Opportunity to discover a deeper potential in myself by exploring my nature's wilder aspects and my commitment to them.

Herb Natural ability to use an illuminating opportunity to flavor my outlook so I can stimulate my enthusiasm in a healthy way.

Herbal remedy Ability to use natural power and strength to successfully resolve a situation that has been making me feel ill at ease.

Herd Instinctive ability to gather my creative resources so I can use them to accomplish a achieve productive outcome.

Here Situation where I can be completely present in the moment so I can fully understand the significance of my position.

Heritage site Situation where I can explore a variety of influences on my development so I can arrive at a better understanding of myself.

Hermaphrodite Aspect of my character that embodies the power of my creativity with the strength to assert it with wisdom and empathy.

Hermit Aspect of my character that happily maintains my personal boundaries so I can devote my time to helping other people.

H

Hermitage Situation where I can quietly explore my inner potential so I can choose the most appropriate way to share it with people.

Hermit crab Instinctive ability to protect my emotional space so I can confidently come out of my shell when the time is right.

Hernia Essential opportunity to contain my deeper feelings so I can make a big effort to heal any potentially emotional tensions.

Hero Aspect of my character that courageously chooses to always do the right thing, even though it may place me in jeopardy.

Heroin Ability to healthily resolve one of my fundamental needs rather than being consumed by what others appear to need from me.

Heroine Aspect of my character that can draw on my deeper reserves of strength so I can step into my power and transform the situation.

Heron Instinctive ability to step into an emotional situation so I can fulfill my ambitions by getting to the point.

Herpes Essential opportunity to feel confident in my creative abilities rather than just spreading unsubstantiated rumors.

Herring Instinctive ability to immerse myself in my deeper emotions and just go with the flow so that I can fulfill my ambitions.

Hesitation Realization that I have the confidence to take action right now rather than doubting my abilities to make a big decision.

Hex Opportunity to express what I think in a positive and supportive way instead of blaming unfortunate circumstances.

Hexagon Ability to shape my circumstances by structuring specific boundaries so I can consistently be efficient and supportive.

Hexagram Ability to understand a number of different points of view so I can decide the outcome rather than leaving it to fate.

Hibernation Opportunity to listen to my rhythms so I can take time to recover rather than idly going through the motions.

Hiccups Essential opportunity to take full control of my source of inspiration instead of feeling embarrassed by any temporary setbacks.

Hidden Opportunity to be more open about my ambitions so I can discover some of my talents that I was previously unaware of.

Hide Ability to feel comfortable about openly sharing my vulnerabilities rather than feeling I always have to be thick-skinned.

Hide-and-seek Opportunity to play around with ways of discovering my natural talents, even though it may take time to reveal them all.

Hideous Realization that I can use my unique talents to attract people toward me instead of worrying that I will unsettle them.

Hiding Opportunity to be much more open about my talents rather than trying to conceal them in case people might criticize them.

Hieroglyph Ability to clearly illustrate my strength of character by communicating what I need to say in an obvious and direct manner.

Hi-fi Ability to specifically understand the significance of my particular experiences so I have complete faith in what I say.

Higgs boson Ability to give weight to my theories by taking the time to pay attention to an elusive but particularly significant detail.

High Realization that I can raise my level of understanding much farther than I think so I can gain a more elevated perspective.

High chair Ability to maintain my habitual viewpoint on a situation, even though it may seem rather childish to the people around me.

High explosive Ability to control my energetic talent for creating powerful transformations instead of allowing it to blow up unexpectedly.

H

High heels Ability to take a series of decisive steps to elevate my status, even though it can sometimes leave me feeling vulnerable.

High jump Opportunity to make the most of an emerging possibility by letting go of any potential criticism that may be holding me back.

High maintenance Realization that I need to consistently develop my talents rather than hoping that others will look after them for me.

High-pitched Realization that I can decide an uncertain outcome by really listening for what I am trying to express at a deeper level.

High priest Aspect of my character that provides me with the spiritual authority to connect with an elevated understanding of my situation.

High risk Realization that I need to increase my confidence in my undoubted abilities rather than feeling I have to play them down.

High school Situation where I can achieve a more complete understanding of my talents so I can examine what I really know about myself.

High school musical Situation where I can flamboyantly display what I have learned without worrying that others will judge me.

High-speed Ability to make rapid progress with a particular plan, even though I feel I may not be able to completely control the outcome.

High tide Opportunity to experience the full range of my emotions rather than always trying to maintain them at a certain level.

Highway Situation where I can use a widely accepted procedure to fast-track my ambitions as I make progress toward my goal.

Highway code Ability to indicate my intentions to the people around me so we can safely work together to reach a collective result.

High-wire Ability to make a really strong connection with other people so I can raise my confidence in negotiating tense situations.

Hijack Opportunity to seize the initiative so I can take control of my ambitions rather than being diverted by other people's needs.

Hike Opportunity to use self-motivation and energy to rise to any approaching challenges so I can consistently move forward.

Hiker Aspect of my character that makes a sustained effort to achieve my objective by taking a series of steps that lead to success.

Hiking trail Situation where I can follow a particular path that will lead to success, even though it may require effort along the way.

Hilarious Opportunity to resolve any of my inner tensions so I can feel more relaxed rather than taking myself too seriously.

Hill Situation where I can commit to making a consistent, sustained effort to widen my perspective and elevate my understanding.

Hillside Situation where I can understand my inclination to follow a particular route so I can continue to make definite progress.

H

Hilt Ability to grasp my sense of power so I can run through challenges and confusion right up to the end.

Hind Instinctive ability to be proud of the wilder aspects of my nature so I can explore a range of creative possibilities.

Hindquarters Instinctive ability to stand up for my creativity so I can choose my future direction and take the steps I need to.

Hinge Ability to be more flexible in my approach so I can open up new possibilities and experience a definite turning point.

Hint Opportunity to successfully resolve a challenge by getting a flavor of my own needs rather than trying to control other people.

Hip Essential ability to make a spontaneous connection that can get things moving, even though it may not seem too stylish.

Hip flask Ability to safely contain my emotions so I can take a more spontaneous approach to dealing with a confusing situation.

Hippie Aspect of my character that gives me the freedom to understand my deeper self rather than rejecting conventional values.

Hippopotamus Instinctive ability to feel comfortable in the using the power and strength of my emotions without wallowing in them.

Hire Opportunity to fully recognize the value of my skills and experience, even though it apparently may be for only a short time.

Hiss Opportunity to direct my attention to some emerging thoughts and feelings instead of showing my disapproval of them.

Historical costume Ability to present my self-image in a way that shows my accumulated experience and the real depth of my character.

Historical event Opportunity to become more aware of the significance of my previous actions so I can be more decisive about future choices.

Historical figure Aspect of my character that understands the value of my expertise rather than worrying about my current circumstances.

Historical reconstruction Opportunity to reflect on past experiences so I can rebuild my sense of identity and resolve any inner tensions.

History Opportunity to understand the series of events that led to my current situation so I can build on my experiences.

Hit Opportunity to suddenly make a powerful connection by using the natural strength of my talents to achieve a real impact.

Hitch Ability to stay connected to my chosen outcome without becoming overly attached to it or feeling I'm holding myself back.

Hitchhiker Aspect of my character that can make fast progress toward my objective by drawing on the ambition and drive of others.

Hitchhiking Opportunity to reach my goal by making the best use of the resources around me without feeling I'm getting a free ride.

Hit man Aspect of my character that is trying to kill off one of my developing talents to quickly please the people around me.

Hit squad Aspects of my character I may be unacquainted with but which can make a positive impact on developing my future skills.

Hive Ability to exchange ideas with other people so I can make constructive progress rather than just trying to appear busy.

Hoard Ability to make consistent use of my accumulated wisdom and expertise rather than trying to conceal it from other people.

Hoarse Essential opportunity to speak out clearly so I can make myself heard rather than thinking I'm unable to voice my feelings.

Hoax Opportunity to share my real story with others rather than feeling that sharing my feelings will be of no real value.

Hob Ability to use some of the peripheral benefits of my creative powers so I can keep satisfying my hunger for results.

Hobbit Aspect of my character that has the ability to achieve fantastic results, even though I feel I may not be up to the task.

Hobble Opportunity to make progress by taking a series of decisive steps rather than holding myself back with some limp excuses.

Hobby Opportunity to understand my real vocation in life rather than just toying with pastimes that help to keep me amused.

Hobo Aspect of my character that can understand my fundamental value by exploring my inner life rather than restlessly moving around.

Hockey Opportunity to use my skill to play around with ways of achieving my goals so I can produce a straightforward outcome.

Hod Ability to convey the fundamental aspects of a potentially character-building experience so I can feel more secure in myself.

Hoe Ability to methodically work through some issues in a down-to-earth manner so I can weed out any unwanted developments.

Hog Instinctive ability to get stuck in a potentially messy situation without feeling I am being too selfish about it.

Hoist Ability to remain solid and supportive so I can raise my level of effort and achieve a more elevated understanding.

Hold Ability to have a firm grasp of my inner power so I can use it to maintain my position without any reservations.

Holding Opportunity to provide support for others as I wait for my chance to demonstrate the strength of my capabilities.

Holding pattern Opportunity to take my time so I can choose how to take the best approach in a prevailing atmosphere that may be unclear.

Holdup Opportunity to forcefully declare my value rather than continually trying to delay proceedings until people acknowledge it.

Hole Situation where I can understand my deeper capacity for success by looking more profoundly into what really motivates me.

Holey Realization that I have almost accomplished what I set out to do instead of feeling I have to continually criticize my efforts.

Holiday Opportunity to make time for myself so I can work on an issue that has great personal significance for me.

Holiday camp Situation where I can take the time to relax and explore unfamiliar aspects of my character and play around with them.

Holiness Aspect of my awareness that helps me understand the significance of what I believe and how I can use it in everyday life.

Hollow Situation where I can succeed by going deeper into my ideas and experience instead of thinking I have no talent inside me.

Holly Natural ability to open up to my more immediate spiritual growth rather than always glossing over it in a prickly manner.

Hologram Ability to clearly observe how a situation is shaping up by using my creativity to illuminate it in a more coherent manner.

Holy Realization that I can devote some of my time to understanding the nature of my beliefs and the connections I make with them.

Home Situation where I am happy to stay in my comfort zone so I can feel most relaxed with all the different aspects of my identity.

Home brew Ability to process some possibly confusing emotions without feeling I will have to go too far out of my comfort zone.

Home delivery Opportunity to convey my feelings about a promise I have made so others will open up about their commitments.

Home help Aspect of my character that understands how much I value safety and security to consistently care for my well-being.

Home improvement Opportunity to develop my skills and abilities so I can understand the different aspects of myself.

Home invasion Opportunity to set firm personal boundaries rather than feeling overwhelmed by others' intrusive demands.

Homeless Opportunity to resolve an uncomfortable situation by taking decisive action to reconnect with my fundamental sense of identity.

H

Homesick Opportunity to feel more at home with myself by reconnecting with an aspect of my identity that used to make me feel uneasy.

Homework Opportunity to achieve my chosen ambition by taking my time and making the effort to connect with my true purpose in life.

Home wrecker Aspect of my character that can repair my confidence in my creative abilities instead of being self-destructive.

Homosexual Aspect of my character that can draw people toward me by having a deeper understanding of my most attractive qualities.

Homunculus Aspect of my character that contains all my potential, even though I belittle my talents and play down my achievements.

Honest Realization that I can achieve much greater awareness by speaking my truth instead of trying to keep other people happy.

Honey Potential to fulfill an ambition by busily coordinating a wide range of activities to ensure a smooth and pleasing outcome.

H

Honeymoon Opportunity to enjoy the pleasures of a long-term commitment so I can happily prepare myself for future challenges.

Honeysuckle Natural ability to open up to my blossoming creative talents rather than getting too wrapped up in how I might support myself.

Honor Realization that I owe it to myself to act with integrity instead of worrying about how my actions might appear to others.

Honor killing Opportunity to transform a set of beliefs that no longer serve me so I can display my integrity in a kind, graceful way.

Hood Ability to present my self-image to others in a way that allows me to conceal my beliefs and protect my point of view.

Hoodie Aspect of my character that likes to keep my viewpoint private, even though it may seem furtive to other people.

Hoodlum Aspect of my character that can use my expertise in a more open manner instead of forcing others to acknowledge my value.

Hoof Instinctive ability to stay firmly grounded so I can take powerful, practical steps to quickly move into action.

Hook Ability to quickly catch on to what I need to do rather than feeling I'm stuck with unwanted responsibilities.

Hooker Aspect of my character that can engage more powerfully with my unique creative talents instead of cheapening them.

Hooligan Aspect of my character that can creatively use my powerful instincts rather than indulging in self-destructive behavior.

Hoop Ability to hold a situation together so I can understand the surrounding context more clearly and use it to my advantage.

Hoot Opportunity to loudly draw attention to an approaching challenge rather than appearing apathetic to the people around me.

Hooter Ability to make my presence felt so I can prevent a potential mishap instead of appearing to be sticking my nose in.

Hope Realization that I can take decisive action that will help me realize my aspirations rather than just relying on fate.

Hopeless Realization that pursuing my ambitions will always lead to a valuable outcome, however futile my efforts may seem.

Hopping Opportunity to take a more individual approach to achieving my chosen outcome, even though it may seem unbalanced.

Horde Aspects of my character that can powerfully combine to make a strong, concerted effort to push through to my objective.

Horizon Situation where I can bring my thoughts and theories down to earth so I can be more definite about future possibilities.

Horizontal Opportunity to explore my wider experience so I can take a more relaxed approach to achieving a broader understanding.

Hormonal Essential ability to influence how I respond to a situation by being more aware of how I can channel my moods and emotions.

Horn Ability to sound out some potential opportunities so I can draw other people's attention to the progress I am making.

Hornet Instinctive ability to obviously make my presence felt in a big way instead of feeling stung by other people's criticism.

Horrible Realization that I can resolve any unexpected challenges by responding positively and creatively rather than just becoming upset.

Horrible accident Opportunity to realize the power of my deeper intentions so I can create a positive outcome from any unpredictable situation.

Horror Opportunity to courageously show my inner beauty by being as gracious as possible rather than being afraid to take action.

Horror movie Opportunity to transform my personal story by becoming more aware of the positive, healthy influences in my life.

Horse Instinctive ability to harness my unconscious strength so I can use my natural power to drive forward with my ambitions.

Horseback Situation where I can use underlying strength to support me to instinctively make progress toward my objective.

Horse-drawn Realization that I am making strong and steady progress, even though it may seem to others as if I am just plodding along.

Horseshoe Ability to take definite steps to protect my instinctive strength and power rather than leaving it to good fortune.

Hose Ability to consistently channel my feelings so I can convey the deeper value of my emotions to the people around me.

Hosiery Ability to present my self-image to other people in a way that helps me feel comfortable with taking self-motivated action.

Hospice Situation where I can use my natural strength and determination to decisively resolve an unhealthy situation once and for all.

Hospital Situation where I can take a healthier approach to resolving inner tensions that may have been causing me discomfort or pain.

Hospitality Opportunity to be more welcoming and receptive to my talents rather than dismissing them in a cold, distant manner.

Host Aspect of my character that chooses to look after the needs of people without allowing them to become too reliant on me.

Hostage Aspect of my character that has the courage to make my own choices rather than feeling trapped by my doubts and fears.

Hostel Situation where I have the security and support to understand my value so I can become more comfortable with it.

Hostile Realization that I welcome any challenges to my way of thinking so I can use them as a way of exploring my deeper beliefs.

Hostilities Opportunity to openly declare what is making me feel tense so I can achieve a lasting sense of peace and optimism.

Hot Realization that I can use my passion to increase my chances of success rather than taking a cooler, more calculated approach.

Hot air balloon Ability to use expansive thinking to elevate my level of awareness and rise above it all instead of using empty words.

Hotel Situation where I can check in with myself about what I need so I can feel more at home with my identity on a permanent basis.

H

Hothouse Situation where I can achieve a clearer understanding of my natural abilities by going through some intense self-development.

Hot spring Situation where I can immerse myself in my more heated emotions so I can take a down-to-earth approach in working with them.

Hot tub Ability to feel comfortable with some of my more volatile feelings so I can be open to making the most of whatever emerges.

Hot water tank Ability to contain heated feelings that have been building up so I can channel them in the most effective way.

Hound Instinctive ability to show my unconditional loyalty and affection for particular people without continually harassing them.

Hour Opportunity to take my time so I can understand the significance of what I am trying to do and how long it will take.

Hourglass Ability to have a very clear view of how long I need rather than being concerned that time is running out.

House Situation where I have the security and support I need so I can comfortably explore all aspects of my inner and outer lives.

House alarm Ability to alert myself to any unwelcome thoughts intruding on my plans so I can stay calm and take decisive action.

House arrest Opportunity to slow a fast-moving situation so I can take the time to explore my inner self without limitations.

Houseboat Situation where I can maintain my emotional stability by using my learning and experience to give me security and support.

Housebound Opportunity to make a big step forward in a character-building development rather than feeling I am holding myself back.

Household item Ability to identify a specific quality of my individual talent so I can use it to consistently connect with another person.

Household of three Opportunity to become more intimately aware of my talent for creatively conceiving new ideas with a number of others.

Housemate Aspect of my character that feels comfortable in openly sharing some of my innermost feelings with the people around me.

House sitter Aspect of my character that helps me step outside my comfort zone so I can look after different aspects of my inner life.

Housetrained Ability to develop aspects of my inner self by being open to outside advice and having the discipline to commit to it.

Housewarming Opportunity to get my personal development moving by putting more energy into it rather than trying to appear cool.

Housework Opportunity to express my fundamental value so I can make the effort to connect with a more secure sense of identity.

Housing estate Situation where I can surround myself with like-minded people to make progress in a more down-to-earth manner.

Hovel Situation where I can have a character-building experience so I can make a huge transformation in how other people see me.

Hovercraft Ability to use the power of my ideas to rise above more practical concerns so I can negotiate a complex emotional situation.

Hovering Opportunity to use my powerful thinking to make a definite decision and move on rather than just floating about aimlessly.

Howl Instinctive opportunity to confront an uncomfortable situation so I can draw attention to it by giving voice to how I really feel.

Hub Ability to make consistent progress by keeping my mind centered rather than feeling that everything else revolves around me.

Hubbub Opportunity to be clear about what I am trying to communicate rather than letting it get lost in the noise.

Hubcap Ability to look after what fundamentally motivates me and take good care of it without doing it for the sake of appearances.

Huddle Opportunity to get in closer contact with the people around me so we can mutually reassure one another other about our value.

Hue Mood that can color my perspective by reflecting my range of emotions so I can have a deeper understanding of how I feel.

Hue and cry Opportunity to pursue one of my ambitions by speaking up powerfully so I can draw public attention to my special talents.

Huff Opportunity to display my unique expertise to other people, even though some of my skills may appear quite insubstantial at first.

Hug Opportunity to get much closer to a powerful aspect of my nature by embracing it instead of trying to keep it at arm's length.

Huge Realization that my talents are far more significant than I thought and that I can use them to bring me an abundance of success.

Hula hoop Ability to keep myself centered so I can take a more dynamic approach in influencing what is happening around me.

Hulk Ability to rediscover a large part of myself I have been neglecting so I can continue to explore my emotional life.

Hull Ability to positively displace emotional concerns I may have so I can navigate some potentially complex sentiments.

Hullabaloo Opportunity to make a big noise about my unique talents rather than always having others clamoring for my attention.

Hum Opportunity to speak the words I need to rather than feeling I'm just droning on endlessly in the background.

Human Realization that the most effective way to take advantage of complex unfamiliar situations is just to be myself.

Human cannonball Aspect of my character that has the power to be more direct in my aims rather than throwing myself at a challenge.

Humane killer Ability to take direct action to positively transform my creative situation instead of feeling uncomfortable about the past.

Human trafficking Aspect of my character that needs to make my own decisions rather than feeling others are using me for their own ends.

Humanitarian mission Opportunity to be clear about what my goals are so I can resolve emerging tensions about long-term ambitions.

Humanoid Aspect of my character that can embody my true humanity rather than revealing myself as everyone would like me to.

Human shield Ability to feel secure about what I believe in so I can defend my deepest principles against outside challenges.

Human voice Essential ability to identify with my deeper source of inspiration so I can say what I mean to other people.

Humble Realization that I should take more pride in my skills and abilities instead of feeling I need to keep a low profile.

Humid Realization that I may be allowing my sentiments and experiences to cloud my judgment in a potentially sticky situation.

Humidifier Ability to create a more emotional atmosphere so I feel better about working with some apparently dry subject matter.

Humiliated Realization that I can achieve more respect for my work by having the confidence to behave in a dignified manner.

Hummingbird Instinctive ability to rise above practical concerns and colorfully make my point to encourage my talents to blossom.

Humor Realization that I should take myself a bit less seriously rather than relying on other people to lighten my mood.

H

Humorless Realization that I can reveal some serious truths by always being more open to seeing the funny side of the situation.

Humorous Realization that I can gain profound insight into a situation by seriously examining some of its more ludicrous aspects.

Hump Ability to rise to an obvious challenge and successfully get beyond it rather than allowing myself to feel depressed in any way.

Humpback bridge Situation where I can resolve a dilemma by creating an obvious connection between two apparently distinct areas of my life.

Hunch Ability to shape my preferred outcome by making a straightforward decision rather than feeling I have to rely on my intuition.

Hunchback Aspect of my character that stands up for what I believe in rather than feeling I have to change my views just to fit in.

Hundred Ability to acknowledge that I have accomplished my original intentions and feel confident about fulfilling any future challenges.

Hung Realization that I can take a more practical, down-to-earth approach rather than leaving the eventual outcome up in the air.

Hunger Essential opportunity to fulfill my appetite for success by understanding my most fundamental drives and deepest desires.

Hunger strike Opportunity to feed my need for recognition so I make an impact rather than causing myself prolonged discomfort.

Hung over Realization that I need to let go of past confusion so I can do some clear thinking and enjoy my developing awareness.

Hunk Aspect of my character that can be a big attraction to other people, even though they can't take in all my qualities at once.

Hunt Opportunity to search for my true self and find out who I really am rather than just being involved in meaningless pursuits.

Hunted Realization that I need to track down a valuable part of my potential talent I often unconsciously conceal from myself.

Hunter Aspect of my character that follows my creative instincts so I can track down and identify what makes me most fulfilled.

Hunting Realization that I need to be clear about what I am looking for rather than just going through a series of highs and lows.

Hunting horn Ability to sound out my true calling by drawing attention to my different pursuits so I can choose the most valuable.

Huntress Aspect of my character that pursues my creative ambitions by using my powerful instincts and intuition to decide my future aims.

Hunt saboteur Aspect of my character that can make a positive transformation to my professional pursuits rather than disrupting them.

Huntsman Aspect of my character that embodies the individual strength and power I need to meet my target and pursue ambitions.

Hurdle Ability to quickly overcome a barrier in my path so I can continue to take powerful steps in pursuit of my ambitions.

Hurl Opportunity to forcefully get rid of something I no longer need so I can continue to influence events from a distance.

Hurricane Opportunity to channel my energy in a heated situation so I can stay calm rather than getting carried away by it all.

Hurry Opportunity to take my time and consider what I need so I can quickly move to a deliberate, successful outcome.

Hurt Opportunity to heal a painful situation by healthily resolving it instead of continuing to allow myself to needlessly suffer.

Hurtle Opportunity to direct my ambition so I can achieve my goal in a more controlled way instead of getting carried away.

Husband Aspect of my character that embodies long-term commitment to developing strength and power for achieving my dreams.

Husk Natural ability to let go of some old defensive layers so I can develop an idea into something much bigger and more powerful.

Husky Instinctive ability to show my unconditional loyalty and affection for particular people so we can make smoother progress.

Husky voice Opportunity to speak from a place of deeper inspiration so I can express feelings that will resonate with people.

Hustle Opportunity to forcefully express my fundamental value to people by energetically making positive changes as quickly as I can.

Hut Situation where I have the security and support I need so I can explore a specific aspect of my inner and outer lives.

Hutch Situation where I can look after my abundant creativity by making sure I can protect myself from any harmful challenges.

Hybrid Ability to use two of my specific qualities to creatively produce a more valuable outcome in a resilient and innovative way.

Hybrid being Aspect of my character that can blend two of my talents so I can step into my power and take the action I need to.

Hybrid car Ability to use a range of influences to motivate my progress so I can achieve my objective in a more efficient manner.

Hybrid plant Natural ability to use an illuminating opportunity to vigorously develop a variety of ideas in a down-to-earth way.

Hydra Instinctive ability to use a number of ideas to heal hurt feelings so I can develop a much healthier self-image.

Hydrant Ability to quickly channel emotions so I can influence creative developments that appear to be getting out of control.

Hydration Opportunity to use my experience and learning to get a good feel for a situation so I can continue to maintain it in a healthy way.

Hydraulic Realization that I can use emotions to produce a much more powerful outcome rather than using physical effort alone.

Hydroelectric plant Situation where I can use my accumulated experience to provide a powerfully emotive force I can convey to others.

Hydrogen bomb Ability to safely contain the potential energy I need for a life-changing transformation so I can choose how to use it.

Hydrotherapy Opportunity to relieve an unhealthy situation by resolving emotional tensions I may have not been attending to.

Hyena Instinctive ability to show unconditional loyalty and affection rather than being concerned that I won't be taken seriously.

Hygiene Realization that I can work through any inner conflicts I may have by maintaining a healthy outlook on any challenges.

Hymen Essential ability to fully open up to my capacity for individual creativity so I can naturally bring my concepts to life.

Hymn Ability to instinctively communicate with my spiritual self by giving voice to an evocative display of how I feel.

Hype Ability to authentically communicate my fundamental value rather than feeling I have to appear larger than life to other people.

Hyper Realization that I may have to place more emphasis on my unique expertise instead of always taking a more subtle approach.

Hyperactive Opportunity to take a calmer approach to a situation so I can take decisive action instead of keeping myself busy.

H

Hyperlink Ability to quickly connect a number of vital pieces of information together without becoming too attached to any of them.

Hypermarket Situation where I can display my huge talent and have its value recognized so I can choose from a wide number of options.

Hyperventilating Essential opportunity to use the power of my deeper inspiration rather than getting dizzy about an exciting new possibility.

Hypnosis Opportunity to profoundly immerse myself in how I see the world so I can create a deeper understanding of my place in it.

Hypnotist Aspect of my character that has the power to deepen my understanding of how I can turn my aspirations into accomplishments.

Hypochondriac Aspect of my character that takes a healthy approach to my well-being rather than worrying about inner tensions.

Hypocrite Aspect of my character that stands up for what I believe in instead of always trying to keep other people happy.

Hypothetical Realization that I need to take practical action to ensure my chosen outcome rather than assuming everything will be perfect.

Hysterectomy Opportunity to create the space I need to develop some of my concepts so I can continue to nurture my ambitions.

Hysteria Opportunity to take a more considered approach so my emotional power can achieve a valuable practical outcome.

Hysterical Realization that I can look at a challenging situation in a more lighthearted way, even though others may not find it funny.

H

Ibex Instinctive ability to play around with my strength and vitality so I can make the sheer effort required to stay at my peak.

Ibis Instinctive ability to step into a potentially messy situation so I can sift through my feelings and deal with any tensions.

Ibuprofen Ability to take specific action so I can positively transform a painful situation rather than trying to ignore it.

Icarus complex Aspect of my character that can be distracted by the brilliance of my own talent, even though it can be very liberating.

Ice Ability to use my warmth and vitality to keep a situation moving rather than feeling I'm trying to play it too cool.

Ice age Opportunity to powerfully reshape my current situation by drawing on my extensive accumulated experience over time.

Ice ax Ability to take a series of decisive actions that will help me come to grips with a potentially precarious situation.

Iceberg Situation where I can coolly connect with some of my deeper emotions so I can become more aware of their powerful presence.

Icebox Ability to fulfill my ambitions in a fresh, healthy way by taking a cool and considered approach to my personal boundaries.

Icebreaker Ability to make myself feel more at ease in awkward situations by knowing that I have the power to work through my emotions.

Ice bucket Ability to calmly fulfill one of my emotional needs by using my accumulated experience to consistently carry me through.

Ice climber Aspect of my character that can coolly raise my level of understanding by taking the time to chip away at a major challenge.

Ice cream Potential to fulfill a short-term ambition by trying to appear cool without paying attention to possible long-term gains.

Ice-cream cone Ability to shape my circumstances by being able to contain my short-term ambitions so I can get a grip on them.

Ice cube Ability to take a more refreshing approach to how I fulfill my emotional needs by being very clear about the shape I am in.

Iced tea Potential to fulfill an emotional need by taking a cooler and more relaxed approach so I can stimulate my creative processes.

Ice hockey Opportunity to use my skill to play around with ways of achieving my goals rather than just trying to skate over any challenges.

Ice hotel Situation where I can take a less emotional approach to understanding my value so I can become more comfortable with it.

Ice pack Ability to coolly gather the resources I need so I can take the heat out of a potentially uncomfortable situation.

Ice pick Ability to quickly get to the point so I can experience the value of my accumulated learning in much greater detail.

Ice rink Situation where I can gracefully explore some deeper feelings rather than skimming over them superficially.

Ice skater Aspect of my character that can use my energy and self-motivation to help me make progress by using a balanced approach.

Ice skates Ability to apply direct pressure to keep a situation moving in a graceful manner rather than letting it slip away.

Icicle Ability to clearly see how my emotions naturally build up so I can keep them under control and always get to the point.

Icing Potential to fulfill an ambition by attracting others to go beyond surface appearances so we can make a breakthrough.

Icon Ability to clearly see the outcome I'm looking for so I can consistently point myself in the right direction.

Idea Essential opportunity to form a clear understanding of how I see my current situation so I can easily develop it further.

Ideal Realization that I don't have to completely fulfill my ambitions to be perfectly happy with the results.

Identity Essential awareness of who I am and my potential for using my different characteristics to take meaningful action.

Identity card Ability to be clear about the actions I need to take so I can consistently achieve individual recognition.

Identity check Opportunity to examine my behavior in more detail so I can reach a clearer understanding of who I want to be.

Identity parade Opportunity to proudly display the different aspects of my expertise so I can pick out my most valuable talents.

Identity tag Ability to make a stronger connection to who I really am so I can consistently communicate my value to other people.

Identity theft Opportunity to take responsibility for the value of my individual talents rather than letting people take credit for them.

Ideogram Ability to directly express my ideas in an open, honest manner so I can make my mark with the people around me.

Idiom Ability to express myself in a much more powerful way, even though it may not be immediately obvious to the people around me.

Idiot Aspect of my character that is happy to make mistakes in order to reach a successful outcome, even though it may appear foolish.

Idiot savant Aspect of my character that has an incredible talent for dealing with the most complex situation in a deceptively simple way.

Idle Realization that I can use my self-motivation to get one of my ambitions moving instead of letting it idle.

Idol Aspect of my character that needs other people to admire my qualities so I can develop into who I want to be.

Idyllic Realization that my circumstances do not have to be entirely pleasant and peaceful for me to completely enjoy the experience.

Igloo Situation where I can shape my circumstances to feel more comfortable, even though the prevailing mood can be quite chilly.

Ignition Opportunity to use my creative spark to get fired up so I can direct my energy toward a successful outcome.

Ignition key Ability to unlock a specific aspect of my potential that will help me make powerful progress with my ambitions.

Ignorance Realization that I can gain valuable experience by understanding that I perhaps don't know as much as I thought I did.

Iguana Instinctive ability to express my fundamental creativity so I can feel more at home with my natural spiritual growth.

Ill Essential opportunity to use my natural strength and power to resolve an unhealthy situation rather than feeling uneasy about it.

Illegal Realization that I have ultimate responsibility for my behavior instead of always allowing others to judge my actions.

Illegible Realization that I can clearly make my mark on a situation by spelling out exactly what information I need from other people.

Illegitimate Realization that I am responsible for the outcomes of my actions rather than feeling I have to conform to expectations.

Illicit Realization that it is up to me to make the most of my resources instead of always denying myself the opportunity to succeed.

Illiterate Realization that developing my ability to communicate clearly is one of the most effective ways to achieve my ambitions.

Illness Essential opportunity to have a healthy awareness of my own needs instead of always feeling something is wrong with me.

Illuminate Opportunity to understand a situation with greater awareness by using the power of my creativity and wisdom to clarify it.

Illusion Realization that I am being honest about my abilities and know what to do instead of feeling my mind is somehow tricking me.

Illusionist Aspect of my character that has a firm grasp of the underlying practicalities rather than just appearing to be in control.

Illustration Ability to see the bigger picture by clearly understanding some of the less obvious aspects of what is happening.

Illustrator Aspect of my character that can vividly express my insights rather than just having a sketchy idea of what is going on.

Image Ability to understand what I am looking for so I can clearly picture the outcome that I would like to see.

Imagination Essential opportunity to create valuable outcomes in the world by having the power to create them in my mind first.

Imbalance Opportunity to observe how fairly I attend to my various commitments rather than blowing the situation out of all proportion.

Imbecile Aspect of my character that helps me to further develop my mental strength when dealing with potentially difficult challenges.

Imitation Opportunity to make a difference by doing original work rather than feeling I have to copy everyone else.

Immature Realization that I can continue to develop my ripening confidence instead of feeling I lack the deeper experience I need.

Immediate Opportunity to realize how close I am to achieving my ambitions rather than thinking I always have to act without delay.

Immense Realization that I have almost limitless opportunities to develop my huge talent instead of feeling options are minimal.

Immersion Opportunity for a profound learning experience by going deeper into my emotions rather than feeling I'm getting in over my head.

Immersion heater Ability to become excited about the current situation so I can direct my energy to powerfully transforming it.

Immigrant Aspect of my character that permits me to explore what is foreign and unfamiliar so I feel much more at home with it.

Imminent Realization that I can easily identify new opportunities that are approaching instead of worrying about what will happen next.

Imminent disaster Opportunity to use an ongoing transformation to my advantage rather than allowing it to get out of control.

Immobility Opportunity to use my strength and power to take a series of decisive steps so I can get things moving again.

I

Immoral Realization that I always know the right thing to do rather than feeling I have to conform to the expectations of other people.

Immortal Realization that I can use my enduring talent to help me stay vitally aware of emerging opportunities for my creativity.

Immune response Opportunity to quickly establish firm personal boundaries by taking active steps to protect what's most important to me.

Immunity Opportunity to understand how privileged I am rather than feeling vulnerable to the whims of other people.

Imp Aspect of my character whose mischievous nature can help me develop a seemingly minor skill into something more valuable.

Impact Opportunity to use my power to make a definite transformation without feeling I have to be too forceful about using it.

Impacted tooth Essential opportunity to confidently display my power to others rather than feeling forced into uncomfortable action.

Impaired Opportunity to powerfully draw on hidden reserves of strength and vitality instead of feeling weak and vulnerable.

Impala Instinctive ability to make an enormous intuitive leap so I can use my natural creativity in a variety of new areas.

Impaled Opportunity to get to the point where I can make my own decisions instead of feeling pinned down by the demands of other people.

Impassable Opportunity to reach my objective by finding my way through rather than being concerned about any potential obstacles.

Impatience Realization that I can achieve my chosen outcome more quickly by slowing everything down to see the bigger picture.

Impediment Ability to use my unique talents to make a difference instead of

thinking that circumstances may be holding me back.

Impenetrable Opportunity to open up and make myself more accessible so I can go beyond just having a superficial relationship.

Imperfect Realization that I can use my individual approach to make a difference instead of being concerned about the exact outcome.

Impersonal Opportunity to achieve faster results by taking a more informal approach rather than thinking I have to keep my distance.

Implant Ability to firmly immerse myself in an emerging opportunity instead of letting just the thought of it get under my skin.

Implanted electrode Ability to become more aware of my current way of thinking so I can take practical action rather than internalizing it.

Import Opportunity to bring myself into contention by understanding the value of some ideas that may initially seem unfamiliar to me.

Important Realization that some apparently trivial details can turn out to be far more significant than I had previously imagined.

Impossible Realization that exploring unfamiliar situations in greater detail can give me a far better idea of what is actually possible.

Impossible architecture Situation where I can create the space to explore unusual possibilities so I can constructively make the most of them.

Impossible outcome Opportunity to successfully reach my chosen result by understanding how I can use my unconscious power to influence the outcome.

Impossible task Opportunity to use my expertise to make my choices instead of feeling I will never be appear good enough to others.

Impostor Aspect of my character enabling me to be my true self rather than just manifesting myself in a way that keeps others happy.

Impotence Essential opportunity to stimulate my natural creativity so I can firmly assert my beliefs and stand up for them.

Impound Opportunity to unleash my creative instincts rather than feeling I have to keep them locked away out of sight.

Impregnable Realization that I have the power to bring my more fertile ideas to life by having the courage to go beyond surface appearances.

Impression Opportunity to make my mark so I can use my influence to help me to decide the outcome of my current situation.

Imprisoned Opportunity to break out of my self-imposed limitations rather than feeling trapped by the beliefs of those around me.

Improper Realization that I can use my judgment to decide a suitable course of action instead of being concerned about criticism.

Improvisation Opportunity to respond to the needs of the people around me rather than making it up as I go along.

Improvement Opportunity to develop my skills and talents so I can advance my understanding of my talents and how to use them.

Imprudent Realization that I need to quickly take appropriate action rather than spend a lot of time thinking about the consequences.

Impulse Opportunity to consistently motivate myself by observing my instinctive responses and how they can change my perspective.

Impurity Ability to use a variety of influences to achieve my chosen outcome rather than worrying about imperfections in my approach.

In Opportunity to feel at home with what is emerging for me so I can decide whether to develop it or just let it go.

Inability Realization that making my own decisions gives me the power to fully achieve what I originally intended to accomplish.

Inability to move Opportunity to reach a much deeper understanding of my emotions and the power they have to fundamentally motivate me.

Inability to speak Opportunity to honestly express my feelings to those around me instead of thinking it is not up to me to say anything.

Inaccessible Opportunity to successfully reach my objective by being more approachable to others rather than trying to keep my distance.

Inaccurate Realization that I don't need all the facts to understand precisely what I need to realize what feels right for me.

Inadvertent Realization that I will achieve a better understanding of my real intentions by being open to potentially unpredictable outcomes.

Inanimate Realization that I can bring my ambitions back to life by revitalizing a creative talent that I may have been neglecting.

Inappropriate Realization that I instinctively know the right thing to do and say, even though I may sometimes feel uncomfortable about it.

Inappropriate clothing Opportunity to display myself as the person I want to be instead of always trying to fit in with other people's expectations.

Inappropriate intimacy Opportunity to get in touch with my individual creativity rather than continually trying to contain my passion and excitement.

Inarticulate Realization that the best way to communicate what I need from others is to be flexible in how I voice my needs.

Inauguration Opportunity to formally recognize my ability to make powerful decisions and have them respectfully acknowledged by others.

I

Incandescent Realization that I can use powerful energy to illuminate what is happening rather than feeling angry with myself.

Incantation Ability to clearly spell out my deeper truth to others instead of hoping that everything will work like a charm.

Incapacitated Opportunity to realize the huge amount of learning and experience I can draw on rather than feeling completely helpless.

Incarcerated Opportunity to break free from any self-imposed limitations instead of feeling that others are taking liberties with me.

Incendiary device Ability to use individual passion to make a creative transformation and then ensure I keep it under control.

Incense Ability to transform a situation by creating a much more favorable atmosphere rather than getting really angry about it.

Incentive Ability to motivate myself by realizing how I can use this opportunity to increase the value of my talents in the future.

Incest Opportunity to become more intimately connected with my creative power by understanding the importance of my familiar qualities.

Inch Ability to make consistent progress by paying attention to the smaller details and how they can add up into larger results.

Incident Opportunity to choose my preferred outcome by taking firm, decisive action rather than seeing what might occur to me.

Incinerator Ability to use my creative energies to transform the aspects of a situation that are no longer of any practical use to me.

Incisor Essential ability to use my power and confidence in a really decisive way so I can consistently make definite choices.

Incline Situation where I may need to make more of an effort to reach my objective, even though I am really motivated to achieve it.

Incognito Realization that I need to be honest about the value of my expertise rather than allowing others treat me like a nobody.

Income Ability to have my real value consistently recognized by other people so I can welcome any approaching opportunities.

Income tax Ability to honestly declare the true value of my talents instead of just burdening myself with unnecessary obligations.

Incongruous Realization that I need to adapt my surroundings to my preferences rather than always feeling I am out of place.

Incredible Realization that I have the potential to achieve amazing results, even though I may find it difficult to believe at the moment.

Incubator Ability to work with a fertile idea that is just beginning to form so I can develop it in a caring, consistent manner.

Incubus Aspect of my character that can assert my creative power in an open, gentle way rather than trying to conceal my intentions.

Incurable Realization that I have the strength and vitality to remedy an unhealthy situation by resolving to take immediate action.

Indecent assault Opportunity to resolve a conflict by vigorously protecting my creative space so I can conceive a peaceful solution.

Indecent exposure Opportunity to develop my creative potential in private instead of revealing every aspect of it to those around me.

Indecisiveness Opportunity to choose what I find most meaningful by stepping into my power and standing up for what I believe in.

Independence Realization that I have the freedom to ask for help when I need it rather than feeling that I always have to go it alone.

Indestructible Realization that I can maintain my enduring sense of purpose by always being open to any transformational possibilities.

Index Ability to reach a much better understanding of what I'm looking for instead of always searching randomly.

Index finger Essential ability to identify the actions I need to take so I'm always able to point myself in the right direction.

Indicator Ability to identify what my unconscious intentions are so I can choose the direction I need to progress in.

Indigenous Essential opportunity to always feel at home with my choices by understanding how my surroundings can shape my decisions.

Indigestion Essential opportunity to thoroughly process any recent experiences so I can absorb their real value in a healthy way.

Indignant Realization that I can feel much happier by just pleasing myself rather than getting worked up about the actions of others.

Indignity Realization that I can attract more respect for my achievements by having the confidence to behave in an honorable manner.

Indigo Mood that can color my perspective by reflecting the profound nature of my spiritual explorations and the awareness they reveal.

Indiscreet Realization that I always say just the right thing when I speak from my heart instead of feeling I am revealing too much.

Indistinct Opportunity to clearly understand what my intentions are rather than relying on vague beliefs for guidance.

Individual Aspect of my character that can use my unique perspective to develop a more universal understanding of the world.

Indoors Situation where I can go beyond my comfort zone and explore aspects of my inner life that may have seemed closed to me.

Indulgent Realization that I can gratify some of my more challenging desires by having the discipline to take a stricter approach.

Industrial Realization that I can achieve success on a much larger scale by organizing myself to make more effective use of my skills.

Industrial action Opportunity to make a long-term commitment to a valuable outcome instead of walking out on what I have achieved so far.

Industrial espionage Opportunity to be open about the value of my expertise rather than always trying to disguise my underlying talent.

Industrial plant Situation where I can consistently develop a valuable outcome on a worthwhile basis by using talent and dedication.

Industrial strength Realization that concentrating on my powers of self-motivation will help me achieve my chosen outcome.

Industry Ability to make a systematic effort so I can enterprisingly use my raw talent to achieve a consistently valuable outcome.

Inebriated Opportunity to take a more sober and clearheaded approach to a situation rather than feeling confused by my emotions.

Inert Realization that the only way I can make a fundamental transformation is to become more animated about my involvement in it.

Inevitability Realization that my individual actions can create a positive outcome rather than constantly hesitating to make a change.

Inevitable conflict Opportunity to decisively resolve a tension between two apparently opposing needs to achieve a successful result.

Inevitable disaster Opportunity to realize I can use my power to make a difference rather than feeling everything is getting out of control.

Inevitable outcome Opportunity to decide the final result I would like to see instead of always allowing others to choose it for me.

Infant Aspect of my character that embodies my uniquely precious talents and holds all my potential for supportively developing them.

Infantry Aspects of my character that have the courage and discipline to take the steps I need to peacefully defend my beliefs.

Infection Opportunity to express healthy personal boundaries so I can maintain strong relationships instead of just feeling ill at ease.

Inferno Situation where I can keep my cool by using my emotional capacity to ensure I don't get carried away by my creative passion.

Infidelity Opportunity to strengthen my confidence in the value of my talents rather than feeling they may no longer seem attractive.

Infinity Situation where everything seems to be possible and I have the time and space to choose my preferred outcome.

Infinity pool Situation where I can immerse myself in my emotions and realize there is no limit to how much learning I can accumulate.

Inflamed Essential opportunity to resolve an increasingly uncomfortable feeling by using my passion and creativity in a healthier way.

Inflate Opportunity to use my expansive thinking to give shape to a bigger idea rather than apparently blowing up for no reason.

In-flight entertainment Ability to keep my attention focused as I make progress with a complex project, even though I feel my options may be limited.

Influential people Aspects of my character that have the power and authority to help me choose the outcome that will work best for me.

Information Ability to understand my way of thinking about a situation so I can use my ideas to reach my intended objective.

Informer Aspect of my character that can objectively observe my behaviors, even though I may not choose to show them to others.

Ingot Ability to use my fundamental strength to channel the power of my creative energies so I can shape a definite outcome.

Inhaling Essential ability to use the prevailing atmosphere to keep myself inspired so I can continue to stay fully motivated.

Inheritance Ability to understand the creative power of my wiser self so I can realize the value of a fundamental transformation.

Inhuman Realization that the most effective way to successfully deal with unfamiliar and unsettling situations is to be myself.

Initiation Opportunity to cross a threshold so I can align my identity with a larger group and find out more about who I really am.

Initiative Realization that I have the confidence to take the first step instead of feeling I have to wait for someone else to do it for me.

Injection Opportunity to introduce a higher level of enthusiasm by using my penetrating awareness to get beyond surface impressions.

Injunction Opportunity to make my own choices about what to do rather than feeling I am constantly being judged by others.

Injured Realization that I can naturally develop much healthier relationships instead of feeling that other people can be hurtful.

Injured animal Opportunity to remove influences that may be harmful to my creativity so I can instinctively achieve a healthier result.

Injured person Opportunity to use my individual power to make a positive change rather than worrying it might damage my reputation.

Injured soldier Opportunity to use courage and discipline to deal with any ongoing inner tensions so I can peacefully resolve them.

Injury Opportunity to take action so I can prevent an unhealthy situation instead of leaving myself open to criticism from others.

Injustice Realization that I know the right thing to do rather than blaming my apparent lack of choice on those around me.

Ink Ability to channel my feelings so I can permanently make my mark on a situation and emphasize my unique value to people.

Inkblot Ability to use my imagination so I can clearly see the bigger picture in what originally may have seemed to be a mistake.

In-law Aspect of my character that embodies my wider commitment to developing and exploring the less familiar aspects of myself.

Inlet Situation where I can achieve a deeper emotional insight into the practical realities that are surrounding my progress.

Inn Situation where I can feel more comfortable with what I have achieved so far by taking some time out to consider my progress.

Inner Realization that I can gain a great deal of insight by opening myself up to the strength and power of my individual talents.

Inner tube Ability to maintain my comfortable progress with an ambition without being too concerned about dealing with outside pressures.

Innocence Realization that giving myself the freedom to question my intentions is far more powerful than blaming myself for outcomes.

Inoculation Opportunity to absorb what has been making me feel ill at ease so I can develop a healthy and positive response to it.

Inquest Opportunity to examine why I have been neglecting my talents so I can look at ways of revitalizing them in the future.

Inquiry Opportunity to discover how I feel by asking myself what I need to make the most of my potential ambitions.

Inquisition Opportunity to honestly examine my deeper motivations by having the courage to ask myself some challenging questions.

Insane Essential opportunity to rationally explore some unusual possibilities that may seem like complete madness to other people.

Inscription Ability to use my creative talents to carve out a name for myself so I can make my mark with the people around me.

Insect Instinctive ability to make the most of emerging opportunities in arduous circumstances so I can thrive in any situation.

Insecurity Realization that having the courage to step outside my comfort zone will make me feel far more secure in my future experiences.

Insensitive Realization that opening myself up to unfamiliar challenges will help me achieve a much better feel for what I really need.

Inside Situation where I can open myself up to some exciting new possibilities by making the commitment to develop my inner potential.

Inside job Opportunity to be really honest with myself so I can gain access to the hidden potential I often keep locked away.

Insignia Ability to identify what I find most significant about a situation so I can recognize its value and take meaningful action.

Insignificance Realization that I can make a vital contribution to a successful outcome instead of feeling my actions are of no consequence.

Insomnia Essential opportunity to really wake up to what makes me feel happiest rather than always trying to stay in my comfort zone.

Inspector Aspect of my character that explores how to develop my skills and expertise instead of just critically examining my abilities.

Inspirational Opportunity to experience my passion and vitality so I can powerfully express my thoughts and theories to other people.

Instant Opportunity to take immediate action so I can achieve my ambitions right now rather than delaying my decision any longer.

Instructions Ability to understand the steps I can freely take instead of always waiting for someone else to tell me what to do.

Instructor Aspect of my character that always encourages me to develop my special skills and has the discipline to continue my learning.

Instrument Ability to gauge how well I feel that I am performing so I can get a clear indication of how I am measuring up.

Instrumental Ability to Instinctively communicate with others by expressing myself in a way that provides a fundamental understanding.

Instrument panel Ability to clearly understand what is happening around me, even though it may not seem obvious at first sight.

Insulation Ability to stay in my comfort zone by using accumulated knowledge to distance myself from a potentially challenging situation.

Insult Opportunity to honestly display my pride in my achievements rather than always jumping on my lack of self-confidence.

Insurance policy Ability to protect myself from any future mishaps by believing in the value of my talents and success in using them.

Insurmountable Realization that I have the power to move beyond self-limiting beliefs so I can continue my progress to my goal.

Insurmountable obstacle Situation where I need to tackle an issue as soon as possible so I can move into a new area of opportunity.

Intelligence Realization that I have a larger capacity for learning than I previously realized instead of just thinking that I may be ignorant.

Intelligence gathering Opportunity to become more aware of what I have learned so I can demonstrate the full range of my expertise and experience.

Intelligence officer Aspect of my character that gives me permission to step into my power so I can share by unique insights with others.

Intense Realization that staying as calm as possible can be the most powerful way to identify my deeper purpose and connect with it.

Intensive care Opportunity to take a healthier approach to resolving inner tensions instead of worrying about them around the clock.

Intentions Realization that I have the talents and resources to turn my ideas into action so I can achieve consistently successful results.

Intercom Ability to clearly listen to my internal dialogue so I can speak out and openly share my feelings with the people around me.

Intercourse Opportunity to become more intimately connected with my creative power so I can conceive new channels for my passions.

Interest Ability to turn my attention toward steadily increasing my value instead of being indifferent to any emerging opportunities.

Interface Ability to bring a number of areas of my expertise together so I can make some positive choices about my preferred outcome.

Interference Opportunity to minimize my participation in a potentially confusing situation so I can express my feelings more coherently.

Interior Situation where I can achieve powerful insights by being more open to exploring feelings and ideas emerging for me.

Internal organ Essential ability to consistently perform a special task by being instinctively aware of what feelings I really need to process.

Internet Ability to connect with wider aspects

of my knowledge by becoming more aware of my thought processes and what develops.

Internet troll Aspect of my character that has the courage to honestly and openly express my feelings rather than remaining anonymous.

Interpreter Aspect of my character that helps me understand what is happening in an unfamiliar situation so I can promptly respond.

Interrogation Opportunity to ask myself powerful questions so I can have the honesty to be open to whatever answers might emerge.

Interrupted Opportunity to resolve unexpected challenges that might break my concentration so I can successfully continue my progress.

Interrupted intimacy Opportunity to connect more deeply with my individual talent rather than allowing others to intrude on my creative process.

Intersection Situation where I can align a number of my conflicting intentions by making a definite decision to follow a particular path.

Interval Opportunity to pause so I can reflect on what I have achieved so far and ensure that I can continue with my success.

Interview Opportunity for me to question my deeper motives so I can clearly give voice to what I need from other people.

Intestinal flora Essential ability to work with the germ of an idea so I can use it to open up to my creative talents and help them blossom.

Intestines Essential ability to digest my experiences and assimilate what I have learned so I can continue to fulfill my ambitions.

Intimacy Opportunity to connect with who I really am so I can be much more confident about sharing my deeper motivations.

Intimacy with boss Opportunity to become much more aware of my powerful ability to make confident decisions so I can successfully act on them.

Intimacy with colleague Opportunity to become more aware of my ability to develop professional characteristics I deeply admire.

Intimacy with friend Opportunity to reacquaint myself with one of my creative talents so I can use it to conceive new ideas.

Intimate embarrassment Realization that I need to take more pride in my creative achievements so I can openly share them with the people around me.

Intimate encounter Opportunity to become more profoundly aware of one of my creative talents that could prove to be unexpectedly valuable for me.

Intimate meal Opportunity to digest the full significance of a creative collaboration so I can use the experience to satisfy my ambitions.

Intimate partner Aspect of my character that helps me understand my creative potential so I can be more confident in openly sharing it.

Intimate relationship Opportunity to connect with my creative self at a deeper level so I can explore undiscovered aspects of my talent.

Intimate situation Opportunity to create some personal space where I can confidently develop my talent and become more aware of its unique qualities.

Intimidating Opportunity to courageously confront a potentially challenging situation rather than being fearful of my potential.

Intolerant Realization that I need to give myself permission to act freely instead of appearing narrow-minded in my beliefs.

Intoxicated Opportunity to keep a clear head in a very exciting situation rather than getting carried away by exhilarating feelings.

Intravenous Essential opportunity to directly connect with my natural passion and vitality so I can convey exactly how I am feeling.

Intruder Aspect of my character that needs to set firm personal boundaries instead of allowing others to interfere with my life.

Intuition Essential opportunity to directly experience how I feel so I can use my insight to achieve my preferred result.

Invalid Aspect of my character that has the power to make a valid contribution rather than always neglecting my hidden strengths.

Invalid documentation Opportunity to identify what I need to make my next move instead of always trying to justify myself to other people.

Invasion Opportunity to set a firm personal boundary in a situation where I feel I am being overwhelmed by the demands of other people.

Invention Opportunity to use my unique understanding to create something original rather than making things up to keep people happy.

Inventor Aspect of my character that uses my curiosity and insight to create unique solutions to whatever challenges I might encounter.

Inversion Opportunity to clearly look at the other side of an argument instead of feeling that my world has been turned upside down.

Investigation Opportunity to explore my self-motivation and examine my behaviors so I can continue to develop my potential.

Investment Opportunity to make time for myself so I can develop my unrealized talents into something much more valuable for me.

Invincible Realization that I can use my courage to overcome any major challenge I encounter instead of always feeling powerless.

Invisibility cloak Ability to present my self-image in a more confident way rather than

getting wrapped up in my lack of recognition.

Invisible Opportunity to openly show up as I really am so I can clearly reveal my obvious capabilities to those around me.

Invisible ink Ability to clearly communicate what I need to say rather than trying to hide my true feelings in case I upset others.

Invisible person Aspect of my character that encourages me to make myself more visible so others can recognize my unique value.

Invitation Opportunity to make a more formal commitment to personal development by taking time to openly explore my needs.

Invoice Ability to clearly speak out so that other people can fully recognize the value of my contribution to a successful outcome.

Involuntary Realization that I can make my own decisions about an emerging opportunity instead of always responding in the same way.

Invulnerable Realization that I can always feel confident in my actions by having the courage to consistently open up to other people.

Iodine Elemental ability to clear up any unseen challenges by taking a positive and healthy approach to how I express my talents.

iPad Ability to grasp what I need to do so that I can take action instead of just making a gesture to please other people.

iPod Ability to listen to what other people are trying to say to me rather than just hearing what I want to hear from them.

Iris Natural ability to quickly get to the point so I can open up to my creative opportunities and encourage them to blossom.

Iron Ability to use my fundamental strength to shape a powerful outcome without feeling that I have to be too hard and unyielding.

Ironing Opportunity to methodically smooth out any inconsistencies in the way

I present my self-image to the people around me.

Iron lung Ability to use external assistance to provide me with inspiration so I can powerfully express my thoughts and ideas.

Irrational Realization that I can take a more logical approach to resolving a challenge, even though it may initially seem to make no sense.

Irrigation Ability to channel my accumulated experience so I can develop potentially fertile ideas in a challenging situation.

Irrigation channel Situation where I can draw on my deeper experience and keep it flowing so I can be far more productive in what I create.

Irritation Opportunity to feel content and comfortable with my own needs rather than being oversensitive to outside influences.

Island Situation where I feel stable and secure by choosing to remain detached from complex emotions that are occurring around me.

Issue Ability to frequently display my talents on a more widespread basis rather than just being obsessed by one specific point.

Itch Opportunity to identify any deeper emotions that may be influencing me instead of just resolving superficial irritations.

Item Ability to identify a specific aspect of my individual talent so I can use it to consistently connect with another person.

Itemized bill Ability to clearly balance the value of a collective achievement with the personal cost of pursuing individual objectives.

Itinerary Ability to achieve a successful outcome by motivating myself to methodically explore a wide variety of specific viewpoints.

Ivory Ability to confidently display my creative instincts to people rather than feeling that I have to conceal my precious talents

Ivory tower Situation where I can consolidate my creative talent and raise it to a higher level instead of trying to appear above it all.

Ivy Natural ability to take my time so I can develop a healthy perspective rather than just trying to cling to whatever I can.

I

Jabbering Opportunity to clearly and consistently communicate my viewpoints instead of going on and on senselessly.

Jack Ability to raise my commitment to a higher level so I can make progress by fully engaging with a heavy responsibility.

Jackal Instinctive ability to transform a situation by using my natural persistence and intelligence to work my way through it.

Jackboot Ability to present my self-image to people by taking gentler steps instead of trying to stamp my authority on the situation.

Jackdaw Instinctive ability to recognize the value of my talents so I can spread my ideas by communicating them to other people.

Jacket Ability to present my self-image to people in a way that shows my more public characteristics while still concealing my privacy.

Jack-in-the-box Ability to quickly spring into action and potentially surprise myself with the emerging value of my expertise and abilities.

Jack plug Ability to make a definite connection with someone close to me so I can powerfully communicate how I feel.

Jackpot Opportunity to use my accumulated knowledge and wisdom so I can make a huge breakthrough in how people see my value.

Jacuzzi Situation where I can immerse myself in my emotions and feel relaxed and comfortable with whatever ideas bubble up.

Jade Ability to attract other people to my transformational abilities by using my charitable nature in a wise and kind manner.

Jagged Realization that I need to take a smoother, more even approach to a challenge instead of feeling torn between two decisions.

Jaguar Instinctive ability to confidently assert my need for greater independence so I can focus on my passions and drives.

Jail Situation where I can give myself total freedom to move on from any self-limiting beliefs that may be barring my progress.

Jailbreak Opportunity to use inner strength to transform some of the habitual behavior patterns that may have been holding me back.

Jailer Aspect of my character that gives me permission to act freely rather than basing my actions on what people may believe about me.

Jam Potential to fulfill an ambition by squeezing in as many experiences as possible so I can achieve a fruitful outcome.

Jamboree Opportunity to improve my mood by recognizing I need to make much more of a noise about my unique talents and experiences.

Jammed Opportunity to release myself from unnecessary commitments rather than always trying to pack too much into my life.

Janitor Aspect of my character that takes care of my most fundamental needs so I have the time and space to fulfill my ambitions.

Jar Ability to shake myself out of complacent feelings so I can preserve my options rather than trying to contain my enthusiasm.

Jargon Ability to clearly communicate my needs in a direct and honest manner instead of trying to hide behind any technicalities.

Jaundice Essential opportunity to understand my personal biases by taking a more positive approach rather than always feeling angry.

Jaunt Opportunity to take a more relaxed approach to how I view a situation by motivating myself to explore a different perspective.

Javelin Ability to decide an uncertain outcome by decisively getting to the point so I can get straight down to the practical aspects.

Jaw Essential ability to have a firm grasp of what is happening so I can speak my truth in a determined, forceful way.

Jawbone Essential ability to give a fundamental structure to what I need to say so I can use my strong beliefs to support my opinions.

Jay Instinctive ability to rise above more practical concerns so I can spread my ideas rather than chattering about them incessantly.

Jaywalker Aspect of my character that pursues my ambitions by following my own path instead of persisting with a more recognized procedure.

Jazz Ability to use my improvisational skills to create a really moving experience and powerfully communicate it to other people.

Jealousy Realization that I have huge potential to succeed rather than feeling resentful about what other people may have achieved.

Jeans Ability to present my self-image to other people in a relaxed and comfortable way that shows my levels of self-motivation.

Jedi Aspect of my character that courageously harnesses my unconscious powers so I can give myself the creative freedom I need.

Jelly Potential to fulfill an ambition by taking a firmer approach to an experience that is making me feel shaky and vulnerable.

Jelly beans Potential to fulfill a short-term ambition that seems attractive instead of taking a consistent approach to self-development.

Jellyfish Instinctive ability to have healthier relationships by being more emotionally supportive instead of just drifting about.

Jeopardy Opportunity to boldly play around with an uncertain outcome rather than feeling as if I am in danger of risking everything.

Jerkin Ability to present my self-image to others by having the confidence to clearly signal my intentions and then take action.

Jerking Opportunity to make smooth and steady progress with my ambitions instead of always feeling I am lurching out of control.

Jerky Potential to fulfill an important ambition by preserving my raw strength and power so I can produce a more substantial result.

Jerry can Ability to contain my raw creative spirit so I can use it to powerfully maintain my drive for success in achieving my goal.

Jersey Ability to present my self-image to others in a manner that shows my willingness to comfortably accommodate their needs.

Jester Aspect of my character that can see the unexpected value in a situation rather than always trying to please other people.

Jet Opportunity to concentrate on a particularly powerful idea so I can add my creative input to get it quickly moving forward.

Jet airliner Ability to direct my creative power so I can rapidly make collective progress on a major project with a variety of other people.

Jet engine Ability to consistently use my creative spirit in a measured way so I can continue to thrust forward with my ambitions.

Jet lag Opportunity to wake up to a rapidly approaching opportunity rather than feeling I am trying to play catch up.

J

Jetsam Ability to stay on top of a potentially emotional situation by making the choice to let go of what is no longer valuable to me.

Jet ski Ability to powerfully make my way through a potentially complex emotional situation rather than just skimming the surface.

Jettisoned Opportunity to decisively let go of what I no longer need so I can make much faster progress toward my objective.

Jetty Situation where I can stay grounded in practical reality and feel secure as I push forward into an emotionally complex situation.

Jewel Ability to attract other people to the value of my brilliance by consistently performing in a smooth and polished manner.

Jeweler Aspect of my character that can identify the most valuable facets of my talents so I can present them in an attractive way.

Jewelry Ability to display the aspects of myself that I find most valuable and reflect on how I can use them to attract people to me.

Jewelry box Ability to feel safer and more secure by setting boundaries around the qualities that make me most attractive to others.

Jig Opportunity to motivate myself in a lively and spontaneous manner so I can consistently reach my preferred outcome.

Jigsaw Opportunity to make sense of a situation by piecing together the areas that interest me so I can see the bigger picture.

Jimmy Ability to powerfully lever my developing skills and abilities so I can successfully open myself up to new opportunities.

Jinx Opportunity to take positive action to reach my preferred result rather than always blaming my misfortune on my circumstances.

Jitters Opportunity to calmly deal with an emerging challenge by taking the time to coordinate my actions in a thoughtful manner.

Job Opportunity to connect with my life purpose by demonstrating how I can create value by fulfilling the needs of other people.

Jockey Aspect of my character that can harness my unconscious energy, even though it seems lightweight and inconsequential.

Jockstrap Ability to present my self-image to others by supporting my creative potential so I feel more secure about using it.

Jodhpurs Ability to present my self-image to people in a way that helps me harness my unconscious energies and show my motivation.

Jogger Aspect of my character that can quickly reach my objective by using my self-motivation to take a series of consistent steps.

Jogging Opportunity to make steady and consistent progress toward my goal by taking time to recall some of my past experiences.

Join Opportunity to make a stronger connection to one of my deeper aspirations so I can successfully develop my potential.

Joiner Aspect of my character that is very skillful at using my habitual behaviors to shape outcomes in a practical manner.

Joint Ability to maintain my levels of motivation by staying flexible and being open to sharing my resources with others.

Joke Opportunity to resolve an apparently trivial dilemma by using an unexpected approach so I can take the situation seriously.

Joker Aspect of my character that can turn the situation around and create the desired effect by behaving in an unexpected manner.

Jolly Realization that I need to be happily satisfied with my motivations instead of going along with what everyone else wants.

Jotter Ability to make mental notes of the valuable points that are emerging for me so I can take practical action with them.

J

Journal Ability to regularly reflect on some of my personal experiences so I can gain a clearer understanding of their deeper value.

Journalist Aspect of my character that can eloquently communicate my current beliefs as I explore a variety of different viewpoints.

Journey Opportunity to make a major transformation in how I view a situation by motivating myself to explore a variety of perspectives.

Jowl Essential ability to express my fundamental opinions so I can give my side of the story in an honest and direct manner.

Joy Realization that I need to spend more time happily satisfying my ambitions instead of always trying to please other people.

Joyrider Aspect of my character that takes a more serious approach to achieving ambitions instead of allowing people to influence me.

Joystick Ability to reach my chosen outcome in a satisfactory manner by happily guiding myself along the path I have chosen.

Judge Aspect of my character that weighs my responsibilities and commitments by giving me a verdict on how well I am meeting them.

Judgment Opportunity to confidently make my own decisions rather than always waiting for other people to choose my actions for me.

Judo Opportunity to resolve any of my inner conflicts by using my fundamental power in a balanced way that minimizes any impact on me.

Jug Ability to get a handle on my emotions so I can happily share them rather than letting them messily pour out.

Juggernaut Ability to employ some extremely powerful drives that will ensure my success in eventually reaching my chosen objective.

Juggler Aspect of my character that can expertly deal with a rapidly changing situation rather than leaving it all up in the air.

Juggling Opportunity to successfully keep a number of commitments moving forward, even though it may leave me feeling on edge.

Jugular Essential ability to keep my natural passion and vitality flowing so I can powerfully express my heartfelt emotions.

Juice Potential to fulfill an emotional need by positively extracting the fullest value of my accumulated learning and experience.

Jukebox Ability to show my value by making a definite choice so I can share my experiences with others in a powerful way.

Jumble Ability to be clear about my fundamental needs instead of feeling I have to sort out what is confusing for other people.

Jumping Opportunity to make the most of an emerging possibility by releasing myself from any obligations that may be holding me back.

Jump lead Ability to conduct myself in a powerful way so I can bring vital energy to a situation and get charged up about it.

Jump-start Opportunity to get powerfully connected to fundamental drives and ambitions so I can get myself moving again.

Junction Situation where I can bring a number of my projects together so I can choose how to make further progress with them.

Jungle Situation where I can explore the great diversity and huge growth capacity of all the unexplored aspects of my character.

Junk Ability to work my way through an emotional situation by using traditional methods rather than feeling they have no value.

Junkie Aspect of my character that can resolve an unhealthy situation by injecting a positive outlook into my need for self-discipline.

Junk mail Ability to communicate my needs in a clear, concise way instead of needlessly trying to get the attention of other people.

J

Junk shop Situation where I can display my unique value to people by making a specific choice to let go of what I no longer need.

Junkyard Situation where I can give myself the space to be much more open about my opportunities for making a personal transformation.

Juror Aspect of my character that can make my own decisions instead of always allowing the opinions of other people to influence me.

Jury Opportunity to judge my strength of character rather than feeling I always have to wait for the verdict of other people.

Just Realization that I can quickly get to exactly where I need to be by using a fair and impartial approach to reach my objective.

Justice Realization that I am the best judge of my current situation rather than permitting other people to make my decisions for me.

Justification Ability to be consistently confident in my own decisions instead of feeling I always have to give my reasons.

Juvenile delinquent Aspect of my character that needs to take personal responsibility for my emerging potential rather than lapsing into inactivity.

J

K

Kale Potential to fulfill an ambition by having a healthy awareness of all the little wrinkles required to make my ideas happen.

Kaleidoscope Ability to imaginatively work through my habitual behavior patterns and see how they color my thinking in different ways.

Kamikaze Aspect of my character that can help me transform my life by getting an idea off the ground and then successfully landing it.

Kangaroo Instinctive ability to make a powerful creative leap forward while using past experience to help me make balanced progress.

Karaoke Opportunity to use my unique creativity to express what I need to say rather than playing along with someone else's idea.

Karate Opportunity to rapidly resolve any of my inner conflicts by being open and honest rather than worrying about my vulnerabilities.

Kayak Ability to use my self-motivation and energy to individually navigate my way through a potentially complex emotional situation.

Kazoo Ability to clearly express some of my more unusual ideas rather than feeling I'm droning on endlessly about them.

Keel Ability to maintain my emotional stability as I work my way through an unpredictable situation that might throw me off course.

Keen Realization that I can use my great enthusiasm to cut through any confusion so I can understand what is happening.

Keep Opportunity to feel more secure about the levels of experience I have accumulated so I can retain my overall perspective.

Keep fit Opportunity to maintain my unique expertise and skills so I can shape my preferred outcome in a positive and healthy manner.

Keepsake Ability to understand what memories are most precious to me so I can ensure I will always be able to treasure them.

Keg Ability to use my accumulated experience to get right to the bottom of a situation so I can provide some deeper insight.

Kelp Natural ability to make practical use of my feelings so I can thrive in any emotional situation, no matter how adverse it is.

Kennel Situation where I can feel comfortable and at home with my instinctive loyalty rather than feeling I've ended up in the doghouse.

Kernel Potential to fulfill an ambition by coming out of my shell so I can understand the value of my fundamental qualities.

Kestrel Instinctive ability to use my quick thinking to pursue a specific goal rather than feeling I am hovering around.

Ketchup Potential to fulfill an ambition by taking some time out so I can understand the true flavor of what is happening.

Kettle Ability to contain my feelings in an emotionally heated situation so I can share them with other people in a friendly way.

Key Ability to give myself the specific freedom to open up to new possibilities that will help me unlock my hidden potential.

K

Keyboard Ability to know which emotional buttons to press so I can successfully achieve my chosen outcome in a complex situation.

Key code Ability to open up to a potentially valuable opportunity by being able to clearly express myself in a very specific manner.

Key cutter Ability to take decisive action so I can give myself much more freedom to shape the outcome that I would like to see.

Keyhole Ability to understand a private situation that is usually concealed so I can open up the possibility of exploring it further.

Keyhole surgery Opportunity to deal with inner tensions by following a specific procedure to understand what is going on inside me.

Keyphone Ability to get my message through to other people so they can pick up on what I'm trying to say to them.

Khaki Mood that can color my perspective by sweeping away misconceptions so I can take a much fresher and more optimistic approach.

Kick Opportunity to use my self-motivation and energy to take immediate action so I can make the most of an exciting challenge.

Kid Aspect of my character that embodies my uniquely precious talents and holds a serious amount of potential for continuing growth.

Kidding Opportunity to demonstrate how I seriously feel rather than always playing around to keep everyone else happy.

Kidnap Opportunity to transform my situation by giving myself the freedom to take deliberate action rather than feeling like a victim.

Kidnapped by a gang Opportunity to make my own choices so I can liberate myself from feeling restricted by the expectations of others.

Kidnapper Aspect of my character that has the courage to take decisive action rather than being held hostage to my doubts and fears.

Kidney Essential ability to clarify my feelings about a situation so I can filter out any harmful and unhealthy influences.

Kidney stone Essential opportunity to break down specific discomforting issues so I can be clear about my feelings.

Kill Ability to take direct action to positively transform my situation by choosing to let go of the past and step into the future.

Killer Aspect of my character that can revitalize one of my neglected talents so I can use it to create a profound transformation.

Killer whale Instinctive ability to immerse myself in my emotions so I can generate a huge opportunity for a deeper transformation.

Killing Opportunity to transform a behavioral pattern that no longer serves me so I can continue my growth and development.

Kiln Ability to get fired up about an opportunity so I can use it to turn some possibilities into practical certainties.

Kilner jar Ability to retain a clear idea of what I need to fulfill my ambitions rather than allowing any other thoughts to intrude.

Kilt Ability to present my self-image to people by freely opening up to the wilder aspects of my creativity and how I can assert them.

Kilter Realization that I can make faster progress by lining up further opportunities rather than being thrown off balance.

Kin Aspects of my character that are most familiar to me and consistently support me by sharing my fundamental passion and vitality.

Kindergarten Situation where I can carefully nurture a variety of creative projects by taking the time to see them through fresh eyes.

Kindling Ability to ignite a creative transformation by drawing on my knowledge and trying not to become too emotionally involved.

K

Kindness Realization that generously sharing my creative gifts with others usually opens up valuable opportunities for me to explore.

King Aspect of my character that has the maturity to use my gifts wisely so my power can be widely recognized by other people.

Kingdom Situation where I can use my wider influence to make the most of my talents and resources so I can develop their full potential.

Kingfisher Instinctive ability to be immersed in my emotions so I can capture a fleeting feeling and transform it into a colorful idea.

Kinky Opportunity to straighten out a challenge by taking a different approach, even though it may deviate from normal procedure.

Kiosk Situation where I can demonstrate my value by giving myself the opportunity to publicly say what I am privately feeling.

Kipper Potential to fulfill an ambition by preserving my more emotional approach rather than allowing confusion to cloud the issue.

Kiss Essential opportunity to make a much more intimate connection so I can sensitively communicate some of my deeper feelings.

Kissing boss Opportunity to become more deeply aware of my ability to make powerful decisions and confidently express them.

Kissing colleague Opportunity to develop my own potential by speaking more openly about the professional characteristics I deeply admire.

Kissing friend Opportunity to openly express some of my deeper feelings so I can begin to reacquaint myself with my creative talents.

Kit Ability to collect my thoughts together so I can use my experiences and resources to construct a more valuable outcome.

Kit bag Ability to look after the personal resources that will help me work my way through any particularly challenging situations.

Kitchen Aspect of myself that provides the capacity to nurture myself and others, even when the situation is becoming a bit heated.

Kitchen cupboard Ability to open up to the personal resources I can use to look after my well-being instead of shutting myself off.

Kitchen sink Ability to deal with a specific challenge that may be draining energy, rather than feeling I have to deal with everything.

Kitchenware Ability to put my nurturing skills to practical use so I can create a result instead of feeling I'm just hanging around.

Kite Ability to float one of my ideas so I can play around with it rather than feeling I am stringing myself along.

Kitten Instinctive ability to feel relaxed and comfortable about myself so I can playfully develop my growing independence.

Klaxon Ability to quickly sound out some approaching opportunities so I can alert other people to the progress I am making.

Kleptomaniac Aspect of my character that should accept my value in a healthier way instead of feeling I always have to take something for it.

Knapsack Ability to access the resources I need so I can maintain my levels of self-motivation without feeling too weighed down.

Kneading Opportunity to work my way through aspects of a valuable opportunity so I can achieve the most satisfying outcome.

Knee Essential ability to take the steps I need by staying flexible, even though it can make me appear weak and vulnerable.

Kneeling Opportunity to stand up for what I believe in rather than feeling that others' needs are more important than my own.

K

Knell Opportunity to alert myself to a potentially fundamental transformation that is slowly beginning to make more sense for me.

Knickers Ability to present my self-image in a way that allows me to reveal my unique creative talents and become more intimate with them.

Knife Ability to assert my individuality by decisively cutting through any uncertainty and ensuring that I keep my mind sharp.

Knight Aspect of my character that courageously harnesses instinctive energies so I can give myself the creative freedom I need.

Knitting Opportunity to use my creative skills to connect different aspects of my story so I can feel more comfortable about them.

Knob Ability to fully grasp the significance of a specific turning point that will help me open up a new range of opportunities.

Knock Ability to focus my attention on how I can make an immediate impact instead of feeling anxious about potential failures.

Knocking Opportunity to decisively respond to an approaching opportunity rather than dismissing it as being of no consequence.

Knockout Opportunity to use my power to take a single decisive action that will wake me up to a whole new range of possibilities.

Knoll Situation where I can rise to prominence by making a little bit of effort by widening my perspective and elevating my awareness.

Knot Ability to hold a complicated situation together, so I can release myself from any commitments that prevent my progress.

Know-how Ability to understand the fundamental purpose of what I am trying to do rather than just considering the practical aspects of it.

Know-it-all Aspect of my character that is always open to new learning experiences rather than feeling I've seen it all before.

Knowledge Ability to understand that using a more emotional approach can often reveal that I know far more than I think I do.

Known Realization that I am attracted to what I find most meaningful, even though I am not consciously aware of it at the time.

Knuckle Essential ability to grasp what is happening so I can meet the challenge rather than feeling anxious about it.

Knuckleduster Ability to shape my chosen outcome in a powerful and decisive way, even though it may limit my freedom to take further action.

Koala Instinctive ability to use my natural skills to thrive in arduous conditions rather than trying to be cute about my talents.

Kohl Ability to emphasize my particular viewpoint and make it more attractive to other people, even though it may seem quite exotic.

Komodo dragon Instinctive ability to motivate myself so I can make a fundamental transformation without being too cold-blooded about it.

Kryptonite Ability to understand the fundamental element of what makes my personal story so strong instead of feeling vulnerable about it.

Kumquat Potential to fulfill an ambition by preserving a variety of resources so I can always achieve a fruitful and positive outcome.

Kung fu Opportunity to use my power to reach out to people rather than feeling vulnerable about the steps they are taking.

K

Lab coat Ability to present my self-image to others in a way that gives them confidence in my clean and methodical way of working.

Label Ability to consistently identify what I need from the people around me so I can communicate my preferences to them.

Labia Essential ability to open up to my capacity for unique creativity so I can honestly express some of my intimate feelings.

Labor Opportunity to productively work my way through a set of challenges rather than feeling that my efforts are of no consequence.

Laboratory Situation where I can find the correct solution to a dilemma by experimenting with a number of controlled, logical approaches.

Laboratory animal Instinctive ability to examine habitual behaviors to understand how they sometimes make me feel trapped.

Labor camp Situation where I can explore the practical aspects of unfamiliar challenges without feeling I am being forced into it.

Laborer Aspect of my character that is willing to make a consistent effort to develop my potential expertise and perfect my skills.

Labyrinth Situation where I can understand some of my behavior patterns by exploring my deeper identity and all the power it contains.

Lace Ability to clearly see through the more intricate details of a situation so I can take a softer and more open approach to it.

Laceration Opportunity to heal some painful feelings so I can gain healthy closure rather than feeling torn apart by the situation.

Laces Ability to carefully shape how I appear to the people around me so I can make myself feel more secure and comfortable.

Lacing Opportunity to use my emotions to influence a situation so I can bring two aspects of my self-image closer together.

Lack Opportunity to realize that I have more than enough natural talent instead of feeling I need to resolve any apparent inadequacies.

Lacquer Ability to be clear about what is happening at a deeper level rather than trying to superficially gloss over it.

Lacrosse Opportunity to stick to a particular way of working so I can use my skill to play around with how I can achieve my goals.

Lactose-intolerant Essential opportunity to look after my emotional needs by giving myself permission to act in a free and healthy manner.

Lad Aspect of my character that confidently asserts my youthful ambitions and has the potential to develop my strength and power.

Ladder Ability to use a particular series of steps to achieve a specific ambition so that I can continue to perform at a high level.

Ladle Ability to use my capacity for nurturing the needs of other people so I can share my wisdom and feel emotionally fulfilled.

Lady Aspect of my character that can gracefully embody my talent for using my creativity in a charming, attractive manner.

Ladybug Instinctive ability to use my passion and vitality to spot opportunities for happiness so I can thrive in any situation.

L

Lag Realization that I need to take decisive action right now instead of feeling I am continually trying to play catch-up.

Lager Potential to fulfill an emotional need by sharing some possibly confusing feelings that may take time to become clear.

Lagging Ability to maintain my feelings of warmth by keeping my emotions flowing rather than always becoming too wrapped up in them.

Lagoon Situation where I can take a relaxed view of my emotional experiences instead of feeling I have to go into them more deeply.

Lair Situation where I can feel relaxed and secure in my ability to get my teeth into any opportunity that comes along.

Lake Situation where I can draw on my accumulated experience so I can reflect on my deeper emotions and my learning from them.

Lamb Instinctive ability to think for myself and make my own choices instead of innocently conforming to other people's expectations.

Lame Opportunity to stand up for myself and move straight to a series of decisive steps rather than responding limply.

Lamp Ability to use my natural energy and the power of my wisdom to illuminate an uncertain situation so I can bring clarity to it.

Lamppost Ability to lift a potentially dark mood by using my creativity and energy to illuminate the situation and help raise awareness.

Lamprey Instinctive ability to immerse myself in my emotions and go with the flow rather than letting myself feel drained of any vitality.

L

Lampshade Ability to influence my creative output so I can see the bigger picture instead of dazzling myself with my own brilliance.

Lance Ability to make my point by taking short, sharp action rather than feeling I have to go on about it at length.

Land Situation where I can take a more practical and down-to-earth approach with the confidence that I can support my progress.

Landfill site Situation where I can completely let go of behaviors I no longer need rather than trying to bury them out of sight.

Landing Opportunity to successfully complete a complex plan by taking a down-to-earth approach that keeps me in touch with reality.

Landing craft Ability to use the ebb and flow of my emotional life to establish a more practical way of using my drives and ambitions.

Landing gear Ability to successfully land the value of one of my bigger ideas by using my practical skills to their fullest extent.

Landlady Aspect of my character that can help me feel relaxed and at home with myself by demonstrating the value of my creativity.

Landline Ability to consistently communicate what I need to say by always taking a more down-to-earth and practical approach.

Landlord Aspect of my character that can help me feel more comfortable for a period of time by recognizing the strength of my skills.

Landmark Situation where I can clearly see how much progress I have made so I can give myself the opportunity to celebrate it.

Land mine Ability to safely deal with any potentially explosive feelings rather than trying to bury them in a superficial manner.

Landscape Situation where I can explore the underlying situation that provides fundamental support for different aspects of my nature.

Landslide Opportunity to safely transform the realities of a situation by letting go of any aspects that I have no further inclination for.

Lane Situation where I can take a narrower and more defined route for self-exploration, although it may not seem obvious to begin with.

Language Ability to communicate what I need to say, even though I may not always use the vocabulary others would like.

Lantern Ability to guide myself through an uncertain episode by using the light of my previous experience to illuminate the way.

Lap Ability to feel relaxed and comfortable in my current position rather than feeling I have to go around my viewpoints again.

Lap dancer Aspect of my character that is becoming more aware of the value of my talent and can take creative steps to bring it to life.

Lapdog Instinctive ability to show my unconditional loyalty for particular people rather than taking their support for granted.

Lapel Ability to present my self-image to other people by showing that I have more than enough material to make me feel comfortable.

Lap of honor Opportunity to repeatedly act with integrity so I can honestly celebrate my continuing success in achieving my goals.

Laptop Ability to balance my creative energies with my commitment to my work so I can quickly decide the best choice to make.

Larch Natural ability to develop my long-term spiritual growth by taking a more enduring approach to any tough challenges I encounter.

Lard Potential to fulfill an ambition by taking a fresh approach and exercising a healthy perspective so I can get stuck in it.

Larder Aspect of myself that has the capacity to nurture my ambitions by taking a methodical approach to building up my resources.

Large Realization that I am able to use some of my huge talent rather than worrying about the potential size of any challenges.

Lark Instinctive ability to joyfully rise above the more mundane aspects of a situation and play around with some inspiring ideas.

Larva Instinctive ability to consistently fulfill a series of ambitions so I can prepare myself for a fundamental transformation.

Lasagna Potential to fulfill an ambition by looking at the different levels where I can use my fertile ideas and practical experience.

Laser Ability to create a lot of excitement by taking a more coherent approach so I can focus my powerful insights more precisely.

Laser pointer Ability to attract attention to a specific detail in my way of thinking so I can clearly demonstrate the power of my ideas.

Laser printer Ability to quickly connect to a particular way of thinking so I can clearly spell out what I am trying to communicate.

Lash Opportunity to immediately take positive and forceful action instead of feeling I have to defend myself from any criticism.

Lasso Ability to make a stronger connection to my creative instincts so I can harness the power of my unconscious energies.

Last Realization that I can achieve success by taking a more enduring approach rather than worrying that I will never succeed.

Last-minute Opportunity to choose exactly the best moment to take action by taking time to understand some of the smaller details.

Latch Ability to quickly understand what is happening so I can feel more secure without becoming too attached to the outcome.

Late Realization that I need to quickly commit to taking meaningful action rather than involving myself in meaningless activity.

Late for exam Opportunity to understand what makes me feel happiest instead of endless self-examination.

Late for school Opportunity to take action so I can immediately use what I have learned rather than always trying to be perfect the first time.

L

Late for wedding Opportunity to fully commit to a major decision rather than trying to slowly work my way through a series of compromises.

Late for work Opportunity to immediately involve myself in purposeful action instead of busying myself with meaningless activity.

Lathe Ability to create a productive result by feeling confident in my abilities and knowing that I can turn my hand to anything.

Lather Ability to make a fresh start in how I deal with my emotions instead of getting worked up about my situation.

Latrine Situation where I can attend to my personal needs by being more open about the thoughts and feelings that no longer nourish me.

Latte Potential to fulfill an emotional need by stimulating a conversation that helps me to look after other people in a healthy way.

Lattice Ability to make a number of strong connections that provide different viewpoints rather than relying on my judgment and bias.

Laughing Opportunity to use my deeper inspiration to resolve a dilemma so I can release any tension I have been feeling.

Laughter Ability to take a potential opportunity more seriously rather than feeling my talents are of no real practical value.

Launch Opportunity to get a new initiative off the ground so I can use it to pursue my ambitions in a powerful and direct manner.

Launchpad Situation where I can powerfully raise my levels of awareness by directing my energy toward the fundamental practicalities.

Launderette Situation to gain a clearer understanding by resolving superficial disagreements that may be coloring my viewpoint.

Laundry Ability to freshen up my self-image by using my emotional awareness to clearly understand how I might appear to other people.

Laurel Natural ability to consistently develop my creative powers so I can use them to help other people recognize my achievements.

Laurel wreath Ability to celebrate a triumphant transformation and have it recognized by others without becoming too wrapped up in it.

Lava Ability to channel intensely passionate emotions that can often bubble up from nowhere, rather than being consumed by them.

Lavatory Situation where I can open up about my feelings and clearly state my needs rather than allowing it to become too messy.

Lavender Natural ability to maintain a dignified equilibrium so I can open up to my spiritual growth and encourage it to blossom.

Law Ability to give myself permission to choose how I behave in my wider social circle rather than feeling guilty about my actions.

Law court Situation where I can sum up the different feelings I have so I can permit myself to take positive and powerful action.

Lawn Situation where I can cultivate my social skills in a healthy, considered manner rather than just letting myself behave wildly.

Lawn mower Ability to consistently maintain the level of my social skills so I can use them as a basis for my continuing healthy growth.

Lawsuit Opportunity to present my personal choices to people in a formal, authoritative manner that provides me with more freedom.

Lawyer Aspect of my character that always tries to do the right thing instead of trying to live up to the expectations of people.

Laxative Ability to truly express my needs and let go of something that has been troubling me, even though it might turn out messy.

Layabout Aspect of my character that chooses to take a more relaxed, less obvious approach to pursuing long-term ambitions.

L

Layer Ability to use my accumulated levels of experience to feel more comfortable with what is happening just below the surface.

Lazy Realization that I can be highly motivated and industrious when working with a challenge that has personal significance for me.

LCD Ability to display my unique abilities by getting consistently excited about my emotions and illuminating my clear potential.

Lead Ability to conduct myself in a powerful way by understanding the impact I can make rather than feeling weighed down by it.

Leader Aspect of my character that can create future possibilities for myself and other people by exploring my undiscovered qualities.

Lead guitarist Aspect of my character that can take my instinctive creativity in both hands so I can create new possibilities for my ideas.

Leading Opportunity to consistently guide myself in the right direction by using my unique achievements to plan a winning strategy.

Leading lady Aspect of my character that can gracefully display my talent for using my creativity in a powerful and attractive manner.

Leading man Aspect of my character that obviously embodies my individual strength and power so I can skillfully create a unique result.

Lead poisoning Opportunity to choose how I react to heavy commitments rather than opening up an unhealthy situation.

Lead weight Ability to decisively immerse myself in my emotions without feeling too weighed down by any heavier responsibilities.

Leaf Natural ability to absorb the power of my creative talent so I can use it to raise awareness of my long-term spiritual growth.

Leaflet Ability to share my viewpoint with a wide range of people, even though it may not initially seem too substantial to them.

League Ability to combine a number of my talents so I can successfully work toward an objective that may seem quite distant.

League table Ability to use habitual relationships with others as a way of mutual support and working toward a common goal.

Leak Opportunity to be more emotionally self-contained so I can resolve a situation that might leave me feeling drained.

Leaking house Opportunity to build trust so I can feel more secure in myself rather than allowing any outside emotions to intrude.

Leaking roof Opportunity to maintain a rational approach to thought processes instead of allowing myself to be influenced by feelings.

Leaking toilet Opportunity to openly share my personal needs with others rather than allowing them to slip out unexpectedly.

Leaking walls Opportunity to establish firm personal boundaries with other people so I don't become too involved in their emotions.

Lean Essential opportunity to take care of myself by using a healthy approach rather than feeling I need other people to support me.

Leaning Opportunity to understand my inclination toward a course of action, even though it may require outside support.

Leap Opportunity to immediately release myself from any current obligations so I can make the most of an emerging possibility.

Leap year Opportunity to quickly make the most of an emerging possibility rather than reacting predictably to the current situation.

Learning Opportunity to find out more about myself so I can develop my unique talents and understand the best way to make use of them.

Lease Opportunity to transform my situation by confidently demonstrating some of my valuable properties to the people around me.

L

Leash Ability to consistently control and direct my instinctive energies rather than letting myself just be carried away by them.

Least Realization that I can make the most of a possibility by exploring details that are more significant than they appear to be.

Leather Ability to protect my inner self by making myself comfortable with the boundary between my inside and outside worlds.

Leave Opportunity to make time for myself so I can work on an issue that has great professional significance for me.

Leaving Realization that I have accomplished what I originally set out to do and that it is time to move on to the next opportunity.

Lecherous Realization that I can use my creative urges far more effectively rather than indiscriminately indulging myself in them.

Lecture Opportunity to share my expertise and experience with a wider audience rather than being self-critical of my achievements.

Lecturer Aspect of my character that is happy to share my knowledge when it is required rather than continually going on about a subject.

LED Ability to persistently illuminate a number of possibilities so I can choose a firm direction for my current situation.

Led Opportunity to confidently choose my own direction rather than always feeling that other people are just stringing me along.

Ledge Situation where I can relax in the knowledge that my sheer effort has helped me attain a much higher level of achievement.

Ledger Ability to be more open about the wealth of my accumulated knowledge rather than worrying that others won't value it.

Leech Instinctive ability to firmly hold on to my personal boundaries so I don't end up feeling drained of passion and vitality.

Leek Potential to fulfill an ambition by taking a more straightforward approach that allows me to draw on my deeper resources.

Leeway Opportunity to give myself enough room to maneuver so I can continue to stay on course with one of my ambitions.

Left Natural awareness of the more instinctive side of my character that intuitively enables me to express my unconscious potential.

Left luggage Situation where I can temporarily let go of my bigger hopes and ambitions rather than allowing them to weigh me down.

Leftovers Potential to fulfill an ambition by using resources I have accumulated from previous projects and putting them to good use.

Leg Essential ability to stand up for my individual viewpoint so I can confidently motivate myself and take decisive action.

Legacy Ability to draw on the wealth of knowledge and experience I have accumulated so people will recognize my talents.

Legacy system Ability to realize the value of my previous expertise and experience rather than abandoning it in favor of something new.

Legal Realization that I am ultimately responsible for how I behave instead of always wondering if I am doing the right thing.

Legal tender Ability to declare my confidence in my individual talents so my value can be formally acknowledged by other people.

Legend Ability to identify a more powerful universal pattern so I can have a deeper understanding of the purpose of my own story.

Legendary Realization that I am comfortable with my story rather than always feeling I have to appear larger than life to other people.

Leggings Ability to present my self-image to people in a way that shows my readiness to take action so I can shape my chosen outcome.

L

Legion Aspect of my character that offers me countless opportunities to confidently assert my individual talents in unfamiliar situations.

Legroom Ability to occupy a relaxed and comfortable viewpoint without feeling that the people around me might be cramping my style.

Legume Natural ability to pick up on a number of seemingly minor opportunities that can help me to achieve a long-held ambition.

Leisure Opportunity to free myself from any unnecessary obligations so I can actively work on a challenge that is meaningful to me.

Leisure center Situation where I can work at getting my plans into shape rather than staying in my comfort zone and taking it easy.

Lemming Instinctive ability to pursue my path to a deeper transformation rather than following everyone else around me.

Lemonade Potential to fulfill an emotional need by allowing my optimism to bubble up rather than leaving myself feeling flat.

Lemon color Mood that can color my perspective by naturally stimulating my thought processes so I can create some fresh ideas.

Lemon fruit Natural ability to fulfill an ambition by using a fresh and clean approach that will result in a happy and fruitful outcome.

Lemur Instinctive ability to understand my natural creativity by being inquisitive about how I can bring my talents fully to life.

Lend Opportunity to share a valuable insight and have it acknowledged rather than feeling that my skills are being taken for granted.

Length Ability to use my extensive experience to successfully further my ambitions by taking the time to go the distance with them.

Lens Ability to clearly focus my attention on a specific subject so I can understand more about my particular point of view.

Lentil Potential to fulfill an ambition by collecting a number of ideas that I can use to create a more substantial plan.

Leopard Instinctive ability to embody my need for much greater independence without feeling I have to change my nature in any way.

Leotard Ability to present my self-image to people in a way that shows my commitment to expressing my individual freedom.

Leper Aspect of my character that can fully embody all my unique talents instead of feeling that I am being rejected by other people.

Leprechaun Aspect of my character that may seem quite elusive but has apparent potential to open me up to a golden opportunity.

Leprosy Essential opportunity to use my power rather than rejecting my personal talents and allowing self-doubt to eat away at me.

Lesbian Aspect of my character that can help me become more intimately aware of how I can embody my qualities of empathy and wisdom.

Lesson Opportunity to learn something new and add to my extensive experience instead of feeling that I am being judged by other people.

Lethal Realization that being deadly serious about my intentions will inevitably lead to a powerful and positive transformation.

Lethal injection Opportunity to introduce a much more powerful transformation by using my penetrating awareness to get beyond superficial concerns.

Lethal injury Opportunity to make a deeper, more honest connection with someone close rather than becoming complacent about them.

Lethargy Realization that I can consistently raise my level of self-motivation by directing my energy into actions that really excite me.

Letter Opportunity to become more aware of an important insight so I can increase my fundamental understanding of my character.

L

Letter bomb Ability to safely contain some potentially explosive ideas so I can always open myself up to working with new opportunities.

Letterbox Ability to be more expansive in how I convey my thoughts and theories rather than appearing to be limited in my overall vision.

Lettuce Potential to fulfill an ambition by taking a cool and crisp approach that may result in a variety of healthy outcomes for me.

Leukemia Essential opportunity to convey my passion and vitality in a healthy way rather than allowing it to grow out of control.

Level Opportunity to take an equable approach to dealing with the ups and downs of a challenge that may have thrown me off balance.

Level crossing Situation where I can resolve potential conflicts between my driving personal ambitions and the career track I am on.

Level-headed Realization that taking a calm, considered approach to a new challenge can help me understand where my inclinations lie.

Lever Ability to make a major difference in the outcome of a situation by taking a small but decisive action to influence it.

Levitating Opportunity to rise above it all by actively letting go of any weighty obligations rather than always just hanging around.

Levitation device Ability to release myself from any heavy commitments so I can rise above challenges that I have been encountering.

Liar Aspect of my character that can become more aware of my deeper truths by having the courage to express myself openly and honestly.

Libel Opportunity to be openly confident in my unique talents instead of always listening to other people's opinions of my performance.

Liberation Opportunity to break through self-limiting beliefs that have been holding me back so I can act with much greater freedom.

Liberty Realization that I can confidently make the most of emerging opportunities rather than feeling I have no authority to do so.

Librarian Aspect of my character that can quietly concentrate on continually gaining more knowledge so I can always rely on my skills.

Library Situation where I can steadily accumulate a huge amount of knowledge so I can consistently make use of it at any time.

Lice Instinctive ability to let the minor details look after themselves rather than allowing them to constantly drain my vitality.

License Ability to give myself the freedom to pursue my chosen ambition instead of thinking that I need permission from other people.

Lichen Natural ability to form fundamental relationships that will always inspire me to succeed in the most challenging conditions.

Lick Opportunity to quickly connect in a tasteful and eloquent manner so I can deal with any potentially messy challenges.

Licorice Potential to fulfill an ambition in an initially pleasing manner that will eventually help me to get things moving.

Lid Ability to contain my feelings about a situation rather than thinking I always need to open up my deeper emotions to people.

Lie Realization that I need to express myself openly and honestly so I can be true to myself and stand up for what I believe in.

Lie detector Ability to understand what is going on by paying attention to my inner truth and not feeling guilty about my actions.

Lie-in Opportunity to stay in my comfort zone for a while longer so I can feel more relaxed about any challenges that may emerge for me.

L

Lieutenant Aspect of my character that can skillfully maintain my position by ensuring that I listen to the advice of people around me.

Life Opportunity to use my creativity so I can understand who I actually am and become the person I want to be.

Life and death Opportunity to use my power and vitality to transform my situation so I can let go of the past and step into a new future.

Lifeboat Ability to emotionally reconnect with a precious talent rather than allowing myself to be overwhelmed by my deeper feelings.

Life buoy Ability to use powerful thoughts and theories to prevent me from sinking too deeply into an emotionally upsetting situation.

Life coach Aspect of my character that can help me progress toward my career objectives by being more open to guidance from others.

Life form Natural ability to give shape to my creative instincts so I can display the range of my talents to the people around me.

Lifeguard Aspect of my character that can help me think clearly about my feelings and ensure I am not overwhelmed by my emotions.

Life imprisonment Opportunity to give myself permission to escape from self-limiting beliefs that have left me feeling trapped for some time.

Life insurance Ability to consistently accumulate valuable experience so I can make the most of any transformative opportunity.

Life jacket Ability to draw on other sources of inspiration so I can navigate some complex feelings without being overwhelmed by them.

Lifeless Essential opportunity to revitalize a creative talent that may have seemed lost to me so I can display my practical skills.

Lifeline Ability to stay powerfully connected to my firm belief in myself as I work my way through an emotionally challenging situation.

Life-or-death battle Opportunity to accept my apparent flaws and vulnerabilities so I can become stronger by working with weaknesses.

Life raft Ability to use my inspiration to pump up my confidence in my abilities so that I can navigate some of my more primitive emotions.

Life ring Ability to surround myself with some powerful ideas that will stop me from sinking too far into an emotionally upsetting situation.

Life sentence Opportunity to clearly and honestly state what I need rather than feeling that others always punish me for it.

Life-size Realization that the scale of my larger ambitions is fully dependent on how successfully I can embody my creative instincts.

Lifestyle Realization that I can become more aware of the instinctive expertise that makes me unique so I can fashion a successful outcome.

Life support Opportunity to take really good care of myself so I can maintain my level of creativity during a challenging episode.

Life-threatening Opportunity to challenge habitual anxieties by decisively stepping into my power and positively transforming my situation.

Lifetime Realization that I can use my accumulated wisdom to give me the experience to decide my future and make long-term plans.

Liftoff Opportunity to successfully launch a plan I have been working on so I can get one of my ideas off the ground.

Ligament Essential ability to connect all aspects of myself so I can take coordinated action and stay flexible to change.

Ligature Ability to securely tie up some loose ends so I can use my passion and vitality to make a much stronger connection.

L

Light Ability to understand a situation with much greater clarity by using the power of my wisdom to illuminate what is happening.

Lightbulb Ability to use a new idea to switch on to a sudden awareness that will shed some light on a previously unresolved challenge.

Lighter Ability to spark a creative transformation that will help me ease the burden of issues that have been weighing on my mind.

Light-headed Essential opportunity to achieve a clearer understanding of the gravity of the situation so I can make a definite decision.

Lighthouse Situation where I can use the power of my wisdom to illuminate the best way to reliably navigate through complex emotions.

Lighthouse keeper Aspect of my character that can maintain higher levels of creativity by spending time at the edge of what I know.

Lighting Opportunity to clearly see the different shades of meaning in a situation so I can understand how they reflect my mood.

Lightning Natural ability to sense the prevailing atmosphere so I can create a spark of brilliance that illuminates my understanding.

Lightning conductor Ability to attract powerful thinking so I can direct it to a successful outcome in a down-to-earth manner.

Lightning strike Opportunity to immediately take decisive action so I can use the power of my ideas to achieve more consistent results.

Light saber Ability to assert my power by choosing one side or the other rather than feeling that people are trying to keep me in the dark.

Light show Opportunity to display the brilliance of my talents to others by using my unique expertise to clearly illuminate my value.

Light switch Ability to make a creative decision that immediately illuminates a much wider range of possibilities for using my talents.

Light-year Opportunity to use the power of my wisdom to achieve greater clarity by taking a long-term view of some distant possibilities.

Like-minded Opportunity to understand how I create my perceptions of the world so I can realize how to make a difference in it.

Lilac Natural ability to awaken my creative talents so I can encourage them to blossom while recognizing my responsibilities.

Lily Natural ability to open up to my spiritual awareness so I can encourage it to blossom while staying grounded in reality.

Limb Essential ability to use my power to reach out to other people so I can take the steps I need to connect with them.

Limber Essential opportunity to stay flexible about my plans so I don't feel overstretched when new possibilities emerge for me.

Limbo Situation where I can make a definite decision about the direction I want to take rather than lowering my expectations.

Limbo dancer Aspect of my character that can take a more flexible approach in dealing with limitations that might prevent my progress.

Lime Natural ability to fulfill an ambition by taking a refreshingly healthy approach that will accomplish a fruitful outcome.

Limelight Ability to take some steps that will enable me to display the brilliance of my talents rather than letting them waste away.

Limit Situation where I can progress beyond any self-imposed boundaries so I can open myself up to greater possibilities.

Limited edition Ability to create a number of opportunities to display my expertise rather than feeling that I will have only one chance.

L

Limousine Ability to use my personal drive and ambition to help me extend my power and influence as I progress toward my objective.

Limp Realization that I need to stiffen my resolve and stand up for what I believe in rather than becoming too complacent.

Limpet Instinctive ability to completely adhere to the fundamental realities rather than being swept away by powerful emotions.

Limpet mine Ability to contain potentially explosive feelings I may be hanging on to as I work my way through some complex emotions.

Limping Opportunity to take a series of powerful and decisive steps instead of feeling people are impairing my progress.

Line Ability to align my skills and resources so I can understand how I might progress while maintaining my personal boundaries.

Line dancing Opportunity to display my talents by taking a series of steps that allow me to express myself within certain limitations.

Line drawing Ability to draw on my skills and experience so I can create an outline of how I see my future emerging before me.

Linen Ability to display my elegance and composure to the people around me by using my good manners and being naturally gracious.

Liner Ability to indulge myself by exploring some of the less familiar areas of my emotional life in a relaxed and comfortable manner.

Lingerie Ability to present my self-image to other people in a way that openly attracts attention to my more obvious creative talents.

Lingering Opportunity to decisively move on to some new possibilities rather than trying to hang on to my previous experiences.

Linguist Aspect of my character that can understand what I am trying to say and has the skill to help me express how I feel.

Lining Ability to always feel comfortable with the self-image I present to other people, even though I may not always show it.

Link Ability to stay connected with what I find to be most meaningful in a certain situation, without becoming attached to it.

Linnet Instinctive ability to rise above more practical concerns so I can communicate with other people in a very cheerful way.

Lintel Ability to strongly support my personal boundaries so I can keep myself open to any new possibilities that are opening up.

Lion Instinctive ability to feel relaxed and comfortable about displaying my creative talents so I can take great pride in what I do.

Lioness Instinctive ability to feel confident in the power of my creativity so I can fulfill any ambitions I choose to pursue.

Lip brush Ability to emphasize my individual opinion by making it more presentable to the people around me rather than just dismissing it.

Lip gloss Ability to be clear about what I want to say so I can easily attract other people to my particular point of view.

Lip liner Ability to clearly outline the feelings I want to express so I can make my opinion more attractive to other people.

Liposculpture Opportunity to give more structure to my ambitions by taking a healthier approach so I can shape a success-ful outcome.

Liposuction Opportunity to take a fresh approach to fulfilling my appetite for success by reducing external pressures I may be feeling.

Lip-read Opportunity to listen to what is being said rather than responding to any of the opinions being voiced.

Lips Essential ability to shape how I appear to people by having the confidence to honestly express some of my intimate feelings.

L

Lip salve Ability to express some soothing words in a potentially uncomfortable situation rather than behaving in an uncaring manner.

Lipstick Ability to draw attention to what I want to say so I can make my opinions more attractive to the people around me.

Lip-sync Opportunity to give voice to what I feel instead of mouthing off about what appears to be happening around me.

Liqueur Potential to fulfill an emotional need by indulging myself in the sweet taste of success after happily realizing an ambition.

Liquid Ability to let my feelings and emotions flow so I can reflect on my mood regardless of the shape I might feel I am in.

Lisp Essential opportunity to clearly share my perspective with the people around me rather than worrying about how I might sound.

List Ability to be very specific about the challenges I face so I can understand any positive leanings I have toward them.

Listening Opportunity to clearly understand what other people are trying to say so I can become more aware of my deeper feelings.

Listening device Ability to use a specific procedure that will help me hear what is most important to me so I can take decisive action.

Listening post Situation where I can become more aware of an important understanding I need to confidently communicate to others.

List price Ability to publicly declare the value of my unique talents instead of continually discounting my individual contribution.

Litany Opportunity to bring my experiences fully to life rather than always going on about them in the same old predictable way.

Liter Ability to deal with a potentially emotional situation in a measured, consistent manner that helps me contain my feelings.

Literary agent Aspect of my character that can open me to the wealth of my accumulated knowledge so I can publicly share it.

Literature Ability to reflect on my accumulated knowledge and experience in a structured way so I can acknowledge what I have learned.

Lithe Essential opportunity to stay flexible in my ambitions so I can quickly respond to any new challenges that emerge for me.

Lithium Ability to conduct myself in such a way that I can use my fundamental power to help me lighten my mood and stabilize it.

Lithograph Ability to demonstrate my creative skills by taking a firm and practical approach that enables me to see the bigger picture.

Litigation Opportunity to reach my own decision about what I need to do instead of being influenced by forceful opinions.

Litmus paper Ability to take a more colorful approach that clearly shows the strength of my feelings and how I should respond to them.

Litter Ability to convey my thoughts and ideas in a consistently supportive way rather than allowing them to continually distract me.

Little Realization that I can achieve great success by taking a seemingly insignificant talent and developing its full potential.

Little black dress Ability to present my self-image to others in a way that gives me the freedom to display my confidence in my power.

Little finger Essential ability to finely control my actions and delicately shape my future so I can point myself in the right direction.

Little toe Essential ability to motivate myself to take the steps I need, even though they might be quite small to begin with.

Littoral Situation where I can gain a firmer understanding of my feelings by experiencing the full range of my emotional ups and downs.

L

Liturgy Opportunity to realize a deeper wisdom about who I really am by permitting myself to publicly acknowledge my new experiences.

Live Essential opportunity to use my power and energy to make the transformations that will enable me to use my passion and vitality.

Live audience Opportunity to confidently display my unique expertise and experience rather than always keeping my talents to myself.

Lived-in Realization that I can be more comfortable with myself by moving beyond superficial behavior patterns that may hold me back.

Livelihood Opportunity to bring my talents to life so I can develop my expertise and experience to connect with my true purpose.

Lively Opportunity to use my energy to bring one of my ambitions to life rather than just playing around with a variety of activities.

Liver Essential ability to process the valuable and more challenging aspects of my power so I can fulfill my ambitions in a healthy manner.

Liver spot Essential opportunity to stay in touch with my real feelings rather than being concerned about blemishes on my reputation.

Liver transplant Opportunity to work through different ways of dealing with my powerful needs instead of automatically rejecting them.

Livery stable Situation where I can realize the value of my instinctive energies by consistently harnessing them to provide a positive outcome.

Livestock Instinctive ability to gather my creative talents so I can continue to develop them and realize their full value.

Live wire Ability to make an energetic connection with other people by using my fundamental power to communicate how I feel.

Living Opportunity to make every moment count so I can enjoy my life to its fullest extent and feel completely fulfilled by it.

Living room Aspect of myself that helps me to feel relaxed and comfortable with sharing my talents and opening up to their possibilities.

Lizard Instinctive ability to motivate myself so I can express my fundamental creativity without appearing too cold-blooded about it.

Llama Instinctive ability to think for myself and make my own choices so I can explore opportunities that are unfamiliar to me.

Load Ability to convey how I feel rather than always burdening myself with self-imposed obligations and responsibilities.

Load-bearing wall Ability to maintain firmly established boundaries to consistently cope with the weight of my commitments.

Loaded Opportunity to use my accumulated knowledge and experience so I am always prepared to deal with any weighty challenges.

Loaf Potential to look after my basic needs and fulfill my ambitions by using my knowledge and ideas rather than just lying around.

Loan Opportunity to understand the value of my skills and abilities to the people around me rather than feeling I am worthless.

Loan shark Aspect of my character that can help me to fulfill my deeper purpose by using my unique talents in a very single-minded way.

Lobby Aspect of myself where I have the space to explore a variety of opportunities so I can use my power to influence their outcome.

Lobotomy Opportunity to make a deeper connection that will focus my mental efforts rather than letting a situation get on my nerves.

Lobster Instinctive ability to protect my rich emotional life by taking a more colorful approach rather than feeling a bit nippy.

L

Lobster pot Ability to immerse myself in my emotions so I can capture some instinctive urges and use them to fulfill my ambitions.

Local Ability to use my personal experiences to deal with an unfamiliar challenge without needing to feel completely at home with it.

Local anesthetic Ability to specifically deal with a situation that is making me feel uncomfortable rather than numbing myself to it.

Location Situation where I can find a more definite understanding of who I really am and how I fit into the larger scheme of things.

Locator beacon Ability to identify exactly what I need so I can use my insight and understanding to successfully achieve my objective.

Loch Situation where I can draw on my accumulated experience so I can reflect on my wilder emotions and my learning from them.

Lock Ability to keep myself feeling secure in an unfamiliar situation so I can stay open to the possibility of choosing my outcome.

Lock and key Ability to give myself the specific freedom to open up to new possibilities while maintaining a level of personal security.

Locked Realization that becoming stuck in habitual ways of thinking can be a barrier to my future success, even though it feels secure.

Locker Ability to be quite guarded about some of my personal skills and experiences so I use them only when I choose to.

Locket Ability to attract attention to one of my more significant experiences so I can always keep its value close to my heart.

Lock keeper Aspect of my character that helps me to safely channel my feelings so I can always negotiate emotional ups and downs.

Locksmith Aspect of my character that can help me to pick my way through a combination of choices so I can access new opportunities.

Locomotive Ability to use my personal drive and ambition to keep my career on track so I can become a driving force in my profession.

Locust Instinctive ability to deal with a large number of small and persistent challenges that can eat away at my greater ambitions.

Lodestone Ability to choose the direction I need to take with an unfamiliar challenge by using a practical, down-to-earth approach.

Lodge Situation where I can feel safe and comfortable in hunting for new opportunities so I can make the most of what they offer.

Lodged Opportunity to remove any obstacles to my progress rather than always complaining I am stuck in my current position.

Lodger Aspect of my character that may initially seem unfamiliar but can open me up to opportunities that will always stay with me.

Lodging house Situation where I have the security and support to explore aspects of my inner and outer lives over a specific period.

Loft Aspect of myself where I can explore some of my higher-level thinking so I can reconnect with forgotten plans and ideas.

Lofty viewpoint Situation where I can be open to raising my level of understanding rather than feeling people may look down on me.

Log Ability to provide habitual support for my creative activity and continuing achievement by making a record of my development.

Logbook Ability to clearly demonstrate the wealth of my accumulated knowledge so I can use it to recognize the progress I have made.

Log cabin Situation where I feel comfortable and safe as I explore some habitual behaviors so I can I become more familiar with them.

Logical Realization that I can take a more creative approach to resolving a challenge, even though it may seem irrational to other people.

L

Log in Opportunity to clearly confirm the value of my individual talents by knowing the right words to use in any situation.

Logistics Ability to understand how I can make best use of my skills so I can take advantage of any opportunities that really move me.

Logjam Opportunity to use the power of my emotions to work my way through some habitual patterns so I can continue to progress.

Logo Ability to clearly make my mark so I can demonstrate my value to other people and have it instantly recognized by them.

Log out Opportunity to feel secure in the knowledge that I can move on from my current situation and return to it when I need to.

Loincloth Ability to present my self-image to others in a way that shows how comfortable I am with my potential for creativity.

Loitering Opportunity to take some time to decide where I want to go instead of feeling like I am always hanging around.

Lollipop Potential to fulfill a short-term ambition that seems very attractive, even though it may end up in quite a sticky situation.

Loneliness Realization that I have the time and space to become more intimately acquainted with potentially valuable aspects of myself.

Lonely Opportunity to explore all the different valuable aspects of my character so I can achieve a deeper understanding of myself.

Loner Aspect of my character that is happy to pursue my individual ambitions instead of feeling I need the support of other people.

Lone wolf Instinctive ability to show my fierce loyalty to those closest to me, even though it means following a different path than they do.

Long Realization that I am committed to going the distance in pursuing my ambitions, even though it may take me quite some time.

Longbow Ability to reach my target in a tense situation by making a powerful decision that is fully aligned with my original aims.

Long-distance runner Aspect of my character that takes steps to pursue a long-term ambition and has the energy and self-motivation to succeed.

Long haul Opportunity to stay fully committed to successfully completing an important project, even though it may take a considerable time.

Long-lost Opportunity to reacquaint myself with a valuable personal quality my previous circumstances had forced me to let go of.

Long-range Ability to make my presence felt from a distance so I can explore a number of options and display the depth of my experience.

Long-sighted Essential opportunity to take a much closer look at my present situation rather than being too focused on some future events.

Loofah Natural ability to deal with a potentially messy situation by immersing myself in my feelings and absorbing criticism.

Look Opportunity to purposefully direct my attention to one of my particular interests so that I can examine it in greater depth.

Look-alike Aspect of my character that reminds me of a quality I need to display so my talents can be genuinely recognized.

Looking Opportunity to openly seek emerging opportunities rather than always feeling I am missing something of importance to me.

Lookout Aspect of my character that is confident to go to the edge of my comfort zone so I am fully aware of future possibilities.

L

Lookout post Situation where I can observe what is emerging in my unconscious awareness so I can alert myself to new opportunities.

Loom Ability to collect a variety of my different stories so I can weave them together into some far more substantial material.

Looming Realization that a big opportunity is approaching for me, even though it may currently seem indistinct and slightly threatening.

Loon Instinctive ability to go beyond more practical concerns so I can become more aware of what my true calling is in life.

Loop Ability to stay connected to my long-term ambitions rather than feeling I am just going through the same procedure again.

Loophole Ability to look more deeply into the habitual behaviors that motivate me rather than always taking the easy way out.

Looping the loop Opportunity to playfully explore one of my loftier ideas from a variety of viewpoints so I can shape my chosen outcome.

Loose Opportunity to give myself freedom in how I approach a challenge while maintaining a firm connection to my wider ambitions.

Loose-tongued Ability to speak freely in a tasteful and eloquent manner without always feeling I have to reveal my deepest feelings.

Loose tooth Essential opportunity to stay firmly connected to my fundamental power and confidence rather than feeling I can't speak up.

Loot Ability to openly recognize the value of the skills and experience I have accumulated rather than trying to conceal them.

Looting Opportunity to openly display the value of my talents to the people around me without worrying I will get too carried away.

Lopsided Realization that I can balance my commitments by standing up for what I believe in and taking a more straightforward approach.

Lord Aspect of my character that is very comfortable with my achievements instead of feeling I need to constantly display them.

Lore Ability to draw on the valuable experience I have accumulated so I can share a unique insight with the people around me.

Lorry Ability to use my powerful drive to convey the value of my ambitions to others so I can access the resources that I need.

Lorry driver Aspect of my character that directs my powerful motivation so I can convey the value of my intentions to other people.

Losing Opportunity to decisively let go of anything that may be holding me back so I can discover what will fulfill me.

Losing battle Opportunity to take decisive action and move on by letting go of a tension that has been causing conflict for me.

Losing car Opportunity to be more decisive in my ambitions so I can regain my individual motivation and drive myself forward.

Losing car keys Opportunity to be more open to approaching possibilities so I can unlock a specific aspect of my personal ambition.

Losing clothing Opportunity to reveal my natural talents to those around me rather than always trying to be modest about my abilities.

Losing face Opportunity to reveal myself as the person I want to be rather than trying to maintain a facade for the people around me.

Losing job Opportunity to discover my true life purpose instead of feeling I use my talents only for the benefit of other people.

Losing keys Opportunity to open myself up to some new possibilities so I can regain my freedom and continue to unlock my potential.

Losing license Opportunity to regain

L

confidence in freely pursuing a chosen ambition rather than feeling I need permission.

Losing purse Opportunity to rediscover my sense of individual identity and be confident I can continue to make a worthwhile contribution.

Losing shoes Opportunity to realize the practical steps I need to take to reestablish my social standing in a particular situation.

Losing teeth Opportunity to regain my self-confidence by acting in a more self-assured manner, even though I may feel wobbly inside.

Losing wallet Opportunity to rediscover my sense of self-worth by having the confidence to convey my expertise to others.

Loss Opportunity to add to my accumulated experience rather than feeling disappointed that I seem to be missing out somewhere.

Loss of a valuable Opportunity to recover my fundamental sense of self-worth so I can reestablish how worthwhile I am to other people.

Loss of control Opportunity to use my wider influence to guide the situation in my chosen direction instead of trying to handle every detail.

Lost Realization that I am in the right place to discover exactly who I am rather than feeling unsure about the steps I need to take.

Lost at sea Opportunity to understand the ups and downs of my emotional life so I can get back on course instead of just drifting along.

Lost in a city Opportunity to use my accumulated knowledge and wisdom to successfully achieve an ambition that once seemed completely beyond me.

Lost in a desert Opportunity to reconnect with my deepest emotions and open up to them so I can naturally resolve some seemingly hard choices.

Lost in a forest Opportunity to make the most of my natural growth potential so I can clearly continue my journey of self-exploration.

Lost in a house Opportunity to explore the undiscovered aspects of myself so I can feel at home with my character-building experiences.

Lost in a labyrinth Opportunity to explore a wide range of possibilities rather than feeling I am being forced to follow a particular path.

Lost in a shop Opportunity to rediscover the value of my expertise instead of feeling I'm not being truly valued by the people around me.

Lost in the countryside Opportunity to understand less familiar aspects of my nature so I can discover valuable opportunities they offer.

Lost property Ability to fully reclaim confidence in my talents so I can reconnect with some of my unrealized hopes and ambitions.

Lot Ability to measure the large amount of value I have to offer so I can understand the size of the contribution I can make.

Lotion Ability to gently use my empathy to connect more easily so I can smooth over a rough patch and resolve any hard feelings.

Lottery Opportunity to recognize the huge value of my talents by making a definite commitment to them rather than leaving it to chance.

Lotus flower Natural ability to open up to a blossoming awareness of how I can transform my position and encourage my talents to bloom.

Loud Realization that I need to place much more emphasis on an important message I am trying to communicate to myself.

L

Loud hailer Ability to attract attention to what I need to say so I can powerfully speak my truth and have it fully acknowledged.

Loudspeaker Ability to stay connected to my deeper feelings so I can share them with other people and get my message across.

Lounge Aspect of myself that helps me feel relaxed and comfortable with my social connections so I can be more open with them.

Loupe Ability to closely observe some of my habitual behaviors so I can understand how they attract other people toward me.

Louse Instinctive ability to always do the right thing rather than allowing myself to be distracted by an irritating minor detail.

Lout Aspect of my character that can use my graciousness and empathy to influence people rather than feeling I am just too loud.

Love Realization that my capacity to profoundly connect with other people can also reflect a much deeper understanding of myself.

Love affair Opportunity to resolve any loss of confidence in my attractiveness by taking the time to reach a deeper awareness of my value.

Lovebird Instinctive ability to rise above any practical concerns so I can communicate with other people in a really attractive way.

Love child Aspect of my character that embodies my powerful creativity and holds wonderful potential for the continuing growth of my talent.

Loved one Aspect of my character that helps me achieve a profound level of self-awareness so I can express unspoken talents.

Love handles Essential opportunity to indulge myself in my creative abilities by taking a fresh approach and exercising a healthy perspective.

Love-hate Realization that I can resolve my creative tensions by using passionate intensity in a more positive and balanced manner.

Love-in Opportunity to honestly connect with the people around me rather than feeling I am taking only a superficial approach.

Lovemaking Opportunity to become more deeply connected to my creativity so I can conceive new plans and ideas with others.

Love nest Situation where I can comfortably conceive fertile new ideas rather than sitting around waiting for something to happen.

Lover Aspect of my character that can connect at a deeper level and that helps me become more intimately aware of my creative potential.

Love triangle Opportunity to shape an outcome by understanding my deeper needs so I can identify the connection I must make.

Low Realization that I can use an experience to achieve a much deeper understanding rather than feeling a bit down about it.

Low altitude Situation where I can stay much closer to practical concerns I may have rather than getting carried away by a flight of fancy.

Low earth orbit Opportunity to take a closer look at my powerful attraction to a particular situation and why I keep coming back to it.

Lower Opportunity to reach a more profound understanding of myself rather than feeling I have to decrease my standards in any way.

Low tide Opportunity to go with the natural rhythm of my emotions so I can explore the fundamental realities that they reveal.

Loyalty Realization that I need to believe in myself by having true faith in my own talents and complete confidence in my abilities.

Loyalty card Ability to closely observe the choices I take to fulfill myself so I can see the bigger picture in my habitual behaviors.

Lozenge Ability to shape my chosen outcome so I can fulfill a short-term ambition rather than worrying about long-term effects.

L

LSD Opportunity to open up my thinking to a different level of awareness by relying on my talent instead of any outside influences.

Lubricant Ability to use a more emotional approach so I can reduce any relationship friction and help everything run smoothly.

Lucid Realization that I can make much more powerful decisions by having a clearer understanding of what I want to happen.

Luck Opportunity to achieve my ambitions through hard work and practicing my skills rather than leaving my success to chance.

Luge Ability to quickly progress toward my objective by using the outcome of accumulated work in a cool, professional manner.

Luggage Ability to clearly convey my hopes and ambitions so I can keep myself motivated as I explore some different points of view.

Lugworm Instinctive ability to make my way deep into the practical aspects so I can eventually achieve a much bigger ambition.

Lukewarm Opportunity to use energy and passion to increase my chances of success rather than appearing indifferent to the outcome.

Lull Opportunity to take some time to myself so I can gently relax and calmly prepare myself for any approaching challenges.

Lullaby Ability to instinctively communicate the value of one of my concepts rather than feeling I will quickly lose interest.

Lumbar Essential ability to connect at a deeper level so I can stand up for what I believe in and make sure that I can back it up.

Lumber Ability to use my practical skills to produce a straightforward outcome rather than feeling weighed down by any obligations.

Lumbering Opportunity to use my experience to make fast and decisive progress instead of feeling that my habits are holding me back.

Lumberjack Aspect of my character that can realize the full value of my long-term spiritual growth rather than cutting myself off from it.

Luminous Ability to illuminate an unfamiliar situation by using my natural brilliance and taking the time to reflect on what I see.

Lump Ability to gather all my skills and experiences together so I can make a big difference and really rise to prominence.

Lump sum Ability to realize the full value of my knowledge and learning so I can use it to immediately make a real difference.

Lunar eclipse Natural opportunity to reflect on my intuitive talents so I can take some time to understand my fundamental brilliance.

Lunar lander Ability to take a more practical approach to understanding my unexplored talents and how I can continue to reflect on them.

Lunar module Ability to fully connect with my intuitive brilliance so I can take some steps to help me achieve my creative ambitions.

Lunar orbiter Ability to understand my powerful attraction to a potentially emotional situation and why I intuitively keep coming back to it.

Lunatic Aspect of my character that helps me to understand the irrational nature of my intuition and how I can use it more consistently.

Lunch Opportunity to fulfill my appetite for power by keeping myself going as I progress toward a greater sense of achievement.

Lunch break Opportunity to reflect on one of my habitual behaviors so I can understand how to fulfill one of my larger ambitions.

Lunchtime Opportunity to explore some emerging possibilities for personal fulfillment so I can decide how to use them in the future.

L

Lung cancer Essential opportunity to express my deeper feelings about an unhealthy situation rather than letting it grow out of control.

Lung disease Essential opportunity to resolve some chronic tension so I can feel more at ease with my source of deeper inspiration.

Lungs Essential ability to embody the source of my inspiration so I can use it to powerfully express my insight and ideas to people.

Lurching Opportunity to make steady and predictable progress by taking the specific steps I need to directly pursue my ambitions.

Lure Ability to purposely draw my deeper feelings to the surface so I can make a more powerful connection with my emotions.

Lurking Opportunity to be open about my viewpoint rather than trying to conceal it in case people criticize me.

Lust Opportunity to become more powerfully aware of what I deeply desire so I can successfully fulfill my creative ambitions.

Lute Ability to take my instinctive creativity in both hands so I can express my ideas, even though they may sound old-fashioned.

Luxury Realization that indulging in my passions lets me be much more comfortable with the wealth and richness of my talents.

Lychee Potential to fulfill an ambition by working through any perceived vulnerabilities so I can achieve a fruitful outcome.

Lying Opportunity to stand up for what I believe in so I can speak my truth by communicating how I feel.

Lying prone Opportunity to stay close to practical considerations so I can comfortably take a much more down-to-earth approach.

Lymph gland Essential opportunity to powerfully resolve unwelcome feelings instead of opening myself up to an unhealthy situation.

Lynching Opportunity to support my highest principles rather than just hanging around and feeling that I will always let myself down.

Lynch mob Opportunity to identify individual aspects of my character and understand their needs so I can resolve any potential tensions.

Lynx Instinctive ability to feel relaxed and comfortable about my levels of independence so I can quickly spring into action.

Lyrics Ability to express myself powerfully and evocatively so I can clearly give voice to a beautiful and deeply felt message.

L

Macabre Realization that I can revitalize a seemingly hopeless situation rather than worrying about how it might go horribly wrong.

Macaroni Potential to fulfill an ambition by giving myself the space to develop a number of fertile ideas over a long period.

Mace Ability to defend my instinctive expertise by using the strength of my practical abilities to get my message across.

Machete Ability to assert my power by decisively cutting through any uncertainties I encounter so I can clearly see where I stand.

Machine Ability to produce an outcome of great practical value by using my unique skills rather than just going through the motions.

Machine gun Ability to continually assert my power in a forceful manner so I can communicate my aims to people from a safe distance.

Machinery Ability to provide a consistent performance that gives me the confidence to continually create predictably effective outcomes.

Machinist Aspect of my character that can consistently influence the outcome of a challenging situation by observing my behaviors.

Macho Realization that I can use my power for a variety of purposes instead of allowing my thoughts to be dominated by a single idea.

Mackerel Instinctive ability to immerse myself in my emotions so I can have a clearer understanding of my behavioral patterns.

Mackintosh Ability to present my self-image to people in a way that makes it easier for me to shrug off any unwelcome emotional influences.

Macrobiotic Potential to fulfill one of my long-term ambitions by having a healthy regard for my talents and knowing how to sustain them.

Macrocosm Situation where I can become more aware of an incredible range of possibilities to explore my huge potential.

Mad Realization that I can use my unique methods to explore possibilities that might seem quite insane to the people around me.

Madam Aspect of my character that can help me set some secure personal boundaries around how I employ my individual creativity.

Mad cow disease Opportunity to resolve an unhealthy situation by taking a radically different view of how I look after myself.

Made-to-order Ability to present my self-image to others in a way that suits me rather than trying to fit in with them.

Madhouse Situation where I have the security and support I need to explore new possibilities, even though they seem quite irrational.

Madman Aspect of my character that is desperately trying to assert my individuality so I can use the power of my personal expertise.

Madness Opportunity to objectively focus on some of my wildest ambitions so I can see how to make them happen in reality.

Madwoman Aspect of my character personifying the wisdom of my creativity and crying out for my talent to be noticed.

Maelstrom Opportunity to become more centered in my deeper feelings rather than being overwhelmed by ongoing emotional conflict.

Maestro Aspect of my character that encourages me to develop my unique talents to communicate in a fundamentally powerful way.

Mafia Aspects of my character that can resolve tensions with those closest to me by openly proving my unconditional loyalty to them.

Magazine Ability to communicate plans and ideas by clearly laying them out in a colorful manner so I can share them with other people.

Magenta Mood that can color my perspective by reflecting how I can resolve any deeper emotional tensions I may be feeling.

Maggot Instinctive ability to transform a situation that was apparently lifeless rather than allowing my anxieties to eat away at me.

Magic Ability to make a fundamental transformation by using my imagination to create a practical, positive result in reality.

Magical Realization that I can conjure up my own powerful ideas instead of feeling I have to conform to conventional thinking.

Magical animal Instinctive ability to express my creative nature so I can use it to transform my situation in a profoundly practical way.

Magic bullet Ability to achieve the ambition I'm aiming for by taking a single decisive action rather than just waiting for a miracle.

Magic carpet Ability to be comfortable about where I stand in a situation so I can convey some of my wilder ambitions to other people.

Magician Aspect of my character that shows real potential for my dramatic transformation without needing to continually delude myself.

Magic mushroom Natural ability to rapidly develop the resources I have rather than getting carried away by my colorful imagination.

Magistrate Aspect of my character that has the power to consider my day-to-day actions rather than allowing other people to judge me.

Magma Ability to shape a firm outcome by understanding the intensely passionate emotions bubbling away just under the surface.

Magnesium Ability to conduct myself in such a way that I can use my fundamental power to impress everyone with my dazzling talents.

Magnesium flare Ability to immediately use a flash of brilliance to illuminate my talents so I can attract attention to my unique creativity.

Magnet Ability to strongly attract the attention of other people to my point of view, even though I may be polarizing their opinions.

Magnetic field Situation where I am being drawn to a viewpoint that will allow me to realize the value of my accumulated knowledge.

Magnetic storm Natural opportunity to channel the energy from a variety of conflicting possibilities so I can attract a successful result.

Magnificence Realization that I can use my wonderful talents to create a splendid result that will gladly be acknowledged by other people.

Magnifying glass Ability to closely observe what is happening for me in my situation without allowing it to be blown out of proportion.

Magnolia Natural ability to let my talents blossom so I can display my creative abilities while staying grounded in reality.

Magnum Ability to draw on my huge reserves of accumulated experience so others can acknowledge my courage and resourcefulness.

M

Magpie Instinctive ability to see a situation in black and white rather than being drawn toward some superficially attractive ideas.

Maharaja Aspect of my character providing the opportunity for my emerging wisdom to be more widely acknowledged by other people.

Mahogany Natural ability to build up my practical skills and essential strength so I can habitually produce an enduring outcome.

Maid Aspect of my character that serves my creative skills and provides support in fulfilling my ambitions and realizing my dreams.

Maiden Aspect of my character that embodies my potential to develop the empathy and wisdom I need to fulfill my aspirations.

Mail Ability to communicate my needs in a clear and concise way, although the potential for fulfilling them may seem quite distant.

Mailbox Ability to feel safe and secure in how I communicate my needs, even though it may take me some time to become aware of them.

Mail order Ability to make a specific choice about my preferred outcome so I can achieve an ambition that once seemed quite distant.

Mail-order bride Aspect of my character that can get me closer to my instinctive creativity, even though my requirements might be exacting.

Maimed Opportunity to reconnect with my fundamental strengths so I don't end up feeling cut off from any new possibilities.

Main course Opportunity to achieve a major ambition by absorbing my recent experiences and using them to fulfill my appetite for success.

Maintaining Opportunity to consistently develop my talents in a practical manner rather than neglecting them and just standing still.

Maintenance Ability to take good care of the skills and expertise I have accumulated so they are always available when I need them.

Maintenance man Aspect of my character embodying the individual strength and power I can use to keep progressing toward my goal.

Maintenance payment Ability to have the full value of my creativity accepted by others rather than trying to keep things as they are.

Major Aspect of my character that can provide a substantial increase in my level of understanding by keeping me well organized.

Majority verdict Opportunity to honestly speak my truth and say how I feel instead of letting myself be influenced by others' opinions.

Make believe Realization that I create my own perceptions of the world and that my opinions and perspectives are based on these.

Makeover Opportunity to transform how I habitually see myself so I can leave the past behind and step into new opportunities.

Makeshift Opportunity to make a more permanent shift in my understanding rather than trying to temporarily work out a solution.

Makeup Ability to resolve tension by facing up to it instead of trying to cover up my perceived flaws in the eyes of other people.

Making love Opportunity to become more intimately aware of my talent for creatively conceiving new plans and ideas with others.

Malady Opportunity to resolve an unhealthy situation by taking positive action rather than blaming my habitual behavior patterns.

Malaise Opportunity to feel much better about myself by having a healthy regard for my well-being instead of feeling anxious about it.

Malaria Opportunity to deal with some minor irritations so I can healthily resolve a situation that often makes me feel hot and bothered.

M

Male Realization that I can firmly assert my ambitions and achieve my dreams by decisively choosing how I use my strength and power.

Male chauvinist Aspect of my character that can be far more open to the unique qualities of others rather than habitually dismissing them.

Male model Aspect of my character that can give the appearance of being powerful and assertive though I may feel quite vulnerable.

Malevolent Realization that I can use my unconscious power in a really positive way instead of feeling it has a bad influence on me.

Malformed Realization that I can achieve a perfect outcome and reshape my ambitions by clearing up any distortions in my perspective.

Malfunction Opportunity to change the way I communicate with other people rather than always trying to fix my relationships with them.

Malfunctioning machine Opportunity to maintain the quality of my relationships with other people instead of waiting until they unexpectedly break down.

Malicious Realization that I can achieve much greater success by being kind and benevolent instead of being petty and small-minded.

Malignant Realization that I can take a more benign approach by expressing my frustrations, rather than letting them grow out of control.

Malignant growth Essential opportunity to realize what has been emerging for me so I can immediately cut out any unhealthy behaviors.

Malingerer Aspect of my character that is open and honest about the work I want to do instead of apparently avoiding my commitments.

Mall Situation where I can look through a variety of outlets for displaying my skills so I can have my value recognized by more people.

Malleable Opportunity to shape a situation more to my liking by working through practical aspects until I feel comfortable with them.

Mallet Ability to consistently knock my plans into shape by taking my time and using my power to produce a breakthrough result.

Malnourished Opportunity to fulfill my hunger for success by being open to new experiences instead of starving myself of fulfillment.

Malpractice Opportunity to use my skills to do the right thing rather than neglecting my talents and losing confidence in my abilities.

Maltreated Opportunity to sensitively handle an emotional conflict instead of abusing my power and appearing inconsiderate to others.

Malware Ability to reach a definite outcome by using my own process rather than being led astray by any corrupting influences.

Mamba Instinctive ability to transform my long-term spiritual awareness by discarding a self-image that is no longer useful to me.

Mammal Instinctive ability that embodies all aspects of my creative nature and gives me the motivation to express my natural warmth.

Mammogram Ability to observe how I am able to learn from my experiences so I can be proud of my skills in nurturing other people.

Mammoth Instinctive ability to use my huge range of accumulated experience so I can deal with any weighty obligations that emerge.

Man Aspect of my character that embodies the individual strength and power I need to assert my ambitions and achieve my dreams.

Manacles Ability to become more aware of my freedom of action so I can release myself from any apparent restraints on my behavior.

Manager Aspect of my character that tries to exert control over how I assert my strength and power so I can work in a disciplined way.

M

Manatee Instinctive ability to immerse myself in my emotions so I can explore my abundant creativity in a peaceful and gentle way.

Mandala Ability to explore my inner world so I can see the bigger picture and realize how everything eventually comes full circle.

Mandarin Aspect of my character that gives me the permission to take decisive action rather than feeling I have no power to act.

Mandolin Ability to take my instinctive creativity in both hands so I can strike the right tone, even though I may be fretting about it.

Mandrake Natural ability to use my human instincts so I can give form to my ideas, even though they might be confusing to begin with.

Mane Ability to develop some ideas that emerge from my fundamental style of thinking so I can harness their power to make progress.

Man-eater Aspect of my character that can attract me toward a creative opportunity that may devour a huge amount of time and effort.

Maneuvering Opportunity to turn a situation around by having a firm grasp of where I am trying to get to and what I must achieve there.

Manger Ability to fulfill my ambitions by taking a more relaxed approach to exploring my creative urges and how I can nurture my talent.

Mangled Opportunity to shape an outcome in the best way I can instead of thinking I may be distorting its apparent value.

Mango Potential to fulfill an ambition by achieving a fruitful and healthy result rather than always ending up in a bit of a pickle.

Mangrove swamp Situation where I can experience the ebb and flow of my emotions so I can move on from details that are overwhelming me.

Mangy Realization that I need to take care of how I appear to other people rather than just being irritated by them all the time.

Manhole Situation where I can explore my deeper capacity for success by understanding how to assert my individual strength and power.

Manhunt Opportunity to search for a way to successfully fulfill my ambitions rather than being involved in meaningless pursuits.

Maniac Aspect of my character that instinctively knows how to reach my chosen outcome, even though others may think I'm insane.

Manic depression Opportunity to take a positive, realistic approach to achieving my deepest ambitions rather than feeling a bit hollow inside.

Manic episode Opportunity to choose the path I want to take rather than blaming my changing mood on life's ups and downs.

Manifestation Opportunity to make an idea happen in practical reality, even though it may not seem entirely obvious how I will do it.

Manifold Ability to bring a number of my skills and experiences together so I can share my abundance of talent in a variety of ways.

Manipulated Opportunity to control my actions so I can shape my own future rather than feeling that others are influencing me.

Manna Potential to fulfill my spiritual ambitions by satisfying my longing for success and nourishing my continuing creativity.

Mannequin Aspect of my character that can embody my inner beauty and bring it to life instead of feeling stuck in one place.

Mannerism Opportunity to observe my habitual patterns so I can become more aware of how to communicate what I need to say.

Manners Realization that I can choose my behavioral patterns rather than feeling that I have to behave in a particular way.

M

Mansion Situation where I can realize my potential by being far more expansive in how I explore all aspects of my inner and outer lives.

Manslaughter Opportunity to transform my feelings of vitality by embodying the strength and power I need to assert my ambitions.

Manta ray Instinctive ability to immerse myself in my emotions so I can make powerful progress without getting into much of a flap.

Mantelpiece Ability to keep my creative ideas organized and accessible so I can get my plans off the ground rather than disposing of them.

Mantle Ability to present my self-image to people by opening up to new possibilities instead of being too wrapped up in my concerns.

Mantra Ability to spontaneously communicate my spiritual awareness rather than feeling I have to say the same thing again and again.

Mantrap Situation where I can clearly see where I am holding myself back so I can use my strength and power to realize my ambitions.

Manual Ability to open up to my wealth of accumulated knowledge so I can put it into practical use and shape my preferred outcome.

Manufacturer Aspect of my character that uses my abundance of raw talent to consistently produce valuable results to share.

Manure Ability to encourage healthy growth by using the wisdom and experience I have accumulated through dealing with my needs.

Manuscript Ability to understand the different aspects of my story by communicating them very clearly in a consistent, considered manner.

Many Realization that I have an abundance of natural talent and can use it to make the best choice from a variety of options.

Map Ability to use my previously accumulated experience to navigate my way through an unfamiliar and potentially complex situation.

Map reference Ability to understand my position by looking at the bigger picture and recognizing how I can navigate through it.

Maple Natural potential for my long-term spiritual growth by taking some time to examine the shadier aspects of a situation.

Maracas Ability to take my instinctive creativity in both hands so I can shake things up and get everything moving again.

Marathon Opportunity to use my self-motivation and energy to successfully reach my chosen ambition by committing to it in the long run.

Marauder Aspect of my character that needs to have my talents recognized by other people instead of just getting carried away by events.

Marble Ability to steadily maintain a solid presence by understanding all the possible variations rather than scattering my efforts.

Marching Opportunity to assertively pursue one of my ambitions by using self-motivation and discipline to take the steps I need.

Mare Instinctive ability to harness my creative energies so I can use my intuitive power to drive forward with my ambitions.

Margarine Potential to fulfill my ambitions by spreading my resources so I can make a situation more palatable for everyone involved.

Margin Ability to give myself enough space to comfortably explore my options rather than always feeling I am completely on edge.

Marijuana Ability to face up to the realities of a challenging situation in a relaxed manner instead of trying to escape from them.

Marina Situation where I can consistently relax and enjoy emotional security for myself and other people by staying closely connected.

M

Marine Ability to feel at home with my emotional life so I can have a much profounder understanding of what really moves me.

Mark Ability to clearly achieve my chosen level of success by ensuring that I continue to make a good impression on other people.

Market Situation where I can choose from a number of options by displaying my various talents so I can have their value recognized.

Marketplace Situation where I can explore particular aspects of my character so I can understand the value I offer to people.

Marksman Aspect of my character that creates a clearer understanding by powerfully communicating my ambition and how I aim to achieve it.

Markswoman Aspect of my character that can powerfully convey my intentions to others so I can assert my specific aims to them.

Marlin Instinctive ability to immerse myself in my emotions so I can cut through any approaching challenges and get to the point.

Marmalade Potential to fulfill an ambition by preserving my optimism and enthusiasm so I can always achieve a fruitful outcome.

Maroon Mood that can color my perspective by reflecting how I can attract attention to my practical skills and my passion for them.

Marooned Opportunity to use my self-motivation to fulfill my ambitions rather than feeling I must rely on the efforts of others.

Marquee Situation where I can feel relaxed and comfortable as I develop new relationships, although they may only be temporary in nature.

Marriage Opportunity to make a more balanced commitment to some of my fundamental needs, even though it may require some compromises.

Marriage certificate Ability to have my unique skills formally acknowledged by others so I can feel confident about a long-term commitment.

Marriage guidance Opportunity to use my experience and instinct to know which direction to commit to in order to achieve my objective.

Marriage of convenience Opportunity to quickly fulfill a short-term ambition by appearing to be quite happy with making a long-term commitment.

Marrow Essential ability to develop my passion and vitality by using my inner strength to consistently support myself in my actions.

Marsh Situation where I need to get on a firmer footing and take some decisive steps rather than feeling inundated by my emotions.

Marsh gas Ability to understand the pervasive nature of my ideas and how I can sometimes get myself stuck in certain ways of thinking.

Marshmallow Potential to fulfill a short-term ambition that seems very attractive, without taking the time to actually chew it over.

Marsupial Instinctive ability that embodies all aspects of my creative nature and enables me to provide fertile new opportunities.

Martial art Opportunity to resolve any of my inner conflicts by using the strength and power of other people in a balanced and graceful way.

Martial law Opportunity to show my authority in public by behaving as I choose rather than feeling guilty about how people see my actions.

Martyr Aspect of my character that can revitalize my prospects by changing viewpoints instead of falling victim to my habitual beliefs.

Martyrdom Opportunity to invite other people to help me achieve my ambitions rather than feeling I always have to suffer in silence.

M

Marvelous Realization that I should display my excellent talents and abilities more often instead of being astonished by my success.

Marzipan Ability to take the kernel of an idea and skillfully use it as the basis to mix a variety of my skills and experiences.

Mascara Ability to accentuate the attractiveness of my particular point of view so I can draw people toward my way of thinking.

Mascot Ability to use my creative instincts to powerfully influence the outcome of a situation rather than trusting to good luck.

Masculine Realization that I can use my strength and power to firmly assert my ambitions so I can decisively achieve challenging objectives.

Mashed potato Potential to fulfill an ambition by breaking down any difficult challenges so I can continue to sustain my progress.

Mash up Opportunity to mix a variety of influences so I can use my unique talent to create a whole new perspective.

Mask Ability to present my self-image to people in a way that will help me reveal my true feelings rather than trying to conceal them.

Masked ball Opportunity to take some steps that will help other people to become more aware of my talent, instead of trying to hide it.

Masking tape Ability to maintain personal boundaries so I can be clear about outside influences that may be coloring my perspective.

Masochism Opportunity to stop beating myself up over inconsequential details so I can take much more pleasure in fulfilling my needs.

Masochist Aspect of my character with the opportunity to step into my power and take charge rather than causing myself unnecessary pain.

Mason Aspect of my character that can shape my circumstances by chipping away at a hard challenge until I begin to feel comfortable.

Masonry Opportunity to assemble the building blocks to provide me with a consistently solid, supportive sense of belonging.

Masquerade Opportunity to be open and honest about the steps I need to take rather than feeling I have to conceal my needs.

Mass Ability to use accumulated experience to bring my skills together and successfully deal with any potential responsibilities.

Massacre Opportunity to take great care in removing particular influences from my life so I achieve my chosen objectives.

Massage Opportunity to exert some gentle and persistent pressure so I can work through any anxieties and release any built-up tensions.

Masseur Aspect of my character that can use my strength and power to resolve any tensions so I can take a more relaxed perspective.

Masseuse Aspect of my character that is in touch with my empathy and wisdom so I can ease frictions that may be causing tension.

Mass grave Situation where I can prepare the ground for a major life transformation by letting go of the habits that no longer serve me.

Mass murderer Aspect of my character that feels I have to eliminate all my creativity so I can fit in with others' wider demands.

Massive Realization that I need to make a huge effort to develop my colossal talents rather than feeling that they are inconsequential.

Mass-produced Ability to use my individual creativity to shape a unique outcome instead of going through the motions like everyone else.

Mass spectrometer Ability to understand

the most important aspects of a complex situation by identifying small but significant details.

Mass uprising Opportunity to courageously stand up for my wider beliefs by making a fundamental change to some habitual behaviors.

Mast Ability to support my decision-making process so I can capture some of my current way of thinking and convey its power.

Mastectomy Opportunity to realize I have great capacity to look after other people instead of trying to cut myself off from them.

Master Aspect of my character that gives me the permission to assert my strength and power so I can use the skills I have developed.

Master class Opportunity to learn more about my unique talents so I can give myself permission to use my strengths and stand out.

Master key Ability to give myself the freedom to open up to a huge range of possibilities that will unlock my hidden potential.

Master of ceremonies Aspect of my character that can encourage others to actively participate in helping me to achieve my individual ambitions.

Masterpiece Ability to use my individual skills and talents to create a unique outcome that will be gratefully acknowledged by other people.

Master switch Ability to make a single decision that will influence all my other choices so I can quickly accomplish my chosen outcome.

Mastiff Instinctive ability to show the strength of my unconditional loyalty and affection in a persistently determined manner.

Mastodon Instinctive ability to use my huge amount of accumulated wisdom so I can deal with any challenges that emerge from my past.

Masturbation Essential opportunity to imagine a variety of successful outcomes so I can intimately explore my potential for creativity.

Mat Ability to know where I stand on a situation so I can clearly communicate my position, even though it may have its limitations.

Matador Aspect of my character that can successfully challenge me to deal with pent-up aggression that may be causing me to see red.

Match Opportunity to make a creative connection by having a clear idea of what I am looking for so I can achieve my chosen outcome.

Matchbox Ability to set boundaries around my individual creative resources, even though they may seem quite small and limiting for me.

Matches **Ability to strike up some opportunities** by using my head to provide a creative spark, even though it may involve some friction.

Matchmaker Aspect of my character that can choose who I want to be with rather than leaving it to the decisions of other people.

Mate Aspect of my character that I am very comfortable with and can always rely on to consistently support my current ambitions.

Material Ability to provide a substantial basis for my thoughts and feelings so I can shape them into something that is more tangible.

Maternal Realization that I have an endless capacity for unconditional love and affection that provides me with empathy and wisdom.

Maternity leave Opportunity to take time out from my normal routine so I can develop a particular plan that is very precious to me.

Mathematician Aspect of my character that can figure out the best solution by understanding that sometimes everything doesn't always add up.

M

Math Ability to make logical sense of a situation by understanding its relative magnitude so I can work through it precisely.

Matriarch Aspect of my character that is familiar with my qualities and uses my power and wisdom to shape my preferred outcomes.

Matrix Ability to use my relationships to provide a firm foundation for my creativity so I can see what opportunities may emerge.

Matron Aspect of my character that takes care of my fundamental qualities in an efficient manner that makes me feel more at ease.

Matter Realization that I can make a difference by doing something more substantial and showing what I'm made of.

Matter-of-fact Realization that I can create a tangible outcome by using the power of my imagination rather than limiting myself in other ways.

Mattress Ability to support my need for rest and relaxation so I can stay within my comfort zone as I explore my creative urges.

Mature Realization that I can use my ripening confidence to make a major decision rather than feeling as if I don't have the experience.

Maul Ability to defend myself from sharply pointed criticism rather than allowing it to drive a wedge between me and someone else.

Mauve Mood that can color my perspective by reflecting how I can confidently use my wisdom in a gentle, considered manner.

Maverick Aspect of my character that reveals new opportunities by challenging traditional methods so I can assert my individuality.

Maximum Realization that I have the power to increase my level of awareness rather than feeling I am going beyond my limits.

Mayday Opportunity to use my own resourcefulness to resolve a sudden challenge rather than feeling I always need to ask for help.

Mayfly Natural ability to make the most of the briefest opportunities so I can continue to develop a more sustainable ambition.

Mayonnaise Opportunity to achieve an ambition by doing a substantial deed rather than trying to embellish it in an unfulfilling way.

Mayor Aspect of my character that takes responsibility for looking after my wider achievements so I can fulfill my ambitions.

Maypole Situation where I can celebrate a point that needs to be recognized rather than continually going in circles.

Maze Situation where I can work my way through my habitual behavior patterns and reach an understanding of their root cause.

Me Essential awareness that gives me the individual ability to take independent action so I can understand who I really am.

Meadow Situation where I can cultivate my knowledge in a healthy way by using accumulated experiences to naturally grow my expertise.

Meager Realization that my talents are more than sufficient to work with the available resources so I can produce high-quality results.

Meal Opportunity to fulfill my appetite for success by taking in new experiences so I can digest their real significance.

Mean Realization that my generosity helps me understand more about who I am rather than feeling I have nothing to give.

Meandering Opportunity to explore an emotional situation by looking at a variety of viewpoints without feeling I have to be direct.

Meaning Ability to understand what I am trying to say rather than feeling that there is no point in trying to express myself.

Meaningful Realization that I can become much more aware of who I really am by understanding the significance of particular actions to me.

M

Measles Essential opportunity to clearly communicate my needs so I can deal with minor points that have been really irritating me.

Measurement Ability to precisely gauge my performance so I can see how closely it compares with what I originally intended to do.

Meat Potential to fulfill an ambition by using my raw strength and power to produce a result of great substance and importance.

Meat cleaver Ability to cut my way through surface appearances and produce a powerful outcome, even though my actions may seem quite divisive.

Meat hook Ability to quickly catch on to how I use my strength and power rather than feeling I have been left hanging around.

Mechanic Aspect of my character that is familiar with all the intricacies of how I can produce an outcome of great practical value.

Mechanism Ability to produce a specific outcome by having a fundamental understanding of how other people are influenced by my actions.

Medal Ability to display my true courage in dealing with challenging situations rather than feeling that my efforts are unrewarded.

Medallion Ability to draw the attention of other people to my deeper desires rather than trying to impress them in a superficial way.

Meddling Opportunity to maintain a respectful distance in a challenging situation, unless I have been invited to participate in it.

Medevac Opportunity to resolve troubling thoughts by discharging myself from emotional commitments that no longer serve me.

Media Ability to communicate my thoughts and feelings to a wider audience so I can influence how I appear to other people.

Media baron Aspect of my character that has the potential to hold great power and can use it wisely to motivate the people around me.

Media circus Situation where I can influence people by attracting attention to my instinctive creativity rather than trivializing my talents.

Media darling Aspect of my character that can use my influence in a more subtle manner instead of trying to be the center of attention.

Media event Opportunity to become more aware of the significance of my wider actions so I can become more influential with others.

Media hype Ability to authentically communicate my value to others instead of continually attempting to attract attention to myself.

Medic Aspect of my character that can immediately respond to an unhealthy situation so I can resolve it in a short period of time.

Medical Opportunity to become more aware of my inner tensions so I can successfully deal with them and reach a healthy outcome.

Medical certificate Ability to recognize my confidence and competence so I can have a healthy regard for my skills and how I use them.

Medical examination Opportunity to understand what I have learned about my inner tensions rather than criticizing myself for admitting them.

Medication Ability to take consistent action to work my way through a challenge instead of feeling that life is treating me badly.

Medicine Ability to remedy an unhealthy situation by making the decision to deal with any tensions rather than feeling ill at ease.

Medicine cabinet Ability to accumulate useful learning and access valuable memories instead of becoming too upset about an outcome.

Medicine man Aspect of my character that can resolve inner tensions in a healthy manner by making an instinctive connection to my wiser self.

M

Medieval Opportunity to use my basic skills so I can understand my fundamental purpose in life instead of spending ages trying to find it.

Mediocre Realization that I have some unique talents and experiences so I can use them to make my individual value stand out.

Meditation Opportunity to reflect on how I can connect the potential value of my inner world to the practical realities of the outer world.

Medium Realization that I can make a large difference by attending to the small details so I can convey my value to other people.

Meerkat Instinctive ability to observe what is happening around me so I can quickly share it with those closest to me.

Meeting Opportunity to become more acquainted with the different aspects of my character so I can integrate their various needs.

Mega Realization that my talents are far more extraordinary than I thought so I can use them to bring me an abundance of success.

Megalith Ability to always be firm and practical so I can make the greatest use of my monumental talent and ensure I stand out.

Megalomaniac Aspect of my character that instinctively knows how to use my abundant talents, even though others may think I'm insane.

Megalopolis Situation where I can connect with the huge potential of my wider social network so I can access the resources I need.

Megalosaurus Instinctive ability to use my massive power to transform any of my threatening emotions so I can respond in a much warmer way.

Megaphone Ability to powerfully speak my truth so I can always make myself heard without feeling that I have to raise my voice.

Megastore Situation where I have a large number of options to share the value of my wide expertise with all the people around me.

Melancholy Realization that I can raise my spirits by illuminating some new opportunities rather than feeling that everything is gloomy.

Melanoma Essential opportunity to get in touch with my feelings so I can be incisive about an unhealthy situation.

Mêlée Opportunity to resolve any inner conflicts I may have by getting a grip on the situation so I can shape the outcome.

Mellow Realization that I can easily resolve any unnecessary stress by drawing on my accumulated experience and ripening maturity.

Melodrama Opportunity to deepen my learning by understanding the intensity of my emotions rather than feeling I'm losing the plot.

Melody Ability to instinctively communicate with other people in a powerful way by giving voice to my feelings with an air of confidence.

Melon Potential to fulfill an ambition by having a healthy awareness about how I can make the most of a juicy opportunity.

Meltdown Opportunity to keep my cool in a situation where I may feel powerless so I can contain my energy and use it wisely.

Melting Opportunity to take a more fluid approach to dealing with a challenge rather than rigidly attempting to stick to my opinions.

Melting point Opportunity to free myself from old behavior patterns and emotional blockages by taking a much more warmhearted approach.

Melting pot Ability to fulfill a potential ambition by gathering a variety of warmth and wisdom so I can create something fresh.

M

Meltwater Opportunity to immerse myself in the powerful clarity of my emotions rather than freezing myself out of a valuable possibility.

Member Aspect of my character that enjoys having a real sense of belonging and support instead of feeling I am out on a limb.

Membership card Ability to demonstrate my commitment to successfully achieving a collective outcome by allowing other people to use my resources.

Membership fee Ability to have other people recognize the value of my commitment instead of feeling that my efforts are taken for granted.

Member only Realization that I can give myself permission to display my talents rather than feeling excluded from any new opportunities.

Membrane Essential ability to stay flexible in setting my personal boundaries so I can decide how open I can be with other people.

Memento Ability to remind myself of how I successfully resolved a previous challenge so I can put my current situation into perspective.

Memo Ability to draw attention to the value of my individual awareness, even though I may not be able to act on it immediately.

Memoir Ability to intimately observe my habitual behavior patterns so I can reach a better understanding of who I really am.

Memorabilia Ability to display what I have learned from an accumulation of significant experiences so I can share their wider value.

Memorial Ability to honor a significant experience from my past so I can understand its fundamental value in my present situation.

Memorize Opportunity to make a heartfelt commitment so I can remember the true value of a relationship instead of forgetting about it.

Memory Essential ability to recreate my experience so I can apply it to the current situation and achieve my chosen outcome.

Memory card Ability to communicate the value of my experiences to others in a succinct, specific manner that they will understand.

Memory stick Ability to stay with what I know so I can use the strength of my experience to communicate my message to others.

Men Aspects of my character that collectively embody the individual strength and power I need to successfully realize my ambitions.

Menace Aspect of my character that challenges my fears by stepping into my power rather than causing myself any further anxiety.

Menagerie Ability to bring a wide range of my creative instincts together so I can proudly display them to the people around me.

Mending Opportunity to create some new value by making the effort to repair a situation that initially appeared to be of little use.

Menopause Opportunity to transform my creative potential from an individual awareness into an experience that will be widely recognized.

Menstruation Essential opportunity to experience my potential for creative transformation rather than allowing it to cramp my style.

Mental Realization that I can use original thinking to deal with a new challenge instead of going crazy about the situation.

Mental block Opportunity to make progress by thinking up some solid ideas rather than allowing myself to be obstructed by others.

Mental cruelty Opportunity to be kind and gentle about my emerging awareness instead of causing myself a lot of pain and anxiety.

Mental illness Essential opportunity to use the strength of my ideas to resolve an unhealthy situation rather than just feeling uneasy about it.

M

Mention Opportunity to proudly recognize my contribution to a collective effort instead of always trying to keep quiet about it.

Mentor Aspect of my character that uses my accumulated experience to intuitively guide me toward a much greater understanding.

Menu Opportunity to make specific choices about what will fulfill my appetite for success so I can digest their significance.

Mercenary Aspect of my character that has the courage and discipline to engage with my inner conflicts so I can openly realize my value.

Merchandise Ability to see the real value of my talents so I feel more confident in displaying my skills and abilities to others.

Merchant Aspect of my character that values my capabilities and actively encourages other people to openly recognize them.

Merciless Realization that I can be kinder in dealing with some of my most precious aspirations rather than trying to eliminate them.

Mercury Ability to conduct myself in such a way that I can use my power to resolve any heavy emotions and potentially toxic outcomes.

Mercy Opportunity to be more compassionate about how I realize my ambitions rather than leaving it to the whims of other people.

Mercy killing Opportunity to transform a behavioral pattern that no longer serves me by being more compassionate about my fundamental needs.

Merganser Instinctive ability to rise above more practical concerns so I can immerse myself in my emotions and get a grip on them.

Merger Opportunity to combine two of my distinct talents into a quality that can help me to be much more powerful and recognizable.

Merit Realization that I need to acknowledge the brilliance of my efforts rather than feeling that I have somehow been at fault.

Merkin Ability to confidently reveal the bald facts instead of trying to appear wildly creative with some unrealistic ideas.

Mermaid Aspect of my character that naturally immerses myself in my emotions so I can fulfill my aspirations and realize my dreams.

Merman Aspect of my character that can strongly assert my deepest ambitions by naturally immersing myself in my powerful imagination.

Merry Realization that I can always improve my mood by recognizing how I can actively use my special talents to raise my spirits.

Merry-go-round Situation where I can use my power and energy to decide my direction rather than feeling I am going in circles.

Mesa Situation where I can consolidate the higher levels of success I have attained so I can make my achievements more prominent.

Mesh Ability to make a number of strong connections with other people so we can work together in a really coordinated way.

Mesmerized Realization that I can profoundly raise my level of understanding by completely immersing myself in my thoughts and feelings.

Mesolithic Opportunity to use my natural instincts and creativity to shape my preferred outcome, even though it may seem quite basic.

Mess Realization that I can use my natural instincts to clear up an apparently complex situation by using a less structured approach.

Message Ability to increase my self-awareness by communicating how I feel rather than assuming everyone else thinks the same way.

Message board Ability to make my thoughts and feelings more apparent to other people by having the confidence to share them in public.

Message box Ability to feel safe and secure

M

about what I want to say by being clear about personal boundaries with people around me.

Messenger Aspect of my character that can help me increase my levels of self-awareness by having the motivation to change my perspective.

Messiah Aspect of my character that needs to express a powerful spiritual truth so I can deliver on my promises to other people.

Messiah complex Realization that I need to change my perceptions of the world instead of always trying to change the world for other people.

Metabolism Essential ability to use my power and energy as a way of enabling my passions to emerge into existence and continually evolve.

Metal Ability to conduct myself in such a way that I can use my fundamental power to shape a definite outcome and support it.

Metal detector Ability to understand what is going on by paying attention to the value of what might be concealed below surface appearances.

Metalworker Aspect of my character that expresses my value to other people by conducting myself in a way that allows me to shape an outcome.

Meteor Ability to understand the practical implications of a sudden flash of inspiration so I can use it in a down-to-earth manner.

Meteor shower Opportunity to track a number of illuminating ideas so I can clarify my thoughts and inspire myself even further.

Meter Ability to measure my progress by taking a more objective view so I can be more aware of how to reach my chosen outcome.

Methadone Ability to deal with one of my fundamental needs rather than trying to substitute it by dealing with the needs of others.

Methane Ability to use the potential value

of some volatile thoughts and theories rather than allowing them to debilitate me in any way.

Method Ability to observe myself as I work my way through an unfamiliar situation so I can resolve any habitual behaviors.

Method acting Opportunity to be who I really am rather than feeling I have to always reveal myself in a particular way to meet expectations.

Methodical Realization that I need to work my way through the outcomes I would like to achieve by setting firm intentions and goals.

Meticulous Realization that I need to be extremely clear about my wider intentions without becoming too obsessed by minor details.

Metro Ability to easily connect with the wider aspects of my social circle so I can convey my deeper understanding to them.

Metronome Ability to become more consistently aware of my internal rhythms so I can choose exactly the right time to take action.

Metrosexual Aspect of my character that balances my masculine and feminine energies so I can proudly display my power and creativity.

Mexican wave Opportunity to respond to a number of demands for my attention so I can show my appreciation in consistent and coherent way.

Mice Instinctive ability to deal with any small anxieties that may been gnawing away at me so I can take firm and positive action.

Microbe Instinctive ability to resolve an unhealthy situation by removing any minor influences that are making me feel ill at ease.

Microburst Natural opportunity to stay on track with a particular project, even though I feel that the atmosphere has suddenly changed.

M

Microchip Ability to rapidly integrate a large number of different thought processes so I can confidently provide a definite answer.

Microcosm Situation where I can have a much wider appreciation of the bigger picture by taking time to explore the smaller details.

Microfilm Ability to expand on what I want to say to other people rather than feeling I always have to conceal it from them.

Microphone Ability to confidently express myself by sharing passions with a wider audience instead of feeling no one is listening.

Microprocessor Ability to quickly work through a variety of seemingly insignificant tasks that will soon add up to a major achievement.

Microscope Ability to clearly focus on some very specific details so I can understand how they contribute to the overall situation.

Microsurgery Opportunity to resolve inner tensions by opening up and being specific about what is making me feel uncomfortable.

Microwave Opportunity to reach a satisfying outcome by using the intensity of my thought processes to powerfully signal my intentions.

Microwave meal Ability to rapidly fulfill my appetite for short-term success, even though the experience could have been more fulfilling.

Microwave oven Ability to quickly fulfill my raw ambition by intensively focusing my energy so I can satisfy my hunger for results.

Midday Opportunity to naturally illuminate what has recently been emerging into my conscious awareness so I can develop it further.

Middle Situation where I feel centered and fully involved in what I am doing without needing to go to extremes to enjoy myself.

Middle finger Essential ability to control my actions and shape my future by ensuring I can always stand out from the people around me.

Midge Instinctive ability to decisively deal with a number of minor irritations rather than letting them continually sap my energy.

Midget Aspect of my character that has huge potential and helps me hold my head high instead of habitually belittling my achievements.

Midnight Opportunity to naturally discover a deeper understanding of myself by exploring what is emerging from my unconscious awareness.

Midnight feast Opportunity to fulfill some of my greatest ambitions by going deeper into my unconscious self and sharing my experiences.

Midnight sun Opportunity to consistently illuminate a situation with the power of my creativity so I can take my time to understand it.

Midriff Essential ability to connect my emotions and my actions so I can use my core beliefs to support the steps I need to take.

Midstream Situation where I am in the midst of connecting with my feelings so I can use them to accumulate more learning and experience.

Midwife Aspect of my character that can help me successfully deliver a labor of love that I have been developing for some time.

Midwinter Opportunity to surround myself with the practical resources I need to prepare myself for some emerging possibilities.

Migraine Essential opportunity to relieve myself of some mental stress by letting go of some ideas that have been challenging me.

Migrant Aspect of my character that periodically makes a major shift in my viewpoint so I can understand what works for me.

Migration Opportunity to spread my influence by leaving an area I have been uncomfortable with so I can move into new possibilities.

M

Mild Realization that I may have to take a harder-edged approach to achieve the results that will make a difference to me.

Mildew Ability to contain my emotions so I can identify opportunities for transformational growth that I may have been neglecting.

Mile Ability to go the distance so I will soon be able to connect with a long-held desire that once seemed quite far away.

Milestone Ability to measure my progress toward my objective by maintaining a solid presence so I can always be firm and practical.

Military Realization that I can be more disciplined in how I approach a situation so I can deal with any self-destructive behaviors.

Military police Aspects of my character that take full responsibility for my individual actions so I can maintain my level of discipline.

Milk Potential to fulfill my emotional needs by looking after people in a healthy way rather than always going off on my own.

Milk float Ability to gently maintain my levels of drive and ambition by quietly looking after my needs in a healthy way.

Milk shake Potential to fulfill an emotional need by taking a firmer approach to consistently achieve more definite results for me.

Milk tooth Essential ability to increase my feeling of confidence and maturity rather than thinking there will be an inevitable fallout.

Milky Way Ability to open to a more universal awareness as I continue to move toward a deeper, wider understanding of myself.

Mill Situation where I can refine my practical skills by working my way through them rather than wandering around aimlessly.

Milliner Aspect of my character that helps me present my individual viewpoint to other people so it seems more attractive to them.

Million Ability to acknowledge that I have accomplished much more than I originally thought I could and feel fulfilled beyond measure.

Millionaire Aspect of my character that realizes the wealth of my accumulated knowledge so I can use it to assert my true value.

Millipede Instinctive ability to take things one step at a time so I can keep progressing steadily toward my chosen objective.

Millpond Situation where I can take a calmer approach so I can reflect on the potential power of my accumulated experience.

Millstone Ability to grind out the results I need by being firm and practical rather than feeling I am a liability.

Mime Opportunity to speak up so other people can hear my truth rather than just hoping they will understand my intentions.

Mime artist Aspect of my character that needs to give voice to my concerns rather than letting others suffer in silence.

Mimic Opportunity to speak my individual truth instead of continually repeating what I think others would like to hear from me.

Mince Potential to fulfill an ambition by using my raw strength and power rather than feeling unable to take the steps I want to.

Mincemeat Potential to fulfill an ambition by using a variety of resources I have been preserving for a particularly special occasion.

Mincing machine Ability to produce an outcome of great practical value by working through a challenge and breaking it down into smaller pieces.

Mind Essential opportunity to understand how I create my perceptions of the world so I can be more aware of emerging opportunities.

Minder Aspect of my character that helps me maintain my status in a social situation so I can always feel safe and secure.

Mind reader Aspect of my character that

M

understands my needs and how I can fulfill them rather than deceiving myself.

Mine Situation where I can dig deeper into the practical experience I have accumulated so I can reveal my hidden talents.

Mine clearance Opportunity to safely process any potentially explosive feelings so I can create a practical, positive transformation.

Mine detector Ability to locate a potentially volatile response that may be hidden just below the surface so I can safely deal with it.

Minefield Situation where I can steadily work my way through any concealed challenges by being careful about the steps I take.

Miner Aspect of my character that has the courage to go much deeper into my sense of self so I can bring my raw power to the surface.

Mineral Ability to use my raw talent to create an outcome of great value, even though it may require some effort to bring it into reality.

Mine shaft Situation where I can directly connect to my deep experience and profound awareness so I can convey my power and strength.

Minesweeper Ability to safely navigate my way through my emotional highs and lows so I can deal with potential dangers.

Miniature Realization that I can achieve success on a far greater scale by attending to the details and understanding their significance.

Mini-me Aspect of my character that embodies my potential for individual growth rather than feeling I have to copy everyone else.

Minimum wage Ability to have my value recognized by other people instead of thinking that my contribution will never be worthwhile.

Mining Opportunity to reach a profounder

awareness by making a sustained practical effort and not being afraid to get my hands dirty.

Miniskirt Ability to present my self-image to other people in a way that draws their attention to the steps I plan to take.

Minister Aspect of my character that provides me with the spiritual awareness to connect with a wider understanding of my situation.

Mink Instinctive ability to boldly push forward with my ambitions instead of ferociously asserting my need for comfort and luxury.

Minnow Instinctive ability to immerse myself in a particular emotion, even though it may seem quite insignificant compared to others.

Minority Opportunity to honestly speak my truth and feel secure in my viewpoint rather than being influenced by the weight of numbers.

Minotaur Aspect of my character that can safely access my raw strength and power by patiently working through my deeper awareness.

Minstrel Aspect of my character that has the presence to evoke my deeper feelings rather than just wandering from place to place.

Mint Potential to fulfill an ambition by using my taste to take a fresh approach that will result in the creation of new value for me.

Minus Realization that I can be a positive influence in a situation by adding my skills instead of feeling I will somehow diminish it.

Minute Opportunity to take my time to understand some of the tiniest details so I can choose the best moment to take action.

Miracle Opportunity to fundamentally transform a situation by using my abundant creativity rather than following an obvious procedure.

M

Miracle cure Opportunity to remedy an unhealthy feeling by trusting in my potential for change instead of thinking I have no options.

Mirage Opportunity to reflect on what is happening rather than being distracted by my vivid imagination in the heat of the moment.

Mire Situation where I can really get stuck in some messy practicalities instead of becoming bogged down in specific details.

Mirror Ability to gain a much clearer sense of self-awareness by reflecting on who I am instead of just copying other people.

Mirror image Ability to look at my situation from a different perspective so I can understand how my actions may appear to others.

Mirth Realization that I can joyfully celebrate my achievements so I can gleefully understand how to overcome any difficult challenges.

Misbehaving Opportunity to do something meaningful by taking full responsibility for my actions rather than blaming other people.

Miscarriage Opportunity to let go of any misconceptions so I can still use my fertile imagination when I feel the time is right.

Miscellany Ability to use all the different elements of my skills so I can take a more coherent approach to dealing with a challenge.

Mischievous Realization that I can use my creative talents to provide a positive outcome rather than thinking I am annoying people.

Misdiagnosed Opportunity to identify the real cause of an unhealthy situation so I can take decisive action to permanently deal with it.

Miser Aspect of my character that often undervalues my accumulated wisdom and can conceal my talent rather than generously sharing it.

Miserable Realization that I feel happiest and most fulfilled when I am involved in meaningful work that is challenging for me.

Misfortune Realization that I have far more control over my intended outcome than I think instead of feeling I am always unlucky.

Misprint Ability to clearly communicate what I want to say to other people so I can make my mark without being misinterpreted.

Miss Opportunity to relax and let go of any foregone conclusions so I can understand how to successfully reach my target.

Missed approach Opportunity to use a more down-to-earth method so I can complete a complex project rather than leaving it in the air.

Missed connection Opportunity to take immediate action to fulfill a personal ambition instead of busying myself with habitual activity.

Missile Ability to powerfully assert my beliefs and exert my influence by concentrating my energies so I can get really fired up.

Missile shield Ability to defend myself against any outside threats to my beliefs by carefully tracking the thoughts that are emerging for me.

Missile silo Situation where I can assert my individual power by ensuring I can use my accumulated resources to cover any eventuality.

Missing Realization that I need to attend to a vital aspect of my development by staying really present so I can resolve any challenges.

Missing a bus Opportunity to make consistent progress toward my professional objectives by taking on board what I need to do.

Missing a plane Opportunity to raise my involvement in a powerful idea so I can get it off the ground and make progress with it.

Missing a train Opportunity to embark on a particular professional path instead of trying to decide where I want my career to go.

M

Missing body part Opportunity to understand the unique contribution I can make to a situation so I can take immediate action.

Missing teeth Opportunity to display the power of my talents to other people rather than feeling that I have lost confidence in myself.

Missing the target Opportunity to clearly understand my aims so I can deliberately focus my actions on getting closer to my ultimate ambition.

Missing the tide Opportunity to become more aware of the ebb and flow of my emotions so I can use their power instead of trying to control them.

Mission Opportunity to be clear about what my goals are so I can always stay fully committed to achieving my objective.

Missionary Aspect of my character that is keen to move into unfamiliar areas so I can share my beliefs and describe my position.

Mission statement Ability to declare how I feel about a situation so other people can understand how I will reach my objective.

Misspelling Realization that I can clearly communicate what I want to create without feeling that others are judging my performance.

Mist Natural opportunity to clarify any slightly confused thinking in the prevailing mood so I can see the way ahead more clearly.

Mistake Opportunity to learn from experience so I know how to do the right thing instead of feeling that my skills have no value.

Mistletoe Natural ability to create a space where I can connect with my talents so I can share them with the people around me.

Mistress Aspect of my character that tries to appear committed, even though I may only be concealing my more exciting creative abilities.

Misunderstanding Realization that I need to explore my viewpoint in greater detail rather than trying to keep everyone else happy.

Miter Ability to present my self-image by drawing attention to my spiritual perspective instead of adopting a different angle.

Mittens Ability to present my self-image to people in a way that shows my warmth and commitment as I shape and direct my future.

Mixed marriage Opportunity to make a more balanced commitment to some of my fundamental needs, even though they may appear to be quite different.

Mixer Ability to blend a number of my basic skills together so I can produce an outcome that holds much greater value for me.

Mixing Opportunity to move into unknown and unfamiliar areas so I can openly absorb a variety of valuable new influences.

Mixing desk Ability to instinctively communicate with others by choosing just the right level to make sure I connect with them.

Mixture Ability to make a difference by realizing that I will have to use a range of my skills to achieve a particular result.

Moat Situation where I can proudly display my more powerful characteristics rather than always trying to hide behind my emotions.

Mob Opportunity to identify individual aspects of my character so I can understand their qualities and resolve any conflicting needs.

Mobile launcher Ability to powerfully assert my beliefs and strongly exert my influence at any time and place I feel is appropriate.

Mobile phone Ability to clearly communicate what motivates me, even though I may not be viewing the situation from a firm perspective.

Mobster Aspect of my character that can be intimidated by my close relationships rather than having the confidence to assert my value.

M

Moccasin Ability to present my self-image to other people by taking steps to display how relaxed I am in using my instinctive creativity.

Mochaccino Potential to fulfill an emotional need by indulging in a rewarding, short-term ambition that will stimulate further conversation.

Mocking Opportunity to truly commend myself for my achievements rather than allowing others to be contemptuous of my efforts.

Mockingbird Instinctive ability to rise above more practical concerns so I can really spread my ideas rather than always belittling them.

Mockumentary Opportunity to investigate my real motives and behaviors rather than playing along with people's expectations.

Model Aspect of my character that may appear to possess perfect qualities instead of using my power to achieve an ideal outcome.

Model aircraft Ability to give some shape to a plan by playing around with how it might look so I can control its progress and direction.

Model railway Ability to play around with my professional career path so I can have more control of how to stay on track with it.

Modem Ability to form my opinion so I can communicate my needs in a specific manner rather than just accepting the facts.

Moderation Opportunity to indulge in my talents and explore how I can successfully use them instead of feeling I have to hold back.

Modern Realization that I can use my accumulated experience to take action right now rather than reverting to old habits.

Modesty Realization that I need to proudly display my talents to other people instead of thinking it is more worthwhile to conceal them.

Modified Realization that I have the skill and ingenuity to shape my chosen outcome rather than just accepting the current situation.

Module Ability to use my skills and expertise as a way to fulfill a bigger ambition instead of thinking I just don't fit in.

Moist Realization that I am relaxed and comfortable about my emotions rather than feeling they are intruding into my thoughts.

Moisture barrier Ability to establish a personal boundary so I don't end up being too influenced by the emotions of the people around me.

Moisturizer Ability to stay in touch with my real feelings by carefully maintaining the boundary between my inner and outer worlds.

Molar Essential ability to confidently work my way through the finer details of my ambitions without it becoming too much of a grind.

Molasses Potential to fulfill an ambition by releasing myself from a sticky situation that once seemed to offer instant gratification.

Mold Ability to consistently shape a successful outcome by ensuring I always remain aware of the value of the surrounding context.

Moldy Natural opportunity to make a fresh start by looking at some aspects of my talents that I may have been neglecting.

Mole Instinctive ability to immerse myself in the practical aspects of a situation so I can clearly make independent progress.

Molecule Ability to understand the smallest details so I can understand the attraction that they hold for my continuing creativity.

Molehill Ability to make practical progress through consistent effort rather than blowing the difficulties out of all proportion.

Mollusk Instinctive ability to protect my feelings so I can immerse myself in emotions without appearing vulnerable to others.

M

Monarch Aspect of my character whose splendor and refinement is widely recognized and has the maturity to use them wisely.

Monastery Situation where I can reflect on the more spiritual aspects of my life and commit to experiences I always vowed I would do.

Money Ability to declare my confidence in my undoubted talents so I can have my value genuinely recognized by other people.

Money laundering Opportunity to reappraise my talents by working my way through any emotional tensions that may influence my apparent value.

Mongoose Instinctive ability to deal with any challenges that may prevent me from discarding a self-image that is no longer useful to me.

Mongrel Instinctive ability to freely mix my creative instincts so I can embody them in a more robust and resilient manner.

Monitor Ability to observe what is happening in a complex situation so I can decide to take action when the timing is right.

Monitor lizard Instinctive ability to take a more detached view of my fundamental creativity without being too cold-blooded about it.

Monk Aspect of my character that is devoted to the more spiritual aspects of my life and gives me the time for self-reflection.

Monkey Instinctive ability to understand my natural creativity by being impulsive and inquisitive as I play around with the situation.

Monocle Ability to look more closely at a situation so I can understand other viewpoints apart from my perspective.

Monolith Ability to steadily maintain a single-minded presence by always being firm and practical as I use my accumulated experience.

Monologue Opportunity to share my perspective so I can clearly state my beliefs without feeling I have to go on at length.

Monotonous Realization that I can introduce a lot more excitement into a situation by drawing on the rich variety of my experiences.

Monsoon Natural opportunity to use my powerful ideas to release pent-up emotions that may have been clouding my thoughts.

Monster Instinctive ability to make the most of a huge opportunity rather than allowing my anxieties to grow out of all proportion.

Month Opportunity to use my natural sense of rhythm to consistently understand some of the possibilities that regularly emerge for me.

Monument Situation where I can reconnect with a significant experience from my past that has had a lasting influence on how I see myself.

Mood Realization that I can be more effective in achieving consistent results by understanding that my feelings may change over time.

Mood music Ability to instinctively communicate with others in a fundamentally powerful way by understanding what is often unspoken.

Mood room Aspect of myself that has the capacity to help me explore unseen opportunities so I can develop potential skills.

Moon Elemental ability to reflect on my intuitive talents and all the unexplored possibilities that they can illuminate for me.

Moonlight Ability to understand a situation with much greater clarity by using my intuitive power to illuminate what is often unseen.

Moon phase Opportunity to reflect on what is emerging for me so I can understand some unseen possibilities and how they might evolve.

Moonstone Ability to attract people to my viewpoint by reflecting some clear thinking that may illuminate a variety of new possibilities.

Moorland Situation where I can raise my awareness by having greater freedom

M

to open myself to a much wider range of possibilities.

Moose Instinctive ability to feel at home in the deeper reaches of my unexplored self rather than continually hunting for fulfillment.

Mop Ability to quickly clean up a messy situation that has resulted from the outpouring of potentially uncontrollable emotions.

Moral Ability to use my sense of right and wrong to honestly speak my truth so other people understand the power of my story.

Morass Situation where I can make tangible progress by freeing myself from any confusion that may prevent me from taking further steps.

More Realization that I can increase my levels of awareness by opening up to new possibilities rather than minimizing my involvement.

Morgue Situation where I can examine my neglected talents and look at ways of revitalizing them rather than leaving them lying.

Morning Natural opportunity to open up to a wider understanding of myself by illuminating my needs and seeing what emerges from them.

Morphine Ability to take direct action to positively transform a painful situation instead of trying to numb myself to its influence.

Morsel Potential to fulfill an ambition by being able to take in the significance of some small but particularly valuable details.

Mortal Realization that I have the opportunity to use my energy and self-motivation to make a fundamental difference to my situation.

Mortal danger Opportunity to go to the edge of my comfort zone so I can transform a finely balanced situation and use it to my advantage.

Mortar Ability to take decisive action to cement a relationship together rather than just taking potshots at it from a distance.

Mortar bomb Ability to safely contain my potentially explosive feelings so I can choose the action that will have the greatest impact.

Mortar tube Ability to consider the variety of angles that I can take to consistently convey the power of my feelings to other people.

Mortgage Ability to make a valuable commitment to my long-term personal development by using a potentially character-building experience.

Mortuary Situation where I can respectfully acknowledge a once-vital aspect of my past behavior so I can peacefully lay it to rest.

Mosaic Ability to become more aware of the intricacies of my behavioral patterns and the colorful ways in which they are connected.

Mosque Situation where I can reflect on the spiritual aspects of my life and how they call me to explore all facets of my beliefs.

Mosquito Instinctive ability to decisively deal with any minor irritations rather than letting them sap my vitality in an unhealthy way.

Moss Natural ability to thrive in the most arduous of conditions, even though I may feel stuck between a rock and a hard place.

Most Realization that I can take greatest advantage of my potential by exploring topics that usually don't interest me in the least.

Moth Instinctive ability to trust in my potential to undergo a transformation rather than dazzling myself with my brilliance.

Mothball Ability to maintain a certain aspect of the self-image I present to other people, even though it may no longer be relevant.

Mother Aspect of my character embodying my capacity for creativity and wisdom by providing me with unconditional love and affection.

M

Mother-in-law Aspect of my character that can provide me with access to unfamiliar resources rather than merely judging my level of commitment.

Mother's death Opportunity to reconnect with a part of myself that may have seemed lost so I can embrace and embody its loving qualities.

Motion Opportunity to change my viewpoint so I can make some definite progress in exploring my options as I move forward.

Motion blur Realization that I can make things clearer for myself rather than feeling that the situation is moving too quickly for me.

Motion detector Ability to understand what is going on by paying attention to my deeper motivations instead of routinely ignoring them.

Motion sensor Ability to identify what is happening beyond my immediate awareness so I can quickly move to a more measured response.

Motion sickness Opportunity to resolve an unhealthy situation by making a decisive movement rather than just worrying and feeling ill at ease.

Motivation Opportunity to make decisive progress with my ambitions by choosing the direction I want to go in and consistently following it.

Motivational trainer Aspect of my character that has the discipline to make a continuing commitment to ensuring powerful progress with my ambitions.

Motor Ability to drive my ambitions forward by consistently using my creative energies in a measured way to reach a powerful outcome.

Motorbike Ability to express my individual freedom so I can feel motivated to follow my path and go wherever I want to go in life.

Motorboat Ability to navigate complex and unpredictable feelings by using my personal power and drive to maintain my emotional stability.

Motorcycle Ability to use my personal ambition and drive so I can freely pursue my choices as I progress rapidly toward my objective.

Motorcyclist Aspect of my character that gives me a great degree of individual freedom in making powerful choices about my chosen direction.

Motor home Ability to feel relaxed with all the different aspects of myself so I can continue to expand my comfort zone.

Motorway Situation where I can use a widely recognized method as a way of pursuing my ambitions and progressing toward my objective.

Motorway junction Situation where I can powerfully bring a number of my ambitions together so I can choose how to make further progress with them.

Motorway pile-up Opportunity to use my personal drive to keep my individual ambitions moving instead of allowing my commitments to accumulate.

Motorway services Situation where I can look after my professional needs by openly encouraging others to look after my needs.

Mound Situation where I can raise my level of competence and really stand out by accumulating a great deal of practical skill.

Mountain Situation where I can gain a much wider perspective by making a committed and sustained effort to heighten my understanding.

Mountain bike Ability to use my strength and power to make self-motivated progress as I work my way through the ups and downs of a situation.

Mountaineer Aspect of my character that can heighten my awareness by making a committed, sustained effort to step outside my comfort zone.

Mountain goat Instinctive ability to attain a particular standing in my social circle by

M

making people aware of the effort I put in.

Mountain lion Instinctive ability to display my creative talents by proudly showing how comfortable I am with the heights I have achieved.

Mourner Aspect of my character that helps me understand what makes me unique so I can let go of what I no longer need.

Mourning Opportunity to happily move on by revitalizing a talent I have been neglecting or deciding to finally lay it to rest.

Mouse Instinctive ability to make my feelings obvious so I can deal with any small anxieties that may have been gnawing away at me.

Mouse mat Ability to take a softer approach so I can clearly communicate my position, even though it may have its limitations.

Mousetrap Ability to quickly and decisively deal with any minor concerns that may have been limiting my wider freedom to take action.

Mousse Potential to fulfill an ambition by whipping up some enthusiasm instead of trying to appear consistently cool to other people.

Mouth Essential ability to give voice to what I am presently experiencing so I can speak up and honestly express my feelings.

Mouth guard Ability to protect my confidence from any unforeseen impacts so I can defend myself from any threats to my power.

Mouthwash Ability to open up about my feelings so I can come clean and take a fresh approach in expressing what I need.

Movement Opportunity to make progress by being committed to my purpose so I can continue to make significant advances.

Movie Situation where I can become more aware of my personal story and how I can use it to transform what matters to me most.

Moving Opportunity to shift my perspective by having a deeper understanding of my emotions and the power they can convey for me.

Moving house Opportunity to transform how I view myself by taking the time to understand what will make me most at home with how I feel.

Mowing Opportunity to maintain the level of my practical skills so I can use them as a basis for my continuing healthy growth.

MP3 Ability to give voice to how I feel by neatly encapsulating what I am instinctively trying to communicate to other people.

Muck Ability to go beyond superficial appearances by getting stuck in a messy opportunity so I can realize its value.

Mucus Essential ability to protect some of my sensitive issues and ensure that everything runs smoothly without causing too much mess.

Mud Situation where I can take a firmer approach by staying down-to-earth and trying to minimize my emotional involvement.

Muddle Opportunity to be specific about what I need rather than always trying to resolve any confusion for other people.

Mudflat Situation where I can explore the rich variety of my emotional experiences without getting too bogged down in the details.

Mudguard Ability to remain clear about my intentions as I use my energy and self-motivation to progress toward my chosen objective.

Muesli Potential to fulfill my ambitions by using a variety of vital resources I have built up over a long period.

Muffin Potential to fulfill short-term ambition in a pleasing and comfortable way without allowing any of my needs to just spill out.

Mug Ability to fulfill an emotional need by allowing myself to take in a particular experience so I can face up to its value.

Mugger Aspect of my character that needs to recognize the value of my relationships rather than feeling guilty about my actions.

M

Mugging Opportunity to have the value of my expertise recognized by other people instead of feeling that I'm forcing myself on them.

Muggy Natural opportunity to lighten an oppressive mood by making my feelings obvious to others so I can clear the air.

Mulberry Natural ability to provide support for my personal stories, even though they may seem quite lightweight to other people.

Mule Instinctive ability to harness my unconscious energy so I can carry a heavy responsibility without questioning the outcome.

Multicolored Mood that can color my perspective by reflecting how I can use my range of talents to clearly understand my various options.

Multistory parking garage Situation where I may have to leave a personal ambition at a certain level until I have the opportunity to drive it forward again.

Multitasking Opportunity to make rapid progress by using a wide variety of talents rather than limiting myself to an individual option.

Multitude Ability to identify one significant aspect of my talents, even though I have a wide range of experience to choose from.

Mumbling Opportunity to speak up clearly instead of trying to minimize the power of what I need to say to other people.

Mummy Ability to display my unique talent so I can transform my situation rather than always trying to keep it under wraps.

Mural Ability to apply a new perspective to a situation so I can use it to strongly support my beliefs and maintain my privacy.

Murder Opportunity to profoundly transform my creativity by taking powerful and decisive action so I can bring it to life.

Murder cover-up Opportunity to reveal a creative talent that I may have been hiding to keep everyone else happy.

Murdered Realization that I can revitalize a talent that I have been neglecting rather than feeling I have been forced to eliminate it.

Murderer Aspect of my character that is trying to kill off one of my vital strengths so I can fit in with the demands of other people.

Murderess Aspect of my character that is attempting to get rid of one of my creative talents because people are challenged by its power.

Murder suspect Aspect of my character that has unshakable belief in my talents, even though other people may confess to doubting my capabilities.

Murky Realization that I need to make my feelings extremely clear rather than being a bit obscure in how I communicate them.

Murmur Opportunity to become more aware of what is happening around me instead of continually having a distinct feeling of uneasiness.

Murmuration Opportunity to make other people more aware of their collective purpose so we can work together in a more instinctive manner.

Muscle Essential ability to have my own strength of purpose and the power to use it wisely instead of feeling antagonized by people.

Muscular Realization that I always have the potential to motivate myself and take action rather than feeling that I am weak willed.

Museum Situation where I can understand my continuing value by revisiting my greatest achievements and revitalizing my inner resources.

Mushroom Natural ability to rapidly develop using the resources I have rather than expanding uncontrollably in shadier circumstances.

Music Ability to instinctively communicate with people in a fundamentally powerful way so I can give voice to what is often unspoken.

Musical Realization that I can achieve a pleasing outcome by taking a more harmonious approach that resonates with others.

Musical chairs Opportunity to achieve an ambition by moving away from my habitual viewpoint rather than feeling left out by others.

Musical instrument Ability to skillfully communicate how I feel, even though I may not able to use the powerful words I want to.

Musical theater Situation where I can flamboyantly step into my variety of talents so I can display my abilities to a wider audience.

Musician Aspect of my character that instinctively shares my deeper feelings and can strike just the right tone in emotional situations.

Musket Ability to assert my power in a forceful manner so I can communicate my aims, even though my methods may seem old-fashioned.

Mussel Instinctive ability to safeguard my feelings by sticking with the practicalities whenever I immerse myself in my emotions.

Mustache Essential opportunity to powerfully assert my authority rather than trying to conceal my feelings by keeping a stiff upper lip.

Mustard Ability to stimulate my appetite for success by becoming really enthusiastic about an apparently difficult challenge.

Mustard seed Natural ability to use my keen awareness to develop a seemingly insignificant plan into something much bigger and more powerful.

Muster Opportunity to gather together all the various aspects of my talents so I can use them to coordinate a successful outcome.

Mutant Natural ability to shape a successful outcome by choosing to behave differently rather than revealing myself in the same old way.

Mute Opportunity to listen for my inner voice so I use it to honestly express my feelings in a strong and confident manner.

Mute button Ability to listen for what is going on by calmly taking a specific action and knowing when I need to stay quiet.

Mutilated Ability to powerfully reach out to other people so I can connect with them in a healthy way rather than just cutting myself off.

Mutilated body Ability to use my creative instincts to make sense of my situation instead of feeling that my world is falling apart.

Mutiny Opportunity to give myself the emotional freedom I need by creating a fundamental change rather than resisting it.

Mutton Potential to fulfill an ambition by using my raw strength and power to make my own choices instead of conforming to expectations.

Myopia Essential opportunity to see the bigger picture by observing a situation from closeup rather than just being narrow-minded.

Myrrh Ability to create a much more favorable atmosphere so I can share a special experience with the people around me.

Myself Essential awareness that gives me the opportunity to understand my viewpoint so I can step into my power and take action.

Mysterious Realization that I can discover my potential by taking definite action to explore the unknown and unfamiliar aspects of myself.

Mysterious corridor Situation where I can step into the unknown and take a more straightforward approach to opening up any new opportunities.

Mysterious forest Situation where I can explore the healthy diversity and natural growth potential of the unfamiliar aspects of my character.

Mysterious house Situation where I have the security and support I need so I can comfortably investigate unknown and unfamiliar aspects of myself.

M

Mysterious lover Aspect of my character that helps me connect at a deeper level so I can become more intimately aware of my potential.

Mysterious man Aspect of my character that embodies the individual strength and power I need to courageously explore my undiscovered talent.

Mysterious woman Aspect of my character that embodies the emerging value of the all unknown and unfamiliar aspects of my developing creativity.

Mystery Opportunity to explore the unknown and unexplained aspects of myself so I can discover how to express my unique talents.

Mystery shopper Aspect of my character that can be open about my value rather than secretly hoping that someone else will discover it.

Mystic Aspect of my character that can transcend my normal level of understanding by being more open to what is unknown and unfamiliar.

Mystical Realization that I can discover a deeper level of truth by taking practical steps to transform my vaguer aspirations into reality.

Myth Opportunity to connect my individual story to a much more powerful universal pattern rather than dismissing it as fiction.

Mythological Realization that I can use the classic behaviors of other people to truly understand my own habitual behavioral patterns.

Mythology Ability to understand how my individual story connects to the individual stories of everyone else and forms a much bigger story.

M

N

Nadir Situation where I can observe what is happening in my deepest self instead of feeling completely down about the situation.

Nagging Opportunity to decisively resolve an uncomfortable situation rather than always finding faults with my performance.

Nail Ability to go deeper so I can make a long-lasting connection without feeling I'm just trying to drive my point home.

Nail-biting Opportunity to decisively assert my confidence and power in a tense situation rather than causing myself gnawing anxieties.

Nailing Opportunity to take forceful action to make my point instead of always trying to hammer out an agreement with other people.

Nail polish Ability to protect my skills in shaping outcomes so I can ensure my efforts will continue to shine and attract interest.

Nail scissors Ability to look at both sides of a situation so I can continue to grow in confidence rather than thinking I must cut back.

Nail varnish Ability to smooth over any rough patches so I feel confident pointing out any challenges as I continue to shape my future.

Naked Opportunity to openly display my unique talents, even though it makes me feel exposed and vulnerable to people's judgment.

Naked in public Opportunity to uncover my need to express my talents rather than trying to conceal them from the criticisms of others.

Name Ability to understand what I find most meaningful in life so I can identify how I can communicate my uniqueness to other people.

Name badge Ability to declare who I really am rather than feeling I should reveal myself as the person that others want to see.

Name-calling Opportunity to connect with other people at a much deeper level instead of making fun at their skills and experience.

Nameless Realization that I can make my feelings known to others rather than feeling I am a nobody whose opinion doesn't count.

Nameless threat Ability to clearly identify an approaching opportunity instead of always thinking that the future is filled with danger.

Nanny Aspect of my character that gives me the authority to develop a complex plan instead of expecting other people to take care of it.

Nanobot Ability to get right down into the smallest details of a situation so I can consistently deal with a much bigger challenge.

Nanotechnology Ability to use a tiny part of my skill set to make a big difference rather than feeling I have to make a more obvious effort.

Nap Opportunity to smooth a situation over so I can take a more relaxed approach to exploring some of my future ambitions.

Nape Essential ability to confidently communicate my most personal thoughts and ideas rather than trying to leave them behind.

Napkin Ability to take preemptive action so I can deal with some of the unintended consequences of fulfilling a personal ambition.

Napping Opportunity to just let go and relax so I can explore my deeper potential instead of always trying to catch myself.

N

Nappy Ability to ensure my behavior doesn't seem childish to other people so they will help me through any messy emotions.

Narcissist Aspect of my character that has the opportunity to let my talents bloom rather than becoming fixated how I appear to people.

Narcissus Natural ability to open up to my creative expertise so I can display it to people while staying firmly grounded in reality.

Narcotic Ability to sharpen my awareness so I can use my natural creativity rather than feeling that any opportunities are just dull.

Narrative Ability to understand my personal perspective by reflecting on my significant life events and the role I played in them.

Narrator Aspect of my character that can understand where my story is going rather than just describing a specific episode in my life.

Narrow Situation where I am focused on a specific goal, although my choices may seem constrained by limitations I impose on myself.

Narrow boat Ability to navigate a well-defined emotional situation by understanding my objective and proceeding in a calm and consistent way.

Narrow path Situation where I can take steps to understand my direction in life instead of feeling my wider opportunities are limited.

Narrow road Situation where I can use a recognized procedure as a way of pursuing ambitions, even though it may have limitations.

Narwhal Instinctive ability to immerse myself in my emotions so I can pursue a large opportunity and get to the point.

Nasty Realization that I can deal with a challenging situation in a pleasant and graceful manner rather than finding it offensive.

Nasty smell Essential awareness that helps me identify the mood that is currently in the air so I can resolve any unpleasantness.

Nation Aspects of my character that work together to make me feel secure so I can understand where I'm coming from.

Native Realization that I feel naturally at home in a new situation, even though it may have initially seemed quite foreign to me.

Native speaker Aspect of my character that can fluently express the most natural, fundamental qualities of what makes me unique.

Natural Realization that I can use my essential talents to achieve a healthy outcome rather than trying to follow an artificial process.

Naturalist Aspect of my character that observes my behavioral patterns and how they reflect different parts of my fundamental nature.

Nature Ability to instinctively connect with my deeper and wider self so I can use it to explore the value of my undiscovered qualities.

Nature trail Situation where I can use a recognized process to understand the value of some of my less familiar skills and abilities.

Naturist Aspect of my character that is always keen to explore my natural creativity and is happy to openly share it with other people.

Naughty Realization that I am happy to create a positive outcome rather than feeling I need to do what other people tell me to.

Nausea Essential opportunity to rid myself of a feeling of unease so I can choose a more practical way to achieve an ambition.

Nautical Realization that I have the skills and experience to deal with any complex emotional challenge I may potentially encounter.

Naval Realization that I can use my strength and power to assert my feelings so I can defend myself against any emotional threats.

Naval base Situation where I can use my established expertise to provide the essential resources I need to explore complex emotions.

Nave Situation where I can bring different aspects of my spiritual awareness together without having to go on about it at length,

Navel Essential ability to contemplate where I originally came from so I can see my fundamental connection to those closest to me.

Navigable Opportunity to use my current emotional state to safely reach deeper objectives rather than leaving myself high and dry.

Navigator Aspect of my character that can help steer me through challenging, uncertain situations by ensuring I don't lose the plot.

Navy Ability to organize my emotional life in a powerful and disciplined way so I can navigate any potentially conflicting situations.

Navy blue Mood that can color my perspective by reflecting my deeper emotional outlook in a profoundly calm, self-assured manner.

Neanderthal Aspect of my character that can use my fundamental power to create new opportunities rather than always looking backward.

Near Situation where I can stay close to achieving my ambitions practically rather than thinking they are just remote possibilities.

Nearly Realization that I am very close to achieving a successful outcome instead of thinking that such a result is beyond me.

Near miss Opportunity to relax and let go of foregone conclusions so I can understand how to get closer and closer to my goal.

Near-sighted Essential opportunity to widen my understanding by looking to the future rather than becoming fixated on specific details.

Neat Realization that my structured approach is proving very effective instead of feeling I have to dilute my efforts in any way.

Nebulae Situation where I can explore a huge range of creative possibilities, even though they can sometimes seem quite distant and vague.

Necessity Ability to understand my fundamental needs by being specific about what my purpose is in this situation.

Neck Essential ability to confidently communicate my personal thoughts and emotions, even though it can make me feel vulnerable.

Necklace Ability to attract other people by displaying my wealth of thoughts and feelings and the way in which I can communicate them.

Necktie Ability to present my self-image in a way that shows my more formal approach to expressing my range of ideas and emotions.

Necropolis Situation where I can reconnect with my wider social network so I can revitalize a talent that may have seemed lost to me.

Nectar Natural ability to achieve a successful outcome by opening up to a blossoming awareness of how I can use my specific skills.

Need Realization that I can create huge value by becoming more aware of my deeper purpose and how I can definitively fulfill it.

Needle Ability to use my penetrating awareness to get under the surface without having to be too pointed in my criticism.

Needlework Opportunity to painstakingly use some of my probing insights to go a bit deeper so I can make some creative connections.

Negative Opportunity for me to take some positive action so I can turn the situation around and see what is happening.

N

Neglect Realization that I need to be more attentive to looking after my skills rather than disregarding their true value to me.

Neglected animal Instinctive ability to voice my concerns so others can understand my needs and help me feel more fulfilled.

Negligee Ability to present my self-image to people in a very intimate and appealing manner that clearly displays my creative talents.

Negligence Opportunity to take more care of a talent I have abandoned so I can reconnect with all the satisfaction it can offer.

Negotiator Aspect of my character that can help others understand my specific needs so we can mutually agree on a way forward.

Neighbor Aspect of my character that accommodates my needs by being comfortable in setting boundaries in personal relationships.

Neighborhood watch Ability to observe my personal boundaries so I can deal with intrusions into my privacy in a relaxed, open way.

Neolithic Opportunity to move on from hard challenges by using my natural instincts to produce a wide range of fertile ideas.

Neon sign Ability to create an illuminating idea by identifying one of my unspoken needs, even though it may not be initially obvious.

Nephew Aspect of my character that cheerfully expresses my impetuous, playful side, even though it can sometimes seem a bit unfamiliar.

Nerd Aspect of my character that understands how to resolve a situation rather than feeling I have to be completely obsessed about it.

Nerve Essential ability to make sense of what is happening around me so I can boldly choose the best action for me to take.

Nerve center Situation where I can gather my thoughts together so I can have a sense of the best course of action for me to take.

Nerve gas Ability to defend my beliefs and assert my viewpoint rather than feeling paralyzed by other people's criticisms.

Nerve-wracking Opportunity to restore my confidence in my creative abilities instead of abandoning myself to self-destructive thinking.

Nervous Realization that I can calmly deal with an ongoing challenge rather than feeling apprehensive about the potential outcome.

Nest Situation where I can comfortably develop fertile new talents instead of sitting around waiting for something to happen.

Net Ability to capture some vital information and protect it, even though it might mean hanging on to some old habits and feelings.

Nettle Natural ability to confront an irritating situation by grasping the initiative instead of waiting to be stung into action.

Network Situation where I can take the invitation to share my accumulated experience and connect with wider aspects of my own talent.

Neurosurgeon Aspect of my character that can decisively resolve an unhealthy situation by making sense of what is happening around me.

Neurotic Realization that I create my own emotions and can positively influence them rather than becoming obsessed by them.

Neutered Realization that I need to protect my creative instincts instead of letting myself be cut off from my source of inspiration.

Neutral Realization that I need to make a commitment rather than feeling I can remain detached from a developing situation.

Never Realization that I can use this opportunity to open up to a wider variety of possibilities instead of closing down my options.

New Opportunity to reflect on how I habitually see myself so I can become more aware of the different aspects of my character.

Newbie Aspect of my character that has no preconceptions about my skills and abilities and is more open about what I need to achieve.

Newborn Aspect of my character that has the resources to revitalize one of my valuable concepts so I can use it to make a fresh start.

News Opportunity to understand what possibilities are currently emerging for me so I can make best use of the information.

Newsagent Aspect of my character that can display my emerging awareness so I can have it more widely recognized by other people.

News broadcaster Aspect of my character that enables me to become much more aware of my own story so I can announce my progress.

News bulletin Opportunity to give a brief account of my latest experiences to others rather than going on about them at length.

News conference Opportunity to listen to the different aspects of what has been emerging for me so I can understand my range of needs.

Newsfeed Ability to instantly become much more aware of my own story and understand how my ambitions are routinely seen by others.

Newsflash Ability to suddenly understand what is happening so I can use my creativity to illuminate a larger opportunity.

Newspaper Ability to express the different layers of my emerging awareness so I can use them to take full advantage of a situation.

Newt Instinctive ability to immerse myself in my emotions so I can express my creativity without feeling too cold-blooded about it.

Next Realization that I can create my own future by understanding what is currently happening and building on previous experience.

Next door Situation where I feel comfortable setting boundaries in my personal relationships so I can move into new opportunities.

Next of kin Aspect of my character that consistently supports me and helps me to work through major life challenges I encounter.

Nib Ability to uniquely express my talents by channeling my creativity so I can get straight to the point and make my mark.

Nibbles Potential to fulfill an ambition by committing to a big decision instead of always worrying about biting off more than I can chew.

Nice Realization that I sometimes just need to please myself rather than being concerned about other people disagreeing with me.

Niche Situation where I feel that I naturally fit into what is happening around me and have access to all the resources I need.

Nick Opportunity to make my mark just in time rather than feeling I will dent my confidence and end up feeling guilty about it.

Nickel Ability to conduct myself in such a way that I can shape a powerful outcome, even though people may not initially seem to value it.

Nickname Ability to feel very comfortable with my unique skills and abilities instead of having other people trivialize my expertise.

Nicotine patch Ability to resolve an unhealthy personal situation by taking powerful action rather than trying to cover up my true feelings.

Niece Aspect of my character that cheerfully expresses my creative wisdom, even though it can sometimes seem slightly unfamiliar.

Night Opportunity to discover a deeper understanding of myself by exploring aspects that are not obvious to my conscious awareness.

Nightclub Situation where I can explore the reflections of my unknown and unfamiliar self and how they illuminate my creative potential.

N

N

Nightgown Ability to present my self-image to people in a way that makes me feel relaxed and comfortable about my wider creative freedom.

Nightingale Instinctive ability to rise above any practical concerns so I can give voice to my creative ideas in a beautiful way.

Nightmare Essential opportunity to explore my accumulated wisdom so I can step into my own power and choose who I want to be.

Night-vision goggles Ability to gain a much clearer understanding of some of my less familiar qualities by being more open and sensitive to them.

Nightwear Ability to present my self-image to people in a relaxed and comfortable way so I can always be open to new possibilities.

Nihilist Aspect of my character that can create a healthy, positive future rather than indulging in self-destructive behavior.

Nil by mouth Opportunity to speak up and openly express my feelings instead of thinking it will prevent me from fulfilling my ambitions.

Nimble Realization that I can quickly respond to any emerging challenges so I can turn them into exciting opportunities.

Nimbus Natural opportunity to lift my spirits and rise above it all rather than wrapping myself in an array of conflicting emotions.

Ninja Aspect of my character that can stealthily achieve my ambitions by using my vast range of powerful skills and abilities.

Nip Opportunity to quickly move on from an uncomfortable situation rather than being constantly critical of my circumstances.

Nip and tuck Opportunity to feel happy in my own skin instead of trying to conceal aspects of myself so I can cut out any criticism.

Nipple Ability to consistently connect to a source of emotional support that will sustain me as I open up to some long-term ambitions.

Nipple ring Ability to demonstrate individual commitment to providing a strong, supportive partnership that will develop over time.

No Opportunity to define some personal boundaries so I can take a positive approach to resolving any individual conflicts.

Nobody Aspect of my character that can transcend my physical limitations rather than feeling I have nothing substantial to offer.

Nocturnal Realization that it feels quite natural to explore aspects of my unfamiliar self that are not obvious to my conscious awareness.

Nod Opportunity to acknowledge an idea that is emerging for me so I can go ahead with it rather than letting it fade away.

No-fly zone Situation where I can release myself from weighty commitments instead of feeling I have no freedom to explore new ideas.

Noir Mood that can color my perspective by illuminating some contrasting opportunities that are beginning to open up for me.

Noise Realization that I need to be clear about what I am trying to communicate rather than becoming too disturbed by it.

Nomad Aspect of my character that can feel at home anywhere by taking the time to comfortably explore all aspects of my inner self.

No-man's-land Situation where I can resolve an ongoing conflict by removing egotistical influences and taking a down-to-earth approach.

Nondescript Realization that I have a remarkable talent rather than feeling my skills and expertise are of no significance to anyone.

None Realization that everything starts to make sense when I remove any preconceptions I may have about a particular situation.

Nonsense Realization that I can make perfect sense of my situation by understanding what is emerging for me at an unconscious level.

Nonstick Ability to fulfill one of my ambitions in a quick, convenient manner rather than feeling I have to adhere to any traditions.

Noodles Potential to fulfill an ambition by using a narrow range of ideas and practical experience to consistently shape the outcome.

Nook Situation where I have reached a turning point in understanding how my present position fits into my wider ambitions.

Noon Opportunity to continue accumulating skills and experiences rather than feeling I have reached a high point in my creativity.

No one Aspect of my character that has the potential to develop into who I want to be instead of feeling completely insignificant.

Noose Ability to quickly catch on to how I sometimes express myself in a self-defeating way rather than getting too hung up about it.

Normal Realization that I can use my talents to create something extraordinary instead of feeling I have to conform to expectations.

North Natural opportunity to become more aware of the direction I am taking so I can build up some practical resources.

Nose Essential ability to follow my instinctive awareness so I can sniff out opportunities, even though it may seem intrusive to people.

Nosebleed Essential opportunity to find some healthy channels for my creative passions instead of feeling that they are unwelcomed.

Nosedive Opportunity to take time to understand the prevailing atmosphere rather than impetuously jumping into it headfirst.

Nostalgia Realization that I can bring some of my learning and experience back to life, instead of feeling sentimental about the past.

Nostril Essential ability to keep myself open to any emerging opportunities so I can continue to inspire myself in a healthy way.

Note Ability to remember the significance of my current actions so I can understand how to deal with any future challenges.

Notebook Ability to observe the significant points emerging from my habitual behaviors so I can consciously attend to them.

Noteworthy Opportunity to understand the significance of my intentions so I can use my evident talents to do something exceptional.

Nothing Ability to realize the developing value of my limitless potential rather than always feeling there is something missing.

Nothingness Realization that I need to bring everything back to its original state so I can understand the true significance of my skills.

Notice Opportunity to pay attention to what is happening right now so I can prepare myself for what might emerge in the future.

Notion Opportunity to be extremely clear in my understanding rather than basing my intended actions on some vague assumptions.

Nourishment Ability to fulfill a long-term ambition by looking after my fundamental needs so I can confidently sustain my progress.

Novel Ability to understand the significance of any new situations I encounter so I can weave them into my continuing story.

Novelist Aspect of my character that understands my deeper desires and can help me open up exciting new chapters in my life.

Novice Aspect of my character that can develop my huge potential by being open to new experiences and learning from them.

Now Opportunity to take immediate action in the present rather than always living in the past or fantasizing about the future.

Nowhere Situation where I can open myself up to a huge range of possibilities rather than feeling I have made no progress at all.

Nozzle Ability to clearly express the thrust of what I am trying to convey rather than letting my feelings spill out aimlessly.

N

N

Nuclear bomb Ability to control the massive amount of energy I have for a potentially life-changing transformation rather than overreacting.

Nuclear bunker Situation where I can defend my most powerful thoughts and ideas by using individual resources I often conceal.

Nuclear disarmament Opportunity to deal with unresolved tensions by stepping into my power and transforming relationships with others.

Nuclear explosion Opportunity to control the energy needed for a fundamental personal transformation rather than wasting it in needless conflict.

Nuclear radiation Opportunity to use my natural energy in a positive manner so I can absorb the fallout from other people's conflicts.

Nuclear reactor Ability to use my elemental energy to create a brighter future rather than allowing my hard work to go to waste.

Nuclear shelter Situation where I can permanently feel safe and secure so I can protect myself from a fundamentally uncertain outcome.

Nuclear war Opportunity to resolve an ongoing tension once and for all by declaring what I need rather than trying to avoid conflict.

Nude Opportunity to proudly display my natural abilities even though it can make me feel vulnerable to other people's criticism.

Nudge Opportunity to gently draw attention to my individual efforts so I can continue to push forward with my personal ambitions.

Nudist beach Situation where I can go to the edge of my comfort zone by confidently opening up and showing others who I really am.

Nudity Realization that I can openly show my unique talents and feel comfortable with exposing them to the judgment of others.

Nugget Ability to dig a bit deeper so I can identify a practical piece of wisdom that will allow me to shape a definite outcome.

Nuisance Realization that I can step into my power and resolve an irritating situation rather than allowing it to continually annoy me.

Nuisance caller Aspect of my character that has the capability to speak my truth instead of feeling annoyed with myself for not doing anything.

Numbed Opportunity to deal sensitively with a potentially painful situation rather than continuing to feel uncomfortable about it.

Number Ability to make the most of a variety of opportunities instead of thinking I have to count on anyone in particular.

Number plate Ability to recognize my personal ambition and drive so I can be certain in my choices as I make progress toward my goal.

Numbers Ability to understand the magnitude of my emerging potential so I can begin to take specific steps to measure my progress.

Numbness Opportunity to get my passion and vitality flowing again so I can understand how I feel about a particular situation.

Nun Aspect of my character that can sometimes seek to conceal my unique creative potential rather than joyfully embracing it.

Nuptials Opportunity to make a more balanced commitment to some of my fundamental needs and have them acknowledged by other people.

Nurse Aspect of my character that makes me feel more at ease by taking care of fundamental needs in a healthy, efficient manner.

Nursery Situation where I can safely bring together a number of ideas I have been playing around with so I can develop them.

Nursery rhyme Ability to convey how well versed I am in my fundamental understanding, even though it may make no sense to other people.

Nursery school Situation where I can learn valuable lessons by playfully exploring a variety of ideas and displaying my expertise to people.

Nursing home Situation where I can feel relaxed with the different aspects of myself by taking care of my basic needs in a healthy way.

Nurturing Opportunity to take care of my unspoken needs so I can develop the capacity to look after the needs of others.

Nut Potential to fulfill an ambition by choosing to come out of my shell more so I can open up to a variety of challenges.

Nut and bolt Ability to make a fundamental connection by using a practical skill that matches up exactly with an obvious opportunity.

Nutcracker Ability to deal with a particularly tough problem by taking strong and decisive action that will bring me out of my shell.

Nutmeg Potential to spice up an ambition by taking time to work my way through what would make it more exciting for me.

Nutshell Ability to successfully sum up the particular challenge I have been encountering rather than being defensive about it.

Nylon Ability to generate some plausible material, even though my creative process might seem somewhat artificial to other people.

Nylons Ability to present my self-image to other people in a way that gives me the freedom to take smooth, self-assured action.

Nymph Aspect of my character that has a very creative nature, although it can be challenging to capture and pin down.

Nymphomaniac Aspect of my character that has a fundamental desire to be completely free of any limitations on my creative instincts.

O

Oaf Aspect of my character that can use my skill and dexterity to influence people instead of feeling I am clumsy and stupid.

Oak tree Natural potential for my long-term spiritual growth so my wisdom can mature and provide an impressively strong legacy.

Oak wood Situation where I can take a more mature approach to my spirituality by exploring my natural potential for long-term growth.

Oar Ability to work my way through a challenging emotional situation by using my energy and self-motivation to stick with it.

Oarlock Ability to keep myself feeling secure in an unfamiliar situation by relying on my self-motivation and energy to support me.

Oasis Situation where I can use my emotions to develop some fertile new ideas rather than feeling that nothing is happening around me.

Oath Opportunity to show my full commitment to a situation by having the confidence to openly and honestly speak my truth about it.

Oatmeal Potential to fulfill an ambition in a wholesome and natural way so I can use it to sustain me on an everyday basis.

Oats Natural ability to share lots of my ideas with the people I meet in the hope that some substantial possibilities will take root.

Obedience Realization that I need to be loyal to my own needs rather than feeling I have to always seek permission from other people.

Obedience school Situation where I can learn valuable lessons about my faith in my abilities instead of waiting for instructions.

Obelisk Situation where I can remind myself of an important realization from my past that still stands out prominently for me.

Obese Essential opportunity to take action outside my comfort zone so I can actively experience the healthy fulfillment I seek.

Obituary Opportunity to unquestionably recognize my fundamental need for personal transformation so I can clearly express it.

Object Ability to identify a valuable resource available to me in this situation so I can use it to achieve a particular goal.

Objection Opportunity to express my unspoken talent rather than automatically accepting others openly criticizing my efforts.

Obligation Opportunity to liberate myself from preconceptions by committing to transform a situation that has been holding me back.

Oblique Realization that I can approach a challenge from quite a different angle instead of using a more straightforward procedure.

Obliterated Opportunity to use energy and motivation to create a new future for myself rather than feeling continually wiped out.

Oblivion Opportunity to remember all my accumulated expertise and experience so I can express the real value of who I actually am.

Oblong Ability to shape an outcome by being able to make sense of an irregular situation without always going on about it at length.

Obnoxious Realization that I can use my skills to positively influence others rather than worrying I will drive them away.

Oboe Ability to take my instinctive creativity into both hands so I can channel my thoughts and evocatively express them.

Obscene Realization that I can express my fundamental creative instincts in a gracious and discreet manner without appearing offensive.

Obscenity Opportunity to behave in an open-minded and appropriate manner rather than giving my ambitions an indecent amount of exposure.

Obscured Opportunity to make my intentions obvious to other people instead of always appearing to have an ulterior motive.

Observation post Situation where I can take a closer look at some familiar habits so I can understand how they may influence my future.

Observatory Situation where I can see what emerges as I reflect on my deeper connections with a more universal understanding.

Observing Opportunity to remain detached in a challenging situation so I can see the bigger picture and take action when I need to.

Obsession Opportunity to directly connect to my fundamental power so I can use it to open up a whole new range of possibilities.

Obsolete Realization that I can develop my skills to make them relevant to my situation rather than feeling I am out-of-date.

Obstacle Ability to take a stand on an issue that challenges me so I can use it to overcome any self-limiting beliefs I may hold.

Obstetrician Aspect of my character that can help me to successfully deliver a creative concept I have been developing for some time.

Obstinate Realization that I can persistently determine my chosen outcome by staying open to possibilities rather than digging my heels in.

Obstruction Ability to decisively resolve any challenges to my continued progress instead of standing in the way of my own success.

Obvious Realization that I can clearly understand subtleties of an ambiguous situation by looking beyond conventional evidence.

Occasion Opportunity to choose the most favorable time to display my value to other people so they can recognize my contribution.

Occult Ability to reveal my unique talents by illuminating my unconventional approach rather than feeling overshadowed by others.

Occupation Opportunity to make the effort to connect with my true purpose in life without allowing it to take over everything else I do.

Occurrence Opportunity to make the most of an emerging situation rather than waiting for it to develop more favorably for me.

OCD Opportunity to resolve some unhealthy behaviors by paying close attention to my habitual patterns and how I can influence them.

Ocean Situation where I can voyage into a wider understanding of my deeper emotional self, experiencing its moods and rhythms.

Ocelot Instinctive ability to embody my need for continuing independence without feeling I have to change my behavior in any way.

OCR Ability to identify my most valuable characteristics so other people can recognize the value of what I can communicate.

Octagon Ability to shape my chosen outcome by looking at a number of different angles and how they can transform my way of thinking.

Octopus Instinctive ability to stop myself from becoming too wrapped up in a deep emotional entanglement that might drag me down.

Odor Instinctive awareness that can help me to understand the prevailing mood and make more sense of any emerging opportunities.

Odyssey Opportunity to explore my unsung self so I can discover my potential by motivating myself to look at a range of perspectives.

O

Off center Opportunity to align my talents with the current situation so I can move closer to experiencing the source of my inspiration.

Off-color Realization that I can make myself feel better by shifting my perspective to reflect the emotional intensity of the situation.

Offense Opportunity to take responsibility for my own actions rather than making assumptions about the real intentions of others.

Offensive Opportunity to deal with any potential conflict by choosing how I respond to the apparently threatening advances of others.

Offer Opportunity to openly share my talents with other people so I can invite them to recognize the value of my expertise.

Office Situation where I can have my individual talents formally recognized by other people so I can ensure I am fully valued.

Office bearer Aspect of my character that can embody my unspoken power and influence so I can use it to achieve my wider ambitions.

Officer Aspect of my character that gives me full permission to step into my power so I can take action to resolve a challenge.

Official Realization that I have the authority to take responsible action rather than feeling I have to meet the demands of other people.

Official secret Opportunity to explore the fundamental mysteries of what I need so I can take action to make the most of them.

Off-line Situation where I can give myself the time to reflect on what I need rather than feeling disconnected from future possibilities.

Off-ramp Situation where I can follow my personal inclinations so I can choose a more individual route to achieve my objective.

Off-road Situation where I can fulfill personal ambitions by moving away from recognized procedures into less familiar territory.

Offshore Situation where I can avoid dealing with specific practicalities, even though it may involve more emotional ups and downs.

Offspring Aspect of my character embodying my talents, enabling me to take immediate action by using accumulated knowledge.

Offstage Situation where I can progress to the next level by developing my skills in private rather than drawing attention to them.

Ogre Aspect of my character concerned about being consumed by my enormous hunger for power as I try to assert my ambitions.

Ogress Aspect of my character that uses my enormous creativity to meet the challenge of feeding my massive appetite for success.

Oil Ability to keep a complex situation moving by smoothing over potentially troubling emotions and preventing any future conflict.

Oil drum Ability to contain some of my more volatile emotions so I can use their power when I really need to fuel my creativity.

Oil field Situation where I can use my accumulated experience to draw on the depths of my practical skills so I can realize their value.

Oil refinery Situation where I can use my natural energy and resourcefulness to process my raw talent and distil motivational learning.

Oil rig Situation where I can explore my deepest reserves of energy and resourcefulness and safely channel them into productive activity.

Oil rig worker Aspect of my character that can safely deal with pressures of maintaining energy levels and potential to motivate myself.

Oilskin Ability to feel very comfortable when I immerse myself in my feelings and explore the boundary between my inner and outer worlds.

Oil tanker Ability to navigate an emotional situation by feeling secure in what motivates my drive for success as I progress to my goal.

Oil well Ability to consistently connect with aspects of my deeper wisdom so I can channel their power and create a transformation.

Ointment Ability to deal with an unhealthy situation, even though it seems a superficial irritation with no deeper consequences.

Okapi Instinctive ability to raise my overall awareness by taking a more prudent approach rather than sticking my neck out.

Old Opportunity to rejuvenate some of my habitual behaviors so I can make fresh progress by developing them in a new direction.

Old-age pensioner Aspect of my character that can draw on my accumulated wealth of experience to keep myself consistently motivated and energized.

Old car Ability to reflect on my extensive expertise so I can revitalize my personal ambition as I progress toward my objective.

Old clothes Ability to present my self-image to other people by being comfortable about sharing my practical experiences with them.

Olden times Opportunity to draw on my experiences so I can explore the exciting new possibilities offered by my future development.

Old-fashioned Realization that I can create new value by using my wealth of accumulated experience in a contemporary situation.

Old flame Aspect of my character that can transform a situation by spontaneously reigniting fundamental passions and natural creativity.

Old friend Aspect of my character that I am well acquainted with and can always rely on to provide me with valuable experiences.

Old house Situation where I have the security and support I need to comfortably explore all aspects of my character-building experiences.

Old machine Ability to produce an outcome of practical value by using unique experiences rather than just going through the motions.

Old man Aspect of my character that can rejuvenate my ambitions by always having the courage to involve myself in new opportunities.

Old regiment Aspects of my character that are always willing to defend my basic needs and resolve inner tensions I may be experiencing.

Old school Situation where I can revisit some of the lessons I have learned so I can use them to succeed with a current opportunity.

Old-timer Aspect of my character that can use my past experience to give me the power to take action right now so I can decide my future.

Old woman Aspect of my character that can revitalize my creative talent by using my extensive experience to make the wise choices I need.

Old workplace Situation where I can revisit some of my professional experiences so I can fully understand the true value of my skills.

Oligarch Aspect of my character that can use my great power and influence to create positive change rather than appearing selfish.

Olive branch Natural ability to resolve accumulated tension by reaching out to others so I can share some of my spiritual wisdom.

Olive color Mood that can color my perspective by inspiring me to use natural wisdom to take a more peaceful, harmonious approach.

Olive drab Ability to draw attention to my natural talents by displaying them more colorfully rather than feeling I have to conceal them.

Olive fruit Natural ability to fulfill an ambition by using a gentle, peaceful approach that will usually result in a fruitful outcome.

Olive grove Situation where I can use my deeper understanding of spiritual growth as a way of resolving conflicts involving others.

O

Olive oil Potential to fulfill an ambition by smoothing over any troubling emotions so I can help prevent any future tensions.

Olive tree Natural potential for my long-term spiritual growth by dealing with tensions rooted in my everyday behaviors.

Omelet Potential to fulfill an ambition by decisively breaking some barriers so I can open up to a variety of fertile new ideas.

Omen Opportunity to decide my future by making a firm decision rather than looking for information that supports my personal biases.

Ominous Realization that I can challenge any fears I have about the future by stepping into my power instead of just feeling anxious.

On board Ability to use my personal resources and abilities as a way of helping me make progress toward my particular objective.

Oncologist Aspect of my character that can identify the source of an unhealthy situation rather than allowing it to grow out of control.

One Ability to single-mindedly pursue my personal development by realizing I am a unique individual embodying significant talent.

One-armed bandit Ability to take action by using my individual power to produce a fruitful outcome rather than just leaving it to chance.

One-man band Aspect of my character that can dynamically coordinate a wide variety of skills and talents to create a unique outcome.

One-night stand Opportunity to become more intimately aware of my continuing creative brilliance rather than feeling it might be a one-off.

Onesie Ability to present my self-image to people in a way that shows how comfortable and relaxed I am with the surrounding situation.

One-way street Situation where I can convey the value of my contribution to people around me so we can build a stronger relationship.

One-way ticket Ability to demonstrate my commitment to others by giving myself permission to display unique abilities to them.

On hold Opportunity to have a firm grasp of my inner power so I can make progress rather than just waiting for events to happen.

Onion Potential to fulfill an ambition by taking time to understand the different layers of meaning so it doesn't end in tears.

Online Situation where I can easily connect with an almost infinite array of possibilities, even though some may seem quite distant.

Onlooker Aspect of my character that observes my habitual behavior patterns so I can understand what is going on for me.

On stage Situation where I can step into an opportunity for development by having a platform to share talents with a wider audience.

Onyx Ability to attract other people to the value of my talents by displaying how I can use the lighter and darker aspects of my work.

Ooze Opportunity to display my confidence rather than feeling I can't prevent my emotions from spilling out and making a mess.

Opal Ability to show the transformational value of my talents by using them to nurture other people in a smooth and polished manner.

Opaque Ability to clearly understand what is happening by being transparently honest rather than trying to obscure the issue.

Open Realization that I am free to explore a number of possibilities instead of closing myself off from any new opportunities.

Open air Situation where I am surrounded by a number of fresh opportunities, although I can feel vulnerable to changing moods around me.

Open day Opportunity to welcome new possibilities into my life so I can illuminate a situation that may have been unclear for me.

Open door Ability to access different aspects

of my character so I can cross the threshold into working with some new possibilities.

Open-heart surgery Opportunity to resolve romantic tensions by opening up about feelings so I can understand what is going on inside me.

Opening Opportunity to step into a new area that holds great possibilities for me instead of closing myself off from future growth.

Opening night Opportunity to discover a deeper understanding of myself so I can realize what initially attracts other people to me.

Open marriage Opportunity to have more freedom in the commitments I make to myself instead of always feeling I have to make compromises.

Open-mike night Opportunity to openly speak up about my talents rather than feeling I always have to listen to others' advice.

Open prison Situation where I can give myself permission to easily escape from self-limiting beliefs that may be holding me back.

Open sea Situation where I can journey into a much wider understanding of my deeper emotional self and the opportunities it holds.

Open secret Opportunity to explore the deeper mystery of who I am so I can have the freedom to reveal hidden skills and talents.

Opera Opportunity to bring together different aspects of my character so I can use my various talents in a more dramatic way.

Opera glasses Ability to look more closely at a situation so I can form a much clearer opinion about dramas I may be involved in.

Opera house Situation where I have the security and support I need so I can express what dramas are currently playing out for me.

Opera singer Aspect of my character that can clearly give a powerful and dramatic voice to how I feel about a situation.

Operating table Ability to feel comfortable and solidly supported as I open up to others

and share my innermost feelings with them.

Operating theater Situation where I can fully step into the various aspects of my talents so I can resolve any undesirable tensions.

Operation Opportunity to resolve a potentially unhealthy situation by taking incisive action to deal with it in a professional manner.

Operations center Situation where I can bring together a number of my talents so I can use them to experience deeper self-awareness.

Operative Aspect of my character that can really make things happen by using my deeper expertise in a talented, individual manner.

Operator Aspect of my character that can produce a valuable outcome by using unique skills, rather than going through the motions.

Opinion Opportunity to step more fully into my own perspective so I can become more aware of the qualities others see in me.

Opossum Instinctive ability to look after my most precious ideas rather than appearing to have no interest in developing them.

Opposing Opportunity to transform any inner conflicts into a positive outcome rather than feeling antagonistic toward other people.

Opium Ability to temporarily avoid dealing with some of my fundamental needs rather than just letting my natural talents blossom.

Opposite Realization that I can invariably achieve a fundamental insight by directly reflecting on another person's point of view.

Optical Ability to stay focused on how I can achieve my personal vision so I can illuminate any emerging opportunities.

Optical illusion Realization that I have a clear understanding of what is happening rather than just seeing what I want to see.

Optician Aspect of my character that can help bring a situation into focus for me so I can see emerging opportunities in a new light.

O

Optimism Realization that I can always achieve a positive outcome by making the best use of my talents rather than feeling hopeless.

Opulent Realization that I have an abundance of talent and can use it to help me feel more comfortable about a challenging situation.

Oracle Aspect of my character that helps me to ask questions about my spirituality rather than always appearing to be a know-it-all.

Oral cancer Opportunity to speak up about an unhealthy situation so I can deal with it, instead of allowing it to grow out of control.

Oral hygienist Aspect of my character that maintains my feelings of confidence and power so I can clearly express what I need to say.

Orange color Mood that can color my perspective by warmly reflecting my generous spirit and how I can use it to make positive change.

Orange fruit Natural ability to fulfill an ambition by using a sunny, optimistic approach, which will always result in a fruitful outcome.

Orange juice Potential to fulfill an emotional need by taking a fresh perspective rather than feeling I am being squeezed by people.

Orange tree Natural potential for my long-term spiritual growth by keeping grounded so I can enjoy the fruits of my labors.

Orangutan Instinctive ability to understand my natural creativity by happily asserting my individual power and confidently taking action.

Orb Ability to shape my circumstances so I can have a well-rounded understanding about what is happening in my sphere of influence.

Orbit Opportunity to understand why I am so powerfully attracted to a particular situation and why I always keep coming back to it.

Orchard Situation where I can develop my natural potential for spiritual growth and make the most of the abundantly fruitful outcome.

Orchestra Aspects of my character that can integrate a variety of my creative talents in a powerful and harmonious way.

Orchid Natural ability to open up to a seemingly exotic opportunity so I can encourage a variety of rarer talents to bloom.

Order Opportunity to bring a more organized structure to a challenging situation by giving myself the authority to act decisively.

Ordinary Realization that I can use my unique talent to make an extraordinary transformation rather than feeling as if I'm nothing special.

Ore Ability to dig deeper so I can reach my fundamental power and use it to shape a definite outcome in a more refined manner.

Organ Ability to channel my creativity so I can use my natural skills and abilities to consistently perform a special task.

Organism Natural ability to organize myself so I can use my raw talent to fulfill my fundamental needs and thrive in any situation.

Organist Aspect of my character that can strike just the right tone when pitching some of my spiritual awareness to other people.

Organization Aspects of my character that coordinates all my skills and abilities so I can use them to achieve a more structured success.

Orgasm Opportunity to enjoy a feeling of intense excitement as I become more intimately aware of how to reach the peak of my talents.

Orgy Opportunity to openly share my creative talents with a wider variety of other people without necessarily conceiving anything new.

Orient Opportunity to make myself familiar with a situation so I can feel confident in exploring some unfamiliar aspects of myself.

Oriental Realization that I can broaden my understanding by looking at a situation from a variety of different perspectives.

Orienteering Opportunity to navigate my way through a challenge by taking powerful steps to energetically pursue one of my ambitions.

Origami Opportunity to shape a pleasing outcome by turning over a new leaf so I can express different layers of my creative talents.

Ornament Ability to confidently add my individual touch to a situation rather than feeling I always have to embellish my exploits.

Ornamental garden Situation where I can cultivate deeper relationships instead of hoping they will somehow just blossom around me.

Orphan Aspect of my character that can give me permission to lovingly nurture myself rather than abandoning my potential growth.

Orphanage Situation where I feel safe and secure in developing my uniquely precious talents and the potential that they hold for me.

Orthodontist Aspect of my character that always behaves correctly so I can brace myself for any challenges to my confidence and power.

Oryx Instinctive ability to use my intuition and get straight to the point, even though I may be concerned about a risky outcome.

Oscilloscope Ability to clearly see how my mood periodically changes with time so I can understand natural fluctuations in my emotions.

Osteopath Aspect of my character that sensitively aligns my inner strength of purpose with the fundamental structure of my beliefs.

Osteoporosis Opportunity to resolve a potentially fragile situation by consistently using my inner strength to support me in my actions.

Ostrich Instinctive ability to keep my big ideas grounded in reality rather than trying to avoid the attention that they attract.

Otherworldly Realization that I can use the power of my imagination to develop new opportunities that have previously seemed beyond me.

Otter Instinctive ability to immerse myself in my emotions and play around with them so I can fulfill some of my deeper ambitions.

Ottoman Ability to express my habitual perspective in a relaxed and easy manner so I can raise any steps I might need to take.

Ouija board Ability to creatively express my spirituality to other people rather than feeling I have to spell it out all the time.

Out Opportunity to move away from my comfort zone so I can take the time to explore some new possibilities for inner growth.

Outbreak Opportunity to take some time to transform one of my habitual behaviors rather than having it continually plague me.

Outburst Opportunity to reflect on what I need to say instead of suddenly venting my feelings in an uncontrolled manner.

Outcast Aspect of my character that can live by my own rules rather than feeling that my viewpoints are always rejected by others.

Outcome Opportunity to successfully achieve my chosen result by understanding the consequences of all possible actions I can take.

Outcry Opportunity to speak up powerfully and draw other people's attention to my special talents so I can take immediate action.

Outdoors Situation where I can step outside my comfort zone and open to some new possibilities that may have seemed closed to me.

Outer Ability to understand that what is happening in my inner life will be tangibly reflected in my achievements in my outer life.

Outer space Situation where I can open up to any of my perceived limitations by exploring the infinite possibilities available to me.

O

Outfit Ability to present my self-image to other people in a way that shows my willingness to fit in and coordinate my overall efforts.

Outhouse Situation where I can explore some less familiar areas of my inner and outer lives so I can keep everything in perspective.

Outlaw Aspect of my character that lives by my own rules instead of feeling that I have to conform to the expectations of other people.

Outline Ability to sketch out what I need so I can understand the bigger picture rather than getting lost in the details.

Outnumbered Realization that I have more opportunities available than I can use so I will have to choose the ones I want to pursue.

Out-of-body Opportunity to raise my awareness so I can step outside immediate concerns and see them from a different perspective.

Out of control Opportunity to decide a specific outcome by using my influence instead of feeling I must be in command.

Out-of-control car Opportunity to take a more relaxed approach as I steer my way through a challenging situation so I can continue to make progress.

Out-of-control plane Opportunity to consider where one of my plans is heading so I can take a more down-to-earth approach to ensure its success.

Out-of-control train Opportunity to make a decision about my professional direction instead of feeling I am going off the rails.

Outpatient Aspect of my character that can resolve an unhealthy situation by taking steps to move beyond it rather than just lying around.

Outpost Situation where I can observe some of my less familiar behaviors and take appropriate action if they seem threatening.

Outrage Opportunity to use my powerful energy to create a positive outcome instead of feeling offended by the actions of people.

Outside Situation where I can step outside my comfort zone so I can have a clear understanding of how I really feel inside.

Outsider Aspect of my character that may seem unfamiliar but has the presence to offer a valuable new perspective on the situation.

Outskirts Situation where I can explore wider issues involved in a new opportunity rather than trying to make my way around them.

Oval Ability to shape my circumstances by pursuing my own direction rather than feeling I have to take a more straightforward approach.

Ovary Essential ability to consistently produce a whole range of fertile possibilities that will help me conceive practical outcomes.

Oven Ability to patiently contain my raw ambition so I can use my creativity to get fired up and satisfy my hunger for results.

Oven glove Ability to comfortably protect my individual power so I can fittingly direct my future in an intensely creative situation.

Over Realization that I can raise my level of understanding more than I think so I can use it to reach a successful outcome.

Overacting Opportunity to become consciously aware of some subtly powerful aspects of my character that often remain unspoken.

Overalls Ability to present my self-image to other people in a very workmanlike manner so I can deal with some messy practicalities.

Overboard Situation where I can make the choice to immerse myself in some complex emotions rather than jumping in feet first.

Overcast Natural opportunity to make a clear breakthrough in my thinking instead of feeling limited by the current level of my emotions.

Overclocking Opportunity to speed up an intricate process by choosing the precise moment to quickly take action on my previous decisions.

Overcoat Ability to present my self-image to others in a more formal way that may conceal the real depth and variety of my talents.

Overcooked Opportunity to maintain a fresh and stimulating approach to my ambitions so I can make the best use of my raw talent.

Overdo Opportunity to make the right amount of effort to reach my objective instead of spending too much time pursuing an ambition.

Overdose Opportunity to remedy an unhealthy situation by listening to my fundamental needs rather than being influenced by others.

Overdraft Ability to have a clear understanding of my value instead of feeling limited by accounts of how others may see me.

Overdressed Opportunity to display some different aspects of my self-image, even though it may not seem entirely appropriate at the time.

Overdrive Ability to raise my levels of motivation and energy so I can progress more quickly as I pursue one of my ambitions.

Overdub Opportunity to understand what sentiments others are really expressing, even though it seems to make no sense at the time.

Overgrown Opportunity to develop unrealized potential so I can increase my value instead of feeling I have to cut back on everything.

Overgrowth Opportunity to clearly understand my basic needs so I can direct energy and resources more efficiently.

Overhang Situation where I have to face up to the impending effort required rather than letting everything get on top of me.

Overhaul Opportunity to make faster progress than I had previously imagined

was possible by taking the time to look after myself.

Overhead Situation where I can raise my level of understanding by bringing together a range of ideas without worrying about the cost.

Overload Opportunity to let go of some of myself-imposed obligations and responsibilities rather than feeling weighed down by them.

Overnight Opportunity to successfully accomplish an ambition by understanding aspects of myself that I am often not consciously aware of.

Overnight bag Ability to look after my fundamental needs as I take time to explore a deeper understanding of my more expansive ambitions.

Overpass Situation where I can raise the level of my ambitions higher than I think so I can use them to reach a successful outcome.

Overpowering Realization that I have the capacity to fulfill my needs and keep myself fully motivated rather than feeling overwhelmed.

Override Opportunity to step into my power and make my own decisions so I can speed up my progress toward my eventual objective.

Overseas Situation where I can experience a wider understanding of my less familiar aspects and how these affect my moods and perceptions.

Overseer Aspect of my character that observes my habitual behaviors so I can understand how to use my expertise more effectively.

Overshadow Opportunity to clearly illuminate my talents so I can display them instead of feeling my efforts are being put in the shade.

Overshoot Opportunity to quickly communicate my intended aims to other people, even if it seems I may be going too far this time.

O

Overspending Opportunity to become more aware of how I openly share my talent and how I can have my value recognized more by others.

Overtake Opportunity to use my motivation and drive to move beyond a particular challenge so I can decisively leave it behind me.

Overthrow Opportunity to use my power and strength to assert my ambitions rather than feeling the situation is somehow beyond me.

Overtime Opportunity to use my experience to make the best use of my talents and stay present to what I plan to accomplish in the future.

Overwhelming Opportunity to effectively channel my power and energy so I can raise my profile and impress the people around me.

Overworked Opportunity to express my fundamental value to other people rather than feeling they are taking my efforts for granted.

Overwrite Opportunity to let go of the past by clearly communicating the nature of my character so I can make my mark in the future.

Ovulation Opportunity to choose exactly the right time to develop one of my potential talents so I can move into a fertile new area.

Owe Opportunity to declare my value of my unique talents to other people instead of feeling I am indebted to them in any way.

Owl Instinctive ability to use my wisdom to seek out fulfilling opportunities rather than just taking a dim view of any challenges.

Own Opportunity to be more self-possessed by taking full accountability for my actions instead of feeling I am not responsible.

Owner Aspect of my character that possesses the ability to step into my power so I can effectively use my resources.

Owner's manual Ability to open up to my wealth of accumulated knowledge so I can use my personal resources to shape my preferred outcome.

Own goal Opportunity to successfully reach one of my objectives by choosing the specific direction I want to strike out in.

Ox Instinctive ability to use my great power to make sustained progress, even though I feel I lack the courage and audacity I need.

Oxygen Ability to use my pure inspiration to convey the power of my thinking so I can always breathe new life into any challenges.

Oxygen mask Ability to stay motivated by using a persistently inspiring idea rather than feeling I am making a last-gasp effort.

Oxygen tent Situation where I can feel relaxed and comfortable by maintaining an inspiring atmosphere in challenging circumstances.

Oyster Instinctive ability to make the most of a potentially irritating truth by turning it into a statement of pure desire.

Pacemaker Ability to stimulate my passion and vitality by getting charged up about the potential for using my energy in an exciting way.

Pacifier Ability to take comfort in my thoughts so I can provide quiet reassurance for people instead of just spitting my ideas out.

Pack Ability to gather the resources I need so I can carry out my commitments rather than feeling weighed down by them.

Package Ability to be receptive to new opportunities and whatever value they may offer instead of becoming too wrapped up in myself.

Packed lunch Opportunity to fulfill my appetite for power by carrying out my obligations as I progress toward a greater sense of achievement.

Packet Ability to clearly communicate my needs by being precise about my requirements and the assistance I hope to receive.

Packing Opportunity to convey the value of my accumulated knowledge to other people so I can confidently move into new areas.

Packing case Ability to prepare for a personal transformation by containing my enthusiasm so I can methodically gather my resources.

Pact Ability to recognize tensions caused by potentially conflicting aspects of my character so I can use them more agreeably.

Padded bra Ability to support my capacity for nurturing other people by presenting my abilities to them in an open and honest manner.

Padded cell Situation where I can take firm steps to break out of my limiting patterns instead of feeling I'm bouncing off the walls.

Padding Ability to make myself feel more comfortable by being firm and fair rather than surrounding myself with any ambiguities.

Paddle Ability to use my energy and self-motivation to work through an emotional situation without going into it too deeply.

Paddleboat Ability to navigate a relatively calm emotional situation by using my self-motivation and energy to keep everything moving.

Paddle steamer Ability to navigate complex, unpredictable feelings by working through any powerful emotions that may be building up.

Paddling pool Situation where I can play around with some of my emotions rather than feeling I have to immerse myself in them.

Paddy field Situation where I can pool my accumulated experience with others so we can cultivate our knowledge and realize its value.

Padlock Ability to keep a specific aspect of my character feeling secure, even though it may become an obstacle to greater fulfillment.

Padre Aspect of my character that takes a more disciplined approach that encourages me to assertively develop my deeper connections.

Pagan Aspect of my character that has a natural connection to the deeper power of my elemental creativity, joyfully acknowledging it.

Page Ability to gather my ideas in one area so I can communicate exactly what I need to say to other people.

Pageant Opportunity to proudly display my accumulated expertise so other people can support me as I continue to move forward.

Pagoda Situation where I can examine the structure of my beliefs by exploring the different layers of learning I have accumulated.

Pail Ability to get a handle on a potentially emotional situation so I can use my accumulated experience to carry me through it.

Pain Essential opportunity to confront an uncomfortable situation and satisfactorily deal with it rather than chronically avoiding it.

Painkiller Ability to take direct action to positively transform an uncomfortable situation so I can decisively resolve my feelings.

Pain reliever Ability to stand out from people by taking a more relaxed approach to how I deal with habitually uncomfortable situations.

Paint Ability to colorfully express my instinctive feelings about a situation so people can see it from a different perspective.

Paintball Ability to play around with a potentially successful outcome so I can make my mark with the people who are close to me.

Paintbrush Ability to clear up any confusion by applying a fresh perspective to a situation so it can be seen in a different light.

Painter Aspect of my character that can create a different point of view by using my natural talents rather than covering them up.

Painting Opportunity to take a more colorful approach to how I habitually view a situation so I can see it in a fresh light.

Paintings Ability to clearly see different perspectives on a situation so I can become more aware of how to express my viewpoint.

Pair Ability to see both sides of a situation so I can clearly understand how they each contribute to supporting each other.

Palace Situation where I can explore the different aspects of my rich creativity and have my obvious talents recognized by other people.

Pajamas Ability to present my self-image to other people in a relaxed way so I can feel comfortable and at home with myself.

Palate Essential ability to judge the flavor of a situation so I can use my experience to speak up and express my feelings.

Palaver Opportunity to communicate how I feel by maintaining my commitment rather than going on and on with no real purpose.

Pale Realization that I can revitalize a situation by showing my passion for it rather than letting it fade away into insignificance.

Paleontologist Aspect of my character that explores the origins of my instinctive creativity rather than feeling my future is set in stone.

Palette Ability to clearly see how my different moods can color my perspective so I can use them to change my overall outlook.

Palimony Opportunity to make a commitment to maintaining my sense of self-worth and independence rather than having to rely on friends.

Pallbearer Aspect of my character that helps me convey how I feel about my neglected ambitions instead of forgetting about them.

Pallet Ability to gather together some of my resources so I can provide a consistent and stable support for a new opportunity.

Palliative care Opportunity to nurture my natural talents and strengths so I can decisively resolve an unhealthy situation once and for all.

Palm Essential ability to grasp that my future is in my hands and I can shape any outcome by being open to new opportunities.

Palm tree Natural potential for my long-term spiritual growth by taking a more relaxed perspective as I stay rooted in the practicalities.

Palpitations Opportunity to take courageous and decisive action rather than halfheartedly leaving the eventual outcome to chance.

Pampa Situation where I can naturally grow my skills so I can use them with the wider possibilities spreading out in front of me.

Pamphlet Ability to honestly open up about one of my individual beliefs so I am able to publicly share it with other people.

Pan Ability to fulfill a potential ambition by gathering some of my knowledge and experience and cooking up something new.

Pancake Potential to fulfill an ambition that may require me to do a stack of work without feeling I have to go completely flat.

Pancreas Essential ability to maintain my levels of power and energy so I can continue to fully digest the value of my experiences.

Panda Instinctive ability to see a situation in black and white rather than feeling I have to chew over my decision at length.

Pane Ability to remain clear about a potentially fragile situation so I can understand how I currently see the successful outcome.

Panel Ability to clearly define my personal boundaries so I can raise some issues for further discussion with other people.

Panel game Opportunity to discuss ways of achieving my goals, even though the outcome may seem uncertain to those around me.

Panic Opportunity to take a deep breath so I can calmly observe a situation that seems to be suddenly stifling my progress.

Panic attack Opportunity to engage with a sudden challenge by taking forceful action to maintain composure rather than feeling defensive.

Panic button Ability to calmly take specific action so I can continue to make progress rather than feeling stuck in the same spot.

Panic-buying Opportunity to ensure that my talents are fully recognized by other people instead of suddenly feeling I have no real value.

Pannier Ability to make self-contained progress toward my objective by using motivational skills to keep commitments balanced.

Panorama Ability to open up my beliefs and broaden my knowledge so I can see the bigger picture and understand a wider perspective.

Pansy Natural ability to open up to the healthy variety of my creative talents so I can happily encourage them to blossom.

Pant Essential opportunity to calmly inspire myself by taking my time as I exercise my power in a potentially challenging situation.

Panther Instinctive ability to embody my need for greater independence, even though I may have to temporarily conceal my real motivation.

Panties Ability to present my self-image to people in a way that helps me retain modesty about my deeper creative talents.

Pantomime Opportunity to do something new rather than habitually going through old routines and exaggerating their importance.

Pantomime horse Ability to harness my unconscious strength so I can bring new ideas to life rather than taking the same old steps.

Pantry Aspect of myself that gives me the capacity to fulfill my potential ambitions by consistently supplying the resources I need.

Panty girdle Ability to present my self-image to people in a way that helps me shape an outcome by defining my creative potential.

Pantyhose Ability to present my self-image to people in a way that helps me to smoothly support my need for self-motivated action.

Paparazzi Aspects of my character that can become too focused on trivialities rather than trying to accurately portray my deeper purpose.

P

Papaya Potential to fulfill an ambition by being healthily optimistic about how I can make the most of a really juicy opportunity.

Paper Ability to express the different layers of my creative expertise by turning over a new leaf so I can make my mark.

Paperback Ability to open up to the wealth of my accumulated knowledge so I can convey the different levels of what I have learned.

Paper bag Ability to collect some of my thoughts so I can quickly open up to any new possibilities that grab my attention.

Paper clip Ability to collect some of my plans and ideas so I can share them with other people instead of feeling bent out of shape.

Paper cup Ability to fulfill an emotional need by making the most of any passing experience rather than trying to permanently hold on to it.

Paper plate Ability to make the most of a convenient opportunity to fulfill my appetite for success without buckling under the strain.

Paperwork Ability to have a clear understanding of my fundamental value rather than being frustrated by unnecessary procedures.

Papier-mâché Ability to blend emotional experiences with the different layers of my creativity so I can shape my chosen outcome.

Papyrus Ability to express ancient wisdom in a pithy manner so I can use my accumulated learning to straighten the situation out.

Parachute Ability to maintain my progress by collecting a range of ideas so I can use them in a more down-to-earth manner.

Parachutist Aspect of my character that can step away from some of my loftier ambitions so I can use my talents in a more grounded way.

Paracosm Situation where I can make sense of what is going on around me by developing my potential for continuing growth and love.

Parade Opportunity to proudly put all my talents on display so people can recognize how I am driving forward with my ambitions.

Parade ground Situation where I can take a practical, down-to-earth approach as I display my talents so they can be fully acknowledged.

Paradise Situation where I can finally understand what will make me happiest in life so I can move toward a brighter fulfillment.

Paradox Situation where I can decisively reconcile my different perspectives so I can move forward into a new area of opportunity.

Paraffin Ability to refine my raw talent so I can use my instinctive creativity to illuminate the wilder edges of my understanding.

Paraglider Ability to warm to some current ways of thinking so I can use them to convey my own ideas and achieve one of my ambitions.

Parakeet Instinctive ability to confidently voice any minor concerns rather than always repeating the ideas of other people.

Paralympian Aspect of my character that can motivate me to achieve great success instead of feeling limited about my apparent abilities.

Paralysis Opportunity to use my self-motivation and energy to free myself from a fear that has been limiting my freedom.

Paramedic Aspect of my character that can ensure my continued well-being by reacting quickly in a situation where I feel threatened.

Paramilitary group Aspects of my character that are surprisingly organized and have the discipline to challenge self-destructive behaviors.

Paranoia Opportunity to listen to my inner voice and make my own decisions rather than always letting other people tell me what to do.

Paranormal Realization that I can use instinctive creativity to shape an outcome instead of attempting to follow a rational procedure.

Parapet Ability to defend my beliefs by powerfully standing up for them rather than feeling I have to keep my head down.

Paraphernalia Ability to surround myself with all the skills and resources I need to produce an outcome of great practical value.

Paraplegic Aspect of my character that has the self-motivation to meet any challenge rather than feeling I can't stand up for myself.

Parasail Ability to capture some prevailing thoughts and theories so I can use them to raise my overall level of understanding.

Parasite Instinctive ability to deal with anyone who might be feeding off my energy and creativity so I can remove their influence.

Parasol Ability to get a handle on the prevailing mood so I can minimize the effect of any outside influences on my personal plans.

Paratrooper Aspect of my character that has the courage and discipline to bring my ideas down to earth so I can use them practically.

Parcel Ability to be receptive to new opportunities and whatever value they hold rather than getting wrapped up in the present.

Parcel bomb Ability to safely contain any potentially explosive feelings so I can always handle how I open up to new opportunities.

Parchment Ability to stay in touch with my real feelings by being comfortable with expressing the different layers of my creative talents.

Parent Aspect of my character that embodies my fundamental sense of security and gives me authority to lovingly develop my potential.

Parfumier Aspect of my character that helps me to create an attractive atmosphere so I can remind others of special experiences.

Park Situation where I can stand back from any of my social responsibilities and open myself to a wider range of opportunities.

Parka Ability to present my self-image to other people in a way that shows my willingness to work through any arduous challenges.

Park-and-ride Situation where I can briefly step out of my individual ambitions so I can join others in creating a collective success.

Parking lot Situation where I may have to temporarily postpone an individual ambition until I have the opportunity to drive it forward again.

Parking meter Ability to give myself time to look at ways of fulfilling my ambitions so I can make more measured progress.

Parking space Situation where I can spend a bit of time-out so I can take some steps to look at different ways of achieving my ambitions.

Parking ticket Ability to use drive and ambition to show my value to others rather than allowing them to routinely block progress.

Parkour Opportunity to energetically negotiate a series of major obstacles by quickly motivating myself to take some powerful steps.

Parliament Situation where I can contemplate choices available to me and have other people support the wisdom of my decisions.

Parole Opportunity to take complete responsibility for my freedom rather than feeling that other people are limiting my actions.

Parole officer Aspect of my character that takes full accountability for releasing me from any self-limiting behaviors.

Parquet flooring Ability to support the fundamental principles I stand for so I feel comfortable in showing my habitual opinions.

Parrot Instinctive ability to confidently voice my original thoughts rather than always repeating others' ideas.

Parsley Natural ability to clarify my ambitions to other people so I can get a flavor of the resources available to me.

P

Parsnip Potential to fulfill an ambition by using resources that require careful preplanning and the willingness to get my hands dirty.

Part Ability to understand how my individual needs and ambitions fit into a wider process so I can help to create something bigger.

Partially sighted Essential opportunity to look beyond the more obvious aspects of a situation so I can stay aware of the bigger picture.

Participant Aspect of my character that can achieve my chosen outcome by actively engaging with a challenge rather than just observing it.

Particle Ability to understand the bigger picture by taking the time to pay attention to a small but particularly significant detail.

Particle accelerator Ability to clearly understand the impact of a seemingly insignificant detail so I can step into my own power.

Particulate Ability to identify small details that other people may not see so I can filter out influences that may be unhealthy or harmful.

Parting Opportunity to intentionally set up the conditions for achieving a deeper connection by temporarily taking a more detached view.

Partition Ability to allocate my resources in a deliberate and disciplined manner rather than feeling that I am being too divisive.

Partner Aspect of my character that helps me to understand all my idiosyncrasies so I can combine my qualities to achieve success.

Partnership Opportunity to understand my fundamental needs so I can provide a solid platform to support their continuing activity.

Partridge Instinctive ability to use my ideas in a practical, down-to-earth manner, even though I may have to do it very discreetly.

Part-time job Opportunity to fulfill some of my own needs and ambitions by collectively creating value through meeting the needs of others.

Party Opportunity to happily celebrate my special skills and varied talents by inviting other people to recognize my expertise.

Pashmina Ability to present my self-image to people in a way that shows my confidence rather than getting too wrapped up in myself.

Pass Opportunity to openly recognize my levels of knowledge and expertise so I can make a major breakthrough in my progress.

Passage Situation where I can follow a prescribed method to connect with a wider opportunity, although it may initially seem restricting.

Passageway Situation where I can use my habitual behaviors to move beyond restrictions, even though it may seem to be quite limiting.

Pass code Ability to move into a whole new area of possibility by clearly communicating exactly how I feel about a very specific detail.

Passenger Aspect of my character that allows other people to choose the direction I take because it often seems the easiest option.

Passerby Aspect of my character that can provide me with useful information about how to make the next move in my current situation.

Passionate Realization that I can use my deepest emotions to transform a situation without becoming obsessed by it.

Passive Opportunity to step into my own power so I can take specific action to actively fulfill one of my individual ambitions.

Passive smoking Opportunity to clarify my thoughts rather than letting myself be continually drawn into confusing, unhealthy situations.

Pass mark Ability to successfully progress into new opportunities by ensuring that I always make a good impression on other people.

Passport Ability to move into new territory by having my unique talents openly acknowledged and giving myself the permission to use them.

Password Ability to know just the right thing to say so I can open myself up to some wider opportunities where I can feel more secure.

Past Opportunity to reconnect with my accumulated wisdom and experience so I can use it to progress my future ambitions.

Pasta Potential to fulfill an ambition by using a variety of fertile ideas and practical experience to consistently shape the outcome.

Paste Ability to apply a healthy mix of my various skills and experiences so I can hold a potentially sticky situation together.

Pastry Potential to fulfill an ambition by producing fresh ideas that will increase my value instead of just appearing flaky.

Pastry chef Aspect of my character that has the great taste and skill to transform my raw talent so I can develop its potential capacity.

Pasture Situation where I can use my accumulated experience to sustain my creative instincts so I can realize their practical value.

Pasty Potential to fulfill one of my ambitions by containing my enthusiasm rather than becoming too wrapped up in the situation.

Patch Ability to make an obvious connection so I can strengthen my contribution instead of trying to cover up my talents.

Patchwork Ability to bring a variety of influences together so I can connect them into something much larger and more useful.

Patent Opportunity to make my thought processes obvious to other people rather than trying to conceal my actual intentions.

Patent leather Ability to feel comfortable with the boundary between my inside and outside worlds so I have the confidence to shine.

Paternity test Opportunity to judge my performance so I can see how well I embody the loving power and authority that people need from me.

Path Situation where I can take steps to understand my current direction in life and decide where it might be taking me.

Pathologist Aspect of my character that can bring one of my neglected talents back to life rather than continually picking holes in it.

Patience Opportunity to maintain composure so I can draw on my experience and judge the right moment to take decisive action.

Patient Aspect of my character that takes time to consider future steps I can use to improve my situation rather than just lying around.

Patient zero Aspect of my character that can resolve my current feeling of uneasiness by taking time to identify its fundamental source.

Patina Ability to always shine in any situation by feeling comfortable with the layers of experience I have built up over time.

Patio Situation where I can enjoy a close, supportive relationship that helps me to relax by smoothing over any challenges.

Patriarch Aspect of my character that can use my power and wisdom to achieve my chosen outcomes, even though it may require some discipline.

Patrol Opportunity to intentionally open myself up to emerging possibilities rather than feeling I have to be constantly vigilant.

Patter Ability to use my sound judgment to take the steps I need to rather than talking aimlessly about my intentions.

Pattern Ability to see a variety of distinct connections I can use to characterize aspects of myself that may not be obvious.

Pauper Aspect of my character that can use the wealth of my talent to create great value rather than feeling I have nothing to offer.

P

Pavement Situation where I can use my energy and self-motivation to stay safe and secure as I move closer to my wider ambitions.

Pavement artist Aspect of my character that can use natural ingenuity and creative expertise to express myself in a down-to-earth manner.

Pavilion Situation where I can shape my thoughts and ideas so I can feel more comfortable as I open myself to wider awareness.

Paw Instinctive ability to stay firmly grounded in my individual creativity so I can take practical steps to move into action.

Pawn Opportunity to think strategically about the specific moves I need to make rather than feeling that people are controlling me.

Pawnbroker Aspect of my character that helps me to claim my self-esteem by acknowledging my value and letting other people know about it.

Pawnshop Situation where I can reclaim my self-worth and have people acknowledge it, even though I may feel I am of little value.

Pawn ticket Ability to recognize my contribution to others by giving myself permission to display my unique expertise to them.

Pay Opportunity to acknowledge the worth of my individual expertise so I can continue to recognize my value to other people.

Pay-and-display Situation where I can temporarily park an ambition and permit myself to realize the value of exploring other possibilities.

Payback Opportunity to have other people recognize my talents now rather than always referring to past achievements.

Payday Opportunity to wait for just the right time to display the value of my expertise so I can have the most rewarding experience.

Payment Ability to declare the full significance of my creative talents so I can have my value completely accepted by other people.

Pay-per-view Opportunity to choose how I see a particular situation by understanding the value of the contribution I can make to it.

Paywall Ability to strongly support my beliefs and have my value acknowledged by maintaining firm personal boundaries.

Pea Natural ability to develop a number of seemingly similar ideas that can steadily mount up so I can achieve a long-held ambition.

Peace Opportunity to declare inner tensions I am experiencing so I can use their energy to move forward and feel more relaxed.

Peacekeeping force Aspects of my character that can use my strength and discipline to resolve emerging tensions or personal conflicts.

Peach Natural ability to use my healthy, well-rounded optimism to make the best of a situation and achieve a fruitful outcome.

Peacock Instinctive ability to take great pride in a variety of my creative ideas so I can confidently display them to other people.

Peak Situation where I can step up to the challenge and confidently make the sustained effort required to be a high achiever.

Peanut Potential to fulfill an ambition by choosing to come out of my shell rather than feeling my abilities are undervalued.

Peanut butter Potential to fulfill an ambition by opening up to other ideas so I can smooth over rough patches and make them more palatable.

Pear Natural ability to fulfill an ambition by widening my perspective and using my healthy awareness to shape a fruitful outcome.

Pearl Instinctive ability to encapsulate a grain of truth into an expression of pure wisdom rather than feeling irritated by it.

Peasant Aspect of my character that can cultivate my fundamental practical skills so I can create a valuable result for everyone.

Peat Ability to use my accumulated practical experience and down-to-earth approach to get fired up about my natural creativity.

Peat bog Situation where I can use my layers of learning to quickly deal with any messy details that are slowing down my progress.

Pebble Ability to take a well-rounded approach by using solid, specific actions, even though they initially seem insignificant.

Peck Instinctive opportunity to judge the finer points of a situation so I can understand how it may affect my apparent status.

Pecs Essential ability to embody my deeper inspiration so I can use it wisely as I proudly show off my talents to other people.

Peculiar Realization that my talents have a unique value to other people and not worry that I may seem out of place.

Pedal Ability to consistently control progress toward my goal by using my judgment to apply the right amount of pressure.

Pedal steel guitar Ability to take my instinctive creativity in both hands so I can strike the right tone rather than letting things slide.

Pedantic Opportunity to use specific details so I can understand the wider context rather than being restricted by individual procedures.

Pedestal Ability to confidently elevate my status so people can recognize the level of my achievements and the value of where I stand.

Pedestrian Aspect of my character that can use my self-motivation and energy to take a series of deliberate steps to lead to success.

Pedestrian crossing Situation where I can resolve a dilemma between two distinct career paths by making a decision that takes me beyond them.

Pediatrician Aspect of my character that can resolve unhealthy tensions so I can develop my potential for continuing growth and love.

Pedigree Ability to chart the development of my creative instincts so I can achieve a purer understanding of how to use them.

Pedophile Aspect of my character that needs to respect my uniquely precious talents so they can develop without any interference.

Pee Essential ability to release any pent-up feelings that may have been causing me accumulating tension and discomfort.

Peeling Opportunity to understand the nature of a potential ambition by keenly exploring beyond its superficial appearances.

Peephole Ability to look more deeply into what is happening so I can motivate myself to confidently step into an opportunity.

Peeping Opportunity to confidently share my individual clarity of vision rather than feeling that I always have to conceal my talents.

Peering Opportunity to clearly understand an approaching challenge by broadening my perspective rather than trying to close my eyes to it.

Peg Ability to use my habitual behaviors as a reference point so that I can make a connection without becoming too attached to it.

Pelican Instinctive ability to briefly immerse myself in my deeper emotions so I can use my mental capacity to bring feelings to the surface.

Pellet Ability to influence a situation from a distance by taking a well-rounded approach to working out what I need from it.

Peloton Aspects of my character that can combine my talents and balance my different levels of motivation to make significant progress.

Pelt Ability to become more comfortable with ideas that emerge from my instinctive behaviors so I can develop them further.

P

Pelvic floor Essential ability to support the fundamental concepts I believe in so I can continue to exercise my individual judgment.

Pelvis Essential ability to give structure to a concept so I can support my creative potential if I choose to develop it further.

Pen Ability to uniquely express my talents by channeling my creativity so I can direct its flow without feeling restricted.

Penal colony Situation where I can give myself permission to move on from the self-limiting beliefs that may now seem quite foreign.

Penalty Opportunity to recognize the value of my actions to other people rather than punishing myself in case I have upset them.

Penalty shootout Opportunity to rapidly decide a potentially uncertain outcome by having the confidence to step up and give it my best shot.

Pencil Ability to quickly figure out a situation by drawing on my individual learning so I can get straight to the point.

Pencil sharpener Ability to consistently make my point so I can clearly communicate my ideas rather than having my progress blunted.

Pendant Ability to draw other people's attention to my deeper feelings rather than having any hang-ups about my attractiveness.

Pendulum Ability to alternate between seeing both sides of a situation so I can use that awareness to consistently move it forward.

Penetrating stare Opportunity to forcefully get beyond any surface impressions so I can look intensively into what is going on.

Penetration Opportunity to move beyond perceived barriers to my progress so I can become more aware of what is happening inside me.

Penguin Instinctive ability to view my emotional life from a black-and-white perspective rather than indulging in flights of fancy.

Peninsula Situation where I can feel much more independent while still maintaining my firm connection to some wider possibilities.

Penis Essential ability to channel my natural creativity and firmly assert my talents by regularly standing up for what I believe in.

Penitentiary Situation where I can escape from some self-limiting beliefs that may leave me feeling trapped in the long run.

Penknife Ability to quickly achieve an ambition by decisively cutting through any uncertainty so I can assert my individuality.

Pennant Ability to clearly display my individual viewpoint so I can attract the attention of others to the point I am making.

Penniless Opportunity to use my abundance of talent to make a valuable contribution rather than feeling I have nothing to offer.

Pension Ability to fully appreciate the accumulated value of my growing wisdom and realize how my self-worth has matured over the years.

Pensioner Aspect of my character that has the freedom to use my vast wealth of wisdom and experience rather than limiting my involvement.

Pension fund Ability to draw on the rich variety of my accumulated knowledge and experience so I can continue to increase my value to people.

Pentagram Ability to shape an outcome by drawing on a number of points rather than feeling that I have to leave it all to chance.

Penthouse Situation where I can achieve one of my loftier ambitions by comfortably exploring all aspects of my inner and outer lives.

Pent-up Opportunity to honestly express my emotions rather than feeling I have to always confine myself to certain subjects.

Peony Natural ability to display my blossoming creativity so I can resolve any tensions I may be experiencing with other people.

People Aspects of my character that tangibly reflect all my potential abilities and can embody my uniqueness in all its various forms.

Pepper Ability to consistently stimulate my appetite for success by spicing up what otherwise might be a bland experience for me.

Peppermint Ability to flavor one of my ambitions in a fresh, exciting way that gives me the confidence to honestly speak my truth.

Pepper spray Ability to use stimulating ideas so I can define my personal boundaries to other people in a clear and gentle way.

Perch Situation where I can comfortably have an overview of what is happening in my life so I can make plans for my next move.

Percussion Ability to make myself heard in a variety of distinctive ways rather than always banging on about one particular subject.

Peregrine falcon Instinctive ability to dive into an opportunity so I can use my quick thinking to rapidly pursue a specific objective.

Perfect Realization that my apparent flaws and inconsistencies are what make me unique, and I don't need to try to conform to expectations.

Perfect crime Opportunity to have complete confidence in my flawless judgment instead of always punishing myself for appearing clueless.

Perforation Ability to stay detached from any tensions I may be feeling rather than always picking holes in what I am trying to do.

Performance Situation where I can confidently display my unique skills so I can have them appreciated by a wider audience.

Performance anxiety Realization that the best way to understand what I need is to have the courage to display my abilities to other people.

Performance artist Aspect of my character that uses my natural ingenuity and creative instincts to dynamically display my expertise to other people.

Performance poet Aspect of my character that can evoke my deeper feelings by having the courage to share my emotions with a wider audience.

Performing Opportunity to draw attention to my individual expertise and experience so I can become more confident in using them.

Perfume Ability to create an attractive atmosphere that reminds me of a special experience so I can share it with other people.

Peril Opportunity to successfully reach my objective by having the courage to step outside my comfort zone and minimize any hazards.

Perimeter Situation where I can go to the edge of what I know so I can achieve a better understanding of the surrounding context.

Period Opportunity to take my time and explore some options so I can bring a learning experience to a successful conclusion.

Period drama Opportunity to look at my personal situation in an exciting new way rather than feeling I've seen it all before.

Peripheral Ability to make full use of my creative potential by making a firm connection to an opportunity at the edge of my experience.

Periscope Ability to clearly observe what thoughts and plans are emerging as I immerse myself in a complex emotional situation.

Perish Opportunity to decisively engage with a personal transformation rather than trying to stay cool and just let it fade away.

Perjury Opportunity to openly and honestly speak my truth rather than thinking I have to conceal my feelings from other people.

Perm Ability to explore some of the twists and turns in my thinking process rather than always jumping straight to a conclusion.

Permafrost Situation where I can free up some of my deeper practical experience from the past rather than leaving it frozen in time.

P

Permanent tooth Essential ability to remain confident in my continuing power rather than feeling I will lose it at some point in the future.

Permit Ability to give myself full permission to use my talents so they can be formally acknowledged by other people on a wider basis.

Perpendicular Realization that I can straighten things out by making a firm decision rather than leaning one way or the other.

Perpetrator Aspect of my character that takes full accountability for my actions, even though others may not understand my motivations.

Perplexing Realization that I can resolve one of the puzzling aspects of my behavior by taking time to observe my habitual reactions.

Persecution Opportunity to encourage my creative development rather than continually punishing myself for apparently wasting time.

Perseverance Realization that I can achieve consistent success by continuing to make an effort rather than feeling I'm making no progress.

Persistence Realization that I have an enduring belief in my own abilities and that my presence will continue to be felt by others.

Persistent vegetative state Essential opportunity to have a healthy awareness of my talents, even if there continues to be no response from other people.

Person Aspect of my character that helps to develops my conscious awareness by reflecting the variety of roles that I play in my life.

Personal assistant Aspect of my character that understands my motivation and takes care of my unique needs as I pursue an individual ambition.

Personal computer Ability to use my mind to quickly and precisely work out the different ways I can influence the outcome of a situation.

Personality disorder Essential opportunity to use my creativity to solve an apparently upsetting problem by taking a less structured approach.

Personal shopper Aspect of my character that recognizes my true value and is happy to display my unique qualities in the way that serves me best.

Personal stereo Ability to create my own personal space so I can hear both sides of a situation and keep myself open to new possibilities.

Perspex Ability to remain clear about a situation so I can see through any inconsistencies in the complex ideas that created it.

Perspiration Essential ability to resolve any emotional frictions by choosing to cool things down, instead of letting my feelings leak out.

Pervert Aspect of my character that has the power to make the right choice rather than allowing other people to influence my morals.

Pescatarian Aspect of my character that can fulfill my appetite for success by immersing myself in my emotions and going with the flow.

Pessimism Opportunity to understand how I can step into my personal power and use it to achieve desirable and pleasant outcomes.

Pest Instinctive ability to directly deal with the source of a situation that is annoying me instead of allowing it to plague me.

Pestle Ability to use my power to smooth out a potentially rough situation rather than allowing other people to constantly wear me down.

Pet Instinctive ability to nurture an idea that is close to my heart so I can give it my unconditional care and attention.

Petal Natural ability to open up to some illuminating ideas so I can attract other people to a more colorful way of thinking.

Pet bird Instinctive ability to nurture some plans and ideas that are close to my heart so I can develop them with love and affection.

Petition Ability to attract the support of other people by clearly communicating my needs and specifically stating my beliefs to them.

Petri dish Ability to be receptive to a variety of cultures so I can observe how they each develop their particular beliefs.

Petrified Opportunity to courageously take some practical, down-to-earth action rather than feeling everything is too hard for me.

Petrol Ability to refine my raw creative spirit so I can use it to powerfully fuel my drive for success in achieving my ambitions.

Petrol bomb Ability to safely contain my potentially explosive feelings so I can create a positive transformation in a volatile situation.

Petrol pump Ability to consistently channel my spirited creativity so I can always achieve my ambitions in a high-pressure situation.

Petrol station Situation where I can conveniently access my creative spirit so I can use it to help drive a personal ambition forward.

Petrol tanker Ability to employ powerful resources that will help me convey the value of my creativity as I progress with an ambition.

Petticoat Ability to present my self-image to people by being more openly confident so I can reveal the layers of my natural creativity.

Petty cash Ability to have my value quickly and easily recognized by people rather than feeling my contribution is insignificant.

Pew Ability to share a relaxed and comfortable viewpoint with people as we become more aware of how we support our mutual beliefs.

Pewter Ability to bring a number of different aspects of my fundamental power together so

I can use them to provide a valuable outcome.

Phallus Essential ability to display my natural creativity and firmly assert my power by standing up for my beliefs.

Phantom Aspect of my character that I need to finally lay to rest or bring back to life, even though I thought it was dead and buried.

Phantom limb Essential opportunity to have the confidence I need in my presence of mind so I can use my power to reach out to others.

Phantom pregnancy Essential opportunity to become more aware of the growing presence of my creative abilities rather than having any misconceptions.

Pharaoh Aspect of my character that has the power and authority to take immediate action instead of always living in the past.

Pharmacist Aspect of my character that has the formula for successfully resolving an unhealthy situation, rather than just dispensing advice.

Pharmacy Situation where I can see the value of using a prescribed process to deal with an unhealthy situation and improve it for everyone.

Phase Opportunity to become more aware of what is emerging for me so I can bring it into existence and then evolve it further.

Phaser Ability to assert my power in a forceful manner by focusing my energies as I communicate my aims to those around me.

Pheasant Instinctive ability to leave concerns behind and quickly raise my game so I can get a colorful idea off the ground.

Phenomenon Opportunity to create a really impressive performance by observing my natural talents so I can use them more consistently.

Philanderer Aspect of my character that loves to connect at a deeper level so I can continue to have faith in my creative talents.

P

Philanthropist Aspect of my character that can create abundant opportunities by consistently being supportive of my developing expertise.

Phlegm Essential ability to clearly communicate my thoughts and feelings by being able to remain as calm and composed as possible.

Phobia Essential opportunity to become more aware of who I really am so I can courageously resolve any of my habitual anxieties.

Phoenix Apparent ability to produce transformative ideas by using my creativity to let go of the past so I can rise to new challenges.

Phone Ability to communicate what I need to say to another person by knowing how to press just the right buttons with them.

Phone book Ability to open up to the wealth of my accumulated knowledge and learning so I can communicate what I need to say.

Phone-in Opportunity to participate in a wider discussion with other people, even though I may initially feel quite distant from them.

Phone sex Opportunity to become much more intimately aware of how I can communicate my plans so I can bring them into reality.

Phony Realization that I can make genuinely profound connections with other people by being honest and open about my emotions.

Photograph Ability to consistently capture a unique perspective so I can use it to reliably remind me of a valuable area of expertise.

Photographer Aspect of my character that has the talent to see things in a different way so I can open my eyes to new possibilities.

Photon Ability to understand a situation with much greater clarity by illuminating the tiniest details and the effect they can have.

Photocopier Ability to use my talents to create original work rather than feeling I have to duplicate the efforts of people.

Photo finish Opportunity to evidently see the tiny details that can make all the difference as I drive forward with one of my ambitions.

Photofit picture Ability to piece together the various aspects of who I really am so I can identify the ambitions I need to pursue.

Photo shoot Opportunity to display my power and influence in an assertive manner so I can quickly share my ambitions with other people.

Phrase book Ability to say just the right thing to people by confidently opening up to the wealth of my accumulated knowledge and learning.

Physician Aspect of my character that sympathetically examines my general behavior and can help me remedy unresolved tensions.

Physicist Aspect of my character that understands my fundamental qualities and how I can consistently apply them to real-world situations.

Physiotherapist Aspect of my character that has a healthy regard for my well-being and helps me maintain my powers of self-motivation.

Piano Ability to take my instinctive creativity in both hands so I can express the higher thoughts and deeper emotions that I feel.

Pibroch Ability to instinctively communicate with other people in a profoundly evocative way that will resonate with them.

Piccolo Ability to take my instinctive creativity in both hands so I can channel some of my higher ideals in a graceful manner.

Pick Opportunity to choose my preferred outcome from a range of options so I can successfully fulfill a fundamental desire.

Pickax Ability to take a series of powerfully decisive actions that will help me open up to the strength of some of my deeper feelings.

Picket line Aspects of my character that can help me to strike out on my own instead of feeling restricted by the needs of other people.

Pickle Potential to fulfill an ambition by trying to preserve a more natural approach rather than allowing it to end up in a mess.

Pickled Opportunity to make the most of a fresh and exciting possibility right now instead of planning to save it for the future.

Pickpocket Aspect of my character that can easily access concealed resources by being more open and honest about my intentions.

Picky Realization that I need to make a decisive choice rather than fussing over minor details that may prove inconsequential.

Picnic Opportunity to make things easier and more pleasant for myself by naturally spreading out various ways of fulfilling my ambitions.

Picture Ability to frame my individual perspective so I can use it as a way of clearly presenting my personal point of view.

Picturesque Realization that I can connect with a deeper understanding of my power by taking the time to look beyond surface appearances.

Picture window Ability to understand my individual perspective on a situation so I can clearly see through concerns I may have.

Pie Potential to easily fulfill one of my ambitions by carefully dividing the responsibilities and sharing them with other people.

Piece Ability to make the wider connection to how I fit in to a larger effort so I can understand what I am contributing to it.

Pied-à-terre Situation where I can explore aspects of my character in a more relaxed manner, even though I don't feel entirely at home.

Pier Situation where I can go a long way to understanding my wider emotions while

keeping my feet firmly planted on the ground.

Piercing Opportunity to cut through any superficial awareness and really get to the point, although it may initially prove painful.

Pig Instinctive ability to get stuck in a potentially messy situation and enjoy intelligently mucking about with it.

Pigeon Instinctive ability to home in on an idea and communicate it to other people, although they may initially seem quite distant.

Pigeonhole Ability to be more receptive to what really motivates me rather than feeling I have to conform to specific expectations.

Piggy bank Ability to steadily accumulate a wealth of wisdom and experience, even though my initial contributions might seem quite small.

Pigment Ability to clearly change my current mood by understanding how my individual experiences might be coloring my perspective.

Pike Instinctive ability to immerse myself in my feelings so I can understand my fundamental ambitions and how to satisfy them.

Pilchard Instinctive ability to fulfill my deeper ambitions by taking a well-rounded approach so I can appear to just go with the flow.

Pile Ability to accumulate an impressive amount of practical skills so I can use them to rise to prominence among other people.

Pile driver Ability to make a sustained effort that provides a deeper level of support for my plans so I can confidently build on them.

Pile-up Opportunity to take control of a developing situation and choose the outcome rather than letting it all get on top of me.

Pilgrim Aspect of my character that is willing to devote all my time and effort to achieve an ambition that means the world to me.

P

Pilgrimage Opportunity to achieve a much deeper understanding of my needs by persistently motivating myself to fulfill a significant ambition.

Pill Ability to follow a prescribed process so I can take specific action to help resolve a potentially unhealthy situation.

Pillar Ability to staunchly support fundamental aspects of my character development that may initially seem above and beyond me.

Pillar box Ability to collect my thoughts and plans together so I can convey them to others and communicate how I feel.

Pillbox Situation where I can comfortably defend my opinion, even though I may have to widen my perspective at some point.

Pillion passenger Aspect of my character that can use the personal ambition and drive of others to help me progress toward my objective.

Pillory Ability to take decisive action to deal with any criticism rather than feeling that I am firmly locked in to a single perspective.

Pillow Ability to provide gentle, consistent support for my emerging ideas so I can feel more relaxed and comfortable with them.

Pillow fight Ability to resolve inner tensions I may have by taking a softer, gentle approach rather than beating myself up about them.

Pillow talk Opportunity to become much more intimately aware of what I need to say so I can feel more comfortable about it.

Pilot Aspect of my character that can see the bigger picture so I can get my ideas off the ground and then successfully land them.

Pilot light Ability to maintain my creative spark so I can immediately respond to any new opportunities that might require my input.

Pimp Aspect of my character that can realize the fundamental value of my creative talents instead of always trying to show them off.

Pimple Essential opportunity to realize that

an apparent blemish on my character is only superficial and can be easily dealt with.

Pin Ability to use my penetrating awareness to get under the surface of a situation so I can make a definite decision.

PIN Ability to quickly access my wealth of expertise and experience so I can demonstrate my specific value to other people.

Pinball Opportunity to play around with a potentially successful outcome by having a clear strategy rather than just bouncing around.

Pincer Instinctive ability to have a strong feel for both sides of a situation so I can quickly grasp an emerging opportunity.

Pinch Opportunity to openly recognize the value of my talents rather than trying to minimize their real contribution to my success.

Pincushion Ability to be comfortable in accepting a number of different points of view so I can absorb any criticism from other people.

Pineapple Potential to fulfill one of my ambitions by taking it piece by piece until I achieve the fruitful outcome I am looking for.

Pinecone Natural ability to protect the small seeds of some ideas so I can eventually develop them into something much stronger.

Pine marten Instinctive ability to work my way through a number of spiritual opportunities before I decide which one to branch out into.

Pine tree Natural potential for my long-term spiritual growth, which can make me long for some wilder and more evocative experiences.

Ping Opportunity to quickly test the strength of my ongoing relationships so I can immediately alert myself to sudden changes.

Ping-Pong Opportunity to knock some ideas backward and forward so I can demonstrate my skills and get my point across.

Pink Mood that can color my perspective by

reflecting how the soft and gentle nature of my approach can always keep me healthy.

Pinkie finger Essential ability to control my actions and shape my own future, even though my contribution may appear quite small.

Pinnacle Situation where I can become a high achiever by firmly grasping the practicalities and understanding the sheer effort involved.

Pins and needles Essential opportunity to get my passion and vitality flowing again rather than feeling quite numb about the situation.

Pint Potential to fulfill an emotional need by happily sharing my feelings with other people rather than bottling them up.

Pioneer Aspect of my character that has the courage to confidently explore new opportunities that take me to the edge of what I know.

Pip Ability to take a seemingly insignificant idea and realize that this is the time to develop it into something more powerful.

Pipe Ability to contain my emotions by consistently channeling my feelings so I can convey their deeper value to other people.

Pipeline Ability to reliably communicate the power of my feelings to other people, even though they may appear to be quite distant.

Piper Aspect of my character that takes my instinctive creativity in both hands and uses it to explore my wilder hopes and ambitions.

Piranha Instinctive ability to immerse myself in my emotion, st I can connect with the fundamental basis of my ambitions.

Pirate Aspect of my character that needs to honor the power of my feelings and the deeper value that they can convey for me.

Pistol Ability to get something started by clearly communicating my aims to others without having to be too forceful about it.

Piston Ability to consistently deal with a series of high-pressure situations so I can use them to power a sustained drive for success.

Pit Situation where I can venture deeper into the fundamental aspects of an opportunity so I can uncover previously unseen value.

Pitch Situation where I can decide an uncertain outcome by using a number of different angles to display my expertise to others.

Pitcher Ability to convey some of my emotions and experiences so I can share them with people in a much more satisfying manner.

Pitchfork Ability to quickly pick up on what I need to do, even though it may seem like it will require a lot of effort from me to succeed.

Pit stop Opportunity to take a brief pause in my drive to achieve a particular ambition so I can use the time to remotivate myself.

Pity Realization that I have the opportunity to celebrate my talents rather than being disdainful of what I have achieved so far.

Pivot Ability to understand the point of what I'm doing so I can use it to turn the situation around to my advantage.

Pixel Ability to see the much bigger picture by taking the time to understand all the small but significant details that produce it.

Pixelated Realization that expressing myself openly and honestly can help me to be clearer about how to completely resolve a challenge.

Pixie Aspect of my character that may seem quite whimsical but whose mischievous nature can often develop creative opportunities.

Pizza Potential to fulfill an ambition by carefully dividing the responsibilities so I can easily share them with other people.

Placard Ability to clearly demonstrate my needs by having the confidence to openly communicate my feelings to those around me.

P

Place Situation where I can experience particular aspects of my character so I can understand how they fit into the larger scheme.

Placebo Ability to remedy an unhealthy situation by deciding to resolve tensions rather than feeling that my actions are of no value.

Placenta Essential ability to take care of one of my developing concepts by instinctively understanding what is needed to support it.

Plague Opportunity to resolve an unhealthy situation I have been avoiding, although it has been affecting all aspects of my life.

Plaice Instinctive ability to immerse myself in my emotions so I can use my practical talents without being too obvious about it.

Plain Situation where I can see all possibilities spread out before me in a very straightforward way that leads to obvious choices.

Plainclothes officer Aspect of my character that gives me permission to fully explore the power of my talents without drawing attention to myself.

Plait Opportunity to carefully align various strands of my thinking so I can weave them together into a strong and healthy outcome.

Plan Ability to achieve a successful outcome by drawing on my knowledge and experience so I can see the bigger picture.

Plane Ability to carefully shape my habitual behaviors so I can smooth out inconsistencies and find the best fit for my talents.

Planet Situation where I can fully embody my world of life experience so I can use it to understand what is going on all around me.

Planet Earth Situation where I can make a world of difference by using my self-awareness to understand what is going on all around me.

Plane tree Natural potential for my long-term spiritual growth by carefully shaping my choices while staying rooted in the practicalities.

Plank Ability to support a fairly narrow set of beliefs that may eventually lead to a sudden realization about how I feel.

Plankton Natural ability to immerse myself in my emotions so that I can fulfill an ambition rather than drifting aimlessly.

Planning permission Opportunity to develop some valuable aspects of my character rather than feeling restricted by self-imposed limitations.

Plant Natural ability to use an illuminating opportunity as a way of absorbing enriching ideas in a practical, down-to-earth way.

Plantation Situation where I can produce a valuable outcome by cultivating my natural abilities, even though it may require some effort.

Planting Opportunity to carefully nurture the developing aspects of my natural expertise by providing practical support and resources.

Plasma screen Ability to clearly understand how a situation currently appears to me so I can use experience to make a quick decision.

Plaster Ability to smooth over the rougher aspects of any situation so I can resolve underlying tensions and minimize discomfort.

Plasterer Aspect of my character that takes a more level-headed approach so I can smooth out any ups and downs I may be feeling.

Plastic Ability to synthesize a complex variety of ideas that I can mold into an outcome that will have the most practical value.

Plastic bag Ability to collect some practical resources together so I can always be open to any new opportunities that may emerge.

Plastic bullets Ability to decisively assert my power from a distance rather than bouncing around ideas that may prove quite painful.

Plastic explosive Ability to control my powerful talent for creating sudden change by molding my talents to the surrounding circumstances.

Plasticine Ability to play around with some of my practical skills so I can use my range of experiences to shape a specific outcome.

Plastic surgery Opportunity to cut out my self-critical nature and just be who I am rather than trying to reshape myself to please others.

Plastic wrap Ability to hang on to what I need so I can clearly see what habits and behaviors I can let go of.

Plate Ability to be receptive to the variety of ways in which I can fulfill my appetite for success without feeling overloaded.

Plateau Situation where I can consolidate the higher levels of success I have attained so I can make even faster progress.

Plate-glass window Ability to clearly understand my individual perspective on a situation so I can be more receptive to how other people see it.

Plate rack Ability to rank my opportunities so I can remain clear about how I can continue to fulfill my appetite for further success.

Platform Situation where I can raise my level of awareness by being able to solidly support my beliefs as I share them with other people.

Platform ticket Ability to demonstrate my value to other people so I can permit myself to examine a number of approaching opportunities.

Platinum Ability to use my fundamental strength to let my value shine through so I can continue to be a catalyst for further activity.

Platitude Realization that honestly voicing my opinion is far more valuable than always trying to appear profound to other people.

Platonic Realization that tensions can generate stronger growth rather than thinking that my relationships should always be ideal.

Platoon Aspects of my character that can quickly react to any unforeseen challenges by responding with a firmly structured approach.

Platter Ability to widen the scope of my ambitions and spread my influence so I can serve up a variety of new opportunities.

Platypus Instinctive ability to sensitively navigate some of my murkier emotions, even though some of them can seem quite primitive.

Play Opportunity to observe different aspects of my character and see how I can resolve tensions that may emerge between them.

Playboy Aspect of my character that can take more responsibility for developing my strength and power rather than just amusing myself.

Player Aspect of my character that actively engages in exploring a number of opportunities, even though the outcome may be uncertain.

Play girl Aspect of my character that gives me freedom to openly speak my mind so I can fulfill my ambitions and realize my dreams.

Playground Situation where I can play around with different aspects of my character and experience their range of skills and abilities.

Playgroup Situation where I can learn valuable lessons and begin to develop my unique talents by displaying them to the people around me.

Playing Opportunity to decide my preferred outcome by working my way through a number of possibilities and seeing what emerges.

Playing cards Ability to deal with my feelings in a really open and honest way rather than always trying to stack the odds in my favor.

Playlist Ability to spontaneously give voice to my feelings instead of constantly trying to plan ahead so I can deal with any eventuality.

Playpen Situation where I can develop some of my fundamental ideas while being able to keep them separate from my other projects.

P

Playroom Aspect of myself where I can develop a variety of colorful new ideas without feeling anyone is judging my efforts.

Playwright Aspect of my character that can develop my communication skills so I can convey the fundamental power of my personal story.

Plea bargain Opportunity to have my value recognized by other people instead of punishing myself for not making the most of my chances.

Pleasant Realization that I am happiest when engaging with a difficult challenge rather than doing something that is unacceptable to me.

Pleasure Realization that fulfilling my deepest ambitions may require some effort instead of always trying to amuse myself.

Plectrum Ability to pick my words carefully so I can strike just the right tone when dealing with a tense and drawn-out situation.

Pledge Opportunity to make a firm commitment to developing my unique talents and abilities so I can fulfill all my natural promise.

Plethora Realization that I have a wealth of experience and more than enough talent to bring a situation to a successful outcome.

Pleurisy Opportunity to resolve an un‐ healthy situation by being clear about what I need rather than getting all fired up about it.

Pliers Ability to the get a grip on a potenti‐ ally delicate situation so I can use my skill to shape a successful outcome.

Plimsoll mark Ability to clearly gauge my ability to navigate a complex emotional situa‐ tion by routinely observing the buoyancy of my mood.

Plinth Ability to provide solid and stable support for one of my unique talents so I can openly display it to other people.

Plodding Opportunity to steadily pursue one of my ambitions by using my self‐ motivation and persistence to take the steps I need.

Plot Ability to plan the next stage in my story by understanding my ambitions and the measures I can take to achieve them.

Plotting Opportunity to openly share my ambitions with other people so I can use our collective resources to help me succeed.

Plow Ability to take a decisive and down-to-earth approach so I can open up some of my practical resources to ensure future growth.

Plowing Opportunity to consistently open up to my accumulated expertise so I can reap the benefits of my efforts at a future date.

Pluck Opportunity to quickly get a firm grip on a situation so I can use my courage and decisiveness to pull off a great success.

Plug Ability to contain my enthusiasm by carefully controlling the flow of my emotions and energy so they don't just drain away.

Plug hole Situation where I can look deeply into what motivates me rather than feeling drained of any ambition and energy.

Plum Potential to fulfill one of my ambitions by picking the best approach so it will result in a fruitful outcome.

Plumage Instinctive opportunity to display the colorful nature of my ideas and the distinctive patterns that often emerge from them.

Plumber Aspect of my character that knows how to work with the various pressures of my emotional life so I can avoid messy experiences.

Plumbing Ability to channel my feelings and emotions so I use them to fulfill specific needs rather than losing control of them.

Plume Ability to explore my thoughts and theories by taking pride in the soft and gentle approach I use when displaying them.

Plummet Opportunity to go much deeper into my ideas so I can let everything fall into place and achieve a profounder understanding.

Plump Opportunity to feel comfortable with my accumulated experience rather than feeling as if I am being forced to make a choice.

Plunder Opportunity to have the full value of my talents recognized by other people without allowing myself to get too carried away.

Plunge Opportunity to decisively commit to future success by having the courage to wholeheartedly immerse myself in my emotions.

Plunge pool Situation where I can immediately reflect on my accumulated learning and experience so I can explore it in greater depth.

Plunger Ability to clear up an emotional frustration by drawing out what has been blocking me from clearly expressing my feelings.

Plutonium Ability to conduct myself in such a way that I can use my fundamental power and energy to prevent any unnecessary conflict.

Plywood Ability to build up different layers of knowledge so I can use my practical abilities to produce a straightforward outcome.

Pneumatic drill Ability to use the concentrated power of my ideas to go deeper into the practicalities so I can break up any potential obstacles.

Pneumonia Essential opportunity to be clear about my sources of inspiration so I can resolve a potentially unhealthy situation.

Poached egg Potential to fulfill an ambition by breaking into a fertile new area so I can use my creativity to make something of it.

Poacher Aspect of my character that needs to recognize the value of my creative instincts rather than always trying to conceal them.

Pocket Ability to feel more secure about my personal capacity to provide the resources I need to comfortably achieve my ambitions.

Pocketbook Ability to open up to the wealth of my accumulated knowledge and experience so I can share their value with other people.

Pocketknife Ability to assert my individuality by decisively cutting through any uncertainty so I can display my individual expertise.

Pocket money Ability to declare my confidence in my unique abilities so I can ensure my individual value is genuinely acknowledged.

Pod Ability to shape an outcome by carefully containing my ambitions until the time is ripe for me to share them with other people.

Podcast Opportunity to share my thoughts and feelings with a wider audience rather than feeling I am just talking to myself.

Podium Situation where I can raise awareness about my levels of achievement so I can encourage other people to support me.

Poem Ability to express myself powerfully and evocatively so other people can feel a much deeper connection with my story.

Poet Aspect of my character that can really evoke my deeper feelings, even though it can sometimes seem to be without rhyme or reason.

Poetry Ability to use my unique creativity to express exactly how I feel rather than always trying to be completely matter-of-fact.

Poetry slam Opportunity to say what I feel about what is happening right now instead of feeling I should always listen to other people.

Pogo stick Ability to use the strength of my practical skills to move forward rather than feeling I'm using my energy just to stand still.

Point Ability to be specific in how I express my needs so other people will be able to support my particular opinion.

Point-blank Opportunity to increase my chances of success by refusing to be put off by other people ignoring my immediate objectives.

Pointing Opportunity to demonstrate my chosen direction so I can use my power and strength to achieve my preferred outcome.

Pointing device Ability to attract attention to my specific way of thinking so I can have my plans and ideas acknowledged by other people.

Poison Ability to choose how I react to any unwelcome feelings rather than opening myself up to a potentially unhealthy situation.

Poison gas Ability to resolve an unhealthy situation by openly and honestly expressing my thoughts so that I can quickly clear the air.

Poison ivy Natural ability to take my time and develop a healthy perspective instead of just creeping around and making rash decisions.

Poke Opportunity to make myself more open to different points of view rather than always trying to get my individual point across.

Poker Ability to get to the heart of a creative transformation so I can keep it moving to maintain the most valuable output.

Poker face Essential opportunity to show my true feelings instead of trying to conceal them when I feel the emotional stakes are high.

Poker game Opportunity to choose my preferred outcome by understanding what is often left unspoken so I can successfully deal with it.

Polar bear Instinctive ability to use my wisdom to stay cool when dealing with a challenge so I can powerfully protect my loved ones.

Polar explorer Aspect of my character that keeps a cool head so I can have a warm feeling about venturing into unknown, unfamiliar areas.

Polar ice cap Situation where I can use my warmth and vitality to keep things moving without feeling I must go to the ends of the earth.

Pole Ability to clearly draw attention to a point that needs to be recognized at some

higher level without going crazy about it.

Polecat Instinctive ability to achieve greater independence by using my talents rather than ferreting around for other opportunities.

Pole dancing Opportunity to open up to other people so I can attract attention to how I can use my expertise at a higher level.

Pole position Opportunity to use my drive and ambition to position myself for future success rather than feeling I have to work flat-out.

Pole-vaulter Aspect of my character that can become a high achiever by taking a more direct approach so I can raise my game.

Police Opportunity to take full responsibility for my individual actions so I can continue to maintain myself in good order.

Police car Ability to give myself permission to pursue my personal ambitions so I can make rapid progress toward my objective.

Police dog Instinctive ability to show my unconditional commitment to achieving a result by pursuing it in a persistently determined manner.

Policeman Aspect of my character that gives me the permission to fully assert the power of my talents and the strength of my ambitions.

Police station Situation where I can take a more disciplined approach to dealing with my commitments without feeling restrained.

Police uniform Ability to present my self-image to people in a way that permits me to use my power in an authoritative manner.

Policewoman Aspect of my character that has the authority to display the power of my creativity and permits me to use my deeper wisdom.

Policy Ability to respond spontaneously to an emerging opportunity rather than feeling that I always have to follow an agreed procedure.

Polio Essential opportunity to resolve any unhealthy tensions by showing my passion for them instead of feeling crippled by indecision.

Polish Ability to attract the interest of people by continually refining my talents and ensuring that my efforts continue to shine.

Polite Realization that the most powerful way to shape an outcome is to be gracious rather than experiencing a rude awakening.

Political prisoner Aspect of my character that needs to take responsibility for my opinions instead of feeling trapped by self-limiting beliefs.

Political rally Opportunity to bring all the aspects of my beliefs together so I can concentrate my efforts on a particular outcome.

Political refugee Aspect of my character that has the courage to stand up for my beliefs rather than running away from any disagreements.

Politician Aspect of my character that has the power to make a choice and act on it but often tries to gain favor by being more diplomatic.

Pollen Natural ability to spread some of my fertile ideas more widely so they have the opportunity to blossom in other areas.

Pollen count Opportunity to make the most of my blossoming creativity rather than allowing myself to be irritated by the prevailing mood.

Polling booth Situation where I can decide how I would like to proceed by considering a number of options that will enable me to make my mark.

Polling station Situation where I can make a commitment to my future by exploring a number of choices to help me put my plans into practice.

Pollution Realization that I can take a much healthier approach that will help me think more clearly rather than wasting my effort.

Polo Opportunity to harness my unconscious

energies so I can play around with different ways of achieving my eventual goals.

Polonium Ability to conduct myself in such a way that I can use my fundamental power to prevent a potentially unhealthy situation.

Polyester Ability to provide a substantial basis for my thoughts and feelings, even though it may initially appear to be quite artificial.

Polygamy Opportunity to make a more balanced commitment to a variety of my basic needs, although it may require a number of compromises.

Polygon Ability to shape my circumstances so I can see the various sides presented by each point of view and understand all the angles.

Polygraph Ability to understand what is going on by paying attention to my unspoken feelings rather than just feeling guilty.

Polystyrene Ability to let a complex variety of ideas bubble up to the surface so I can mold them into an outcome of practical value.

Polythene Ability to clearly see what is happening at a deeper level for me rather than getting too wrapped up in superficialities.

Pomegranate Natural ability to have a healthier awareness of how I can transform a relationship so I can achieve a really fruitful outcome.

Pomp Realization that I can display my skills and experience in a very practical manner rather than continually parading them.

Pompous Realization that I need to be more open about sharing my unique talents instead of worrying that I will appear too egotistical.

Pond Situation where I can take a more relaxed approach as I reflect on my accumulated experiences in a familiar social setting.

Ponderous Realization that I can release myself from some weighty obligations rather than having to continuously think about them.

P

Pontoon bridge Situation where I can resolve an emotional dilemma by quickly creating a connection between two areas of my life.

Pony Instinctive ability to harness my unconscious energy so I can use it to carry me through some familiar situations.

Ponytail Essential opportunity to bring together some ideas so I can use them to display the style of thinking that shapes my plans.

Poodle Instinctive ability to be honest and open with other people rather than feeling I always have to pander to their whims.

Pool Situation where I can reflect on my accumulated learning and experience so I have the opportunity to go deeper into my emotions.

Pool table Situation where I can decide to deal with any uncertainties by working out all the angles so I can give it my best shot.

Pooper scooper Ability to deal with loyalties and affections that were once vital for me but are now no longer of any real value to me.

Poor Realization that I have a great wealth of accumulated talent and experience rather than feeling that I have little to offer.

Poorly Opportunity to openly deal with the source of my inner tensions so I can have a much healthier appreciation of my needs.

Pop Opportunity to suddenly let go of any tension so I can draw attention to my work and have it appreciated by a wider audience.

Popcorn Potential to fulfill an ambition by acknowledging the achievements of people rather than getting too puffed up about their methods.

Poplar tree Natural potential for rapid spiritual development while having the presence to remain rooted in everyday practicalities.

Poppy Natural ability to let my talents blossom by remembering the courageous aspects of myself I can sometimes forget.

Popsicle Potential to fulfill a seemingly attractive short-term ambition, even though I have to move quickly to make the most of it.

Pop star Aspect of my character that enjoys publicly displaying my powerful talents so they can be appreciated by a wider audience.

Popular Realization that I am often happiest looking after my own needs rather than always looking to other people for their approval.

Populated area Situation where I can fully explore the wider range of my own talents and give myself the space to concentrate on them more.

Porcelain Ability to conceal any fragile emotions that I may be feeling by presenting an apparently impenetrable exterior to others.

Porch Aspect of myself where I can openly enjoy time and space to consider the connections between my inner and outer lives.

Porcupine Instinctive ability to clearly make a number of points rather than being habitually defensive and responding in a prickly manner.

Pore Essential ability to open up about my feelings by being comfortable with the boundary between my inner and outer worlds.

Pork Potential to fulfill an ambition by using my raw strength and power to get stuck into a potentially messy situation.

Pornography Realization that my creativity is most powerful when I engage with it rather than trying to observe it from a distance.

Porpoise Instinctive ability to immerse myself in my feelings and use my deeper emotional awareness in an intelligent and purposeful way.

Porridge Potential to fulfill an ambition by freely giving myself a variety of options rather than seeing what my choices may boil down to.

Port Situation where I can connect with some wider learning and experience and access the resources I need to fulfill my ambitions.

Portable building Situation where I can temporarily feel comfortable as I explore some of the unknown, unfamiliar aspects of my character.

Portable crib Ability to convey my excitement about a personal labor of love so I can share how I have been developing it for the future.

Portable toilet Situation where I can conveniently attend to my personal needs, even though they may only seem to be quite temporary in nature.

Portage Opportunity to make a sustained practical effort so I can continue to make progress with my emotional explorations.

Portcullis Ability to defend my beliefs against any criticism so I can decide what other perspectives I am willing to accommodate.

Porter Aspect of my character that can successfully carry out my intentions by not burdening myself with too many responsibilities.

Portfolio Ability to convey how I see a situation so I can clearly communicate the breadth of my knowledge and experience.

Porthole Ability to clearly understand my individual perspective so I can see how to navigate an emotionally complex situation.

Portion Ability to take a more measured approach to how I can fulfill my ambitions by understanding the size of my overall contribution.

Portrait Ability to reflect on my unique characteristics so I can draw my own conclusions about how they shape my identity.

Pose Opportunity to adopt a particular stance that genuinely supports my beliefs rather than just posturing to impress people.

Position Situation where I can spend some time reviewing my progress so far so I can understand the best way to move into the future.

Positive Realization that I can affirm my talents by taking definite steps to share them rather than being uncertain about their value.

Posse Aspects of my character that can work together to help me pursue an ambition if I give myself the permission to use them.

Possessed Realization that I need to own my habits and behaviors rather than becoming obsessed by how other people may be controlling me.

Possessions Ability to maintain my composure so I can really own my habits and behaviors as I objectively decide my chosen outcome.

Possibility Opportunity to take a chance so I can explore some of the options for making my ambitions actually happen in reality.

Possum Instinctive ability to control my actions so I can shape my future rather than pretending to have no interest in moving forward.

Post Opportunity to confidently communicate an important message that may have taken some time for me to become fully aware of.

Postage stamp Ability to convey the value of what I have to say by communicating in a measured way so I can stick to my message.

Postcard Ability to communicate a brief but important message about future possibilities, even though they may seem quite distant.

Poster Ability to draw attention to my needs by having the confidence to openly communicate my feelings to those around me.

Postman Aspect of my character that helps me to deliver the promises I make by being able to communicate how I really feel.

P

Postmortem Opportunity to revitalize one of my neglected ambitions rather than just picking it apart to understand why I abandoned it.

Post office Situation where I can communicate the value of my talents to a much wider audience by addressing frustrations I may have.

Posture Essential ability that enables me to show people my levels of confidence in my unique talents and how they can support me.

Post-traumatic stress Opportunity to let go of an unhealthy situation that has upset me in the past so I can confidently step into a new future.

Pot Ability to fulfill a potential ambition by gathering some of my knowledge and experience so I can create something fresh.

Potato Potential to fulfill my ambition and sustain my progress by using my natural abilities in a practical and healthy manner.

Potent Realization that I am far stronger and more powerful than I think and not weak and ineffective.

Pot plant Natural ability to use an illuminating opportunity as a way of absorbing new ideas so I can create a fresh perspective.

Potpourri Ability to remind myself of a special experience by collecting colorful ideas so I can create an attractive atmosphere.

Potshot Opportunity to decisively assert my power and influence in a forceful manner rather than being vague and misleading in my aims.

Potter Aspect of my character that is receptive to how I feel about a situation so I can use my skills to actively shape the outcome.

Pottery Situation where I can use my instinctive creativity and practical skills to form some plans that people will be receptive to.

Potty Situation where I can attend to my personal needs by choosing to let go of childish behaviors that may be driving me crazy.

Potty trained Essential opportunity to use my self-discipline so I can make a continuing commitment to looking after my individual needs.

Pouch Ability to look after personal expertise I will always want to retain while still being open to learning new methods.

Poultry Instinctive ability to consistently provide fertile ideas so I can use them to fulfill a variety of potential ambitions.

Pounce Opportunity to suddenly grasp a potentially fulfilling aspect of my deeper self so I can make a powerful connection with it.

Pound Opportunity to take decisive action so I can use the weight of my experience to make a real impact and demonstrate my value.

Pouring Opportunity to channel my emotions by controlling how I share them with others rather than being too self-contained.

Pouting Opportunity to confidently express some of my more intimate feelings instead of trying to appear displeased or ungrateful.

Poverty Realization that I have an abundance of accumulated expertise and experience rather than feeling I am a poor performer.

Powder Ability to make some dry subject matter come to life by carefully adding my specific learning and experience to the mix.

Power Natural capacity to fulfill my needs and understand my greater purpose by using my energy to keep myself fully motivated.

Power breakfast Opportunity to wake up to a new way of feeding my appetite for success by continuing to develop my vital purpose in life.

Power lines Ability to convey my capacity to generate new opportunities so I can use it to meet the needs of others in the future.

Power nap Opportunity to take a more relaxed approach to understanding the deeper purpose of some of my future ambitions and aspirations.

Power outage Opportunity to become more aware of my own inner power and strength rather than having to rely on external sources.

Power shower Situation where I can come clean about an emotional situation and clarify my purpose by clearly showing how I feel about it.

Power station Situation where I can use my raw talent to generate a variety of opportunities that will help me convey my purpose to people.

Powwow Opportunity to become more acquainted with any conflicting aspects of my character so I can peacefully resolve any tensions.

Pox Opportunity to resolve an unhealthy situation by making a series of breakthroughs in how I can stay in touch with my feelings.

Practical Realization that I can decide whether making a particular effort is worthwhile rather than listening to some unrealistic advice.

Practice Ability to accumulate valuable expertise, by displaying my skills instead of feeling I'm constantly repeating myself.

Prairie Situation where I can open up to the vast scale of what I can develop from my fertile and productive imagination.

Praise Opportunity to take great pride in my unique talents and skills rather than looking to other people for recognition and approval.

Pram Ability to convey a concept that I feel very strongly about so I can take a series of steps to keep pushing it forward.

Prank Opportunity to create a valuable outcome by using my intelligence rather than feeling that other people will think I'm stupid.

Prankster Aspect of my character that is keen to display my deeper talents instead of showing off with some tricks of the trade.

Prawn Potential to fulfill an ambition by

making the most of my abilities, even though they may seem small and insignificant to people.

Prayer Ability to communicate my fundamental belief in myself so I can express my spiritual connection to a more universal truth.

Praying Opportunity to trust in my own wisdom and experience rather than giving responsibility to outside beliefs that seem beyond me.

Praying mantis Instinctive ability to devour small pieces of knowledge and information so I can use them to support my basic beliefs.

Preacher Aspect of my character that can openly and honestly show my beliefs rather than trying to change how other people think.

Precious Realization that my talents and experience are uniquely valuable instead of lacking confidence and just appearing too fussy.

Precipice Situation where I am on the edge of a sudden and potentially major transformation that will require me to take immediate action.

Precise Realization that I need to be extremely clear about my broader intentions rather than appearing to be too exacting.

Precision tool Ability to use my specific talents to shape my circumstances so I can take direct action to create my chosen outcome.

Precognitive Essential opportunity to become more aware of how my inner life can sometimes appear to actually emerge into practical reality.

Predator Instinctive ability to pursue a potentially fulfilling aspect of my deeper self so I can connect with it more powerfully.

Predicament Opportunity to resolve an apparently impossible situation by using my wider awareness to make a more fundamental connection.

P

Prediction Opportunity to openly state my intentions so I can make a conscious decision about what is going to happen.

Predictive text Ability to express my unique thoughts and ideas rather than feeling that others are trying to put words in my mouth.

Preemptive strike Opportunity to robustly defend my position by taking immediate action to forcefully demonstrate the strength of my beliefs.

Preening Opportunity to straighten out my thoughts and theories rather than continually being concerned about how I appear to others.

Prefect Aspect of my character that provides me with the authority to explore my unique talents so I can develop my expertise.

Preference Opportunity to openly express my choice by honestly sharing my feelings rather than feeling that my options are limited.

Preflight check Opportunity to deal with a number of practical concerns before launching into a wider exploration of my plans and theories.

Pregnant Essential opportunity to develop a concept that is precious to me so I can create a uniquely wonderful outcome.

Prehistoric Opportunity to fully connect with my ancient power so I can understand how it informs my most basic urges and drives.

Prejudice Realization that I can achieve my ambitions more easily by understanding the context rather than holding any preconceptions.

Preliminary exam Opportunity to thoroughly prepare myself for success instead of feeling I have something to prove to everyone else.

Premature Realization that I need to pay more attention to what is emerging in the present rather than focusing on an idealized future.

Premium Realization that I need to embrace my exceptional qualities rather than feeling that always being original comes at a price.

Premenstrual tension Opportunity to resolve any stresses I experience when using my passion and vitality to work with some fertile ideas.

Premolar Essential ability to work my way through some larger aspects of a potential ambition before chewing it over in finer detail.

Prenuptial agreement Ability to openly express the value of my talents before I make a deeper commitment that may require a number of compromises.

Prepared Opportunity to always ready myself for success so I can take full advantage of any possibilities that may emerge for me.

Prescription Ability to resolve an unhealthy situation by using my ingenuity instead of hoping someone else will make me feel better.

Presence Realization that I can reveal myself as the person I want to be now rather than being occupied by more distant concerns.

Present Opportunity to open up to my creative gifts and talents so I can use them immediately by sharing them with other people.

Presentation Opportunity to get my message across by speaking honestly rather than being too concerned about how I appear to people.

Preservative Ability to maintain my sense of purpose by keeping my ambitions alive rather than neglecting them until they fade away.

Preserve Opportunity to continually develop my specific area of expertise instead of feeling that I always need to maintain my status.

President Aspect of my character that permits me to step into a greater sense of my own power so I can ultimately make my own decisions.

Press Ability to clearly get my message across by using a steady and forceful manner rather than letting any concerns weigh on me.

Press conference Situation where I can listen to different aspects of my character so I can understand what is going on for me right now.

Press release Opportunity to let go of any of my inhibitions so I can open up to a wider audience and share what I am feeling.

Pressure Realization that I can achieve an outcome by exerting a persistent force rather than trying to meet people's expectations.

Pressure cooker Ability to satisfy my hunger for results by responding rapidly instead of always getting too worked up about the situation.

Pressure suit Ability to present my self-image to people in a way that shows my capacity to thrive, even if the mood is particularly hostile.

Pressure vessel Ability to contain some of my more volatile emotions so I can transform my situation rather than overreact to it.

Pressure washer Ability to open up about my feelings by powerfully channeling my emotions so I can come clean and take a fresh approach.

Prestigious Realization that I need to celebrate my talents instead of feeling I have to live up to the expectations of others.

Pretending Opportunity to understand what I believe, even though it may turn out to be quite different from my initial impressions.

Pretense Realization that I can achieve much more by being open and honest rather than trying to deceive myself about my feelings.

Pretentious Realization that I am being too modest about openly displaying my expertise and need to have greater self-belief in my abilities.

Pretty Realization that I can attract other people by using my talents instead of doing something I may find much less appealing.

Pretzel Potential to fulfill an ambition by using my good taste to stay grounded rather than appearing to get myself tied in a knot.

Preventative Realization that I can resolve an unhealthy situation by instigating vital action instead of just waiting for it to be fixed.

Preview Opportunity to explore some of my beliefs so I can understand them more fully before I take a definite viewpoint with them.

Previous house Situation where I can rediscover some fundamental qualities so I can create the space to develop their true potential.

Previous offense Opportunity to take responsibility for my actions so I can let go of assumptions I may be holding about others.

Prey Instinctive ability to powerfully connect with a potentially fulfilling aspect of my deeper self instead of feeling fearful of it.

Price Ability to publicly declare the value of my unique talents so they can be acknowledged and accepted by other people.

Price tag Ability to confidently make my mark so other people can acknowledge my abilities and understand the value of my skills.

Prick Opportunity to quickly get beyond superficial appearances so I can adjust my previous expectations to the actual reality.

Pride Realization that I can swell my opportunities by honestly showing my confidence in my abilities and displaying them openly.

Priest Aspect of my character that provides me with the spiritual authority to connect with a wider understanding of my situation.

Priestess Aspect of my character that intuitively connects me with my deeper level of wisdom so I can share my creative power.

Prim Realization that I need to communicate exactly what I need rather than continually fussing around with all the available options.

Prima donna Aspect of my character that can attract unconditional support and affection by having a greater awareness of how I appear.

P

Primal Realization that I have the inner vitality to achieve my deepest aspirations rather than waiting for my life to begin.

Primary Realization that I have the power to choose my priorities instead of feeling that my needs are secondary to everyone else's.

Primary school Situation where I can learn fundamental lessons about life and put them into practice by demonstrating them to others.

Primate Instinctive ability to understand my natural creativity by grasping opportunities and then successfully directing the outcome.

Prime Realization that placing more importance on developing my talents makes it much more likely that they will successfully flourish.

Prime minister Aspect of my character that embodies my power for confident and decisive change so I can make a significant transformation.

Primer Ability to carefully prepare the ground so I can colorfully express my instinctive feelings about a particular situation.

Primeval Realization that I often create my most original work when I take the opportunity to reconnect with my fundamental instincts.

Primitive Aspect of my character that understands my fundamental purpose in life, even though I may not have fully developed it yet.

Primrose Natural ability to open up to my creative talents so I can be encouragingly optimistic while staying grounded in reality.

Prince Aspect of my character that provides the opportunity for my emerging power and strength to be more widely acknowledged.

Princess Aspect of my character that gives me the opportunity to develop my creativity and wisdom and have them more widely recognized.

Principle Realization that I have a funda-

mental set of beliefs I use to guide my actions, even though I am often unaware of them.

Printed Realization that I need to clearly communicate what I want to say so I can consistently make my mark on a more permanent basis.

Printer Ability to clearly spell out what I am trying to communicate to other people so we can all share the same perspective.

Priorities Realization that I need to fully commit my efforts to achieving my ambitions instead of trying to work in a different way.

Prism Ability to perceive a situation by with much greater clarity by understanding how my various moods can color its outcome.

Prison Situation where I can give myself permission to escape from the self-limiting beliefs that can often leave me feeling trapped.

Prison camp Situation where I can go beyond my perceived self-limitations and explore some of the unfamiliar aspects of my character.

Prison cell Situation where I can step into a much wider freedom by having the courage to break out of any beliefs that may be limiting me.

Prisoner Aspect of my character that needs to take responsibility for my freedom instead of feeling trapped by self-limiting beliefs.

Prisoner of war Aspect of my character that needs to take responsibility for my freedom instead of feeling trapped by an ongoing inner conflict.

Prison officer Aspect of my character that gives me the permission to freely go beyond the boundaries and limitations I impose on myself.

Prison warden Aspect of my character that takes responsibility for looking after my sense of freedom and the opportunities it provides.

Private Situation where I can attend to my

individual needs by having the confidence to establish some firm personal boundaries.

Private investigator Aspect of my character that examines my habitual behaviors and observes my self-motivation so I can continue to progress.

Private land Situation where I can take a practical, down-to-earth approach to defining my personal boundaries so I can attend to my needs.

Privet Natural potential for my more immediate spiritual growth by creating a relaxing, more private space for my development.

Prize Ability to use my unique talents in a potentially rewarding situation so I can ensure they are acknowledged by other people.

Probation Opportunity to trust in my own talents and abilities rather than constantly trying to check up on my performance.

Probation officer Aspect of my character that ensures I can put my learning and experience to good use instead of feeling limited by my past.

Probe Ability to take a more direct approach so I can investigate what is actually happening and explore the available options.

Problem Ability to resolve a challenge by using my natural skills and abilities rather allowing it to become an obstacle to my progress.

Problem child Aspect of my character that embodies a uniquely valuable lesson and holds great potential for developing my understanding.

Procedure Opportunity to achieve my preferred outcome by deciding the actions that I am going to take and committing to them.

Process Opportunity to observe myself as I work my way through a situation so I can resolve challenges I am uncomfortable with.

Processing plant Situation where I can

produce a valuable outcome by taking the time to consistently work my way through my raw emotions.

Procession Opportunity to put my skills on display so I can constantly develop them and steadily drive forward with my ambitions.

Proctologist Aspect of my character that rationally examines my behaviors so I can take more decisive control of fundamental needs.

Prod Opportunity to move into action at a point of my own choice rather than feeling other people are trying to push me along.

Prodigal Realization that I have an abundance of natural talent instead of being concerned about trying to use my skills more prudently.

Produce Opportunity to bring some of my plans and ideas into existence so I can demonstrate the value of what I can contribute.

Production line Situation where I can align skills and resources to reach my preferred outcome rather than going through the motions.

Professional authority Aspect of my character that has great confidence in my practical abilities and gives me permission to share them with people.

Professional football player Aspect of my character that can use my expertise to build up some professional connections so I can achieve my goals.

Professor Aspect of my character that has a deep, fundamental understanding rather than just declaring myself to be an expert.

Proficiency badge Ability to display my achievements to other people so they can formally acknowledge my level of skill and dedication.

Profile Ability to outline what I need by being able to see both sides of a situation and what they actually represent to me.

P

Profiterole Potential to fulfill an ambition by choosing the easiest, most luxurious way to quickly indulge my need for immediate success.

Profound Realization that I have a great depth of understanding about a situation rather than feeling my knowledge is just superficial.

Program Ability to make a clear plan of action that has a specific outcome so I can display my expertise to a wider audience.

Progress Opportunity to keep advancing my ambitions by being open to new learning and experiences rather than living in the past.

Prohibited Opportunity to give myself complete permission to explore unfamiliar aspects of my character instead of always holding back.

Project Ability to transport myself into the future by carefully planning what I am going to achieve and identifying the resources I need.

Projectile Ability to achieve the ambition I am aiming for by taking a single decisive action rather than throwing my chances away.

Projector Ability to share an illuminating story with others so I can draw attention to my achievements and let my talents shine.

Prolong Opportunity to take my time so I can understand what is happening instead of going on about it at length.

Promenade Opportunity to proudly display my self-motivation and energy so I can comfortably take the steps I need to succeed.

Prominence Ability to raise my profile and attract attention to what I have achieved by proudly sticking up for what I really believe in.

Promiscuous Realization that I can achieve a much profounder level of creativity by being selective about what I involve myself in.

Promise Realization that I can deliver the full potential of my talents instead of letting myself down by losing my confidence.

Promontory Situation where I can feel secure about where I stand as I make my way forward into an emotionally complex situation.

Promotion Opportunity to become more aware of my emerging talents so I can use them to progress in my ambitions.

Prone Essential opportunity to stay close to the practical considerations while keeping myself open to any unexpected outcomes.

Prong Ability to get stuck in a challenge so that I can shape the outcome rather than feeling that I am missing the point.

Proof Realization that I have all the evidence I need to understand my beliefs and can simply shrug off any criticism from other people.

Prop Ability to support my ambitions by standing up for my beliefs instead of feeling that other people are always holding me up.

Propaganda Ability to clearly communicate my wider intentions in an open and honest way rather than allowing others to mislead me.

Propeller Ability to use the general thrust of my ideas and feelings to powerfully drive me forward instead of just going round and round.

Proper Realization that I can take the appropriate action by listening to my emotions rather than always trying to please other people.

Property Ability to own my habits and behaviors instead of becoming too self-possessed about my aspirations and ambitions.

Property developer Aspect of myself that helps me to become involved in character-building activity so I can develop my unrealized potential.

Prophet Aspect of my character that helps me voice my intentions for the future by openly expressing my wider spiritual awareness.

Proportion Realization that I need to keep a situation in perspective so I can take a more measured approach to fulfilling my ambitions.

Proposal Opportunity to make a deeper connection by understanding my needs and how they can influence the needs of others.

Prosecution Opportunity to take committed action so I can follow a particular plan all the way through to a successful conclusion.

Prospect Opportunity to achieve a valuable outcome by digging a bit deeper rather than anticipating an effortless success.

Prostate Essential ability to use my emotional drive so I can assert my feelings and make the most of a fertile opportunity.

Prosthesis Ability to openly and honestly show how I miss being involved rather than behaving in a way that appears artificial to me.

Prostitute Aspect of my character that can become more intimately aware of my unique creative talents rather than cheapening them.

Prostrate Realization that I need to be much more down-to-earth about the practical aspects of a situation so I can study it at length.

Protection Opportunity to be open to new possibilities while safely maintaining personal boundaries so I can ensure healthy relationships.

Protégé Aspect of my character that looks after my welfare so I can develop my talents in a more relaxed and secure manner.

Protein Ability to assemble the fundamental building blocks that will give me the strength and power to fulfill much bigger ambitions.

Protest Opportunity to actively express how I feel about a situation rather than just thinking that I should passively accept the outcome.

Proud Realization that I can make myself stand out by openly showing my confidence in my personal expertise more prominently.

Prove Opportunity to emphatically confirm my skills and abilities by reflecting on the successful results I have achieved.

Providence Realization that I can provide myself with all the encouragement I need rather than waiting for assistance from others.

Provocation Opportunity to take positive action so I can achieve a successful outcome instead of feeling that people are goading me.

Prowler Aspect of my character that has an instinctive understanding of my needs, although it can often seem quite threatening to me.

Prozac Ability to take some individual action to raise my aspirations rather than always relying on other people to make me happy.

Prude Aspect of my character that openly delights in displaying my creative expertise instead of trying to modestly conceal it.

Prudent Realization that I have the experience to take care of myself rather than always feeling that no one really cares about me.

Prudish Realization that I instinctively understand the proper way to act rather than having to conform to other people's procedures.

Prune Opportunity to healthily fulfill one of my ambitions by making a decisive choice to cut out habits that no longer serve me.

Psychiatrist Aspect of my character that seeks to bring some order to the way I think, even though it may influence my creativity.

Psychic Aspect of my character that has the ability to shape an outcome by making a specific choice rather than leaving it to fate.

Psychological Realization that I can achieve my deepest ambitions and highest aspirations by becoming more aware of habitual patterns.

P

Psychologist Aspect of my character that instinctively observes my behaviors so I can achieve a deeper understanding of who I am.

Psychopath Aspect of my character that has the power to connect my expertise to my ambitions rather than trying to eliminate them.

Ptarmigan Instinctive ability to rise above more practical concerns and spread my ideas, even though conditions may be quite arduous.

Pterodactyl Instinctive ability to use my primal power so I can transform any threatening emotions into strong thoughts and plans.

Pub Situation where I can comfortably fulfill my emotional needs by taking a relaxed viewpoint as I reacquaint myself with my talents.

Pubic hair Essential ability to develop ideas that emerge from my fundamental creativity so I can use them to shape my concepts.

Public Realization that I can achieve more success in the wider community by taking time to explore the private aspects of my inner life.

Public embarrassment Opportunity to show other people how proud I am of my achievements rather than always feeling self-conscious about them.

Public holiday Opportunity to make some time for myself so I can work on a private issue that has great personal significance for me.

Public lavatory Situation where I can open up about my inner feelings without feeling ashamed about expressing them to others.

Public official Aspect of my character that gives me permission to act on my behalf instead of following the demands of others.

Public performance Opportunity for me to fully recognize and accept my own talents rather than looking to others for approval.

Public toilet Situation where I can attend to my personal needs instead of feeling I always have to look after the needs of other people.

Puck Ability to happily shape my circumstances by using my layers of knowledge to play around with a potentially successful outcome.

Pudding Potential to fulfill a short-term ambition that seems very attractive so I can pay more attention to a long-term accomplishment.

Puddle Situation where I can splash out by using a specific personal experience to help me reflect on my accumulated learning.

Puff Opportunity to take more pride in one of my ideas, even though it may seem quite insubstantial and inconsequential to others.

Puffin Instinctive ability to rise above any practical concerns so I can immerse myself in my emotions and express them very colorfully.

Pull Opportunity to be drawn toward the powerful aspects of my nature so I can understand what makes me attractive to people.

Pulley Ability to easily lift my mood by using my ingenuity to release myself from a weighty obligation that has been holding me back.

Pulling Opportunity to understand what is attracting me toward a particular choice so I can direct my efforts to making it happen.

Pullover Ability to present my self-image to people in a way that can quickly make me feel comfortable and relaxed about my situation.

Pulp Ability to blend my practical skills and emotional experiences so I can use them to shape an outcome in a different way.

Pulpit Situation where I can share my viewpoint with others as a way of raising awareness of the fundamental power of my story.

Pulse Essential ability to put my finger

on what makes the situation tick by understanding what is happening below the surface.

Puma Instinctive ability to confidently assert my independence and freedom in an effortless way that naturally attracts people to me.

Pump Ability to consistently channel my thoughts and feelings so I can deliver what is needed in a high-pressure situation.

Pumpkin Potential to fulfill an ambition by using my ingenuity to dig a bit deeper so I can illuminate what is really happening.

Pun Ability to clearly communicate my intentions rather than causing any ambiguity, even though it may initially appear amusing.

Punch Opportunity to forcefully assert my power and influence by taking decisive action to shape a definite outcome for myself.

Punching bag Ability to easily absorb any challenges from other people rather than feeling that I am the target of their frustration.

Puncture Opportunity to keep progressing an ambition, even though I may need to get more pumped up and keep the pressure on myself.

Punished Opportunity to take pleasure in making my own choices instead of constantly doubting my ability to reach a happy outcome.

Punishment Ability to give myself the permission to do something I will enjoy rather than always giving myself a hard time.

Punt Ability to navigate complex, unpredictable feelings by giving myself the chance to use my powerful instincts and experiences.

Puppet Ability to see how other people might be trying to manipulate my actions rather than always allowing them to pull my strings.

Puppeteer Aspect of my character that can control the outcome of a story by staying connected to what is happening for me.

Puppy Instinctive ability to playfully realize my potential for unconditional love and affection so I can develop my relationships.

Purchase Opportunity to get a grip on what is happening so I can use my valuable skills to acquire some practical experience.

Pure Realization that I can experience my true self by taking authentic action rather than worrying about any apparent imperfections.

Purge Opportunity to eliminate any of my behaviors that are no longer useful rather than bringing up my concerns all the time.

Purple Mood that can color my perspective by reflecting how I can use my wisdom and power in a gracious and considered manner.

Purpose Realization that the most powerful way to fulfill my needs is to create unique value by using my special talents.

Purse Ability to feel more secure in my identity by carefully developing my self-worth and staying close to my ambitions.

Pursued by animal Opportunity to take more control of instinctive impulses so I can use their power to naturally create exceptional results.

Pursued by authorities Opportunity to assert one of my talents by taking full responsibility for it rather than trying to avoid any commitment.

Pursued by boat Opportunity to positively influence my deeper emotions instead of feeling my current situation is beyond control.

Pursued by car Opportunity to take control of my drive and ambition rather than feeling I am being forced to behave in a certain way.

Pursued by children Opportunity to spend more time developing one of my talents instead of playing around with some ideas I have.

Pursued by gang Opportunity to develop my talents by asserting my individuality rather than giving in to the demands of other people.

P

Pursued by killer Opportunity to revitalize one of my neglected talents so I can use it to create a profound transformation in my life.

Pursued by lorry Opportunity to use my powerful drive to convey the value of my ambitions instead of feeling overwhelmed by the possibilities.

Pursued by men Opportunity to develop my strength and power so I can assert my talents and successfully realize ambitions.

Pursued by monster Opportunity to connect with one of my raw, powerful talents so I can refine it and make the most of a huge possibility.

Pursued by storm Opportunity to channel energy from my conflicting turmoil of emotions so I can use it to positively clear the air.

Pursued by tank Opportunity to be more open about my ambitions instead of consistently being defensive about what my intentions are.

Pursued by vampires Opportunity to assertively look after my vital needs rather than feeling that others are draining my energy.

Pursued by werewolves Opportunity to fundamentally transform my situation by powerfully asserting my fierce loyalty to the people closest to me.

Pursued by women Opportunity to develop my individual empathy and wisdom so I can passionately express my unique creativity.

Pursued by zombies Opportunity to revitalize a unique talent I have been neglecting so I can breathe some new life into my creative efforts.

Pursuit Opportunity to follow through with an emerging possibility so I can use it to achieve one of my long-held ambitions.

Pus Essential opportunity to resolve some unhealthy feelings by dealing with the deep-rooted anxieties that may be causing them.

Pushing Opportunity to keep moving forward so I can overcome a challenge, even though my efforts may be met with some resistance.

Push-start Opportunity to motivate myself by making a stronger effort, even though it may take a while to start making real progress.

Putrefaction Opportunity to revitalize my situation and achieve healthy growth by breaking down what I've learned and using it to grow.

Putrid Realization that I can use my enthusiasm to instil a new vitality into my work rather than feeling that it is just falling apart.

Putter Ability to take some decisive action to reach a specific objective rather than feeling that I am wandering along aimlessly.

Putty Ability to feel more secure in my viewpoint rather than allowing other people to shape my opinions too easily.

Puzzle Opportunity to solve one of the more mysterious aspects of my behavior by taking my time to intuitively work through it.

Pygmy Aspect of my character that can hold my head high by instinctively understanding how the small details make a big difference.

Pylon Ability to provide strong support for the particular message I want to convey so I can communicate it really powerfully.

Pyramid Ability to shape an outcome by making a strong, sustained effort to elevate my awareness so I can gain a wider perspective.

Pyre Situation where I can use my accumulated talent to let go of habitual patterns so I can heighten my developing creativity.

Pyromaniac Aspect of my character that can make considered creative choices rather than being overwhelmed by all-consuming passions.

Pyrotechnics Ability to use some flashes of inspiration to illuminate my creative skills so I can display my fundamental passions.

Python Instinctive ability to transform a potentially hurtful situation by letting go rather than getting too wrapped up in it.

P

Quack Opportunity to draw attention to some deeper ideas I am working with instead of dismissing them as being of no value.

Quadrangle Situation where I can take a practical and down-to-earth approach in sharing what I have learned with the people around me.

Quadriplegic Aspect of my character that has the self-motivation to reach out to any challenge so I can always stand up for myself.

Quadruplets Aspect of my character that embodies how I can healthily develop my fundamental characteristics in an even and consistent manner.

Quagmire Situation where I can really get stuck into some messy practicalities rather than allowing them to slow down my progress.

Quaich Ability to celebrate an emotional commitment by fully acknowledging a shared feeling instead of just letting it spill out.

Quail Instinctive ability to use my ideas in a practical, down-to-earth manner so I can to make a courageous choice.

Quail's eggs Natural ability to develop the wealth of my talents so I can break into fertile new areas instead of sitting on my potential.

Quaking Opportunity to prepare myself for action so I can move quickly and consistently instead of feeling a bit shaken up.

Qualifications Ability to have my accomplishments fully acknowledged by those around me so I can create more value with my expertise.

Quality Ability to become more aware of the personal characteristics that naturally enable me to consistently show my individual value.

Quality control Opportunity to make choices about how I employ my valuable talents rather than allowing others to decide for me.

Qualm Realization that I need to have more confidence in my expertise so I can trust myself to resolve any unfamiliar tensions.

Quandary Opportunity to take full advantage of an uncertain situation by understanding what I need to make me feel fulfilled.

Quantity Ability to recognize the value of my accumulated expertise and experience so I can always measure up to any challenges.

Quantum Ability to specifically understand the huge effect that some tiny details can have so I can use them to their fullest extent.

Quantum leap Opportunity to make the most of a new possibility by understanding the difference a seemingly insignificant detail can make.

Quarantine Opportunity to take precautions about a potentially upsetting feeling rather than relying on my infectious enthusiasm.

Quark Ability to piece together some valuable observations, even though they seem to make little sense in isolation from each other.

Quarrel Opportunity to resolve a tense situation by squaring up to the facts instead of feeling I just have to accept the situation.

Quarry Situation where I can pursue a more valuable prize by using my strength of character to dig down deep into my reserves.

Quarryman Aspect of my character that uses my strength and power to make hard decisions so I can make constructive developments.

Quarter Realization that I can achieve much wider fulfillment by wholeheartedly embracing whatever makes me feel the most contented.

Quarterback Aspect of my character that has the power to influence an uncertain outcome by taking the steps to courageously engage with it.

Quartermaster Aspect of my character that can use my experience and resourcefulness to support me so I can deal with inner conflicts.

Quartet Aspects of my character that can bring together a number of my acknowledged creative talents in a stable, structured manner.

Quartz Ability to tune in to what is happening so I can be crystal clear about a decision I need to make.

Quashed Opportunity to courageously stand up for what makes me truly unique rather than allowing other people to always put me down.

Quay Situation where I can safely embark on emotional explorations with the security of always being able to return to solid ground.

Quayside Situation where I can become more accustomed to emotional involvement by having the feeling I am always on a firm footing.

Queasy Opportunity to resolve unhealthy emotions by working my way through them rather than worrying and feeling ill at ease.

Queen Aspect of my character whose refinement is widely recognized by other people and has the maturity to use it graciously.

Queer Realization that my unusual approach has huge potential for success, even though it may seem quite unnatural to other people.

Quell Opportunity to transform any anxieties that I have about an uncertain situation instead of allowing them to overwhelm me.

Quench Opportunity to completely satisfy my need for emotional fulfillment so I can quickly take the heat out of a situation.

Quest Opportunity to transform a situation by asking myself questions about what I need and being open to exploring them further.

Question Opportunity to discover unknown potential by asking myself what I need so I can step into some new possibilities.

Questionnaire Ability to follow an agreed process so I can take a series of decisive steps that can change the situation for me.

Queue Opportunity to observe my levels of motivation and take decisive action when the moment comes rather than standing around.

Quiche Potential to fulfill an ambition by understanding what my various responsibilities are so I can share them with other people.

Quick Realization that I can take a more measured approach to achieving my chosen outcome instead of responding immediately.

Quicksand Situation where I can stay calm and extricate myself from a messy situation so I can get myself onto a much firmer footing.

Quiet Opportunity to hear what I need to say so I can clearly express my feelings without their becoming lost in the noise.

Quill Ability to seemingly pluck an idea out of thin air so I can use it to convey a message that allows me to make my mark.

Quilt Ability to feel relaxed and comfortable by covering my vulnerabilities and surrounding myself with a sense of loving warmth.

Quinine Ability to remedy an unhealthy situation that may be cramping my style rather than continuing to feel hot and bothered about it.

Q

Quinquereme Ability to use layers of learning and experience to keep myself fully motivated as I navigate a complex emotional situation.

Quintessence Ability to concentrate on the most significant aspect of a situation to understand the value of my fundamental character.

Quintuplets Aspects of my character that embody how I can healthily develop my fundamental possibilities in a variety of ways.

Quip Opportunity to draw attention to a much deeper connection rather than trying to appear clever to the people around me.

Quirky Realization of the unique value of one of my individual characteristics instead of worrying that it may just appear eccentric.

Quiver Ability to shake off any feelings of indecision by understanding what my aims

are so I can get straight to the point.

Quiz Opportunity to ask myself what I want in life so I can question whether I am permitting myself to make the right choices.

Quizmaster Aspect of my character that gives clues to help me understand what success looks like for me and how I can achieve it.

Quotation Ability to clearly express the value of what I can provide instead of always looking to óthers to speak up for me.

Quote Opportunity to spontaneously speak from my heart instead of feeling that my words will have no significance for other people.

Rabbit Instinctive ability to be abundantly creative, even though I may communicate too enthusiastically about my good fortune.

Rabbit hole Situation where I can understand my capacity for success by going deeper into the practical aspects of my fertile imagination.

Rabbit warren Situation where I can explore the range of possibilities I can conceive rather than letting myself be crowded out.

Rabble Aspects of my character that can help me bring order to one of my creative urges rather than feeling continually distracted by it.

Rabid dog Instinctive ability to show my unconditional loyalty and affection without behaving in a maniacal, extreme manner.

Raccoon Instinctive ability to seek out resources in an unobtrusive manner so I can take care in how I choose to work with them.

Race Opportunity to use my self-motivation to reach my preferred outcome instead of waiting for other people to finish things for me.

Race car Ability to use my personal ambition and drive to choose my ultimate objective rather than going in circles.

Race driver Aspect of my character that directs my motivation so I can successfully steer my way through challenges I encounter.

Racehorse Instinctive ability to harness my unconscious strength so I can use my natural power to quickly reach my chosen outcome.

Racetrack Situation where I can achieve my objective by following my own path instead of becoming caught up in a cycle of competition.

Rack Ability to arrange my priorities so I can have a clear understanding of the resources I require and when I can use them.

Racket Opportunity to make a big noise that draws attention to my abilities so I can use them in an open and honest manner.

Racketeer Aspect of my character that can use unconventional methods to acquire the resources I need to demonstrate my value.

Raconteur Aspect of my character that can draw the attention of others to the strengths and challenges of my particular perspective.

Raconteuse Aspect of my character that can attract the attention of others to the wisdom and creativity of my perspective.

Racquet Ability to serve up an opportunity that may take me beyond formally recognized boundaries as I aim to get my point across.

Radar Ability to become much more aware of what is usually unseen and unspoken before it starts to appear over my horizon.

Radar gun Ability to point out self-limiting beliefs that may be holding me back so I can continue to make rapid progress.

Radar screen Ability to clearly see approaching opportunities so I can look at possible outcomes and reduce potential conflicts.

Radar trap Situation where I can move beyond habitual behaviors that may have prevented me from quickly achieving my objective.

Radiant Ability to illuminate a situation with my unique energy so I can feel brighter about the prospects for using my brilliance.

R

Radiation Opportunity to widen my sphere of influence by using my natural energy to absorb the powerful creativity of other people.

Radiation sickness Opportunity to use my natural energy to protect myself from the potentially damaging side-effects of any unresolved tensions.

Radiator Ability to safely channel my more heated emotions so I can continue to provide warmth and comfort for myself and others.

Radio Ability to share thoughts and ideas with others who are on my wavelength, although they may seem quite distant to begin with.

R

Radioactive Realization that I can use natural power to deal with a potentially unhealthy situation that may seem too hot to handle.

Radio-controlled Ability to influence a specific event from a comfortable distance so I can achieve the outcome I've been thinking about.

Radio telescope Ability to clearly see apparently distant possibilities by observing how they align with my personal vision.

Radiotherapist Aspect of my character that can help me resolve unhealthy tensions by directing my thoughts toward a specific area.

Radish Potential to fulfill an ambition by getting to the root of the experiences that add flavor to my life and that I relish most.

Radome Ability to shape my ideas so I can create a well-rounded perspective and become more aware of what is often unseen.

Raffle Opportunity to acknowledge the value of my abilities by buying into them rather than leaving anything to chance.

Raft Ability to navigate some of my more primitive emotions in a basic, instinctive way that opens up new possibilities for me.

Rafters Ability to safely support my wider sense of identity so I can continue to explore the various aspects of my inner life.

Rag Ability to clear up my awareness of how I might appear to other people by always being open to using whatever material I can.

Rage Realization that I can use my powerful energy to create a positive outcome rather than just feeling angry about other people.

Ragged Opportunity to tidy up any loose threads so I can present a coherent process instead of allowing others to pull it apart.

Raid Opportunity to respond to a sudden challenge by taking forceful action to assert my ambitions rather than just being defensive.

Rail Ability to align my perspectives so they can support how I would like to progress instead of allowing people to criticize me.

Railcar Ability to communicate my value to others so I can be more open about the career path I would like to follow.

Railing Ability to easily hold on to my chosen personal boundaries so I can use them to consistently support my motivations.

Railway Ability to follow a particular professional path that provides me with the guidelines to consistently stay on track with it.

Railway bridge Situation where I can resolve a professional dilemma by creating a lasting connection between two areas of my career.

Railway cutting Situation where I can take decisive action by making the effort to work my way through obstacles to my career progression.

Railway siding Situation where I can take time out to reflect on the career path I would like to take rather than feeling shunted about.

Railway station Situation where I can make a choice to embark on a professional path that will have a predictable, timely outcome.

Railway train Ability to follow a set of guidelines that keeps me on the straight and narrow as I make progress with my professional ambitions.

Rain Natural opportunity to release emotions that may have been clouding my thoughts so I can use them to shape my chosen outcome.

Rainbow Opportunity to use the prevailing atmosphere to illuminate the full spectrum of connections between my thoughts and feelings.

Raincoat Ability to present my self-image to people in a way that helps me feel more secure about minimizing my emotional involvement.

Raindrop Ability to decisively let go of an emotion that is no longer useful to me rather than always leaving things up in the air.

Rain forest Situation where I can explore the incredible diversity and huge growth potential of all the unknown aspects of my character.

Rainstorm Natural opportunity to let go of conflicting emotions that have been clouding my judgment so I can clear the air.

Raisin Potential to fulfill an ambition by collecting a bunch of fruitful opportunities and letting them develop in their own sweet time.

Raising Opportunity to increase my level of understanding so I can fully acknowledge my value and recognize my elevated status.

Rake Ability to sort through an area of expertise I have been cultivating so I can clear up any misunderstandings.

Rally Opportunity to bring all the aspects of my talents together so I can concentrate my efforts on a particular result.

Ram Instinctive ability to be persistent and force my viewpoint rather than conforming to the expectations of others.

Rambler Aspect of my character that finds value in exploring a variety of opportunities without always going on about them at length.

Ramp Situation where I can understand my inclination to reach a particular objective so I can increase my efforts accordingly.

Rampage Opportunity to use my powerful energy to create a positive difference rather than destroying confidence in my own abilities.

Rampant Realization that I can raise my profile by using my spirited energy to attract others toward my perspective.

Rampart Situation where I can elevate my status, by understanding my strengths and establishing a firm personal boundary.

Ram raid Situation where I can use my drive and ambition to make a personal breakthrough in how I perceive the value of my skills.

Ramrod Ability to use my power in a straightforward and disciplined manner rather than feeling I have to push it down everyone's throat.

Ramshackle Realization that I can use any challenge as a character-building experience instead of feeling continually run-down about it.

Ranch Situation where I can produce a valuable outcome by expanding my horizons and giving free rein to my natural instincts.

Rancher Aspect of my character that can establish creative boundaries that give me the freedom to develop my Instinctive talents.

Random Realization that I can specifically decide what I would prefer the outcome to be rather than just leaving it to chance.

Range Situation where I can explore a number of options by using my wide experience to display the extent of my knowledge.

Range finder Ability to get a clear indication of the effort needed to connect with a distant opportunity so I can make my mark.

Rank Realization that I can transform my standing with other people by resolving underlying tensions that may be upsetting them.

R

Ransom Opportunity to freely declare my value and have it recognized rather than feeling I am being victimized by other people.

Ransom note Ability to give myself the freedom to express myself openly and honestly so I can clearly communicate my value to people.

Ransom payment Ability to openly declare the full significance of my creative talents rather than thinking I owe a debt to anyone else.

Ranting Opportunity to convey how I feel in a calm, consistent manner instead of getting all worked up about the situation.

Rap Opportunity to decisively strike out on my own rather than taking the hit for something I was not originally involved in.

Rape Opportunity to take full control and responsibility for my creative power by setting firm personal boundaries around it.

Rape alarm Ability to become more aware of the power of my creativity so I can take decisive steps to set firm boundaries around it.

Rapid Realization that I can make a positive change within a very short time rather than feeling my progress is too slow.

Rapid fire Opportunity to quickly assert my power from a distance so I can defend my perspective and create a vital transformation.

Rapids Situation where I can experience a sudden transformation rather than getting quickly carried away in a rush of emotions.

Rapist Aspect of my character that needs to take full responsibility for my creative instincts by recognizing clear personal boundaries.

Rappelling Opportunity to stay connected during a sudden transformation so I can gently let myself down without any real risk.

Rapper Aspect of my character that can powerfully communicate how I feel without being confined to traditional methods.

Rapport Realization that I can achieve a close personal connection that brings me back to earlier experiences so I can share them.

Rapture Realization that I can really elevate my spirits by just pleasing myself so I can take huge enjoyment in what I do.

Rare Realization that I can perform exceptionally well by having the confidence to use my talents on a more consistent basis.

Rarefied atmosphere Situation where I can use my prevailing mood to surround myself with inspiring ideas rather than scattering them.

Rare steak Potential to fulfill an ambition by avoiding any unnecessary preparations so I can experience my raw strength and power.

Rash Opportunity to resolve an unhealthy situation by attending to a thoughtless decision that is starting to get under my skin.

Rasp Opportunity to shape an outcome by getting below the surface so I can see what is going on, without sounding off about it.

Raspberry Potential to fulfill an ambition by gathering a number of ripening possibilities rather than showing my displeasure.

Rat Instinctive ability to do the right thing by resourcefully dealing with a powerful anxiety that may be gnawing away at me.

Ratchet Ability to make steady progress by continually engaging with a challenge so I can maximize the outcome of my efforts.

Rate Opportunity to measure how well my development is going so I can judge when I will achieve a successful outcome.

Rationality Realization that I can take a more reasonable approach to dealing with a challenge instead of taking an unrealistic viewpoint.

Rations Potential to fulfill my ambitions by making full use of the resources I have rather than feeling my opportunities are limited.

Rattle Ability to draw my attention to a

R

situation that is not progressing as smoothly as it should without being too concerned about it.

Rattlesnake Instinctive ability to transform how I appear to others rather than becoming too concerned about apparent threats to me.

Raucous Realization that I can place more emphasis on an important message by taking a gentler, more pleasant approach to it.

Ravaged Realization that I can protect an opportunity of great value to me by peacefully resolving any emotional conflicts.

Rave Essential opportunity to express a passion I am mad about without feeling I have to be extravagantly enthusiastic.

Raven Instinctive ability to grasp an idea that is emerging from my deeper awareness so I can use it to transform my thinking.

Ravenous Opportunity to fulfill my huge appetite for success by understanding my fundamental ambitions and what I desire from them.

Ravine Situation where I may find progress difficult because I keep taking the path of least resistance when channeling my emotions.

Ravishing Realization that I have the confidence to share the incredible value of my talents without getting too carried away.

Raw Natural opportunity to communicate how I really feel in an honest and healthy way rather than overprocessing my emotions.

Raw food Potential to fulfill my ambitions by preparing myself properly so I can satisfy my fundamental appetite for success.

Raw sewage Ability to process unhealthy feelings and habitual behaviors so I can let go of them once and for all.

Ray Ability to positively direct my energy and understanding so I can illuminate an opportunity that seemed quite distant.

Ray gun Ability to assert my power in a forceful manner so I can communicate my aims to people by positively channeling my energy.

Razor Ability to get much closer to the basis of my ideas by using my finely honed judgment to confidently take precise action.

Razor blade Ability to use the power of my acute awareness to cut through confusion so I can sense what is happening.

Razor wire Ability to clearly define my personal boundaries without being too sharp or cutting in how I communicate with others.

Reaching Opportunity to firmly grasp an idea or concept so I can connect with possibilities that currently seem beyond me.

Reaction Opportunity to understand what my fundamental motivation is in this situation so I can choose the best way to respond to it.

Reactionary Aspect of my character that has the opportunity to embrace positive change rather than strongly fighting against the new.

Reactor Ability to tap into a vital source of energy by understanding how to successfully mix some of my different qualities together.

Reading Opportunity to understand different aspects of my character by using accumulated knowledge and digesting its significance.

Ready Realization that I can be completely prepared for any eventuality by always having much more confidence in my abilities.

Ready meal Opportunity to fulfill my appetite for achievement by preparing myself to succeed so I can easily absorb my experiences.

Ready-to-wear Ability to present my self-image to people in a way that shows I am prepared to fit into whatever opportunities I find.

R

Reality Realization that I create my own perceptions of what I consider to be possible and can build on these to create practical value.

Reality television Opportunity to observe habitual behavior patterns so I can use the power of my imagination to make a decision.

Reality TV star Aspect of my character that is desperate to show my true identity rather than revealing myself as others want to see me.

Realization Opportunity to become more aware of how I can put plans into action so I can receive tangible benefits from their success.

Realm Situation where I can extend my sphere of influence so I can successfully achieve outcomes that may have seemed impossible.

Reaping Opportunity to realize the value of my fertile imagination by collecting the results of some ideas that I previously planted.

Rear Situation where I can gain an understanding of what is behind my chosen outcome rather than letting it emerge unexpectedly.

Rearguard action Opportunity to identify the circumstances that have led to a potential inner conflict so I can confidently resolve it.

Rearranging Opportunity to change priorities in an existing situation by examining my various needs and how they are interdependent.

Rearview mirror Ability to gain a much clearer sense of self-awareness by reflecting on my progress in developing my personal ambitions so far.

Reasonable Realization that I can resolve a confusing challenge by taking a more rational approach instead of behaving inconsistently.

Reasonable force Opportunity to use the power of my talent to exert my influence

so I can take a more measured approach to resolving conflict.

Reasonable suspicion Realization that rationally acknowledging my personal skill and unique insight makes me less likely to doubt my eventual success.

Reassurance Opportunity to take action so I can restore my confidence in my abilities rather than waiting for others to encourage me.

Rebel Aspect of my character that challenges traditional methods by asserting my individuality and recognizing my uniqueness.

Rebellion Opportunity to rise to the occasion so I can create a fundamental change rather than putting up any resistance to it.

Rebirth Opportunity to make a new beginning by bringing some of my previous plans to life, even though I conceived them some time ago.

Reboot Opportunity to take a fundamental step that will transform a frustrating situation and allow me to start all over again.

Rebound Opportunity to bounce back from the hard realities of a situation so I can use my energy to choose my own direction.

Rebuild Opportunity to use my basic abilities and experience as a foundation for learning some new skills that will increase my value.

Rebuke Opportunity to applaud my efforts and the courage I have shown instead of being self-critical of how I might appear to people.

Recall Opportunity to examine my previous successes so I can apply my experience to my current situation and recognize its value.

Recapture Opportunity to reconnect with my instinctive talent so I can use it in a more specific manner to develop new possibilities.

Receipt Ability to deliver a performance that demonstrates my true value so I can have it formally acknowledged by other people.

Receptacle Ability to contain emotions and feelings so I can be open to how I can use them to shape my situation in the best possible way.

Reception Opportunity to acknowledge the value I provide so I can understand how my contribution is being received by others.

Receptionist Aspect of my character that is always open to listening to who I really am and what I need in any eventuality.

Recess Situation where I can withdraw from everyday activity so I can concentrate my attention on establishing my niche.

Recession Opportunity to develop valuable skills so I can demonstrate my worth to other people rather than appearing withdrawn.

Recharge Opportunity to build my energy again so I can use the potential of my talents and have my value powerfully recognized.

Recipe Ability to fulfill one of my ambitions by following a recognized procedure that will consistently result in a successful outcome.

Reciprocating Opportunity to use the power of alternate perspectives instead of feeling I am switching between different viewpoints.

Recital Opportunity to bring my experiences to life so I can confidently communicate the value of my learning to other people.

Reckless Realization that I can make the most of an opportunity by taking time to look after myself and ensuring I always feel secure.

Reckoning Opportunity to work out what I need and how I can achieve it rather than trying to use assumptions and guesswork.

Reclaimed Situation where I can build on past experiences and use them to solidly support the development of a range of new skills.

Recluse Aspect of my character that can quietly maintain my personal boundaries so I can explore interests and develop them further.

Recognition Opportunity to identify what is most meaningful for me so I can decide the actions I need to take to truly acknowledge it.

Recoil Opportunity to use my energy to spring forward again so I can engage with a challenge rather than shrinking away from it.

Recollection Opportunity to understand what action I should take by drawing on my learning and using the experience I have built up.

Recommendation Opportunity to acknowledge the confidence I have in my talents rather than waiting for people to show their approval.

Reconciliation Opportunity to deal with my inner tensions instead of resigning myself to thinking I can't do anything about them.

Recondition Opportunity to renew my sense of self-worth by taking time to work my way through a talent I may have been neglecting.

Reconnaissance Opportunity to inspect my behavioral patterns so I can prepare myself to make the most of any new opportunities.

Reconstructive surgery Opportunity to rebuild my sense of identity and resolve my inner tensions by opening my deeper feelings to others.

Record Ability to capture the outcomes of my habits and behaviors so I can recognize the unique value of my individual performance.

Record breaker Aspect of my character that can free myself from habitual patterns of behavior so I can achieve a successful outcome.

Record deal Opportunity to acknowledge the value of my talents so that I can use them to agree to a beneficial outcome with other people.

Recorder Ability to become more aware of future possibilities by having clear understanding of the basis of past behaviors.

R

Recording artist Aspect of my character that uses my natural ingenuity and creative instincts to consistently achieve recognized outcomes.

Record player Ability to get to the center of some of my habitual behavior patterns rather than appearing to go round and round.

Recovery Opportunity to restore capabilities I thought I had lost so I can continue to make progress with my ambitions.

Recreation Opportunity to take time out so I can conceive a variety of new ideas and play around with them at my leisure.

Recruitment agency Situation where I can gain clearer understanding of my individual talents to decide where best to apply them.

Recruitment center Situation where I can understand the attraction my talents have for others so I can recognize my unique value.

Rectangle Ability to shape my circumstances by using specific boundaries to provide some structure without going on about it at length.

Rector Aspect of my character that can inspire me to study complex life lessons so I can learn how to apply them in everyday life.

Rectum Essential ability to take control of my needs by deciding the best time to let go of what is no longer useful to me.

Recumbent bicycle Ability to take a more laid-back approach to my ambitions by using my energy and self-motivation to keep my commitments balanced.

Recuperating Opportunity to resolve an unhealthy situation by taking the time to rediscover my passions and what they mean to me.

Recurrent Opportunity to make a new start by understanding my fundamental behavioral patterns rather than becoming stuck in them.

Recycle Opportunity to make the most of my expertise and abilities by recognizing their continuing value to the people around me.

Red Mood that can color my perspective by reflecting my passionate outlook in a vital and exciting way that raises my spirits.

Redacted Opportunity to understand what I need to communicate instead of being vague and allowing people to fill in the blanks.

Red carpet Ability to be comfortable about displaying my unique talents rather than feeling that I have to conceal them from other people.

Red dwarf Elemental ability to have my passion and vitality recognized by other people in a way that naturally attracts them to me.

Redeeming Opportunity to use my valuable skills to restore equilibrium instead of feeling I have to compensate for any shortcomings.

Redemption Opportunity to take time out so I can rediscover one of my neglected talents without making myself feel guilty about it.

Red eye Essential opportunity to achieve a clear understanding of the actions I need to take by taking time to reflect on my ambitions.

Red giant Elemental ability to naturally attract other people toward me as they recognize how expansively I have developed my passions.

Redhead Ability to present my thinking in an apparently passionate and emotional style that other people often find very attractive.

Red-hot Realization that I can use my passion and vitality to increase my chances of success rather than taking a cooler approach.

Red light Ability to understand the situation with much greater clarity by stopping myself from becoming too personally involved in it.

Red-light district Situation where I can set personal boundaries around how I share my particular type of creativity with other people.

Redress Opportunity to present my self-image to other people in a way that enables them to recognize how I can balance their needs.

Reduce Opportunity to distill the essence of my experience so my contribution will be more powerful and require less overall effort.

Redundancy Opportunity to employ my unique skills in a different way so I can have their value fully recognized by other people.

Reed Natural ability to grow my skills in a healthy manner so I can continue to use them as a way of supporting my development.

Reed bed Situation where I can feel comfortable and at home with developing my abilities while staying rooted in everyday experience.

Reef Situation where I can use accumulated skills to immerse myself in my experience and make a difference to my surroundings.

Reek Opportunity to see evidence of a fundamental creative transformation, even though it may initially appear quite unpleasant.

Reel Ability to take in what is happening so I can give myself a chance to unwind rather than feeling a bit off balance.

Refectory Situation where I can provide the space and resources to achieve my collective ambitions by openly sharing them with others.

Referee Aspect of my character that helps me to reach a winning result by ensuring that I fairly balance all of my opposing needs.

Reference Ability to understand my position by looking at the bigger picture so I can recognize how I can successfully fit into it.

Reference number Ability to make the most of a specific opportunity rather than feeling I have to count on a number of other options.

Referred pain Essential opportunity to confront an uncomfortable situation by understanding the original tension that caused it.

Refinery Situation where I can consistently produce results by taking the time to process what makes my raw talent so valuable.

Reflection Opportunity to take time to see myself as I really am so I can have a clearer understanding of my expertise and experience.

Refresher course Opportunity to make continued progress by using my accumulated achievements to make further advances in my chosen direction.

Refreshing Opportunity to take a different approach so I can become more aware of my emotions and what they can help me to achieve.

Refreshment Potential to revitalize my ambitions and emotional needs by building on smaller achievements to reach greater success.

Refrigerator Ability to stay cool and preserve my composure as I choose how to use my resources to fulfill some long-term ambitions.

Refuel Opportunity to channel my creative power so I can use it to motivate my continued drive for success in a spirited manner.

Refueling truck Ability to employ powerful drives that will provide the resources to catalyze a valuable shift in my long-term ambitions.

Refuge Situation where I can temporarily feel safe and secure by stepping into my own power and defending myself from any criticism.

Refugee Aspect of my character that has the courage to stand up for what I believe in rather than running away from any conflict.

Refund Opportunity to realize a valuable outcome by being more persistent rather than feeling I have spent all my effort on nothing.

Refurbish Opportunity to take a fresh look at how I habitually use my skills so I can make them more inviting to other people.

R

Refuse Ability to set some personal boundaries so I can decisively process what I no longer need and can gracefully let it go.

Regal Realization that I need to acknowledge my qualities of wisdom and grace before they can be recognized by other people.

Regalia Ability to present my self-image to other people in a manner that displays the level of power and refinement I have achieved.

Regatta Opportunity to navigate complex and unpredictable feelings myself rather than waiting for others to process them for me.

Regenerate Opportunity to use my creative flow to bring one of my talents back into existence so I can use my skills in a new way.

Regime change Opportunity to transform how I habitually take action so I can make best use of my resources to achieve my objectives.

Regiment Aspects of my character that can defend my basic needs and deal with any inner tensions by taking a firmly structured approach.

Region Situation where I can continue to develop my power by giving myself the space to understand any feelings of self-limitation.

Register Ability to take notice of particular events so I can understand their significance in achieving a successful result.

Registrar Aspect of my character that formally acknowledges my needs and ensures I can receive recognition on a wider basis.

Registration plate Ability to clearly identify my individual motivation so it can be easily recognized as I display it to those around me.

Registry office Situation where I can make a more balanced commitment to some fundamental needs by announcing them to others.

Regret Realization that I have the talent to achieve success in the future rather than feeling disappointed about my past performances.

Regular Realization that I can use my natural talent and normal routine to take some unusual steps that will provide a breakthrough.

Rehab Opportunity to transform some of my habitual behaviors by understanding how I routinely deal with my fundamental needs.

Rehab center Situation where I can step into my true power by transforming my relationship with behaviors that aren't the real me.

Rehearsal Opportunity to achieve a successful outcome by developing my talents more fully rather than just going through the motions.

Rehearsal studio Situation where I can use natural ingenuity and creative instincts to more fully develop my potential talents and abilities.

Reheated Opportunity to use my vitality to quickly increase my chances of success rather than slowly warming to a new opportunity.

Reignite Opportunity to use my creative spark to get fired up about some powerful possibilities I thought had fizzled out.

Reincarnation Opportunity to revitalize myself so I can make a new beginning and open up to the possibilities of a better life.

Reindeer Instinctive ability to thrive in arduous conditions and provide the motivation for people to generously share their resources.

Reinforced concrete Ability to emphasize the firmness of my viewpoint by maintaining my set opinion based on the weight of available evidence.

Reins Ability to harness unconscious energy and control its direction rather than feeling I have to slow down and limit my progress.

Reinvent Opportunity to use my unique insight to transform perceptions of who I am instead of trying to keep people happy.

Rejection Opportunity to be more accepting of myself by recognizing my talents rather than denying I have any special abilities.

Rejection letter Ability to acknowledge my unique expertise to increase my fundamental understanding of my characteristic qualities.

Rejection slip Ability to firmly grasp the challenges I will need to deal with instead of letting any opportunities just slide away.

Rejuvenate Opportunity to rediscover self-motivation and energy by drawing on experience rather than appearing jaded to others.

Rekindle Opportunity to ignite a creative transformation in a situation where I previously may have been too emotionally involved.

Relapse Opportunity to use my vitality to fully recover from an unhealthy situation rather than sliding back into my old habits.

Relationship Opportunity to see undiscovered aspects of myself reflected in another person so I can connect more profoundly with them.

Relative Aspect of my character that helps me become more familiar with my unique qualities and how I habitually associate with them.

Relaxation Opportunity to take time to resolve accumulated tension so I can keep making progress without slacking off.

Relaxation therapy Opportunity to relieve an unhealthy situation by letting go of chronic tensions I may not have been attending to.

Relay race Opportunity to use my self-motivation to reach my preferred outcome so I can hand over responsibility to a colleague.

Release Opportunity to free up my time and resources rather than feeling I have to confine my efforts to achieving a certain result.

Relegated Opportunity to let go of some commitments and obligations so I can step into a league of my own and raise my game.

Relentless Opportunity to make a sustained effort to achieve a successful outcome rather than putting myself under too much pressure.

Relic Ability to pay attention to an important part of my past so I can understand its value in my present situation.

Relief Opportunity to stand out from people by taking a more relaxed approach to how I deal with any habitual tensions and conflicts.

Religion Realization that I need to look beyond my everyday world to connect myself back to who I am and what I believe.

Religious icon Ability to clearly see the bigger picture by making a deeper spiritual connection to the outcome I am really looking for.

Relish Potential to fulfill an ambition by approaching it with great enthusiasm without feeling I have to lay it on too thick.

Relive Opportunity to use my experience to make the right choice in an unfamiliar situation without causing myself any anxiety.

Relocation Opportunity to feel more centered in a new environment to continue to develop my character and progress in my ambitions.

Reluctance Realization that I can successfully engage with a new opportunity by displaying my talents, even if I feel disinclined to do so.

Remainder Ability to participate by making the best use of all my resources rather than feeling that my contribution will be left out.

Remains Ability to use the evidence of a creative transformation as a way of understanding how I can embody skills and abilities.

Remand center Situation where I can experience the source of who I am by allowing myself to escape from self-limiting beliefs.

Remark Opportunity to observe how I can use my individual talent in a unique way rather than allowing other people to judge me.

R

Remedy Ability to identify what is specifically troubling me so I can resolve a situation that has been making me feel ill at ease.

Remembering Opportunity to re-create an experience so I can apply it to my current situation and recognize its full significance.

Remembrance garden Situation where I can cultivate relationships and interests so they help me recall my experiences in the future.

Reminder Realization that I need to remember the value of my accumulated experience rather than letting other people criticize me.

Reminiscent Realization that I can use my learning to achieve a successful outcome, even though I have no direct experience of it now.

Remnant Ability to use a seemingly limited resource to successfully achieve an ambition instead of feeling that I am being left behind.

Remorseful Realization that I can use my learning to achieve a successful outcome rather than feeling guilty about letting myself down.

Remortgage Opportunity to take full credit for how I have developed my character so I can continue to expand my future ambitions.

Remote Realization that I can influence my chosen outcome by taking personal action rather than always trying to keep my distance.

Remote control Ability to influence a situation and change the possible outcome without feeling I have to become too involved in it.

Remote sensor Ability to clearly understand what might be influencing my current situation so I can provide a measured response to it.

Removal van Ability to employ my personal drives and resources so I can convey my most valuable skills and expertise to other people.

Removing Opportunity to make a real difference by letting go of what I no longer need and without detracting from my chances.

Renaissance man Aspect of my character that embodies my wide variety of accomplishments and talents by giving me the power I need to succeed.

Render Opportunity to collect a range of my ideas and experiences together so I can create a more coherent and substantial outcome.

Rendezvous Opportunity to connect with particular aspects of my character so I can use their qualities to resolve a situation.

Renegade Aspect of my character that has faith in my deeper motivations rather than feeling I have betrayed myself in any way.

Renewable Ability to consistently recover my energy levels so I can continue to use my power in a positive and healthy manner.

Renovate Opportunity to renew my ambitions by building on what I have learned already rather than thinking I have to make a fresh start.

Rent Ability to feel relaxed and at home with myself by being able to demonstrate my value to other people for a period of time.

Reopen Opportunity to explore a possibility in greater depth so I can expand my awareness rather than closing myself to it.

Repair Opportunity to restore my confidence in my expertise and abilities rather than just trying to patch things up temporarily.

Repeat Opportunity to emphasize my unique contribution by always being original instead of saying the same thing again and again.

Repel Opportunity to attract other people to me by using my power to maintain my boundaries and drive away what I don't need.

Repertoire Ability to draw on my extensive knowledge and experience to use my personal talents to create a powerful performance.

Repetitive strain injury Opportunity to

take action and prevent an unhealthy situation by being more flexible in how I choose to work.

Replay Opportunity to take a second look at dealing with any tensions that may be emerging between different aspects of my character.

Replicant Aspect of my character that may try to please other people by appearing to go along with how they think I should behave.

Reply Opportunity to take my time and observe what is emerging for me rather than feeling I have to answer immediately.

Report Ability to have a clear understanding about what my needs are so I can express them as honestly as possible.

Report card Ability to communicate my value to others by being more open about my needs rather than feeling I'm being judged.

Reporter Aspect of my character that takes a more objective view of opportunities and can understand their corresponding significance.

Repository Situation where I can feel secure in accumulating a wide range of knowledge I can safely access any time I need to.

Repossession Opportunity to recover my sense of self-worth by valuing my expertise and abilities instead of feeling indebted to people.

Representative Aspect of my character that can reveal itself and be the real me rather than trying to appeal to the expectations of others.

Repression Opportunity to liberate myself from old habits that no longer serve me so I can encourage new opportunities to emerge.

Reprieve Opportunity to create a positive self-transformation by giving myself respite from situations where I treat myself too harshly.

Reprimand Opportunity to speak out about the courage I have shown instead of allowing other people to give me a hard time.

Reproduction Opportunity to conceive a unique idea rather than feeling I have to copy everyone else to be accepted.

Reptile Instinctive ability to express my fundamental creativity so I can use my primitive urges in a less cold-blooded manner.

Repulsive Realization that I can use my talents to attract other people toward me without worrying they will find them distasteful.

Reputation Realization that I can listen to my own opinion rather than feeling I have to live up to the expectations of other people.

Request stop Situation where I can bring a restrictive situation to an end so I can embark on a new stage in progressing with my career.

Requiem Opportunity to celebrate a major transformation by instinctively communicating with people in a fundamentally powerful way.

Requisition Opportunity to understand my personal requirements rather than allowing others to constantly make demands on my time.

Rescue Opportunity to reconnect with a valuable talent I thought I had lost so I can use it to give myself the freedom I need.

Rescued Realization that I can feel secure in being outside my comfort zone because it gives me much more freedom to decide my future.

Research Opportunity to systematically investigate what will make me feel fulfilled rather than engaging in endless self-examination.

Researcher Aspect of my character that takes the time to question my behaviors so I can understand my fundamental needs.

Resemblance Realization that I can make a difference by understanding what my preferred outcome looks like and how close I am to reaching it.

R

Resentment Realization that it is up to me to have my expertise valued by other people rather than feeling my efforts are being ignored.

Reservation Opportunity to set some personal boundaries so I can ensure my participation instead of thinking that I have to hold back.

Reserve Realization that opening up about how I feel will give me access to far more resources than I am normally accustomed to.

Reserved parking Situation where I can make a future commitment to creating definite opportunities for progressing in my professional ambitions.

Reserved table Ability to be open and supportive with others by showing the strength of my commitment to our continuing relationships.

Reservoir Situation where I can draw on my accumulated learning and experience so I can channel it in the direction that I choose.

Residence Situation where I can feel relaxed with the different aspects of myself rather than dwelling on areas I find challenging.

Resident Aspect of my character that feels more at home in certain situations instead of thinking I have to move beyond my comfort zone.

Residue Ability to separate the more valuable aspects of an opportunity rather than being concerned about what I must leave behind.

Resignation Realization that taking responsibility for my actions gives me far more power than giving up on my ambitions.

Resigned Realization that I can pursue new opportunities by making bold decisions instead of letting any valuable chances slip away.

Resigning Opportunity to move on from a situation that is no longer serving me rather than feeling it will always have to be this way.

Resilient Opportunity to bounce back in a challenging situation rather than being too rigid in outlook and seeing it as a setback.

Resin Ability to exude confidence in my accumulated wisdom and creativity instead of feeling I am stuck in habitual behaviors.

Resistance Opportunity to rise to a challenge so I can establish my value rather than conforming to everyone else's demands.

Resonate Opportunity to communicate the full power of what I want to say by ensuring that other people are on the same wavelength.

Resort Situation where I can feel relaxed and comfortable about exploring a variety of options so I can decide which one to choose.

Resources Ability to make the most of any situation and display my value by using the knowledge and experience I have built up.

Respectability Realization that having greater trust in my own abilities makes it easier for me to behave honestly and with real integrity.

Respectable Ability to recognize the value of my thinking so I can hold my head high instead of worrying about how my ideas might appear.

Respirator Ability to be consistently inspired by choosing to reveal my true feelings rather than trying to conceal them from other people.

Respite home Situation where I can come to terms with all the different aspects of myself so I can create a major life transformation.

Response Opportunity to listen to my inner voice so I can make a decision rather than waiting for other people to take action.

Responsible Realization that I can provide the answers I need by being more accountable for my own actions and their outcomes.

Rest Opportunity to refresh my perspective by taking a more relaxed approach rather than worrying about all my other concerns.

Restaurant Situation where I can make choices about how I can fulfill a valuable ambition by letting others care for my needs.

Restaurant critic Aspect of my character that tries to help me fulfill my appetite for success, even though it can sometimes make me doubt my skills.

Restless Realization that I can use my energy and self-motivation to take some decisive action instead of just keeping myself busy.

Restoration Opportunity to renew my enthusiasm by rebuilding faith in my creative abilities so I can produce original work again.

Restraining order Ability to bring a more organized structure to a challenging situation by giving myself the freedom to express how I feel.

Restraint Opportunity to liberate my unique talents rather than feeling I have to hold back in order to fit in with everyone else.

Restricted access Opportunity to give myself permission to explore new possibilities so I can move beyond any of my perceived limitations.

Restricted opening Situation where I can step into a new area that holds great possibilities for me instead of feeling that I might not fit in.

Restriction Opportunity to release myself from any self-imposed limitations so I have more freedom to pursue my higher aspirations.

Restroom Aspect of myself that ensures my emotional privacy so I can take care of my most fundamental needs in a relaxed manner.

Restructuring Opportunity to understand the fundamental basis of some of my behavioral patterns so I can decide how to transform them.

Result Opportunity to understand the consequence of my actions so I can achieve the preferred outcome that I am looking for.

Resurrection Opportunity to raise my spirits be leaving the past behind so I can transform my life by revitalizing my unique abilities.

Resuscitate Opportunity to breathe new life into a project I may have been neglecting so I can begin to feel inspired again.

Retail park Situation where I can explore a variety of outlets for my talents to open myself up to a wider range of opportunities.

Retainer Ability to declare my value to the people around me instead of feeling that they are always trying to put me in my place.

Retaining wall Ability to maintain firm personal boundaries with other people rather than allowing their concerns to creep up and overwhelm me.

Retaliation Opportunity to be forgiving in how I respond to a threatening challenge instead of reflecting the same kind of behavior.

Retardant Ability to slow down a potentially volatile situation so I can have the opportunity to choose how I will react to it.

Retina Essential ability to absorb what is happening so I can be more receptive to any illuminating possibilities.

Retired Realization that I have the freedom to draw on accumulated wisdom and experience rather than just withdrawing into myself.

Retirement Opportunity to use my self-motivation and energy to move into exciting new areas rather than feeling my skills are of no value.

Retreat Opportunity to make a major advance by contemplating my position in peace and quiet before I start to push forward again.

Retrieve Opportunity to regain a talent that I thought I had lost by recovering my self-confidence and my appreciation of my value.

R

Retro Realization that I can accomplish my ambitions in the style I choose rather than feeling that I am living in the past.

Retrospective Opportunity to look into the future so I can decide the result instead of looking in hindsight at what might have been.

Return Opportunity to realize the value of my accumulated knowledge and experience rather than going back over old ground all the time.

Return ticket Ability to demonstrate my value to people by permitting myself to shift their perspectives and transform their viewpoints.

Reunion Opportunity to reconnect with all the different aspects of my character that form the fundamental parts of who I am today.

Revamp Opportunity to take some steps to renew my sense of purpose instead of being too concerned about superficial appearances.

Reveal Opportunity to be open about my abilities rather than trying to conceal them in case they make me feel vulnerable.

Revelation Opportunity to discover a deeper truth by understanding the value of my talents and powerful ways in which I can use them.

Revenge Opportunity to forgive myself about any conflicting emotions I experience rather feeling I have done something wrong.

Reverberation Opportunity to bounce some ideas around so I can sound out other people's thoughts instead of echoing their sentiments.

Reverse Opportunity to reflect on my progress so far so I can explore other perspectives rather than taking any backward steps.

Reverse engineering Opportunity to examine a particular outcome so I can understand how it was shaped by my underlying behavioral patterns.

Reversing Opportunity to withdraw my personal commitment rather than feeling there is no way forward for me in my current position.

Reversing a car Opportunity to release myself from a commitment that is preventing me from making the most of my personal ambition.

Reversing a truck Opportunity to skillfully make my way through a potentially restrictive situation so I can convey the value of my expertise.

Reversing downhill Opportunity to use my accumulated experience to make faster progress instead of letting the situation get out of control.

Revert Opportunity to move on to explore new ways of using my talents rather than going back to habits that no longer serve me.

Revetment Ability to provide substantial protection for my personal boundaries so I can definitely retain my deeper sense of purpose.

Revisited Opportunity to arrive at the same conclusion by using a different approach rather than feeling that I've seen it all before.

Revolution Opportunity to become more centered and step into my power so I can give myself the freedom to turn my situation around.

Revolutionary Aspect of my character that can liberate my talents by boldly breaking out of a situation that has turned full circle for me.

Revolver Ability to repeatedly assert my power in a forceful manner so I can consistently communicate my aims to other people.

Revolving door Ability to step fully into a new opportunity rather than feeling as if I'm going round and round in circles all the time.

Reward Ability to pursue a challenging objective and successfully accomplish it so I can have my true value recognized by people.

Rewind Ability to quickly return to my initial perceptions and run through possible outcomes so I can fast-track my ambitions.

Rheumatism Opportunity to be more flexible in how I connect with people so I can resolve unhealthy tension I may be experiencing.

Rhinestone Ability to display my more valuable facets rather than using superficial appearances to attract attention from others.

Rhinoceros Instinctive ability to make my point by firmly standing my ground so I can happily let any criticism bounce off me.

Rhubarb Potential to fulfill an ambition by sticking up for myself rather than stewing over a situation and feeling sour about it.

Rhyme Ability to convey how well-versed I am in my particular line of work so I can always understand how to make my mark.

Rhythm Opportunity to choose exactly the right time to take definite action rather than repeating myself again and again.

Rib Essential ability to protect my more sensitive side against any hurtful remarks, even though they were only made in jest.

Ribbon Ability to collect my thoughts and ideas together so I can have their value recognized when I share them with other people.

Rib cage Essential ability to safeguard my source of inspiration and maintain my vitality by understanding my fundamental strengths.

Rice Natural ability to cultivate my knowledge by developing the small grains of truth that can provide me with great satisfaction.

Rich Realization of the true value of my accumulated learning and experience so I can use it to add to my wealth of knowledge.

Rickety Opportunity to build up my reputation by being strong and supportive rather than sometimes appearing shaky and unreliable.

Rickshaw Ability to make progress toward my chosen ambition by using the energy and experiences of others to help motivate me.

Ricochet Opportunity to bounce an idea around and see where it ends up rather than feeling I always have to meet my original aim.

Rid Opportunity to move on from a situation that no longer serves me by choosing to let go of some old habits and behaviors.

Riddle Opportunity to quickly find the solution to a situation that has been puzzling me rather than going through it again and again.

Ride Ability to speed up my progress so I can always keep moving toward my objective by using whatever energy and power is available.

Ridge Situation where I can use my accumulated skills to raise my levels of awareness and make a difference in my surroundings.

Ridicule Opportunity to take my achievements more seriously so I can realize their value instead of looking for praise from other people.

Ridiculous Realization that I can use my talents to solve a challenging dilemma rather than worrying about others laughing at me.

Riding Opportunity to trust in myself so I can keep motivated instead of feeling that I am overreliant on external support.

Riff Ability to emphasize my instinctive communication skills rather than just feeling I am repeating myself over and over again.

Rifle Ability to communicate my aims by forcefully asserting my power from a distance instead of hurriedly going through my needs.

Rifle range Situation where I can achieve a much clearer understanding of how to reach the objectives I am aiming for.

Rift Situation where I can resolve an obvious dilemma by making the most of an opportunity that has been open to me for some time.

Rig Ability to use my practical experience to shape and direct a specific outcome rather than feeling that I am being manipulated.

Right Realization that I can always take the most appropriate action, even though it may require questioning my own judgment.

R

Right-of-way Situation where I can follow my chosen path while still being open to any other possibilities I may encounter as I progress.

Rigid Realization that I can still provide solid support by being more flexible rather than feeling that I have to be unyielding.

Rigor mortis Opportunity to revitalize my creative talents by taking a softer and more flexible approach to regain my self-motivation.

Rim Ability to go to the edge of my knowledge and experience so I can take a closer look at my wider capacity for success.

Rime ice Ability to use my warmth and vitality to gain a clearer understanding instead of being brushed off by superficial appearances.

Ring Ability to demonstrate my individual commitment to a strong and powerful partnership that will continue to develop over time.

Ring finger Essential ability to control my actions and shape my own future by showing my commitment to a long-term relationship.

Ringing Opportunity to increase my awareness of an emerging opportunity so I can take actions that will clearly resonate with me.

Ringside Situation where I can objectively observe some of my unresolved inner conflicts rather than continually wrestling with them.

Ring tone Ability to pay more attention to a personal matter that I need to communicate to others rather than just ignoring it.

Ringworm Instinctive ability to release myself from some unhealthy commitments that have been irritating me and getting under my skin.

Rinse Opportunity to be consistently clear about my emotional challenges rather than allowing any messy feelings to build up.

Riot Opportunity to bring some order to my various needs so I can demonstrate them to other people and have them acknowledged.

Rip Ability to take energetic and decisive action so I can open up fresh opportunities and confidently step into a new future.

Rip cord Ability to continue my progress by opening myself up to a wider range of ideas rather than rushing toward any conclusions.

Ripe Opportunity to make full use of the wisdom and experience I have accumulated so I can develop a more fruitful outcome.

Ripple Ability to spread my influence more widely by understanding the power of my deeper emotions and how they appear.

Rise Opportunity to stand up for what I believe in instead of allowing a challenging situation to make me feel down.

Risk Realization that I need to have more confidence in my undoubted abilities rather than feeling I always have to play it safe.

Risotto Potential to fulfill an ambition by cultivating my knowledge and experience so I can continue to nourish my growth.

Risqué Realization that I can use my judgment and take the most creative approach rather than feeling vulnerable to criticism.

Rite of passage Opportunity to follow a clearly defined path that will help me take the first steps to move into a new, exciting future.

Rites Opportunity to make a fundamental transformation by simply taking a spontaneous approach without any traditional commitments.

Ritual Opportunity to realize a deeper wisdom about who I really am by permitting myself to cross a threshold into new experiences.

Rival Aspect of my character that is trying to deal with my competing needs rather than taking advantage of their combined power.

R

River Situation where I can enter into my emotional flow so I can understand the source of my feelings and the course they might take.

River crossing Situation where I can resolve an emotional dilemma by going with the flow until I can achieve a much firmer understanding.

River journey Opportunity to make an ongoing transformation in my emotional life by motivating myself to explore a variety of sentiments.

Rivet Ability to concentrate all my attention on forming a powerful, enduring bond that will provide me with great strength.

Road Situation where I can use a recognized procedure as a way of pursuing my ambitions as I move toward my chosen objective.

Roadblock Situation where I can make progress by understanding self-imposed limitations that may be slowing me down and frustrating me.

Roadkill Ability to use my instinctive creativity to positively transform my progress rather than constantly trying to avoid using it.

Road rage Realization that I can use power-ful motivation to create a positive outcome instead of feeling angry about other people.

Roadrunner Instinctive ability to quickly motivate myself so I can take some steps to energetically pursue some of my fleeting ideas.

Road sign Ability to make meaningful progress with my ambitions by making a significant connection and understanding its importance.

Road trip Opportunity to develop some of my ambitions by exploring a variety of different viewpoints and the perspectives they offer.

Roar Opportunity to communicate how I feel by opening up to my fundamental power and strength so I can convey it to other people.

Roast Opportunity to use my raw strength and power to fulfill a long-term ambition without worrying about any potential criticism.

Roast dinner Opportunity to achieve my main ambitions by taking a more patient approach so I can produce a more substantial result.

Robber Aspect of my character that needs to honor the value of my talents rather than feeling at a loss with my self-confidence.

Robbery Opportunity to have the value of my expertise recognized by other people instead of thinking I'm giving myself away.

Robe Ability to present my self-image to people in a way that shows how comfortable and relaxed I feel with who I am.

Robin Instinctive ability to display the passion I feel for an idea so I can maintain my optimism, even under adverse conditions.

Robot Aspect of my character that may ignore my real feelings and just efficiently go through the motions to keep everyone happy.

Rock Ability to always maintain a firm and practical outlook, even though I may sometimes appear to be unyielding to other people.

Rock climber Aspect of my character that can raise my awareness by getting a firm grip on the situation and being sure where I stand.

Rocket Ability to powerfully thrust myself toward a higher level of awareness by concentrating on my energies and getting fired up.

Rocket scientist Aspect of my character that is experimenting with a variety of possibilities so I can quickly elevate my understanding.

Rockfall Opportunity to relax my grip in a situation and let everything drop into place rather than feeling I always have to be so firm.

R

Rock garden Situation where I can attend to my long-standing relationships so they will continue to naturally blossom around me.

Rocking Opportunity to get a situation moving by understanding how I can get down to the fundamental process that is causing it.

Rocking chair Ability to maintain my habitual viewpoint on a situation, even though I may seem to shift from one perspective to another.

Rocking horse Ability to play with my unconscious energies and their patterns, although it may not take me anywhere in particular.

Rock pool Situation where I can firmly contain a range of emotions in order to reflect on my accumulated learning and experience.

Rockumentary Opportunity to understand the fundamental basis of a formative experience so I can examine my motives and behaviors.

Rocky Situation where I will have to make some hard decisions so I can firmly direct my efforts in order to make continued progress.

Rod Ability to extend my influence so I can use the strength of my practical skills to produce a straightforward outcome.

Rodent Instinctive ability to take the healthier option so I can deal with any concerns that may been gnawing away at me.

Rodeo Opportunity to attract attention to how I can harness my unconscious strengths and use them to drive forward with my ambitions.

Rogue Aspect of my character that can make an unexpected breakthrough by speaking my truth rather than deluding myself about my needs.

Rogues gallery Ability to examine different aspects of my character that can help me become clear about what I believe.

Rogue trader Aspect of my character that can create a huge shift in how I value my talents instead of deceiving myself about my abilities.

Role Ability to embody the particular characteristic that will prove most valuable for me in dealing with a specific challenge.

Role-play Opportunity to observe the different aspects of my character and see how I can use them to resolve any emerging challenges.

Role reversal Opportunity to make progress by reflecting on the value of my different characteristics rather than taking backward steps.

Roll Opportunity to fulfill an ambition by going along with what is happening rather than going over the same ground again.

Rollerblades Ability to quickly motivate myself so I can cut through confusion and continue to decisively move along my chosen path.

Roller coaster Situation where I can feel more in control by making the decision to engage with the ups and downs of any challenges.

Roller skates Ability to maintain levels of self-motivation by pushing forward and applying my efforts in a graceful, precise manner.

Roller towel Ability to continually absorb the learning and experience I gain from dealing with my emotions rather than just giving up.

Rolling pin Ability to fulfill a potential opportunity by applying some direct pressure to straighten out any unexpected challenges.

Rollover jackpot Opportunity to make a huge breakthrough in how others see my value instead of giving up on any chance of success.

Romance Opportunity to explore an unfamiliar situation that fascinates me so I can develop an intriguing creative idea.

R

Roman numerals Ability to make the most of a historic opportunity rather than feeling I always have to look to the future to succeed.

Romantic Realization that I have the capacity to make a profound connection with my creativity without being too fanciful or impractical.

Romantic meal Opportunity to fulfill my appetite for a deeper intimacy by being open to new experiences so I can digest their significance.

Romantic partner Aspect of my character that helps me understand my deepest desires so I can become much closer to fulfilling them.

Romantic situation Realization about how I can make the most of my surroundings to help me understand my potential to make a deeper connection.

Romantic surprise Realization that I can exceed my expectations by being open to the possibility of discovering my desirable qualities.

Rom-com Opportunity to resolve an ongoing emotional dilemma by entertaining a variety of outcomes that will keep everyone happy.

Romp Opportunity to play around with a range of creative concepts so I can move quickly to successfully achieve an ambition.

Roof Ability to keep my sense of identity safe and secure so I can continue to explore the various aspects of my inner life.

Roof rack Ability to use my individual drive and ambition as a way of conveying accumulated expertise and experience to others.

Rooftop Situation where I can raise my awareness and arrive at an overall understanding of what helps me feel safe and secure.

Rook Instinctive ability to pick out a powerful idea that will be deeply transformative rather than deluding myself about my needs.

Rookery Situation where I can use deeper thinking to elevate my awareness of my potential for long-term spiritual growth.

Rookie Aspect of my character with the potential to develop expertise by being open to new experiences and learning from them.

Room Aspect of myself that has the capacity to help me feel comfortable and secure in developing my potential talents and skills.

Roommate Aspect of my character that feels comfortable in sharing some of the private areas of my life with the people around me.

Room service Opportunity to make myself feel more at home by making sure I always attend to my own needs, as well as to others'.

Room temperature Realization that I can influence my capacity to develop my talents rather than appearing to blow hot and cold.

Rooster Instinctive ability to wake people up to a new opportunity so I can assertively tell them about it instead of just being shy.

Root Natural ability to connect to a deeper and more fundamental source of inspiration that will fully support my future growth.

Root canal Essential ability to confidently support my power so I can safely channel my passions in order to achieve my ambitions.

Rope Ability to make a commitment that has enough flexibility to keep me feeling connected without becoming overly attached.

Rope ladder Ability to raise my awareness by using a specific series of steps, even though there may seem to be too much flexibility in them.

Rose Natural ability to open up to my creative talents and encourage them to blossom so I can share them with other people.

Rostrum Situation where I can raise my level of awareness by being able to feel supported as I communicate my ideas to people.

R

Rot Opportunity to use my past experiences to provide a very solid and reliable basis for supporting my future development.

Rotating Opportunity to turn a situation around by achieving a central understanding of the motivations that are causing it to happen.

Rotor Ability to work my way through a range of thoughts and ideas so I can use them to gain a more elevated perspective.

Rotten Realization that I can use my past experiences to provide firm support for a new future by nurturing some of my talents.

Rotten bridge Situation where I can resolve a dilemma by creating a much more solid connection between two apparently distinct areas of my life.

Rotten staircase Situation where I can make steady, incremental progress by having a firmer understanding of connections I need to make.

Rotten tooth Essential opportunity to feel confident in my power rather than feeling that my influence is beginning to fade away.

Rough Realization that I don't always have to take the regular option to keep things smooth and acceptable for other people.

Roughage Potential opportunity to healthily fulfill an ambition by being able to digest some of the less savory aspects of an experience.

Roughneck Aspect of my character that can help me go deeper into my accumulated wisdom so I can use it more resourcefully.

Roulette Opportunity to choose an outcome by taking decisive action rather than just spinning my wheels and leaving it to chance.

Round Ability to shape my circumstances by taking a more natural approach instead of feeling I always have to be sharp and edgy.

Roundabout Situation where I can keep progressing my individual ambitions by choosing my moment rather than taking a more circuitous route.

Roundhouse kick Opportunity to use self-motivation and energy to raise my level of influence and maximize an exciting challenge.

Round table Ability to be very open and supportive with people by sharing my honest feelings about our habitual relationship patterns.

Round-trip Opportunity to experience a variety of perspectives so I can explore other ideas without abandoning my original viewpoint.

Roustabout Aspect of my character that helps me channel my emotions so I can deal with the pressures of maintaining my energy levels.

Route Situation where I can ensure I will reach a positive outcome by choosing the path I need to take to achieve my goal.

Routine Opportunity to understand the value of some of my habitual behaviors rather than constantly searching for novel experiences.

Row Situation where I can align my skills and resources so I can line myself up to make the most of an emerging opportunity.

Rowan Natural potential to display my passion for my long-term spiritual growth while staying rooted in everyday practicalities.

Rowboat Ability to use my self-motivation and energy to navigate through the challenges of complex and unpredictable feelings.

Rowdy Realization that I can use my skill and energy to create a significant difference without having to make a big noise about it.

Rowing machine Ability to produce an outcome of great emotional value by focusing my energy rather than going through the motions.

Royal Realization that I need to recognize my qualities of strength and refinement before they will be acknowledged by other people.

R

Royalty Aspects of my character that have the maturity to use my power wisely so my talents can be widely recognized by other people.

RPG Ability to powerfully assert my beliefs and exert my influence over other people by grasping my capacity to shape the outcome.

Rub Opportunity to exert some pressure so I can achieve my chosen outcome without causing too much friction for other people.

Rubber Ability to stretch my capabilities and remain quite flexible so I can absorb the impact of any unexpected challenges.

Rubber bullet Ability to assert my power from a distance with a degree of flexibility so I can always bounce back from any setbacks.

Rubbish Ability to identify my most valuable qualities so I can decisively process what I no longer need and gracefully let it go.

Rubbish dump Situation where I can let go of behaviors I no longer need instead of allowing them to continually accumulate.

Ruby Ability to be crystal clear in how I communicate my love so I can express my passion in a powerful and attractive manner.

Rucksack Ability to be as self-contained as possible so I can maintain my levels of self-motivation without feeling weighed down.

Rudder Ability to choose a clear direction as I navigate my way through a complex and potentially challenging emotional situation.

Rude Realization that I can be far more considerate with other people when I have a healthy regard for my fundamental value.

Ruffle Opportunity to shake up how I can explore my thoughts and theories in a different way rather than just feeling irritated.

Rug Ability to be comfortable about where I stand in a situation, although I understand the limitations of my perspective.

Rugby Opportunity to use my skill to physically engage with ways of achieving my goals, even though the outcome may seem uncertain.

Rugged Situation where I can use my fundamental strengths to endure challenges I encounter instead of taking the easy option.

Ruined Opportunity to rebuild my self-confidence and make the most of my strengths rather than neglecting them and losing their value.

Ruins Situation where I can revisit my unique qualities so I can continue to build on my accumulated experience and wisdom.

Rule Ability to give myself full permission to do the right thing instead of being concerned about how I measure up to other people.

Rum Potential to fulfill an emotional need by exploring some unusual options rather than clearly connecting with my spiritual self.

Rumble Opportunity to engage with a challenge that resonates with me so I can achieve a much deeper understanding.

Ruminant Instinctive ability to fulfill some of my ambitions in a healthy and natural way by taking the time to chew things over.

Rummage Opportunity to discover some of my potential abilities by taking the time to actively look into my personal development.

Rummage sale Opportunity to work my way through a potentially chaotic situation so I can identify what is of most value to me.

Rumor Opportunity to confirm the value of my talents to other people rather than just hoping that they will be recognized.

Run Situation where I can make much faster progress by using my powerful self-motivation to energetically take the steps that I need.

Runaway car Ability to use my ambition and drive to take control of a challenging situation so I can choose my direction.

R

Runaway child Aspect of my character that needs encouragement in using my unique talents so I can feel more at home with them.

Runaway horse Instinctive ability to grasp the power of my unconscious strength so I can use it to drive forward with my ambitions.

Runaway train Ability to follow a set of guidelines and work to a specific timetable rather than allowing myself to be carried away.

Rune Ability to convey the ancient wisdom embodied by certain aspects of my character rather than leaving the outcome to fate.

Rung Ability to provide some stable and solid support so I can use my self-motivation and energy to steadily make progress.

Runner Aspect of my character that can quickly take steps to meet a challenge and has the energy and self-motivation to succeed.

Runner-up Aspect of my character that is happy to offer support rather than always thinking I have to put my interests first.

Running Opportunity to quickly motivate myself so I can take some powerful steps to energetically pursue one of my ambitions.

Running battle Opportunity to make a stand and deal with conflicting feelings instead of always trying to avoid ongoing inner tension.

Runt Instinctive ability to develop a potentially vital personal ambition, even though it may seem insignificant to other people.

Runway Situation where I can provide clear direction to get a powerful idea off the ground and then take a more down-to-earth approach.

Rupture Essential opportunity to make a real effort to heal any emotional disruptions rather than allowing them to spill out.

Rural Situation where I can explore some of the unfamiliar aspects of my nature and cultivate any of the opportunities that they hold.

Rush Opportunity to take my time to understand how I can make the fastest progress rather than letting myself get carried away.

Rush hour Opportunity to reflect on my professional progress and decide if my career path is taking me where I want to go.

Russian roulette Opportunity to choose an outcome by confidently and forcefully asserting my power rather than leaving it to chance.

Rust Ability to use my fundamental power to shape a definite outcome and support it rather than neglecting my basic strengths.

Rusty car Ability to maintain the fundamental integrity of my driving ambitions instead of feeling that they will inevitably fall apart.

Rusty machinery Ability to maintain the level of my expertise so I can continue to create effective outcomes in a smooth, consistent way.

Rustproof Realization that I have all the integrity I need to understand my basic beliefs so I can defend them against any criticism.

Rut Ability to use my instinctive creativity to make some deeper connections and get moving again rather than just feeling stuck.

Rye Natural ability to nurture my instincts by reaping the benefits of ideas I have steadily accumulated.

R

Sabbatical Opportunity to work toward realizing my deeper life purpose rather than feeling I am taking things too easily.

Sabotage Opportunity to do something constructive instead of constantly undermining my abilities and how other people see them.

Saber Ability to assert my power by choosing one side or the other instead of thinking that I always have to just sit on the fence.

Saboteur Aspect of my character that can subvert my creative instincts rather than using them to make a more positive transformation.

Saccharine Potential to fulfill an ambition by trying to sweeten the short-term outcome, even though it may seem artificial and unsatisfying.

Sachet Ability to maintain my overall mood by ensuring that I look after a number of the smaller details so I can keep them safe.

Sack Ability to collect some resources that will give me a rough idea of how I can progress without losing out on new opportunities.

Sacked Opportunity to decisively make my career choices, even though it may involve stepping well outside my comfort zone.

Sack race Opportunity to take some definite steps to reach my chosen result rather than jumping all over the place to keep people happy.

Sacred Realization that I can devote some of my time to understanding my highest and deepest qualities and how I can embody them.

Sacrifice Opportunity to progress to a new future by stepping into my power and letting go of a way of life that no longer has any value.

Sad Opportunity to happily learn more about what will make me feel satisfied rather than feeling upset that I may have lost something.

Saddle Ability to feel comfortable and in control as I harness my instinctive energies without feeling weighed down by responsibilities.

Saddlebag Ability to be open to new opportunities by harnessing my unconscious energy so I can use it to consistently carry me forward.

Sadism Opportunity to enjoy the freedom to use my individual power instead of always giving myself a hard time about it.

Sadist Aspect of my character that often beats myself up over minor misgivings rather than taking real pleasure in my achievements.

Sadness Realization that I am happiest when I share my feelings instead of having continual regrets about not speaking my truth.

Safari Opportunity to become more familiar with the richness and complexity of my creative instincts so I can get closer to them.

Safe Ability to feel openly secure about the combined value of my creative gifts instead of trying to hide them away from other people.

Safe breaking Opportunity to open myself up to my concealed talent, even though it means I have to be more forceful with other people.

Safecracker Aspect of my character that is trying to find the right combination to open me up to my real value so I can feel more secure.

Safe house Situation where I have the security and support I need so I can examine any of my potentially self-destructive behaviors.

Safe sex Opportunity to become more intimately aware of my creative talents so I can feel much more confident in how I use them.

Safety Situation where I can always feel really secure in my deeper purpose, even when I'm participating in a risky opportunity.

Safety belt Ability to securely maintain my position as I make progress with my ambitions, even though I may meet unexpected challenges.

Safety cage Situation where I can become more aware of my defense mechanisms so I can remove perceived barriers to my progress.

Safety catch Ability to take a calm, objective approach to achieving one of my personal aims so I don't trigger any of my anxieties.

Safety deposit box Ability to feel safe and secure by setting boundaries around my resources so I can limit access to my expertise.

Safety harness Ability to feel more confident in a potentially hazardous situation by maintaining connections with those around me.

Safety net Ability to raise my confidence in dealing with tense situations instead of feeling that my efforts will just fall through.

Safety pin Ability to make a quick connection to the people around me rather than trying to go too deeply beyond surface impressions.

Safety valve Ability to control the flow of my emotions so I can happily vent my frustrations instead of just unexpectedly blowing up.

Saffron Potential to spice up my ambitions by reflecting on my optimism about a situation and how it is brightening my feelings.

Saga Opportunity to understand my deeper motivations and how they encourage me to do the right thing, even though it may seem risky.

Sage Aspect of my character that can help

resolve inner tension by having a healthy regard for my accumulated wisdom and experience.

Sagging Realization that I have the talent to rise above any material concerns instead of feeling constantly let down by my obligations.

Sail Ability to capture some of my prevailing thoughts and theories so I can convey some of the power they have to move me.

Sailboat Ability to navigate complex and unpredictable feelings by using powerful ideas to help me maintain my emotional stability.

Sailing Opportunity to explore the natural rhythm and flow of my emotions by using the power of my ideas to help me make progress.

Sailor Aspect of my character that is very much at home exploring my feelings and can help me work through challenging emotions.

Saint Aspect of my character that can help me rise above everyday concerns and patiently express my loving wisdom and spirituality.

Salad Potential to fulfill an ambition by using a variety of raw materials as a basis for achieving a healthy and successful outcome.

Salamander Instinctive ability to feel at home in situations where I need to immerse myself in my emotions as I work with creative ideas.

Salami Potential to fulfill an ambition by cramming in a lengthy range of experiences so I can always get a slice of the action.

Salary Ability to have my true worth recognized by others by keeping myself grounded and using my good taste to create value.

Sale Opportunity to make the most of my talents and have their value recognized by others rather than just giving myself away.

Sales assistant Aspect of my character that helps me understand my value and nurtures me as I look for the best ways to employ it.

Salesperson Aspect of my character that

looks for opportunities to share the wealth of my talent with people and have it fully acknowledged.

Saliva Essential ability to assimilate my experiences so I can tastefully resolve anxieties I may have about my potential.

Salmon Instinctive ability to recognize my powerful intuition so I can always make my way back to the source of my inspiration.

Salmon ladder Ability to use a specific series of steps to raise my awareness so I can continue to provide inspiration at a higher level.

Saloon Situation where I have the capacity to feel comfortable in developing my potential talents, even though it may seem confusing.

Salopettes Ability to present my self-image to people in a way that helps me to quickly navigate the ups and downs of any situation.

Salt Ability to flavor my approach by using my good taste to stay grounded and ensure that my value is recognized by other people.

Salt cellar Ability to grasp the value of my good taste so I can draw on my experience and use it to support my everyday activities.

Salt lake Situation where I can use my creative input to minimize any emotional influences so I can clearly reveal my deeper value.

Salt marsh Situation where I can explore the continual ebb and flow of my feelings so I can get on a firmer footing with my emotions.

Salute Opportunity to acknowledge my deeper feelings so other people can recognize how much an event has moved me.

Salvage Opportunity to reconnect with a valuable talent I thought I had lost so I can use it to make a worthwhile contribution.

Salvo Opportunity to resolve a conflicting situation by displaying the power of my ideas so I can relieve myself of any obligations.

Sample Ability to examine one specific aspect of how I feel so I can use my wider experience to help me make a bigger choice.

Samurai Aspect of my character that heroically engages with my inner conflicts so I can decisively resolve any potential challenges.

Sanctuary Situation where I can take the time to connect my highest awareness and deepest understanding so I can embody them.

Sand Ability to understand how all the seemingly small events and episodes can help me build up a more concrete life experience.

Sandals Ability to present my self-image to people by taking steps that open up my identity and show how comfortable I am with sharing it.

Sandbar Situation where an accumulation of small events and practical details can become a barrier to navigating an emotional situation.

Sand castle Ability to play with the practical details of my character so I can construct an idea of how things could be for me.

Sand dune Situation where I can use my shifting perspective to understand how lots of small details can build into something bigger.

Sandstorm Natural opportunity to channel the energy from lots of small ideas rather than feeling I have to cover everything up.

Sandwich Potential to fulfill an ambition by understanding different levels of an opportunity and what difference they can make for me.

Sapphire Ability to be crystal clear in how I communicate my intentions so I can express my aspirations in a calm, considered manner.

Sarcasm Realization that I need to communicate how I honestly feel about my abilities instead of always being scornful of my talents.

Sarcophagus Ability to resurrect one of my long-neglected ambitions so I can transform my situation rather than feeling too boxed in.

S

Sap Natural ability to rise to the challenge of my long-term spiritual growth without feeling as if it is depleting my energy.

Sapling Natural ability to give loving care and attention to my long-term spiritual growth while staying rooted in the practicalities.

Sardine Instinctive ability to immerse myself in my emotions and go with the flow rather than trying to cram in lots of experiences.

Sarong Ability to present my self-image in a relaxed way rather than becoming too wrapped up in how I might appear.

Sash Ability to present my self-image to people by being proud of my accomplishments so I can happily display them in public.

Satanic Realization that I can often be tempted by new possibilities, even though I don't necessarily have any burning ambitions.

Satellite Ability to maintain my distance when people are bouncing ideas off me rather than thinking that everything revolves around me.

Satellite dish Ability to be open and receptive to the theories and ideas of other people, even though they may initially seem quite far-fetched.

Satin Ability to provide a more attractive basis for my thoughts and feelings rather than appearing to always gloss over them.

Satisfaction Realization that I can achieve success by understanding what I need rather than being disappointed in my experiences.

Satellite navigation system Ability to see the bigger picture so I can successfully steer myself through unfamiliar and potentially complex situations.

Satsuma Natural ability to fulfill an ambition by taking a sunny and optimistic approach that will often result in a fruitful outcome.

Saturated Opportunity to completely immerse myself in a deeper learning experience so I can fully absorb the fundamental point.

Satyr Aspect of my character that revels in the growth potential of my instinctive nature and unashamedly gives free rein to it.

Sauce Potential to fulfill an ambition by understanding what makes me so special, without feeling I have to lay it on too thick.

Saucepan Ability to fulfill a potential ambition by bringing together my knowledge and experience and creating something new.

Saucer Ability to fulfill a practical need by allowing me to support some quite emotional actions rather than letting them spill out.

Sauna Situation where I can open up about some of my emotional frictions instead of getting all hot and bothered about them.

Sauntering Opportunity to free myself from unnecessary obligations so I can use my self-motivation in a more relaxed manner.

Sausage Potential to fulfill an ambition by packing a variety of influences into a series of experiences and using my connections.

Savage Aspect of my character that draws on the power of my natural instincts so I can calmly cultivate my creative talents.

Save Opportunity to reconnect with my deeper purpose so I can feel more secure in using my talents in uncertain situations.

Savings Ability to acquire deeper wisdom by making responsible choices so I will be able to show my increasing value to other people.

Savings account Ability to clearly understand my rising sense of self-worth and how it influences the stories I share with other people.

Savory Potential to fulfill an ambition by looking for long-term satisfaction rather than being attracted by short-term gains.

Saw Ability to use my power and confidence to consistently cut my way through old behavioral patterns that no longer serve me.

Sawmill Situation where I can transform

my habits by using the power of my practical skills to confidently shape my preferred outcome.

Sawn-off shotgun Ability to influence a wider range of people by powerfully, forcefully, and succinctly communicating my aims to them.

Saxophone Ability to take my instinctive creativity in both hands so I can use it to soulfully express the beliefs that inspire me.

Scab Essential opportunity to heal rather than cover up any hurt feelings by bringing together both sides of an argument.

Scabbard Ability to discreetly convey how I can decisively deal with potential challenges, rather than being openly antagonistic.

Scaffolding Ability to build up my confidence and maintain my self-image by being open to using external support when I really need it.

Scalding Opportunity to cool down an emotionally heated situation before it becomes too painful for everyone who might be involved.

Scale Ability to understand the degree of effort needed to realize a specific ambition rather than seeming to appear defensive.

Scales Ability to weigh up the advantages and disadvantages of any commitments I have made so I can balance my involvement.

Scallop Potential to fulfill an ambition by opening up to what I feel inside rather than presenting a hard outer image to people.

Scalp Essential ability to provide a basis for sharing my thoughts and ideas with other people so I can help them to succeed.

Scam Opportunity to make a fundamental transformation by having the confidence to declare my goals and how I plan to achieve them.

Scandal Opportunity to take charge of my own instinctive behavior and be proud of it rather than behaving as people might like me to.

Scanner Ability to methodically observe what is often unseen so I can use it to reveal a deeper and wider understanding of myself.

Scantily dressed Ability to present my self-image to people in a way that shows how comfortable I am with displaying my creativity.

Scapegoat Aspect of my character that always takes responsibility instead of letting other people blame me when there is a lot at stake.

Scar Essential ability to heal old wounds so I can share the experience with other people rather than continuing to feel uncomfortable.

Scarcity Opportunity to realize the abundance of my talents instead of feeling I lack the expertise to do what I need to.

Scarecrow Ability to cultivate my ambitions and keep an eye on them so they are not jeopardized by any interfering influences.

Scared Realization that I can make a courageous and transformative choice by using my power to boldly pursue what I need.

Scarf Ability to present my self-image by warmly communicating my most personal ideas and emotions without feeling vulnerable.

Scarlet Mood that can color my perspective by reflecting my passionate outlook in an intensely exciting way that raises my spirits.

Scary Opportunity to realize that I can make the most of any uncertain and unfamiliar situation by trusting in my own abilities.

Scary shadows Ability to throw some light on the less familiar aspects of my character so I can become more comfortable with my talents.

Scattered Opportunity to spread my influence widely by concentrating my efforts rather than allowing myself to be distracted by others.

Scavenger Aspect of my character that can pick up on any talents I have been neglecting so I can use them to transform my progress.

S

Scenario Opportunity to outline what I need so I can see the bigger picture and everything that might be involved in it.

Scene Situation where I can become more aware of what motivates me by understanding the background to my habitual behaviors.

Scenery Situation where I can see the underlying nature of my character and explore how it supports different aspects of my nature.

Scent Essential awareness that helps me to get back on track as I explore my feelings, rather than feeling thrown by circumstances.

Scepter Ability to demonstrate the strength of my practical abilities so other people will recognize my wisdom and refinement.

Schedule Ability to make the most of future opportunities by reflecting on my commitments to myself and understanding what I need.

Scheme Opportunity to give some form to my ideas by methodically exploring different ways in which I can shape their outcome.

Schizophrenic Aspect of my character that can bring a number of different areas of my identity together so I can understand who I am.

Scholarship Ability to develop my wider understanding of my potential talents by starting to value the knowledge I have gained already.

School Situation where I can learn valuable lessons and examine what I know by publicly demonstrating talents and experience.

Schoolbag Ability to be open to new information so I can quickly access all I need to learn about some emerging possibilities.

School cafeteria Situation where I can make the most of lessons I have learned by working through choices about what I need.

Schoolchild Aspect of my character embodying my unique, precious talents and holding potential for developing true awareness.

School playground Situation where I can play with different aspects of my character so I can learn about my talents and experiences.

Schoolteacher Aspect of my character that encourages me to develop my unique expertise and gives me authority to continue exploring.

Schooner Ability to navigate complex, unpredictable feelings by using prominent ideas to maintain my emotional stability.

Sciatica Opportunity to resolve a painful experience by courageously taking action rather than always letting it get on my nerves.

Science Ability to systematically study who I am, what I need, and what I believe so I can gain a wider understanding of myself.

Science fiction Ability to explore all potential outcomes of a situation instead of feeling that some of my plans seem too far-fetched.

Scientific equipment Ability to create a result that will have a great practical value by methodically working my way through a number of options.

Scientific experiment Opportunity to make valuable progress by systematically studying my future needs and being open to outcomes.

Scientist Aspect of my character that is constantly experimenting with a variety of possibilities so I can understand my situation.

Scissors Ability to look at both sides of a situation so I can quickly cut through any confusion and get straight to the point.

Scone Potential to fulfill an ambition by gathering some of my thoughts and ideas together and digesting them in a relaxed way.

Scoop Ability to come up with an original idea by using my deeper level of experience rather than thinking I have nothing to offer.

Scooter Ability to use my personal ambition and drive so I can happily play around with my choices as I progress toward my goal.

S

Scorch Ability to use my creative passion to transform how a situation appears to me, even though it may initially seem quite damaging.

Score Opportunity to judge my performance in a challenging situation by playing around with different ways of achieving my goals.

Scoreboard Ability to be open and honest about how well I feel I am performing rather than letting people decide if I make the grade.

Scorn Realization that I need to honestly communicate my deeper motives instead of being dismissive of other thoughts and ideas.

Scorpion Instinctive ability to take the sting out of a situation by keeping a healthy awareness rather than feeling defensive and short-tempered.

Scouring Opportunity to get to the bottom of a messy situation so I can ensure that my individual efforts will continue to shine.

Scout Aspect of my character that observes my behavior so I can understand how to assertively develop my strength and power.

Scowling Opportunity to face up to my own brilliance instead of feeling I have not managed to live up to other people's expectations.

Scrabble Opportunity to use my skill to try to make a number of important points, even though I may end up sending mixed messages.

Scramble Opportunity to quickly take action by being really clear about my fundamental needs and the sheer effort involved to succeed.

Scrambled eggs Potential to fulfill an ambition by breaking into some fertile new areas and mixing them up to reach a satisfying outcome.

Scrambled message Ability to increase my self-awareness by systematically working through what I need so I can communicate it to other people.

Scrap Ability to transform a situation by picking up on a number of small but valuable details so I can use them in a new way.

Scrapbook Ability to collect a variety of ideas and experiences so I can assemble them into a more valuable understanding.

Scrape Opportunity to get below the surface so I can see what is going on without causing myself any deeper discomfort.

Scrap heap Situation where I can create value by applying my accumulated practical experience rather than feeling over the hill.

Scrap-metal dealer Aspect of my character that recognizes fundamental value in my talents and can use them to shape a definite outcome.

Scrap yard Situation where I can give myself the space to work through areas of expertise that can provide me with unexpected value.

Scratch Ability to make a new start by dealing with an important surface detail instead of thinking I can always gloss over it.

Scratch card Ability to recognize the huge value of my talents by looking beyond surface appearances rather than leaving it to chance.

Scrawl Opportunity to clearly make my mark in a graceful and elegant manner instead of feeling as if I am somehow out of place.

Scrawny Realization that I have the power to increase my wider influence rather than feeling my contribution is deficient in any way.

Scream Opportunity to alert myself to an approaching opportunity by understanding an important message I am trying to communicate.

Scree Situation where I can create a more coherent outcome by using different aspects of the sheer effort I have made to succeed.

Screeching Opportunity to take a gentler and more pleasant approach that will resonate more deeply with what I am trying to express.

Screen Ability to establish a personal boundary by being quite selective about the people I choose to share my story with.

Screen saver Ability to maintain my viewpoint without becoming fixated on a particular opinion that might end up with me feeling burned-out.

S

Screen shot Opportunity to capture a clearer understanding of my thought processes so I can decide the best options for me to take.

Screen test Opportunity for me to judge how well I am displaying myself rather than letting others decide if I make the grade.

Screen wash Ability to open up about my feelings so I can clearly see my way forward as I make progress in my chosen direction.

Screenwriter Aspect of my character that is aware of how I may appear to others so I can understand how to reach my chosen outcome.

Screw Ability to go deeper so I can make a long-lasting connection without feeling that I'm going round and round.

Screwdriver Ability to consistently engage with the practical aspects of a deeper connection so I can drive home my point.

Scribble Realization that I can make my mark in a much more consistent manner by looking after myself and ensuring that I feel safe.

Script Ability to shape my ambitions and direct my future actions by making a specific choice about the outcome I would like to create.

Scriptwriter Aspect of my character that can successfully resolve any emotional tensions instead of feeling I am losing the plot.

Scroll Ability to convey some of my accumulated wisdom by opening up to how I feel rather than appearing to be too wrapped up.

Scrotum Essential ability to be open to new opportunities so I can bring out my best in a creatively challenging situation.

Scrounger Aspect of my character that can make full use of my valuable talents rather than feeling I have to copy other people.

Scrub Opportunity to make an effort and come clean about my sentiments instead of feeling that I just have to abandon my progress.

Scrubland Situation where I can take a more practical, down-to-earth approach rather than feeling I should just give up right now.

Scruffy Realization that I can tidy up some misconceptions about how I appear to people by being careful with how I express myself.

Scrum Opportunity to move beyond a deadlock and start making progress again, even though the eventual outcome may be uncertain.

Scrunchie Ability to pull together some of my wilder thoughts and ideas so I can have a much clearer view of the way forward.

Scrutinize Opportunity to give careful attention to my habits and behaviors rather than allowing others to be critical of them.

Scuba diver Aspect of my character that can safely explore some of my deeper emotions by thinking in a powerful, self-contained way.

Scuffle Opportunity to be clear about any inner conflicts I may have rather than trying to meet people's vague demands.

Scullery Situation where I have the room to nurture myself and others so we can see what plans and projects we can cook up together.

Sculpting Opportunity to take the more practical aspects of my life in both hands so I can use them to help shape my ambitions.

Sculpture Ability to understand how I can give more structure to my ambitions so I can definitely shape a successful outcome.

Scum Ability to stay clear about my deeper emotional needs rather than feeling I should skim over the top of them.

Scurry Opportunity to reach a successful outcome by making slow, steady progress rather than feeling I should rush into things.

Scurvy Essential opportunity to resolve an unhealthy situation by taking a fresh approach that uses the fruits of my experience.

S

Scuttle Ability to carry myself through a challenge by using a solid creative skill that has accumulated over a long period of time.

Scuttling Opportunity to open up to the power of my emotions rather than trying to conceal them by letting them sink without a trace.

Scythe Ability to use my power and strength to transform a situation by cutting through any confusion so new ideas can emerge.

Sea Situation where I can voyage into a wider understanding of my deeper emotional self and how I experience my moods and rhythms.

Sea anchor Ability to maintain a sense of emotional stability rather than feeling as if I am drifting aimlessly in my current situation.

Sea anemone Instinctive ability to open up to some of my emotions so I can explore them in more depth while staying grounded in reality.

Seabed Situation where I can feel fully supported in my emotional life so I can take a more relaxed approach to my passing feelings.

Seabird Instinctive ability to rise above any emotional concerns so I can spread my ideas by communicating them to other people.

Sea breeze Natural opportunity to use a simple idea to work through an emotional challenge with far greater ease than I had thought possible.

Sea eagle Instinctive ability to use the power and strength of my feelings to lift myself higher so I can clearly see the bigger picture.

Seafood Potential to fulfill my ambitions by satisfying my need for emotional fulfillment so I can nourish my continued growth and vitality.

Seagull Instinctive ability to feel at home with the emotional and practical aspects of a situation so I can rise above any concerns.

Seahorse Instinctive ability to immerse myself in my emotions so I can stand up for myself rather than just going with the flow.

Seal Instinctive ability to be warm and playful with my emotions and feelings so I can be happy making a deeper commitment to them.

Sealant Ability to make a definite emotional commitment so I can resolve a situation that has been leaving me feeling drained.

Sealed orders Ability to open myself up to making my own decisions rather than feeling I have to wait for the approval of other people.

Sealing wax Ability to clearly shape the message I want to communicate to others so I can make my mark with them.

Sea lion Instinctive ability to play around with some possibilities so I can feel good about making deeper commitments to them.

Seam Ability to increase my material benefits by bringing together some of my different skills so I can use their combined value.

Sea monster Instinctive ability to make the most of a huge opportunity rather than allowing myself to be overwhelmed by my emotions.

Seamstress Aspect of my character that can maintain my self-image and hold it all together in the face of criticism from other people.

Seamy Realization that I need to be more open about the self-image I present to other people so they can see the real me.

Séance Apparent opportunity to reconnect with a number of different aspects of my character I thought I'd managed to lay to rest.

Seaplane Ability to come up with a powerful idea so I can attract the emotional support I need to achieve my higher ambitions.

Search engine Ability to reach a successful outcome by looking inside myself for a meaningful answer about part of my life.

Searching Opportunity to discover how I feel about an unfamiliar situation by exploring a wide variety of different viewpoints.

S

Searching for car Opportunity to choose the professional direction I need to take so I can regain my personal drive and ambition.

Searching for home Opportunity to reveal myself in the way that makes me feel most comfortable instead of always looking for ways to please other people.

Searching for keys Opportunity to gain a firm grasp of what appears to be preventing my progress so I can unlock my hidden potential.

Searching for toilet Opportunity to attend to my personal needs rather than feeling I always have to look after the needs of other people.

Searching for work Opportunity to take action that demonstrates my fundamental value instead of waiting for others to discover my expertise.

Searching for workplace Opportunity to rediscover my purpose in life rather than feeling my expertise and experience is valueless.

Searching in city Opportunity to explore my wider social connections so I can access valuable resources I was previously unaware of.

Searching in countryside Opportunity to explore some unfamiliar, undiscovered aspects of my nature so I can see their possibilities.

Searching in cupboards Opportunity to reconnect with some personal behaviors and experiences I may been closed to so I can open up to their value.

Searching in distant land Opportunity to take a more practical, down-to-earth approach to achieving much more than I thought was remotely possible.

Searching in house Opportunity to explore the different aspects of my inner and outer lives so I can comfortably feel more secure in myself.

Searchlight Ability to use the power of my wisdom to illuminate what is happening so I can understand it with greater clarity.

Search party Aspects of my character committed to reconnecting with my forgotten talents so I can discover their true value.

Sea serpent Instinctive ability to heal any emotions that have been hurt by so I can quickly move on from my current situation.

Seashell Ability to feel much more safe and secure in my emotional life by taking the time to listen to my deeper feelings.

Sea sickness Opportunity to resolve an unhealthy emotional situation by bringing up my concerns rather than just feeling ill at ease.

Seaside Situation where I can edge toward a firmer, more grounded understanding of what will make me feel most emotionally fulfilled.

Season Opportunity to understand my natural instincts and rhythms so I can experience how they can flavor my wider awareness.

Season ticket Ability to demonstrate my value to people by giving myself permission to display my unique skills and abilities to them.

Seat Ability to occupy a relaxed and comfortable viewpoint and become more aware of how I can continue to support my position.

Seatbelt Ability to safely maintain my habitual viewpoint as I make progress with my ambitions through some unexpected challenges.

Seat of the pants Opportunity to make sense of what is happening so I can become more aware of how to consistently support my position.

Sea urchin Instinctive ability to present an impenetrable outer appearance to other people as a way of protecting my deeper feelings.

Seaweed Natural ability to make healthy use of my feelings so I can thrive in any emotional situation, no matter how adverse it is.

Seaworthy Ability to work my way through a complex emotional situation by realizing the respect that others have for my expertise.

Secluded Opportunity to subtly maintain personal boundaries without withdrawing from new connections that may emerge.

Second Opportunity to offer my support in an instant rather than always thinking that I should have to put my own interests first.

Secondary school Situation where I can learn some of life's bigger lessons so I can examine my needs and how I can achieve them.

Secondhand Realization that I can draw on the value of accumulated knowledge rather than feeling I must always do something new.

Secret Opportunity to explore the deeper mystery of who I really am so I can reveal the great potential I often hide from people.

Secret agent Aspect of my character that regularly tries to disguise some of my hidden talents and has passions I attempt to conceal.

Secretary Aspect of my character that routinely helps me to communicate my deeper purpose so I can be clear about my intentions.

Secret headquarters Situation where I can gather together a number of my ideas so I can become more aware of their previously unrealized value.

Secretion Essential ability to influence my emotions and convey how I feel so I can relieve myself from any messy obligations.

Secret police Aspects of my character that takes full responsibility for my actions instead of always feeling I am checking up on myself.

Secret room Aspect of myself that has huge undiscovered potential, even though I may often try to conceal it from the people around me.

Sect Aspects of my character that hold a particular set of beliefs and can use them as a basis for pursuing a specific ambition.

Secure Realization that being more certain about the value of my skills and abilities can make me feel less threatened by any challenges.

Secure area Situation where I can define my personal boundaries so that I can give myself the space to develop without any interference.

Secure line Ability to open up and express what I need to say instead of worrying that I will give away too much about how I feel.

Secure room Aspect of myself that feels comfortable in exploring my innermost feelings so I can understand their deeper value to me.

Security box Ability to feel safe and secure in the value of my expertise rather than closing myself off from any opportunities to use it.

Security check Opportunity to examine my behavior in greater detail so I can be more open about any feelings I may be trying to conceal.

Security guard Aspect of my character that feels responsible for protecting my deeper needs, though it can reduce available options.

Security procedure Opportunity to achieve my preferred outcome by working my way through my motives so I can be clear about them.

Security scanner Ability to methodically observe what is often unseen so I can have a clearer understanding of my deeper motivations.

Security van Ability to make committed progress toward my goal by understanding the value of my personal drive in a professional capacity.

Sedated Opportunity to stay calm so I can wake up to the actions I need to take to maintain my level of self-motivation.

Sedative Ability to take a calmer approach to healthily resolving a challenging situation rather than becoming overly agitated by it.

Sediment Ability to feel more settled by slowing down the rush of my feelings and emotions and allowing a clearer picture to separate out.

S

Seduction Opportunity to connect with my creative talents at a more intimate level so I can make them appear even more attractive.

Seductress Aspect of my character that can intentionally open me up to a creative opportunity that I am often tempted to pursue.

Seed Natural ability for a seemingly insignificant idea or plan to potentially grow into something much bigger and more powerful.

Seedling Natural ability to give careful attention to my long-term spiritual growth while staying rooted in the basic practicalities.

Seeing Opportunity to understand what is going on by focusing on some details to see if they fit in with my overall vision.

Seeking Opportunity to discover a greater truth by asking myself what I want and realizing how I can step into new possibilities.

Seeping Opportunity to open up a little more about my feelings so I can absorb the full significance of the emotions I experience.

Seer Aspect of my character that uses my deeper unconscious awareness to visualize my preferred outcome so I can plan accordingly.

Seesaw Ability to resolve the ups and downs of a particular situation by playing around with how I can balance my expectations.

Seething Opportunity to let my more passionate feelings bubble up to the surface so I can let off steam and bring things to a head.

Seismic activity Opportunity to become more aware of a potentially major break through so I don't find myself caught off balance in the future.

Seismometer Ability to gauge the potential extent of a personal upheaval so I can break new ground instead of feeling shaken up.

Seized Opportunity to get things moving smoothly again by taking control and getting a real grip on what is actually happening.

Seizure Essential opportunity to open up and release myself from any restrictions rather than behaving in a more convoluted manner.

Selector Ability to make a definite choice by understanding my preferences and using my unique power to act decisively on them.

Self Essential awareness that gives me the opportunity to understand who I am, what I need, and what I believe.

Self-addressed envelope Ability to understand more about who I am by ensuring I am always receptive to whatever emerges from my awareness.

Self-catering Opportunity to make some time to explore my unspoken needs so I can understand how to fulfill my appetite for success.

Self-confident Opportunity to trust in my unique talents so I can have complete faith in being able to reach a successful outcome.

Self-contained Ability to feel secure in my personal beliefs so I can be more open about sharing them with the people around me.

Self-defense Opportunity to achieve a deeper feeling of security by having the courage to engage with potentially threatening behavior.

Self-destructive Opportunity to use my unique talent to create the life I want instead of feeling that my expertise has no real value.

Self-harm Opportunity to open myself up to a healthy new awareness rather than constantly indulging myself in self-destructive behaviors.

Self-help book Ability to listen to my needs so I can happily satisfy them instead of always taking the advice of other people.

Self-identity Essential opportunity to become more aware of who I am so I can take meaningful action to affirm my individuality.

Self-improvement Opportunity to individually develop my expertise and experience so I can make the most of my potential talents.

Self-indulgent Opportunity to take a stricter approach to how I gratify my desires so I can have the discipline to achieve better results.

Selfish Realization that I can achieve much greater individual success by devoting more time to understanding the needs of others.

Self-medicating Opportunity to remedy an unhealthy situation by making a personal commitment to my future rather than just feeling ill at ease.

Self-pity Opportunity to celebrate my accomplishments with other people instead of being disdainful of what I have achieved so far.

Self-portrait Ability to reflect on a particular aspect of my character so I can clearly identify how I can fit into the bigger picture.

Self-preservation Opportunity to maintain my sense of purpose by keeping my ambitions alive rather than allowing my confidence to be eroded.

Self-protection Opportunity to be open to new possibilities while safely maintaining my personal boundaries against possible threats.

Self-sacrifice Opportunity to progress into a new future by realizing my power so I can let go of a way of life that no longer has any value.

Self-service Opportunity to attend to my needs so I am satisfied that I can look after the needs of the people around me.

Self-storage Situation where I can consistently accumulate my experience and expertise so I can easily access it at any time.

Self-timer Ability to decide my preferred outcome by using my past experience to understand how a situation may eventually work out.

Sell-by date Ability to fulfill an ambition by making the most of a specific opportunity rather than allowing it to go to waste.

Selling Opportunity to realize how worthwhile some of my talents are so I can have their value recognized by other people.

Sell-out Opportunity to use my valuable talents to attract other people to my particular viewpoint rather than just trying to be popular.

Semaphore Ability to communicate my feelings by flagging up some real concerns rather than indulging in pointless arm waving.

Semen Essential ability to use my competitive urges and take assertive action so I can make the most of a fertile opportunity.

Semiconscious Opportunity to wake up to what is happening around me rather than feeling I can never see the bigger picture.

Semidetached house Situation where I have the security and support to take an objective view as I explore my inner and outer lives.

Seminar Opportunity to develop my awareness of what motivates me and understand how it influences my deeper behavioral patterns.

Semtex explosive Ability to control my unresolved fears about my self-destructive behavior rather than allowing it to blow up unexpectedly.

Send Opportunity to connect with some wider possibilities by being able to convey my feelings about how receptive I am to them.

Senile dementia Opportunity to resolve an unhealthy situation by keeping my mind on what matters rather than living in the past.

Sensation Realization that I can make the most of an exciting new opportunity by opening up to feelings I'm not usually aware of.

Sense Realization that I can achieve a more complete understanding by being more open to feelings I would usually ignore.

Sensible Realization that I can use my judgment to decide the best course of action rather than being influenced by other people.

Sensible shoes Ability to present my self-image by taking steps to display my personal expertise and how comfortable I am with it.

S

Sensitivity Opportunity to tune in to what is happening so I can understand the finer details of what is required.

Sensor Ability to clearly understand what is happening beyond surface appearances so I can definitely provide a measured response.

Sensory deprivation Opportunity to explore my inner life so I can create my own opportunities rather than always feeling left out by others.

Sensual Realization that I can become more intimately aware of my talents by being open to possibilities that I might usually dismiss.

Sentence Ability to clearly and independently state what I need without feeling that other people will continually punish me for it.

Sentenced Opportunity to specifically communicate my future plans rather than feeling I am committing myself to stay in the same place.

Sentimental Realization that I sometimes need to tell others how I feel about them rather than appearing to be overemotional.

Sentinel Aspect of my character that looks beyond surface appearances so I can understand what is going on for me.

Sentry Aspect of my character that looks out for any challenges to my privacy so I can forcefully guard my personal boundaries.

Sentry box Situation where I can feel comfortable in setting personal boundaries and can look out for any challenges to my security.

Separate Ability to pursue my individual ambitions so I can maintain firm personal boundaries without my actions being divisive.

Separation Opportunity to rediscover a neglected talent by reconnecting with an aspect of my character that has become distant.

Sepia Mood that can color my perspective by reflecting on a more nostalgic outlook that can sometimes cloud my deeper emotions.

Septic Opportunity to decisively deal with any harmful influences by taking a healthy approach to resolve any underlying conflict.

Sequence Opportunity to choose my preferred outcome by deciding what I would like to happen next rather than following convention.

Sequins Ability to encourage my talents to shine by skillfully putting them into action so I can sparkle in any situation.

Serenade Ability to instinctively communicate my creativity by giving voice to a beautiful and deeply felt message about my feelings.

Serendipity Realization that I can use my wealth of talent to create valuable opportunities rather than discovering them by accident.

Serenity Ability to create a peaceful resolution in an effortless manner by understanding my underlying need for tension and drama.

Serf Aspect of my character that can gain more freedom by establishing personal boundaries rather than trying to please others.

Sergeant Aspect of my character that has the authority and discipline to take charge of my inner conflicts and peacefully resolve them.

Serial Opportunity to experience the different aspects of my individual story so I can understand the value of the eventual outcome.

Serial killer Aspect of my character that repeatedly tries to kill off one of my talents because others are challenged by my ingenuity.

Serial number Ability to consistently display an individual talent to other people rather than counting on anyone else to do it for me.

Serious Opportunity to make a commitment to thinking more deeply about my situation so I can make light of some of my obligations.

Sermon Opportunity to share my personal perspective with other people so they can understand the fundamental power of my story.

S

Serpent Instinctive ability to heal any hurt feelings by moving on from a self-image that is no longer healthy for me.

Serrated edge Ability to make a definite difference by consistently cutting my way through old behavioral patterns that no longer serve me.

Serum Essential ability to protect myself, by being really clear about my feelings and how they provide support for my passions.

Servant Aspect of my character that habitually tries to please people by feeling that I should routinely put their needs before my own.

Serve Opportunity to understand what I need by taking decisive action rather than waiting around for someone else to look after me.

Server farm Situation where I can produce a valuable outcome by developing my thought processes and cultivating my professional connections.

Service Realization that the most effective way to look after other people's needs is to make sure that I always attend to my own needs.

Service charge Ability to make decisive progress by asserting my needs rather than just hoping that others will automatically accept me.

Service station Situation where I can have easy access to resources that will enable me to maintain my progress with a personal ambition.

Servo-assisted Ability to stay in control of my drive and ambition by using my accumulated experience to apply just the right pressure.

Session Opportunity to bring different aspects of my expertise together so I can achieve a decisive outcome in a shorter time.

Set Ability to bring together all my skills and talents so I can make a definite decision about the direction I need to take.

Setback Opportunity to make a major advance by using my accumulated experience rather than feeling disappointed about options.

Set square Ability to clearly express my personal boundaries rather than always feeling that I should draw the line somewhere.

Settee Ability to share a relaxed and comfortable viewpoint with others so I can be aware of how we support one another's positions.

Setting Situation where I can relate my needs to my immediate surroundings so I can understand my potential for development.

Setting concrete Opportunity to take a firm stance in my viewpoint instead of feeling I am unable to take the steps I need to support it.

Setting sun Natural opportunity to reflect on the power of my creativity so I can prepare for the next idea that will dawn on me.

Settlement Situation where I can conveniently connect with my friends on a more permanent basis so I can decide my chosen outcome.

Settling Opportunity to consolidate what will make me feel secure instead of feeling that my confidence is starting to subside.

Set-top box Ability to be receptive to a variety of possible outcomes so I can use the power of my imagination to make a decision.

Setup Opportunity to organize my procedures to achieve an ambition instead of thinking I'm doing other people's work for them.

Severance package Ability to step into a more worthwhile future by being receptive to new possibilities and whatever value they contain.

Severe Realization that I can achieve more by taking a gentler approach rather than being uncompromising and unnecessarily extreme.

Sewage Ability to let go of unhealthy feelings and habitual behaviors that no longer serve me so I can get rid of them more easily.

S

Sewage works Situation where I can separate out my healthy emotions by working my way through the outcomes of my habits and behaviors.

Sewer Situation where I can explore a deeper understanding of my unhealthy emotions so I can channel them into positive activity.

Sewing Opportunity to piece together the various aspects of my self-image so I can present it to other people more consistently.

Sewing machine Ability to use a recognized procedure as a way of consistently presenting a more coherent self-image to those around me.

Sex Opportunity to become much more intimately aware of my talent to conceive a special ambition and bring it fully into being.

Sex aid Opportunity to support what I want to accomplish with my creativity rather than allowing any anxieties to hold me back.

Sex change Opportunity to transform my situation by understanding how to use my creative talent to make a difference in how I feel.

Sex crime Opportunity to have more confidence in my creative instincts instead of punishing myself when I feel I have let other people down.

Sex drive Ability to use my motivation to make progress with my powerful talent for bringing ideas to life and developing them.

Sex maniac Aspect of my character that uses my creative instincts to reach my chosen outcome, even though other people may think I am crazy.

Sex offender Opportunity to take responsibility for channeling my creativity instead of expecting other people to control it for me.

Sexual infection Opportunity to maintain healthy creative boundaries so I can develop the germ of an idea without feeling ill at ease.

Sexual intercourse Opportunity to become more intimately aware of my instinctive talent for creatively conceiving new ideas with others.

Sex worker Aspect of my character that can freely express my creative value to other people rather than feeling I have no real purpose.

Shabby Realization that I can express myself more powerfully by taking loving care of some aspects of myself I have been neglecting.

Shack Situation where I am comfortable in spending some time exploring some of the unknown, unfamiliar aspects of my character.

Shackles Ability to use my unique power to liberate myself from an uncomfortable situation rather than always trying to hold myself back.

Shade Situation where I can take a cooler and more relaxed perspective so I can see how my mood can sometimes color my viewpoint.

Shades Ability to protect my unique insight so I can filter out any glaring distractions in an otherwise illuminating situation.

Shadow Ability to see the contrast between the familiar aspects of my character and the unexplored, unfamiliar aspects.

Shadowy figure Aspect of my character that can help me to clearly see the value of my fundamental talents instead of worrying how I may appear.

Shady character Aspect of my character that can identify the qualities I find most meaningful rather than always doubting myself.

Shaft Ability to directly connect my practical skills and experience so I can use them to consistently convey my power and strength.

Shaggy Ability to constantly produce lots of healthy ideas, even though they may require some work to make them more presentable.

Shaky Realization that I can achieve a more consistent outcome by taking a firmer approach that will achieve definite results.

Shallow Realization that I can achieve a profounder understanding of what I need by going deeper than surface appearances.

Shallow grave Situation where I need to explore my needs in much greater depth as I prepare the ground for a major life transformation.

Sham Opportunity to make a difference by fully engaging with any challenges instead of just being concerned about my appearance.

Shaman Aspect of my character that instinctively makes a profoundly healthy connection to the power of my wiser and experienced self.

Shame Realization that I need to respect my emotions and take pride in them rather than feeling embarrassed about my behavior.

Shampoo Ability to make my thoughts and ideas more presentable by cleaning up conflicting feelings as I work through them.

Shandy Potential to fulfill an emotional need by allowing my optimism to bubble up so I don't leave myself feeling too confused.

Shape Ability to form an idea of the outcome I would like to see so I can begin to use my expertise to make it happen.

Shape-shifter Aspect of my character that can naturally adapt to different challenges by understanding the deeper context of what is happening.

Shape wear Ability to present my self-image by confidently showing off the best aspects of my character in a more controlled way.

Share Ability to see the bigger picture so I can understand the most effective way to allocate my practical skills and resources.

Shark Instinctive ability to channel my emotional power into a fundamental purpose, even though it can seem threatening to others.

Sharp Realization that being open and honest is the best way to understand what is happening, even though it may feel uncomfortable.

Sharpshooter Aspect of my character that can create a clearer understanding by powerfully communicating my aims to the people around me.

Shattered Opportunity to deal more robustly with any challenging experiences rather than always feeling that I will end up in bits.

Shaver Ability to work my way through some ideas I have been developing so I can use them to shape my style of thinking.

Shaving Opportunity to take a closer look at some ideas I have been sharing so I can choose which ones I no longer need.

Shawl Ability to present my self-image to others by covering up my vulnerabilities and surrounding myself with loving security.

Sheaf Ability to reap the value of my previous efforts by collecting all the results so I can make a bundle from them.

Shears Ability to look at both sides of a situation so I can quickly get to the point and take decisive action to transform it.

Sheath Ability to discreetly convey how I can decisively deal with any wounding criticism without having to be opening aggressive.

Shed Situation where I can access a variety of skills and experiences so I feel comfortable in working with any challenges.

Sheep Instinctive ability to think for myself and make my own choices instead of conforming to the vague expectations of other people.

Sheepdog Instinctive ability to show commitment to my creativity by making my individual choices in a persistently determined manner.

Sheep tick Instinctive ability to let small, unnecessary formalities look after themselves rather than letting them drain my energy.

Sheet Ability to have my material needs well covered so I can take a more relaxed, comfortable approach to my creativity.

S

Sheet music Ability to instinctively communicate my fundamental needs to others so we can all give voice to what is often unspoken.

Shelf Ability to keep my resources organized and accessible so I can get an idea off the ground rather than neglecting it.

Shell Ability to present an apparently impenetrable outer appearance to people as a habitual way of protecting my inner vulnerability.

Shellfish Instinctive ability to protect what I am feeling inside by presenting an apparently invulnerable outer image to other people.

Shell suit Ability to present my self-image to people in a way that shows my casual approach and apparently invulnerable appearance.

Shelter Situation where I can temporarily feel safe and secure and am able to protect myself from a potentially uncertain outcome.

Shelving Ability to raise my level of awareness about the value of my widespread resources so I can use them in a more structured way.

She-male Aspect of my character embody both my masculine and feminine attributes, allowing me to powerfully express my creativity.

Shepherd Aspect of my character that can look after my more traditional talents by taking care to protect them from my wilder urges.

Shepherdess Aspect of my character that can gather some vague ideas and use them to produce a range of valuable material.

Shepherd's crook Ability to reach out and take control of wayward thinking so I can concentrate all my creative ideas in one place.

Sheriff Aspect of my character that has a clear sense of what is right and wrong and always aims to hold me fully accountable to it.

Shield Ability to protect my inner life from any possible dangers so I can defend myself

from outside threats to my deeper feelings.

Shift Opportunity to experience a personal transformation by changing my perspective rather than abandoning my situation.

Shift worker Aspect of my character that can consistently transform my raw talent into a valuable outcome just by putting the hours in.

Shimmering Opportunity to reflect on my emerging talent by taking a firm, unwavering approach that will really allow me to shine.

Shin Essential ability to stand up for my more fundamental viewpoints so I can be at the forefront of any decisive action.

Shine Ability to use the power and energy of my creativity to illuminate any potential opportunities I encounter.

Shingle Situation where I can take a well-rounded approach to connecting my accumulated knowledge with my wider emotional experience.

Shin guard Ability to protect any vulner-abilities that may be just below the surface as I take steps to achieve my objective.

Shining Opportunity to use the unique power of my wisdom to illuminate the possibilities of a situation with much greater clarity.

Ship Ability to explore my emotional highs and lows and navigate them safely so I can maintain my preferred course of action.

Shipbuilder Aspect of my character that can develop a solidly structured sense of who I am so I can navigate any emotional challenges.

Shipwreck Situation where I can raise myself from the depths of an overwhelming emotional experience and plot a new course of action.

Shipyard Situation where I can be more open about my personal ambitions and the resources I need to resolve any emotional challenges.

Shire horse Instinctive ability to harness

my unconscious strength so I can use my great power to keep plodding on with my ambitions.

Shirt Ability to present my self-image to people in a way that allows them to recognize the value of my material ambitions.

Shiver Essential opportunity to use my inner vitality to keep things moving, even when other people appear to be cool and distant.

Shoal Instinctive ability to collect my feelings so I can go with the flow without getting too caught up in my deeper emotions.

Shock Realization that I have an unexpectedly powerful ability to change my circumstances without it being a complete surprise.

Shock absorber Ability to keep a level head as I negotiate some surprising ups and downs I may encounter when pursuing an ambition.

Shoe Ability to present my self-image to people by taking steps to display my personal status and how comfortable I am with it.

Shoe box Ability to set some personal boundaries so I will be able to maintain my status in a way that feels comfortable for me.

Shoelaces Ability to feel more secure about the steps I am taking instead of worrying that I will somehow lose my personal status.

Shoemaker Aspect of my character that helps me stay motivated and supports the steps I take to display my personal status to people.

Shooting Opportunity to use my power and influence in an assertive manner so I can quickly communicate my intended aims to others.

Shooting star Opportunity to understand a sudden flash of inspiration from my higher awareness so I can use it in a more down-to-earth manner.

Shop Situation where I can make a worthwhile choice by displaying my specific value and having it recognized by other people.

Shop assistant Aspect of my character that helps me understand and acknowledge my value so I can choose the best ways to use it.

Shopkeeper Aspect of my character that looks after all my special gifts so I can ensure their value is recognized by other people.

Shoplifting Opportunity to recognize the increasing value of my talents rather than forcefully trying to conceal them from others.

Shopping Opportunity to discover what others recognize as my unique talents so I can make some choices to realize my value.

Shopping mall Situation where I can explore a variety of outlets for my skills so I can have their value recognized by more people.

Shop window Ability to clearly understand my viewpoint on my most valuable assets so I can see how I am currently using them.

Shopworn Opportunity to use the value of my skills to break down some hard challenges so I can continue to support my future growth.

Shore Situation where I can edge toward a firmer, more grounded understanding of the continual ebb and flow of my emotions.

Short Realization that I can reach out and quickly convey how I feel without being too abrupt or going on about it at length.

Short-changed Opportunity to realize my value by transforming my relationships instead of allowing others to take me for granted.

Short-circuit Opportunity to take my time and be clear what I am trying to communicate rather than getting my wires crossed.

Shortcut Situation where I can take decisive action to leave any unwelcome aspect of the past behind so I can step into a new future.

Shorthand Ability to have a firm grasp of my inner power so I can use it to quickly convey the full impact of my deeper understanding.

S

Short-sighted Essential opportunity to see the bigger picture by opening up to wider possibilities instead of being narrow-minded.

Short-tempered Realization that I can consistently achieve long-term success by taking a more equable approach when dealing with my emotions.

Shot Opportunity to assert my power and influence in a forceful manner so I can quickly communicate my intentions to people.

Shot-blasting Opportunity to channel some of my most powerful thoughts and ideas so I can strip away any superficial misconceptions.

Shotgun Ability to influence a much wider area by asserting my power in a more forceful manner as I communicate my aims to people.

Shoulder Essential ability to display my levels of strength and confidence to people so I can continue to provide support for them.

Shoulder bag Ability to be open to new opportunities so I can continue to provide strong support for my accumulated skills and resources.

Shouting Opportunity to attract the help and support of other people by raising my concerns and being vocal about what I need.

Shovel Ability to dig deeper into my practical resources so I can make an honest effort to reveal what is going on.

Shoving Opportunity to keep forcibly moving forward so I can overcome a challenge that may be causing a lot of resistance for me.

Show Opportunity to display my talents to other people by performing a unique skill and having its value more widely recognized.

Shower Situation where I can come clean about an emotional situation and clarify where I stand by letting my feelings flood out.

Showering Opportunity to stand up for myself and open up more to my emotions so I can become clearer about how I feel.

Showgirl Aspect of my character that can display my growing wisdom and that has the talent to keep developing my creativity and intuition.

Show jumper Aspect of my character that can harness my unconscious strength and power so I can make progress in leaps and bounds.

Showreel Ability to reflect on the opportunities where I perform best so I can share my developing ambitions with other people.

Showroom Situation where I feel comfortable and secure in displaying the resources that will help me develop potential talents.

Shredder Ability to transform some accumulated behavioral patterns so I can move on from an episode that has been pulling me apart.

Shrew Instinctive ability to deal with any small anxieties that may have been gnawing away at me rather than losing my temper with them.

Shriek Opportunity to take a gentler and less vocal approach that will have a deeper resonance with those I am trying to attract.

Shrill Realization that I can take an approach that will resonate more deeply with me rather than feeling I am being too intense.

Shrimp Instinctive ability to make the most of a personal ambition, even though it may seem small and insignificant to other people.

Shrine Situation where I can devote my effort to understanding the qualities that I find most powerful so I can learn how to embody them.

Shrink Opportunity to expand my levels of awareness by narrowing my overall focus and objectively observing what is emerging for me.

Shrink-wrap Ability to protect myself from any emotional upset by having a clear view of the practical value of my talents.

Shriveled Opportunity to soak up the surrounding atmosphere and absorb the full value of my experiences to make a fresh start.

S

Shroud Ability to prepare for a major transformation in my life by ensuring I don't get too wrapped up in concealing my talents.

Shrubbery Situation where I can open up more to my more immediate spiritual growth by exploring what seems unknown and unfamiliar to me.

Shuddering Opportunity to make a situation run more smoothly by resolving any frictions and not worrying about possible outcomes.

Shuffling Opportunity to take some deliberate steps to successfully reach my objective instead of feeling that I am dragging my heels.

Shut Opportunity to achieve closure in a challenging situation by opening myself up to the reality of what is actually happening.

Shut off Opportunity to open myself up and communicate how I feel to other people rather than closing myself off from them.

Shutter Ability to be very firm about the aspects of my private life that I share with other people, without completely closing myself off.

Shuttle Ability to make decisive change in my point of view rather than feeling that I'm always going backward and forward with it.

Shuttlecock Ability to knock some loftier ideas back and forth so I can raise some points that will help decide an outcome.

Shy Realization that I need to be more confident in displaying my expertise rather than avoiding any opportunities to share it.

Sibling Aspect of my character that enables me to become more familiar with the strength of my creativity without being too demanding.

Sick Opportunity to resolve an unhealthy situation by taking decisive action rather than worrying or feeling ill at ease.

Sick bag Ability to be open to new opportunities by taking a healthy approach so I can bring up any issues of no practical value.

Sick bay Situation where I can explore my feelings of uneasiness in relative calm so I can be more receptive to my deeper emotions.

Sick leave Opportunity to make some time for myself so I can resolve a personal issue that has great professional significance for me.

Sick note Ability to understand the significance of my current actions so I can give myself permission to deal with any other tensions.

Sick pay Opportunity to acknowledge the value of my expertise so I can maintain healthy relationships with others.

Sickle Ability to shape my future and take control of it by choosing to cut through personal confusion so new ideas can emerge.

Sickness Opportunity to resolve some uneasy feelings so I can decide on a healthier way to successfully accomplish my ambitions.

Side Situation where I can get to the center of what is happening rather than feeling I have to choose one specific viewpoint.

Sidebar Ability to understand some peripheral issues that may have a major influence on how I get to the center of the situation.

Sidecar Ability to make progress toward my objective by staying close to someone who has the freedom to pursue ambitions.

Side effects Realization that the influence of my actions on the people around me can often have a more powerful outcome than I intended.

Sideline Situation where I can align my skills and resources with an emerging opportunity instead of feeling that people are ignoring me.

Side mirror Ability to gain a clearer understanding of what is behind my chosen pursuit by reflecting on wider aspects of my situation.

Side street Situation where I can build stronger relationships by using an alternative route to get to the center of what is happening.

S

Sideways Realization that I have to be straightforward in how I approach a challenge rather than allowing myself be knocked off balance.

Siege Opportunity to strongly resist a challenge to my security by being open to new possibilities rather than isolating myself.

Sieve Ability to separate out the more valuable aspects of my accumulated experience without putting too much of a strain on myself.

Sifting Opportunity to work my way through the finer details so I can closely examine what I should keep and what I should let go.

Sight Essential opportunity to focus on a particular objective so I can set some goals while staying aware of the bigger picture.

Sightseeing Opportunity to explore a number of areas that are of significant interest to me so I can continue to widen my awareness.

Sign Ability to explore a more meaningful aspect of my character by making a significant connection and understanding its importance.

Signal Ability to communicate what I need to say by taking direct action rather than just making some ineffective gestures.

Signal box Situation where I can decisively change my career path by levering my knowledge and experience to make the right choice.

Signature Ability to make my mark so other people can recognize my unique identity and acknowledge my individual value.

Signature tune Ability to instinctively communicate my unique value to other people in a familiar way that will resonate with them.

Signet ring Ability to make an impression on people by demonstrating my commitment to the healthy development of a continuing partnership.

Significant Realization that I have the power to take meaningful action rather than feeling that my actions are of no consequence.

Significant other Aspect of my character that embodies my commitment to understanding how I can make a difference to people.

Sign language Ability to communicate what I find most meaningful to other people rather than feeling I always have to stay silent.

Signpost Ability to raise my awareness of a significant connection so I can choose to follow a path that will bring me closer to it.

Silage Ability to use my natural enthusiasm so I can raise my levels of awareness while staying rooted in everyday practicalities.

Silence Opportunity to listen for my inner voice and hear what I need in this moment rather than letting my voice get lost in the noise.

Silencer Ability to assert my power by forcefully getting rid of anything I no longer need in a discreet and effective manner.

Silhouette Ability to outline what I need by using contrasting perspectives rather than taking a flat, two-dimensional approach.

Silk Ability to provide a material basis for some of my more delicate feelings so I can fashion them into something more tangible.

Silkworm Instinctive ability to create a strong thread for my personal story, even though it may seem quite lightweight to other people.

Sill Ability to strongly support the firm basis of one of my viewpoints in an unobtrusive and self-effacing manner.

Silly Realization that I can make a serious contribution to a challenging situation instead of feeling as if people will laugh at me.

Silo Situation where I can accumulate individual power by ensuring that some of my more valuable resources are fully protected.

Silt Ability to steadily accumulate practical knowledge by using my learning and experience to convey some of the finer details.

Silver Ability to use my fundamental strength to truly reflect my value so I can have my great achievements mirrored by other people.

Silver birch Natural potential for my long-term spiritual growth by using my grace and flexibility to reflect my deep-rooted value.

Silver bullet Ability to resolve a potentially energy-sapping situation by taking decisive action rather than leaving it to superstition.

Silver star Ability to show my confidence in dealing with challenging situations instead of feeling my efforts will be unrewarded.

SIM card Ability to identify the beliefs I most regularly subscribe to so I can consistently communicate them to those around me.

Similarity Realization that I can make a difference by understanding how some of my unique qualities correspond to those in others.

Simmering Opportunity to take the lid off how I feel rather than letting my feelings continue to bubble up uncontrollably.

Simple Realization that I can achieve a decisive outcome by taking a straightforward approach instead of overcomplicating the situation.

Simulator Ability to commit myself to following a definite course of practical action rather than appearing to go through the motions.

Sin Realization that I am responsible for attending to my moral behavior instead of allowing anyone else to judge me on it.

Sincerity Realization that I can achieve my ambitions by being honest about my intentions rather than trying to please other people.

Sinew Essential ability to stay fundamentally connected by remaining powerfully flexible instead of feeling that I am under any strain.

Sing-along Opportunity to work together with a group of other people so we can give voice to what will make us feel most inspired.

Singed Realization that I can completely transform my creative talent rather than just superficially working around the edges of it.

Singer Aspect of my character that can give voice to my deepest and most powerful feelings by speaking passionately from my heart.

Singing Opportunity to draw on my powerful source of inspiration so I can be vocal about what I need from others.

Single Realization that I have the power and independence to make my own decisions rather than looking for permission from others.

Single parent Aspect of my character that embodies my potential for individual development and gives me the authority to be myself.

Sinister Realization that I have the power to always do the right thing rather than feeling continually threatened by lurking anxieties.

Sinister lover Aspect of my character that can connect at a deeper level by creating a more intimate awareness of what I feel is right for me.

Sinister stranger Aspect of my character that may appear unfamiliar but can give me deep insight into how to take exactly the right action.

Sink Ability to contain my emotions about a particular situation so I can clear up some aspects that have been draining my energy.

Sinking Opportunity to voluntarily immerse myself in deeper emotions and feelings instead of allowing the situation to drag me down.

Sinking feeling Opportunity to raise my levels of awareness by understanding what I am intuitively sensing rather than being overly objective.

Sinking ship Opportunity to remove unwanted emotional influences so I can keep myself on an even keel and continue my progress.

S

Sinuous Realization that I can achieve a graceful outcome by being more straightforward instead of going through twists and turns.

Sinus Essential ability to create the space that helps support my viewpoint rather than getting too choked up about a situation.

Sip Potential to fulfill an emotional need by taking things one small step at a time instead of feeling completely drained.

Siphon Ability to convey how I feel by being open and direct rather than continually behaving in a closed and convoluted manner.

Siren Ability to draw my attention to a potentially dangerous situation that may result in an unexpected series of events for me.

Sister Aspect of my character that enables me to share my creativity and wisdom in familiar situations without being too demanding.

Sister-in-law Aspect of my character that has helped me make a commitment to sharing my creativity and wisdom in less familiar situations.

Sitar Ability to take my instinctive creativity in both hands so I can express my feelings in an exotic and evocative manner.

Sitcom Opportunity to resolve a fundamental dilemma by taking a relaxed and comfortable viewpoint that invariably keeps everyone happy.

Site Situation where I can explore the basis of some of my plans so I can take specific action to achieve my chosen outcome.

Sitting Opportunity to take a relaxed and comfortable viewpoint and become more aware of how I can continue to support my position.

Situation Realization about my potential for personal development by understanding how I can relate my needs to my immediate surroundings.

Six-pack Essential ability to feel really connected to my strongest core instincts instead of constantly worrying about my appearance.

Six-shooter Ability to consistently assert my power in a forceful manner so I can repeatedly communicate my aims to others.

Size Realization that the scale of my ambitions will influence the amount of effort required to accomplish my desired level of success.

Size zero Realization that I need to restore my appetite for life by being more self-indulgent rather than worrying about how I appear.

Sizzling Realization that I can potentially fulfill an ambition by using my creativity and passion to increase my chances of success.

Skateboard Ability to use my self-motivation and energy to balance my options so I can skillfully navigate my way through a situation.

Skating Opportunity to apply direct pressure to keep a situation moving in a graceful manner rather than trying to slip away.

Skating rink Situation where I can play around with the more tangible aspects of my accumulated experience without feeling overwhelmed.

Skeleton essential Ability to understand the bare bones of a situation by having the fundamental strength to stand up for my beliefs.

Skeleton key Opportunity to open myself to a variety of possibilities that will give me wider freedom to unlock my hidden potential.

Sketch Ability to outline some of my basic thoughts and ideas so I can develop them further rather than acting too hastily.

Sketchbook Ability to open up to the wealth of my accumulated knowledge and learning so I can develop an outline for the future.

Sketch map Ability to use my previously accumulated experience to outline the main characteristics of a potentially complex situation.

Skewer Ability to fulfill a potential ambition by lining up a number of possibilities so I can understand the point of them all.

Ski Ability to make rapid progress by using by expertise and experience to weigh the options so I can balance my commitments.

Skid Ability to keep a weighty situation moving smoothly forward rather than letting it go out of control and ending up in disarray.

Skidding Opportunity to maintain progress with an ambition by responding immediately to unforeseen circumstances and keeping a light touch.

Skid pan Situation where I can become more comfortable with resolving unforeseen challenges as I progress in my chosen direction.

Skiing Opportunity to quickly navigate the ups and downs of a situation by using some solid learning from my accumulated experience.

Ski instructor Aspect of my character that encourages me to embark on a steep learning curve and helps me avoid any potential pitfalls.

Ski jump Opportunity to make the most of an emerging possibility by using my accumulated expertise to release myself from obligations.

Ski lift Ability to heighten my awareness and elevate my level of understanding so I can use my experience to make rapid progress.

Skill Ability to decide on my chosen outcome and successfully accomplish it rather than feeling that I am unable to contribute.

Skilled labor Opportunity to decisively work my way through a set of challenges instead of thinking that my efforts are of no consequence.

Skillet Ability to fulfill a potential ambition by gathering some of my knowledge and experience and quickly applying it.

Ski mask Ability to present my self-image

to other people in a way that helps to feel more comfortable with any sudden changes in mood.

Skim milk Potential to fulfill my emotional needs in a healthy way by dividing my time equally between myself and others.

Skimobile Ability to use my personal drive and ambition so I can make my way through certain facets of my learning and experience.

Skin Essential ability to stay in touch with my feelings by being comfortable with the boundary between my inner and outer worlds.

Skin cancer Essential opportunity to get in touch with my feelings rather than allowing them to grow unhealthily out of control.

Skin complaint Essential opportunity to deal with an unhealthy situation by openly sharing feelings instead of just moaning ineffectively.

Skin diver Aspect of my character that enjoys openly immersing myself in my emotions so I can stay in touch with my deeper feelings.

Skinny Essential opportunity to increase the value of my perspective rather than letting people think that I am just a lightweight.

Ski plane Ability to use my accumulated expertise to get a powerful idea off the ground so I can accomplish my highest ambitions.

Skipper Aspect of my character that has the familiarity of experience to safely steer my way through an uncertain emotional situation.

Skipping Opportunity to reach a more valuable outcome by taking definite steps instead of trying to quickly miss them out.

Skirmish Opportunity to take decisive action and make a bold stand rather than skirting around a potentially tense encounter.

Skirt Ability to present my self-image to people in a way that gives me the wider freedom to take the steps I choose to.

S

Ski tow Ability to use my motivation to keep my learning moving in the right direction without feeling that I'm being pushed into it.

Skulduggery Opportunity to honestly express my ideas in a truthful way so people will be encouraged to share what they think.

Skulking Opportunity to be openly proud about the value of my ideas rather than trying to conceal them in case others criticize me.

Skull Essential ability to safeguard my instinctive intelligence so I can fundamentally support my personal way of thinking.

Skull and crossbones Ability to signal the power of my emotions to others and draw their attention to the feelings I am trying to convey.

Skunk Instinctive ability to use my common sense so I can take a black-and-white approach rather than feeling I have to kick up a stink.

Skunkworks Situation where I can use my ingenuity to accomplish an apparently impossible task instead of trying to hide my talent.

Sky Situation where I can open up my higher levels of awareness so I can encompass a wider variety of thoughts and theories.

Sky burial Opportunity to lay to rest some old ways of thinking so I can use my ideas to move into the future in a more gracious manner.

Skydive Opportunity to immerse myself in a rush of exciting ideas so I can work my way through them to reach a successful conclusion.

Skydiver Aspect of my character that is bold enough to confidently jump at an exciting idea and bring it successfully down to earth.

Skylark Instinctive ability to play around with some inspiring thinking so I can happily rise above some weighty commitments.

Skylight Ability to clearly understand my individual perspective by using the power of my wisdom to illuminate what is happening.

Skyscraper Situation where I can fully step into the various aspects of my professional self so I can raise the scale of my ambitions.

Skywriting Opportunity to share some of my higher aspirations by communicating them clearly to people and ensuring I make my mark.

Slab Ability to make a significant contribution by using my entire range of talents rather than restricting myself to one area.

Slack Opportunity to give myself some room to maneuver instead of feeling as if I am restricting myself or behaving irresponsibly.

Slag heap Situation where I can accumulate some appreciable skills so I can use a more refined approach to make myself stand out.

Slalom Opportunity to quickly navigate the twists and turns of a situation by using some solid learning from my accumulated experience.

Slam Opportunity to achieve closure in a challenging situation by taking a gentle approach instead of trying to be too forceful.

Slanderous Realization that I need to take responsibility for some of my own behaviors rather than allowing other people to judge me.

Slang Ability to express what I feel about my situation, even though other people may not completely understand me to begin with.

Slanting Opportunity to understand my inclination toward a particular course of action instead of sloping away from any responsibility.

Slap Opportunity to resolve a potentially conflicting situation by showing my hand rather than allowing it to come to blows.

Slapstick Opportunity to take a more considered approach instead of behaving predictably in an obvious attempt to please others.

Slashed Opportunity to make some sweeping changes by taking decisive action rather than feeling too cut up about what has happened.

S

Slate Ability to keep my sense of identity safe and secure instead of being too hard on myself in regard to some specific details.

Slaughter Opportunity to use my raw talent to transform my vitality rather than indiscriminately cutting myself out of any challenges.

Slaughterhouse Situation where I can transform my habitual behaviors by choosing what I value the most and what I can safely dispose of.

Slave Aspect of my character that has the opportunity to master a new skill so I can use it to gain more freedom of action.

Slave driver Aspect of my character that directs my motivation and energy so I can take a more liberated approach to choosing an outcome.

Slave labor Opportunity to liberate more of my time by freely making the decision to productively work my way through a set of challenges.

Slavery Realization that I can achieve a much greater sense of liberation by choosing to take more responsibility for my actions.

Slave trader Aspect of my character that can free up a great deal of my time by ensuring that my value is fully recognized by other people.

Slay Opportunity to use my power and strength to deal with a sudden conflict so I can continue my growth and development.

Sleazy Realization that I have the moral power to always do the right thing, rather than allowing people to judge me on my actions.

Sledge Ability to smoothly progress toward my objective by using the outcome of my accumulated work in a cool, consistent manner.

Sledgehammer Ability to produce a definite result by taking the time to persistently use my strength and power to shape the outcome.

Sleep Opportunity to realize that I can explore my most powerful ambitions and highest aspirations by letting go and just relaxing.

Sleeper cell Aspects of my character that have the surprising power to challenge my unresolved fears by being open about them.

Sleeping bag Ability to open myself up to new opportunities by going into unfamiliar territory so I can explore my wider ambitions.

Sleeping pill Ability to follow a prescribed process so I can work my way through my options and resolve a potentially unhealthy situation.

Sleeping policeman Ability to smooth out any challenges to my continuing progress instead of feeling that others are always trying to slow me down.

Sleepwalk Opportunity to directly pursue one of my ambitions by taking a more relaxed approach to exploring some unfamiliar territory.

Sleeve Ability to present my self-image to people in a way that protects my power to take action rather than concealing my intentions.

Sleigh Ability to use the result of my accumulated efforts to smoothly progress toward my objective in a cool and connected manner.

Slender Realization that my flexibility is a great personal strength, instead of feeling that my contribution is lacking in some way.

Sleuth Aspect of my character that can investigate my real needs by closely tracking my habitual behaviors and how I act on them.

Slice Ability to fulfill one aspect of my ambitions by getting myself involved in the action and then taking it one step at a time.

Slick Realization that I can make a situation run more smoothly by trusting in my skills rather than just glossing over my abilities.

Slide Opportunity to continue developing my wider ambitions by letting myself go now and again and seeing where it takes me.

Slide rule Ability to work my way through to the most pleasing outcome for me instead of worrying about how I measure up to others.

S

Sliding door Ability to easily access different aspects of my character so I can explore choices and their potential outcomes.

Slightest Realization that my expertise and efforts will make a huge difference rather than feeling that they will have very little effect.

Slim Realization that I can indulge in my appetite for success by taking a fresh approach instead of feeling that I may not succeed.

Slime Ability to clear up some messy emotions by being clear about my feelings rather than letting the chance just slip away from me.

Slimy Ability to minimize any frictions with the people around me instead of allowing the situation to become messy and unpleasant.

Sling Ability to provide support for my actions so I can decide what I need to let go of rather than just suspending my activities.

Slingshot Ability to assert my power and influence in a forceful manner so I can quickly make my presence felt to other people.

Slip Opportunity to maintain the resilience of my balanced approach rather than becoming fixated on possible failures that may occur.

Slipped disc Essential opportunity to shape my circumstances by using my underlying strength to stand up for what I believe in.

Slippers Ability to present my self-image to people by taking steps to display how relaxed I am with all the different aspects of myself.

Slippery Opportunity to get a grip on my ambitions so I can use my influence to smoothly guide them to reach my chosen outcome.

Slipping Opportunity to easily achieve an ambition by relaxing my need for control and allowing everything just to slide into place.

Slip up Opportunity to restore a more balanced viewpoint so I can continue to increase my level of understanding and ensure success.

Slipway Situation where I can easily enter into an emotionally challenging situation so I can navigate it safely and comfortably.

Slit Ability to look more deeply into what really motivates me, even though my choices may seem restricted by self-limiting beliefs.

Slither Opportunity to move ahead in an indirect manner rather than taking definite steps to successfully reach my intended objective.

Sliver Ability to grasp a small piece of information that allows me to understand the bigger picture and the possibilities it holds.

Slob Aspect of my character that can help me to indulge my ambitions by taking a fresh approach and exercising a healthy perspective.

Slog Opportunity to persistently pursue one of my ambitions by using my self-motivation and determination to take the steps I need.

Slogan Ability to express myself consistently by communicating a message that will help other people to understand me more easily.

Slop Opportunity to contain my emotions so I can share how I feel about a situation instead of dealing with it carelessly.

Slope Situation where I can understand how inclined I am to reach my objective rather than trying to shrug off any responsibility.

Sloppy Realization that I can easily clear up any misunderstandings by taking a more considered approach to a messy situation.

Slot Ability to look deeper into my ambitions so I can be more receptive to a new opportunity and see where I fit in.

Sloth Instinctive ability to take a more relaxed approach instead of feeling that I always have to turn everything upside down.

Slouch Opportunity to display my talents for standing up for what I believe in rather than just letting my standards drop.

Slovenly Realization that I can take a more structured approach in looking after myself

S

so I can achieve more consistent success.

Slow Realization that I can take my time and choose the best way forward rather than feeling I'm being rushed into making a decision.

Slow cooker Ability to use my creative powers in a calm and considered way so I can consistently satisfy my appetite for success.

Slow down Opportunity to ensure fast progress by taking decisive action rather than rushing around and keeping myself busy.

Slow motion Opportunity to become more aware of my natural rhythms so I can use them to support my actions and speed up progress.

Slow puncture Opportunity to keep confidently progressing with an ambition rather than being anxious that others will let me down.

Sludge Ability to get to the bottom of what I'm currently feeling by taking a firmer approach so I can stay down-to-earth.

Slug Instinctive ability to take my time as I pursue my chosen path, even though I may appear vulnerable to any heavy-handed action.

Sluggish Opportunity to respond really quickly so I can use my energy and motivation to successfully bring my ambitions to life.

Sluice gate Ability to control the flow of my feelings so I can be more aware of emotional boundaries and securely maintain them.

Slum Situation where I can have a character-building experience by reconstructing my identity in a way that I will be proud of.

Slumber party Opportunity to realize that I can achieve my highest aspirations by inviting other people to recognize my unique expertise.

Slum dweller Aspect of my character that has the strength and power to tear down self-limiting behaviors and build on my experience.

Slump Opportunity to increase my commitment by being strong and supportive instead of letting my efforts collapse.

Slur Opportunity to clearly say what I feel rather than feeling hurt that other people seem to be ignoring my efforts.

Slurp Opportunity to fulfill an emotional need by avoiding any obvious challenges that may be absorbing too much of my attention.

Slush Ability to use certain facets of my accumulated experience as a way of helping a learning opportunity to run more smoothly.

Slut Aspect of my character that can become more intimately aware of my creative talents by setting some boundaries around them.

Sly Realization that I can solve a challenging problem by using my natural intelligence rather than appearing devious.

S

Smack Opportunity to be suddenly struck by a particular possibility and how I can explore all the potential value it suggests.

Small Realization that I can achieve huge success by attending to the apparently minor details as I develop my skills and expertise.

Small change Ability to make a major transformation by understanding the value of skills I thought were of no real consequence.

Smallpox Opportunity to resolve an unhealthy situation by making a major breakthrough in how I can stay in touch with my feelings.

Small print Ability to clearly spell out what I am trying to communicate to other people so we can all share the bigger picture.

Small talk Opportunity to speak up and tell other people how I feel so we can make a major advance in our wider relationship.

Smarmy Realization that I can honestly communicate what I am feeling to other people rather than trying to flatter their attentions.

Smart Realization that I can intelligently demonstrate my insight to people without worrying that it might be a painful experience.

Smart card Ability to use my characteristic ingenuity as a way of accessing a number of resources I was previously unaware of.

Smash Opportunity to make a major breakthrough that I feel happy about rather than letting myself fall to pieces.

Smash and grab Opportunity to suddenly realize my value by breaking down barriers and getting a real grip on what I can contribute.

Smash hit Opportunity to suddenly make a powerful connection with a bigger audience by using the strength of my natural talent.

Smear campaign Opportunity to make my mark by speaking my truth so I can expand public awareness without using any dirty tricks.

Smear test Opportunity to judge the health of my creative potential rather than letting other people judge if I can make the grade.

Smell Essential awareness that helps me to identify the mood that is currently in the air so I can sniff out any opportunities.

Smile Essential opportunity to show my feelings of power and confidence as I face up to a challenge rather than turning it down.

Smirk Realization that I can confidently step outside my comfort zone and achieve powerful success rather than just appearing smug.

Smithereens Ability to piece together the tiniest details so I can have a greater understanding of the scale of my ambitions.

Smitten Opportunity to realize how struck I am by one of my creative talents so I can understand how to make the most of it.

Smock Ability to present my self-image to people in a way that may appear workmanlike but can cover up some of my other talents.

Smog Opportunity to clear up any vague feelings about the prevailing mood as it seems to be clouding the issue and causing confusion.

Smoke Opportunity to see evidence of a fundamental creative transformation, even though it may seem confusing and can cloud the issue.

Smoke alarm Ability to alert myself to rapidly transforming a situation so I can stay calm in order to minimize any potential confusion.

Smoke bomb Ability to safely contain any explosive feelings so I can create a positive transformation with minimum disorientation.

Smoke jumper Aspect of my character that can keep a cool head in a potentially confusing situation so I can clearly see my way forward.

Smoker's cough Opportunity to speak up so I can draw attention to a confusing situation and clear up a consistently irritating tension.

Smokescreen Ability to make my intentions extremely clear to the people around me instead of leaving them confused about my ambitions.

Smoke signal Ability to communicate what I need to say by taking creative action rather than just making ineffective gestures.

Smoking Opportunity to keep a clear head rather than allowing myself to be continually drawn into confusing and unhealthy situations.

Smoking gun Opportunity to take full responsibility for the assertive way in which I have been communicating my aims to the people around me.

Smoking jacket Ability to present my self-image to others in a way that shows how relaxed I am with a potentially confusing situation.

Smoldering Opportunity to use my creative abilities to transform a situation without allowing my passionate nature to cloud the issue.

Smooch Opportunity to get much closer and more comfortable with an aspect of my nature so I can express some of my deeper feelings.

Smooth Opportunity to effortlessly resolve a challenge by remaining unruffled so I can consistently remove any obstacles.

Smoothie Potential to fulfill an ambition by easily extracting my best qualities so I can blend them together in a healthy manner.

Smorgasbord Potential to fulfill an ambition by understanding the different levels of opportunity and being open to a variety of options.

Smother Opportunity to courageously express what I think by drawing on my inspiration rather than allowing other people to take over.

SMS Ability to increase my understanding by quickly communicating what I think instead of feeling limited in my vocabulary.

Smudged Opportunity to be clear about how I can fundamentally transform a situation by demonstrating how I will make my mark.

Smug Realization that I can achieve more by stepping outside my comfort zone rather than being complacent about my efforts.

Smuggler Aspect of my character that has the opportunity to be open about what I can contribute rather than trying to conceal my gifts.

Snack Opportunity to sustain my appetite for success by being content with a smaller achievement that will lead to a bigger result.

Snack bar Situation where I can make choices about how I can fulfill some minor ambitions so I can make progress with some larger ones.

Snail Instinctive ability to take my time to pursue my chosen path without making myself too vulnerable to outside criticism.

Snake Instinctive ability to discard a self-image that is no longer useful to me so I can heal any hurt and transform my situation.

Snake charmer Aspect of my character that can attract all the attention I need to help me let go of a self-image I no longer require.

Snap Opportunity to quickly break out of one of my habitual patterns so I can immediately make a much stronger connection.

Snap fastener Ability to immediately make a firm connection with a new opportunity without feeling I am permanently committed to it.

Snare Ability to release myself from a situation that has been holding me back by using some creative instincts that I was unaware of.

Snarl Instinctive ability to powerfully express how I feel rather than getting caught up in a continuing lack of confidence.

Snatch Ability to seize a sudden opportunity and grasp its significance so I can use it to support my actions and help shape my future.

Snatch squad Aspects of my character that can grasp the significance of an unseen opportunity so I can become more acquainted with it.

Sneak Opportunity to be open and honest about my intentions rather than feeling I have to behave in a furtive, underhanded manner.

Sneakers Ability to present my self-image to people by taking casual steps to display my talent and how comfortable I am with it.

Sneeze Essential opportunity to quickly get some minor concerns off my chest instead of feeling continually irritated by them.

Sniff Opportunity to quickly inspire myself rather than feeling upset that other people seem to be quite disdainful of my actions.

Sniffer dog Instinctive ability to identify the mood that is in the air so I can continue in a persistently determined manner.

S

Snigger Opportunity to be more open about a dilemma I am facing rather than worrying that other people are disrespectful of my efforts.

Sniper Aspect of my character that can powerfully communicate my aims in a precise manner, even though people may be critical of me.

Snob Aspect of my character that has great confidence in my abilities instead of always worrying what others think of me.

Snooker Opportunity to examine all the angles in a situation so I can give it my best shot rather than just feeling frustrated.

Snooper Aspect of my character that has a unique understanding of my deeper needs, although it can often seem quite intrusive to me.

Snooze Opportunity to just let go and relax so I can happily explore my most powerful ambitions and highest aspirations in comfort.

Snore Essential opportunity to give voice to what's emerging from my unconscious awareness rather than just sounding off about it.

Snorkel Ability to keep thinking clearly by using a specific theory, even though I may be immersing myself in an emotional situation.

Snort Opportunity to let go of some ideas I no longer need rather than attempting to express my feelings of indignation.

Snot Essential ability to protect my instinctive awareness so I can ensure everything runs smoothly without causing any mess.

Snout Instinctive ability to follow my natural awareness so I can sniff out opportunities, even though it may seem intrusive to people.

Snow Ability to crystallize certain facets of my learning and experience so they can accumulate into something more substantial.

Snowball Ability to play around with a potentially successful outcome so I can become more aware of how to share my experiences.

Snowball fight Opportunity to resolve an inner conflict by communicating my experiences to the people around me in a playful and gentle manner.

Snowboard Ability to make rapid progress by using my expertise and experience to skillfully carve my way through any potential challenges.

Snowdrift Situation where I can choose to accumulate specific expertise instead of going where my mood seems to take me.

Snowdrop Natural ability to open up to my creative talents so I can encourage any emerging possibilities while staying grounded in reality.

Snowfield Situation where I can use the experience I have built up as a way of making fast progress through some ups and downs.

Snowflake Ability to take a particular aspect of how I feel so I can use it to understand my deeper emotions without going crazy.

Snow leopard Instinctive ability to gracefully deal with apparently arduous conditions without feeling I have to change my nature in any way.

Snowman Aspect of my character that is happy to take a cool and considered approach, although I may find it difficult to take action.

Snowmobile Ability to use my personal drive and ambition so I can quickly make the most of my accumulated experience and learning.

Snowplow Ability to quickly cut through any frustrating experiences so I can take a more decisive and down-to-earth approach.

Snowshoe Ability to present my self-image to other people by taking confident steps to show how my accumulated expertise can support me.

Snowstorm Natural opportunity to channel what I have learned from my conflicting experiences so I can calmly make substantial progress.

Snuff Ability to deal with a potentially unhealthy situation rather than condescendingly observing that it doesn't meet my standards.

Snuffling Instinctive opportunity to draw on my deeper inspiration so I can clearly identify the mood that is currently in the air.

Snug Opportunity to move outside my comfort zone and get much closer to a challenge so I can see how I might fit into it.

Snuggling Opportunity to feel comfortable with a possibility that I have been trying to get much closer to for some while now.

Soaking Opportunity to immerse myself in a learning experience without allowing myself to be emotionally overwhelmed by it.

Soap Ability to make a fresh start by releasing myself from any behavioral patterns that don't allow me to show myself at my best.

Soap opera Opportunity to say what I feel rather than overdramatizing my emotional life as a way of attracting attention.

Soaring Opportunity to rise above any weighty obligations so I have the freedom to heighten my awareness and explore my ideas.

Sobbing Opportunity to show how I feel by taking a deep breath and releasing any emotions that have been holding me back.

Sober Opportunity to raise my spirits by taking a clear-headed and healthy approach without any potentially distracting influences.

Soccer Ability to play around with a potentially successful outcome so I can achieve some collective goals with people close to me.

Social Realization that one of the best ways to discover more about myself is to spend time with other people and find out about them.

Socialite Aspect of my character that can make a prominent contribution to those around me rather than appearing decorative.

Social media Ability to find out more about myself by understanding how others reflect the various aspects of my character.

Social network Ability to make deeper connections with my unique talents by openly sharing my viewpoints with the people around me.

Social worker Opportunity to express my fundamental value to others by making the effort to take care of their unspoken needs.

Sock Ability to present my self-image by being able to stand up for what I believe in and show how comfortable I am with it.

Socket Ability to make a deeper connection so I can achieve a much profounder awareness of my capacity for more prominent success.

Socket set Ability to explore a range of different ways to make connections so I can decide which one will be the most fitting.

Soda Potential to fulfill an emotional need by observing what bubbles up rather than feeling I immediately have to look for a solution.

Sodden Opportunity to make the most of an immersive learning experience without allowing myself to be emotionally overwhelmed.

Sofa Ability to share a softer and more relaxed viewpoint with people so we can become more aware of how to support one another.

Soft Realization that I can often resolve tough challenges by taking a more flexible approach in how I make my presence felt.

Soft furnishings Ability to feel comfortable with my habitual behaviors so I can use them in a coordinated way to support my viewpoints.

Soft shoulder Situation where I can take time out to reflect on my progress without allowing myself to become bogged down in the details.

S

Software Ability to reach a definite outcome by using particular thought processes that I can adapt and apply to different situations.

Soggy Realization that I need to take a more practical approach to reaching an outcome rather than becoming too absorbed in my emotions.

Soil Ability to work with my ideas and emotions to break down some hard challenges so I can use them to support my future growth.

Soirée Opportunity to discover a deeper understanding of myself by inviting others to celebrate my special skills and talents.

Solar eclipse Natural opportunity to demonstrate my continuing brilliance rather than feeling that I am being left alone in the dark.

Solar energy Natural capacity to use my individual brilliance to keep myself fully motivated so I can achieve my chosen outcome.

Solar flare Ability to draw immediate attention to my unique creativity so I can illuminate my passions and open up to them more.

Solar panel Ability to absorb the wider value of my continuing brilliance so I can use it to make the most of my current situation.

Solar plexus Essential ability to digest the significance of my experiences so I can boldly choose the best action for me to take.

Solar power Ability to use my creativity to keep myself fully motivated so I can understand my greater purpose and fulfill my needs.

Solar wind Natural opportunity to understand the incredible value of my creative energy and how it can have the power to move me.

Solder Ability to bring different aspects of my fundamental power closer together so I can continue to shape a valuable outcome.

Soldier Aspect of my character that has the courage and discipline to engage with my inner conflicts and peacefully resolve them.

Soldier of fortune Aspect of my character that can accumulate a wealth of experience by having the courage and discipline to deal with any tensions.

Sole Essential ability to know the fundamental basis of where I stand, even though I may be the only person with that viewpoint.

Solemn Realization that I can make serious progress by taking a more lighthearted approach rather than making any heavier commitment.

Solenoid Ability to get the current situation moving by attracting the attention of others to how I am personally conducting myself.

Solicitor Aspect of my character that helps me understand my sense of right and wrong and how it influences my urges.

Solid Ability to shape my circumstances by consistently maintaining my practical skills rather than always outlining my ideas.

Solidified Opportunity to keep myself in better shape by getting my emotional life flowing again so I can learn about new solutions.

Solitaire Opportunity to work my way through an unpredictable situation by taking a chance instead of accepting the hand I've been dealt.

Solitary Realization that I have the combination of talents to support my decisions rather than always trying to please other people.

Solitary confinement Opportunity to look beyond my immediate limitations so I can transform my situation instead of feeling stuck with who I am.

Solitude Opportunity to become more aware of a presence much bigger than myself without becoming too attached to preconceived outcomes.

Solo Opportunity to emphasize my abilities

S

by demonstrating my talents to other people rather than using them on my own.

Solstice Opportunity to observe my natural creative awareness by remaining centered as I reach out to the edge of my understanding.

Solution Ability to use my emotional capacity to dissolve any hard feelings so I can find the answer I have been looking for.

Somebody Aspect of my character that has the motivational ability to clearly stand out rather than feeling like I am a nobody.

Someone else driving Opportunity to take full control of my direction rather than thinking I am being driven by others' demands.

Somersault Opportunity to quickly see a situation from another angle instead of feeling I have to turn everything upside down.

Something Ability to identify what I need to make the most of my practical skills so I can achieve a successful outcome.

Sometime Opportunity to use past experience and future vision to take immediate action, as this may be a now-or-never chance for me.

Somewhere Situation where I can understand what is happening around about me so I can choose the direction I want to take.

Son Aspect of my character that embodies my playful curiosity and that I can encourage to assertively develop my real potential.

Sonar Ability to take a profounder look into the emotions I am experiencing so I can understand the depth of my feelings.

Sonata Opportunity to use my instinctive creativity to express what moves me rather than just sounding off about my present situation.

Song Ability to instinctively communicate with people by giving voice to a beautiful and deeply felt message about how I feel.

Songbird Instinctive ability to rise above any

of my practical concerns so I can evocatively express an outpouring of my emotions.

Songbook Ability to open up to the wealth of my accumulated experience and emotions so I can publicly share them with other people.

Songwriter Aspect of my character that can convey the power of my understanding by creating a moving, deeply felt message to others.

Sonic boom Realization that I can move beyond a self-limiting belief and make a real impact, though I may be under great pressure.

Soon Opportunity to step into a new future so I can take immediate action rather than always feeling that I am falling behind.

Soot Ability to look beyond the superficial messiness resulting from a creative transformation so I can sweep away any misconceptions.

Soothe Opportunity to feel more at ease when I step outside my comfort zone rather than constantly looking to people for reassurance.

Soprano Aspect of my character that can give voice to my highest and most inspired feelings by speaking passionately from my heart.

Sorbet Potential to fulfill short-term ambition by trying to stay cool so I can always take a fresh approach to further challenges.

Sorcerer Aspect of my character that can independently decide my preferred outcome instead of superstitiously leaving it to fate.

Sorcery Opportunity to reach a decisive outcome through my own efforts rather than thinking it's just a spell I'm going through.

Sordid Realization that I can move beyond any superficial appearances by having the moral strength to always do the right thing.

Sore Essential opportunity to take a positive and healthy approach to a sensitive situation so I can resolve any distress.

S

Sorrow Opportunity to cheerfully gain more experience instead of feeling disappointed that I seem to be losing out somewhere.

Sorry Opportunity to happily share my honest emotions rather than having continuing regrets about not saying what I feel.

Sort Opportunity to decide what kind of outcome will suit me best so I can work my way through a variety of possible options.

Sortie Opportunity to go out of my way to deal with a challenge rather than feeling that I am being continually harassed by other people.

Sorting office Situation where I can choose the type of message I need to communicate and decide whom I should be addressing it to.

SOS Opportunity to communicate my feelings of distress by taking the time to spell out the long and the short of the situation.

Soufflé Potential to fulfill an ambition by taking some fertile ideas and combining them without getting too puffed up about my success.

Sought-after Opportunity to make other people much more aware of my unique talents rather than constantly searching for praise.

Souk Situation where I can gather valuable insight and resources, even though the process may seem quite foreign and unfamiliar to me.

Soul Essential opportunity for me to understand who I really am by inspiring myself to connect with my emotions at a deeper level.

Soul mate Aspect of my character that is comfortable sharing my feelings and that I can always rely on to consistently support me.

Sound Instinctive awareness that brings my attention to an event that resonates with me and helps me identify emerging opportunities.

Soundalike Aspect of my character that says the right thing to keep other people happy but may not truly express my genuine beliefs.

Sound barrier Opportunity to courageously break through a self-limiting belief so I can get beyond the influence of any critical voices.

Sound bite Opportunity to use my power and confidence to sum up what I need to say so I can take some decisive action.

Sound effects Ability to change my overall mood by understanding how different circumstances can shape how I might appear to others.

Soundproof Ability to speak out about what I believe so I can defend myself against criticism rather than always keeping quiet.

Soundtrack Ability to bring a situation to life by listening out for what is usually unspoken and realizing how it can anticipate my mood.

Soup Potential to achieve my ambitions by satisfying my need for emotional fulfillment so I can nourish my continuing growth.

Sour Essential ability to use my personal taste to get the flavor of a situation rather than feeling disappointed by the result.

Source Situation where I can make a new beginning by exploring where I'm coming from so I can decide my preferred outcome.

Source code Ability to understand exactly how I feel about a specific detail so others can help me achieve my chosen objective.

South Natural opportunity to become more aware of the direction I am taking so I can use my passion for my creative talents.

Souvenir Ability to remind myself of the great value of my accumulated experience, even though it may seem quite trivial at the time.

Sou'wester Ability to present my self-image in a way that protects my way of thinking and lets me shrug off intrusive emotions.

Sow Instinctive ability to use my creativity and wisdom to nose out any hidden value by rooting around in the practicalities.

Sowing Opportunity to plant some ideas in my fertile imagination so I can carefully nurture them and reap their valuable benefits.

Soy milk Potential to fulfill an emotional need by looking after myself in a healthy way so I can keep my finger on the pulse.

Spa Situation where I can feel healthy and refreshed by being relaxed and comfortable about exploring the source of my emotions.

Space Situation where I can expand on any perceived limitations by giving myself enough room so I can see the bigger picture.

Space age Opportunity to reflect on my experience so I can take a more universal approach to my continuing development.

Space bar Ability to create some room so I can have a clear understanding of my various characteristics and how I communicate them.

Space capsule Ability to contain my sense of adventure by understanding my needs so I can go beyond any perceived self-limitations.

Spacecraft Ability to use my ambition and drive to put me in a unique position that enables me to demonstrate my special expertise.

Space flight Opportunity to make a major commitment to elevating my awareness so I can explore universal concepts and theories.

Space hopper Ability to play around with some big ideas rather than sitting on them and feeling they are taking me nowhere.

Spaceman Aspect of my character that embodies the individual power and ambition that will take me far beyond apparent limitations.

Space opera Opportunity to explore unfamiliar aspects of my character so I can use their various talents in a dramatic way.

Space rocket Ability to use my drive and ambition to concentrate my energies to thrust myself toward a higher level of awareness.

Spaces Situation where I can make the most of a number of emerging opportunities rather than feeling that something is missing.

Spaceship Ability to explore remote possibilities that may be hugely valuable for me so I can maintain my preferred course of action.

Space station Situation where I can boost the next stage of my professional progression to a higher level so I can explore new horizons.

Space suit Ability to present my self-image to people in a way that reflects my commitment to exploring the unknown and the unfamiliar.

Space telescope Ability to explore future possibilities by carefully examining how my personal vision aligns with the bigger picture.

Spacewalk Opportunity to pursue one of my ambitions by stepping outside my comfort zone and immersing myself in a huge opportunity.

Spacewoman Aspect of my character that embodies the creativity and wisdom I need to expand my awareness to a more universal level.

Spade Ability to explore the practicalities of a situation in greater depth so I can definitely uncover what is really going on.

Spaghetti Potential to fulfill an ambition by using fertile ideas and practical experience, even though it may seem never-ending.

Spam Opportunity to connect with other people in a much more meaningful way instead of feeling there is no substance to my ideas.

Spambot Ability to communicate how I feel rather than just going through the motions to try to gain everyone's acceptance.

Span Ability to use the extent of my practical experience to create a lasting connection between two different areas of my life.

Spandex Ability to be flexible and accommodating in how I appear to others so I can always maintain my power to make progress.

Spaniel Instinctive ability to sniff out new opportunities so I can show my continuing loyalty and affection in a determined manner.

S

Spanking Opportunity to get to the bottom of any apparently childish behavior rather than feeling I have to keep punishing myself.

Spanner Ability to take direct action so I can feel more secure about a situation and open myself up to a range of possibilities.

Spare Ability to keep some of my strength and energy in reserve, even though it means restraining my urges and being quite frugal.

Spare part Ability to keep making progress by drawing on accumulated expertise rather than feeling I am unable to make a difference.

Spare tire Ability to let go of any weighty obligations that may be slowing me down so I can continue to progress with my ambitions.

Spark Ability to ignite my enthusiasm so I can get fired up about a new creative idea that is kindling my interest.

Sparkle Opportunity to shine by using my individual brilliance in drawing attention to the talents of the people around me.

Spark plug Ability to motivate my drive for success in a more spirited manner by releasing the potential energy of my deeper inspiration.

Sparring partner Aspect of my character that can play around with some of my unresolved inner conflicts and encourage me to overcome them.

Sparrow Instinctive ability to develop an important everyday idea that usually goes unnoticed so I can share it with other people.

Sparrow hawk Instinctive ability to carefully observe a situation so I can quickly pounce on an idea and use it to fulfill an ambition.

Spartan Realization that indulging in my needs and ambitions enables me to use my wealth of talent in a much more courageous manner.

Spasm Essential opportunity to consistently use my strength and power in an uncomfortable situation without feeling twitchy about it.

Spate Opportunity to powerfully channel my emotions so I can quickly transform my circumstances by making a quick decision.

Spatula Ability to stir up some enthusiasm by mixing a variety of influences together so I can fulfill a potential ambition.

Spawn Natural opportunity to use my deeper emotions and fertile imagination to produce a large number of potentially valuable ideas.

Speaker Ability to convey some of my current thinking into some powerful and energetic ideas that can move the people around me.

Speaking Essential opportunity to honestly express my feelings and share them with other people so I can get my message across.

Speaking clock Ability to look ahead and choose the precise moment to say what I need to so I can make the most of a big opportunity.

Spear Ability to extend my individual power by decisively getting to the point so I can cut through any approaching challenges.

Spear carrier Aspect of my character that can decisively make a powerful point rather than feeling I'm stuck on the sidelines.

Spear gun Ability to confidently keep my distance so I can communicate my feelings to other people and ensure they get my point.

Spearmint Ability to flavor my approach by using my good taste to create a refreshing influence that will clear up any confusion.

Special Realization that I can use my distinctive characteristics to emphasize my qualities rather than feeling I make no difference.

Special branch Aspects of my character that observe my habitual behavior patterns so I can understand how to make the most of my power.

Special edition Ability to specifically display my unique insight to a wider audience so I can increase my apparent value to them.

Special effects Realization that I can use

my talent to produce some fantastic results without having to rely on any artificial gimmickry.

Special forces Aspects of my character that use the power of my unconscious awareness to resolve challenges that initially seemed impossible.

Species Natural ability to understand the defining characteristics of my various qualities so I can take specific action.

Specific Realization that I can use my viewpoint to identify my special purpose rather than being vague about my intentions.

Specimen Ability to examine a specific aspect of my talents so I can understand how to use my instinctive urges more creatively.

Speck Ability to pay attention to a small but particularly significant detail that will allow me to understand the bigger picture.

Spectacle Opportunity to display my impressive talents without feeling concern I'm making an exhibition of myself.

Spectacles Ability to look more closely at a situation so I can easily see the bigger picture and form a clear opinion about it.

Spectacular Realization that I can display my expertise on a much wider scale by always being prepared to take on bigger challenges.

Spectator Aspect of my character that observes my behaviors so I can participate more successfully in some larger opportunities.

Specter Aspect of my character that appears when I have the opportunity to resurrect a neglected talent and bring it back to life.

Spectrum Ability to illuminate some powerful feelings by reflecting on the wider range of moods that can often color my emotions.

Speculator Aspect of my character that considers my future progress so I can make the most of any opportunities I create.

Speech Opportunity to share my personal perspective with other people so I can clearly state my beliefs and future intentions.

Speechless Opportunity to reflect on what emotions are emerging for me rather than thinking I constantly have to express how I feel.

Speech therapist Aspect of my character that can help me resolve unhealthy tensions by clearly stating personal beliefs and intentions.

Speechwriter Aspect of my character that can convey the deeper power of my understanding by specifically sharing my personal perspective.

Speed Ability to get a situation progressing quickly, even though I feel I may not be able to ultimately control its eventual outcome.

Speedboat Ability to quickly navigate complex, unpredictable feelings by using my experience to maintain my emotional stability.

Speed bump Opportunity to swiftly dislodge myself from feelings of complacency so I don't always have to experience a rough ride.

Speed camera Ability to quickly frame a particular perspective and reflect on my beliefs rather than letting people instantly judge me.

Speed dating Opportunity to give myself permission to choose whom I want to be with instead of leaving it up to others.

Speed dial Ability to achieve a successful outcome by facing up to the facts so I can quickly communicate what I need to say.

Speeding ticket Ability to quickly demonstrate my value to others rather than waiting for their permission to display my talents to them.

Speed limit Situation where I can adjust my progress to a more ambitious level by quickly progressing beyond self-imposed boundaries.

Speedometer Ability to instantly measure my progress so I can gauge how swiftly I can take advantage of a fast-approaching opportunity.

S

Speed-reading Opportunity to understand different aspects of my character by using my accumulated knowledge to reach a rapid conclusion.

Spell Opportunity to clearly communicate what I want to create within a certain time frame without feeling influenced by others.

Spellbinding Opportunity to stay fully connected without feeling I will become distracted and end up limiting future options.

Spell-checker Opportunity to examine my behavior in more detail so I can understand if I am communicating as clearly as possible.

Spend Opportunity to become more aware of how openly I distribute my talent and the value I receive in recognition of it.

Sperm Essential ability to convey my feelings by taking assertive, competitive action to make the most of a fertile opportunity.

Sperm bank Situation where I can draw on a wealth of wisdom and experience so I can use it to make the most of an abundant opportunity.

Sperm count Opportunity to take time to understand the full value of my abundant creativity to make the most of my potential.

Sperm donor Aspect of my character that commits to providing unconditional support in helping people take advantage of fertile opportunities.

Spew Opportunity to bring up an issue that is of no practical value in realizing my ambitions so I can take a healthier approach.

Sphere Ability to shape my circumstances so I can create a well-rounded perspective and understand the extent of my influence.

Sphincter Essential ability to control my natural instincts so I can choose the experiences I would like to participate in.

Sphinx Ability to recognize that the transformative power of my wisdom can consolidate my talents and lead to a valuable opportunity.

Spice Ability to use my good taste to add a sense of excitement so I can influence how others experience my distinctive qualities.

Spider Instinctive ability to release myself from an emotional entanglement that may have been causing me a lot of anxiety and fear.

Spiderweb Ability to maintain my emotional resilience by making powerful connections instead of feeling entangled in complex relationships.

Spigot Ability to contain my emotions so I can make the best use of my accumulated experience rather than always feeling drained.

Spike Ability to consistently make my point instead of thinking that my elevated level of influence might be quite short-lived.

Spilling Opportunity to contain my emotions so I can convey how I feel about a situation rather than dealing with it messily.

Spinach Potential to fulfill an ambition by having a healthy regard for my strength and power so I can always use it wisely.

Spinal column Essential ability to stand up for what I believe in by demonstrating the underlying strength of my character.

Spin doctor Aspect of my character that can get straight to the point of the central issue rather than always going round and round.

Spin dryer Ability to stay centered in my opinions instead of becoming too absorbed with my emotions and getting in a tangle.

Spine Essential ability to have the fundamental strength to firmly stand up central to them.

Spine-chilling Opportunity to warm to an approaching possibility rather than feeling anxious about the potential outcomes.

Spinning Opportunity to remain in control by staying centered, even though it seems as if everything is moving too fast around me.

Spinning top Ability to keep myself moving so I can stand up for my beliefs rather than allowing other people to push me around.

Spinning wheel Ability to draw a variety of story threads together so I can achieve a valuable outcome that will lead to other opportunities.

Spiral Ability to shape my circumstances by being remaining centered as I continue to move toward a wider, deeper understanding.

Spiral dive Opportunity to straighten out my approach to a particular situation so I can deal with it in a more level-headed manner.

Spiral staircase Situation where I can make steady progress with achieving an ambition rather than feeling I'm going around in circles.

Spire Situation where I can understand the fundamental point of my beliefs so I can share them more prominently with other people.

Spirit Realization that I can powerfully connect with my higher, wiser self by courageously exploring the unknown and unfamiliar.

Spirit level Ability to take a more even-handed approach in dealing with unfamiliar ups and downs as I explore an unknown challenge.

Spiritual Realization that I can connect with strength and powers that may often seem beyond me but which I actually create myself.

Spit Essential opportunity to immediately share the emotional impact of what I'm trying to say rather than attempting to contain it.

Spiteful Realization that I can succeed in spite of any challenge by being good-natured rather than appearing malicious and small-minded.

Splash Opportunity to experience the positive impact of a sudden emotional change rather than being concerned about it becoming messy.

Splashdown Opportunity to reconnect

with my deeper emotions after spending some time in the rarefied atmosphere of abstract theories.

Spleen Essential ability to rediscover my passion and vitality so I can use any potentially negative feelings in a healthy manner.

Splice Opportunity to join two threads of a story together so I can create a stronger and more enduring string of accomplishments.

Splint Ability to support my fundamental beliefs so I can continue to strengthen them rather than just having a breakdown.

Splinter Ability to separate out the most valuable qualities of my habits and behaviors instead of letting them be a source of irritation.

Split Opportunity to make a distinct choice about leaving a situation that no longer serves me so I can step into a new future.

Spoil heap Situation where I can prominently increase my value by disposing of habitual behaviors that might diminish my standing.

Spoiling Opportunity to increase my fundamental value rather than diminishing it in any way by engaging in unnecessary conflicts.

Spokes Ability to remain centered by connecting firmly to the edge of my understanding so I can continue to make balanced progress.

Sponge Ability to empathetically absorb how other people are feeling so I can soak up any criticism from a potentially emotional situation.

Sponsor Aspect of my character that takes responsibility for displaying the value of my talents so they can be more widely recognized.

Spoof Opportunity to state my intentions and say how I feel rather than trying to distract other people and throw them off track.

S

Spook Aspect of my character that can make a difference by openly sharing my talents instead of feeling frightened by them.

Spooky Realization that I have an uncanny ability to identify emerging possibilities rather than leaving everything to fate.

Spooky attic Aspect of myself that embodies a unique talent I had almost forgotten about but now seems hauntingly familiar to me.

Spooky house Situation where I have the security and support to explore areas of my expertise I had built up and forgotten about.

Spool Ability to take in what is happening so I can make continual progress and give myself the chance to unwind.

Spoon Ability to work through a potential ambition by choosing the most fulfilling aspects and dealing with them one at a time.

Sporadic Realization that I can achieve more consistent success by having the confidence to regularly display my skills to other people.

Spore Natural ability to take the germ of an idea and then use the prevailing mood to spread the seeds of my success far and wide.

Sport Opportunity to achieve my personal ambitions by combining my individual talents, even though the outcome may be uncertain.

Sporting Realization that I always have a chance to decide my chosen outcome, even though I can never be certain about it.

Sports bra Ability to support my capacity for nurturing other people so I can use it to make the most of an emerging possibility.

Sports car Ability to use my personal ambition and drive to make my own decisions so I can rapidly progress toward my objective.

Sportsman Aspect of my character that embodies the individual strength and power I need to make the most of uncertain challenges.

Sportsperson Aspect of my character that

can develop my influence in challenging situations by reflecting the variety of roles I play.

Sportswoman Aspect of my character that embodies the individual empathy and wisdom that enables me to fulfill my most challenging aspirations.

Spot Ability to identify how I can make a big difference rather than feeling concerned about possibly blemishing my reputation.

Spot-check Opportunity to specifically identify particular aspects of my behavior that may be preventing me from making further progress.

Spotlight Ability to focus my power and energy so I can draw wider attention to my creative talents and allow them to shine.

Spots Realization that I sometimes need to look beyond surface imperfections instead of trying to ensure that everything is perfect.

Spouse Aspect of my character that embodies my commitment to exploring and developing the unknown, unfamiliar aspects of myself.

Spout Ability to direct the flow of my emotions by clearly communicating how I feel rather than going on and on about them.

Sprain Essential opportunity to stay connected to my goal by remaining flexible instead of putting myself under too much of a strain.

Sprat Instinctive ability to immerse myself in my emotions and understand their importance rather than feeling they are inconsequential.

Sprawling Opportunity to spread my influence in a graceful manner instead of feeling that I may appear all over the place to other people.

Spray Ability to channel some of my feelings by using the power of my ideas to convey them to other people in a clear and gentle way.

Spray gun Ability to assert my opinions in a forceful manner so I can communicate how I

S

feel to the people around me.

Spray paint Ability to colorfully express how I Instinctively feel about a situation so I can clearly convey my mood to other people.

Spray tan Ability to take a more natural approach in the way I show my feelings rather than trying to conceal my emotions.

Spread Opportunity to expand my levels of awareness by exploring wider possibilities without stretching myself out too thin.

Spread betting Opportunity to use insight to confidently stick my neck out to decide on the range of possible outcomes in a situation.

Spread-eagled Opportunity to stretch myself in a challenging situation so I can understand the extent of my personal influence.

Spree Opportunity to celebrate my talent by taking a more considered approach rather than appearing to be self-indulgent.

Spring Ability to take immediate action by using my accumulated knowledge instead of feeling like I'm just going around in circles.

Springboard Situation where I can take a more energetic approach before immersing myself in a potentially overwhelming emotional experience.

Spring-cleaning Opportunity to let go of habitual behavior patterns I no longer need so I can welcome a variety of new possibilities.

Spring season Opportunity to understand my natural instincts and rhythms so I can encourage my creative talents to positively blossom.

Spring water Potential to fulfill an emotional need by taking a purer approach so I can draw on my deeper feelings of inspiration.

Sprinkle Opportunity to influence a situation by maintaining a gentle and persistent presence rather than being heavily emotional.

Sprinkler Ability to cultivate my skills in a healthy, consistent manner by using an emotionally light touch as I encourage their growth.

Sprinter Aspect of my character that can rapidly take steps to meet a short-term challenge and has the self-motivation to succeed.

Sprocket Ability to produce a practical outcome by using my power and confidence to stay engaged with some individual relationships.

Sprout Opportunity to quickly develop a particular aspect of my unrealized potential so I can use it to fulfill one of my ambitions.

Spruce Natural potential for my long-term spiritual growth by making the time and effort to look after how I appear to other people.

Spume Ability to let go of some less substantial feelings by understanding the power of my emotions and how they can ebb and flow.

Spur Ability to drive myself on to even greater ambitions by being able to make my talent stick out at just the right moment.

Spurt Opportunity to make the most of a burst of activity by containing my emotions rather than openly gushing about everything.

Sputnik Ability to signal my intentions by launching a new initiative instead of thinking that a situation constantly revolves around me.

Spy Aspect of my character that can make a difference by openly sharing my passions rather than watching from a distance.

Spyhole Situation where I can look more deeply into what motivates me instead of feeling that others are always watching me.

Spying Opportunity to be open about what I am searching for rather than trying to always disguise my underlying intentions.

Spymaster Aspect of my character that has an overall awareness of my habitual behavior patterns so I can use them more effectively.

Spy ring Ability to provide myself with a powerful variety of individual resources so I can make a deeper commitment to my future.

Squabble Opportunity to widen my perspective so I can see the bigger picture rather than continually trying to defend my viewpoint.

Squad Aspects of my character that I may be unacquainted with but that can work together to provide some organized power.

Squadron Ability to coordinate a number of my more powerful ideas so I can use them to forcefully assert my way of thinking.

Squalid Realization that I have all the resources I need to look after myself rather than feeling abandoned by everyone.

Squall Natural opportunity to channel some of my more powerful thoughts and feelings so I can use them to quickly make a difference.

Square Ability to shape my circumstances by structuring specific boundaries in a traditional way so I can face up to any challenges.

Squashed Opportunity to give myself more room to maneuver instead of suddenly feeling restricted by my weightier commitments.

Squash plant Potential to fulfill an ambition by making the most of my raw talent so I can continue to sustain my creative progress.

Squat Opportunity to raise my levels of awareness so I can comfortably achieve an ambition, enabling me to stand proud and tall.

Squatter Aspect of my character that should feel more at home with my talents instead of feeling unentitled to any security or comfort.

Squawk Opportunity to take my time so I can say what I feel in a calm and considered way rather than just making a noise about it.

Squeak Opportunity to widen my perspectives and reduce any underlying friction by having the courage to speak out strongly and clearly.

Squeaking hinge Opportunity to take a smoother approach so I can open up new possibilities and experience a turning point.

Squeal Opportunity to lower my expectations rather than deliberately trying to heighten the tension and being caught by surprise.

Squealing brakes Ability to stay in control of my drive and ambition instead of feeling I have been caught by unexpected circumstances.

Squeamish Opportunity to be bold and courageously engage with a messy situation rather than becoming irrationally upset by it.

Squeeze Opportunity to take the initiative and get a tighter grip on the situation instead of feeling under pressure from other people.

Squelch Opportunity to take the necessary steps in a potentially messy situation rather than thinking I need to show some restraint.

Squib Ability to draw the attention of other people to a talent I am developing without allowing them to dampen my enthusiasm.

Squid Instinctive ability to express some of my deeper feelings by spelling them out instead of feeling that I am clouding the issue.

Squint Opportunity to clearly approach a challenge in a honest and upright manner rather than trying to close my eyes to it.

Squirm Opportunity to give myself more room to maneuver instead of feeling too uncomfortable about self-imposed restrictions.

Squirrel Instinctive ability to discover new opportunities by taking a more agile approach and making sure that always I plan ahead.

Squirt Opportunity to concentrate on a specific sentiment so I can make progress without feeling as if I am being forced to do it.

Stab Opportunity to assert my individuality by decisively cutting through any uncertainty instead of feeling wounded by criticism.

Stable Situation where I can keep everything as it should be by looking after my instinctive energies and harnessing them when needed.

Stab wound Ability to deal with a hurtful

S

point of view by bringing both sides of the argument together so I can gain healthy closure.

Staccato Ability to instinctively communicate with people in a precise, detached manner without letting myself become disconnected.

Stack Ability to rise to prominence by using my accumulated knowledge and experience in a methodical and orderly manner.

Stadium Situation where I have a huge opportunity to play to my strengths and have my talents recognized by a wider audience.

Staff Aspects of my character that work together in a supportive and organized way to successfully reach a collective outcome.

Staff room Situation where I can feel comfortable and secure in using my talents to achieve a collectively agreed-upon result.

Stag Instinctive ability to be proud of the wilder aspects of my nature without feeling that other people are watching me all the time.

Stage Situation where I can progress to the next level in my ambitions by having a platform from which to share my talents with a wider audience.

Stagecoach Ability to harness my unconscious energies so I can use them to make definite progress toward my career objectives.

Staged accident Opportunity to be open to a variety of emerging possibilities rather than trying to draw attention to a specific incident.

Stage diving Opportunity to immerse myself in my emotional life so I can appreciate how much others can support and care for me.

Stage door Ability to have a direct awareness of how I can share my talents by developing possibilities that may have seemed closed.

Stage fright Opportunity to confidently open up my talents to a wider audience by having the courage to make a bold, transformative choice.

Stage presence Realization that I can use my natural abilities to reveal myself as I really want to be instead of being distracted by others.

Stage whisper Opportunity to listen to my inner voice rather than trying to draw attention to my point of view.

Staggering Opportunity to directly pursue an ambition by taking the specific steps I need instead of allowing myself to be overwhelmed.

Stagnant Opportunity to continue my learning and keep my development moving by opening up and providing an outlet for my feelings.

Stag night Opportunity to discover a deeper understanding of myself by exploring the wilder aspects of my nature and my commitment to them.

Stain Opportunity to clear up any emotional confusion and resolve superficial disagreements that may be coloring my viewpoint.

Stained glass Ability to piece together the potentially fragile aspects of a situation so I can see what may be coloring my perspective.

Stainless steel Ability to use my fundamental power to strongly shape a definite outcome so my reputation continues to remain untarnished.

Stair Ability to take a series of steps so I can steadily progress between my higher levels of awareness and my deeper emotions.

Staircase Situation where I can make steady and incremental progress in connecting some of my higher aspirations and deepest desires.

Stair lift Ability to connect my different levels of wisdom and experience without going through the effort of making individual steps.

Stake Ability to make my mark by using the strength of my practical abilities rather than just claiming to have some experience.

Stalactite Ability to extend my fundamental understanding of my character by steadily accumulating practical skills and knowledge.

S

Stalagmite Ability to become more aware of prominent aspects of my practical abilities and how I progressively build them up over time.

Stale Realization that I can create fresh opportunities by using a different approach rather than staying in the same old situation.

Stalemate Opportunity to take a more colorful approach to breaking a deadlock instead of just seeing it from a black-and-white viewpoint.

Stalk Natural ability to extend my freedom of action so I can keep supporting my development rather than trying to conceal it.

Stalked by predator Opportunity to pursue a potentially fulfilling aspect of my deeper self instead of falling prey to any feelings of anxiety.

Stalker Aspect of my character that identifies my concealed talents and keeps track of them so I can proudly bring them into the open.

Stall Opportunity to reengage with my instinctive drives so I can continue to progress with an ambition rather than delaying it.

Stallion Instinctive ability to harness my unconscious strength so I can use my natural power to achieve my wildest ambitions.

Stammering Essential opportunity to transform how I express my feelings by speaking out clearly rather than feeling stuck in old habits.

Stamp Ability to use my impressive authority so other people can recognize the value of what I want to communicate.

Stamp collecting Opportunity to stay calm and gather my thoughts so I can impressively communicate what I want to say.

Stamped, self-addressed envelope Ability to understand what I feel by ensuring I am always receptive to whatever emotions emerge from my awareness.

Stampede Opportunity to control my

creative instincts by proceeding in an orderly manner rather than rushing headlong into a situation.

Stand Situation where I can make my viewpoint more prominently known to the people around me so I can attract their collective support.

Standard Realization that I can establish the basis for a new way of working by choosing to take a different and more creative approach.

Standby Opportunity to step forward so I can display my unique expertise rather than just being there to keep everyone else happy.

Stand-in Aspect of my character that can use my talents to claim my rightful place rather than always standing on the sidelines.

Standing Opportunity to maintain my status by taking a firm stance so I can become more aware of how I can support my viewpoint.

Standing stone Ability to steadily maintain a solid presence by linking my wider spiritual awareness to a firm grounding in reality.

Standstill Opportunity to use my self-motivation to get a situation moving again rather than feeling I can't continue my progress.

Staple Ability to make a fundamental connection that can provide me with the security to access the necessary information I need.

Staple gun Ability to assert my power in a forceful manner so I can make a fundamental connection that will help me retain my position.

Star Elemental ability to have the brilliance of my creativity recognized by people in a way that naturally attracts them to me.

Starch Potential to fulfill an ambition by storing up personal resources so I can stiffen my resolve and sustain my progress.

Starfish Instinctive ability to immerse myself more deeply in my emotions in a way that allows me to reach out to current opportunities.

S

Staring Opportunity to look more intensively into the bigger picture rather than becoming fixated and missing the obvious answer.

Stark Realization that I can discover my fundamental power by taking a softer approach in how I present myself to other people.

Starling Instinctive ability to rise above more practical concerns and spread my ideas by being more gregarious with other people.

Starring in film Opportunity to make others more aware of my story so I can use it to draw attention to my brilliance.

Star shape Ability to shape my circumstances by having the presence to make a number of points that appear attractive to others.

Start Opportunity to get myself moving so I can choose my preferred outcome instead of being confronted with a sudden realization.

Starting pistol Ability to clearly communicate my aims to other people as a way of triggering my self-motivation and getting myself on track.

Startled Realization that I know a surprising amount about what is going on and just need to stay calm to make the most of it.

Starving Opportunity to fulfill my hunger for success by understanding my fundamental ambitions rather than trying to deny their value.

Stash Ability to demonstrate an impressive range of practical skills to other people rather than trying to hide my talents.

State Situation where I can explore my overall condition so I can make a clear declaration of what I need from other people.

Stately home Situation where I can be far more expansive in exploring my inner and outer lives so others can recognize my value.

Statement Opportunity to declare how I feel about the situation so other people can understand the value of my opinion.

Static electricity Ability to get charged up about using my potential energy rather than allowing others to rub me the wrong way.

Statin Ability to remain centered in my emotions by courageously reducing barriers to the healthy and vital flow of my passions.

Station Situation where I can embark on the next stage of my professional progression and take on board the resources I may need.

Stationary Opportunity to take some time to reflect on my next move instead of constantly feeling restless about my current position.

Stationery Ability to gather the basic resources I need to express myself so I can make my mark with other people.

Stationery cupboard Ability to open myself up to the resources I have accumulated rather than trying to shut myself away from them.

Station wagon Ability to use personal ambition and drive to convey my accumulated experience so I can make progress toward my goal.

Statistician Aspect of my character that can make a real difference by seeing the bigger picture instead of thinking I am average.

Statistics Ability to use my unique talents to work through a challenge rather than feeling I probably can't make a difference.

Statue Ability to proudly stand up and have my past achievements recognized by other people so I can keep moving into the future.

Status Realization that I can transform my standing with other people by being aware that I have much more influence than I think I do.

Status symbol Ability to identify the principles I stand for instead of constantly trying to impress the people around me.

Stave Ability to stick up for what I believe in so I can make sure I prevent any unforeseen incidents from occurring.

S

Staying Opportunity to be relaxed and comfortable within myself, though my external circumstances may be changing dramatically.

Steady Realization that I can keep my sense of equilibrium by standing firm in my viewpoint as I progress toward a specific outcome.

Steak Potential to fulfill an ambition by using my raw strength and power to produce something of rare substance that I do well.

Stealing Opportunity to have other people openly recognize the value of my talents rather than creeping around and concealing them.

Stealth plane Ability to make powerful progress with an idea that seems obvious to me, even though other people seem to be unaware of it.

Stealth ship Ability to navigate my way through a complex emotional problem by taking a more discreet direction that may go unnoticed.

Stealthy approach Opportunity to use my discretion as I quietly fulfill one of my ambitions instead of making a song and dance about it.

Steam Opportunity to vent some of my more volatile emotions so I can keep moving ahead rather than just feeling under pressure.

Steamboat Ability to navigate complex and unpredictable feelings by containing powerful emotions that may be building up.

Steam engine Ability to channel the relentless power of my emotions so I can use them to consistently help me accomplish my ambitions.

Steam iron Ability to use my emotional awareness to firmly smooth out inconsistencies in how I present myself to other people.

Steampunk Aspect of my character that can creatively channel my powerful emotions so I can make my far-fetched plans happen.

Steamroller Ability to smooth over a rough patch and keep moving ahead by using the weight of my accumulated learning and experience.

Steam train Ability to follow a set of guidelines enabling me to use my emotional power to make consistent progress toward my objective.

Steel Ability to use my fundamental power to shape a definite outcome without feeling that I have to be too rigid and unyielding.

Steel bars Ability to use my strength of purpose to work through any self-imposed limitations so that I can feel more secure.

Steelworks Situation where I can work with my creative strengths to transform my fundamental power so I can shape a definite outcome.

Steep Situation where I will have to make an effort to negotiate a challenging and rapid transformation so I can soak up any criticism.

Steeple Situation where I can provide prominent support for my higher beliefs so I can make them more obvious to other people.

Steer Opportunity to take control of a fast-moving situation so I can quickly make some choices about my intended outcome.

Steering column Ability to maintain support for my chosen direction so I can make progress by keeping myself on the straight and narrow.

Steering wheel Ability to influence my future by taking it in both hands so I can direct where my drives and ambitions are taking me.

Stem Natural ability to heighten my levels of awareness so I can continue to support my development and not hold anything back.

Stem cell Essential ability to understand my potential for self-renewal so I can naturally break out of any self-limiting behaviors.

Stench Instinctive awareness that helps me nose out the underlying value in a particular situation instead of just feeling offended.

Stencil Ability to consistently outline my impression of a situation in a manner that will be clearly recognized by other people.

Stent Ability to open up to any emotional frustrations I am experiencing so I can get my passion and vitality flowing again.

Step Ability to use my self-motivation and energy to take decisive and positive action that will enable me to make steady progress.

Step backward Opportunity to work my way through a sequence of previous events so I can use self-motivation to keep moving forward.

Stepbrother Aspect of my character that enables me to assert my strength and power in less familiar situations without being too overbearing.

Stepchild Aspect of my character embodying some of my less familiar talents and has great potential for continuing to develop them.

Stepfamily Aspects of my character that are less familiar to me and can provide continuing support and motivation for my development.

Stepfather Aspect of my character that embodies my loving power and authority and can assert my wisdom in unfamiliar situations.

Step forward Opportunity to make a positive change in my circumstances by understanding how to balance some future commitments.

Stepladder Ability to raise my awareness in a specific series of stages so I can continue to increase my performance at a higher level.

Stepmother Aspect of my character that embodies my capacity for creativity and wisdom and can develop qualities that are unfamiliar to me.

Stepping stone Ability to resolve an emotional dilemma by maintaining a solid presence so I can progress through a series of specific stages.

Steps Ability to understand my different levels of motivation so I can progress between my higher awareness and my deeper emotions.

Stepsister Aspect of my character that enables me to share potential talents and abilities by understanding my less familiar qualities.

Stereo Ability to listen to two different perspectives so I can understand what is happening and establish my position.

Stereotype Aspect of my character that has a fixed outlook and may appear two-dimensional rather than embodying my uniqueness.

Sterile Realization that I can use my fertile imagination in a fruitful way instead of feeling impotent and unable to connect.

Sterilization Opportunity to make a clean start so I can minimize any undesirable influences and prevent unexpected outcomes.

Stern Realization that I can move on from a complex emotional situation by taking a more disciplined approach to sharing my feelings.

Steroids Ability to influence how I respond to a situation by becoming more aware of how I can naturally develop my strength and power.

Stethoscope Ability to listen deeply to my innermost feelings so I can resolve tensions by conveying my most heartfelt emotions.

Stew Potential to fulfill an ambition by taking the time to develop a variety of influences rather than getting all worked up.

Steward Aspect of my character that assists in my professional progress by looking after my resources and taking care of my needs.

Stewardess Aspect of my character that tends to my professional needs by taking responsibility for my welfare and ensuring my comfort.

Stick Ability to stay with what I know so I can use the strength of my practical skills to produce a straightforward outcome.

S

Sticker Ability to stay connected and identify what I need so I can share it with other people by indicating my preferences.

Sticking Opportunity to maintain my viewpoint, even if it means that I have to let go of some habits I no longer require.

Sticking plaster Ability to resolve superficial conflicts by adhering to surface impressions rather than feeling I have to go deeper.

Stick insect Instinctive ability to thrive in any situation by naturally displaying my practical skills instead of trying to conceal them.

Stickleback Instinctive ability to immerse myself in my emotions without becoming too involved in the scale of the challenge.

Stickler Aspect of my character that tries to adhere to a set of specific guidelines, even though they may sometimes hold me back.

Sticky Ability to maintain my composure and hold a challenging situation together, even when it appears it may fall apart completely.

Stiff Realization that I may need to take a more flexible approach rather than being too rigid in the methods I am using.

Stifling Opportunity to draw on my individual inspiration and say what I feel instead of continuing in an oppressive atmosphere.

Stigmata Ability to heal some painful feelings by taking decisive action rather than appearing to have gained some closure.

Stile Ability to get over a self-imposed limitation so I can discover my potential by exploring a different field of knowledge.

Stiletto Ability to assert my individuality by decisively cutting through any uncertainty so I can make a very specific point.

Stiletto heel Ability to elevate my status by taking decisive steps to leave the past behind, even though it can leave me feeling vulnerable.

Still Opportunity to reflect on my next move by becoming more aware of the prevailing mood so I can stay calm and take my time.

Stillbirth Opportunity to make a major creative transformation by revitalizing a labor of love I presumed had no further potential.

Stillborn Realization that I can use one of my earlier concepts to make a new beginning, even though I was unable to develop it previously.

Stilts Ability to take some steps to raise my awareness, even though I may feel awkward about how I communicate my elevated status.

Stimulant Ability to speed up a challenging process by giving myself an incentive that will restore my levels of self-motivation.

Sting Instinctive ability to take the heat out of a situation rather than feeling defensive and being sharply critical of other people.

Stingray Instinctive ability to immerse myself in my emotions without always feeling I have to pointedly criticize other people.

Stingy Realization that I can be more generous with the wealth of talent I can offer to people rather than undervaluing myself.

Stink Instinctive awareness that helps me to sweeten the prevailing mood by resolving any underlying tensions that may be upsetting me.

Stink bomb Ability to contain any potentially explosive feelings so I can create a positive transformation rather than feeling offended.

Stir Opportunity to influence the outcome of a situation by creating some excitement that will get other people moving.

Stir-fry Potential to fulfill my appetite for success by taking a fresh approach that will motivate me to take a healthier perspective.

Stirrup Ability to quickly give myself a leg up so I will find it easier to harness my unconscious strength and spur myself on.

Stitch Opportunity to make a firm and

S

long-lasting connection by making a series of small but penetrating insights.

Stoat Instinctive ability to keep pushing forward by boldly speaking my truth and encouraging others to communicate honestly.

Stock Ability to use my wealth of accumulated knowledge and experience, even though their value may seem quite commonplace to me.

Stockade Situation where I can guard against unwelcome behavior by establishing firm personal boundaries without being too defensive.

Stockbroker Aspect of my character that can choose from a number of options so I can continue to accumulate valuable experience.

Stock cube Potential to quickly fulfill an ambition by using my good taste to help me produce an outcome of great substance and importance.

Stockings Ability to present my self-image to other people in a way that gives me the freedom to take smooth and individual action.

Stock market Opportunity to make the most of ups and downs by displaying my wealth of knowledge and having its value recognized.

Stocks Ability to free myself from any restraints to my creativity rather than feeling that I have to work within a rigid framework.

Stock-taking Opportunity to count on my natural talent and understand the value of my wealth of accumulated knowledge and experience.

Stolen Realization that I need other people to openly recognize the value of my skills rather than feeling guilty about displaying them.

Stolen car Opportunity to show other people the value of my ambition instead of feeling guilty about losing my motivation.

Stomach Essential ability to digest the significance of my experiences so I can use them to fulfill my appetite for success.

Stomachache Opportunity to deal with an underlying tension by extracting maximum

benefit from a situation that may have been hard to swallow.

Stomach complaint Opportunity to resolve a challenging situation by fully absorbing the value of my experiences instead of just moaning about them.

Stomach pump Ability to consistently channel my thoughts and feelings so I can move on from experience that no longer motivates me.

Stone Ability to steadily maintain a solid presence by always being firm and practical, even though I may appear hard-edged.

Stone circle Ability to consistently shape my circumstances by being firm and practical as I reach out to the edge of what I know.

Stonemason Aspect of my character that can provide me with the building blocks I need to establish my presence and viewpoint.

Stony path Situation where I can take some steps to understand my current direction in life so I can easily make some hard choices.

Stool Ability to occupy a particular viewpoint, even though I may not feel entirely comfortable in continuing to support my position.

Stoop Opportunity to proudly stand up for what I believe in rather than feeling that it might somehow be beneath my dignity.

Stop Opportunity to bring an end to a challenging situation so I can come to a conclusion about my preferred outcome.

Stopcock Ability to control the flow of my emotions so I can keep developing my character rather than keeping myself in check.

Stopover Opportunity to take some time to reflect on my progress as I explore a variety of viewpoints so I can see a way forward.

Stoppage time Opportunity to decide an uncertain outcome by taking the time to gauge my levels of experience and the best way to apply them.

S

Stop press Opportunity to clearly get my message across by using a steady, forceful manner, even if it means halting everything else.

Stopwatch Ability to take my time so I can gauge my performance rather than feeling I have to conform to an unrealistic deadline.

Storage Situation where I can feel secure in my accumulated wisdom and experience by having the knowledge I can access at any time.

Storage device Ability to bring together my thoughts and ideas in a structured manner so I can use them to provoke a specific response.

Store Situation where I can have my value recognized by sharing it with other people instead of trying to keep my talents in reserve.

Store card Ability to give myself full credit for my accumulated knowledge and wisdom rather than feeling I owe them to anyone else.

Storefront Situation where I can promote the value of my skills and talents so I can explore them in greater depth with my colleagues.

Storeroom Aspect of myself that has the capacity to help me feel secure and comfortable in accessing the knowledge I have built up.

Storing Opportunity to lay aside challenges so I can draw on my wisdom and experience and use it to resolve any tension.

Stork Instinctive ability to rise above practical concerns by sticking my neck out so I can bring a particular idea into being.

Storm Natural opportunity to keep myself calm by continuing to channel the energy from my turmoil of conflicting ideas and emotions.

Stormbound Opportunity to fully connect to my natural energy without feeling that I'm trapped in a situation that may limit my actions.

Storm cloud Situation where I can calmly draw on accumulated learning and experience as a way of resolving approaching conflict.

Storm drain Ability to rid myself of powerfully conflicting emotions rather than allowing myself to be suddenly overwhelmed by them.

Storm lantern Ability to guide myself through powerful emotional tensions by illuminating them in the light of previous experience.

Story Ability to share my unique perspective by understanding my deeper motivations and the role I play in them.

Storyteller Aspect of my character that has the wisdom to act on my deeper motivations rather than telling tales about them.

Stove Ability to use my creative energy in a warm and comfortable manner so I can keep satisfying my appetite for success.

Stowaway Aspect of my character that needs to be open about my efforts to help other people rather than giving them a free ride.

Strafing Opportunity to swiftly assert the power of my ideas in a forceful manner so I can communicate my aims to other people.

Straggler Aspect of my character that has the self-motivation to follow my path rather than feeling that I have to tag along.

Straight Realization that I need to be more direct in expressing how I feel instead of always going round and round in circles.

Straightforward Opportunity to successfully work through a sequence of events by looking at the less obvious aspects of the situation.

Strain Realization that I will put myself under much less pressure by being more relaxed about achieving a successful outcome.

Straitjacket Ability to free up one of the less rational aspects of my creativity so I can get my arms around it without driving myself crazy.

Stranded Opportunity to use my self-motivation to follow my chosen direction rather than feeling I've been left high and dry.

S

Strange Realization that even the most unusual occurrences have a fundamental familiarity that I can feel very much at home with.

Strange animal Instinctive ability that embodies all aspects of my wider creativity and gives me motivation to express natural talent.

Strange event Opportunity to become more aware of the significance of my habitual actions to transform my potential for success.

Strange light Ability to understand a situation with greater clarity by using my natural wisdom to illuminate what is happening.

Strange man Aspect of my character that embodies some of the unfamiliar qualities I need to assert ambitions and achieve dreams.

Strange noise Realization that I need to be specific about what I am trying to communicate instead of just being disturbed by it.

Strange occurrence Opportunity to make the most of an emerging situation rather than waiting for it to turn out the way I would like it to.

Stranger Aspect of my character that may seem unknown and unfamiliar but can give me the deepest insights into who I want to be.

Strange room Aspect of myself that has the potential capacity to help me feel more comfortable and secure in developing my unspoken talents.

Strange town Situation where I can go beyond my usual social circle so I can access unfamiliar resources that will help me succeed.

Strange vehicle Ability to make progress toward an unfamiliar goal by using personal drive and ambition to keep me moving forward.

Strange woman Aspect of my character embodying the unique empathy and wisdom I need to realize the power of undiscovered talents.

Stranglehold Opportunity to fundamentally transform my freedom of expression by having a firm grasp of my thoughts and feelings.

Strangler Aspect of my character that can profoundly transform how I express my feelings instead of preventing me from voicing them.

Strangulation Opportunity to open up to what I feel so I can use it to voice my inspiration rather than becoming all choked up.

Strap Ability to keep myself connected to the outcome of a situation without feeling that I am overly attached to it in any way.

Strategy Ability to understand what unconsciously motivates me at a deeper level so I can choose the best tactics for success.

Straw Natural ability to connect to my potential for emotional fulfillment so I can channel feelings and feel comfortable with them.

Strawberry Natural ability to have a healthy awareness of where my passions lie so I can serve up a more fruitful outcome.

Stray Opportunity to be far more direct in demonstrating what I need rather than becoming distracted by taking care of others.

Streak Opportunity to make my mark by moving really quickly, even though it might make me feel exposed and vulnerable to others.

Stream Situation where I can connect with my feelings and use them to get into the flow of accumulating more learning and experience.

Street Situation where I can use a recognized route to build stronger relationships with other people so I can share their perspectives.

Streetcar Ability to make progress toward my wider professional objectives by ensuring my colleagues are all on the same track.

Street lamp Ability to use my natural energy and the power of my wisdom to illuminate how I can continue to connect with other people.

S

Street peddler Aspect of my character that understands the value of making a deeper connections with others rather than just avoiding them.

Streetwalker Aspect of my character that can become more intimately aware of how I can use my creativity to connect with others.

Strength Essential opportunity to use my powers of self-motivation to demonstrate my commitment to achieving a specific outcome.

Stress Opportunity to strongly emphasize the power of my underlying talents instead of worrying about any of my unjustified fears.

Stretch Opportunity to extend the range of my creativity rather than pursuing an unrealistic goal for too long a time.

Stretcher Ability to convey how I feel so I can move forward to a healthier outcome instead of getting carried away.

Stretcher-bearer Aspect of my character that can give me the full support I need and convey how I feel so I can keep moving forward.

Stretch marks Opportunity to realize my capacity for conceiving valuable ideas instead of feeling I may have gone too far with them.

Stricken Opportunity to realize how struck I am by a particular opportunity so I can understand how I can make the most of it.

Strict Realization that I can be much more flexible in how I achieve success rather than feeling I have to behave in a specific way.

Stride Opportunity to proudly use my self-motivation and energy to take the steps I need so I can rapidly make a major advance.

Strident Realization that I can use a quieter approach that will have a more powerful result instead of just feeling I am too intense.

Strike Opportunity to take decisive action so I can rapidly make an impact rather than causing myself prolonged discomfort.

Strikebreaker Aspect of my character that can achieve a greater understanding of my value by choosing to take time out.

Striking Opportunity to publicly reveal the power of my unique talents so I can make an immediate impact on the people around me.

Strimmer Ability to work at the edge of my natural expertise so I can continue to cultivate it in a healthy and considered manner.

String Ability to stay firmly connected to the outcome of a situation without feeling that I am just going along with everyone else.

Strip Opportunity to uncover what is happening by taking a narrower perspective so I can concentrate my attention on it.

Stripe Ability to see the contrast between my work and the efforts of other people so I can understand the difference I make.

Stripper Aspect of my character that is confident enough to open up about vulnerabilities and share them with others.

Strippergram Aspect of my character that can convey my intentions to others by having the confidence to reveal some hidden aspects.

Strip light Ability to understand my current situation with much greater clarity by taking a much narrower perspective as I explore it.

Strip mining Situation where I can dig deeper into practical experience I have accumulated so I can reveal my concealed value

Strip poker Opportunity to choose my preferred outcome by confidently showing my vulnerabilities, not trying to cover them up.

Strip search Opportunity to discover how I feel about an unfamiliar situation by opening up to different perspectives.

Striptease Opportunity to methodically work my way through a display of my talents rather than worrying about how I appear to others.

Strobe Ability to use my accumulated wisdom so I can be consistently illuminating instead of just showing the odd flash of brilliance.

Stroke Opportunity to keep in touch by using a gentle and relaxed manner rather than getting too worked up about the situation.

Stroll Opportunity to use my self-motivation and energy in a more relaxed manner so I take the necessary steps to succeed.

Stroller Ability to use my self-motivation to take definite steps and make relaxed progress with a new idea I care about.

Strong Realization that I have an abundance of self-motivation that I can easily use to achieve a powerful and fulfilling outcome.

Strongbox Ability to feel openly secure about the strength of my talents by having the confidence to set personal boundaries around them.

Stronghold Situation where I have a firm grasp of my inner strength so I can use it to maintain my position without any real challenges.

Struck Opportunity to realize the potential impact of my actions so I can use my power in a way that rings true.

Structure Ability to examine the various aspects of my inner and outer self so I can see the different ways in which they support me.

Struggle Opportunity to stay engaged with a challenge in the knowledge that I will eventually succeed rather than just giving up.

Strut Opportunity to give myself the support I need to confidently take the required steps as I pursue one of my ambitions.

Stubbornness Realization that I can successfully determine my chosen outcome by staying open to possibilities rather than by being obstinate.

Stuck Opportunity to release myself from any unnecessary obligations so I can move forward rather than feeling I am being held back.

Stuck in mud Opportunity to move on by taking a firmer approach that helps me stay down-to-earth and minimizes my emotional involvement.

Student Aspect of my character that studies my motivations and behaviors so I can achieve a better understanding of myself.

Studio Situation where I can use my natural ingenuity and creative instincts to help me develop my potential expertise and abilities.

Studio apartment Situation where I can bring different aspects of my character together so I can understand my potential for development.

Study Aspect of myself that has the capacity to help me feel comfortable and secure as I take time to learn more about who I really am.

Studying Opportunity to continually add to my accumulating experience and wisdom so I can make the most of what I have learned.

Studying a menu Opportunity to explore possibilities about what will fulfill my appetite for success so I can digest their significance.

Studying a timetable Opportunity to make the most of future possibilities by having a firm understanding of the outcome I want to achieve.

Stuff Ability to gather my thoughts and feelings in a more concentrated way so I can shape them into something more substantial.

Stuffed animal Ability to bring my creative instincts back to life so I can always be inspired to embody and express my natural wisdom.

Stuffy Opportunity to directly open myself up to some less oppressive ways of thinking that may seem like a breath of fresh air to me.

Stumbling Opportunity to take the confident steps I need to pursue an ambition instead of being concerned about any potential obstacles.

Stump Ability to have a firm and proven basis for redeveloping my skills and talents rather than feeling frustrated and cut off.

S

Stung Realization that I need to be open about my intentions rather than concealing them by being sharply critical of other people.

Stun grenade Ability to contain my potentially explosive feelings so I can influence the situation instead of feeling devastated by it.

Stun gun Ability to confidently communicate my aims to other people by observing some behaviors I am not usually conscious of.

Stunned Opportunity to observe what is emerging from my unconscious instead of being overwhelmed by what is happening.

Stunning Realization that I can attract other people toward me by having the confidence to share my talents and reveal my deeper value.

Stunt Opportunity to display my remarkable talents to other people rather than feeling that my potential growth is being hindered.

Stuntman Aspect of my character that courageously embraces creative risks so I can assert my ambitions and achieve my dreams.

Stunt pilot Aspect of my character that can get some potentially risky ideas off the ground by having the skill to successfully land them.

Stuntwoman Aspect of my character that embodies the courage and wisdom I need to make the most of any creative risks.

Stupid Realization that I know much more than I often think I do and need to make myself more aware of opportunities to use my talents.

Stupor Realization that I can use my unconscious awareness to become more self-motivated and energetic instead of ignoring it.

Stuttering Essential opportunity to fluently and coherently express my feelings by taking a more relaxed approach instead of tensing up.

Style Ability to become more aware of the distinct talents that make me unique so I can use them to fashion a successful outcome.

Stylist Aspect of my character that can bring out my best qualities by taking the time to look beyond how I normally reveal myself to people.

Styrofoam Ability to work with a variety of ideas that may be bubbling up so I can then mold them into something more practical.

Suave Realization that using my raw creative power can sometimes be just as effective as attempting to be more sophisticated.

Subatomic particle Ability to understand what is going on by understanding the tiniest details and the attraction they hold for me.

Subject Ability to study a particular aspect of my character so I can understand the specific qualities that make me unique.

Sublime Realization that I have the power to transfer my ideas directly into practical action without becoming too emotionally involved.

Submarine Ability to confidently explore the depths of my emotions and navigate them safely instead of cracking up under pressure.

Submarine canyon Situation where I can naturally go deeper into my emotions, even though it may involve my dealing with extra pressure.

Submarine meadow Situation where I can healthily develop deeper emotional skills by using my accumulated expertise to naturally support me.

Submariner Aspect of my character that is at home in exploring deeper feelings and can help me work through challenging emotions.

Submerged Opportunity to be open about my emotions rather than trying to conceal them in case people are overwhelmed by my feelings.

Submersible Ability to gain a profounder awareness of my emotional life by studying a variety of my behavioral patterns in depth.

Submissive Realization that I have the power to make my own decisions rather than feeling I have to give in to the demands of people.

S

Subscription Ability to consent to a course of action by promising to contribute something of value and underwriting the outcome.

Subsidence Opportunity to have a firmer basis for my viewpoints by letting things settle instead of feeling that I'm sinking out of sight.

Substance Ability to provide a material basis for my thoughts and feelings so I can shape them into something more meaningful.

Subtitle Ability to communicate what I need to say to other people in a situation that may seem foreign or unfamiliar to me.

Substitute Ability to use my unique skills to be original rather than feeling as if I'm filling in to keep everyone happy.

Suburb Situation where I can access the resources I need to fulfill my individual ambitions without becoming too set in my ways.

Subway Situation where I can routinely go deeper into practical considerations as a way of quickly reaching my objective.

Subway platform Situation where I can raise my level of awareness by embarking on a process that will take me deeper into the practical aspects.

Subway ticket Ability to demonstrate my value to people by giving myself permission to display to them the depths of my expertise.

Success Opportunity to achieve my chosen outcome by having confidence in my individual abilities and trusting in my personal talents.

Succubus Aspect of my character that has the confidence to reveal some of my deeper desires instead of trying to conceal my intentions.

Succumb Opportunity to overcome a major challenge rather than surrendering to my anxieties and feeling that I should give up.

Suck Opportunity to fulfill an emotional need by reducing any external pressures that may be absorbing too much of my attention.

Sudden Realization that I can transform my circumstances more quickly than I believed possible just by making a quick decision.

Sudoku Opportunity to solve the reason for one of my recurring behavioral patterns by taking the time to patiently work through it.

Suffering Opportunity to resolve an uncomfortable situation by exploring what would make me feel happy rather than just dismissing it.

Suffocating Opportunity to freely express what I think by drawing on my inspiration instead of allowing others to stifle my creativity.

Sugar Potential to fulfill an ambition by trying to sweeten the short-term outcome without paying any attention to long-term gains.

Suggestion Opportunity to successfully influence an outcome by understanding my needs rather than telling others what to do.

Suicide Opportunity for me to make a major life transformation by revitalizing my ambitions and making a healthy commitment to my future.

Suicide attack Opportunity to make a definite transformation by challenging my unresolved fears and potentially self-destructive behaviors.

Suicide bomber Aspect of my character able to contain my potentially explosive feelings so I can create a positive transformation.

Suicide pact Opportunity to make a deeper commitment to my life ambitions by recognizing any tensions in conflicting aspects of my character.

Suit Ability to present my self-image to other people in a formal and authoritative manner that matches my overall understanding.

Suitcase Ability to convey what I need to help me fulfill an ongoing ambition without weighing myself down with emotional baggage.

S

Suite Ability to use my habitual behaviors and memories in an organized way so I can develop my potential talents and experience.

Sulk Opportunity to realize a happy outcome by displaying my unique expertise to other people rather than trying to conceal it.

Sullen Realization that I can achieve my chosen outcome by taking a positive approach instead of brooding over any missed chances.

Sulphurous Instinctive awareness that helps me identify my potential for creative transformation rather than just feeling a bit sour.

Sultana Potential to fulfill an ambition by collecting a bunch of fruitful opportunities and preserving their value for the future.

Sum Ability to use the full extent of all my knowledge and experience, even when my present situation doesn't seem to add up.

Summer Opportunity to understand my natural instincts and rhythms so I can become more aware of some ripening possibilities.

Summerhouse Situation where I can feel comfortable in exploring my inner life so I can make the most of some developing possibilities.

Summer lightning Natural opportunity to sense the prevailing atmosphere so I can take a warmer approach to developing my creativity.

Summer solstice Opportunity to fully illuminate my creative awareness by remaining centered as I reach out to the edge of my understanding.

Summit Situation where I can reach a much higher level of achievement by committing myself to a sustained period of practical effort.

Summon Opportunity to make my presence felt by drawing on my reserves of courage rather than dismissing my unique contribution.

Sumo wrestler Aspect of my character that can indulge in my appetite for success by

grappling with the practicalities of a major challenge.

Sump Ability to create some space where I can collect my feelings so I am able to convey my emotions much more effectively.

Sumptuous Realization that understanding the value of my expertise enables me to be much more comfortable with my wealth of talent.

Sun Elemental ability to illuminate a situation with the power of my creativity and naturally attract other people into my orbit.

Sunbathing Opportunity to take a more relaxed outlook by immersing myself in the power of my creativity and soaking up the atmosphere.

Sunbeam Ability to provide creative support for my thinking by staying positive so I can provide an illuminating perspective.

Sunbed Situation where I can feel more at home with my talents so I can take a relaxed approach to absorbing my creative urges.

Sunburn Opportunity to use creative passion to stay in touch with my real feelings, even though it seems painful at the time.

Suncream Ability to protect my artistic sensitivities rather than feeling I am exposing myself to too many creative influences.

Sundae Potential to fulfill a short-term ambition by trying to stay cool, even though it may result in a sticky outcome in the long run.

Sundial Ability to use my natural creativity to illuminate the best time to make the most of an opportunity without any shadow of a doubt.

Sunflower Natural ability to open up to my wider creative talents so I can encourage them to blossom while staying grounded in reality.

Sunflower seed Natural ability for a seemingly insignificant creative talent to potentially grow into something much bigger and more powerful.

Sunglasses Ability to protect my unique insight so I can filter out any distractions in an otherwise highly illuminating situation.

Sunken Opportunity to explore my feelings and emotions in greater depth rather than allowing them to bring me down in any way.

Sunken bath Situation where I can feel most relaxed and at home with my emotional life rather than feeling down about my situation.

Sunlight Natural opportunity to illuminate the power of my creativity so I can understand a situation with much greater clarity.

Sun ray Ability to positively direct my fundamental creativity so I can illuminate an opportunity that may seem quite distant.

Sunrise Natural opportunity to become more aware of my increasing capabilities so I can use them to make the most of a new beginning.

Sunroof Ability to open up to a wider awareness of my creative possibilities so I feel more motivated to explore them.

Sunscreen Ability to establish some personal boundaries around my creative opportunities so I don't expose myself to painful criticism.

Sunset Natural opportunity to reflect on the successful completion of a creative project so I can prepare for the next one.

Sunshade Ability to take a cooler and more relaxed perspective so I don't end up feeling dazzled by my own creative brilliance.

Sunshine Opportunity to use the power and energy of my natural creativity to illuminate any valuable possibilities that I may encounter.

Suntan Ability to display my creativity in a healthy way by understanding how many of my feelings I want to expose to other people.

Suntan cream Ability to stay in touch with my deeper feelings by carefully looking after the boundary between my inner and outer worlds.

Sun visor Ability to protect my creative perspective so I can work on the details instead of being distracted by the glaringly obvious.

Super Natural realization that I can use my essential creativity to shape an outcome instead of trying to follow a rational procedure.

Superbug Ability to realize the power of an apparently insignificant idea so I can use it to resolve a potentially unhealthy situation.

Supercomputer Ability to use my unconscious awareness to intuitively work through the permutations that can influence a successful outcome.

Supercooled Ability to take the heat out of any volatile emotions so I can immediately communicate to other people how I feel.

Superficial Realization that I have the skill to explore an issue in greater depth rather than being content with surface appearances.

Superglue Ability to create a long-lasting bond in a close relationship instead of feeling that I am permanently stuck in some old habits.

Superhero Aspect of my character that can transform the outcome of a situation by always courageously choosing to do the right thing.

Superheroine Aspect of my character that can draw on my hidden reserves of strength so I can use my unseen power to transform the situation.

Superhuman Realization that just being myself is the most effective way to transcend any apparent limitations I may encounter.

Super-injunction Opportunity to openly make my choices about what I want to do rather than feeling I will be judged by others.

Supermarket Situation where I can choose from a variety of options for displaying my talents so I can have their value be recognized.

Supermodel Aspect of my character that can use my unspoken power to achieve an ideal outcome rather than just worrying about how I appear.

S

Superstar Aspect of my character that can naturally attract others toward me by sharing the brilliance of my creativity with them.

Superstore Situation where I can have my value be more widely recognized by others so I can open myself up to more choices.

Superstition Realization that I can use practical evidence to decide on my chosen outcome rather than feeling I must leave it to fate.

Supertanker Ability to navigate a potentially complex emotional situation so I can convey what is needed to fuel my long-term ambitions.

Supervillain Aspect of my character that always tries to bring out the best in others, even though my intentions may not be too obvious.

Supervisor Aspect of my character that has a higher awareness of what I am trying to do, without having to constantly watch over me.

Supper Opportunity to achieve my main ambitions in a relaxed manner so I can absorb recent experiences and take time to digest them.

Supple Essential opportunity to make the most of a situation by adapting to new circumstances rather than appearing inflexible.

Supplement Ability to add my individual contribution in a way that increases the overall value of a larger and more complex situation.

Supplier Aspect of my character that can successfully fulfill one of my specific needs by conveying what I honestly feel.

Supply Ability to draw on my accumulated expertise and experience so I can provide myself with all the resources I need.

Support Ability to maintain a definite structure to my activities so I have the capacity to look after the needs of other people.

Supporter Aspect of my character that reinforces the value of my abilities and is always happy to sing my praises to those around me.

Supposed Realization that I always need to speak my truths rather than assuming that others' beliefs are correct.

Suppressed Opportunity to openly encourage my individual abilities rather than trying to conceal them as a way of keeping others happy.

Supreme being Aspect of my character that embodies all the unlimited wisdom and undeveloped potential I can use to create my unique life.

Surcharge Ability to make decisive progress by realizing that my value is above and beyond what other people usually give me credit for.

Sure Realization that I am more certain of achieving a successful outcome if I take the time to deeply question my motivations.

Sure-footed Ability to question how I motivate myself so I can take the right steps to accomplish my chosen outcome.

Surf Opportunity to get to the edge of my emotional experience so I can let ideas bubble up to the surface and see them more clearly.

Surface Situation where I can achieve a profounder understanding by exploring my feelings in greater depth as they rise from inside.

Surface-to-air missile Ability to powerfully assert my beliefs so I can defend my way of thinking against others who bombard me with their ideas.

Surfboard Ability to have a firm basis for playing around with the ups and downs of my emotions instead of feeling overwhelmed by them.

Surfer Aspect of my character that can use the deeper power of my emotions to make the most of unexpected breaks I encounter.

Surfing Opportunity to carve my path through the ups and downs of an emotional situation that is just beginning to break.

Surge Opportunity to powerfully move forward by understanding my deeper emotions and how I can use their continual ebb and flow.

Surgeon Aspect of my character that can decisively resolve a potentially unhealthy situation by taking specific and incisive action.

Surgery Opportunity to resolve inner tensions by opening up my feelings to people so they can understand what's going on inside me.

Surge tank Ability to safely contain my more powerful emotions by giving myself room to consistently maintain my personal boundaries.

Surly Realization that I can assert my power in a kind and gentle manner rather than feeling I have to be rude and bad-tempered.

Surprise Realization that I can exceed my expectations by always being open to the possibility of using my undiscovered talents.

Surreal Realization that I can often gain practical insight by exploring the unseen connections between apparently separate events.

Surrender Opportunity to conquer emerging fears and anxieties that I may have instead of immediately resigning myself to defeat.

Surreptitious Opportunity to be open and obvious about my intentions rather than trying to achieve my goal more clandestinely.

Surrogate mother Aspect of my character that can take an idea someone else has conceived so I can nurture and develop it as if it were my own.

Surrounded Opportunity to break out of familiar circumstances and patterns that may be holding me back so I can center myself.

Surveillance Opportunity to observe my habitual behavioral patterns rather than feeling that other people are watching me all the time.

Surveillance drone Ability to observe my thought patterns as they emerge so I can choose to conceal them from others if I want.

Survey Opportunity to take a more comprehensive view of my wider ambitions and deeper desires so I can estimate my current progress.

Survival Opportunity to maintain my progress after a major life transformation so I can happily continue to thrive and prosper.

Survival kit Ability to use my accumulated expertise and experience to always reach a happy outcome, even though the process may seem arduous.

Survivor Aspect of my character that can draw on my inner resourcefulness and use my experience to thrive on meeting new challenges.

Suspect Aspect of my character that has unshakable faith in my capabilities though others may confess to doubting my talents.

Suspended Opportunity to stay connected to my higher aspirations without becoming too attached to an outcome that will happen anytime soon.

Suspension bridge Situation where I can resolve a dilemma between two areas of my life by maintaining my level of elevated awareness.

Suspicious Realization that I am less likely to doubt my success if I can have more trust in my unique talents and accumulated wisdom.

Suspicious activity Opportunity to reach a definite outcome by taking specific action instead of always doubting the value of what I am doing.

Suspicious character Aspect of my character that can help me identify some of my valuable qualities, even though they initially may seem unfamiliar.

S

Suspicious package Ability to be receptive to new opportunities and the value they might offer rather than becoming too wrapped up in my doubts.

Suture Ability to bring together both sides of an argument so I can gain healthy closure instead of continuing to feel wounded.

Swab Ability to quickly clean up a potentially messy outcome by taking time to understand the nature of the underlying situation.

Swag Ability to feel comfortable with my accumulated experience rather than trying to have it acknowledged by forcing it on to people.

Swagger Opportunity to make one of my big ideas actually happen by confidently taking the required steps to achieve a splendid outcome.

Swallow Instinctive ability to rise above more practical concerns so I can spread my ideas without having to go to great lengths.

Swallowing Opportunity to take in the wider implications of a situation so I can fully digest their deeper significance for me.

Swamp Situation where I can release myself from minor details that are overwhelming me and may be beginning to bog down my progress.

Swan Instinctive ability to powerfully transform my natural way of thinking by elegantly connecting my thoughts and emotions.

Swap Opportunity to let go of some habitual behaviors that no longer serve me in exchange for maintaining my overall progress.

Swarm Natural opportunity to gather all my various skills and abilities so I can use them to achieve a specific outcome.

Swarthy Realization that I can show how I feel about a situation that is darkening my mood, instead of just trying to smooth over it.

Swastika Opportunity to make a significant connection rather than getting bent out of shape by misunderstanding the situation.

Swat Opportunity to openly show my hand so I can decisively deal with some minor anxieties that have been bugging me.

Swathe Opportunity to clear away any possible barriers to my progress rather than becoming too wrapped up in the overall situation.

Sway Opportunity to clearly understand what might be influencing my opinion instead of just moving from one viewpoint to another one.

Swearing Opportunity to declare a firm commitment to developing my potential and achieving success rather than cursing my luck.

Sweat Essential ability to show how I feel about a situation instead of getting all worked up and causing a lot of friction.

Sweater Ability to present my self-image to people in a way that seems more comfortable, even though my initial reception may be cool.

Sweating Essential opportunity to resolve any emotional frictions by cooling down the situation rather than getting heated up about it.

Sweeping Opportunity to make a clean start by looking at a wide range of possible outcomes and quickly deciding how I can achieve them.

Sweepstake Opportunity to contribute to a successful outcome by making a definite commitment rather than leaving it to chance.

Sweet Essential ability to use my personal taste to get the flavor of a situation so I can make sure that everyone is happy.

Sweetheart Aspect of my character that can help me become more aware of some of the qualities that people find most pleasing in me.

Sweet potato Potential to fulfill an ambition and sustain my progress by getting back to my roots in a pleasing and healthy manner.

Swelling Essential opportunity to reduce

S

some of my commitments rather than starting to feel uncomfortable because of increasing strain.

Sweltering Opportunity to welcome a breath of fresh air rather than trying to continue any heated discussions in an oppressive atmosphere.

Swept away Opportunity to stay fully connected to my long-term objective instead of allowing other people to suddenly sweep me off my feet.

Swerve Opportunity to stay on my chosen career path rather than permitting other people to force me to suddenly change direction.

Swim lanes Situation where I can work through an emotional challenge by staying within the suggested guidelines.

Swimmer Aspect of my character that can fully commit to being in an emotional situation rather than just dipping my toes in the water.

Swimming Opportunity to immerse myself in an emotional challenge and work through it by using my self-motivation and energy.

Swimming baths Situation where I am happy to immerse myself in my emotions, even though I may have to contain some deeper feelings.

Swimming pool Situation where I can share the depth of my professional experience without feeling I have to contain my emotions.

Swimwear Ability to present myself to other people by showing my readiness to open up and immerse myself in deeper emotions.

Swine Instinctive ability to root around in a potentially messy situation so I can find some valuable items of information.

Swing Ability to playfully work my way backward and forward through a wide range of different perspectives as I make up my mind.

Swipe Opportunity to take decisive action so I can openly demonstrate my value rather than allowing other people to diminish it.

Swipe card Ability to access valuable areas of my expertise in a challenging situation by giving myself permission to take decisive action.

Swiss army knife Ability to assert my individuality in a useful manner by using my wide range of skills to cut through uncertainty.

Swiss bank account Ability to accumulate a heightened sense of self-worth by having the confidence to display the value of my talents.

Switch Ability to make a specific decision so I can choose my desired outcome without spending too much time making up my mind.

Switchboard Ability to make the specific connection I need so I can communicate what I need to say to a particular person.

Swivel chair Ability to maintain my habitual viewpoint on a variety of aspects instead of taking action by stepping outside my comfort zone.

Swollen Realization that I may be feeling uncomfortable because I have taken on too much rather than decreasing my obligations.

Swoop Opportunity to suddenly realize that I can achieve a profounder understanding by going deeper into a certain style of thinking.

Sword Ability to assert my power by decisively running through potential challenges so I can slice through any uncertainty.

Swordfish Instinctive ability to immerse myself into my emotions so I can express my deeper feelings and get to the point.

Sycamore Natural opportunity for my long-term spiritual growth by widely distributing my ideas while staying rooted in the practicalities.

Syllable Ability to make myself more easily understood by being specific about what I am trying to communicate to other people.

S

Symbol Opportunity to connect my awareness to a much deeper and wider understanding of what is meaningful for me.

Sympathy Realization that I am able to have more influence on those around me by becoming more aware of my deeper feelings.

Symptom Ability to understand what is happening by having a healthy appreciation of what is emerging from my unconscious awareness.

Synchronicity Opportunity to connect my past experience to future aspirations while using resources I currently have.

Synchronized swimmers Aspects of my character that can connect my previous experiences with how I would like events to shape up in the future.

Synthesizer Ability to take my instinctive creativity in both hands so I can use my ideas to generate a wide variety of new perspectives.

Synthetic Realization that one of my most valuable attributes is my ability to show my genuine feelings rather than appearing artificial.

Syringe Ability to draw on my experience so I can resolve a potentially unhealthy situation by injecting my enthusiasm into it.

Syrup Potential to fulfill an ambition by pursuing a seemingly short-term emotional gratification that may have a sticky outcome.

System Ability to organize my knowledge and experience in a structured manner so I can consistently create valuable outcomes.

System operator Aspect of my character that can produce a valuable outcome by using my unique skills rather than just going through the motions.

S

Table Ability to be open and supportive with other people by sharing my thoughts and feelings about our habitual relationships.

Tablecloth Ability to provide a pleasant basis for sharing thoughts and feelings about relationships rather than trying to conceal them.

Tablet Ability to resolve a potentially unhealthy situation by communicating my ideas in a more substantial manner.

Tablet computer Ability to shape my future and quickly decide an outcome by using my mind to precisely work out various possibilities.

Tabloid journalist Aspect of my character that feels comfortable with sharing my talents and experience rather than trying to sensationalize them.

Taboo Realization that I have the power to decide what is acceptable to me rather than permitting other people to tell me what to do.

Tachograph Ability to chart my daily progress toward my objective as I employ my powerful drive to provide a valuable shift in my ambitions.

Tack Ability to choose a specific direction and then stick to it rather than becoming overly attached to a particular outcome.

Tackle Opportunity to seize a creative ambition with both hands so I can land it instead of trying to avoid the issue.

Tacky Realization that I need to use my refinement and experience to choose my outcome rather than adhering to other guidelines.

Tactless Realization that I can achieve much more consistent outcomes by using my insights in a much more caring and thoughtful way.

Tadpole Instinctive ability to transform my situation by developing my inspirational skills and finding different ways to motivate myself.

Tag Ability to make the connection to what I need so I can consistently show my preferences to other people.

Tail Instinctive ability to become more aware of what might follow and how it may eventually end, based on my past experience.

Tail fin Ability to maintain my direction as I explore some loftier thoughts and plans so I can align them with my wider purpose.

Tail gunner Aspect of my character that forcefully asserts my power so I can defend myself from any previous criticisms.

Taillight Ability to understand a situation with much greater clarity and illuminate what is happening so people can follow my example.

Tailor Aspect of my character that is attentive to how I measure up in the views of other people and adjusts my behavior accordingly.

Takeoff Opportunity to get one of my ideas off the ground so I can successfully launch a plan I've been working on.

Takeout Opportunity to fulfill my appetite for success by containing my wider ambitions so I can use a more convenient approach.

Tale Ability to share a unique insight into my personal experiences so I can display the power of my imagination to other people.

T

Talent Realization that I have a natural ability to create value and it has the potential to be widely recognized by other people.

Talent scout Aspect of my character that observes my behavior so I can understand how to develop my natural abilities and aptitudes.

Talent show Opportunity to proudly display my creative skills to other people so my unique abilities can be more widely recognized.

Talent-show judge Aspect of my character that takes responsibility for showing my natural expertise instead of being critical of my efforts.

Talisman Ability to use my creative talents to powerfully influence the outcome of a situation so I can ensure that it works like a charm.

Talk show Opportunity to have my unique talents widely recognized by other people and be comfortable in expressing how I feel.

Talk show host Aspect of my character that can ask just the right question to help me understand my unique talents and how I can share them.

Talking Opportunity to speak up and tell other people how I feel so I can clearly express what is often left unsaid.

Talking animal Instinctive ability embodies my creative nature, giving me the motivation to honestly say what is often left unspoken.

Talking photo Ability to express a particular perspective that is often overlooked so I can remind myself of a valuable experience.

Talk show Opportunity to openly display my abilities to others by having the confidence to speak up and tell them how I really feel.

Tall Realization that I can increase my standing and raise my perceived status with people by confidently declaring my high ambitions.

Tall ship Ability to use the prevailing mood to explore my emotional highs and lows so I can rise above any current concerns.

Talon Instinctive ability to dig my heels in about a creative idea so everyone can grasp the potential ambition that I am pursuing.

Tambourine Ability to draw attention to my instinctive creativity so other people are more likely to supportively play along with me.

Tame Realization that I can use the power of my creative instincts to achieve an ambition instead of trying to keep them under control.

Tamper Opportunity to take a more relaxed approach by leaving things as they are rather than feeling that I constantly have to fix them.

Tampon Ability to channel my passion and vitality so I can stay in control of a creative transformation without it being too messy.

Tan Ability to color my mood in a healthy and optimistic way by understanding how much of my feelings I can expose to people.

Tandem Ability to make progress toward my chosen ambition by staying connected in a close relationship so I can balance my commitments.

Tangent Realization that I can use my current situation to go in a new direction rather than just touching on the possibility.

Tangle Opportunity to work my way through some of the confusion surrounding a situation so I have a clearer understanding of it.

Tank Ability to contain my more powerful emotions by strongly maintaining personal boundaries, even though it may seem quite defensive.

Tankard Ability to fulfill an emotional need by letting myself take in a particular experience rather than feeling confused about it.

Tanker Ability to employ some powerful resources that will help me motivate my drive for success as I progress toward my goal.

Tantric sex Opportunity to become more intimately aware of my ability to conceive something special without going on about it at length.

Tantrum Opportunity to voice my frustrations so I can make a real breakthrough in resolving some of my self-limiting behaviors.

Tap Ability to gently make my presence felt by demonstrating how I can control my feelings rather than just going with the flow.

Tape Ability to make a strong connection so I can align my skills and resources while maintaining my personal boundaries.

Tape measure Ability to precisely understand the scale of any of my self-limiting perceptions so I can use my talents accordingly.

Tape recorder Ability to listen for what makes an experience particularly significant for me so I can use that awareness in the future.

Tapestry Ability to creatively connect a variety of story threads so I can weave together a bigger picture of what may have happened.

Tapir Instinctive ability to follow my natural awareness so I can sniff out promising opportunities and get stuck into them.

Tar Ability to deal with a potentially messy emotional situation by tenaciously maintaining my deeper composure.

Tarantula Instinctive ability to release myself from an emotional entanglement that may have been causing me to have anxious thoughts.

Target Ability to clearly understand my aims so I can adjust my chosen direction and get much closer to my ultimate ambition.

Tarmac Ability to pave the way for my future success by taking a much smoother approach that consolidates all my practical skills.

Tarn Situation where I can make a sustained and committed effort so I can reflect on my accumulated learning and experience.

Tarnished Realization that I can polish my skills and allow my talents to shine through rather than appearing dull to other people.

Tarpaulin Ability to take a more practical approach to protecting my material assets, even though I may have to temporarily conceal them.

Tart Potential to fulfill an ambition by taking an open and honest approach that may seem a bit sharp and undisciplined to other people.

Tartan Ability to shape my wilder urges into something more substantial by providing a material basis for my thoughts and feelings.

Tarzan Aspect of my character that courageously explores the great diversity and huge growth capacity of my creative instincts.

Task Opportunity to connect with my life purpose by taking responsibility for my talents rather than feeling obliged to other people.

Taste Essential ability to judge the flavor of a situation so I can use my sense of refinement to create my preferred outcome.

Tasteless Realization that I am happy to speak out about sensitive subjects instead of always appearing bland to the people around me.

Tattered Opportunity to tidy up any loose threads so I can let go of the past rather than continually feeling I have to pull it apart.

Tattoo Ability to proudly display a belief that is of great personal significance and which has made an indelible impression upon me.

Taunting Opportunity to communicate how I honestly feel about the value of my talents rather than always making fun of my abilities.

Taut Opportunity to pull on my resources and strictly follow my ambitions without allowing myself to become too tense about it.

Tavern Situation where I can fulfill my emotional needs by taking a relaxed view as I reacquaint myself with my professional abilities.

Tax Ability to be fully accountable for realizing the value of my talents rather than burdening myself with unnecessary commitments.

T

Taxi Ability to make progress with a personal ambition by defining my intended outcome so I can access the knowledge I need.

Taxidermist Aspect of my character that can bring my creative instincts back to life so I can proudly display them to other people.

Taxi driver Aspect of my character with a deeper knowledge of my intended objective and how valuable the experience might be.

Tax inspector Aspect of my character that explores how to develop my skills and experience rather than trying to limit my potential value.

Tax return Ability to clearly communicate the fundamental value of my expertise rather than just trying to make a creative statement.

Tea Potential to fulfill an emotional need by taking a more relaxed approach so I can easily stimulate my creative processes.

Tea bag Ability to understand the special qualities I bring to a situation rather than always landing myself in hot water.

Tea break Opportunity to observe my habitual behavior patterns so I can choose to take some time out and refresh my overall outlook.

Teacher Aspect of my character that encourages me to develop my unique talents and gives me permission to continue learning about myself.

Teacup Ability to fulfill an emotional need by reflecting on a particular feeling so I can take the time to enjoy it.

Team Aspects of my character that work well together by complementing each other so I can achieve more than I imagined I could.

Team challenge Opportunity to actively question my deeper motives so I can inspire myself to use a wider variety of my different talents.

Team player Aspect of my character that actively engages in exploring opportunities so I can coordinate their outcomes.

Team sport Opportunity to achieve a collective ambition by being open about my individual talents, even though the outcome may be uncertain.

Teapot Ability to fulfill a potential need by taking the time to build up my strength rather than immediately pouring my feelings out.

Tearful Realization that I am happy to show how I feel so I can clearly resolve some emotions that are leaving me feeling drained.

Teargas Ability to maintain my levels of inspiration instead of allowing myself to be upset by any unwelcome and irritating ideas.

Tearing Opportunity to take decisive action by leaving the past behind rather than allowing conflicting emotions to pull me apart.

Tearjerker Opportunity to share my unique personal perspective by understanding my deeper emotions instead of trying to play on them.

Tears Essential opportunity to maintain my clarity of vision by letting my genuine emotions flow so I can see the bigger picture.

Tease Opportunity to carefully work my way through some ideas rather than allowing myself to be distracted by some petty annoyances.

Teaspoon Ability to work my way through an emotional need so I can feel more fulfilled by choosing the aspects that stir me the most.

Tea towel Ability to feel more fulfilled by absorbing the learning and experience I gain from dealing with my emotions.

Technician Aspect of my character that can use my acknowledged technical skills as a firm basis for displaying my creative talents.

Technique Ability to successfully demonstrate my individual talents to other people by having the confidence to apply just the right touch.

Technology Ability to use my creativity in a practical manner so I can achieve outcomes

T

I previously thought were impossible.

Teddy bear Ability to get more comfortable with my natural wisdom and resourcefulness so I can play around with how I can use them.

Teenage boy Aspect of my character that is confidently asserting my strength and power so I can develop my playful curiosity.

Teenage girl Aspect of my character that is rapidly developing my empathy and intuition so I can become more aware of my creativity.

Teeter Opportunity to make a firm decision to follow one of my particular inclinations rather than letting myself be thrown off balance.

Teeth Essential ability to display my power and confidence to other people by showing them how strongly I can assert my basic needs.

Telegram Ability to clearly convey my intentions to others rather than just hoping that they might be on the same wavelength.

Telegraph pole Ability to raise the level of my communication skills so I can convey what I really want to say to a wider audience.

Telemarketer Aspect of my character that has the opportunity to question deeper motivations rather than routinely ignoring my value.

Telepathy Opportunity to clearly express what is on my mind rather than waiting for other people to work it out for themselves.

Telephone Ability to communicate what I need to say to someone, even if they initially seem distant and disconnected.

Telephone booth Situation where I can communicate with somebody by knowing just the right buttons to press, even though my options seem limited.

Telephone call Opportunity to connect with another person at a deeper level so I can understand what I need to say to them.

Telephone directory Ability to communicate a powerful message by having an initial idea about the person I need to speak to.

Telephone exchange Situation where I can work my way through my habitual styles of communication so I can let go of any that no longer serve me.

Telephone line Ability to make a direct connection with another so I can communicate what is happening for me in the moment.

Telephone number Ability to know what buttons to press to get my message across instead of feeling I have to count on anyone in particular.

Telephone operator Aspect of my character that can help me make a stronger connection with another who can recognize my value.

Teleporter Ability to immediately establish my credibility, even though I appear not to have the remotest idea of what I am talking about.

Telepresence Ability to reveal myself as the person I want to be in this moment rather than being occupied by any distant concerns.

Teleprompter Ability to remind myself of what I need to say to get my message across instead of making it up as I go along.

Telesales Opportunity to make the most of my talents by questioning my needs rather than always listening to other people.

Telescope Ability to take a more objective view of future possibilities by examining how they align with my personal vision.

Telescopic sight Ability to focus on a particular objective so I can clearly see how to successfully reach it and achieve my wider aims.

Teleshopping Opportunity to share my unique creative talent with a wider audience rather than feeling I am just another commodity.

Telethon Opportunity to achieve my chosen ambition by committing to it in the long run instead of worrying about how I appear.

Television Ability to communicate how a

T

situation appears to me so I can use the power of my imagination to make a decision.

Television station Situation where I can gather resources to share the products of my imagination with a wider audience.

Teller Aspect of my character that communicates my value to others by accepting that they are also valuable individuals.

Temper Realization that I can consistently achieve effective results by taking a more equable approach rather than losing my cool.

Temperature Realization that I can influence how passionately I feel about a situation instead of always appearing to blow hot and cold.

Tempest Natural opportunity to channel the energy from a turmoil of conflicting thoughts and feelings so I can shift the prevailing mood.

Template Ability to become more aware of my habitual behavior patterns so I can use them to guide myself through an unfamiliar situation.

Temple Situation where I can examine the structure of my beliefs and trust that the people around me will give me the space I need.

Temporary Realization that I can make a permanent contribution toward my continuing development by making the most of this period.

Temptation Realization that I have complete power to make the correct choice about the best way to pursue one of my deepest desires.

Tempting Opportunity to understand what attracts me about a particular choice so I can achieve a feeling of healthy fulfillment.

Temptress Aspect of my character that can attract me toward a creative opportunity that will have a powerful influence on me.

Tenant Aspect of my character that can often feel more at home with myself by being able to demonstrate my value to other people.

Tenderness Realization that I can often

achieve a stronger result by speaking from the heart rather than worrying I will end up feeling hurt.

Tending Opportunity to take good care of my developing potential so I can use it to make the most of my creative inclinations.

Tendon Essential ability to connect my strength of purpose to the fundamental understanding I use to support my viewpoint.

Tendonitis Essential opportunity to resolve any tension by using my passion in a healthy way rather than feeling I have to be antagonistic.

Tennis Opportunity to get my point across and achieve a decisive outcome rather than just knocking some ideas back and forth.

Tenpin bowling Opportunity to keep myself on the straight and narrow so I can ensure my actions will have an immediate, obvious impact.

Tension Ability to use my individual power to achieve my chosen outcome instead of always feeling stressed out by other people's actions.

Tent Ability to feel relaxed and comfortable in an unfamiliar situation by using my self-motivation to help me feel more secure.

Tentacle Instinctive ability to use my power to reach out to the people around me instead of becoming too wrapped up in my own emotions.

Tent peg Ability to take a down-to-earth approach about my sense of security so I can feel more relaxed in an unfamiliar situation.

Tent pole Ability to support my need for privacy in an unfamiliar situation so I can comfortably establish personal boundaries.

Tenuous Realization that I can make a strong connection by getting a firmer grip on what is happening so I can influence the outcome.

Tepid Realization that I can use my passion and energy to get a situation moving instead of just appearing indifferent to it.

Term Opportunity to make the most of an emerging possibility so I can clearly express what will bring me the greatest fulfillment.

Terminal Situation where I can explore possibilities for my future development rather than feeling it is the end of the line for me.

Terminal illness Essential opportunity to use my natural strength and power to decisively resolve an unhealthy situation once and for all.

Termination Opportunity to bring an unsatisfactory situation to a decisive conclusion so I can create the conditions for a new beginning.

Terminator Aspect of my character that can potentially change my future by relentlessly pursuing a goal and ensuring I achieve it.

Terminus Situation where I can reach a definite conclusion about my professional progress so I can plan my long-term intentions.

Termite Instinctive ability to thoroughly deal with an old habit that may be eating away at me rather than allowing it to plague me.

Tern Instinctive ability to rise above any emotional concerns so I can spread my enduring ideas by communicating them to others.

Terraced house Situation where I am surrounded by the security and support I need to comfortably explore all aspects of my inner and outer lives.

Terra-cotta Ability to preserve a potentially fragile situation by using my practical skills to shape the outcome so I can be receptive to it.

Terraform Opportunity to create a whole new world of experience so I can use it to understand what is going on all around me.

Terrapin Instinctive ability to move slowly and steadily through an emotional situation by always seeing it from a fresh perspective.

Terrible Realization that I can confront any unexpected challenges by staying composed rather than becoming agitated and distraught.

Terrier Instinctive ability to show my unconditional loyalty and affection by pursuing my objective in a persistently determined manner.

Territory Situation where I keep my feet firmly planted so I can defend my beliefs and have the space to develop them further.

Terror Opportunity to courageously step into my true power by staying as calm as possible so I can make a transformative choice.

Terrorist Aspect of my character that has the surprising power to challenge my unresolved fears and potentially self-destructive behaviors.

Terrorist attack Opportunity to surprise myself by dealing with unresolved anxieties rather than feeling threatened by them.

Test Opportunity to judge my performance in a challenging situation instead of allowing others to decide if I make the grade.

Test bed Ability to take a more relaxed approach so I can experiment with how I can achieve my intended levels of performance.

Test drive Opportunity to explore different ways of using my motivation and energy as I make plans to pursue an individual ambition.

Test flight Opportunity to explore the edges of some of my loftier thoughts and plans so I can understand how to raise my performance.

Testicles Essential ability to use my accumulated courage and audacity to bring out my best in a creatively challenging situation.

Test paper Ability to express the different layers of my knowledge and experience rather than allowing other people to judge me.

Test pilot Aspect of my character that is willing to take a chance to get my ideas off the ground in a practical, down-to-earth manner.

T

Test tube Ability to contain the complex feelings that may be compounding an emotional situation, so I can avoid over-reacting.

Test-tube baby Aspect of my character that embodies a unique quality that requires careful nurturing to develop to its true potential.

Tethered Opportunity to release myself from any limiting commitments while retaining enough flexibility to keep me feeling connected.

Text Ability to communicate in a clear and consistent manner so I can describe exactly what is needed to other people.

Textile Ability to weave together the various strands of my thoughts and theories so I can shape them into something more tangible.

Texting Opportunity to immediately share how I feel with the people around me so I can quickly get my message across to them.

Text message Ability to increase my self-awareness by communicating how I feel rather than feeling limited in what I can say.

Texture Ability to get a feel for what is happening at a deeper level by getting a sense of what is happening on the surface.

Thankful Realization that I can draw on my huge reserves of resourcefulness to achieve success rather than feeling obliged to others.

Thatched roof Ability to keep my sense of identity safe and secure so I can continue to explore the various aspects of my inner nature.

Thaw Opportunity to release some of my accumulated experience by taking a warmer approach so I can get back into the flow.

Thawing Opportunity to use my energy to bring passion back into a relationship that has become stuck in a habitual emotional pattern.

Theater Situation where I can fully step into the various aspects of my talents so I can display my abilities to a wider audience.

Theft Opportunity to be firm and fair about the value of my individual talents rather than allowing people to take credit for them.

Theory Ability to have enough self-belief in myself to realize that I can do anything I want rather than always thinking about it.

Therapist Aspect of my character that can help me resolve unhealthy tensions by drawing my attention to my own powers of healing.

Therapy Opportunity to remedy an unhealthy situation by dealing with inner tensions I may have not been fully attending to.

There Situation where I can understand where I am trying to get to so I can fully realize the significance of my current position.

Thermal Ability to raise my levels of understanding by warming to some current ways of thinking and using them to lift my spirits.

Thermal imager Ability to identify the areas in my life I am most passionate about so I can connect with them at a deeper level.

Thermals Ability to present myself to those around me by showing how comfortable I am dealing with challenging situations.

Thermic lance Opportunity to use my intense passion to cut through perceived limitations so I can open up to my true value.

Thermometer Ability to clearly gauge the prevailing mood of a situation so I can influence the outcome by making a measured response.

Thermostat Ability to make myself comfortable in an unpredictable situation rather than appearing to blow hot and cold about it.

Thick Realization that I can make a big difference by using my depth of natural resourcefulness rather than feeling confused.

Thicket Situation where I can concentrate on developing the much wider growth potential of a range of my natural talents.

Thickset Realization that I have an inner presence that can make a big difference

T

instead of feeling I only have a slight influence.

Thief Aspect of my character that needs to recognize the value of my talents rather than feeling guilty about openly displaying them.

Thigh Essential ability to stand up for myself and have the strength of self-motivation to take necessary and decisive steps.

Thimble Ability to protect my creative skills so I can shape my future instead of feeling I'm being needled by other people.

Thin Realization that I have a substantial number of personal strengths rather than thinking my contribution is deficient or weak.

Thing Ability to make sense of what I need to do to make the most of my skills and create a successful outcome.

Thinking Essential opportunity to develop a rational awareness of what is happening without getting overly emotional about it.

Thinking time Opportunity to use my past experience to create a number of different possibilities so I can make the most of them.

Thirst Essential opportunity to understand my fundamental need for emotional fulfillment so I can satisfy my deeper desires.

Thistle Natural ability to thrive in arduous conditions and defend my independence, even though I may seem quite prickly to others.

Thong Ability to present my self-image to other people in a way that draws attention to my creative potential and my connection to it.

Thorn Natural ability to deal with an unwelcome intrusion by making a spur-of-the-moment decision rather than being defensive.

Thoroughbred Instinctive ability to harness my unconscious strength so I can use my pure talent to drive forward with my ambitions.

Thoroughfare Situation where I can directly pursue ambitions by easily seeing the way forward as I move toward my chosen objective.

Thought Essential ability to construct a clear understanding of what is happening without getting too emotional about it.

Thought bubble Ability to work with an emerging idea that seems quite substantial rather than feeling it's going over my head.

Thought control Opportunity to use my ideas to decide my chosen outcome instead of thinking that others are in charge of how my plan progresses.

Thought crime Opportunity to have confidence in my plans and ideas rather than punishing myself when I feel I have let people down.

Thought police Opportunity to take full responsibility for my plans and ideas so I can continue to develop them in an orderly manner.

Thought reader Aspect of my character that understands my unseen, unspoken motivations rather than just trying to guess my intentions.

Thrashed Realization that I need to be more confident in how I display my talents rather than continually beating myself up about them.

Thread Ability to stay connected to the outcome of a situation without feeling I am just hanging on to keep everyone happy.

Threadbare Ability to be open and honest about my intentions rather than appearing to others to be unresourceful and poorly informed.

Threat Ability to make the most of an approaching opportunity instead of habitually feeling that the future is filled with danger.

Threatened by an animal Opportunity to connect with my instinctive creativity so I can give myself the confidence to express my natural wisdom.

Threatened by a stranger Opportunity to understand an unfamiliar aspect of my character that can give me a powerful insight into who I want to be.

Threatening Opportunity to challenge my

T

fears by decisively stepping into my power rather than inflicting potential anxieties on myself.

Threatening letter Opportunity to become more aware of my hidden strengths so I can use them to powerfully express what I need.

Three-dimensional Ability to understand all the different aspects of my ambitions instead of feeling flat about my potential prospects.

Threshing machine Ability to sustain a series of potential ambitions by using unique expertise rather than going through the motions.

Threshold Situation where I can understand more about who I really am by giving myself the permission to step into a new opportunity.

Thrift Realization that I can create more value by displaying my talents in an extravagant manner rather than trying to appear prudent.

Thriller Opportunity to become excited about a potential possibility, even though the outcome continues to appear uncertain.

Throat Essential ability to always remain inspired by ensuring I can connect my heartfelt emotions to my level-headed thinking.

Throb Opportunity to become comfortable with an increasingly powerful force so I can channel it into achieving my chosen outcome.

Throne Ability to occupy a relaxed and comfortable viewpoint as I become more aware of my enduring qualities of strength and wisdom.

Throng Aspects of my character that can demonstrate my unique qualities, even though there may be a lot of demands on my attention.

Throttle Ability to influence my levels of motivation by clearly communicating my thoughts and emotions rather than choking them back.

Through Realization that I have the power and self-motivation to deal with a challenging situation so I can reach a successful outcome.

Throwaway Realization that I can create lasting value by making a long-term commitment to plans instead of leaving them to chance.

Throwback Opportunity to become more aware of the value of my fundamental behaviors, even though some of them may seem quite primitive.

Throwing Opportunity to use my power and strength to influence events from a distance without becoming too closely involved in them.

Thrush Instinctive ability to rise above more practical concerns so I can spread my ideas rather than continually feeling irritated.

Thrust Opportunity to get my message across so I can keep pushing forward with a fundamentally powerful way of thinking.

Thruster Ability to forcefully choose the direction my plan will take so I can reach the outcome I originally intended.

Thrust reverser Ability to land a powerful idea in a short space of time by directing all my energies toward a successful outcome.

Thud Opportunity to suddenly make an impact instead of feeling weighed down by commitments that now seem quite dull to me.

Thug Aspect of my character that can use my power in a more refined manner instead of forcing other people to follow my decisions.

Thumb Essential ability to control my actions and shape my future by judging my actions and work against any opposition.

Thumbnail Essential ability to have a firm grasp of my inner power so I can use it to see the bigger picture and shape my own future.

Thumbprint Essential opportunity to have decisions acknowledged by others so I can use my judgment to make my mark with them.

Thumbscrew Ability to make a definite

choice, even when I feel under a lot of pressure, instead of giving myself a hard time about it.

Thump Opportunity to take a softer approach so I can make a more meaningful connection rather than being forceful in my actions.

Thunder Natural opportunity to use a flash of inspiration to resolve any rising tension rather than always sounding off about it.

Thunderbolt Natural ability to focus the power of the prevailing mood so I can illuminate my understanding with a spark of brilliance.

Thunderclap Natural opportunity to show to those around me how I feel instead of just going along with the prevailing mood.

Thundercloud Natural ability to draw inspiration from the feelings that are bubbling up inside me so I can show the power of my ideas.

Thunderstorm Naturally opportunity to express my feelings in a down-to-earth way instead of allowing any discontent to rumble on.

Tiara Ability to present my self-image to people by attracting attention to my viewpoint so I can show its great value.

Tibia Essential ability to give a fundamental structure to my viewpoint so I can be at the forefront of any decisive action.

Tic Essential opportunity to openly express my concerns instead of persistently worrying that I might appear nervous to other people.

Tick Opportunity to acknowledge a specific aspect of my success, even though it may have seemed quite irritating to me at the time.

Ticket Ability to demonstrate my value to other people by giving myself permission to display to them my unique skills and abilities.

Ticket office Situation where I can have my individual talents formally recognized so I feel confident that I can move into new areas.

Ticking Opportunity to actively listen for any emerging possibilities rather than feeling that the time to act is slipping away.

Ticking bomb Ability to safely contain my potentially explosive feelings so I can choose the right time to make the most of their power.

Ticking clock Ability to feel more relaxed by looking ahead so I can choose the precise moment to make the most of an emerging opportunity.

Tickle Opportunity to make a deeper connection by taking a much firmer approach, even though it may initially seem less enjoyable.

Tidal wave Opportunity to understand the power of my emotions so I can safely channel them, even though they may seem to be overwhelming.

Tidal zone Situation where I can clearly see the full range of my ups and downs so I can understand their influence on me.

Tide Opportunity to experience the ebb and flow of my emotions as a natural rhythm rather than feeling that I have to control them.

Tide mark Ability to acknowledge a series of high and low points I have experienced so I can draw a line and move on.

Tide tables Ability to understand the gravity of my current situation so I can predict how it may influence my feelings in the future.

Tidy Realization that taking a methodical approach gives me more time to explore a variety of potentially valuable possibilities.

Tidying up Opportunity to methodically work my way through my experience and expertise so I can use them much more effectively.

Tie Ability to present my self-image to others in a way that shows my upright approach, even though it can be quite restrictive.

Tiebreaker Opportunity to ask myself a question that will help me to decide the most valuable way to use what I have learned so far.

T

Tied Opportunity to remain firm about the value of my commitments rather than feeling they are always holding me back.

Tier Ability to be more aware of the different levels of meaning in a situation so I can understand my particular viewpoint.

Tiger Instinctive ability to fiercely assert my independence so other people can see the powerful difference I can make.

Tight Opportunity to stay firmly connected to my ambitions rather than feeling that my freedom is being restricted in any way.

Tight-lipped Opportunity to honestly express what I need to say instead of worrying that it will prejudice my relationships in any way.

Tightrope Situation where I can resolve any insecurities about a relationship by making a firm commitment without becoming overly attached.

Tightrope walker Aspect of my character that has the talent to tread a fine line in a tense situation by taking a more balanced approach.

Tights Ability to present my self-image to the people around me in a way that conveniently supports my need for self-motivated action.

Tile Ability to take a more regular and repeatable approach so I can consistently deal with any unforeseen emotional outcomes.

Till Ability to have the value of my practical skills acknowledged by other people so I can begin to break some new ground.

Tiller Ability to keep a firm grip on my chosen direction as I navigate my way through a potentially complex emotional situation.

Tilted Opportunity to feel less out of place by taking a more straightforward approach that will help me line up some new possibilities.

Timber Ability to use my natural strength in a practical manner rather than feeling I am stuck in old behavioral patterns.

Time Realization that I can use my past experience to give me the power to decide my future while staying present to my talents.

Time bomb Ability to accumulate a huge amount of potential energy so I can use it constructively when I feel the time is right.

Timekeeper Aspect of my character that can help me become more aware of emerging opportunities so I can make the most of them.

Time lock Ability to keep myself feeling secure during an unfamiliar event so I can decide the right moment for me to open up.

Time machine Ability to use a structured approach to plan my future instead of just hoping I'll be in the right place at the right time.

Timer Ability to take a more considered approach to reaching a successful outcome rather than just hoping for immediate results.

Time-share Situation where I can claim my space more consistently instead of always feeling that other people are intruding into it.

Timetable Ability to make the most of future opportunities by being open and supportive of others and what they need.

Time travel Opportunity to revisit some of my past experiences so I can use them to powerfully influence how the future unfolds for me.

Time traveler Aspect of my character that methodically works my way through my previous experiences so I can be more certain of my future.

Time trial Opportunity to resolve a challenging issue by taking time to reflect on it rather than trying to beat the clock.

Time warp Opportunity to make a fundamental shift in my future plans, even though I may need to bend some universally acknowledged rules.

Timid Realization that I can discover my true potential by actively seeking new opportunities rather than shying away from them.

Timing device Ability to use a specific procedure that will help me positively influence the eventual outcome of any emerging opportunity.

Tin Ability to take a more practical approach that gives me the space to shape my thinking so I can achieve my intended result.

Tinder Ability to bring my passion to some dry subject matter so I can draw on my knowledge and ignite a creative transformation.

Tingling Opportunity to get my passion and vitality moving again by understanding what excites me about a particular situation.

Tinker Aspect of my character that can use my practical skills to make a big difference instead of feeling I am of no value.

Tinkle Ability to draw my attention to some emerging possibilities, even though they may seem quite insignificant to begin with.

Tinted Ability to understand what is coloring my mood rather than always trying to take a more black-and-white approach.

Tiny Realization that I can achieve success on a far bigger scale by attending to the small details and understanding their importance.

Tip Ability to decisively push ahead and make my point so I can have my value recognized by the people around me.

Tipsy Opportunity to take a more clear-headed approach to a situation rather than merrily hoping it will all work out for me. .

Tip-off Opportunity to listen to the feelings that are emerging from my inner self so I can make the most of approaching possibilities.

Tipping Opportunity to take a more balanced approach to declaring my value rather than feeling I am constantly on edge.

Tiptoe Ability to raise my level of awareness so I can take a more discreet approach instead of feeling I am creeping around.

Tire Ability to get a grip on my drive and ambition so I can safely choose my own direction and continue to maintain my progress.

Tired Opportunity to revitalize my enthusiasm by taking time to relax so I can reflect on any new possibilities that are emerging.

Tissue Ability to take care of an emerging emotional situation by working through its different layers so the outcome isn't too messy.

Title Ability to identify what makes me different from other people so I can use this awareness to understand my value.

T-junction Situation where I can decide on the direction of my future progress by choosing between two apparently opposing perspectives.

Toad Instinctive ability to immerse myself in my emotions and use my inspiration rather than expecting people to flatter my thinking.

Toadstool Natural ability to develop perspective and support it by drawing on the emotional circumstances that surround me.

Toast Potential to fulfill an ambition by openly announcing my achievements so my value will be recognized by other people.

Toaster Ability to use my creativity so I can fulfill my ambitions in a more substantial way rather than just having to scrape by.

Tobacco Ability to temporarily avoid dealing with one of my fundamental needs, even though it may be affecting my deeper inspiration.

Tobacco pipe Ability to take a more relaxed perspective on dealing with my needs, even though it may be harmful for me long-term.

Toboggan Ability to speedily progress toward my objective by using the outcome of my accumulated work in a consistently cool manner.

Today Opportunity to take immediate action as soon as possible rather than always thinking about yesterday or what I will do tomorrow.

T

Toddler Aspect of my character that embodies my uniquely precious talents and has the self-motivation to take the steps I need to.

Toe Essential ability to point myself in the right direction so I can stay alert to any new possibilities that are opening up.

Toenail Essential ability to protect my levels of self-motivation so I can choose my direction and take the necessary, practical steps.

Toffee Potential to fulfill a short-term ambition by quickly working my way through a situation without considering the long-term gains.

Tofu Potential to fulfill an ambition by gathering a variety of smaller resources and taking a more mature approach.

Together Realization that I can remain composed about a challenging situation by combining my characteristic qualities.

Toggle Ability to hold a situation securely together by calmly making a specific decision rather than switching back and forth.

Toilet Situation where I can attend to my needs by choosing to let go of the thoughts and feelings that are no longer healthy for me.

Toilet bowl Ability to be more receptive to looking after my personal needs rather than feeling I always need to look after other people.

Toilet cubicle Situation where I can maintain some personal boundaries so I can have the space to take care of my needs.

Toilet paper Ability to healthily address my personal needs rather than feeling they are of little value and have no real substance.

Toilet queue Opportunity to give priority to my needs so I can take decisive action instead of always standing around.

Toilet roll Ability to take comfort in the knowledge that I can deal with any emotional eventuality, though it may become very messy.

Toilet seat Ability to occupy a relaxed, comfortable viewpoint so I can become more

aware of my needs and how I can attend to them.

Token Ability to provide a true representation of my talents rather than just showing up for the sake of appearances.

Tolerance Realization that I am less likely to appear narrow-minded by giving myself more room to maneuver when I take action.

Toll Ability to ring the changes so other people recognize the value of my developing ambitions rather than trying to hinder them.

Toll bridge Situation where I can resolve a dilemma by creating a lasting connection, even though it may initially seem quite costly.

Toll road Situation where I can have my value of my drive fully acknowledged so I can make faster progress toward my objective.

Tomahawk Ability to take a series of powerful decisive actions that will enable me to assert my beliefs and exert my influence over people.

Tomato Potential to fulfill an ambition by reflecting my healthy passion in a vital and exciting way that swells my opportunities.

Tomb Situation where I can recognize my need for a life transformation so I can prepare the ground without letting it get on top of me.

Tombstone Ability to be firm and practical by acknowledging the value of my accomplishments as I enter a life-transforming experience.

Tomorrow Opportunity to achieve success by reflecting on my experience so I can be more aware of what is emerging for me today.

Tone Realization that I can influence the quality of how I express my feelings rather than letting my mood be colored by other people.

Tongs Ability to use my skill and experience to combine two different approaches so I can pick up on what is happening.

Tongue Essential ability to speak my truth in a tasteful and eloquent manner so I can powerfully communicate how I feel.

Tongue-tied Opportunity to say what I need to by releasing myself from any self-limiting beliefs that may be holding me back.

Tonic Potential to fulfill an emotional need by renewing my enthusiasm in an individual activity that always seems to raise my spirits.

Tonight Opportunity to achieve a deeper awareness by reflecting on my recent actions and imagining how to use them in future.

Tonsils Essential ability to maintain my levels of inspiration by realizing that I am immune to the critical words of other people.

Tool Ability to shape my circumstances by using my expertise and abilities to take direct action so I can influence my chosen outcome.

Toolbox Ability to set firm personal boundaries around my talents and experience so I can continue to shape my circumstances.

Tooth Essential ability to confidently display my power to other people rather than feeling that I have to keep it concealed from them.

Toothache Essential opportunity to resolve an ongoing tension by using power and confidence to examine the root causes of the situation.

Toothbrush Ability to maintain my healthy feelings of confidence on a consistent basis by clearing up any uncertainty from past experiences.

Tooth decay Essential opportunity to use my past experiences to healthily develop my talents so I can confidently build on them.

Tooth filling Ability to take action to fully restore my levels of confidence rather than neglecting them and letting them crumble.

Toothpaste Ability to take a fresh approach to working my way through any issues I have with maintaining healthy levels of confidence.

Toothpick Ability to pick out any aspects of my previous experiences I no longer find fulfilling so I can let them go.

Top Situation where I can understand my highest aspirations by elevating my awareness of what is fundamentally important to me.

Top hat Ability to present myself to other people by drawing their attention to the prominent ideas of my individual viewpoint.

Topiary Ability to shape the outcome of my spiritual growth so I can share some of its different insights with the people around me.

Topknot Ability to hold a complicated situation together by aligning my various ideas so I feel more secure about sharing them.

Topless dancer Aspect of my character that embodies my confidence and openness so I am happy to display my unique form of creativity.

Top secret Realization that I can get closer to my higher aspirations by having the confidence to reveal what fundamentally interests me.

Topsoil Ability to work my way through some apparently superficial challenges so I can use them to support my deeper ambitions.

Topsy-turvy Opportunity to view a challenging situation from the opposite perspective rather than allowing it to turn my world upside down.

Torch Ability to shape my future by using the power of my wisdom to illuminate it so I understand it with much greater clarity.

Torchbearer Aspect of my character that can consistently provide support for me by always keeping my creative potential fired up.

Torchlight Ability to understand a situation with much greater clarity by using my insight to directly illuminate what is happening.

Tormented Realization that I can make myself much happier by accepting the behavior of others rather than being annoyed by it.

Torn Opportunity to make a decision so I can make positive progress rather than allowing the current situation to pull me apart.

T

Tornado Natural opportunity to clearly funnel the energy from a turmoil of ideas and emotions rather than getting sucked into events.

Torpedo Ability to assert my emotional power from a distance so I can achieve my deeper aims without experiencing any sinking feelings.

Torrent Situation where I can rapidly enter into the flow of my emotions so I can understand the power and depth of my feelings.

Torrential rain Natural opportunity to completely clear the air by openly sharing some heavy emotions that have been building up.

Torso Essential ability to embody my core beliefs so I can use my power to support my actions and the steps I need to take.

Tortoise Instinctive ability to make progress toward my goal at a slow and steady pace, even though I may not seem too adventurous.

Tortuous Realization that I can take a much more straightforward approach rather than trying to negotiate a more circuitous path.

Torture Opportunity to confront an extremely uncomfortable situation by powerfully speaking my truth rather than suffering in silence.

Torture chamber Situation where I can take a more open approach to expressing painful feelings instead of feeling I must respond in a certain way.

Toss Opportunity to influence events around me by making the most of my resources rather than carelessly throwing them away.

Total eclipse Natural opportunity to observe the source of my creative brilliance rather than temporarily leaving myself in the dark.

Totalitarian state Situation where I can explore what makes me a unique individual by observing the restrictions I place on myself.

Tote bag Ability to take a more casual approach to exploring new opportunities so I can spend some time gathering what I need.

Totem Ability to identify the fundamental source of my creative instincts so I can use them to influence my chosen outcome.

Totem pole Situation where I can powerfully draw attention to my instinctive creativity rather than just making a song and dance about it.

Toucan Instinctive ability to rise above more practical concerns so I can spread my ideas to other people in a colorful way.

Touch Essential opportunity to make sense of a situation by actually connecting with it so I can understand how it can move me.

Touching Opportunity to make direct contact with someone who is very close to me in a moving way.

Touch screen Ability to connect with my thoughts and feelings as they emerge so I can use them to help shape my chosen outcome.

Tough Realization that I can use my natural strength and power to resolve any challenges that may seem difficult and demanding.

Toupee Ability to confidently reveal the bald facts rather than apparently presenting some unrealistic ideas off the top of my head.

Tour Opportunity to observe how clearly I view a situation by motivating myself to explore a variety of different perspectives.

Tourist Aspect of my character that takes great pleasure in exploring opportunities so I can broaden my life experience.

Tournament Opportunity to use my self-motivation to progressively discover my unique talents, even though the outcome may be uncertain.

Tourniquet Ability to take firm action to contain my more passionate emotions so I don't let my vitality needlessly drain away.

Tow Ability to use my motivation to keep a situation moving in the right direction without feeling I'm being pushed into it.

Tow bar Ability to make a firm connection to my extensive resources so I can convey what I need to fulfill my wider ambitions.

Towel Ability to absorb the associated learning and experience from dealing with my emotions rather than just giving up.

Tower Situation where I can consolidate my power and raise it to a higher level by building on my skills without feeling intimidated.

Tower block Situation where I can fully step into the various aspects of my potential so I can understand how to elevate my awareness.

Town Situation where I can connect with my wider social circle and access all the resources I need to fulfill my ambitions.

Towrope Ability to make a flexible commitment to using the drive and ambition of others so I can continue to make progress.

Toxic waste Ability to healthily process any deeply upsetting emotions instead of dumping them on others.

Toxin Instinctive opportunity to choose how I react to any unwelcome feelings rather than opening myself up to an unhealthy situation.

Toy Ability to play around with some of my resources so I can understand their greater importance rather than just amusing myself.

Toy boy Aspect of my character that allows me to play around with my strength and power so I can confidently assert my talents.

Toyshop Situation where I can make specific choices about how I display my unique value to people instead of just amusing myself.

Trace Opportunity to pick up on a small but significant detail that enables me to understand the direction I would like to follow.

Tracheotomy Essential opportunity to always remain inspired, even though it may mean opening up and directly expressing how I feel.

Track Situation where I can achieve my objective by following a route that other people took, even if their approach was a bit rough.

Tractor Ability to use my drive and ambition to draw on my practical skills so I can cultivate a wider range of knowledge.

Tractor beam Ability to attract other people to my way of thinking by staying positive and providing an illuminating perspective.

Trade-in Opportunity to increase my sense of self-worth by making the decision to move on from a situation that no longer serves me.

Trading Opportunity to exchange some perspectives that will help me ensure that my value is fully recognized by other people.

Traffic Opportunity to coordinate my drive and ambition with other people's plans so I can progress toward a specific goal.

Traffic jam Opportunity to free up some of my frustrated drives so I can make faster progress toward achieving a fruitful outcome.

Traffic lights Situation where I can use my wisdom to illuminate the best choice for me instead of always waiting for others' permission.

Traffic warden Aspect of my character that helps me keep to a strict timetable as I take time to look at different ways to achieve my ambitions.

Tragedy Opportunity to make the most of any challenging circumstances instead of thinking that I am responsible for any hardship.

Trail Situation where I can achieve my objective by creating my own route rather than feeling that my progress is falling behind.

Trailer Ability to use my drive to convey my huge resourcefulness instead of feeling I am just tagging along behind.

Train Ability to follow a set of guidelines that motivates me to progress toward my objective along a particular professional path.

T

Train driver Aspect of my character that can help motivate me to follow a career plan so I can reach a previously agreed-on objective.

Trainer Aspect of my character that has the discipline to make a continuing commitment to developing some potentially valuable talents.

Training Opportunity to develop one of my specific skills by always being open to advice and having the discipline to commit to it.

Training seminar Opportunity to learn more about what motivates me so I can use it to influence my deeper behavioral patterns.

Train set Ability to play around with my professional possibilities so I can understand the scale of my ambitions as I plan my career.

Training shoe Ability to present my self-image to others by taking steps to exercise my power and show how comfortable I am with it.

Train spotter Aspect of my character that takes a keen interest in my career options so I can understand my professional opportunities.

Train station Situation where I can embark on a particular professional path that will advance my career so I can reach my objective.

Traitor Aspect of my character that demonstrates faith in my talents by trusting in my decisions rather than letting myself down.

Tramp Aspect of my character that can make much faster and smoother progress by working with my talents rather than neglecting them.

Trampoline Ability to use natural resilience to support me so I can leap at an opportunity and quickly bounce back from any setbacks.

Trance Essential opportunity to profoundly immerse myself in my thoughts and feelings so I can absorb a much deeper understanding.

Tranquil Realization that I can make exciting progress by taking a calmer, more peaceful approach as I observe what emerges.

Tranquilizer Ability to take gentle and quiet action that will help me resolve a potentially tense situation so I can reenergize it.

Tranquilizer dart Ability to rapidly create peace and quiet to help resolve a potentially unhealthy situation and get it moving again.

Transcendent Realization that my natural ability to work with my unconscious awareness far exceeds the limits I normally place on it.

Transcription Ability to clearly spell out what I am trying to communicate to other people rather than leaving it open to interpretation.

Transfiguration Opportunity to completely transform my understanding of a situation by realizing how my actions appear to others.

Transforming Opportunity to fundamentally change how I see my circumstances so I can leave the past and progress into the future.

Transgender Opportunity to independently choose the aspects of my creative instincts that I prefer to become most intimately aware of.

Transit camp Situation where I can temporarily feel at home with the process of change so I can explore new possibilities.

Transition Opportunity to progressively move forward instead of feeling I must completely abandon the past to advance into the future.

Translator Aspect of my character that has the power and skill to communicate my ideas rather than feeling I'm being misinterpreted.

Translucent Ability to illuminate a situation and achieve a better understanding without necessarily having to identify every aspect of it.

Transmission Opportunity to send out a clear message about how I feel so I can understand how my ideas influence others.

Transmitter Ability to be quite specific about what I need to communicate so I can clearly convey it in a powerful and focused manner.

Transparent Ability to clearly understand what is happening by being open and honest rather than trying to cloud the real issue.

Transparent clothing Ability to present my self-image to other people by being very clear about my intentions instead of always trying to conceal them.

Transparent figure Aspect of my character that can be openly confident with others rather than worrying they will see right through me.

Transplant Opportunity to take one of my vital characteristics and use it in a completely different way rather than just rejecting it.

Transport Ability to shift my perspective and make progress by being able to convey the value of my skills and talents to other people.

Transporter room Situation where I can use my imagination to visualize my future, even though it may seem far-fetched to others.

Transsexual Aspect of my character that can conceive something special by becoming more intimately aware of how I choose to use my creativity.

Transvestite Aspect of my character that enjoys exploring how I appear to others so I can become more aware of how to please myself.

Trap Situation where I can understand my wider freedom of choice by being able to clearly see where I may be holding myself back.

Trapdoor Situation where I can suddenly access a different level of self-awareness that may previously have seemed closed to me.

Trapeze Ability to display my talents as I courageously work my way back and forth through a wide range of perspectives.

Trapeze artist Aspect of my character that feels secure in making a creative leap, even though it seems quite precarious to others.

Trapped Opportunity to release myself from any self-limiting behavior by catching unwanted characteristics I may have been unaware of.

Trapped in a cage Opportunity to remove any barriers to my progress rather than always feeling defensive about my perceived limitations.

Trapped in a house Opportunity to make a commitment to exploring all aspects of my inner and outer lives instead of constantly trying to avoid them.

Trapped in an elevator Opportunity to break out of a potentially restrictive career path so I can continue to elevate my level of understanding.

Trapped in a prison Opportunity to escape from any of my self-limiting beliefs, even though they can give me a false sense of security.

Trapped in a room Opportunity to develop a valuable aspect of myself that has the capacity to provide a character-building experience.

Trapped on a train Opportunity to choose my career path rather than feeling I always have to follow a prescribed set of rigid guidelines.

Trapper Aspect of my character that closely tracks my creative instincts so I can capture their uniqueness and realize their value.

Trash Ability to confidently process what I no longer need so I can let it go and create something much more valuable.

Trash can Ability to use a positive and healthy approach to dispose of habits and behaviors that are no longer of any use to me.

Trash collector Aspect of my character that helps me stay healthy and positive by choosing to dispose of behaviors that no longer serve me.

T

Trauma Opportunity to take decisive action and quickly resolve an unhealthy situation rather than continuing to feel bad about it.

Travel Opportunity to explore a range of different perspectives so I can choose the direction I would like to progress in.

Travel agent Aspect of my character that helps me become more aware of the options available to me as I explore my freedom.

Traveler Aspect of my character that is motivated to work through a variety of viewpoints so I can achieve a much wider understanding.

Trawler Ability to navigate complex and unpredictable feelings by capturing what is happening for me at a deeper emotional level.

Tray Ability to support my ambitions so that I can satisfy my appetite for success and catch any slipups I may otherwise miss.

Treacle Potential to fulfill an ambition by getting stuck in a short-term situation that may be difficult to move on from.

Tread Opportunity to take some definite and deliberate steps to maintain firm contact with the practical realities of a situation.

Treadmill Ability to use my energy and self-motivation to prepare for future challenges rather than going through the motions.

Treasure Ability to realize the wealth of experience and knowledge that I've accumulated, though I often try to hide them.

Treasure chest Ability to open up to the potential for using the richness of my talent rather than feeling I have to keep it locked away.

Treasure hoard Ability to make consistently valuable use of my rich expertise instead of always feeling I have to conceal it from others.

Treasure map Ability to use my hidden talent to clearly identify the most valuable aspect of an unfamiliar and potentially complex situation.

Treatment Opportunity to use a recognized procedure to deal with an uncomfortable situation that may be making me feel ill at ease.

Trebuchet Ability to strongly project my personal influence by conveying my specific aims rather than throwing my weight around.

Tree Natural ability for developing my long-term spiritual growth while staying rooted in everyday practicalities.

Tree surgeon Aspect of my character that can decisively resolve a spiritual dilemma by taking specific action to remove any confusion.

Trek Opportunity to make a major shift in how I view a situation by using my self-motivation and energy to take the steps I need.

Trellis Ability to provide a framework for my blossoming talents so I can continue to support them as they successfully bloom.

Trembling Opportunity to achieve more consistent outcomes by taking a firmer approach rather than allowing myself to be shaken up.

Tremor Opportunity to shake off any feelings of indecision I may have by getting a definite understanding of what will move me.

Trench Situation where I can defend my position by making the effort to dig deeper into the practicalities of my viewpoint.

Trench warfare Opportunity to resolve an inner conflict by taking a more understated approach rather than always appearing to go over the top.

Trespasser Aspect of my character that gives me permission to explore areas of my inner life that I seemed to think were out of bounds.

Trespassing Opportunity to fully step into my power so I can go beyond some conceptual boundaries and open up new possibilities.

Trial Opportunity to resolve a challenging

T

issue by trying out a variety of options rather than allowing myself to be judged by people.

Triangle Ability to shape my circumstances by connecting some of my fundamental qualities in a strong and pleasing manner.

Tribal gathering Opportunity to bring fundamental qualities together so I can demonstrate the range of my wisdom and knowledge.

Tribe Aspects of my character that provide me with a continuing sense of support and security that I feel I can always easily relate to.

Tribute band Aspects of my character that can work together harmoniously so I can use a variety of my talents to create a unique result.

Trick Opportunity to make a dramatic transformation that will have an effect on me instead of just continually deluding myself.

Trickle Ability to gently maintain my emotional involvement rather than allowing myself to be overwhelmed by floods of feelings.

Trifle Potential to fulfill a short-term ambition that will have a pleasing outcome, even though it may have very little long-term value.

Trigger Ability to achieve my aims by firmly making an apparently small decision that will inevitably lead to much greater success.

Trimaran Ability to use the prevailing mood to bring a number of my qualities together so I can navigate an emotional situation.

Trimmer Ability to be more effective in the use of my resources rather than always feeling I have to keep cutting back.

Trip Opportunity to change my view of a situation by exploring a number of perspectives, without worrying about stepping out of line.

Triplets Aspects of my character that embody how I can choose to express my characteristic qualities in a number of different ways.

Tripod Ability to provide myself with strong and stable support rather than being concerned that I don't have a leg to stand on.

Tripping Opportunity to regain my composure by making definite steps in a calm, considered manner rather than deluding myself.

Tripwire Ability to define my personal boundaries so I can make a strong connection with others rather than being wary of them.

Triumph Opportunity to celebrate a personal success by understanding the challenges I had to resolve to achieve it.

Troll Aspect of my character that can reach a fundamental understanding of my individuality by honestly exploring my deepest self.

Trolley Ability to fulfill some of my potential ambitions by being able to convey my needs to other people in a clear and practical way.

Trooper Aspect of my character with the courage and discipline to harness my unconscious energies and powerfully direct them.

Trophy Ability to demonstrate how I use my talents to make the most of an opportunity so others can recognize my achievements.

Trophy wife Aspect of my character that displays my commitment to developing my individual creativity so others can acknowledge it.

Tropical Situation where I can comfortably use my creative energy to explore an incredible variety of potential growth possibilities.

Troubadour Aspect of my character that gives me freedom to evoke my deeper feelings so I can communicate wisdom and power.

Trouble Realization that I need to make an effort to feel more at peace with myself rather than being annoyed by my circumstances.

Trough Ability to consistently nurture and develop my creative instincts, even though I currently feel I am at a bit of a low point.

Trouser press Ability to use a steady, forceful manner so I can proudly present my individual viewpoint and get my message across.

Trousers Ability to present my self-image to people in a way that asserts my viewpoint and displays my self-motivation.

Trout Instinctive ability to immerse myself in my emotions so I can always make my way back to the source of my inspiration.

Trove Ability to rediscover my accumulated wealth of experience and knowledge so I can make an effort to reveal its true value.

Trowel Ability to shape an outcome and create deeper value by making a little bit of effort to go beyond surface appearances.

Truant Aspect of my character that takes responsibility for learning valuable lessons rather than always running away from them.

Truce Opportunity to bring an ongoing inner tension to an end by understanding my conflicting needs and declaring to resolve them.

Truck Ability to employ some powerful drives to provide a valuable shift in my ambitions as I make progress toward my objective.

Truck driver Aspect of my character that can direct my motivation and energy so I can make a large advance in achieving my ambitions.

Trudge Opportunity to determinedly pursue one of my ambitions, even though it may require a lot of energy to take the steps I need.

Trumpet Ability to take my instinctive creativity in both hands so I can clearly communicate my achievements to others.

Truncheon Ability to take responsibility for my individual actions without being too short-tempered or giving myself too hard a time.

Trunk Ability to feel safe and secure in my core strengths so I can be open to new possibilities without feeling vulnerable.

Trust Opportunity to have enough self-belief in my ambitions and confidence in my talents to be able to honestly reveal myself as I really am.

Truth Realization that accurately understanding what I believe helps me to fundamentally increase my levels of awareness.

Truth drug Ability to confirm some of my fundamental beliefs rather than trying to avoid dealing with them and just deluding myself.

T-shirt Ability to present my self-image in a way that displays my more casual and relaxed approach to achieving my ambitions.

Tsunami Opportunity to powerfully channel some seemingly uncontrollable emotions that are apparently threatening to overwhelm me.

Tub Ability to securely contain my emotions so I can always be open to using them to make the most of whatever emerges.

Tuba Ability to take my instinctive creativity in both hands so I can express the inspirational power of my deeper thinking.

Tube Ability to consistently connect with other people so I can always effectively convey my thoughts and feelings to them.

Tug Ability to pull myself out of an emotionally confining situation so I can move into areas that hold more possibilities for me.

Tug-of-war Ability to work with the different strengths that push me and pull me in different directions rather than digging my heels in.

Tulip Natural ability to open up to my creative talents so I can encourage them to blossom and make the most of emerging opportunities.

Tumble Opportunity to take a balanced view and make positive steps rather than feeling awkward about possible pitfalls in my approach.

Tumble dryer Ability to resolve an emotional situation by taking a more rounded approach rather than getting involved in a heated argument.

Tumor Ability to incisively identify the source of an unhealthy situation instead of letting it rapidly grow out of control.

Tundra Situation where I can open up to a variety of possibilities, even though there may be no opportunities for spiritual growth.

Tune Ability to instinctively communicate with other people in fundamentally powerful ways that will resonate with them.

Tunnel Situation where I can move into a more fundamental understanding of my character and explore some of my deepest resources.

Turban Ability to present myself to people by drawing attention to my viewpoint without getting too wrapped up in it.

Turbid Realization that I can achieve much greater emotional clarity by being clear about how I feel to the people around me.

Turbine Ability to completely concentrate on a specific idea so I can use my creative energy to produce a valuable outcome.

Turbocharger Ability to efficiently channel nearly all of my energies so I can drive my ambitions forward rather than feeling exhausted.

Turbulence Natural opportunity to make more progress by going with the flow rather than getting too shaken up about the situation.

Turf Ability to stand my ground so I can cultivate my practical skills without becoming too territorial and excluding other people.

Turkey Instinctive ability to fulfill my ambitions by talking openly about them so they will seem more appealing and successful.

Turn Opportunity to demonstrate my aptitude and adaptability by choosing to change my direction so I can continue making progress.

Turning Situation where I can make a definite choice about the path I want to follow rather than feeling I'm going around in circles.

Turnip Potential to fulfill an ambition by having a healthy awareness of my roots so I can use my natural abilities in a practical manner.

Turnoff Situation where I can choose my future direction rather than completely losing interest in making any further progress.

Turnout Situation where I can take time out from pursuing my long-term ambitions while ensuring I stay close to the action.

Turntable Ability to give myself a platform to voice how I feel so I can listen for possibilities to turn my situation around.

Turquoise Mood that can color my perspective by making me more aware of how I can use my natural energy to resolve any inner tensions.

Turret Situation where I can concentrate on an aspect of my power so I can raise it to a higher level without feeling intimidated.

Turtle Instinctive ability to move slowly and steadily through an emotional situation without having to turn everything upside down.

Turtledove Instinctive ability to rise above more practical concerns so I can look at ways of dealing with any romantic tensions.

Tusk Instinctive ability to confidently display my great power and strength to other people so I can get straight to the point.

Tutor Aspect of my character that encourages me to develop my unique talents and gives me the personal privacy to continue exploring.

T

Tutorial Opportunity to develop my awareness of what motivates me so I can understand how it influences my behavior patterns.

Tuxedo Ability to present myself to other people in a more formal manner so they can appreciate how I embody my talents.

Tweet Ability to express myself quickly and succinctly, even though I would often like to say a lot more about how I feel.

Tweezers Ability to pick up on a very specific aspect of a situation I am dealing with so I can extract the maximum benefit.

Twilight Natural opportunity to experience the developing connection between the deeper aspects of my conscious and unconscious awareness.

Twinkling Opportunity to use my optimism and insight in a more consistent manner so I can become more aware of an emerging possibility.

Twins Aspects of my character that embody how I can choose my characteristic qualities in two distinctly different ways.

Twist Opportunity to take a more straight-forward approach rather than getting caught up in some convoluted thoughts and ideas.

Twitter Ability to quickly share whatever passing thoughts come into my mind without feeling I have to go on about them at length.

Two Realization that my instincts have been confirmed so I can have the confidence to explore the value of my wider potential.

Tycoon Aspect of my character that can accumulate a great sense of power so I can use it to create a huge amount of value.

Type Ability to become more aware of my individual characteristics so I can see how they are reflected in the people around me.

Typewriter Ability to methodically gather my thoughts so I can consistently make my mark as I express myself to other people.

Typhoon Natural opportunity to be much calmer and more centered in my thinking, even though the situation may become quite heated.

Typing Opportunity to shape my thoughts and ideas into a more practical form so I can share them with the people around me.

Tyrant Aspect of my character that could be more powerful by freely expressing my talents rather than constantly repressing them.

T

Udder Instinctive capacity to be kind to people by regularly meeting their emotional needs without causing myself too much tension.

UFO Ability to understand more about myself by comfortably exploring an unfamiliar situation that may seem quite alien to me.

Ugly Opportunity to refine my fundamental power and understand its deeper attraction so I can share my inner beauty with people.

Ukulele Ability to take my instinctive creativity in both hands so I can pitch some of my more popular ideas to the people around me.

Ulcer Essential opportunity to healthily fulfill an ambition rather than allowing a challenging situation to eat away at me.

Ultramodern Realization that I can fundamentally transform my situation by taking practical steps to move on from outdated behaviors.

Ultrasonic Ability to communicate my higher levels of awareness rather than feeling that no one ever listens to what I am trying to say.

Ultrasound Opportunity to clearly see all the future possibilities that embody how I can continue to develop them throughout my life.

Umbilical cord Essential ability to fundamentally connect to my wise and loving self so I can continue to nurture my independence.

Umbrella Ability to get a handle on the prevailing mood so I can minimize the effect of emotional influences on my thought processes.

Umpire Aspect of my character that helps me decide the outcome of an uncertain situation by taking a fair and even-handed approach.

Unable Realization that I can always achieve whatever I set out to accomplish by deciding to step into my power and take action.

Unable to breathe Opportunity to regularly inspire myself and others in a healthy way instead of always stifling my creativity.

Unable to decide Opportunity to do what I need to right now rather than delaying action as a way of keeping other people happy.

Unable to defecate Opportunity to let go of possessions that no longer have any value for me instead of allowing unhealthy tensions to build up.

Unable to get home Opportunity to find out who I really am so I can feel more at home with all the different aspects of my character.

Unable to move Opportunity to shift my perspective so I can reach a deeper understanding of my emotions and how they can profoundly move me.

Unable to park Opportunity to look at different ways of achieving my ambitions by taking time out and exploring other options.

Unable to speak Opportunity to open up about how I feel so I can clearly get my message across to the people around me.

Unable to urinate Opportunity to relieve some emotional tension and discomfort by letting go of pent-up feelings that have been troubling me.

U

Unaccommodating Realization that being more open to the beliefs of others can help me feel more safe and secure about my own beliefs.

Unaccompanied Opportunity to achieve individual goals by following my own path rather than feeling I always need people's support.

Unaccounted for Opportunity to feel confident in the actions I have chosen to take rather than feeling I am missing out elsewhere.

Unannounced Opportunity to spontaneously ask for what I need by having the courage to speak up so people can hear my true voice.

Unassailable Opportunity to realize my fundamental strengths and use them positively rather than constantly looking for my weaknesses.

Unassembled furniture Ability to understand how easily I form habitual behavior patterns so I can use them to support my future ambitions.

Unbearable Opportunity to release myself from commitments and obligations that no longer serve me, instead of carrying on.

Unbeatable Opportunity to achieve a successful outcome by deciding what I am willing to let go of in order to make definite progress.

Unborn Opportunity to bring one of my concepts to life, although it may require a great deal of effort to make it happen.

Unborn child Aspect of my character that enables me to bring talents out into the world and embodies my potential for continuing growth.

Unborn children Aspects of my character that embody a variety of wonderful plans that I have the ability to conceive and bring into the world.

Unbreakable Ability to resolve long-term behaviors that no longer serve me by always being flexible and open to positive change.

Uncanny Realization that I should acknowledge my unique talents rather than attributing my success to coincidence and good fortune.

Uncertain Realization that being confident in my abilities will always enable me to definitely decide the outcome of any situation.

Uncharacteristic Realization that I can often discover my unrealized potential by becoming more aware of my habitual behavior patterns.

Uncharted Situation where I can achieve a clearer understanding of the bigger picture by taking time to explore unfamiliar areas.

Unclaimed Opportunity to take action and realize the value of my potential talents rather than waiting for someone to discover them.

Uncle Aspect of my character with familiar wisdom and loving authority that encourages me to happily develop my wider potential.

Unclog Opportunity to really get a situation moving again instead of continually feeling stuck in my habitual emotional responses.

Uncomfortable Opportunity to engage with a challenge that takes me outside my comfort zone rather than trying to find the easy way out.

Unconscious Opportunity to become more aware of my behavioral patterns so I can wake up to the possibilities happening all around me.

Uncontrollable Opportunity to decide my chosen outcome by taking control of the situation instead of feeling it is out of my hands.

Uncooked Potential to fulfill an ambition by properly preparing myself rather than thinking that I can rely on my raw talent.

Uncouth Realization that I need to take a more direct approach instead of doing nothing in case I feel awkward about how I appear.

U

Uncovered Opportunity to reveal my deeper feelings about a situation rather than giving a superficial response to the people around me.

Uncovering a body Opportunity to go beyond surface impressions so I can use my creativity to regain my self-motivation and revitalize my situation.

Uncovering an entrance Opportunity to reveal a possibility so I can take definite steps to explore the potential it holds for me.

Undead Aspect of my character that attracts my attention to my neglected talents so I can revitalize them or lay them to rest.

Under Realization that I can deepen my levels of awareness so I can achieve a profounder understanding of what I need to do.

Undercarriage Ability to consistently use a more down-to-earth approach, enabling me to land the value of my more powerful concepts.

Undercover agent Aspect of my character that can help me to achieve my ambitions by understanding my deeper passions and my need for intimacy.

Undercover policeman Aspect of my character that gives me permission to fully assert my more intimate needs by revealing them to other people.

Undercurrent Ability to powerfully influence the outcome of a situation by using my deeper experience rather than just going with the flow.

Underdeveloped Opportunity to increase my practical value by widening my overall understanding so I can open myself to new possibilities.

Underdog Aspect of my character that can be consistently successful by courageously using my skills in a persistently determined manner.

Underdone Potential to fulfill an ambition by taking time to work my way through any potentially tough challenges I may encounter.

Underdressed Opportunity to show more of the real me to other people rather than feeling I always have to conceal my vulnerabilities.

Underground Situation where I can go deeper into the practical aspects of my circumstances so I can make a fundamental transformation.

Undergrowth Situation where I can gain deeper understanding of my potential by exploring the rich complexity of my natural abilities.

Underneath Situation where I can arrive at a fundamental understanding of the level of support I have for achieving higher ambitions.

Undernourished Opportunity to look after my most basic needs so I can consistently sustain my progress and fulfill my hunger for success.

Underpants Ability to present myself to others in a way that helps me feel comfortable about how I share my creative talents.

Underpass Situation where I can move into a deeper understanding of my ambitions and explore practical methods for achieving them.

Understanding Realization that I need to step into my own perspective before I can own my beliefs and consistently support them.

Undertaker Aspect of my character that makes a firm commitment to my process of personal transformation during any life changes.

Under threat Opportunity to challenge some of my deeper fears by decisively stepping into my power instead of allowing anxieties to rise.

Undertone Ability to powerfully express my feelings rather than allowing my mood to be colored by the actions of other people.

Undertow Opportunity to convey a much deeper emotion in my current situation instead of allowing circumstances to drag me down.

U

Underwater Situation where I can immerse myself in my emotional life so I can explore my deeper feelings and learn from them.

Underwater city Situation where I can connect with my wider social network at a more emotional level so I can access some deeper expertise.

Underwater house Situation where I have the security and support I need to comfortably explore the emotional aspects of my inner and outer lives.

Underwater ruins Situation where I can revisit deeper feelings so I can continue to build on my accumulated experience and wisdom.

Underwear Ability to present my self-image to other people in a way that helps me to draw attention to my potential creative talents.

Underworld Situation where I can achieve a deeper understanding of the choices I make so I can feel confident in my decisions.

Underworld boss Aspect of my character that asserts my ability to make powerful decisions so I can confidently act on my deeper motivations.

U

Under wraps Ability to safely look after what is most valuable to me rather than feeling I have to reveal it to the people around me.

Undesirable Realization that just being myself is always far more attractive than constantly worrying that I might offend other people.

Undetectable Realization that I have an instinctive understanding of actions I need to take, though they may not always seem obvious.

Undetected Opportunity to be open about how I plan to achieve my objectives instead of feeling I always have to conceal my actions.

Undetonated Opportunity to safely release potentially explosive emotions by choosing the right moment to clearly communicate them.

Undisclosed location Situation where I can make my position clear to others instead of worrying about becoming a target for their displeasure.

Undiscovered Opportunity to find out more about my unrealized potential by exploring the mysterious, unfamiliar aspects of my situation.

Undiscovered house Situation where I have the security and support I need to explore all aspects of my developing sense of self-awareness.

Undiscovered money Ability to have more confidence in my hidden talents so my value can be genuinely recognized by others.

Undiscovered room Situation where I can discover my unrealized potential by realizing I have the capacity to develop a unique talent.

Undomesticated Opportunity to freely pursue my wilder creative instincts rather than feeling I always have to remain in my comfort zone.

Undressing Opportunity to open up my real self to the people closest to me so I can connect with them in a more intimate fashion.

Undrinkable Opportunity to draw on my emotional experiences instead of feeling I have to accept how other people think I should feel.

Unearth Opportunity to uncover the fundamental practicalities of my actual situation so I can examine it in much greater depth.

Unearthly Realization that I can use my creative instincts to shape an outcome rather than trying to follow an accepted procedure.

Uneasy Opportunity to resolve some of my unspoken tensions rather than trying to give the impression that everything is normal.

Unemotional Realization that I can have much greater influence in achieving my preferred outcome by opening up about my feelings.

Unemployment Opportunity to develop my individual expertise so I can demonstrate my value and discover my purpose in life.

Unescapable Opportunity to release myself from any self-limiting beliefs rather than feeling perpetually trapped by external constraints.

Unexpected Opportunity to take full advantage of an unforeseen event rather than feeling I have to behave in a predictable manner.

Unexpected birth Opportunity to rediscover an idea I may have conceived some time ago so I can bring a dearly held plan to life.

Unexpected lover Aspect of my character that can help me become more intimately aware of how I can express my surprising creative potential.

Unexploded bomb Ability to safely contain potentially explosive feelings rather than allowing myself to be triggered by external events.

Unexploded booby trap Ability to create a positive transformation by channeling my instinctive energies instead of always trying to trap myself.

Unfaithful Opportunity to trust in my talents so I can have complete confidence in my skills rather than doubting my abilities.

Unfaithful partner Aspect of my character that can give me the confidence to be myself instead of feeling I am betraying my principles.

Unfamiliar Opportunity to explore beyond my habitual behavioral patterns so I can positively connect with my obvious potential.

Unfamiliar city Situation where I can connect with my wider social network so I can become more aware of previously unseen possibilities.

Unfamiliar house Situation where I have the security and support I need to open up my undiscovered potential to explore it further.

Unfamiliar lover Aspect of my character

that can help me become more intimately aware of how I can embody my deeper creative potential.

Unfamiliar room Situation where I can explore a less familiar aspect of my character to understand the potential it holds for me.

Unfamiliar street Situation where I can strengthen an existing relationship by choosing to approach it in a completely different way.

Unfashionable Opportunity to develop fresh perspectives on how I see myself rather than feeling I always have to follow the latest trend.

Unfastened Ability to fully connect with a new opportunity so I can give myself the freedom to feel much more secure in myself.

Unfed Opportunity to fulfill my appetite for success by digesting valuable new information and using it to motivate my progress.

Unfit Opportunity to have a healthy awareness of my underlying potential so I can shape my chosen outcome in a positive way.

Unflattering Realization that I can communicate what I need through actions rather than trying to keep other people happy.

Unfollow Opportunity to choose my path so I can achieve an ambition instead of feeling that I have to copy other people.

Unformed Realization that I can shape my beliefs about a situation so I can become clear about how to turn my ideas into reality.

Unfortunate Realization that I can use my talent to achieve my chosen outcome rather than blaming the result on circumstances.

Unfriend Opportunity to become more acquainted with an unfamiliar aspect of my character that can help me to achieve one of my ambitions.

Unfriendly Realization that I need to become better acquainted with emerging possibilities instead of appearing hostile to them.

U

Unhappy Realization that I am fortunate in being able to influence my future in a variety of ways rather than leaving it to chance.

Unhealthy Opportunity to resolve any inner tensions I may be experiencing so I can use the whole of my unrealized potential.

Unicorn Apparent ability to harness my powerful imagination so I can use my unconscious energy to get to the point.

Unicycle Ability to successfully balance a variety of commitments, even though it means that I have to be constantly on the move.

Uniform Ability to present my self-image to other people in a manner that permits me to consistently show my power and authority.

Uninvited Realization that I need to define some personal boundaries so I can take the time to openly explore my individual needs.

Uninvited guests Opportunity to openly welcome emerging possibilities so I can confidently begin to entertain my wider potential.

Union Opportunity to become connected to a valuable aspect of my character without feeling that I have to be too attached to it.

Unique Realization that I have a viewpoint that enables me to discover hidden potential that other people may be unaware of.

Unit Ability to achieve an ambition by taking a single aspect of my unique experience and using it to develop a more cohesive effort.

Universe Situation where I can gain a clearer understanding of the bigger picture so I can become more aware of my massive potential.

University Situation where I can examine what I know by studying complex life lessons and learning how to apply them in everyday life.

Unknown Opportunity to step into a much wider awareness so I can discover valuable talents I was previously unaware of.

Unknown yet familiar Realization that I can develop my expertise by understanding that I absorb most of my experiences at an unconscious level.

Unlike Opportunity to understand how I can use my unique abilities to make a difference and ensure that I always stand out.

Unlimited Realization that I can make the most of bigger possibilities by having the courage to move beyond self-imposed boundaries.

Unlisted Ability to establish an obvious personal boundary so I can concentrate on working my way through a particular idea.

Unlock Opportunity to pick my chosen outcome so I can open up to new possibilities and take steps to make them happen.

Unlocked door Ability to freely access different aspects of my character so I can develop areas of talents now open to me.

Unmanned Opportunity to make a difference by using my unique expertise rather than ignoring my feelings and going through the motions.

Unmanned spacecraft Ability to use my ambition and drive to greatly elevate my awareness without feeling that I always have to be personally involved.

Unnoticed Opportunity to pay attention to what is emerging from my unconscious awareness so I can prepare myself for future choices.

Unnoticed door Ability to see a potential opening for me to explore valuable areas of talent that I may have been unaware of.

Unoccupied Opportunity to step into my wider potential so I can fully explore it rather than always abandoning my ambitions.

Unofficial Realization that I can achieve recognized success in my way by giving myself permission to take responsible action.

Unplanned Ability to see the bigger picture

U

so I can consistently achieve a successful outcome by making the most of new possibilities.

Unpleasant Realization that I feel most fulfilled during a difficult challenge, even though it may be temporarily uncomfortable for me.

Unprepared Opportunity to successfully improvise with whatever possibilities might emerge rather than feeling I have to plan meticulously.

Unprepared for exam Opportunity to celebrate what I have learned so far instead of being constantly self-critical of my successful achievements.

Unprotected Opportunity to ensure healthy relationships by safely maintaining my personal boundaries while staying open to new possibilities.

Unprovoked Opportunity to reveal some concealed tension so I can take positive action to prevent any further potential conflict.

Unprovoked attack Opportunity to be more honest and open about my intentions in a relationship rather than appearing defensive.

Unqualified Opportunity to increase my understanding of a specific situation by acknowledging the valuable experience I have accumulated.

Unquenchable Realization that I have a profound capacity for emotional transformation rather than feeling never satisfied.

Unravel Opportunity to reveal the fundamental threads of my story so I can be clear about any assumptions and biases I may have.

Unreadable Ability to achieve a clearer understanding of what will fulfill me by taking the time to spell out my needs to other people.

Unready Realization that any time is the right time if I can develop enough confidence in my ability to always perform consistently.

Unreal Realization that my understanding of what is possible is entirely based on my perceptions and how I create them.

Unreasonable Realization that I need to take a more instinctive approach to a confusing challenge rather than trying to be more rational.

Unreciprocated Opportunity to regularly consider two opposing points of view so I am happy to always provide some value in return.

Unrecognizable Opportunity to understand my deeper purpose by identifying specific actions that will make me feel more fulfilled.

Unrehearsed Opportunity to achieve a successful outcome by taking spontaneous action rather than always being stuck in the same routine.

Unrequited love Realization that I need to profoundly connect with a much deeper understanding of myself rather than relying on others.

Unrest Opportunity to stimulate some action by taking a more relaxed approach instead of worrying that it might get out of control.

Unroadworthy Opportunity to understand the more practical aspects of my drives and ambitions so I can continue to maintain my progress.

Unromantic Realization that I can use a more instinctive approach to realistically make a profound connection with my creative potential.

Unruly Realization that I can use my unique talents to make me stand out rather than feeling I have to do everything in a set order.

Unsafe Realization that the best way to make myself feel more secure is to confront any challenges by taking a calculated risk.

Unscheduled Ability to make the most of emerging possibilities by reflecting on my commitments to myself and understanding what I need.

U

Unseaworthy Opportunity to patch up any emotional concerns I may have so I feel more secure in working through complex feelings.

Unseen Opportunity to achieve a much clearer picture of what is happening by observing my habitual behavior patterns.

Unsettling Realization that I can use a more balanced approach to shake up the situation and instigate some positive action.

Unshaven Opportunity to face up to the facts so I can take a closer look at some of my ideas and cut out the ones I no longer need.

Unspoken Opportunity to understand what I need to express so I can share my feelings and really get my message across.

Unspoken space Situation where I can listen to what is not being said to understand the best way to reach my chosen outcome.

Unstable Opportunity to take a more dynamic approach so I can make the most of the situation instead of letting it knock me off balance.

Unsteady Realization that I can make positive progress by having an unshakable belief in my individual skills and abilities.

Unstoppable Realization that I can always achieve my chosen outcome in any situation by positively channeling my instinctive creativity.

Unsurfaced Opportunity to come to grips with my deeper purpose by having the openness to take the rough with the smooth.

Untamable Realization that I need to use the positive power of my creative instincts instead of always trying to keep them under control.

Untidy Opportunity to look at a variety of emerging possibilities so I can take a more methodical approach to achieving success.

Untie Opportunity to resolve a complicated and potentially tense situation by ensuring that I don't become too attached to the outcome.

Untouched Opportunity to make more sense of a situation by connecting with it and understanding how I can use it to make a new start.

Unused Opportunity to develop my potential skills and expertise by taking practical action rather than trying to maintain my position.

Unused food Ability to fulfill some potential ambitions so I can satisfy my appetite for success and nourish my continued growth.

Unused room Aspect of myself that gives me new opportunities to develop potential talents and skills that I may have been unaware of.

Unusual Realization that I can make a huge difference by boldly making my own choices instead of worrying it will make me stand out.

Unusual animal Instinctive ability to embody all aspects of my creative nature rather than always trying to blend in with my surroundings.

Unusual house Situation where I have the security and support I need so I can comfortably explore unfamiliar aspects of my character.

Unusual message Ability to increase my self-awareness by saying how I feel instead of getting stuck in the same old communication patterns.

Unusual person Aspect of my character that helps me develop my true potential by reflecting the variety of roles I play in my life.

Unusual place Situation where I can experience unfamiliar aspects of my character so I can understand the value of their wider potential.

Unusual romance Opportunity to make a profound connection with a valuable aspect of my creative talents that I was previously unaware of.

Unusual room Situation where I can explore my capacity to use my expertise in a different way, even though it may feel unsettling to begin with.

U

Unusual time Realization that I can use my past experience to powerfully transform my future by making the most of an outstanding opportunity.

Unusual vehicle Ability to use my exceptional drive and ambition to take an unconventional route as a way to achieve an extraordinary objective.

Unusual weather Natural ability to sense the prevailing mood so I can make the most of circumstances I may have no control over.

Unventilated Opportunity to bring a breath of fresh air to a situation by using current thinking to introduce some powerful new concepts.

Unwearable Opportunity to become more comfortable with the self-image I present to other people rather than feeling I don't fit in.

Unwittingly Realization that I can use my instincts to resolve a challenging situation instead of feeling I have to intellectually examine it.

Unworldly Realization that I can create practical value by taking a more spiritual approach, allowing me to see new possibilities.

Unworn Opportunity to decide the self-image I would like to share with other people so I can make a fresh start with them.

Unwrap Opportunity to open up to what I want by working my way through the different layers of meaning that surround it.

Unzipped Opportunity to reveal some innermost feelings so I can feel more comfortable about what might be expected from me.

Up Realization that I can achieve my higher ambitions by making the effort to raise my level of understanding in a positive way.

Updraft Opportunity to be inspired by an uplifting idea instead of feeling that I have to control all emerging possibilities.

Upgrade Opportunity to develop my expertise and abilities by taking a specific step that will enable me to achieve the success I need.

Upheaval Opportunity to make an effort so I can raise my level of commitment, even though it may be initially disruptive for me.

Uphill Situation where I can elevate my awareness and widen my perspective, even though it may require considerable effort.

Upholstery Ability to cushion the potential impact of a situation so I can feel much more comfortable in my particular viewpoint.

Uplifting Opportunity to elevate my deeper understanding of my situation so I can directly raise my awareness of my higher potential.

Uplink Ability to stay connected with a higher level of understanding so I can communicate my ideas to a wider audience.

Upload Opportunity to convey my deeper feelings rather than overloading myself with self-imposed responsibilities and obligations.

Upright Opportunity to take the most appropriate action by always making the effort to firmly stand up for what I really believe in.

Uproar Opportunity to speak up confidently and express my pride in my abilities rather than trying to play them down all the time.

Upset Realization that I can use any apparent setbacks as an opportunity to turn my whole situation around so I can make the most of it.

Upside down Opportunity to view my situation from a different angle to understand my deeper motivations and higher aspirations.

Upstairs Situation where I can become more aware of my ability to think up new ideas and feel secure in the support I have for them.

Upstream Situation where I can follow my instincts to make progress toward a clearer understanding of the source of my emotions.

Urban Situation where I can contain my instinctive behavior to access the resources I need to fulfill my ambitions.

U

Urchin Aspect of my character that embodies some of my uniquely precious talents, even though they may take time to fully mature.

Urge Realization that I can drive myself to much higher levels of achievement by having more confidence in my creative instincts.

Urgent Opportunity to take immediate action so I can resolve some chronic tension rather than always trying to avoid it.

Urinal Situation where I can stand up for my personal needs by choosing to let go of any emotions that make me feel uncomfortable.

Urinary infection Opportunity to maintain healthy personal boundaries so I can resolve emotional issues that make me uncomfortable.

Urination Ability to clearly release pent-up emotions that may have been causing me to feel some tension and discomfort.

Urine Ability to let go of emotions that are no longer healthy for me rather than experiencing further discomfort.

Urn Ability to contain my feelings in an emotionally heated situation so I can feel secure in making a deeper transformation.

Useless Realization that I can be of far more value by using my unique expertise rather than feeling that I have nothing to offer.

Useless brakes Opportunity to decisively steer my way through a challenge instead of feeling I am getting carried away by circumstances.

Useless device Ability to take a more human approach to dealing with a challenge rather than feeling I have to evoke a specific response.

User Aspect of my character that can achieve a much clearer understanding of my purpose by being happy to make some effort.

User-friendly Opportunity to become much more acquainted with my deeper purpose so I can feel more consistently supported by it.

User interface Ability to connect with specific qualities of my character that can give me the ability to successfully achieve my ambitions.

User name Ability to open myself up to some wider opportunities so I can identify how I can communicate my unique talents to people.

Usher Aspect of my character that helps me navigate my way through unfamiliar social situations so I can assert my ambitions.

Usual Realization that I need to behave differently if I really want to make a transformation that will make me stand out.

Utensil Ability to take a consistently practical approach to fulfilling my ambitions without feeling I will mess everything up.

Uterus Essential ability to conceive an idea and embody its unique qualities until I am ready to share it with the people around me.

Utility room Aspect of myself that has the capacity to help me feel comfortable in purposefully developing my potential skills and expertise.

Utopia Situation where I can create my best possible future by realizing that it doesn't always have to appear perfect to other people.

Vacant Opportunity to engage more readily with a challenging situation rather than just occupying myself with mindless activity.

Vacation Opportunity to take a more relaxed perspective in my day-to-day activities so I can work my way through a challenge.

Vaccination Opportunity to maintain a healthy perspective in any circumstances by understanding how to make the most my apparent weaknesses.

Vaccine Ability to protect myself from a potentially unhealthy situation by making the choice to take specific preemptive action.

Vacuum Situation where I can breathe new life into an emerging opportunity rather than feeling I am devoid of all inspiration.

Vacuum cleaner Ability to use powerful thought processes to clean up a situation that's been sucking up too much time and energy.

Vacuum flask Ability to maintain my level of passion for emotional fulfillment instead of allowing myself to cool to the idea of it.

Vagabond Aspect of my character that is happy to go where my mood takes me so I can discover unexpected uses for my talents.

Vagina Essential ability to connect with my capacity for unique creativity so I can naturally bring my concepts into being.

Vagrant Aspect of my character that can take steps to realize my value rather than begging for my talent to be recognized by other people.

Vague Realization that I can produce a definite outcome by having a clearer understanding of what I want to achieve.

Vain Realization that I am much more likely to succeed if I make the time and effort to look beyond superficial appearances.

Vain attempt Opportunity to achieve my chosen outcome by using inner strength instead of trying to look good to others.

Valet Aspect of my character that routinely looks after my fundamental needs and can help me enjoy a more orderly existence.

Validated Opportunity to fully recognize the value of my abilities rather than attempting to conceal my potential talents from other people.

Valid paperwork Ability to have a clear understanding of my fundamental value so I can permit myself to go ahead with my chosen action.

Valium Ability to take a more relaxed approach so I can reconnect with my feelings and generate real excitement in a healthy way.

Valley Situation where I can bring together my learning and experience so I can use them as a basis for some fertile thinking.

Valuables Ability to realize the value of the experience I have accumulated, even though I often try to conceal it from other people.

Valve Ability to control the flow of my emotions to keep them in check and open up about my feelings when I need to.

Vamp Aspect of my character that can help me to persistently pursue a creative opportunity that will revitalize my sense of identity.

Vampire Aspect of my character that can often feel drained of emotional energy from obsessively looking after the needs of others.

V

Vampire fangs Ability to confidently display my power and strength so others can feed off my energy and be inspired by it.

Van Ability to employ my personal drives and resources to make committed progress toward my objective in a professional capacity.

Vandal Aspect of my character that can resolve any self-destructive behaviors by using my creative skills for a positive purpose.

Vandalized Opportunity to create a productive and practical outcome rather than feeling that other people will tear my efforts apart.

Vandalized car Ability to confidently maintain the level of my personal ambition instead of feeling that people are putting holes in my efforts.

Vandalized toilets Situation where I can attend to my personal needs without feeling that people are unwittingly intruding on my private space.

Vanilla Ability to fulfill one of my ambitions in a pleasant, straightforward manner that should always suit everyone else's taste.

Vanished Opportunity to have another look at possibilities I may have overlooked rather than feeling that my chances have disappeared.

Vanishing lover Aspect of my character that can connect at a profounder level by making a deeper commitment to my spontaneous creativity.

Vanishing vehicle Ability to make a long-term commitment to one of my individual ambitions rather than hoping that opportunities will appear.

Vanity Realization that I can clearly understand my unique attraction to others by looking beyond the purely superficial.

Vapor Ability to raise my awareness by observing my emerging feelings so I can view them more expansively and objectively.

Vaporized Opportunity to take a more down-to-earth approach rather than thinking that any possibilities have disappeared into thin air.

Vapor trail Ability to see the general thrust of my ideas so I can get an understanding of the direction they are taking me in.

Varicose veins Essential opportunity to keep my instinctive creativity and vitality flowing by being flexible in how I convey my passions.

Variety Ability to make a difference by using a range of approaches rather than feeling I have to do the same thing every time.

Varnish Ability to carefully preserve my valuable experiences and memories so I can smooth over any potential rough patches.

Vase Ability to recognize my capacity for containing my emotions so I can give my talents the opportunity to consistently blossom.

Vast Realization that my opportunities are far more significant than I thought, and I can use them to realize an abundance of success.

Vat Ability to work with my need for emotional fulfillment so I can understand my capacity for accumulating valuable experience.

Vault Situation where I can open up to some of the deeper resources I often conceal so I can unlock my underlying potential.

Veal Potential to fulfill an ambition by using my raw strength and power to nurture my creative talent and fully develop its value.

Veer Opportunity to keep myself on track by staying focused on my objective rather than allowing myself to be distracted and drift off.

Vegan Aspect of my character that can healthily motivate me to fulfill my potential ambitions by using a more natural approach.

Vegetable Natural ability to fulfill my appetite for success by taking the time to develop my skills in a more natural and organic way.

Vegetarian Aspect of my character that has a healthy respect for my raw strength and power rather than relying on my creative instincts.

Vegetation Natural potential for my more immediate spiritual growth by opening up my development to some of the more practical aspects of it.

Vegged out Opportunity to stay fully engaged so I can use my creative instincts rather than fulfilling ambitions for other people.

Vehicle Ability to use my personal drive and ambition as a way of conveying how I plan to make progress toward a particular goal.

Veil Ability to clearly face up to any challenges so I can be much more open about sharing how I feel to other people.

Vein Essential ability to draw on my experience of my rich creativity so I can keep my natural passion and vitality flowing.

Velcro Ability to quickly latch on to a new opportunity without feeling that I will become overly attached to the eventual outcome.

Velvet Ability to use my charm to comfortably smooth over a situation without allowing other people to think that I am just a soft touch.

Vendetta Opportunity to resolve ongoing tensions by being open to new possibilities rather than taking a more familiar approach.

Vending machine Ability to quickly fulfill an ambition by having a clear understanding of my needs and knowing just the right buttons to press.

Veneer Ability to quickly gloss over any challenges in a situation to give the superficial impression that it can run more smoothly.

Venereal disease Essential opportunity to take a more creative approach to resolving any unhealthy tensions that are causing widespread discomfort.

Venetian blind Ability to open up to a wider perspective instead of trying to conceal my talents and feeling I'm being left in the shade.

Vengeance Realization that I need to use my frustrated ambitions in a more positive manner rather than creating more tension for myself.

Venom Instinctive ability to inject a healthy sense of motivation into an apparently poisonous situation so I can resolve tensions.

Vent Opportunity to clearly communicate what I think so I can air some viewpoints I normally keep to myself.

Ventilator Ability to use my way of thinking to bring a breath of fresh air to a situation that may be stifling any emerging ideas.

Ventriloquist Aspect of my character that should be more open about what I need to say rather than trying to conceal my feelings.

Ventriloquist's dummy Aspect of my character that needs to speak up for myself instead of feeling that other people are trying to put words in my mouth.

Venture Opportunity to increase my value by exploring the more unfamiliar aspects of myself, even though the outcome may be uncertain.

Verbal abuse Opportunity to speak graciously from the heart instead of allowing myself to be provoked by any insults from other people.

Verdict Opportunity to honestly speak my truth and say how I feel rather than letting other people judge me in my absence.

Verdigris Ability to feel comfortable with the layers of experience I have built up over time so I can shine when I need to.

Verge Situation where I can make a definite step toward my ambitions rather than always waiting around on the sidelines.

Vermin Instinctive ability to rid myself of any potentially damaging habits and behaviors instead of allowing them to plague me.

V

Vertebra Essential ability to piece together the fundamental aspects of my character that help me to stand up for what I believe in.

Vertical Opportunity to turn a situation around by raising my expectations and having a higher awareness of what I am trying to achieve.

Vertigo Essential opportunity to achieve a clearer understanding rather than allowing my situation to spin out of control.

Vessel Ability to consistently use my capacity for learning so I can safely navigate a potentially complex emotional situation.

Vest Ability to present myself to other people by opening up about my feelings rather than them keeping close to my chest.

Vet Aspect of my character that looks after my natural instincts and creative urges, even when other people are trying to put me down.

Veteran Aspect of my character that uses my long experience to make wise choices, even though they may involve potential conflict.

Veto Opportunity to give myself full permission to take action instead of thinking that people are making my decisions for me.

Viaduct Situation where I can consistently convey my emotions to other people who may prefer to take a more intellectual approach.

Viagra Ability to firmly believe in my creative power rather than always looking for outside support to help me rise to the occasion.

Vial Ability to clearly capture a precious experience so I can begin to understand more about the nature of my emotions.

Vibraphone Ability to take my instinctive creativity in both hands so I can produce a favorable result that resonates with everyone.

Vibration Opportunity to sense what I need to do to make a situation run more smoothly rather than continually letting it shake me up.

Vibrator Ability to get excited about my creative potential so I can become more intimately aware of how to achieve my desires.

Vicar Aspect of my character that graciously attends to my spiritual development by gently conveying the strength of my beliefs.

Vice Ability to firmly grasp my fundamental purpose so I can release myself from the grip of potentially unhealthy behaviors.

Vice president Aspect of my character that supports me as I develop a greater sense of my power so I can ultimately make my own decisions.

Vice squad Aspects of my character that work together to help me identify unwelcome behaviors so I can release their hold on me.

Vicinity Situation where I am much closer to achieving certain success with a distant ambition than I previously thought was possible.

Vicious Realization that I can use my creative power in a much more confident way rather than feeling that everyone is out to attack me.

Victim Aspect of my character that has the courage to fully step into my power and take positive control of an uncertain situation.

Victimized Opportunity to single out the result that will make me feel most fulfilled instead of feeling that other people are out to get me.

Victim support Ability to maintain a definite understanding of my needs so I have the capacity to look after the needs of other people.

Victory Opportunity to celebrate my skill in being able to engage with personal dilemmas so I can courageously resolve inner conflicts.

Video Ability to closely observe my habitual behavioral patterns so I can clearly see how they usually play out for me.

Video camera Ability to frame a particular perspective so I can reflect on my viewpoint and see how I fit into the bigger picture.

V

Video conference Opportunity to clearly understand the different aspects of my character rather than feeling distant and disconnected from them.

Video diary Ability to collect a variety of personal perspectives so I can reflect on them and gain a clearer understanding of who I am.

Video game Opportunity to play around with a variety of different ways of achieving my goals, even though the outcome may seem uncertain.

Video recorder Ability to make the most of a number of emerging opportunities by having a clearer understanding of my previous behaviors.

Viewer Aspect of my character that can help me to see the wider potential for developing my talents beyond my immediate situation.

Viewfinder Ability to get a clearer understanding of the specific area I am interested in rather than allowing myself to be distracted.

Viewpoint Situation where I can understand a variety of valuable perspectives by always remaining open to seeing the bigger picture.

Vigil Opportunity to closely observe what is emerging from my unconscious awareness so I can maintain my healthy progress.

Vigilante Aspect of my character that openly acknowledges my contribution to any tension rather than taking the law into my own hands.

Vile Realization that I am happy to deal with a messy situation instead of worrying that I may offend some of the people around me.

Villa Situation where I can comfortably explore all aspects of my inner and outer lives in a more relaxed and peaceful atmosphere.

Village Situation where I can connect with those closest to me so I can relate to them more openly as I pursue my ambitions.

Villain Aspect of my character that tries to bring out the best in everyone, even though they may seem to be behaving quite badly.

Vine Natural ability to connect with people and have them support my fruitful endeavors while staying rooted in the practicalities.

Vinegar Ability to sweeten up an unhealthy situation rather than making acid remarks and continually feeling sour about it.

Vineyard Situation where I can feel emotionally uplifted by giving myself the space to produce a future that is ripe with possibilities.

Vintage Ability to understand the value of my accumulated experience so I can take a more mature approach to any new challenges.

Vintage aircraft Ability to achieve my highest ambitions by using a more hands-on approach, even though my methods may seem a little old-fashioned.

Vintage car Ability to arrive at a successful outcome by having a clear understanding of the forces that drive my ambitions.

Vintage clothing Ability to present myself by sharing my experiences rather than feeling I always have to be a trendsetter.

Vintage wine Potential to fulfill an emotional need by reflecting on the value of the experiences I have accumulated over time.

Vinyl Ability to synthesize a complex variety of ideas so I can shrug off any unwelcome emotions and clearly make myself heard.

Viola Ability to take my instinctive creativity in both hands so I can achieve a deeper appreciation of the skills I have to offer.

Violation Opportunity to set firm personal boundaries around my talents so I can take full control of and responsibility for them.

Violence Opportunity to use my power and strength to peacefully resolve a sudden conflict instead of allowing it to become too intense.

Violent Realization that I can use my powerful energy to create a much healthier situation rather than letting it go out of control.

V

Violent attack Opportunity to engage with a challenge by taking forceful action to assert my needs instead of feeling defensive.

Violent storm Opportunity to reach a powerful outcome by calmly channeling the energy from my turmoil of conflicting ideas and emotions.

Violet color Mood that can color my perspective by reflecting my natural creativity and my passion for sharing it with other people.

Violet flower Natural ability to open up to my creative talents so I can encourage them to blossom rather than always being modest.

Violin Instinctive ability to take my creativity in both hands so I can express my most heartfelt emotions to other people.

Viper Instinctive ability to feel comfortable in my own skin so I can strike at the heart of a challenge and resolve it in a healthy manner.

Viral Realization that I can rapidly spread my influence by taking time to understand the nature of a seemingly insignificant detail.

Virgin Aspect of my character that can naturally explore new creative possibilities rather than feeling naive and inexperienced.

V

Virginity Opportunity to revitalize a creative situation by using a purer approach so I can naturally bring a concept to life.

Virile Realization that I can use my powerful energy to firmly assert my individual choices and decisively achieve ambitious challenges.

Virtual reality Opportunity to explore my perceptions of what I consider possible so I can build on these to create practical value.

Virtuoso Aspect of my character that can use my expert skill to produce dazzling results instead of feeling I am not good enough.

Virus Ability to instinctively set definite personal boundaries so I can make myself immune from potentially unhealthy criticism.

Visceral Essential opportunity to respond in an instinctive manner so I can always embody my power and passion in a positive way.

Viscous Ability to maintain my emotional composure rather than allowing myself to become stuck in a potentially messy situation.

Visibility Opportunity to clearly understand where I am going so I can confidently reveal my obvious skills to the people around me.

Vision Essential ability to imagine a healthy and positive future so I can understand what I need to do to see it happen in reality.

Visionary Aspect of my character that looks for ways to move beyond more obvious challenges so I can make the most of wider possibilities.

Visit Opportunity to become more acquainted with unfamiliar aspects of myself so I can access them on a more regular basis.

Visitation Opportunity to do something quite extraordinary by unexpectedly connecting to a powerful and unfamiliar aspect of myself.

Visitor Aspect of my character that gives me the open invitation to become aware of new information beyond my immediate experience.

Visor Ability to protect my point of view so I can see the finer details rather than being distracted by the glaringly obvious.

Visual Ability to focus on a particular objective so I can understand how to attain it while staying aware of the bigger picture.

Visualize Essential ability to imagine a healthy and positive future for myself so I can clearly see how to make it happen in reality.

Vitality Realization that I can use my strength and power to motivate myself so I can energetically pursue my ambitions.

Vitamin pill Ability to use some powerful ideas so I can follow a specific process that will ensure consistently healthy outcomes for me.

Vivid Realization that I can bring a much more colorful aspect of myself to life by intensely engaging with a bright new opportunity.

Vixen Instinctive ability to use my intelligence and resourcefulness to make the most of any challenges that require my creative talent.

Vocabulary Ability to communicate my opinion, even though I may not always use the language other people would like me to.

Vocal Opportunity to give voice to my deeper feelings so I can clearly make myself heard without having to shout about it.

Vocal chords Essential ability to strike just the right tone in what I want to say so it resonates with other people in a powerful way.

Vocalist Aspect of my character that can communicate my deepest, most powerful feelings by speaking passionately from my heart.

Voice Essential ability to meaningfully identify with my deeper source of inspiration so I can express what is often unspoken.

Voiceless Opportunity to speak up and have my voice heard by others rather than appearing to agree with what everyone else wants.

Voice mail Ability to communicate my needs clearly and concisely, even though the conversation may initially seem quite one-sided.

Voice message Ability to precisely communicate how I feel rather than assuming that everyone else thinks the same way that I do.

Voice-over Opportunity to discuss what is emerging for me so I can raise my levels of awareness and reach a specific outcome.

Voice recognition Ability to speak out about what is most meaningful for me so I can identify actions I need to take to make it happen.

Void Situation where I can release myself

from any previous commitments instead of feeling empty with nothing else to offer.

Volatile Realization that I can use my restless energy to make a positive change rather than allowing my emotions to bubble up.

Volcano Situation where I can make the effort to safely contain my mounting anger, even though I want to lose my head and blow my top.

Volcanic eruption Opportunity to release pent-up emotions I've been keeping below the surface so I can positively channel my energy.

Vole Instinctive ability to share my creative expertise rather than allowing my lack of recognition to constantly gnaw away at me.

Volleyball Opportunity to reach a definite outcome with my plans rather than constantly knocking ideas back and forth.

Volume Ability to use my capacity for learning as an obvious way to increase my levels of experience and expand my wider awareness.

Volunteer Aspect of my character that has great confidence in the value of my talents rather than needing recognition from others.

Voluptuous Ability to become more intimately aware of my attractiveness by taking the time to involve myself in a pleasurable situation.

Vomit Essential ability to take a healthier approach by bringing up an issue that is of no practical value in realizing my ambitions.

Vomiting Essential opportunity to discharge some responsibilities that have been making me feel unsettled so I can just let them go.

Voodoo Ability to use my power and talent to influence an outcome rather than relying on fearful superstitions.

Voracious Realization that I can satisfy my huge appetite for success by understanding my fundamental ambitions and how to fulfill them.

Vortex Opportunity to stay calm and turn the situation to my personal advantage instead of getting drawn more deeply into it.

Vote Opportunity to show my hand and express how I feel rather than always trying to keep my thoughts to myself.

Vow Opportunity to make a commitment to myself by believing that I can consistently deliver the full potential of my talents.

Voyage Opportunity to explore my unfamiliar self and discover my potential by motivating myself to look at a variety of perspectives.

Voyeur Aspect of myself that can gain a clearer understanding of my creative abilities by observing my habitual behavior patterns.

Vulgar Realization that I can meet my needs more effectively by refining my sense of power and how I communicate it to other people.

Vulnerability Realization that I can feel more secure by having the courage to open up to others and allowing them to see the real me.

Vulture Instinctive ability to creatively transform an idea by picking my way through it rather than just going around in circles.

Vuvuzela Ability to express the collective feelings of a group of people, even though it may sound like I'm droning on interminably.

V

Waders Ability to make comfortable progress in an unpredictable emotional situation by having a firm idea of where I stand.

Wading Opportunity to steadily work my way through a potentially messy emotional situation by taking careful and deliberate steps.

Wading bird Instinctive ability to probe the practical aspects of my deeper feelings so I can spread my ideas on a wider basis.

Wafer Potential to fulfill an ambition by taking a lighter and more delicate approach, even though any support might seem quite thin.

Waffle Potential to quickly fulfill an ambition that will help me get started rather than going on and on about it.

Waft Opportunity to use an apparently inconsequential idea to get a situation moving so I can understand what is going on.

WAG Aspect of my character embodying my commitment to developing my expertise instead of being concerned about how I appear.

Wage Ability to have my value recognized by other people rather than feeling constantly challenged to assert my self-worth.

Wager Opportunity to decide the outcome of a situation by recognizing the value of my expertise instead of leaving it to chance.

Wagging Opportunity to rapidly look at a number of different perspectives on a situation so I can see the funny side of it.

Wagon Ability to hook myself up to a potentially valuable resource so I can use it for support as I drive forward with an ambition.

Wagon train Ability to explore some wider opportunities by connecting to a number of resources rather than just going in circles.

Waif Aspect of my character that can reclaim my feelings of power and security by being far more direct in demonstrating what I need.

Wail Opportunity to draw attention to a deep emotion I need to express rather than feeling it will be painful.

Waist Essential ability to always keep my inner thoughts and feelings connected to the steps I will take to put them into action.

Waistline Ability to align my skills and resources so I can keep making healthy progress while maintaining my personal boundaries.

Waiter Aspect of my character that consistently helps me to strongly assert my ambitions so I can satisfy my appetite for success.

Waiting Opportunity to take immediate action instead of expecting other people to give me the permission to pursue my ambitions.

Waiting at a window Opportunity to choose where I want to go rather than letting myself be influenced by others' apparent expectations.

Waiting by a door Opportunity to take a decisive step so I can immediately open up to a new possibility instead of just thinking about it.

Waiting room Situation where I can take some time to explore an aspect of my character rather than always allowing other people to put me off.

Waitress Aspect of my character that can bring understanding of how I can display my talents and satisfy my hunger for recognition.

Wake Opportunity to celebrate a fundamental transformation by happily laying the past to rest so I can move on into a new future.

Wake-up call Opportunity to understand what moves me by rapidly becoming more aware of how to develop my unrealized potential.

Waking Opportunity to open my eyes to a whole new world of possibilities so I can use my self-motivation to explore them.

Walker Aspect of my character that can steadily progress with one of my ambitions by taking a series of steps that will lead to success.

Walkie-talkie Ability to take steps so I can share my thoughts and ideas with others who are on the same wavelength as I am.

Walking Opportunity to directly pursue one of my objectives by using my self-motivation and energy to take the necessary steps.

Walking frame Ability to get myself motivated again by using a definite framework and support structure to maintain forward progress.

Walking stick Ability to stay with what I know so I can safely rely on some external support to help me take the steps I need to take.

Walking wounded Aspect of my character that can motivate me to progressively heal some painful feelings so I can gain healthy closure.

Walk of shame Opportunity to take steps that show how much I value my freedom rather than feeling embarrassed about my behavior.

Walk-on part Opportunity to express my unseen strength and power so I can eventually give voice to what I want to achieve.

Wall Ability to strongly support my beliefs and establish my privacy by maintaining firm personal boundaries with other people.

Wallaby Instinctive ability to make a series of powerful creative leaps while using my past experience to help me balance my progress.

Wall chart Ability to understand the bigger picture about the support I need so I can use this perspective to choose my direction.

Walled garden Situation where I can set some personal boundaries around my relationships and interests so I can carefully cultivate them.

Wallet Ability to feel more secure in my individual identity by taking care of my sense of self-worth and how I usually convey it.

Wallflower Natural ability to feel personally supported so I can open up to my creative talents and encourage them to blossom.

Wall painting Ability to apply a new perspective to my situation to help me strongly support my beliefs and maintain privacy.

Wallpaper Ability to draw attention to my boundaries rather than just trying to make them superficially acceptable to others.

Walnut Potential to fulfill an ambition by choosing to come out of my shell so I can use my fertile imagination to crack a problem.

Walrus Instinctive ability to assert my strength and confidence so I can show my willingness to immerse myself in my emotions.

Wand Ability to extend my influence so I can use my practical skills to conjure up a creative solution to a particular challenge.

Wanderer Aspect of my character that takes steps to explore the undiscovered aspects of myself so I can achieve very specific aims.

Wandering Opportunity to motivate myself by having a very definite aim rather than allowing myself to be distracted by outside influences.

W

Waning Opportunity to explore the apparently darker side of any opportunity rather than letting my enthusiasm slowly fade away.

Wannabe Aspect of my character that has the creative potential to achieve a unique success that no one else will be able to emulate.

Want Realization that I can achieve my desires by clearly understanding my fundamental needs and how they drive my deeper purpose.

War Opportunity to resolve an ongoing inner tension by declaring what I need rather than continually trying to evade conflict.

War crime Opportunity to have confidence in my good judgment rather than continually punishing myself by trying to avoid the issue.

War cry Opportunity to give voice to how I feel so I can resolve any ongoing emotional conflicts by just speaking my truth.

War dance Opportunity to take some courageous steps that will help me confront unfamiliar tensions I have been experiencing.

Warden Aspect of my character that takes responsibility for looking after my inner life and all the creative instincts it embodies.

Warder Aspect of my character that can unlock my creativity so I can freely pursue all the opportunities that it can provide.

Warding off Opportunity to maintain healthy personal boundaries so I can make deeper connections rather than avoiding other people.

Wardrobe Ability to become aware of different aspects of my self-image so I can choose how I would like to appear to others.

Warehouse Situation where I can safely accumulate a wide range of skills and experiences so I can quickly access them at any time.

Warfare Opportunity to resolve an ongoing inner struggle by always trying to take the

higher ground so I can see the bigger picture.

War game Opportunity to use my courage to play with some of my inner conflicts, even though the eventual outcome may seem uncertain.

War grave Situation where I can acknowledge a sacrifice required to transform inner tensions so I can courageously undertake to do it.

Warhead Ability to resolve any tensions by concentrating on a powerful idea that will enable me to bring the situation to a head.

Warhorse Instinctive ability to harness my unconscious energies so I can use my natural strength to resolve any ongoing conflicts.

Warlock Aspect of my character that can honestly pursue my preferred outcome instead of superstitiously leaving it to fate.

Warm Realization that I can get my plans moving by putting more energy into them rather than appearing cool about them.

Warm-blooded Instinctive ability to convey my passion and vitality in any situation by naturally channeling the flow of my emotions.

War memorial Situation where I can fully acknowledge the monumental effort I have made to courageously resolve a major conflict in my life.

Warning Opportunity to ensure that I honestly listen to my thoughts and feelings so I can make the most of emerging opportunities.

War paint Ability to be clear about what I need to resolve in an inner conflict rather than just putting on a brave face.

Warpath Situation where I can take steps to understand the cause of any potential conflict instead of preparing myself for battle.

Warped Realization that I can take a more straightforward approach to reach my chosen goal instead of always trying to bend the rules.

Warplane Ability to rapidly resolve any

W

conflicting thoughts I may have by powerfully raising my overall awareness of the situation.

War poet Aspect of my character that can express the nature of inner tensions, although they seem to lack rhyme or reason.

Warp speed Opportunity to make a fundamental transformation in my position, though I may need to bend universal rules.

Warrant Realization that I can give myself the permission to behave in a particular way rather than needing it to be authorized by people.

Warrant card Ability to demonstrate my authority to other people instead of thinking I always need permission before I take action.

Warranty Ability to successfully deliver on a promise I have made rather than feeling that I am seeking forgiveness for my behavior.

Warrior Aspect of my character that heroically engages with my inner conflicts and tensions so I can fight for what I believe in.

Warship Ability to courageously explore my emotional highs and lows so I can assertively maintain my preferred course of action.

Wart Essential opportunity to bring an ugly truth to the surface so I can resolve an unhealthy situation by just letting it go.

Warthog Instinctive ability to get stuck in a potentially messy situation so I can honestly open up my deeper feelings.

War zone Situation where I can resolve areas of ongoing tension that are using up my energy and distracting my attention.

Washbasin Ability to contain my feelings so I can face up to any messy situations and look at ways of cleaning up my self-image.

Washing Opportunity to open up about my emotions so I can come clean and take a fresh approach by releasing what I no longer need.

Washing line Ability to bring a fresh

perspective to my self-image rather than feeling like I am hanging around in a bit of a flap.

Washing machine Ability to have a clear understanding of who I am by resolving superficial disagreements coloring my outlook.

Washing up Chance to be clear about how I have fulfilled my appetite for success so I can prepare for future opportunities.

Wasp Instinctive ability to colorfully demonstrate my point to others instead of defending myself by making stinging remarks.

Waste Opportunity to fully realize the value of my talents and knowledge rather than allowing other people to trash them.

Waste-disposal unit Ability to purposefully let go of what I no longer need so I can work out how to fulfill some of my bigger ambitions.

Wasteland Situation where I can take a more practical, down-to-earth approach to a range of possibilities I may have previously ignored.

Wastepaper basket Ability to gracefully let go of plans and projects that are no longer of value to me so I can move on to new opportunities.

Wasting disease Opportunity to feel much more at ease with myself by directing my energy toward vigorously developing my talents and knowledge.

Wastrel Aspect of my character that can achieve great success by stepping into my power rather than always shirking my responsibilities.

Watch Ability to observe my personal rhythms and see how I can use them to choose the best time to take action and influence an outcome.

Watchdog Instinctive ability to show my unconditional loyalty and affection by carefully observing any potential threats to a loved one.

Watcher Aspect of my character that looks beyond any traditional explanation so I can understand what is going on for me.

Watching Opportunity to observe the thoughts and feelings emerging for me so I can consider them before taking any action.

Water Potential to fulfill an emotional need by immersing myself in my feelings so I can go with the flow and gain experience.

Water bed Situation where I can feel most comfortable with my emotional life and can take a relaxed approach to exploring my creativity.

Water bomber Ability to quickly convey the potential emotional impact of the situation so I can create a more positive transformation.

Water buffalo Instinctive ability to draw on my wide experience so I can use my creativity to naturally drive the situation forward.

Water cannon Ability to influence people by gently using my experience rather than trying to overwhelm them with the power of my emotions.

Water cooler Situation where I can take a more sociable approach to working through my feelings rather than trying to chill out.

Watercress Natural ability to nourish myself by healthily developing the seed of an idea that does not require many practical resources.

Waterfall Situation where I can experience a sudden emotional transformation that has the potential to generate a feeling of power.

Waterhole Situation where I can feel emotionally revitalized by looking deeply into my sentiments and understanding their source.

Watering Opportunity to spread what I have learned so I can develop some potentially fertile ideas in a challenging situation.

Watering can Ability to directly use my experience to increase my understanding rather than feeling the subject matter is too dry for me.

Water lily Natural ability to open up to my creative talents so I can encourage them to blossom by drawing on emotions and feelings.

Waterlogged Opportunity to immerse myself in a positive learning experience rather than allowing it to drag me down.

Water main Ability to channel my fundamental emotions so I can share my experiences of what I have learned in a consistent way.

Water meadow Situation where I can healthily cultivate my practical knowledge instead of allowing emotions to suddenly overwhelm me.

Watermelon Potential to fulfill an emotional ambition by having a healthy awareness of how I can make the most of a ripening opportunity.

Water mill Situation where I can use accumulated learning and experience to refine practical skills by steadily working through them.

Water pistol Ability to playfully express my feelings so I feel more relaxed about clearly communicating my aims to other people.

Waterproof Ability to feel comfortable when I immerse myself in my feelings by realizing I can repel any intrusive emotions.

Water spout Natural opportunity to clearly funnel the energy from a turmoil of emotions rather than letting myself get sucked into them.

Water tank Ability to use accumulated experience and learning to contain my emotions, drawing on them whenever I need to.

Waterwheel Ability to go with the flow so I can use accumulated learning and experience to naturally achieve a productive outcome.

W

Waterworks Situation where I can feel more in control of emerging emotions so I can channel them where they will be most effective.

Wave Ability to make a difference by understanding the power of my emotions and realizing how I can use their ebb and flow.

Wavelength Ability to successfully progress through a series of highs and lows by communicating my needs in a clear and coherent manner.

Wavering Opportunity to achieve my chosen outcome by making up my mind and committing myself to engaging with a challenge.

Waving Opportunity to signal my intentions by taking a definite action to draw the attention of other people to my talents.

Wax Ability to polish my creative talents and bring them to life so I can continue to effortlessly expand them.

Wax dummy Aspect of my character that inspires me to become more self-motivated so I can bring my unique talents to life.

Wax museum Situation where I can openly identify a number of my personal attributes so I can use my creativity to bring them to life.

Way Situation where I can consistently work in my characteristic manner by using a recognized method to pursue my ambitions.

Wayside Situation where I can make definite progress by clearly defining my ultimate goal rather than giving up on my achievements.

Weak-kneed Opportunity to contain my excitement so I can take firm steps to attain my ambitions and stand up for what I believe in.

Weakness Realization that one of my main strengths is being open about my potential vulnerabilities so I can use them positively.

Wealth Realization that I have an abundance of accumulated experience and wisdom rather than feeling that I am lacking in value.

Weapon Ability to powerfully assert my beliefs and exert my influence over people, even though it may proven to be a painful experience.

Wearing Opportunity to present myself to other people in a more enthusiastic manner by choosing how I would like to appear.

Weasel Instinctive ability to speak my truth so I can encourage people to communicate honestly rather than appearing slightly devious.

Weather Natural ability to sense the prevailing atmosphere so I can adapt to changing circumstances I may have no control over.

Weather balloon Ability to quickly elevate my level of understanding so I can become aware of where my current thinking might take me.

Weathercock Ability to clearly assert the direction of my current thinking so I can make the most of approaching possibilities.

Weather forecast Ability to use my experience of how my thoughts and feelings normally develop to successfully make the most of any opportunities.

Weatherman Aspect of my character that can illustrate emerging opportunities and point out favorable conditions for achieving my ambitions.

Weather station Ability to gauge the prevailing mood so I can plan ahead and make the most of opportunities that are approaching.

Weathertight Ability to feel secure in an uncertain atmosphere by realizing that I can deal with whatever challenges may emerge.

Weatherwoman Aspect of my character that empathizes with my prevailing mood and can help me understand possibilities that emerge.

Weaver Aspect of my character that can bring together a number of story threads so I can see any patterns that emerge.

Weaving Opportunity to create a substantial amount of material by drawing together a number of threads into more coherent story.

Web Ability to build a resilient network by making powerful connections that lead to a wide array of strong relationships.

Webbed feet Instinctive ability to quickly make progress through an emotional situation so I can decide the next steps I need to take.

Webcam Ability to conveniently observe some of my behavioral patterns so I can form stronger relationships with other people.

Web page Ability to gather together my ideas in a specific area so I can communicate how I feel to a much more extensive audience.

Website Ability to explore the basis of some my plans so I can take specific action to build a variety of strong connections.

Wedding Opportunity to make a major commitment that will fulfill a long-term ambition, although it may compromise my independence.

Wedding cake Potential to fulfill a shared ambition and celebrate a long-term commitment by understanding the required levels of compromise.

Wedding day Opportunity to wait for just the right time so I can gain an understanding of a commitment I have been unclear about.

Wedding dress Ability to present my self-image to other people in a way that celebrates my long-term commitment to accomplishing my ambitions.

Wedding ring Ability to demonstrate my individual commitment to a fundamental partnership that will continue to develop in a healthy way over time.

Wedding veil Ability to clearly face up to any challenges I may have about making new commitments so I can share my feelings.

Wedge Ability to make a big difference by using my wealth of experience to apply a small amount of effort in just the right place.

Weed Natural ability to make the best use of my underlying resourcefulness and thrive in any situation, no matter how adverse it seems.

Weed killer Ability to healthily transform how I develop my natural talents by being selective in how I use my practical resources.

Week Opportunity to use my natural sense of rhythm to work my way through a series of possibilities that regularly emerge for me.

Weekend Opportunity to make the most of my situation by taking time to relax so I can comfortably reflect on my daily routine.

Weeping Opportunity to show how I feel so I can clearly resolve an emotional situation that is leaving me feeling drained.

Weevil Instinctive ability to make the most of emerging possibilities by controlling any self-destructive ideas as I pursue my ambitions.

Weighing Opportunity to acknowledge the gravity of the situation by understanding my responsibilities and balancing my commitments to them.

Weight Ability to use my inner strength and personal power to successfully deal with any heavy responsibilities and obligations.

Weight-bearing Ability to consistently use my strength of purpose to handle my heavier commitments instead of collapsing under the pressure.

Weight lifting Opportunity to raise my awareness by making a commitment to substantial responsibilities rather than trying to make light of them.

Weight training Opportunity to increase my power and strength in dealing with heavy responsibilities by deciding to pull my weight.

Weight-watcher Aspect of my character that can help me fulfill my appetite for success by being measured in making weightier commitments.

Weir Ability to control the flow of my emotions so I can raise my levels of experience and allow my learning to accumulate.

W

Weird Realization that I can reconcile some aspects of my life that may be unsettling me so I can resolve any challenges they create.

Weirdo Aspect of my character that can help me develop some of my more unusual skills rather than feeling I always have to fit in.

Welcome Opportunity to happily explore my needs rather than feeling my behavior may appear unacceptable to other people.

Well Ability to feel much healthier by connecting to the source of my deeper sentiments so I can share them with other people.

Wellington boots Ability to present my self-image to others by showing my willingness to take steps to engage with my deeper emotions.

Well preserved Realization that I can continually develop my interests instead of thinking I need to keep up with current trends.

Well-worn Ability to be comfortable with the image that I present to other people so I can maintain a healthy sense of identity.

Wench Aspect of my character that has an old-fashioned approach to displaying my creative talents rather than being more assertive.

Werewolf Apparent ability to fundamentally transform a situation by powerfully asserting my fierce loyalty to the people closest to me.

West Natural opportunity to become more consciously aware of the direction I am taking so I can see how I might go farther.

Wet Ability to immerse myself in my feelings so I can fulfill my emotional needs by keeping my current situation moving fluidly.

Wetland Situation where I can take a more practical, down-to-earth approach in dealing with any emotional challenges I encounter.

Wet room Aspect of myself that has the capacity to help me feel more comfortable and secure so I can channel how I feel.

Wet suit Ability to present myself to others in a way that allows me to feel comfortable when exploring deeper emotions.

Whack Opportunity to suddenly make a powerful connection so I can use the natural strength of my abilities to make an impact.

Whale Instinctive ability to generate a huge opportunity by immersing myself in my emotions and expressing my deeper feelings.

Whammy Ability to take full control over my preferred outcome instead of continually thinking that I am always unfortunate.

Wharf Situation where I can keep my feet firmly on the ground as I consider various ways to work my way through an emotional situation.

Wheat Natural ability to sustain my ambitions by working my way through some ideas I have sown so I can reap their benefits.

Wheel Ability to make a revolutionary discovery by realizing that I can choose my direction and keep things rolling along.

Wheelbarrow Ability to use my energy and self-motivation to transform the practical aspects of a developing situation in a down-to-earth way.

Wheelchair Ability to keep moving forward with my point of view, even though I may not be able to take the steps I would like to.

Wheel clamp Ability to give myself the freedom to pursue ambitions rather than trying to control a situation I should just let go of.

Wheelie bin Ability to make a positive, healthy choice about what is no longer useful to me so I can quickly remove it from my life.

Wheeze Opportunity to recognize when I feel most deeply inspired instead of always playing around with other people's ideas.

Whet Opportunity to sharpen my skills so I can cut through confusion to fulfill a particular ambition.

W

Whiff Opportunity to instinctively understand what is happening around me so I can decide the most appropriate action to take.

While Opportunity to make the most of an emerging possibility rather than always waiting around for something to happen to me.

Whimper Opportunity to meet a challenge by stepping into my power and speaking up clearly instead of feeling like a victim.

Whine Opportunity to make the situation run more smoothly by taking the time to voice my concerns in a positive and healthy way.

Whip Ability to shape the outcome of a situation by quickly taking assertive action, even though it may involve a painful decision.

Whiplash injury Opportunity to prevent an unhealthy situation by keeping a level head as I resolve unforeseen challenges to my progress.

Whipped Opportunity to take a more consistent approach rather than feeling I have worked myself up and then let myself down.

Whirling Opportunity to straighten out my way of thinking instead of feeling that circumstances are making my head spin.

Whirlpool Opportunity to become more centered in my emotions instead of experiencing the overwhelming feeling of going around in circles.

Whirlwind Opportunity to stay completely calm so I can allow myself to think straight and turn the situation to my advantage.

Whiskers Instinctive ability to sense what is often unspoken in a situation so I can understand how to work my way through it.

Whiskey Potential to fulfill an emotional need by connecting with my wilder spirit and the feelings it evokes and inspires for me.

Whisper Ability to listen to my inner voice so I can clearly hear the subtle messages I may be trying to communicate.

Whispering Opportunity to use a more subtle approach with other people so I can clearly communicate the obvious value of my ideas.

Whistle Ability to quickly direct my attention so I can focus my thinking on how to communicate my ideas in a much clearer way.

Whistleblower Aspect of my character that can inspire others by drawing their attention to how they can communicate much more openly.

Whistling Opportunity to focus my thoughts on an emerging possibility so I can acknowledge its potential value before it disappears.

White Mood that can color my perspective by opening up my spiritual awareness to an apparently limitless range of possibilities.

White-knuckled Essential opportunity to get a firm grip on what is happening so I can be more relaxed about confronting any challenges.

Whiteout Natural opportunity to clearly understand where I need to draw the line rather than allowing myself to become disoriented.

Whitewash Ability to colorfully express my instinctive feelings rather than trying to conceal any of their potentially darker aspects.

Whiz Opportunity to draw attention to my talents by quickly demonstrating them instead of continually sounding off about them.

Whole Realization that I have all the inner resources I need to feel complete instead of always feeling that something is missing.

Whole food Potential to fulfill my ambitions by taking a completely positive and healthy approach to satisfying my appetite for success.

Whoop Opportunity to be more vocal about my need to spend time satisfying my ambitions rather than trying to please others.

Wick Ability to draw on my accumulated resources so I can illuminate my fundamental passions and developing creativity.

W

Wicked Realization that being completely honest and open with myself usually results in my taking powerful and positive action.

Wicket Ability to skillfully deflect any incoming criticism, even though other people may be apparently behaving in an underhanded manner.

Wide Realization that I can open up my skills to a whole new range of possibilities rather than feeling restricted to a narrow choice.

Widget Ability to discover a number of practical uses for my creative expertise that will help me to shape my preferred outcome.

Widow Aspect of my character that provides me with the opportunity to make a fundamental transformation in developing my strengths.

Widower Aspect of my character that can help me work through a transformative change in how I develop my fundamental creativity.

Wife Aspect of my character that embodies my commitment to developing the empathy and wisdom I need to create my dreams.

Wi-Fi Ability to effortlessly communicate how I feel rather than getting needlessly tangled up in all sorts of protocols and procedures.

Wig Ability to present my self-image to other people by assuming a certain style of thinking that may conceal my deeper thoughts.

W

Wigwam Situation where I can use my creative pursuits to help me feel very much at home with a wide range of my wilder instincts.

Wild Realization that I can use the power of my natural abilities to achieve my greatest ambitions without feeling I'm out of control.

Wild animal Instinctive ability that embodies all of my unknown potential and gives me motivation to express my natural wisdom.

Wild-animal attack Opportunity to

engage with a challenge by confidently using natural creativity rather than feeling I need to defend it.

Wilderness Situation where I can step out of my comfort zone to open up to unexplored opportunities and boldly explore them.

Wildfire Opportunity for a vital transformation that can illuminate new possibilities and help me regenerate my developing creativity.

Wildflower Natural ability to open up to my undiscovered talents so I can encourage them to blossom while staying grounded in reality.

Wildwood Situation where I can build up my practical skills and essential strength so I can feel comfortable in exploring the unknown.

Wile Realization that I can use my instinctive intelligence to resolve a challenging situation rather than trying to be devious.

Will Realization that I can take deliberate action based on my choices instead of always trying to please other people.

Will and testament Ability to prepare for a fundamental transformation by acknowledging the relationship most valuable to me.

Willing Realization that I need to engage with some of my challenges rather than happily going along with meeting expectations.

Willow tree Natural ability for developing my long-term spiritual growth while always remaining flexible about everyday practicalities.

Win Opportunity to achieve a successful outcome by using my courage and skill to engage with challenges I feel uncertain about.

Winch Ability to make powerful progress by understanding the connections that move me rather than feeling that I am stuck.

Wind Natural opportunity to understand some of my prevailing thoughts and theories and how they can have the power to move me.

Wind chimes Ability to feel relaxed about emerging opportunities so I can turn my thoughts to an idea that resonates.

Wind farm Situation where I can produce a valuable outcome by cultivating powerful thoughts so I can develop my creative energy.

Wind instrument Ability to channel my thoughts and ideas in an inspired manner so I can express them in a powerful, evocative way.

Windmill Situation where I can take prevailing theories and ideas and use them to refine my skills by steadily working through them.

Window Ability to clearly see through any of my self-imposed limitations so I can understand what my viewpoint actually is.

Window cleaner Aspect of my character that helps me see a situation with a greater clarity so I can confidently share my perspective.

Window ledge Situation where I can strongly support my point of view by understanding the fundamental basis of my viewpoint.

Window shopping Opportunity to make a specific choice so I can display my unique value rather than exploring different perspectives.

Windpipe Essential ability to always remain inspired so I can express my deeper feelings and clearly convey their value to people.

Windshield Ability to clearly see my way forward so I can progress in my chosen direction, successfully accomplishing a personal ambition.

Windshield wiper Ability to remove any emotional influences that may be distorting my perspective so I can clearly see the way ahead.

Wind sock Ability to understand where current thinking is heading so I can choose the best direction to get my idea off the ground.

Windsurfer Aspect of my character that can use the power of ideas to carve a path through the extremes of an emotional situation.

Wind tunnel Situation where I can move into a more fundamental understanding of my plans and explore the different ways they move me.

Wind turbine Ability to capture the power of a particular way of thinking so I can use my creative energy to produce a valuable outcome.

Wine Potential to fulfill an emotional need by relaxing some of my inhibitions and anxieties that I may have kept bottled up.

Wine bottle Ability to use my courage and resourcefulness to draw on my accumulated experience rather than trying to keep it hidden.

Wine cellar Aspect of myself in which I can draw on my deepest experiences and treasured memories to increase my personal value.

Wine glass Ability to become much clearer about my sentiments, although it can make me feel vulnerable to be emotionally transparent.

Winetasting Opportunity to judge the flavor of a situation so I can use accumulated wisdom to decide my preferred outcome.

Wing Ability to rise above it all by using my ideas to clearly differentiate the influence of the different pressures I encounter.

Winged monster Ability to make the most of a huge opportunity by using the strength of my ideas to help me rise above minor concerns.

Wingman Aspect of my character that identifies any potential threats as I focus on pursuing my ambitions in a single-minded way.

Wing-walker Aspect of my character that can steadily progress in my ambitions by having the courage to stand up for my ideas.

W

Wink Essential ability to confidently signal my point of view by taking a brief moment to reflect on my deeper insights.

Winnebago Ability to feel at home with myself as I take a more relaxed approach to making progress with an ambition.

Winner Aspect of my character that can successfully choose the outcome of a situation by having the courage to step into the unknown.

Winning Opportunity to move toward a successful outcome by having the courage to participate rather than worrying about losing face.

Winning a bet Opportunity to use the power of my insight to confidently stick my neck out so I can decide the outcome that I want to see.

Winning a competition Opportunity to use my self-motivation to discover the value of my talents instead of feeling success is beyond me.

Winning a prize Opportunity to feel that my talents are being recognized by others and I am being suitably rewarded for my efforts.

Winning a race Opportunity to use my self-motivation to achieve my chosen outcome rather than feeling my chances of success are over.

Winning at sports Opportunity to accomplish personal ambitions by conquering my doubts and fears so I can achieve consistent success.

Winning shot Opportunity to forcefully assert my power and influence so I can demonstrate my expertise to those around me.

Winning the lottery Opportunity to treasure the huge value of my unique talents instead of hoping that others will notice them by chance.

Winter Opportunity to understand my natural instincts and rhythms so I can prepare myself for some emerging possibilities.

Winter solstice Opportunity to deeply explore my unconscious awareness so I can illuminate emerging creative possibilities.

Winter sports Opportunity to achieve my ambitions by taking a cool and considered approach, even though the outcome may be uncertain.

Wipe Opportunity to clear up a messy situation by dealing with my feelings rather than always trying to forget about them.

Wire Ability to make a strong connection with others by using my fundamental power to communicate exactly how I feel.

Wireless Ability to communicate how I feel to other people who are on my wavelength, even though they seem quite detached to begin with.

Wiretapping Opportunity to listen to what I'm saying so I can be much more open in conveying my feelings to other people.

Wisdom tooth Essential ability to willingly display my deeper awareness rather than feeling that people have to forcibly extract it.

Wise Realization that I can use deeper awareness to understand what's happening around me so I can make the best decision.

Wise man Aspect of my character that helps me to compassionately assert the power and strength of my natural spirituality.

Wise woman Aspect of my character embodying empathy and wisdom that can help me become deeply aware of my ambitions.

Wish Opportunity to use my power and creativity to achieve one of my desires rather than just hoping it will happen.

Wishbone Ability to break with established structures so I can make new opportunities happen instead of just trusting to luck.

Wish fulfillment Opportunity to create significant value by fully connecting with my fundamental needs rather than just talking about them.

W

Wishing well Situation where I can successfully achieve higher aspirations by connecting to the source of my deeper emotions.

Witch Aspect of my character that takes transformative action instead of believing in unfounded superstitions and vague fears.

Witchcraft Ability to use my skills to provide a practical outcome rather than leaving everything to fate and hoping for the best.

Witch doctor Aspect of my character that examines irrational behaviors so I can understand how to resolve an unhealthy situation.

Withdrawal Opportunity to create a difference by making a deliberate choice to move on from a situation where I no longer add value.

Withdrawal symptoms Opportunity to realize what is happening by having a fuller appreciation of what is emerging from my deeper awareness.

Withered Opportunity to revitalize a situation by immersing myself in exciting new experiences that absorb my energy and enthusiasm.

Witness Aspect of my character that can objectively observe my behavioral patterns so I can make rational sense of them.

Witnessing a crime Opportunity to understand my motivations rather than punishing myself when I feel I've let others down.

Witnessing a miracle Opportunity to openly acknowledge my abundant creativity so I can fundamentally transform a seemingly impossible situation.

Witnessing violence Opportunity to peacefully resolve an emerging conflict by observing how my habitual behaviors may be contributing to it.

Witty Realization that I can use my instinctive curiosity to effortlessly make some deeper connections that speak to me.

Wizard Aspect of my character that can make things happen by using my unique expertise to manifest my chosen outcome.

Wobbly Realization that I have the strength to maintain a firm stance in my beliefs rather than allowing events to throw me off balance.

Wobbly writing Opportunity to show the different aspects of my character by taking a more deliberate approach to how I communicate my needs.

Woe Realization that I can use inner strength to make the most of an unexpected challenge instead of becoming distressed about it.

Wolf Instinctive ability to protect those closest to me by being fiercely loyal to them, even though it may sometimes set me apart.

Woman Aspect of my character that embodies the individual empathy and wisdom I need to fulfill my aspirations and realize my dreams.

Womb Essential ability to nurture my ambitions by providing a creative space to develop my concepts and produce a labor of love.

Wombat Instinctive ability to immerse myself in the unexplored aspects of a situation so I can clearly make practical progress.

Wonder Realization that I can use my instinctive curiosity to create a truly amazing outcome instead of doubting my abilities.

Wonky Realization that I can take a much more straightforward approach rather than feeling that I've been knocked off balance.

Wood Natural ability to build up my practical skills and essential strength so I can always produce a straightforward outcome.

Wooden leg Ability to revitalize my feelings of self-motivation rather than allowing myself to be crippled by my habitual patterns.

Woodland Situation where I can take a more practical, down-to-earth approach in exploring aspects of my long-term spiritual growth.

W

Wood louse Instinctive ability to break out of any habitual behaviors rather than allowing myself to be distracted by minor details.

Woodpecker Instinctive ability to understand any challenges to my spiritual growth so I can get to the point and hammer out a solution.

Woodwork Ability to establish enduring skills that emerge from my habitual behaviors so I can use them in a more practical fashion.

Woodworm Instinctive ability to make my way deep into the practical aspects of my behaviors to rid myself of damaging habits.

Wool Ability to develop warmer feelings about some of my fundamental behaviors so I can be much more comfortable with them.

Word Ability to communicate exactly what I need to say to other people so I can begin to deliver on my promising potential.

Word game Opportunity to use my theories to play around with ways of communicating my needs so I can honestly express myself.

Word processor Ability to methodically gather my thoughts so I can work my way through them and express myself more clearly.

Work Opportunity to express my fundamental value to other people so I can make the effort to connect with my true purpose in life.

Workaholic Aspect of my character that has a compelling need to connect with my fundamental purpose in life by consistently making an effort.

Workbench Ability to share a practical and solid viewpoint with other people so I can feel fully supported in my life's purpose.

Work colleague Aspect of my character that can support deeper ambitions by helping me to achieve objectives through developing talents.

Worker Aspect of my character that can help me to achieve my goals by taking a methodical approach to any challenges I encounter.

Workload Ability to consistently convey my purpose rather than burdening myself with self-imposed obligations and commitments.

Workplace Situation where I can experience particularly valuable aspects of my character and how they support my fundamental purpose.

Workshop Situation where I can shape a valuable outcome by displaying my deeper purpose and having it recognized by others.

Worktop Ability to elevate my awareness of what is fundamentally important to me so I can understand my purpose in life.

World Situation where I can understand what is going on all around me by realizing how I create my perceptions of it.

World war Opportunity to engage with an all-encompassing inner conflict that constantly occupies my thoughts so I can peacefully resolve it.

World Wide Web Ability to become more aware of my thought processes and use them to understand everything around me.

Worm Instinctive ability to make my way deep into the practical aspects rather than feeling that my efforts are of little consequence.

Wormhole Situation where I can transcend any apparent limitations of time and space so I can funnel my energies into a whole new area.

Worn Opportunity to realize how I habitually show myself to people around me so I can decide how I would like to appear to them.

Wornout Opportunity to take a fresh approach to how I express myself in public so I can maintain my deeper sense of purpose.

Worry Realization that I can always release myself from any anxieties by honestly sharing my fears and concerns with other people.

Worsening Opportunity to make a rapid improvement in my situation by always confidently performing to the best of my abilities.

W

Worship Realization that I need to celebrate my unique talents rather than feeling that other people provide my ultimate happiness.

Worst Realization that I can use challenging circumstances to bring out the best of my abilities rather than feeling bad about myself.

Worthless Realization that I can use my unique expertise to make a valuable contribution instead of feeling my efforts are futile.

Worthwhile Realization of the value of an emerging possibility so I can use it to make the most of my expertise and experience.

Worthy Realization that other people have a great deal of respect for my abilities rather than always playing down my talents.

Wound Opportunity to heal some painful feelings by bringing both sides of an argument together so I can gain healthy closure.

Wounded Opportunity to deliberately make myself invulnerable to criticism from others instead of responding so sensitively to it.

Wound up Opportunity to prepare myself for future events by taking a relaxed approach rather than allowing myself to get too tense.

Woven Opportunity to see a pattern that has built up over time so I can gain a clearer understanding of all the ins and outs.

Wrack Opportunity to work my way through some apparently chaotic emotions so I can gain a firmer appreciation of my needs.

Wrapping Ability to safely look after what is most valuable to me rather than becoming too involved in the surrounding circumstances.

Wrathful Realization that I should just forgive myself about any conflicting emotions so I can declare my real needs to other people.

Wreak Opportunity to direct my frustrations into positive action rather than indulging in self-destructive behaviors.

Wreath Ability to celebrate my creative talents by having the presence to remain centered rather than becoming too wrapped up in them.

Wreck Opportunity to repair my self-esteem so I can make the most of my skills rather than behaving in a self-destructive manner.

Wreckage Situation where I am powerfully motivated to make further progress instead of feeling that I need to salvage my pride.

Wren Instinctive ability to be vocal about my ideas instead of worrying that they will have no significance for other people.

Wrench Ability to open up to a range of practical possibilities, even though I may have to give up on an opportunity I once held dear.

Wrestler Aspect of my character that enjoys grappling with the practicalities of a challenge rather than feeling thrown by them.

Wretched Realization that I feel at my most content when I am involved in a challenging situation where I can show my value.

Wriggle Opportunity to give myself some more room to maneuver rather than feeling that my options for action may be restricted.

Wring Opportunity to get a grip on a situation by taking a more straightforward approach instead of winding myself up.

Wrinkle Ability to use some inside knowledge to straighten out any minor challenges so I can keep everything running smoothly.

Wrist Essential ability to stay flexible in how I use my strength and power so I can directly shape the outcome of my choice.

Wristwatch Ability to observe personal rhythms so I can remain flexible to emerging opportunities and make every moment count.

Writ Ability to make a definite commitment to following a recognized procedure so people recognize the power of my intentions.

Write-off Ability to move on from a situation that is going nowhere so I can step into new opportunities and make committed progress.

W

Writer Aspect of my character that can convey the power of my understanding and create circumstances to achieve my ambitions.

Writhing Opportunity to give myself freedom to choose my outcome rather than feeling uncomfortable about self-imposed restrictions.

Writing Opportunity to show the different aspects of my character by communicating them clearly and ensuring I make my mark.

Wrong Realization that I have the power and the opportunity to do what I feel is right rather than feeling that I am being led astray.

Wrong button Ability to make a strong connection with another person by taking the time to listen to their needs and understand them.

Wrong car Ability to use my personal drive to pursue my objectives instead of feeling I am trying to meet someone else's needs.

Wrong clothes Ability to present myself to others by showing what makes me different rather than always trying to fit in.

Wrong destination Situation where I need to reach a firm conclusion about where I want to go with my life instead of feeling a bit lost.

Wrong hat Ability to use my different style of thinking to get in the right frame of mind instead of being restricted by conventional ideas.

Wrong house Situation where I have the security and support to explore who I am rather than feeling that I have to put on a front.

Wrong key Ability to give myself the specific freedom to unlock my hidden potential instead of trying to fit in with the needs of others.

Wrong number Ability to figure out a new way to get my message across rather than counting on methods that have worked in the past.

Wrong order Opportunity to take a different approach to achieving a successful outcome instead of using the same method every time.

Wrong paperwork Ability to have my fundamental value recognized by others rather than trying to justify my unique expertise.

Wrong person Aspect of my character that has the capacity to help me feel more comfortable with exploring some unfamiliar areas of my talent.

Wrong procedure Opportunity to achieve my preferred outcome by taking individual action instead of feeling I have to conform to expectations.

Wrong road Situation where I need to define the particular path I want to pursue rather than following other people's advice.

Wrong route Situation where I need to make plans for accomplishing personal success instead of following a recognized procedure.

Wrong shoes Ability to present my self-image by showing how comfortable I am with my status rather than feeling my style is being cramped.

Wrong train Ability to choose my professional path instead of thinking that others are making my career choices for me.

Wrong turning Situation where I can make an independent choice about future commitments rather than feeling obliged to act a certain way.

Wrong way Situation where I can choose to work in my own characteristic manner instead of thinking I have to conform to convention.

W

Xbox Ability to readily engage with a number of specific challenges where I can directly assert my skills in a more playful manner.

X-rated Opportunity to tastefully make a choice by exploring the tensions between my creative urges and my more adult responsibilities.

X-ray Opportunity to make an intense examination of my deep belief structures and understand how I use them to support my actions.

X-ray machine Ability to reveal some crucial information by examining the bare bones of a situation so I can clarify what is happening.

Xylophone Ability to take my instinctive creativity in both hands so I can hammer out a much more favorable result for everyone.

Yacht Ability to comfortably navigate my way through an emotional situation by taking inspiration from prevailing thoughts and ideas.

Yachtsman Aspect of my character that can make the best use of the prevailing atmosphere to steer me toward a particular objective.

Yachtswoman Aspect of my character that instinctively understands the moods of the current situation and can guide me safely through it.

Yak Instinctive ability to use my natural power to complete an arduous task rather than standing around talking about it.

Yam Potential to fulfill an ambition by using my natural ability to dig a bit deeper into the more earthy aspects of the situation.

Yang Opportunity to assert my essential spirituality in a positive manner so it complements my more instinctive feelings.

Yank Opportunity to pull myself out of a restricting situation so I can move into areas that seem to hold much more opportunity.

Yap Opportunity to draw attention to reasons that my loyalty needs to be rewarded rather than just sitting around chatting about it.

Yard Situation where I can give myself the space to be much more open about my personal ambitions and the resources I need.

Y

Yardarm Ability to make the most of prevailing thoughts and ideas by supporting
my capacity for powerful and progressive
thinking.

Yardstick Ability to objectively size up
the situation so I can see how my practical
skills measure up compared to those of
other people.

Yarn Ability to coherently communicate
the most important thread of a story without
allowing it to become too long and drawn out.

Yaw Opportunity to maintain a direction
toward my goal without being distracted by
events that might throw me off course.

Yawn Opportunity to wake up to my need
for fresh inspiration rather than always
falling into the same old boring routines.

Year Opportunity to use my natural sense
of rhythm to take a long-term view rather
than reacting to the current situation.

Yearling Instinctive ability to develop some
of my unconscious energies so I can harness
their power at some point in the future.

Yearning Opportunity to use my creative
power and deeper desires by acting
immediately rather than being confused
by my natural talent.

Yeast Ability to expand my cultural awareness by naturally rising to the occasion and
trying not to getting too agitated about it.

Yeast extract Ability to satisfy my particular
tastes by quickly identifying the cultural
influences that are of most significance to me.

Yell Opportunity to take decisive action
by expressing myself clearly and powerfully
instead of keeping quiet about how I feel.

Yellow Mood that can color my perspective
by reflecting my optimism about my plans
and ideas rather than letting them fade away.

Yelp Opportunity to immediately alert people
to a situation where my loyalty is being ignored,
even though it may be painful to do so.

Yes Opportunity to affirm my unique
expertise so I can take a positive approach
to resolving any challenges and conflicts.

Yesterday Opportunity to reflect on some
of my most recent experiences so I can make
the most of what is emerging in the present
situation.

Yesteryear Opportunity to contemplate
some of my earlier experiences so I can use
my accumulated wisdom to deal with my
current situation.

Yet Opportunity to understand what has
been happening up until now so I can have
a more definite view of future events.

Yeti Aspect of my character that uses my
creative instincts to explore a range of possibilities and their various ups and downs.

Yew tree Natural potential for my long-term
spiritual growth by resurrecting some of my
talents I laid to rest some time ago.

Yield Opportunity to make the most of my
fertile imagination rather than giving up
and always doing what people expect of me.

Yin Opportunity to go deeper into my more
instinctive feelings in a way that complements
how I define my spirituality.

Yips Opportunity to get fully back into the
swing of things by resolving minor tensions
that may be throwing me off balance.

Yodel Opportunity to draw attention to
the effort I have been making in steadily
developing my skills so I can progress
even higher.

Yoga Opportunity to extend my abilities
by balancing opposing aspects of my
character that may have been causing
me some tension.

Yoga teacher Aspect of my character that
learns how to stretch my abilities by staying
flexible and keeping my energies balanced.

Yogi Aspect of my character that asserts my
power by staying flexible and balanced, even
when I'm feeling a bit stretched.

Yogini Aspect of my character that stretches my creativity by staying open to emerging possibilities and keeping them in perspective.

Yogurt Potential to fulfill an ambition by nurturing my talents and having a healthy respect for my growing cultural awareness.

Yoke Ability to harness two potentially opposing outcomes so I can use my instinctive power to connect with my ambitions.

Yokel Aspect of my character that may appear simple and old-fashioned but has a natural understanding of how to develop my expertise.

Yolk Potential to fulfill an ambition by getting right to the center of a fertile idea and using it in an optimistic way.

Yomp Opportunity to use my self-motivation to relentlessly engage with emerging personal conflicts and successfully resolve them.

Yore Opportunity to explore some of the fundamental relationships that have helped shape me into the person I have become.

Young Ability to shape my chosen outcome by nurturing my unique talent and continuing to develop it in a healthy and positive way.

Young animal Instinctive ability to develop the creative aspects of my nature so I can give myself motivation to express my natural wisdom.

Young man Aspect of my character that has a growing awareness of how to assert my ambitions by using developing strength and power.

Young woman Aspect of my character that embodies the developing wisdom I can use to fulfill my aspirations and realize my dreams.

Yowl Opportunity to draw attention to a situation where people need to recognize my loyalty instead of apparently ignoring me.

Yo-yo Ability to play around with a plan or an idea so I can happily understand how I can influence any potential ups and downs.

Zabaglione Ability to take a variety of pleasing thoughts and potentially fertile ideas and concoct a favorable outcome from them.

Zander Instinctive ability to deal with an issue that has been preying on my emotions so I can use it to help me fulfill an ambition.

Zap Opportunity to quickly resolve a challenging situation by focusing on my abilities and using them to make an instant choice.

Zealot Aspect of my character that has a fundament urge to make connections, even though others might be challenged by my methods.

Zebra Instinctive ability to harness both my conscious and unconscious energies rather than seeing everything in black and white.

Zebra crossing Situation where I can motivate myself to take a series of clearly defined steps to safely move between different career options.

Z

Zen Opportunity to become much more enlightened about a challenging situation by taking a more relaxed, contemplative approach.

Zenith Situation where I can use my accumulated spiritual wisdom to reach a personal high point before going deeper into the next phase.

Zephyr Opportunity to gently play around with some ideas that currently please me, even though they might never blow anyone away.

Zeppelin Ability to contain my expansive ideas in a more rigid framework so I can use them to steadily progress toward my objective.

Zero Opportunity to bring everything back to its fundamental state so I can focus on exploring my unlimited potential.

Zester Ability to go beyond surface appearances so I can release my natural enthusiasm and energy in a more fruitful way.

Ziggurat Situation where I can take a series of steps to examine the structure of my beliefs and how I have built them up over time.

Zigzag Opportunity to try a few different tacks before I decide to make a firm commitment to definitely go one way or the other.

Zimmer Ability to remotivate myself by using a definite framework and support structure to steadily maintain my forward progress.

Zinc Ability to protect my fundamental power from any emotional influences that may eat away at my deeper sense of well-being.

Zip code Ability to clearly identify how I feel about a specific aspect of my character so I can deliver on the promise it may hold.

Zipper Ability to quickly conceal my innermost feelings so I can choose to reveal them when I feel it is more convenient to open up.

Zipping up Opportunity to quickly become intimately connected with two apparently separate aspects of how I might appear to others.

Zip wire Ability to make a strong connection so I can make rapid progress with an idea I currently am very excited by.

Zither Ability to habitually take my instinctive creativity in both hands so I can express myself in a simple and vibrant way.

Zombie Aspect of my character soullessly going through the motions in my career, and it feels like I'm wasting my unique talents.

Zone Situation where I can be definite about my personal boundaries so I can direct my attention to an area that interests me.

Zoo Situation where I can safely observe some of my wilder instincts so I can understand how to keep them under control.

Zookeeper Aspect of my character that looks after my wilder creative instincts and ensures that they always feel healthy and fulfilled.

Zooming Opportunity to move quickly by focusing my creative energies on the fastest way to reach a very specific outcome.

Zoom lens Ability to explore different aspects of the bigger picture by quickly changing my perspective so I can focus on the details.

Zorbing Opportunity to play around with some different aspects of a situation so I can clearly see it from a variety of angles.

Zzz's Essential opportunity for me to become comfortable with who I really am so I can consistently put my dreams into action.

Z

ABOUT THE AUTHOR

Ian Wallace is a qualified psychologist with more than thirty years of experience who specializes in dreams and the dreaming process. He is a regular guest on the *Steve Wright Show*, frequently appears in the press and on television, and is the author of the bestselling *Top 100 Dreams*. Ian also works with leading businesses to facilitate change and improve communication. For more information about Ian and his work, visit www.ianwallacedreams.com or follow him on Twitter, @ianwallace.